CRIMINAL INVESTIGATION

THIRD EDITION

Bruce L. Berg
Department of Criminal Justice
California State University

John J. Horgan
Special Agent, Retired
Federal Bureau of Investigation

Glencoe McGraw-Hill

New York, New York   Columbus, Ohio   Woodland Hills, California   Peoria, Illinois

Library of Congress Cataloging-in-Publication Data

Berg, Bruce L.
    Criminal Investigation / Bruce L. Berg and John J. Horgan.—3rd ed.
      p.   cm.
    Rev. ed. of: Criminal investigation / John J. Horgan. 2nd ed. 1979.
    Includes bibliographical references and index.
    ISBN 0-02-800928-2
    1. Criminal Investigation.   I. Horgan, John J.   II. Horgan, John J.
Criminal investigation.   III. Title.
    HV8073.B435   1997
    363.25—dc21
                                               97-13607
                                               CIP

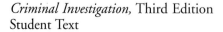

Glencoe/McGraw-Hill

A Division of The **McGraw·Hill** *Companies*

Criminal Investigation, Third Edition
Student Text

Send all inquiries to:
Glencoe/McGraw-Hill
936 Eastwind Drive
Westerville, OH 43081

ISBN 0-02-800928-2

Printed in the United States of America.

1 2 3 4 5 6 7 8 9 10   027   04 03 02 01 00 99 98 97

Brief Contents

Expanded Contents

Preface

The third edition of *Criminal Investigation* presents the basic principles of criminal investigation. It includes current investigative procedures used in the handling of crime scenes, interviewing and interrogating suspects and witnesses, gathering and preserving evidence, conducting surveillance, writing reports, establishing *modus operandi,* and utilizing technical resources. In addition, the text explores concepts, philosophies, and methods related to the prevention and suppression of crimes and the apprehension of criminals.

Criminal Investigation, Third Edition, is written in a practical, down-to-earth style, appropriate for students in career-oriented programs at both the two- and four-year level. Special attention is given to helping students understand the legal aspects of collecting and processing evidence to ensure that their work stands up in court. Relevant court decisions that affect the procedures and guidelines that criminal investigators must follow when doing their jobs are also presented.

Program Components

Our goal for this edition was to provide a complete teaching/learning program suitable for a variety of instructional and learning styles. The *Criminal Investigation,* Third Edition, instructional program includes the following components:

- Student Text
- Study Guide
- Instructor's Manual
- Instructor's Presentation Software
- Interactive Student Assessment System

Textook Features

Complete Student Pedagogy

Each chapter has been completely revised and expanded to promote good instructional practices and increased student comprehension of the concepts presented. **New** to this edition are **chapter learning objectives, bold-faced key terms,** and **key terms definitions in the margins.** An **integrated learning system** ties the chapter objectives from the text material, through to the chapter summaries, and the chapter review questions. These learning aids help students focus on the important concepts to be learned. Within the chapter, content is broken down into appropriately sized sections that students can absorb with ease.

Visual Learning Program

Included in the third edition of *Criminal Investigation* is a **greatly expanded visual learning program.** The chapter-opening photograph sets the stage for learning, while photographs and artwork within the chapter help students visualize the concepts presented. All new two-color charts, graphs, maps, and figures provide students with the latest relevant information. The intext visual learning program is further enhanced through the **multimedia** materials in the Instructor's Presentation Software on CD-ROM.

Flexible Chapter Coverage

For maximum flexibility, the content material is divided into **22 chapters** that can be easily **customized** for **quarter** or **semester** study. New to this edition are chapters on the timely topics of organized crime (19), white-collar crime (20), and terrorism (22).

High-Interest Boxed Features

Also **new** to this edition are **high-interest boxed features** that enhance the instructional impact of the content. These features reinforce and extend the chapter concepts and provide visual interest.

FOCUS ON TECHNOLOGY

Focus on Technology highlights a variety of technologies available to criminal investigators. These technologies range from computerized criminal investigation systems to crime scene sketching software, and from reflective ultraviolet photography to trace explosives detectors. One of these technology features appears in each of the 22 chapters, providing a practical introduction to the wide range of technologies available to help investigators do their jobs.

CAREER FOCUS:

Career Focus presents useful information about employment opportunities for criminal investigators. Included are such careers as police detective, corporate investigator, and foreign service special agent.

FYI (For Your Information) provides interesting sidelights related to the chapter content.

Statistics presents useful data showing trends, developments, and changes.

History focuses on people and events that are an interesting backdrop to the study of the chapter concepts.

Critical Thinking and Investigative Skill-Building Exercises

Newly added to the end-of-chapter materials is a series of **real-world** critical thinking and workplace **skill-building** exercises. These exercises are correlated to the **SCANS** (Secretary's Commission on Achieving Necessary Skills) competency guidelines as applied to the job of a law enforcement officer. They offer opportunities to connect knowledge and skills to the workplace.

CRITICAL THINKING INVESTIGATIVE EXERCISE

Critical Thinking Investigative Exercises require students to analyze a situation and make a choice, develop an hypothesis, reach a conclusion, or propose a solution.

INVESTIGATIVE SKILL BUILDERS

Investigative Skill Builders help students develop investigative skills that can be used on the job. They include such skills as acquiring and evaluating information, participating as a member of a team, allocating time, and teaching others.

Integrity/Honesty Exercises confront students with ethical situations involving clients or fellow officers that can arise in the workplace in which they must make a decision or propose a course of action.

Resources for the Student

Study Guide

Also **new** to *Criminal Investigation,* Third Edition, is the student Study Guide. This learning aid provides independent study and reinforcement of the chapter concepts. The Study Guide contains study outlines, key terms review, concept review, and application exercises. Also included is a section on career development.

Resources for the Instructor

Instructor's Manual

The **new** Instructor's Manual contains a variety of resources to assist both new and experienced instructors. Included are chapter outlines, chapter summaries, discussion questions, learning-by-doing activities, and answers to the end-of-chapter exercises. Also included are course schedules and a correlation of the end-of-chapter exercises to the SCANS competencies for a law enforcement officer. The Instructor's Manual is available in two formats—a print version and as a Microsoft® Word 6.0 for Windows® file on the Instructor's Presentation Software CD-ROM.

Instructor's Presentation Software (IPS)

The **new** Instructor's Presentation Software (IPS) CD-ROM allows the instructor to conduct a multimedia interactive classroom presentation of the concepts in *Criminal Investigation,* Third Edition. The CD-ROM contains the following components:

- **Lecture Presentation and Enhancement Package in PowerPoint Format**
  This presentation package contains over **2500 lecture screens, graphics,** and **full-color images** that can be used to introduce or reinforce the chapter content. Additionally, there are over **30 topical or issues-oriented presentation modules** that go beyond the chapter concepts. These additional modules allow the instructor to enhance class lectures with topical and issues-oriented material not found in the textbook. The PowerPoint Viewer is included on the CD-ROM, so that the instructor need not have the PowerPoint software to use this material in class.

- **Interactive In-Class Student Assessment With Hyperlink**
  A unique software program, called Hyperlink, allows the instructor to access any objective question from the electronic question bank onscreen in the classroom. When used with the optional Glencoe electronic Group Link Student Response System, the instructor can track student responses and generate a report on their performance after every class. This software is a great tool for motivating students and encouraging classroom participation and is integrated with the PowerPoint presentation allowing both programs to run concurrently.

- **Interactive In-Class Criminal Investigation Challenge**
  This Criminal Investigation Challenge, called Hyperchallenge, is designed along the lines of a Jeopardy-style game. Students earn points either singly or as a team for correct answers. As with the interactive assessment system, Challenge can be used with Glencoe's electronic Group Link Student Response System.

- **PowerPoint Lecture Presentation and Instructor's Manual in Microsoft Word Format**
  A Microsoft Word 6.0 DOC file containing the text from all presentation screens, the location of all art and photographs in the presentation, and the complete Instructor's Manual is provided. The instructor can customize and integrate the PowerPoint presentation with the Instructor's Manual material and store all course-related teaching outlines and notes on his or her own computer for future retrieval and updating.

Interactive Student Assessment System (ISAS)

This new testing system allows the instructor to choose from 1100 test items and add, delete, or edit questions as desired to create individual or randomly mixed versions of the test. Tests can be given in class, or can be placed in a computer lab allowing students to take a quiz or a test in the lab without requiring the presence of the instructor. Utilizing this system, instructors need not take valuable class time to give tests and quizzes! The software will grade all objective questions (multiple choice, true/false) in the test and generate a report of each student's performance for the instructor. Alternately, the instructor can set up a series of self-tests as an on-line review for the student, and the students can receive their results upon completion of the self-test.

Acknowledgments

We gratefully acknowledge the contributions of the following individuals who helped in the development of this textbook.

J. Michael Aaron
Forensic Specialist
Camden, NJ

Carl R. Butcher
Missouri Western
  State College
St. Joseph, MO

Brenda Collins
Ohio State
  Highway Patrol
Columbus, OH

Tim Elliget
Newark Police
  Forensic Services
Newark, OH

Alan L. Hart
Northwestern Michigan
  College
Traverse City, Michigan

James C. Helmkamp
National White Collar
  Crime Center
Richmond, VA

Dawn Herkenham
Forensic Science
  Systems Unit
FBI Laboratory
Washington, DC

C. Wayne Johnston
Arkansas State University
State University, AR

Roger Kahn
Ohio Bureau of Crimi-
  nal Identification &
  Investigation
London, OH

John I. Kostanoski
State University
  of New York
Farmingdale, NY

George L. Lawless
South Plains College
Levelland, TX

Mona M. McKinniss
U.S. Postal Inspection
  Service
Columbus, Ohio

Sarah Nordin
Salano Community
  College
Suisun City, CA

Joyce Riggs
FBI Bomb Data Center
Washington, DC

Tim Sweeney
National Law Enforce-
  ment Telecommunica-
  tions Systems, Inc.
Phoenix, AZ

Clarence Terrill
Harford Community
  College
Bel Air, MD

About the Authors

Bruce L. Berg is currently an Associate Professor of Criminal Justice at California State University, Long Beach. Previously, Dr. Berg was a Professor of Criminology at Indiana University of Pennsylvania and a faculty member in the Department of Sociology at the University of Massachusetts, Boston Harbor Campus. He also served as the Internship Director and a faculty member at Florida State University's School of Criminology. Dr. Berg received his Ph.D. in Sociology from Syracuse University. He has published nearly three dozen articles, essays, and book chapters in the areas of criminology, policing, deviance, and research methods. He is also the author of *Qualitative Research Methods for the Social Sciences, Law Enforcement: An Introduction to Policing Methods for the Social Sciences* and is a coauthor of *Research Methods for the Social Sciences: Applications and Practice.* Dr. Berg has been an active member of the American Society of Criminology and the Academy of Criminal Justice Sciences since 1983. He has presented numerous papers and workshops at meetings of these associations, as well as served on several committees.

John J. Horgan is a retired Special Agent of the FBI. He has an extensive background in criminal investigation and related fields. He was a police instructor and conducted numerous police schools for many law enforcement departments in California and other western states. He holds Ph.B. and LL. B. degrees and is a graduate of the FBI National Police Academy, Washington, DC. He initiated and coordinated a Police Science Degree program at San Bernardino Valley College, San Bernardino, CA, where he attained the status of Associate Professor. He served as a Resource Assistant at Alfred North Whitehead College, University of Redlands, Redlands, CA. He is a Life Member of the California Peace Officer Association, the Southern California Robbery Association, and the California Police Educators Association. He has traveled to the British Isles, Ireland, Europe, and Japan to observe police procedures and court systems.

CHAPTER 1

Basic Grounding and Overview

CHAPTER OBJECTIVES

After completing this chapter, you will be able to:

1. Identify and define the nature of crime.

2. Name the sources of criminal law in the United States.

3. Explain the distinction between *felonies* and *misdemeanors*.

4. Summarize the objectives of criminal investigation.

5. Understand the nature of inductive and deductive reasoning in criminal investigations.

CRIME SCENE DO NOT

What Is Crime?

Whenever you read the newspaper, listen to the radio, or watch the news on television, you are confronted with crime—shootings on city streets, robberies of convenience stores, beatings of spouses and children, prostitution, automobile thefts. What exactly is crime, though? If you were to look up the word *crime* in a dictionary, here's one definition you might find:

> An act or the commission of an act that is forbidden or the omission of a duty that is commanded by a public law of a sovereign state to the injury of the public welfare and that makes the offender liable to punishment by the law.[1]

This definition does not tell us what behavior is forbidden or commanded, what constitutes a violation of the law, who is responsible for investigating and locating information about the behavior, or who is responsible for prosecuting the errant behaviors. Edwin Sutherland and Donald Cressey suggest the following four primary factors in classifying a behavior as a *crime:*[2]

- The behavior is offensive to some political authority.
- The behavior is specifically defined both in terms of the offense and the punishment.
- The prohibition is uniformly applied to all.
- The remedy contains penal sanctions enforced by the state.

To summarize Sutherland and Cressey, we can define a **crime** as an offense against the public at large, proclaimed in a law and punishable by an official governing body. The body of law that defines criminal behavior and prescribes the punishment to be imposed for such behavior is **criminal law.** The purpose of criminal law is to prevent harm to society.

Development of Criminal Law

At one time, most people considered crime a private matter. When one person wronged another, the injured party sought compensation or relief in the form of revenge. Unfortunately, this sometimes resulted in bloody feuds between individuals and their entire families. Worse still, the conflict could result from a misunderstanding or mistake by the injured party!

In time, societies evolved into nation-states, and the customs and traditions that had guided individual behavior were replaced with written law. The state, or the government, became the representative of the public at large. Thus, the government became the *plaintiff,* the party that accuses a person of a crime. Usually, the government is referred to as the **prosecutor.** The person who is accused of a crime is called the **defendant.**

Crime   An offense against the public at large, proclaimed in a law and punishable by a governing body.

Criminal law   The body of law that for the purpose of preventing harm to society, defines what behavior is criminal and prescribes the punishment to be imposed for such behavior.

Prosecutor   Name given to the government as the party that accuses a person of a crime.

Defendant   In criminal law, the person who is accused of a crime.

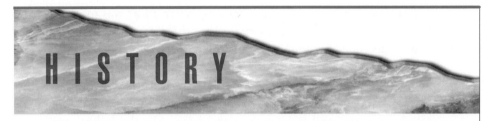

HISTORY

*T*he first written laws (circa 3000 B.C.) were found on clay tablets among the ruins of Ur, one of the city-states of Sumeria (now southeastern Iraq). The laws tried to free poor people from abuse by the rich, and everybody from abuse by the priests. One law forbade the high priest to go into the garden of a poor mother and take wood or fruit from her to pay taxes. Others cut burial fees and forbade the clergy and high officials to share among themselves the cattle that were sacrificed to the gods.

Public sentiment may change about which behaviors should be illegal. For example, until recently, in most jurisdictions of the United States, it was not legally possible for a husband to rape his wife. Also, in 1996 Arizona and California passed laws making it lawful for people with certain medical conditions to smoke marijuana. In any event, no act or behavior can be considered criminal unless it is prohibited by the law of the place where it is committed, and the law provides for the punishment of the offenders. We will now look at the sources of those laws that define what conduct is criminal and prescribe the punishment to be imposed for such conduct.

Sources of Criminal Law in the United States

Each crime must have an exact definition. Crimes are defined in several different bodies of law that govern behavior in the United States. These bodies of law include the following:

- common law
- statutory law
- case law
- administrative law

Common Law   One of the earliest sources of definitions of crimes is the common law. The early American colonists came from England and adopted the law of England as the law of their new land. In the early days of English history, the kings had tried to centralize the English government and establish a court system. Judges traveled in circuits around the countryside, deciding cases based on custom and tradition. They settled disputes in as consistent a manner as possible. The judges maintained this consistency by relying on previous legal decisions whenever they faced a similar set of circumstances. Every effort was made to share the law "in common" with everyone else throughout the country. This body of decisions became known as the **common law.**

Statutory Law Most crimes are defined by **statutory law.** This is the body of laws passed by legislative bodies, including the U.S. Congress, state legislatures, and local governing bodies. On the federal and state levels, these laws are known as *statutes;* on the local level, they may be known as city *ordinances* or town *bylaws.* In many states, the legislature has standardized common-law definitions of such crimes as murder, bur-glary, arson, and rape by defining them in statutes. Other states have cre-ated a separate **penal code,** a collection of statutes that define criminal offenses and specify corresponding fines and punishments. See Figure 1–1 for some examples of state criminal statutes.

Figure 1–1 Examples of state criminal statutes.

California State Penal Code **Section 211:** Robbery
211. Robbery is the felonious taking of personal property in the pos-session of another, from his person or immediate presence, and against their will, accompanied by means of force or fear.
212. The fear mentioned in Section 211 may be either:
    1. The fear of an unlawful injury to the person or property of the person robbed, or of any relative of his or member of his family; or,
    2. The fear of an immediate and unlawful injury to the person or property of anyone in the company of the person robbed at the time of the robbery.

New York State Penal Code **Section 160.00:** Robbery
Sec. 160.00 Robbery; defined.
    Robbery is forcible stealing. A person forcibly steals property and commits robbery when, in the course of committing a larceny, he uses or threatens the immediate use of physical force upon another person for the purpose of:
    1. Preventing or overcoming resistance to the taking of the proper-ty or to the retention thereof immediately after the taking; or
    2. Compelling the owner of such property or another person to deliver up the property or to engage in other conduct which aids in the commission of the larceny.

The distinction between federal and state criminal laws is very important. The U.S. Constitution created a national government with limited powers. One of the limitations is of police power. The federal government has no general police power; it can create criminal statutes only for those areas over which the federal government has jurisdiction. For example, Congress can create laws against counterfeiting because the federal government has the power to coin money. Some federal jurisdiction overlaps with state criminal laws. For example, both the federal government and state governments have statutes that outlaw the manufacture, sale, and use of certain drugs.

On the state level, criminal liability is defined quite specifically. Crimes are considered serious transgressions against the public safety, and conviction of a crime can result in death or imprisonment. Although the criminal statutes of the states generally resemble one another, the exact definitions and penalties may differ from jurisdiction to jurisdiction. The exact charges also may differ; for example, petty larceny in one state may be grand larceny in another.

Case Law   The rules of law announced in court decisions also provide a source of definitions of crime. This **case law** includes the sum total of reported judicial cases that interpret previous decisions, statutes, regulations, and constitutional provisions. Each interpretation becomes part of the law on the subject and serves as a **precedent.** That is, the decision furnishes an example or authority for deciding subsequent cases in which identical or similar facts are presented.

Administrative Law   Legislators and judges cannot do all that is needed to protect the public good. To broaden the power of the law, legislators set up administrative agencies to create rules, regulate and supervise, and render decisions in such areas as communications, labor relations, and working conditions. The decrees and decisions of these agencies are known as **administrative law** and can include criminal penalties for violations. One such example is the regulation dealing with the mailing of obscene material.

Classification of Crimes

Crimes can be classified in a number of ways. One such classification is according to the severity of the criminal behavior. The more serious the crime, the more stringent the punishment. Generally, a **felony** is a relatively serious offense punishable by death or by impris-

Case law   The sum total of all reported cases that interpret previous decisions, statutes, regulations, and constitutional provisions that then become part of a nation's or a state's common law.

Precedent   A decision in a court case that furnishes an example or authority for deciding subsequent cases in which identical or similar facts are presented.

Administrative law   The body of law created by administrative agencies in the form of rules, regulations, orders, and decisions, sometimes with criminal penalties for violations.

Felony   A relatively serious criminal offense punishable by death or by imprisonment for more than a year in a state or federal prison.

onment for more than a year in a state or federal prison. Some felonies are also punishable by a fine. Felony crimes include murder, rape, and assault. A **misdemeanor** is a less serious crime that is generally punishable by a prison sentence of not more than one year in a county or city jail. Disorderly conduct is an example of a misdemeanor. Because crimes may be defined differently in various bodies of law and from one jurisdiction to another, it is important that criminal investigators be familiar with their area's criminal laws.

Misdemeanor A less serious crime that is generally punishable by a prison sentence of not more than one year in a county or city jail.

Criminal investigation The lawful search for people and things to reconstruct the circumstances of an illegal act, apprehend or determine the guilty party, and aid in the state's prosecution of the offender.

What Is Criminal Investigation?

Having defined crime, we will now consider the nature of criminal investigation. **Criminal investigation** is a lawful search for people and things to reconstruct the circumstances of an illegal act, apprehend or determine the guilty party, and aid in the state's prosecution of the offender. Investigators must sift through all available information and determine which pieces can be linked together to accomplish the goal of punishing the criminal responsible for the crime. The primary objectives of a criminal investigation are the following:

1. Deal with emergencies.
2. Determine if a crime has been committed and, if so, what crime.
3. Establish crime scene priorities.
4. Identify suspects.
5. Apprehend the suspects.
6. Gather and preserve evidence.
7. Recover stolen property.
8. Assist in prosecution and conviction of the defendant or defendants.

Now let's see how these objectives were met in a real criminal investigation.[3]

Case Study

Early in the morning of September 20, 1996, the police in Columbus, Ohio, received a report of a gunshot in the Linden area. When officers arrived, they found Anthony C. Kacir alone in a parking lot with a bullet wound in his head. There was no gun on or near the victim. Kacir was transported to the hospital, where he died later that day. The police strongly suspected that a murder had been committed. (Objectives 1, 2, and 3)

From interviews with friends, police investigators learned that Kacir, a 19-year-old college junior, had been returning by car to his northside apartment from his eastside college campus when he was shot. Friends indicated that the caring, well-liked student generally took the same route home. A check of Kacir's bank accounts revealed that he had removed $200 from an ATM at 2:12 A.M. Friday. Investigators theorized that someone had abducted him as he neared his apartment, had forced him back into the car, made him drive to the bank to withdraw the money, and then shot him about 2:20 A.M. and dumped him from the car. (Objectives 4 and 6)

Kacir's car was found Friday afternoon, several blocks from where Kacir had been shot. A search of the car revealed a single set of fingerprints, which the police department's fingerprint identification system matched to a juvenile who had a previous criminal conviction. With this evidence and other information, police were able to connect three juveniles to the crime. Arrested and charged with delinquency counts of aggravated murder and aggravated robbery in the slaying of Anthony C. Kacir were Aubrey Jamison, 15; Lamar A. Coleman, 15; and Harold Lee Riggins, 17. Jamison and Coleman admitted to participating in the crimes and implicated each other and Riggins. (Objectives 4, 5, 6, and 7)

When the suspects were arraigned in court on September 27, evidence gathered by police investigators formed the basis of the charges of aggravated murder and aggravated robbery brought by the prosecuting attorney. The officers and investigators were called on to testify in court regarding all aspects of the investigation. In December, after each defendant had been given a separate hearing, in which additional testimony was presented, the judge ruled that the three would be tried as adults. (Objective 8)

Rights of the Accused

Our previous discussion of criminal law has dealt with **substantive law,** the body of law that creates, defines, and regulates rights and defines crime and its penalties. **Procedural law,** on the other hand, governs the ways in which substantive laws are administered. For the criminal investigator, procedural law covers such subjects as the way suspects can legally be arrested, searched, and interrogated. Thus, procedural law is concerned with **due process of law,** the rights of people suspected of or charged with crimes. Most of the procedural, or due-process, rights of criminal suspects in the United States are found in the Bill of Rights, the first ten amendments to the United States Constitution (see Figure 1–2). These ten amendments were added to the U.S. Constitution soon after it was adopt-

Substantive law The body of law that creates, defines, and regulates rights and defines crime and its penalties.

Procedural law The body of law that prescribes the manner or method by which rights and responsibilities may be exercised and enforced.

Due process of law The rights of people suspected of or charged with crimes, prescribed by the U.S. Constitution, state constitutions, and federal and state statutes.

ed because many felt the Constitution did not adequately protect the people's rights. Other due process rights are found in state constitutions and federal and state statutes. Criminal investigators must know and apply all relevant due-process procedures for their particular jurisdictions.

Figure 1–2 A summary of the Bill of Rights.

Guarantees of Basic Citizens' Rights
First Amendment: freedom of religion, speech, press, assembly, and of the right to petition the government

Protection Against Arbitrary Police and Court Action
Fourth Amendment: prohibits unreasonable searches and seizures

Fifth Amendment: requires grand jury indictment for serious crimes, bans double jeopardy, prohibits having to testify against oneself, guarantees no loss of life, liberty, or property without due process of law

Sixth Amendment: guarantees right to speedy, public, impartial trial in criminal cases, with counsel and right to cross-examine witnesses

Seventh Amendment: guarantees right to jury trial in civil suits

Eighth Amendment: prohibits excessive bail or fines and cruel and unusual punishment

Protection of States' Rights and Other Rights
Ninth Amendment: affirms that rights not listed in other amendments are not necessarily denied

Tenth Amendment: states that powers not delegated to the national government or denied to the states are reserved to the states

Military Protection and Rights
Second Amendment: guarantees the right to organize state militias and to bear arms

Third Amendment: prohibits the quartering of soldiers in homes in peacetime

Requisites of a Successful Criminal Investigator

There are many attributes that a criminal investigator must have. Some of these special qualities are listed in Figure 1–3. One of the most important is the ability to make reasoned connections between the information and evidence gathered from the crime scene and witnesses and a possible suspect in the crime. These connections may be made through either deductive reasoning or inductive reasoning.

Figure 1–3 Characteristics of a successful criminal investigator.

- Curiosity, habitual inquisitiveness
- Observation, using all five senses
- Suspicion and refusal to take anything for granted
- Memory, ability to recall facts and past events
- Ordinary intelligence and common sense
- An unbiased mind
- Avoidance of inaccurate conclusions
- Patience, understanding, and courtesy
- Ability to play a role
- Ability to gain and hold confidence
- Persistence and endless capacity for work
- Knowledge of the essential elements of a crime
- Interest in sociology and psychology
- Ability to recognize criminal activity or operations
- Resourcefulness
- Ability to make friends and secure the cooperation of others
- Tact, self-control, and dignity
- Knowledge of investigative techniques
- Interest in the job and pride of accomplishment
- Loyalty

Deductive Reasoning

Suppose an investigator notices a kitchen knife extending from the back of the victim and also sees a pool of blood beneath the victim. The investigator deduces that the weapon used in the death of the victim was a knife. Moreover, because the knife is stuck in the back of the victim, the investigator further deduces that it was a murder. The investigator is using **deductive reasoning;** that is, he or she begins with a general

Deductive reasoning
The drawing of conclusions from logically related events or observations.

When most people hear the term *criminal investigator,* they generally think of a police detective. Detectives are almost always plainclothes investigators who gather facts and collect evidence in criminal cases. In large police departments, detectives are organized into specialized units such as the homicide division, the narcotics division, or the arson division.

Detectives do some of their work at a desk and some out in the field in a variety of environments. They may be assigned as many as two or three cases a day, and having 30 cases to handle at one time is not unusual. Schedules for detectives often are irregular, and overtime as well as working at night and on the weekend, may be necessary.

To become a police detective, one must first have experience as a police officer. Hiring requirements for police officers vary, but most departments require at least a high school diploma. In almost all large cities, the hiring of police officers follows local civil service regulations. In some departments, a college degree may be necessary for some or all police positions. After gaining three to five years' experience in the department and demonstrating the skills necessary for detective work, a police officer may be promoted to a position as a detective. In some police departments, candidates must first take a qualifying exam. For new detectives there is usually a training program which may last from a few weeks to several months.

Students interested in being a detective should take a diverse course load that includes English, American history, government, business law, psychology, sociology, chemistry, and physics. Also important are courses in journalism, a foreign language, using a computer, and keyboarding. Salaries for police detectives range from about $27,500 to nearly $45,000, depending on location. With experience the salary increases considerably.

explanation of the crime and then tests that formulation against specific available information.

Inductive Reasoning

Inductive reasoning The making of inferences from apparently separate observations or pieces of evidence.

Inductive reasoning moves from examining apparently separate pieces of evidence to drawing an inference or building an explanation of the crime. Suppose the investigator finds a victim lying in a pool of blood and the victim has numerous cuts from what might have been a sharp object. The investigator could, using inductive reasoning, infer that the victim died as the result of wounds inflicted by a knife. However, this is only what the investigator thinks may have happened. More complete analysis of the wounds on the victim's body and additional information and evidence may lead to different conclusions.

Drawing Conclusions

The important point here is not whether investigators use deductive or inductive reasoning. Rather, it is that any conclusions drawn by a criminal investigator should be based on careful reasoning and systematic collection of information and evidence. It is especially important that investigators remain objective and avoid preconceived notions about possible crimes.

Inductions are not always proof of a crime. For example, upon entering a store after receiving a possible-robbery-in-progress broadcast, an officer might observe an unconscious man on the floor, bleeding from an apparent gunshot wound. Inductively, the officer might assume that the man is a victim of a robbery. A moment later, a woman wielding a handgun might come from the back room, crying. After disarming her, the officer might learn that she is the proprietor and that she accidentally shot the customer on the floor while trying to shoot the escaping robber.

The ability to reason based on observation and facts is important to investigators.

By the same token, deductions are not always proof in themselves either. Suppose the officer had walked into the store and found the proprietor standing over the wounded customer on the floor. From these observations, the officer might have deduced that the woman was the robbery victim, but might have mistakenly thought the customer was the robber.

In short, although both induction and deduction are important reasoning skills, investigators still must carefully check the facts of every situation before drawing conclusions.

Case Study

In one case, a California Highway Patrol officer heard over the radio that a fellow officer was chasing a white and blue late-model Cadillac on the interstate. The information indicated that the speeding car had run off the road and into the center divider during the chase. The officer who had heard the radio bulletin saw the suspect Cadillac coming his way, traveling erratically. He followed the car and clocked it on radar at speeds well over the legal limit as it crossed over several lanes of traffic. The officer forced the vehicle to pull over. From his patrol car, the officer observed that the vehicle had Illinois license plates that were old and bent. A check of the license plate number revealed that there was no warrant out for it.

The officer *induced* that the driver was drunk. Because the driver had exhibited symptoms of intoxication while driving and when questioned, the officer administered a series of sobriety tests. The driver performed poorly on the tests, leading the officer to *deduce* that the driver was in fact driving under the influence of an intoxicating beverage.

Even after arresting the man for driving under the influence (DUI), the officer continued to feel the driver was concealing something and induced that there might be more wrong with the situation than met the eye. He checked the vehicle identification number (VIN) and noticed that it was not securely attached to the car as it should be—itself a violation of the law.

The officer opened the hood of the Cadillac and wrote down the engine identification number. This number is cross-referenced with the VIN. A check with the FBI's National Crime Information Center (NCIC) in Washington, D.C., revealed that the car had been stolen and the VIN replaced with another but that the thieves had neglected to replace the engine identification number. A female passenger in the car refused to provide any identification and was placed under arrest, along with the driver, for possession of a stolen vehicle.

The driver told the officer that he had some gold bullion and rare coins in a case in the backseat of the car. He indicated that he did not wish to leave this case in the car unattended. With the suspect's permission, the officer opened the case and indeed found gold bullion. However, the officer also found eight ounces of cocaine, a number of blank Illi-

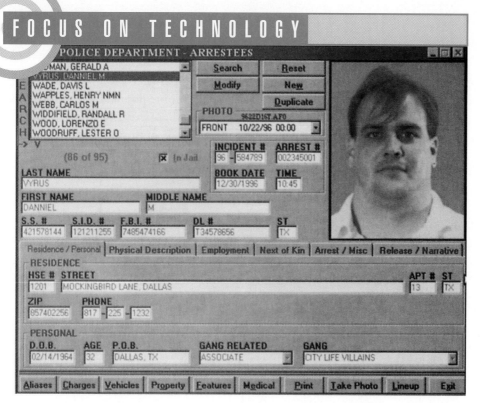

Computerized Criminal Investigation Criminal investigators spend hundreds of hours gathering, recording, reporting, and evaluating information. This tremendous job is made easier by using computers. Criminal investigation systems combine applications such as evidence control, criminal profiling, crime analysis, and case management into one centralized system available to many users.

nois drivers' licenses, several blank social security cards, and other sets of identification. Bank books, safe-deposit keys, and registrations for additional automobiles were also found.

A subsequent FBI fingerprint check revealed that the driver was not the person he claimed to be. He was, in fact, a felon with a record dating back to age 16. He was now 42 years old. His record showed the following arrests: murder of a police officer, assault on a police officer, grand theft, auto theft, smuggling, and possession of narcotics.

As the result of what had begun as a rather routine drunk-driving arrest, officers uncovered a major auto theft ring in Los Angeles and Chicago. The power of inductive and deductive reasoning combined with careful observation and persistence produced a successful police investigation.

SUMMARY BY LEARNING OBJECTIVES

Learning Objective 1

Crime is a behavior that is offensive to some political authority and for which both the offense and the punishment have been specifically defined. The prohibition against the behavior is uniformly applied to all, and the remedy contains penal sanctions enforced by punishments administered by the state.

Learning Objective 2

Criminal law is the body of law that, for the purpose of preventing harm to society, defines what behavior is criminal and prescribes the punishment to be imposed for such behavior. The sources of criminal law are common law, statutory law, case law, and administrative law.

Learning Objective 3

Crimes can be classified by the severity of the criminal behavior and by the punishment for the behavior. A felony is a serious crime, such as murder, robbery, or arson, that is punishable by imprisonment or death. A misdemeanor is a less serious crime that is generally punishable by a fine or by imprisonment for less than one year.

Learning Objective 4

The objectives of criminal investigation include the following: deal with emergencies; determine if a crime has been committed and, if so, what crime; establish crime scene priorities; identify suspects; apprehend the suspects; gather and preserve evidence; recover stolen property; and assist in prosecution and conviction of the defendant or defendants.

Learning Objective 5

It is important for an investigator to be able to make reasoned connections between the information and evidence gathered from the crime scene and witnesses and a possible suspect in the crime. These connections may be made through either deductive reasoning or inductive reasoning. Inductive reasoning moves from apparently separate observations to drawing a general inference. Deductive reasoning reaches a conclusion based on related observable facts.

QUESTIONS FOR REVIEW

Learning Objective 1

1. Define *crime, criminal law, prosecutor, defendant.*
2. What are four primary factors in determining what constitutes a crime?
3. Does public sentiment influence what constitutes a crime? Explain.

4. What are the sources of criminal law in the United States?

5. How did English common law become part of the laws in most American states?

6. Which source of criminal law contains the most definitions of crimes? Explain why.

7. What is meant by the term *precedent* in case law?

8. How can one distinguish between a *misdemeanor* and a *felony?*

9. Is rape a felony or a misdemeanor?

10. What are the primary objectives in any criminal investigation?

11. How do *inductive reasoning* and *deductive reasoning* differ?

12. Why must an investigator not rely solely on inductive or deductive reasoning?

CRITICAL THINKING INVESTIGATIVE EXERCISE

Using the hypothetical facts that follow, test your ability to make inductive inferences and deductive conclusions. Carefully read the facts of the case, and then list what you can reasonably infer or safely deduce from the information provided.

Facts

You have been called to the scene of what appears to be a double homicide. Upon arriving, you receive the following information from the uniformed officer already on the scene:

There are two victims—a man and a woman—both white. The woman is approximately 25 years old, 5 feet 6 inches tall, and 120 pounds. She has blond hair just past her shoulders and is wearing make-up that appears to be smeared. The man is also about 25 years old. He is about 5 feet 11 inches tall and weighs about 175 pounds. His hair is short and light brown. A man walking his dog found the victims on the porch of the house.

The keys to the house are in the door, but the door is locked. Neither victim has any identification. There is a large brown purse open on the ground, with the contents emptied onto the ground. The man's wallet has not been found. Neither victim is wearing any jewelry, although each victim has a light trace of a line on the ring finger of the left hand. The man is fully clothed, but the woman is naked from the waist down.

The man's body has 12 wounds that appear to be stab wounds, and there are several cuts on his hands and forearms. The woman's neck is bruised, and she has a single stab wound just under her sternum, or breastbone.

After an autopsy and a laboratory examination, the following information is provided:

The man had three deep stab wounds to the chest, any of which could have been fatal. Each of these wounds was six inches deep and had severed one or more arteries. In addition, he had nine shallow stab wounds, varying in depth from one inch to two inches, none in lethal locations. The wounds had been made by a single-edged cutting instrument, such as a single-edged knife.

The woman's neck showed signs of fingers imprinted in her bruises. She died from asphyxiation, caused by a crushed windpipe. The single stab wound was six inches deep, but was inflicted after death. The wound was pointed at both ends of the entry, making it consistent with a double-edged cutting instrument, such as a bayonet or a double-edged knife. There was semen in the woman's vagina. Laboratory tests of the semen revealed three separate blood types, including one matching the dead man's blood type.

INVESTIGATIVE SKILL BUILDERS

Acquiring and Evaluating Information

You and your partner answer a radio call to investigate a house burglary. When you arrive, you take a look around the house while your partner talks to the victim. You check ground-level windows and doors. At the back door, you find that the glass pane nearest the door lock has been broken. You look on the floor, but there are very few glass shards there. You look through the door's window and see a pile of broken glass lying on the ground outside the house.

As you continue looking around the house, you note that all the windows in the house are securely locked. In the living room, a large area rug has been rolled back, and a floor safe under it is open. You peer into the safe and see that it is empty. There are several empty jewelry boxes, from rings and bracelets or necklaces, lying around the opening of the safe.

As you reenter the room where your partner is speaking with the homeowner, the victim asks your partner when he should contact his insurance company about the burglary. You observe that the victim seems very calm about the entire situation. At no time does the victim ask whether you or your partner think the burglar will be caught.

1. What might you deduce from the broken pane of glass in the back door?

2. What might you induce about the burglary itself?

3. What kinds of questions might you ask the victim at this point in the investigation?

Integrity/Honesty

You make a routine traffic stop of a woman driving at excessive speed. You obtain her driver's license and begin writing her a ticket. She begins to cry. She tells you it is her third speeding offense and, not only will she probably lose her license, but also her husband will beat her. She begs you not to write the ticket. What action will you take in this situation?

Problem Solving

You have been called to a backyard pool. When you arrive, you see a woman in a bathing suit lying motionless on her back. Emergency medical service (EMS) personnel motion to you. As you near the woman, they inform you that she has drowned. They also say that she has a large bump on the side of her head.

A man is sitting at a metal patio table about six feet from the body. He is wearing casual clothing and sneakers. He is restrained and seems calm. You speak with him and learn that he is the woman's husband and was inside the house when he heard his wife call for help. He tells you, "By the time I got out back, it was too late. She was already dead." He explains that he left his wife's body in the pool and called the EMS, who pulled his wife's body from the water after they arrived.

1. What can you induce about the man's story?

2. What kinds of questions are you going to ask the husband?

ENDNOTES

1. *Webster's Third New International Dictionary* (unabridged), Encyclopaedia Britannica, Chicago, 1995.

2. Edwin H. Sutherland and Donald C. Cressey, *Criminology,* 9th ed., Lippincott, Philadelphia, 1974.

3. Brent LaLonde, "Police: Killing Followed Abduction Near Fairgrounds," *The Columbus Dispatch,* September 25, 1996, p. 4B; "Fingerprints Lead to Slaying Suspects," *The Columbus Dispatch,* September 26, 1996, pp. 1A–2A; Brent LaLonde and Tim Doulin, "3 Suspects Have Criminal Convictions," *The Columbus Dispatch,* September 27, 1996, p. 2A; Tim Doulin, "Third Suspect in Student's Slaying to Be Tried as Adult," *The Columbus Dispatch,* December, 18, 1996, p. 3C.

CHAPTER 2

The Preliminary Investigation

CHAPTER OBJECTIVES

After completing this chapter, you will be able to:

1. Understand the importance of the preliminary investigation.

2. Describe the responsibilities of investigators at the crime scene.

3. Discuss the value of accurate note taking at crime scenes.

4. Explain what is meant by the *corpus delicti* of a crime.

5. Distinguish between *prima facie* and circumstantial evidence.

6. Explain how the rules of evidence affect investigative procedures.

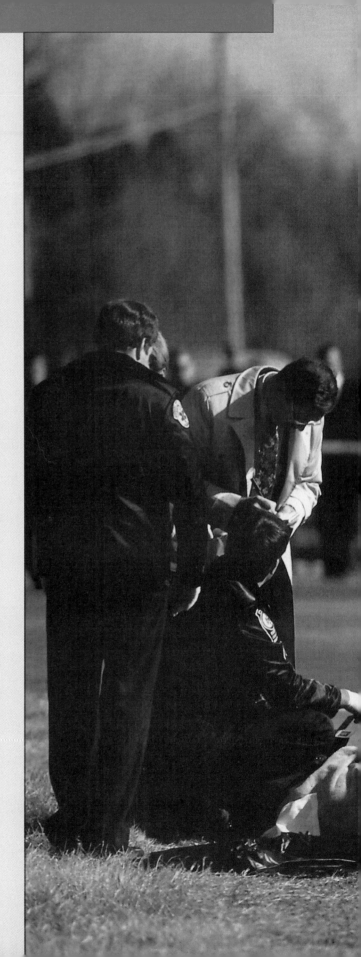

Initial Response

Preliminary investigation
Fact-gathering activities that take place at the scene of a crime immediately after the crime has been reported to or discovered by police officers.

The fact-gathering activities that take place at the scene of a crime immediately after the crime has been reported to or discovered by police officers are all part of the **preliminary investigation.** In most cases, many of these activities are initially undertaken by members of the uniformed patrol of the police agency responding to the call for assistance.[1]

Sometimes a call to the police requires immediate action to save a life or apprehend an offender. It may be a call for a robbery in progress, an assault, a riot, a domestic disturbance, or a prowler. Other types of crimes, such as prostitution, illegal gambling, auto theft, passing bad checks, or various forms of fraud, may not require an immediate response but will be handled in due time.

When responding officers arrive at a crime scene, they often find a situation filled with confusion. The scene of a bank robbery may include frightened or injured customers and employees. At an assault or rape scene, a number of well-meaning people may be watching or comforting the victim. After a burglary, family members may feel unsafe in their home. In any of these situations, the responding officer must remain calm and take charge.

A preliminary investigation may be the prelude to an in-depth investigation. In larger departments, detectives typically carry out the in-depth investigation. They also conduct the follow-up investigation, apprehend the offender, and prepare the case for court. In smaller departments, the responding officer is more often responsible for both the preliminary investigation and the follow-up investigation. The roles and responsibilities of uniformed officers and detectives, therefore, are not always distinguishable. Much will depend on the size of the agency that undertakes the preliminary investigation.

The initial information from the preliminary investigation, regardless of who collects it, provides the foundation for the eventual criminal case against a suspect. The failure to carefully collect, accurately record, and skillfully process all the available information will leave the follow-up investigation without the benefit of all the existing evidence. It may necessitate repeating much of the preliminary investigation and may lead to the loss of valuable evidence.

The partnership of patrol officers and detectives might be compared to that of a baseball team. If the players do not support their pitcher in the field and at bat, they cannot win the ball

STATISTICS

A study of police fast-response times in Florida, Illinois, New York, and California showed that only 2.9 percent of all responses resulted in immediate suspect apprehension. A major reason this rate is so low is that only 25 percent of the calls received concerned crimes in progress, those for which a fast response is critical.[2]

game. Likewise, if errors of omission or commission are made in the handling of an investigation, the case may be lost in court.

The Crime Scene

The scene of the crime is the focus of the preliminary investigation. As part of their preparation on the way to the crime scene, officers should create a list of things to consider upon arriving at the crime scene. Many officers keep a list of things to do at the crime scene in their field notebooks. A checklist like that in Figure 2–1 can ensure that officers do not forget any aspect of the preliminary investigation.

Deal With Emergency Situations

The first responsibility of any law enforcement officer is to protect and preserve the personal safety of the public. When arriving at the scene of a criminal call, the responding officer should quickly determine if anyone is injured or needs medical treatment and should summon the necessary health professionals.

Determine If a Crime Has Been Committed

Officers usually determine if a crime has been committed and what that crime is as soon as possible after arriving on the scene. Doing so requires visual inspection of the area and interviews with any victims and witnesses. Such activities provide the responding officer with information about whether the situation involves a criminal act. Furthermore, the officer can determine if additional assistance is required.

Establish Crime Scene Priorities

When the responding officer arrives, he or she must decide on a plan of action. Sometimes this is dictated by the flow of observed events. If the scene involves an emergency, such as a hit-and-run accident or a shooting, there may be injured persons who need immediate medical attention. In another situation, an officer may arrive and come under fire from unknown assailants. This, of course, would change the officer's plan of action.

Quick thinking and good judgment are essential for responding officers. Sometimes decisions are simple, and there is sufficient time to consider options. Frequently, however, crime scene conditions require split-second decisions. If an officer arrives at the scene of a crime, sees a

Figure 2–1 Crime scene investigation checklist.

Victim

1. Identify and treat the victim, or obtain proper medical care as needed.
2. Interview the victim if he or she is able to speak.
3. Get a description of the offender.
4. Broadcast a general description of the event and the offender's description.

Evidence

1. Determine what type of evidence is present. Are there any specific needs, such as special technical assistance, photography, care in preservation and securing of items, or casting?
2. What elements of real or direct evidence have been found? List and detail each item.
3. What elements of circumstantial evidence are present or identified from interviews?

Witnesses

1. Obtain and confirm the identity of each witness.
2. Separate all witnesses.
3. Conduct a separate interview with each witness.
4. Determine relationships of witnesses with the victim, the offender, and other witnesses.
5. Determine where they were positioned during the incident and what they were doing.
6. Obtain a description from them of the offender.

Method of Operation

1. Indicate how the crime was committed.
2. Indicate the time the crime occurred.
3. Indicate where the crime occurred.
4. Were any weapons used? If so, what weapons?
5. Who was involved in the incident? Indicate all parties.
6. Was anyone injured? If so, indicate the nature and extent of the injuries.
7. How did the offender arrive at and leave the scene?
8. Check with headquarters concerning similar types of crimes occurring recently.

Property Involved

1. Was any property taken? If so, what property?
2. Was any property damaged? If so, what was it, and to what extent was it damaged?
3. What is the value of the property taken or damaged?
4. Are there any identifying marks on any of the items taken?
5. Were any weapons taken?

person shoot another person, and then sees the shooter run away, should the officer tend the injured party or take chase and try to apprehend the shooter? Typically, one would expect the officer to try to save the wounded person's life. The responding officer may have to take a **dying declaration,** a statement given by the victim in anticipation of death. However, if the officer believes nothing can be done to save the wounded person's life, pursuing the assailant is the better alternative. After killing one person, the assailant poses the threat of injuring or killing others.

Identify a Suspect

Officers responding to a call may see a suspect fleeing the scene and give chase. Or the victim and eyewitnesses, if any, may provide a description of the perpetrator. Officers, familiar with crime patterns in the area, may recognize the perpetrator's *modus operandi* (method of operation) and identify a suspect in the crime. If the suspect has fled, the investigator might request a broadcast of the description of the suspect, his or her vehicle, if any, and the direction of flight.

Descriptions should set one person apart from another to make identification and eventual apprehension of the suspect easier. Every characteristic or feature added to a description eliminates suspects, reducing the broad field in which the search is to be made. Remember, though, that witnesses sometimes exaggerate their descriptions. An average-sized man sometimes looks much larger when holding a gun aimed at a victim. Looking up at a criminal who has knocked you down may alter your perspective on height or weight. Furthermore, a person's state of mind during the course of a crime may affect his or her ability to describe a suspect.

To overcome these problems, investigators typically use comparison descriptions. A **comparison description** allows the witness to look at a person whose height is known and note the similarities and differences between that person and the suspect. A comparison can also be obtained by having a witness compare the suspect's height with the height of a doorway or some object in the room. In some convenience stores, managers hang a ruled edge the length of the doorjamb, allowing the clerk to see approximately how tall a person is as he or she passes through the doorway.

In most cases, the witness has seen the suspect only briefly—and that under distressing circumstances. The average witness will not be able to recall all the characteristics in detail. However, with proper interviewing and the use of comparisons, an experienced investigator should be able to draw out a fairly detailed description of the suspect. When there are many witnesses, a **composite description** should be compiled from all the interviews. In other words, if in eight descriptions the height of a suspect is 5′8″, 5′8″, 5′9″, 5′9″, 5′10″, 5′9″ or

Communications/Video Systems LEFT: When every second counts, communications control consoles make it possible for dispatchers to relay critical information to field officers and investigators. RIGHT: A video camera is situated next to the rear-view mirror in this patrol car. A video monitor shows all the action. The videotape supports the officer's observations and report.

10″, 5′10″, and 5′11″, the composite for the suspect's height averages out to approximately 5′8–10″.

At a minimum, the description of a suspect should include the following: race; approximate age; height; weight; build; complexion; color of hair; hairline and hairstyle; speech characteristics; the basic shape of ears, eyes, nose, and mouth; dental features, such as overbite, underbite, or missing or discolored teeth; facial hair; and chin and head shape. An investigator should seek out any peculiarities or features witnesses recall about a suspect. Any single unusual feature, such as a tattoo, scar, or blemish, may eliminate hundreds of suspects. In addition, officers should obtain descriptions of the suspect's clothing. Was the suspect wearing a baseball cap or another kind of hat? What color were the suspect's shirt, pants, and shoes? Did witnesses notice any items of jewelry, such as a watch, pin, necklace, or ring?

Apprehend the Suspect

Apprehending suspects is best accomplished when officers act immediately, as when an arrest is made at the scene of the crime. Unfortunately, this is not typically the case. In fact, research shows that only about 21 percent of all crimes reported to the police are eventually cleared by an arrest. The proportion of cases that result in an arrest at the scene is appreciably smaller. In some cases, as when there is a silent alarm, coincidental observation by officers, or a very fast response, police do arrive on the scene while suspects are still present and can be taken into custody.

When suspects are taken into custody, they are usually "Mirandized," or given a **Miranda warning** informing them of their constitutional rights. **Custody** is loosely defined as a situation in which an officer has deprived a suspect of liberty and the suspect feels he or she is not free to leave. A rule of thumb police officers follow is to Mirandize whenever the conversation with a suspect changes from an interview or questioning to an interrogation. If a suspect is arrested, the *Miranda* warning must be given before interrogation.

In other cases, a suspect may flee just as the officers arrive. Under such circumstances, they may pursue the fleeing suspect. If the suspect leaves the officer's jurisdiction while being pursued, the chase is called a **hot pursuit.** If the suspect has already fled when the officer arrives, the officer should quickly relay descriptive information to other police units.

Miranda warning A cautionary statement to suspects in police custody, advising them of their rights to remain silent and to have an attorney present during interrogation.

Custody Detainment by a police officer; a situation in which a person feels he or she is not free to leave.

Hot pursuit The crossing of jurisdictional lines to chase a suspect.

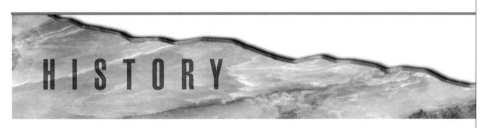

HISTORY

In March 1963, Ernesto Miranda was arrested for the rape and kidnapping of an 18-year-old woman. The victim selected Miranda from a police lineup, and the police questioned him for two hours. During questioning, Miranda was not told that he could remain silent or have a lawyer. Miranda confessed, was convicted, and then appealed. In Miranda v. Arizona (1966), the Supreme Court reversed the conviction.[3] The Court ruled that suspects must be clearly informed of their rights before police question them. Unless they are so informed, their statements may not be used in court. Ernesto Miranda was later retried (under an assumed name) for the same offenses of rape and kidnapping. His original confession was not used, but he was convicted on the basis of other evidence gathered by the police. After serving time in prison, Miranda was released on parole. He was killed in 1972 in a skid row card game in Phoenix, Arizona.

Gather and Preserve Evidence

The crime scene should be protected against interference by unauthorized people. It should remain secured until the investigators have examined it for evidence and have released it. Securing it may require covering suspected items with paper, boxes, or plastic. It may also require setting up barricades around areas or stationing officers to guard pieces of evidence.

Before the physical evidence is gathered, the crime scene should be photographed and sketched. In some cases, a search for latent fingerprints may be undertaken. Casts of footprints, tracks, and tool impressions should be made when these are present. Generally speaking, an item should be considered a piece of evidence if it fits any one of the following categories:

- It has the potential to offer clues to the suspect's identity (fingerprints, footprints, hair, skin scrapings, and so forth).
- It tends to suggest the manner or method in which the crime was committed (weapons, documents, tools, or other instruments).
- It is not usually found at that location. Out-of-place items may have been left or moved by the suspect.

When gathering and preserving evidence, officers should never touch anything with the naked hand or move anything before it has been recorded and cataloged. The investigator's goal is to protect all the evidence and make sure that no one touches, moves, or removes it. After securing the crime scene, investigators can request technical assistance in gathering evidence. Officers and investigators must maintain an irrefutable **chain of custody** for all evidence found, documenting its possession from the time it is discovered until it is produced in court. Procedures for gathering and preserving evidence will be more fully described in Chapters 3 and 4.

Chain of custody Proof of the possession of evidence from the moment it is found until the moment it is offered in evidence.

Recording the Crime Scene

Among the many activities undertaken at the crime scene, one of the most important is note taking. There are several reasons for the critical importance of taking notes in a criminal investigation, particularly at the preliminary stage. First, taking notes requires investigators to commit their observations to writing. Second, it allows them to keep a detailed, chronological record of everything they see and do. It is not unusual for some seemingly unimportant item in the investigator's notes to become

Many states, counties, and cities have criminal investigators who are not assigned to the state, municipal, or sheriff's department. Rather, they are employed by public agencies with specialized regulatory responsibilities with police power. The names and functions of these agencies vary among states and localities, but can include such agencies as alcoholic beverage license and control, gambling and wagering commission, bureau of taxation and finance, environmental conservation, and industrial safety commission. As employees of such agencies, investigators assure that the role of the agency is carried out according to the guidelines established by the state, county, or municipality.

The work may involve investigating and apprehending persons involved in criminal activities as agency employees, as persons doing business with the agency, or as individuals over whom the agency has licensing or regulatory control. For example, an investigator working for the state inspector general's office may investigate the possibility of fraud, waste, and abuse at a financially troubled state university and recommend that school officials face criminal charges. Like other investigators, agency investigators gather information about suspects, study records, set up surveillance, conduct court-ordered wiretaps, execute search warrants, participate in raids, and operate as undercover agents.

Education requirements will vary depending on the location and specific nature of an agency's role. Some positions may require a college degree and related experience, in addition to passing a civil service examination. Training requirements will vary with each agency as will the need for the use of firearms.

a pivotal point in the prosecution of the suspect. Third, carefully prepared records can also provide a mechanism for jogging an investigator's memory when he or she testifies in court.

Field notes should be neat, legible, and comprehensive. Notes that are sloppy or incomplete or have mixed-up chronology can be misinterpreted later or lead to inaccurate descriptions in court. Be as specific as possible in taking notes in the field. For example, avoid saying that a weapon was found *near* a victim. Instead, specify the distance from the victim. Also indicate the time that an item of evidence was discovered. Notes should be complete enough for someone to read them 25 years later and still have a clear idea of what was found and done by investigators at the crime scene.

Whether they are from a preliminary or follow-up investigation, complete and accurate notes are critically important. They should be taken on every call, or contact, made by an officer while conducting an investigation. Each contact should then be followed by an appropriate report. Not only are these reports important for possible use at trial, but they allow the department head to render accurate accounts of officers' time to the city manager, mayor, city council, or board of supervisors.

When creating field notes, officers are often guided by questions concerning *who, what, when, where, how,* and *why.* Answers to these questions, along with other elements of evidence and physical identification, are key pieces of information for later reports. Figure 2–2 shows how these questions might be formulated into a set of guidelines to assist a preliminary investigation.

Figure 2–2 Guidelines for writing field notes.

Who were the people involved (names, ages, residences, businesses, telephone numbers, descriptions)? Who did what to or with whom? Who saw or heard anything of importance? Who handled the evidence? Who discovered the crime? Who had custody of the property last?

What happened? What crime was committed? What time did it occur? What weapon was used? What is the suspect's method of operation? What was the reason for the crime? What was taken? What vehicle, if any, was involved?

When did the crime occur (time of day)? When was the crime discovered? When were the police notified? When was the victim last seen? When was the property last seen?

Where did the crime occur? Where was the victim at the time? Where were the witnesses? Where was the suspect first seen? Where was the suspect last seen? From where was the property taken?

How was the crime committed? How did the suspect get to the scene? How did the suspect leave or make a getaway? How many people were involved? How much money or property was taken?

Why was the crime committed (what events preceded the offense)? Why did so much time elapse before the police were notified? Why was this particular victim attacked? Why was the criminal act committed in this particular way?

Specificity is important in creating field notes. (See Figure 2–3.) Be careful not to accept vague comments, such as "He was young" or "He was old," or even "He was tall" or "He was short." Clarify these comments by asking, "Approximately how old would you say the suspect was?" or, "Approximately how tall was the suspect?" When property has been taken, descriptive data should include the quantity and kind of article taken, the

Figure 2–3 Sample field notes.

```
                                                          03-07-98
              Case # 12345
              Time: 1200 hours
              Burglary - at 5 Klamath, Irvine, CA.
              Victim - Jane Jones
              Tel. # 555-1234

              Victim Jones states she returned home from shopping at
              1100 hours.
              States she found her front door open - but she says she is
              certain it was closed & locked when she left (no sign of
  Window     forced entry).
  may have
  been
  jimmied    Victim Jones states the following items are missing:
              1 - Panasonic Stackable Stereo
                - serial # unknown
                - smoke gray & black in color
                - small chip on left corner (front) of phono dust cover
                - value: $465

              2 - G.E. Color Television
                - wood grain color
                - serial # unknown
                - no special identifying marks
                - value: $249
```

trade name, a physical description, serial numbers, personal identifying marks, any damage, the age, the condition, and the current estimated market value. It is a good idea never to leave the scene of a crime or end an interview until you are satisfied that you have accumulated all available information. For police notes, the operative maxim is "More is better."

Field notes are the major frame of reference and raw source from which operational reports are prepared. Since the demands of a case often require field notes to be taken down out of order or by several people, unavoidable interruptions and sequence problems may occur. To overcome these sorts of problems, many officers rely on a loose-leaf notebook, recording each interview on a separate sheet of paper. A loose-leaf binder allows the investigator to sort pertinent notes together while maintaining chronology. Notes can be organized and reorganized as necessary to prepare operational reports.

Recently, some officers have begun using microcassette recorders to tape-record their field notes. If you choose this route, make a written transcription of your field recordings as quickly as possible to ensure their accuracy. Remember, in most jurisdictions, an officer's field notes—whether written or recorded—can be subpoenaed during a criminal court case. Inaccurate field notes can lose a criminal conviction in the same way that accurate ones might win the case.

It is imperative to maintain a written record of all phases of investigation, including preliminary and follow-up procedures. These notes will be the basis for all reports and may be entered as evidence.

Ideally, once operational reports are complete, field notes or copies of them should be placed in the file of the case to which they relate. Many officers retain copies of their field notes. Notes made at the time of the investigation can be used later to refresh the officer's memory in court. Defense counsel have the right to cross-examine an officer on his or her testimony. Therefore, field notes should be neat, legible, accurate, and written in an understandable fashion. A number of police agencies across the country employ technical writers to train their officers how to keep accurate and literate field notes.

The Legal Significance of Evidence

Responding officers are typically responsible for certain aspects of the preliminary investigation. For example, an officer arriving on the scene of an incident must immediately determine what has happened and whether anyone is injured. The officer must assess whether a crime has been committed and, if so, what type of crime. Should the initial allegations prove unfounded or the acts noncriminal, the matter can be closed with the first report. If, on the other hand, the officer's findings indicate that a criminal law has been violated, then proof of the *corpus delicti* of the particular offense must be established. ***Corpus delicti,*** which is Latin for "body of the crime," is the material facts showing that a crime has been committed. It includes all the physical elements that, taken together, demonstrate that a crime has been committed.

To sustain a conviction, it is necessary to establish that the elements of a crime, as defined in criminal law, have occurred. These elements must be demonstrated. For example, in a murder, it is not the dead body that is the *corpus delicti*. Rather, it is evidence that the death occurred as a result of some criminal act. A broken pane of glass or pry marks on the edge of a door might be the *corpus delicti* in a burglary case. The identity of the perpetrator is not usually an element of the *corpus delicti* in a crime. At each crime scene, investigators must know and keep in mind the requirements to prove that a crime has been committed. They must try to find evidence that meets those requirements.

Sometimes, the *corpus delicti* of a crime can be established on the basis of ***prima facie* evidence,** that is, the evidence is good and sufficient on its face to establish a given fact. Suppose an officer stops a motorist who is driving in an erratic fashion. Noting the driver's slurred speech after having observed the irregular driving pattern, the officer decides to administer a field sobriety test. Failure of this test is taken to mean that the driver's blood alcohol level is at least 0.1 percent, evidence of intoxication in that state. The officer can now arrest the driver for driving under the influence of alcohol, basing the arrest on *prima facie* evidence. In some states, such as Pennsyl-

Corpus delicti All the material facts showing that a crime has been committed; Latin for "body of the crime."

Prima facie evidence Evidence good and sufficient on its face to establish a given fact or chain of facts and, if not rebutted or contradicted, to be proof of that fact; Latin for "on the surface."

vania, drivers who refuse to take a breath or blood analysis for alcohol have their licenses revoked whether they are guilty or not. In effect, refusing to submit to the test constitutes *prima facie* evidence of guilt.

Had the officer in the preceding example used only the driving pattern and the slurred speech to determine that the driver was intoxicated, the officer would have been relying on circumstantial evidence. **Circumstantial evidence** is evidence of associated facts from which deductions can be drawn to show indirectly the facts to be proved. Circumstantial evidence is not always as useful as some other forms of evidence. For example, the driver's erratic driving pattern and slurred speech might be the results of fatigue and a speech impediment rather than alcohol. In many cases, however, any or all of the elements of a crime can be proved by circumstantial evidence. By using *deductive reasoning* (see Chapter 1), the investigator can conclude from a series of known elements that a crime has occurred.

Circumstantial evidence Evidence of other facts from which deductions can be drawn to show indirectly the facts to be proved.

Rules of Evidence

When a suspect is apprehended at the crime scene or shortly thereafter, the evidence collected by the officer in the preliminary investigation becomes the basis of the charges the state then brings against the defendant. Every criminal investigator must have a working knowledge of the **rules of evidence** to ensure that the evidence collected during the investigation will be admissible in court.

Admissibility is the essence of the rules of evidence. Virtually anything may be admitted in court as evidence, provided there is no rule that prohibits its admissibility. Rules concerning the limitation or exclusion of evidence in a court case center on a doctrine known as the **exclusionary rule.** According to this rule, where evidence has been obtained in violation of the rights guaranteed by the U.S. Constitution, that evidence must be excluded at trial. The exclusionary rule is grounded in the Fourth Amendment and is intended to protect citizens from illegal searches and seizures. In practice, it means that police officers and investigators must abide by certain guidelines when searching for and seizing material that may be used as evidence in a court of law.

Three tests—relevancy, materiality, and competency—govern a judge's ruling

Rules of evidence Rules of court that govern the admissibility of evidence at trials and hearings.

Exclusionary rule The rule that evidence that has been obtained in violation of constitutional guarantees against unlawful search and seizure cannot be used at trial.

FYI

A system of rules and procedures for presenting evidence in U.S. courts has developed over the past 200 years. Originally derived from the English legal system, these *rules of evidence* have been significantly amended through federal and state court decisions and legislative actions. Today, the Uniform Rules of Evidence, the Federal Rules of Evidence, and state rules, such as the Maine Rules of Evidence and the California Evidence Code, set the standards of admissibility against which evidence will be judged.

Police investigators must know the guidelines for admissibility of evidence.

on admissibility of evidence. **Relevancy** is the applicability of evidence in determining the truth or falsity of the issue being tried. Relevant evidence relates to, or bears directly upon, the point or fact at issue, from which inferences can be drawn.

Even if the evidence is relevant, it may be denied admissibility if it is such an insignificant point that it will not affect the outcome of the case. **Materiality** is the importance of the evidence in influencing the court's opinion on an issue. In other words, is the evidence important enough to take up the court's time with it?

Finally, evidence must pass the test of competency. **Competency** is the quality of a piece of evidence and/or of a person offering evidence. If the credibility of a piece of evidence or of an individual offering evidence is faulty, the value of the evidence diminishes, and it may be ruled inadmissible.

Suppose, for example, that prosecutors in a case involving a series of letter bombs want to introduce various materials, found in the suspected bomber's home, that could be used to construct bombs. To have

Relevancy The applicability of evidence in determining the truth or falsity of the issue being tried; a requirement for admissibility in court.

Materiality The importance of evidence in influencing the court's opinion because of its connection with the issue; a requirement for admissibility in court.

Competency The quality of evidence, or its fitness to be presented to assist in determining questions of fact; a requirement for admissibility in court; also used to describe a witness as legally fit and qualified to give testimony.

them ruled admissible, the prosecution must demonstrate the relevancy of the materials to the case. In other words, a link between the specific types of bomb-making materials found in the suspect's home and those used in the letter bombs has to be shown. Certainly, items used to make bombs are material to a case brought against a suspected letter bomber. The competency of the evidence can be shown by having officers and forensic scientists with ample training and experience explain the relationship between the materials found at the home and the bombs.

SUMMARY BY LEARNING OBJECTIVES

Learning Objective 1

The information gathered in the preliminary investigation provides the foundation for the eventual court case against a criminal suspect. This information must be carefully collected, accurately recorded, and skillfully processed.

Learning Objective 2

During the preliminary investigation, investigators should fulfill these responsibilities: deal with emergency situations, determine if a crime has been committed, establish crime scene priorities, identify a suspect, apprehend the suspect, and gather and preserve evidence.

Learning Objective 3

Maintaining clear, literate, and accurate field notes during all phases of an investigation is absolutely essential to preparing a good report and a solid case against a defendant. Field notes are the source from which operational reports are prepared.

Learning Objective 4

Corpus delicti, which is Latin for "body of the crime," is the material facts showing that a crime has been committed. It includes all the physical elements that demonstrate that a crime has been committed. To sustain a conviction, the elements of a crime, as defined in criminal law, have to be established and demonstrated.

Evidence collected at a crime scene may be of two types: *prima facie* evidence, which is good and sufficient on its face to establish a given fact, and circumstantial evidence, which is indirect evidence or associated facts from which conclusions can be drawn.

Learning Objective 6

Evidence collected at a crime scene must pass three tests of admissibility in court: relevancy (is it proper to apply it to determining the truth or falsity of the issue being tried?), materiality (is it important enough to influence the court?), and competency (is the quality of the evidence or the witness explaining it free of faults?). Evidence also must be gathered without violating a person's constitutional rights against unlawful search and seizure.

QUESTIONS FOR REVIEW

Learning Objective 1

1. What is a preliminary investigation?

Learning Objective 2

2. Define *dying declaration, comparison description, composite description, hot pursuit,* and *chain of custody.*

3. Enumerate the investigative responsibilities at a crime scene.

4. Why must an officer secure a crime scene upon arrival?

5. What method could you use to help a victim or a witness provide as accurate a description as possible of a suspect?

6. When are suspects generally given a *Miranda* warning, and what is it?

Learning Objective 3

7. List the six basic questions that an investigator's field notes should answer about a crime.

Learning Objective 4

8. What is the meaning and importance of the term *corpus delicti?*

Learning Objective 5

9. With which type of evidence—*prima facie* or circumstantial—would an investigator be most apt to use deductive reasoning?

10. What is meant by the exclusionary rule? Why is it significant for criminal investigators?

11. Identify three tests that a judge might apply to evidence gathered at a crime scene to determine its admissibility in court.

CRITICAL THINKING INVESTIGATIVE EXERCISE

You are a police officer dispatched by radio to assist Officer Murray, already on the scene checking out a suspicious person in a supermarket parking lot. As you turn your cruiser into the parking lot, you hear two gunshots and see Officer Murray falling to the ground as the car he was standing near speeds away with wheels squealing. What actions will you take? Explain your answer.

INVESTIGATIVE SKILL BUILDERS

Acquiring and Evaluating Information

Go around the room and count off, alternating the number one and the number two. Ask the instructor to flip a coin to determine whether the ones or the twos will be the investigators; the other group will be witnesses. Now ask your instructor to leave the room for about 15 minutes. Working in pairs, the investigators should interview the witnesses to obtain a description of the suspect—your instructor. Try to include information about the following characteristics: race; approximate age; height; weight; build; complexion; color of hair; hairline and hairstyle; type of speech; the basic shape of ears, eyes, nose, and mouth; dental features, such as overbite, underbite, or missing or discolored teeth; chin and head shape; facial hair; unusual eyebrows; and scars, blemishes, or tattoos. Also include clothing descriptions. Investigators should record the descriptions as field notes. When your instructor returns, read aloud the descriptions to compare their accuracy.

Integrity/Honesty

You are the first to arrive at the crime scene. After looking around and acquiring the necessary information about victims and witnesses, you begin to secure the scene. While doing so, you unconsciously light a cigarette. When you finish smoking, you casually drop the butt on the ground within the crime scene. Later, you notice that one of the forensic technicians has found, bagged, and tagged your cigarette butt. Will you tell the detective leading the crime scene investigation that it is your cigarette butt? Explain.

Problem Solving

You and your partner arrive on the scene of an armed robbery of a convenience store. It is not clear whether the suspect has fled. There are five people in the store.

1. What do you do upon arriving at the scene?
2. Should you assume the suspect has fled and treat the people as victims?
3. What precautions might you take to protect yourself, your partner, and the victims?

ENDNOTES

1. Bruce L. Berg, *Law Enforcement: An Introduction to Police in Society,* Allyn and Bacon, Boston, 1992.
2. W. G. Spelman, and D. K. Brown, *Calling the Police: A Replication of the Citizen Reporting Component of the Kansas City Response Time Analysis.* Police Foundation, Washington, 1981.
3. *Miranda v. Arizona,* 384 U.S. 436, 444 (1966).
4. "Crime Scene Matters," *FBI Evidence Response Teams,* Department of Justice, Washington, no date (manual used for training in 1996).

CHAPTER 3

Preserving the Crime Scene

CHAPTER OBJECTIVES

After completing this chapter, you will be able to:

1. Discuss the role of evidence in criminal investigation.

2. List the eight basic steps of gathering and preserving evidence at a crime scene.

3. Identify what investigators consider the location of a crime scene.

4. Explain the importance of photography in preserving a crime scene.

5. Tell how crime scene sketches complement still photography, and list the five methods used to prepare sketches.

6. Give the five search patterns from which investigators may choose when conducting a search.

7. Understand the importance of securing and preserving evidence found at a crime scene.

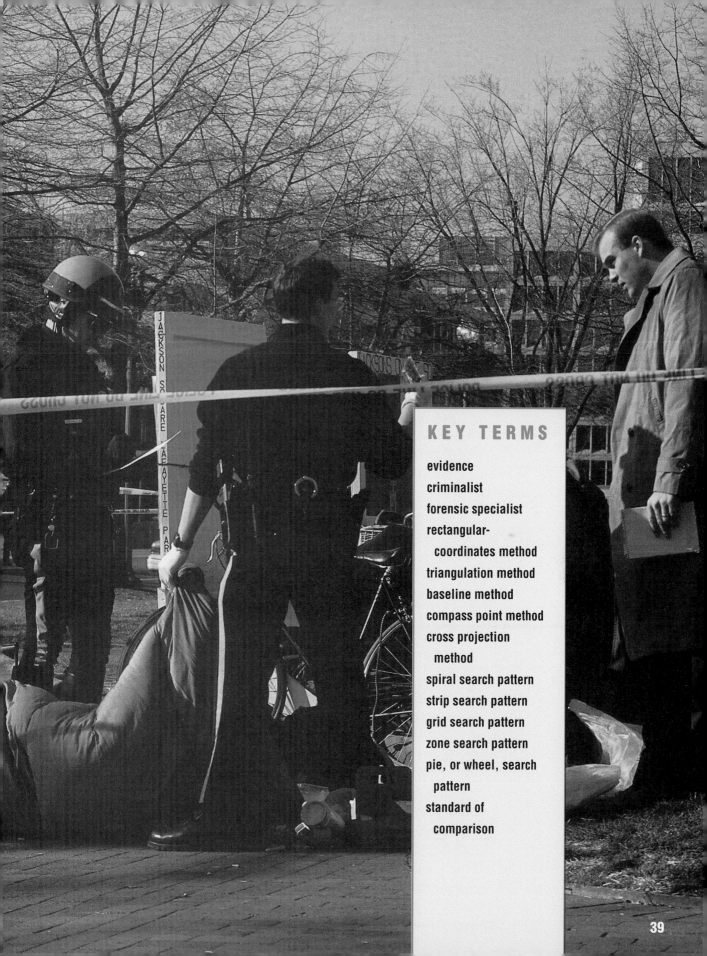

KEY TERMS

evidence
criminalist
forensic specialist
rectangular-
  coordinates method
triangulation method
baseline method
compass point method
cross projection
  method
spiral search pattern
strip search pattern
grid search pattern
zone search pattern
pie, or wheel, search
  pattern
standard of
  comparison

Evidence and the Crime Scene

Evidence   Any item that helps to establish the facts of a related criminal case. It may be found at the scene of the crime or on the victim or taken from the suspect or the suspect's environment.

Criminalist (or forensic specialist)   A person specifically trained to collect evidence and to make scientific tests and assessments of various types of physical evidence.

A criminal investigation must be concerned with both people and things. Together they constitute the field of physical evidence for an investigation and comprise the ingredients that, when combined, may produce a solution to a crime. Utilizing both human testimony and physical evidence, a prosecuting attorney will bring a case against a defendant. The prosecuting attorney can muster a strong case only if the investigators have done their job thoroughly. This means that they have effectively sought and collected *usable* evidence. **Evidence,** in criminal investigation, is any item that helps to establish the facts of a related criminal case. Evidence may be found at the scene of the crime or on the victim or taken from the suspect or the suspect's environment. How that evidence is protected, collected, secured, and transported will affect its later usefulness when introduced in a criminal court case.

Criminalists, or **forensic specialists,** are persons specifically trained to collect evidence and to make scientific tests and assessments of various types of physical evidence. In some jurisdictions, investigators can call on these trained technicians to aid in the search for evidence. In most preliminary investigations, however, the responding officer or investigator must take on the role of the forensic specialist. There are eight basic procedures that the investigator should keep in mind when gathering and preserving evidence at a crime scene.

1. Recognize or discover relevant physical evidence.
2. Examine evidence to determine that it can be tested or compared in a crime laboratory.
3. Collect evidence with care and diligence, according to standard procedures, and in a lawful manner.
4. Carefully handle, package, and label evidence to avoid breakage, loss, contamination, or questionable links in the chain of custody.
5. Carefully record how, where, and by whom evidence was located, to assure that there has been no tampering with or altering of evidence.
6. Carefully transport evidence to a laboratory, maintaining the proper chain of custody and security.
7. Maintain the integrity of the chain of custody from the crime lab to the court after tests have been completed.
8. Present or explain evidence in a court proceeding, substantiate the find, if necessary, and document the chain of custody.

To be effective in gathering evidence at a crime scene, an investigator must know what qualifies or is significant as physical evidence in a particular crime; how to properly collect, preserve, and transport the evidence; and what the crime lab can do with it. The crime laboratory is only as good as the investigator. If the investigator fails to locate adequate evidence, there is little a crime laboratory can do! Generally speaking, there are three main sources of evidence at the disposal of the investigator: (1) the scene of the crime, (2) the victim, if any, and (3) the suspect and his or her environment.

Among the decisions an investigator must make during the preliminary investigation is what constitutes the crime scene. The boundaries must be established so that the entire crime scene can be effectively preserved. The crime scene can be understood to include all areas in which the criminal, any possible victim, and any eyewitnesses moved during the time the crime was committed. Typically, one might expect this to include a fairly stable, limited area. In some crimes, however, the crime scene may actually comprise several different sites. For instance, say that a young girl was abducted from her bedroom one evening. She was then transported by car to a cabin in the woods and sexually assaulted. Following the assault, the abductor shot her to death and carried the body into the woods, where he buried it in a shallow grave. In this example, each location—the bedroom, the car, the cabin, and the area around the grave—is part of the crime scene. The boundaries of a given part of the crime scene, however, are well defined physically and must be preserved.

The ultimate success or failure of a criminal investigation depends on the thoroughness exercised at the crime scene in preserving, collecting, and recording all available information. Very often the position of an article in a room, in a lot, or in a building will convey to the trained eye the events preceding the crime. It is important to repeat, therefore, the rule that nothing at a crime scene should be touched, moved, or altered in any way until it has been identified, photographed, sketched, measured, and recorded.

Pictorial Documentation of the Crime Scene

One of the investigator's most important jobs at the crime scene is to create an accurate, objective visual record of the crime scene before any items or objects are moved or removed as possible elements of evidence. Photographs of the scene of a serious criminal act should be taken as soon as possible after preliminary investigation priorities have been taken care of, before note taking, sketching, or a search for evidence begins.

Photographing the Crime Scene

The role of photographs in a criminal investigation is to present a logical story visually. Nothing in the crime scene should be disturbed before photographs are taken. The pictures should illustrate the original, uncontaminated conditions of the crime scene. Photographs should be taken of the crime scene only, without spectators or police personnel. The photographs then become a comprehensive visual record of the crime scene and, if properly executed, help ensure a thorough investigation and a subsequent prosecution. A series of poorly planned and poorly executed photographs may result in a weak, ineffectual prosecution.

When photographing a crime scene, follow the axiom "More is better." That is, if there is a question whether some object or aspect of the scene should be photographed, it should be. Later, if it becomes apparent that some seemingly innocuous part of the scene was indeed important, but not photographed, it may be too late to photographically preserve it.

To adequately present the crime scene visually, the photographs must form an organized sequence and show all relevant locations and objects. One guideline for taking crime scene photographs is to progress from the general to the specific. This involves using three major types of vantage points: *long-range, mid-range,* and *close-up.* What constitutes a long-range, mid-range, or close-up photograph is somewhat relative. For instance, a long-range photograph of an apartment complex may be an aerial view of the entire area. A long-range photograph of a room may be a view from the doorway to the room. The actual vantage points will depend on the immediate area where the crime was committed and the kind of location involved.

A separate series of photographs should be taken for each distance. For instance, in a homicide investigation, the photographer might snap the following: *long-range* photographs of the overall scene, to show the murder scene as a person would view it from a standing position in the doorway and from different corners of the room, including the victim and all the objects in the room; *mid-range* photographs from different angles about eight or ten feet from the victim, omitting some of the objects shown in the long-range views; *close-up* photographs, taken from about five feet or less from the victim, showing wounds on the victim's body, an arm, leg, or torso, or objects close to the victim's body, such as a gun, empty cartridges, and blood patterns.[1]

Sometimes it may be necessary to include a measurement scale in photographs of objects at a crime scene. This helps those viewing the photographs understand the size and distance relationships depicted. Whenever practical, depending on the subject matter of the photograph, a measuring device should appear in the

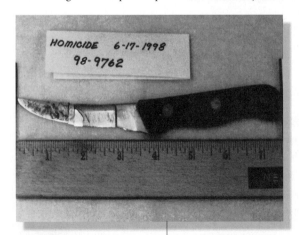

A measuring device helps to depict the size of the object.

HOMICIDE 6-17-1998
98-9762

Chapter 3 *Preserving the Crime Scene*

The progression of photographs from different distances helps to reconstruct the crime that was committed.

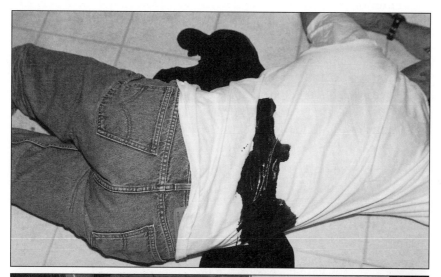

photograph along with the crime scene object. It is critical to note, however, that judges sometimes demand to see crime scene photographs without the clutter of extraneous scaling devices. Therefore, always remember to photograph subject matter at the crime scene as it is originally found. Then repeat the photograph with a scaling or identification marker.

The first photograph on every roll of film shot at the crime scene should be a title card (Figure 3–1) indicating the crime location, date, case identifier, photographer, and roll number. All subsequent photographs taken at the crime scene should be identified by number and entered in the photo log (see Figure 3–1).

Figure 3–1 Photo title card and photo log.

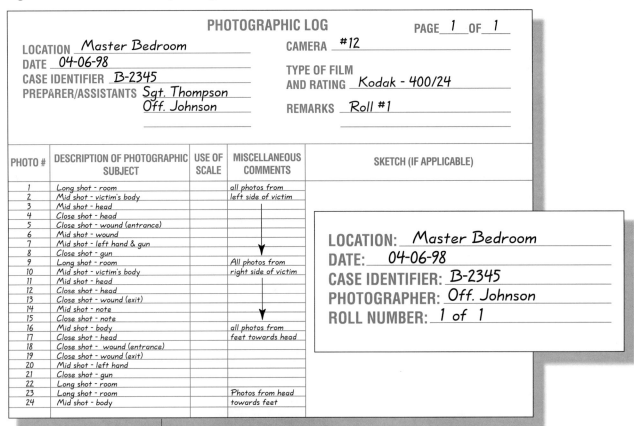

PHOTOGRAPHIC LOG   PAGE _1_ OF _1_

LOCATION _Master Bedroom_   CAMERA _#12_
DATE _04-06-98_
CASE IDENTIFIER _B-2345_   TYPE OF FILM
PREPARER/ASSISTANTS _Sgt. Thompson_   AND RATING _Kodak - 400/24_
Off. Johnson   REMARKS _Roll #1_

PHOTO #	DESCRIPTION OF PHOTOGRAPHIC SUBJECT	USE OF SCALE	MISCELLANEOUS COMMENTS	SKETCH (IF APPLICABLE)
1	Long shot - room		all photos from	
2	Mid shot - victim's body		left side of victim	
3	Mid shot - head			
4	Close shot - head			
5	Close shot - wound (entrance)			
6	Mid shot - wound			
7	Mid shot - left hand & gun			
8	Close shot - gun			
9	Long shot - room		All photos from	
10	Mid shot - victim's body		right side of victim	
11	Mid shot - head			
12	Close shot - head			
13	Close shot - wound (exit)			
14	Mid shot - note			
15	Close shot - note			
16	Mid shot - body		all photos from	
17	Close shot - head		feet towards head	
18	Close shot - wound (entrance)			
19	Close shot - wound (exit)			
20	Mid shot - left hand			
21	Close shot - gun			
22	Long shot - room			
23	Long shot - room		Photos from head	
24	Mid shot - body		towards feet	

LOCATION: _Master Bedroom_
DATE: _04-06-98_
CASE IDENTIFIER: _B-2345_
PHOTOGRAPHER: _Off. Johnson_
ROLL NUMBER: _1 of 1_

Videotaping the Crime Scene

As an adjunct to still photography of the crime scene, some departments and agencies have begun using video cameras and recorders. Videotaping equipment is relatively inexpensive and easy to operate, and it can provide a comprehensive and complete visual record of a crime scene. Provided that the operator is competent to use the video equipment, a videotape may be admissible in court. A videotape of a crime scene also allows the investigative team leader to examine the crime scene into which he or she deployed team members. Furthermore, rookie investigators can use videotapes of crime scenes to learn crime scene investigation techniques.

As with any investigative equipment, the results of videotaping are only as good as the quality of the equipment. A police department or agency considering the purchase of video equipment should buy the best it can afford. Buying inexpensive equipment may burden the agency with video recordings that are not sharp or clear enough to be submitted as evidence in court. It would be wise to assign an officer to thoroughly research the prices and capabilities of available video equipment. It may also be useful to ask other agencies in the area about their experiences videotaping crime scenes.

If your agency or department decides to go the video route, be sure to keep enough batteries and tapes on hand to allow complete recording of crime scenes. It is better to return to headquarters with several blank tapes and unused battery packs than to run short of tapes or lose power in the middle of taping. As a rule of thumb, 30-minute tapes are usually sufficient for videotaping a crime scene, although several may be necessary at some crime scenes. A 30-minute tape is easier to scan for particular segments than a 2-hour tape.

Police agencies should never become too dependent on videotaping, and it should never become a replacement for conventional still photography. Videotaping should augment and enhance sketches and still photography. It can record the continuous flow of investigative activities at a crime scene and serve as an additional check on the chronology of investigative events. Once videotaping has begun, it should continue uninterrupted. Even when the camera is moved from one location at the scene to another, it should continue running. Continuous taping ensures the recording of the chronology of events with no questionable gaps. When tapes or batteries are changed, the operator should indicate in the log the amount of time that elapses. The recording should then return to being continuous.

As with still photography, the first shot on each videotape should be a title card indicating the location and date of the taping, the case identifier, the video camera operator, and the videotape number. Also, as with still photographs, a log should be maintained, indicating what each numbered tape contains.

Videotaping of crime scenes follows the same basic guidelines as still photography. A slow, wide pan of an area furnishes a long-range view of the crime scene. A shot with the lens partially zoomed in offers a midrange view. A tight zoom delivers a close-up shot. When the taping is complete, the cassette should be clearly labeled and secured, as any other piece

FYI

In the Commonwealth of Pennsylvania, owing to privacy laws, it is a felony to audiotape anyone without that person's express permission. This includes the audio portion of videotapes, even those produced by retail surveillance cameras or cameras operated by police agencies.

of evidence is. Most tape cassettes have a tab that can be punched out to prevent recording over or erasing the tape. These tabs should be punched out immediately upon completion of videotaping.

Sketching the Crime Scene

Why, you might ask, should the crime scene be sketched if it has already been photographed or videotaped? Sketches are useful in the questioning of witnesses and suspects or the writing of investigative reports. Sketches are also excellent companions to photographs. Where photographs provide exacting details, sketches offer accurate information about the placement of objects, and they show relationships and distances between things. Sketches can be used to refresh an investigator's memory; to reflect the relationship of objects to the surrounding area; to help the prosecutor, judge, and jury understand conditions at the crime scene; and to supplement photographs of the scene.[2] See Figure 3–2 for a completed sketch of a homicide scene. Note how the sketch preparer depicted the locations of the victim, the gun cartridge cases, and the footprints.

Legally, for a sketch or diagram to be admissible in court, it must meet the following requirements:

- It must be part of a qualified person's testimony.
- It must recall the situation that the preparer saw.
- It must express the place or scene correctly.

Preparing the Sketch

A crime scene sketch complements the notes and photographs taken during the crime scene investigation. The purpose of the sketch is to present accurate information, not necessarily to be artistic. A simple line drawing with accurate measurements is sufficient. Some outdoor measurements may be paced off, estimated, or obtained by using the odometer of a car. However, in a final sketch for a report, precise measurements and accurate reproduction of the crime scene are essential.

Initially, you should take a general look around the scene and decide which details to include in the sketch. Next, decide what scale to use. In general, try to use the largest scale possible. You can determine what scale to use by taking the longest measurement at the scene and dividing it by the longest measurement of your sketching paper. Most reports and records are kept on 8½- × 11-inch sheets of paper. Thus, if your longest measurement at the scene is 100 feet, let 1 inch equal 10 feet so that your drawing will fit comfortably within the 11-inch length of the paper. Using graph paper also makes it easier to draw objects while maintaining scale.

All sketches should include a compass or an orienting compass arrow indicating north; a legend or key to explain letters, numbers, or symbols used; and an indication of the scale used.

Sketching Methods

Several different methods can be used to prepare crime sketches. These methods all establish the location of evidence and other objects.

Figure 3–2 Crime scene sketch.

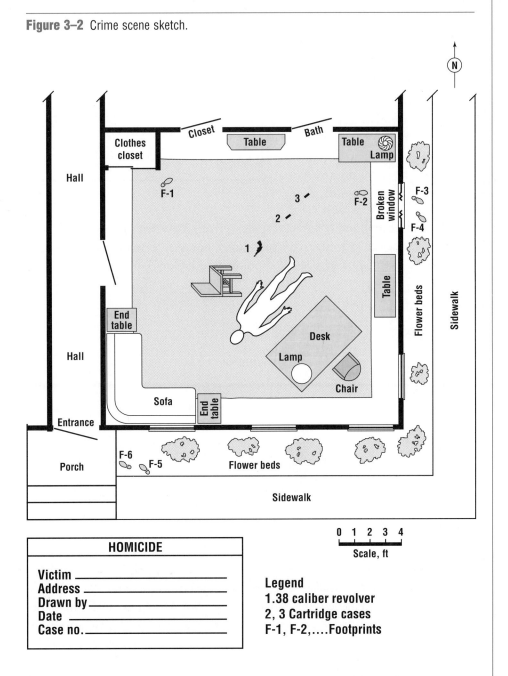

HOMICIDE

Victim _____
Address _____
Drawn by _____
Date _____
Case no. _____

Scale, ft
0 1 2 3 4

Legend
1. 38 caliber revolver
2, 3 Cartridge cases
F-1, F-2,....Footprints

Rectangular-coordinates method A sketching method that involves measuring the distance of an object from two fixed lines at right angles to each other. It is often used to locate objects in a room.

Triangulation method A sketching method that requires measuring the distance of an object along a straight line from two widely separated, fixed reference points.

Baseline method A sketching method that takes measurements along and from a single reference line, called a baseline, which can be established by using a length of string, a chalk line, or some other convenient means.

Rectangular Coordinates The **rectangular-coordinates method** requires two reference lines at right angles to each other. It is often used to locate objects in a room, as depicted in Figure 3–3. Two walls of the room serve as the lines. Distances are measured from the objects to the walls along lines perpendicular (at right angles) to the walls.

Triangulation The **triangulation method** requires measuring the distance of an object from two fixed reference points. This procedure may be used either inside or outside. In a room, the corners are convenient fixed points. The locations of objects strewn about the room are recorded simply by their distances from the two points. For example, in Figure 3–4, Object *A* is 4 feet (1.2 meters) from *Y* and 8 feet (2.4 meters) from *X*. When using this method outside, select two trees or two street corners, a mailbox and a fire hydrant, or any other two fixed points (see Figure 3–4).

Figure 3–3 Rectangular coordinates method.

[Figure 3–3 diagram: Room with object A (4′ from left wall, 8′ from bottom) and object B (10′ from left wall, 3′ from bottom). Reference point X at bottom left corner.]

Figure 3–4 Triangulation method.

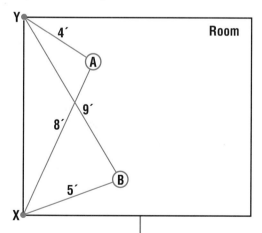

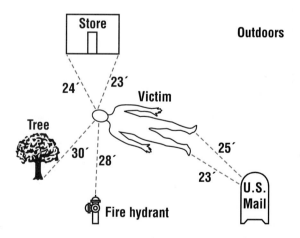

Baseline The **baseline method** requires measurements to be taken along and from a single reference line, called a baseline. The baseline should be established by using a length of string, a chalk line, or some other convenient means. Often you can establish the line between two objects, such as a rock and a tree, or between two corners of a room, as shown in Figure 3–5. The measurements indicating the location of a given object are then taken from left to right along the baseline to a point at right angles to the object being plotted. The distance from the baseline to the object is then indicated on the sketch.

Figure 3–5 Baseline method.

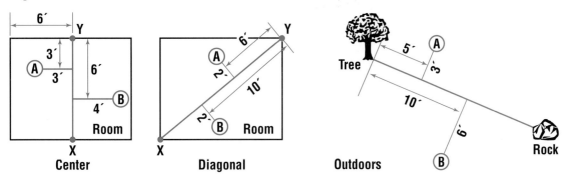

Center   Diagonal   Outdoors

Compass Point

The **compass point method** requires a protractor or some other method of measuring angles between two lines. One point, often the corner of a room, is selected as the point of origin. A line extending from the origin is used as an axis from which angles can be measured. For example, object *A* in Figure 3–6 is lo-cated at a point 10 feet (3 meters) from the origin (the corner point) and at an angle of 20 degrees from the vertical line through the corner point (the axis).

Compass point method
A sketching method that requires a protractor or some method of measuring angles between two lines. One point is selected as the origin, and a line extending from the origin becomes an axis from which angles can be measured.

Figure 3–6 Compass point method.

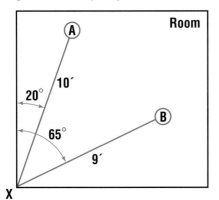

Cross Projection

In the **cross projection method,** the crime scene takes on the appearance of a box opened out. The ceiling opens up like the lid of a hinged box, with the four walls opening utward. In some law enforcement circles, this method is also called an *exploded sketch*. It is an effective way to portray evidence found on or in the walls or ceiling of a room (see Figure 3–7).

Cross projection method
A sketching method in which the ceiling appears to open up like the lid of a hinged box, with the four walls opening outward. Measurements are then indicated from a point on the floor to the wall.

Equipment for Sketches

As in other aspects of crime scene investigation, officers should do advance preparation to have the right equipment available to draw crime

Figure 3–7 Cross projection method.

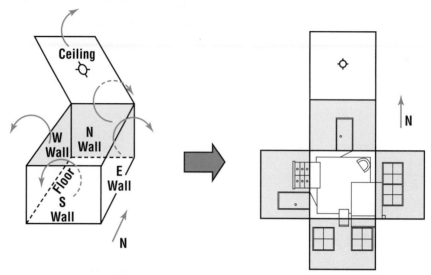

scene sketches. The following are some items an investigator should carry to create sketches at the scene:

- A supply of pencils (medium or hard lead)
- Graph paper and blank paper
- A clipboard or other solid portable drawing surface
- A metal tape measure of at least 50 feet
- A folding ruler, such as the standard 6-foot folding ruler used by carpenters, for short measurements
- A 12- or 15-inch ruler, for drawing straight lines, drawing to scale, or making very short measurements
- A reliable compass or some other means of finding north
- A protractor, for drawing and measuring angles

Discovering and Recognizing Evidence

After the crime scene has been photographed and sketched, you can begin a search. When you search a crime scene, systematically look for physical evidence that may prove useful in establishing that a crime has been committed, determining what method of operation the perpetrator may have used, eliminating suspects, and identifying the perpetrator. Reasoning and experience will help you determine the value and relevance of the evidence you find.

Equipment for Searches

In many departments, a prepared evidence-gathering kit is taken to the crime scene. In some departments, such as the sheriff's department in Tampa, Florida, officers carry a small latent-fingerprint set whenever they are on patrol. It is especially important for patrol officers in small departments to be prepared to conduct crime scene searches. Such officers

FOCUS ON TECHNOLOGY

Computer-Aided Crime Scene Sketching   Sophisticated software makes it possible for investigors to generate professional crime scene drawings as well as reconstructions of motor vehicle accidents. The drawings can be easily manipulated and updated and used in other programs to produce a finished report. Some programs can rescale drawings to enlarge them for courtroom presentations.

should carry in their car trunks an assortment of equipment like the following:

Latex gloves	Compass
Camera, film	String
Rope	Knife
Evidence tags	Steel tape measure
Assorted containers	Ruler
Assorted envelopes	Pens
Pill boxes	Indelible marker
Magnifier	Paper
Test tubes	Fingerprint kit
Plastic bags	Shovel
Bottles	Flashlight, batteries
Cellophane tape	Probing rod
Ax	Wire
Saw	First-aid kit
Wrecking bar	Metal detector
Chalk, chalk line	

In larger departments, investigators can call in forensic specialists to assist with the search.

Search Patterns

Depending on the location or the type of crime, you may choose one of the following five basic patterns for searching a crime scene.

Spiral The **spiral search pattern** is typically used in an outdoor crime scene and is launched by a single investigator. He or she begins at the outermost corner and walks in a decreasing spiral toward a central point (see Figure 3–8). Following the spiral from the outermost edge to the center provides a detailed search. This pattern should not be undertaken in reverse. That is, you should never begin at a central point and spiral outward; in entering the central area to begin, you are likely to trample or destroy evidence.

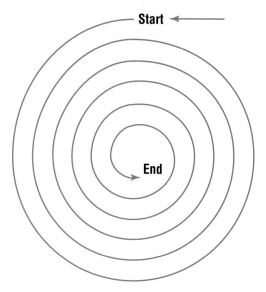

Figure 3–8 Spiral search pattern.

Start

End

Spiral search pattern   A search pattern typically used in outdoor areas and normally launched by a single person. He or she begins at the outermost corner and walks in a decreasing spiral toward a central point.

Strip The **strip search pattern,** like the spiral, is typically used outdoors, but it may be used in large open indoor areas, such as a warehouse or factory, or even in smaller areas, such as a room. Strip searches may be undertaken by a single officer or several officers. This search pattern involves imagining a series of lanes dividing up the entire space to be searched, as depicted in Figure 3–9. The searchers move up and down each lane, continuing until the area has been completely searched. When more than one person is searching and one person finds evidence, all the other searchers should freeze until the evidence has been properly collected. Then they can resume the search from the points where they stopped.

Figure 3–9 Strip search pattern.

Grid The **grid search pattern** begins like a strip search. However, after completing the search by horizontal lanes, the searchers double back at right angles to the original strip search, as shown in Figure 3–10. In effect, the searchers are conducting another strip search, perpendicular to the first. The grid search pattern is both more time-consuming and more thorough. Often, simply looking at the same area from two different angles yields evidence that would be missed in a simple strip search.

Figure 3–10 Grid search pattern.

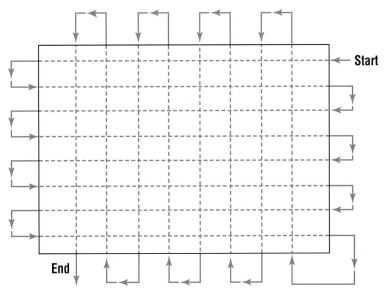

Figure 3–11 Zone search pattern.

Zone A	**Zone B**
Zone C	**Zone D**

Zone search pattern A search pattern in which the area is divided into four quadrants, each of which is then examined with one of the other patterns.

Pie, or wheel, search pattern A search pattern in which the area is divided into pie-shaped sections, usually six in number. Each section is then searched, usually by a variation of the strip pattern.

Zone In a **zone search pattern,** the investigator creates two imaginary axes, which divide the area into four quadrants (see Figure 3–11). Each quadrant can then be examined with one of the previously described patterns. When the area is particularly large, a zone search pattern is sometimes used to create four smaller and more manageable search areas.

Pie or Wheel The **pie search pattern,** like the zone pattern, involves dividing the search area into smaller sections. In the pie pattern, the sections are pie slices, or sections of a wheel, usually six in number, as depicted in Figure 3–12. Each slice of the pie is then searched with a variation of the strip search.

The strip and grid search patterns are most commonly used by investigators. When search areas are very open or large, the spiral, zone, or pie patterns prove productive. The preferred method of searching varies with the crime, the type of evidence sought, and the purpose of the search. Guards should be posted at doors, gates, and other entryways while a search is being conducted.

When searching your assigned section, be alert for areas that appear to have been recently disturbed. Watch for indications of tampering, such as loose moldings, detached light fixtures, uncovered air ducts, splintered floorboards, new nails or screws, and patches in plaster or cement. Also be alert to new paint, fresh stains, soil disturbances, new grass or sod, broken twigs, freshly turned soil, and recent scratch marks on window frames or walls. Unusual arrangements, dust disturbances, outlines from missing wall hangings, and tool marks should all be examined. Also look for special hiding places, such as hidden compartments, false bottoms, hollowed-out objects, and stuffed toys. Obvious places, such as furniture, beds, vacuum cleaners, ice trays, food boxes, and other containers, should not be overlooked.

Figure 3–12 Pie, or wheel, search pattern.

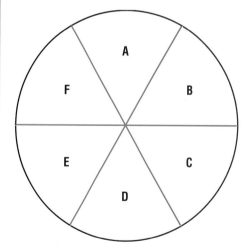

Collecting and Marking Evidence

We have already discussed the importance of legal search and seizure when identifying and collecting evidence. We also know that the evidence presented in court must be material, relevant, and competent. In addition, the court will want answers to the following questions about evidence collected at the crime scene:

- Who found it?
- What did it look like?
- When was it found?
- Where was it found, and what is its relation to other objects at the scene?
- Where was it held from its collection to its presentation in court?

To answer these questions, complete logs and notes of all evidence found during a search must be maintained.

Investigators should handle all evidence carefully and should wear latex gloves to ensure that they leave no accidental fingerprints and to protect themselves from toxic materials and infectious disease. Small items of evidence generally can be lifted and placed directly into a test tube, small bottle, or plastic bag. Large items can be placed in boxes or bags. A fairly common evidence container in use today is a 9 × 12-inch manila envelope.

The investigator who finds the evidence should place his or her personal identifying mark on it. The mark should be permanent and capable of positive identification. In addition, this mark should not be placed on any area that might need to be examined in the lab. A knife can be used to mark hard objects; a pen can be used on absorbent materials. Evidence that cannot be physically marked, such as bird shot or liquids, should be placed in an appropriate container. This receptacle should then be sealed and identified with a label or property tag indicating the title of the case, the officer's name or initials, the date, the time, the specific location where it was found, and the case number, if available. It is preferable to have

HISTORY

One of the first crime laboratories was set up in 1910 in Lyons, France, by a doctor named Edmond Locard. Locard helped develop scientific methods of investigating crimes. The first crime laboratory in the United States was established in Los Angeles in 1923. Today the United States has almost 300 crime laboratories. Some crime laboratories examine only one type of evidence. The FBI crime laboratory, organized in 1932, is one of the best known in the world.

another investigator present at the time the evidence is found, and the name of this investigator also should be recorded on the evidence log.

Some kinds of evidence are more valuable than others. For example, evidence in its original, unaltered state is more valuable than evidence that has been damaged. Also, some types of evidence, such as fingerprints, require a standard of comparison. A **standard of comparison** is a model, measure, or object with which evidence is compared to determine whether both came from the same source. A fingerprint found at a crime scene must be matched with a known print to be of value. A shard of glass found on a suspect's clothing could be compared with glass collected from a broken window at a burglary to provide evidence of the suspect's participation in the crime. Specimens of blood, hair, fibers, soil, bullets, paper, cloth, paint, and so forth must be collected in sufficient quantity to make comparison possible.

As mentioned at the beginning of the chapter, how evidence is protected, collected, secured, and transported affects its value. As an investigator it is your job to ensure that evidence does not lose its value through improper collection, handling, packaging, or identification.

Standard of comparison
A model, measure, or object with which evidence is compared to determine whether both came from the same source.

SUMMARY BY LEARNING OBJECTIVES

Learning Objective 1

Evidence in a criminal investigation is any item that helps to establish the facts of a related criminal case. How evidence is protected, collected, secured, and transported affects its later usefulness when introduced in a criminal court case.

Learning Objective 2

Basic steps in gathering and preserving evidence during a criminal investigation include recognizing and examining relevant physical evidence; carefully collecting, handling, and recording evidence and transporting it to a crime lab; maintaining the security of evidence from the lab to the courtroom; and presenting or explaining evidence in court.

Learning Objective 3

The crime scene includes all areas in which the criminal, any victim, and any eyewitnesses moved during the time the crime was committed. It generally encompasses a limited area, but in some instances may include several sites.

Learning Objective 4

Photography in criminal investigation involves the pictorial documentation of the crime scene and objects at the crime scene before anything is touched. Crime scene photographs are generally taken from long-range, mid-range, and close-up vantage points. In some police agencies, videotaping is used as an adjunct to still photography.

Learning Objective 5

Crime scene sketches are companions to still photographs because they provide accurate information about the placement of objects at the scene and show the actual relationships and distances between things. When preparing sketches, investigators may use one of the following methods: rectangular coordinates, triangulation, baseline, compass point, and cross projection.

Learning Objective 6

Investigators may search for evidence at a crime scene by using the spiral, strip, grid, zone, or pie (or wheel) search pattern. The strip and grid search patterns are most commonly used by investigators.

Learning Objective 7

A complete accounting of evidence found at a crime scene should include who found or collected it, where and how it was transferred for safekeeping, and how it has been protected and stored since its collection.

QUESTIONS FOR REVIEW

Learning Objective 1

1. Define *evidence* and *criminalist*.
2. Name three main sources of evidence.
3. What affects the usefulness of evidence when it is introduced in court?

Learning Objective 2

4. Which of the eight basic steps in gathering and preserving evidence in a criminal investigation is the most important from a forensic specialist's point of view?

Learning Objective 3

5. If a rape was committed in the park, but the victim's unconscious body was found two blocks away behind a grocery store, which is the crime scene?

6. Why should a crime scene be photographed before anything in it is touched or moved?

7. List the three distances from which crime scene photographs should be taken.

Learning Objective 5

8. What purpose does a sketch serve in a criminal investigation?

9. Why must the elements of a crime scene sketch be drawn to scale?

10. Which sketching method is useful for showing items in the walls? For measuring the distance of an object from two fixed lines? For measuring along a straight line from two widely separated reference points?

Learning Objective 6

11. In which search pattern do searchers complete one pattern and then double back at right angles across the area being examined? In which pattern does a searcher move in decreasing concentric circles?

12. Why must you never begin a spiral search pattern from the innermost point and move outward?

Learning Objective 7

13. Define *standard of comparison*.

14. Why is a chain of custody for evidence important to a criminal investigation?

CRITICAL THINKING INVESTIGATIVE EXERCISE

Divide into five groups, one for each of the five sketching methods described in the chapter. Individually prepare a sketch of your classroom, or another room or area that your instructor may designate, using the sketching method assigned to your group. The members of the group may discuss the sketching method and may help one another as appropriate. When your sketch is complete, compare it with the other sketches, and analyze how you might improve your sketch.

INVESTIGATIVE SKILL BUILDERS

Allocating Resources

You have been assigned to lead a team investigating a homicide in a 12-unit apartment building. When you arrive, the uniformed officer tells you that, besides the murder victim, there are no other injured victims.

1. What tasks do you need to perform, and in what sequence?
2. What do you think are the priorities?
3. Estimate how many officers you will need to secure the crime scene and conduct the preliminary investigation.

Integrity/Honesty

You are assigned to videotape a crime scene. Another officer is assigned to take conventional photographs. Later, when reviewing the video log, you notice that times on the log have been altered to suggest that there was no interruption in time during the several minutes you stopped shooting video to change the camera battery.

1. Do you correct these entries on your own initiative?
2. Do you notify the team leader?
3. What are the possible ramifications of your decision for yourself? Your colleague? The victim or the perpetrator?

ENDNOTES

1. Information in this section is drawn from "Photography," *FBI Evidence Response Teams*, Department of Justice, Washington, no date (manual used for training in 1996).
2. "Sketching Crime Scene," *FBI Evidence Response Teams*.

CHAPTER 4

Physical Evidence

CHAPTER OBJECTIVES

After completing this chapter, you will be able to:

1. Explain the role of the crime laboratory in criminal investigation.

2. Relate the correct procedures for collecting various kinds of physical evidence.

3. Understand the importance and application of DNA profiling.

4. Discuss the nature and importance of blood and semen evidence.

5. Explain how hair and fiber evidence may be used to identify suspects.

6. Describe the importance of glass and paint evidence.

7. Explain the importance of firearm evidence in criminal investigation.

8. Describe how to collect comparison specimens of document evidence.

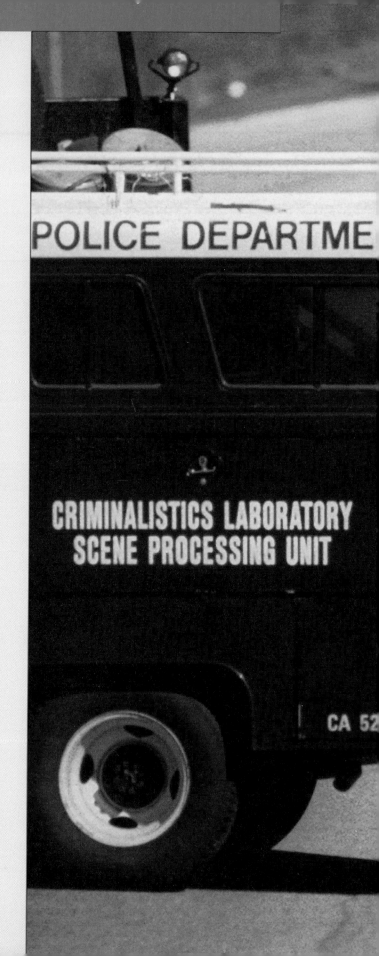

The Crime Laboratory

Crime laboratories work closely with criminal investigators and other police personnel in determining whether a crime has actually been committed, who may or may not have committed it, and—sometimes—how the crime was committed. The crime laboratory uses physical specimens collected by investigators from crime scenes, victims, and suspects to scientifically consider answers to these questions. Scientific examination of physical evidence plays a vital role in the successful prosecution of criminals and in the clearing of persons who are innocent.

Recognizing, collecting, and preserving physical evidence is essential to the work of every criminal investigator. The chain of custody must also be maintained. Officers must know where to look and what to look for, how to collect evidence, how and where to identify it, and how to package and transport it. In addition, they should know the value of microscopic evidence and the scientific examinations that can be applied to the evidence recovered. They must also be familiar with the kinds of assistance that crime laboratories can provide.

The examinations carried out in the laboratory can be described in two words—*identify* and *compare.* An unknown white powder contained in a capsule taken from a suspected drug addict is identified as heroin. A reddish stain in the trunk of a murder suspect's car is identified as human blood, and that stain is compared and matched with the victim's blood. Such examinations assist in convicting the guilty. Crime lab examinations can also ensure protection for the innocent.

A crime laboratory is actually a large group of laboratories under one roof. Each laboratory specializes in its own area or branch of science, such as pathology, toxicology, odontology, or ballistics. Each laboratory, likewise, has its own specialized equipment, ranging from scanning electron microscopes to emission spectrographs, from atomic absorption spectrometers to equipment for thin-layer chromatography and electrophoresis.

DNA Profiling

DNA profiling A procedure in which DNA is extracted from biological evidence samples gathered from crime scenes and from comparison samples collected from victims and suspects. The DNA samples are analyzed and compared to determine whether or not they could have had a common origin.

One of the most important advances in crime lab technologies is **DNA profiling.** DNA (deoxyribonucleic acid) is a molecule present in all life forms. It determines an organism's traits and the way those traits are passed on from generation to generation. It is different for each person, except for identical twins. Forensic scientists can get information about the identity of biological evidence by conducting sophisticated laboratory tests on the DNA. The process begins when DNA is extracted from biological evidence samples gathered from crime scenes and from comparison samples collected from victims and suspects. The scientists will analyze these DNA samples and compare them to determine

Although the first crime lab in America was set up in Los Angeles in 1923, one of the most well-known early forensic laboratories was that set up by Chicago police in 1929. That year, in the St. Valentine's Day Massacre, *four gangsters dressed as police officers gunned down seven rival Chicago gangsters against a brick wall.[1] Colonel Calvin Goddard, an independent forensic consultant, came to Chicago, and with physical evidence collected at the scene of the killings, including photos and various diagrams, he reconstructed the slaying of the seven mobsters. Goddard later published his report in the first issue of the* American Journal of Police Science.[2]

whether or not they could have had a common origin. The final result is a genetic DNA profile which can be used to strongly link a suspect to a crime scene or to a victim or to turn attention away from a suspect.

Suppose blood is the only evidence police have from a murder. If the DNA analysis of the blood collected at the crime scene matches the DNA analysis of the blood of the suspect in the crime, police have a strong link placing the suspect at the crime scene. On the other hand, if the DNA of the suspect's blood does not match the DNA of the samples from the murder scene, police may turn their attention to another suspect.

There are two types of DNA tests—PCR (for Polymerase Chain Reaction) and RFLP (for Restriction Fragment Length Polymorphism). The key to DNA testing is the presence of cells containing DNA (Figure 4–1). Blood, semen, and body tissue are some good sources of such cells, while saliva, urine, and perspiration are poor sources. The investigator or technician needs to collect samples that are likely to contain DNA for DNA testing to be successful. In DNA testing, the samples are consumed and cannot be used later for other purposes.

Submitting Evidence to the Lab

Evidence transmitted to the laboratory for examination should be accompanied by certain information if the laboratory is to make a useful and complete examination. Administrative data—such as the nature of the offense, the date it was committed, its location, the names of the victim and the suspect, and the case number—should be provided. Also included should be a summary of the case, including the crime scene

Figure 4–1 How DNA profiling is performed.

DNA, deoxyribonucleic acid, is the material that carries the genetic pattern that makes each person unique. Scientists in the laboratory can map DNA patterns in samples of skin, blood, semen, or other body tissues or fluids. The DNA patterns can then be analyzed and compared.

There are two main DNA testing procedures used in criminal forensics.

1 Samples are taken of tissue or body fluids at crime scenes. Comparison samples are taken from victims and suspects.

RFLP (Restriction Fragment Length Polymorphism)

2 In the laboratory, DNA genetic material is extracted from the samples and mixed with enzymes to cut the DNA into fragments.

3 The DNA fragments are put in a special gel and exposed to an electrical charge to sort the fragments by size.

4 Genetic tracers are used to search out and lock onto specific fragments of the DNA.

5 The tracers reveal a pattern. Each evidence sample will have a pattern that can be compared with the sample from the victim and the sample from the suspect.

PCR (Polymerase Chain Reaction)

2 In the laboratory, DNA is extracted from the samples.

3 Part of the DNA molecule is amplified in a test tube to produce billions of copies of that part.

4 The amplified DNA is analyzed.

5 The analysis of the evidence sample can be compared with the analysis of the sample from the victim and the sample from the suspect.

Comparing the patterns in the samples results in a DNA profile representing distinctive features of the samples that may or may not match.

Crime evidence	Suspect	Victim
—	—	=
—	—	
Match		

Crime evidence	Suspect	Victim
—	—	=
—	—	
No match		

report, and a list of the articles of evidence submitted and the examinations requested. Finally, the information submitted should include the urgency of the request, the person to whom the evidence should be returned, and the person to whom the report should be directed.

The physical evidence that crime labs analyze can be anything. Glass, paint, soil, bullets, blood, handwriting, paper, capsules, and knives are only a few examples. In size, physical evidence may range from a battleship to a grain of pollen, from an apartment building to a sample of air. We will now take a look at some of the common types of evidence that investigators may encounter at crime scenes. For your convenience, a condensed physical evidence collection guide appears at the end of this chapter.

Blood as Evidence

Blood is among the most common forms of evidence found at the scenes of serious and violent crimes. Blood may be found in trace amounts, puddles, spatters, smears, or droplets. It is useful as evidence whether it is wet or dry. Blood may appear on the floor, walls, ceiling, articles of clothing or furniture, and objects used in the course of the crime or attempts to conceal it. Dried spills or drops of blood are referred to as **bloodstains.** Blood samples may also be collected from suspects and victims for examination and comparison. Blood evidence can help narrow the group of suspects, support the identification of a suspect, and even guide the reconstruction of a crime.

Caution is important in the handling of blood at crime scenes. Although blood is an excellent form of evidence because of its ability to distinguish among individuals, blood can be a serious health hazard—regardless of whether it is wet or dry. Handling hepatitis- or HIV-contaminated blood samples increases your risk of contracting one or the other of these serious diseases. All persons at crime scenes, at autopsies, and in the lab should wear latex, vinyl, or rubber gloves for protection. Also, whenever working around other human specimens, such as stool, urine, saliva, semen, or vaginal secretions, exercise extreme caution. Most police departments have guidelines for correctly and safely handling biological specimens, and these should be scrupulously followed. If you have questions regarding the proper handling or disposal of specimens, consult your local department of health or a qualified health professional.

Blood is an easily visible fluid, and one that is difficult to remove from many fabrics and carpeting. Persons who commit crimes sometimes try to remove the incriminating crimson fluid from weapons and other objects. Forensic technology has advanced to a point, however, where even minute traces of blood may be discerned by the use of any of a number of **reagents,** or substances used to detect or test for the presence of blood. Each of these tests is extremely sensitive, and each has certain advantages and disadvantages. For example, although the reagent *luminol* can detect even very minute traces of blood not visible to the naked eye, it must be used in total darkness. *Benzedine,* on the other hand, is used only in a controlled laboratory setting because it can cause cancer.

Bloodstains Dried spills or drops of blood.

Reagents Substances used to detect or test for the presence of blood, or other substances.

Value in Cases

Following are some cases in which bloodstains would be of value as evidence.

Assault and Murder Blood may be found on both victim and suspect. Clothing, weapons involved, and fingernail scrapings are also common sources of blood evidence. Rags, handkerchiefs, towels, tissues, toilet paper, rugs, or other materials that the perpetrator may have used to wipe off hands or the weapon are potential sources of bloodstains. Additional potential sources include sink traps, floor cracks, and crevices. If the offense occurred outdoors, vegetation or soil from the crime area may contain blood.

Burglary   Broken glass, window and door frames, or walls may reveal evidence of injury to a burglar.

Hit-and-Run   Points of impact and the undercarriage of the vehicle may reveal suspicious stains.

Rape   Undergarments of both the victim and the suspect may be stained with blood, as may bedding, upholstery, and carpeting. If the crime was committed outdoors, soil in the area of the attack may reveal bloodstains.

What Bloodstains Can Reveal

The location, shape, and appearance of blood drops, splashes, or spatters can sometimes provide useful information about how a crime occurred. Spatters of blood may permit determination of the direction of the falling drops that produced them. The shape of blood spots may permit an estimate of the velocity, the impact angle, the distance fallen from the source of the spatter, or all three (see Figure 4–2). The diameter of a blood spot is useful only for the first 5 or 6 feet from impact. Distances beyond 6 feet show little reliable change in the spatter pattern. The degree of spatter from a single drop depends more on the type of surface on which it falls than on the distance it falls. The coarser the surface, the more likely it is that the drop will rupture and spatter rather than land as a round drop.

Conclusions about velocity and impact should not be drawn from a very small bloodstain. Very fine specks of blood may actually represent castoffs, satellites of larger drops of blood. However, when these smaller castoffs appear in great numbers, they may have been caused by an impact. The smaller the diameter of the droplets, the higher the velocity of the impact.

Spatters can indicate the position of a victim and the perpetrator at the time an attack took place. For example, considerable backspatter on walls, furnishings, or objects behind the victim is likely from a gunshot wound. Small, independent spatters usually have a uniform taper, in the shape of a teardrop. In these cases, the tail of the teardrop always points away from the direction of impact. Small castoffs resemble tadpoles and

Figure 4–2 The significance of the shape of blood stains.

a

Blood dropped vertically from a height of 50 inches (1.3 meters) onto a flat surface shows a radiating, or bursting, effect. The stain is 1 inch (2.5 centimeters) in diameter.

b

The same amount of blood as in *a*, but dropped vertically onto a flat surface from a height of 8 inches (20 centimeters), makes a smaller stain (3/4 inch [about 2 centimeters]) with a wavy edge.

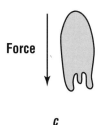

Force

c

Oval stain has spattering showing two or three spikes (splashes). Broad portions of the splashes indicate the point at which the blood first struck obliquely on a flat surface and thus show the direction from which it came.

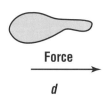

Force

d

Stain shows two oval spots like an exclamation mark and indicates a left-to-right direction of blood drop.

tend to be longer and narrower than the teardrop shape of independent droplets. The sharper end of these stains always points back toward the direction of their impact.

Blood provides fairly uniform patterns, regardless of the age or gender of the victim. Additionally, since blood spattered from a body is at a constant temperature and is normally exposed to environmental conditions for only a short time, atmospheric temperature, pressure, and humidity have little discernible effect on blood's behavior.

Blood-Typing

Blood-typing evidence is useful for eliminating suspects as well as for incriminating them. **Blood-typing** classifies certain aspects of the blood into different categories. There are four major blood groups—A,

Blood-typing Method of classifying blood into four major blood groups—A, B, AB, and O. Another factor, called the *Rh factor,* also helps determine a person's blood type, which is positive or negative for the Rh factor.

B, AB, and O. A person's blood type depends on the presence or absence of certain substances, called *antigens,* in the blood. Another factor, called the *Rh factor,* also helps determine a person's blood type. Most people are positive for this factor, or Rh-positive; that is, their blood contains the factor. Others are negative for the factor, or Rh-negative; their blood does not contain the Rh factor.

Using the just-described classifications, tests can determine whether a particular blood sample could have come from a specific person. Blood type and Rh factor cannot positively link a suspect to a crime, but they can positively rule out a suspect. For example, let's say a sample of blood found at the scene of a murder is A negative. A test of the victim's blood proves it to be B positive. This result shows that the victim is not the source of the blood and any suspect in this murder will have to have A negative blood. If a suspect with A negative blood were apprehended, DNA analysis could then be used to positively link the suspect to the murder scene.

Possible Examination Results

There are three main questions that laboratory examination of blood evidence can answer:

1. Is the substance blood? (If not, what is it?)
2. Is the substance human blood? (If not, from what animal did it come?)
3. If it is human blood, to what blood group does it belong?[3]

Semen as Evidence

Always handle semen stain areas as carefully as possible. Rough treatment will break up any spermatozoa present so that a positive identification may be impossible. Submit all articles for semen stain examination to the laboratory immediately. Do not neglect to submit all swabs, smears, and stains removed from the victim during examination by a physician.

Value in Cases

The victims of certain types of crimes are the most important sources of evidence.

Death   The victim's body and clothing, as well as bedding, towels, and other articles at the scene, may be sources of such stains. Other possible sources of such evidence are suspects and items in their surroundings, such as clothing, handkerchiefs, and automobiles.

Rape and Other Sex Offenses

Semen stains are often, although by no means always, found as physical evidence in sex offenses. Through DNA typing, it is possible to match semen stains with a person's blood sample.

FYI

DNA is a 3-foot-long molecule that is tightly wound inside the 46 chromosomes in each cell of the body. Half of the chromosomes are contributed by the father's sperm and half by the mother's egg. Every cell derived from that fertilized egg will have identical DNA.

Possible Examination Results

Here are three main questions that laboratory examination of semen stains may answer:

1. Does the stain contain human semen?
2. Can the blood group (A, B, O, AB) of the stain be determined? If so, what is it?
3. If a blood specimen from the suspect is available, does it match the DNA present in the semen sample?

Hair as Evidence

Hair is a valuable, though sometimes overlooked, means of personal identification. Human hair grows from follicles in the skin at a rate of about 1/2 inch a month, although this varies. Unlike body fluids and skin, human hair generally retains its structural features for very long periods of time. It is an ideal source of information about an individual and can be used to identify both the sex and the race of a person.[4]

Although hair cannot absolutely identify a particular individual, as a fingerprint can, scientific examination can fairly conclusively rule out a strand's having come from a particular individual. Sometimes eliminating a suspect is as important as identifying one. Furthermore, certain drugs and chemicals will remain in hair for many months. Thus, a 2-inch length of hair taken from a suspect could offer important information about substances that the suspect has ingested during the past 2 years.

Value in Cases

There are certain types of cases in which collecting hair samples should be a regular part of an investigator's routine.

Assault At a crime scene, hair from the victim, the suspect, or both may be found. Clothing, weapons, and the surrounding area are common locations for hair evidence. Individual strands, clumps, or tufts of hair may be grasped in the hand of a victim. Microscopic examination of a hair root may suggest whether it has fallen out or has been forcibly pulled out.

Rape Direct particular attention toward locating and examining hair of all types. Samples of pubic hair, along with vaginal smears for semen, should be taken when rape is believed to have occurred. Pubic hair may be found on undergarments of the victim and the suspect and on bedding, clothing, furnishings, or auto upholstery. Microscopic examination of hairs can aid in determining whether *consent* was given or *nonconsensual force* was used to engage in intercourse. Proof of lack of consent is a key element in successful prosecution of a rape case.

Hit-and-Run The points of impact and the undercarriage of the suspect vehicle may carry hair evidence. When a vehicle strikes a person, hairs and fibers often become imbedded in areas of fresh damage, torn fenders, loose chrome, and bug catchers. If hair is firmly attached to a removable part of the vehicle, remove the part from the vehicle, if possible, rather than the hair from the part.

Death As a matter of routine, collect a sample of about 20 strands of hair from the deceased in all cases of sudden or unusual death.

Possible Examination Results

From a laboratory examination of hair samples, the following questions may be answered:

1. Is the hair sample human or animal?
2. If human, from which part of the body did it originate?
3. If animal, what type of animal was it (dog, cat, deer, wolf)?
4. Are there any indications of the characteristics of the individual from whom it came?
5. Could the hair have come from a particular person, and if so, what is the probability that it did come from that person?
6. Did the hair fall out naturally, was it pulled out, or was it cut by a sharp instrument?
7. Are there any foreign substances adhering to the hair (for example, dye, blood, grease)?

Fibers as Evidence

Fibers occur at crime scenes more frequently than any other type of microscopic evidence. Yet, investigators often overlook this type of evidence because of its extremely small size. Fragments of torn cloth, easily visible to the naked eye, are often collected as evidence in a variety of cases. Fibers, on the other hand, are more difficult to locate. Good investigators know how and where to look for such evidence. Fibers are often transferred from one person's clothing to another's or may be impressed in a bullet that has penetrated a particular garment, fabric, or furnishing. Fibers may even be found under fingernails, at various points of entry in break-ins, or on various parts of a suspect's or victim's body.

If fiber evidence is suspected but not visible, for example on a windowsill, a car bumper, or an article of clothing, use the **adhesive-tape technique** to collect the evidence. Take ordinary transparent tape and cover the area to which fibers may have adhered. When you pull the tape off, any fibers will adhere to the sticky surface of the tape. Then attach the tape, sticky side down, to a clean, smooth, nonabsorbent surface (glass, plastic, or a similar material). Be careful not to contaminate the tape with fibers from your own clothing. Even if it looks as if there are no fibers clinging to the tape, microscopic examination of the tape may reveal the presence of a number of fibers.

Fibers can be classified into four general groups: *mineral, vegetable, animal,* and *synthetic.* Mineral fibers may include various sorts of insulation, glass, and asbestos. Vegetable fibers may include cotton, jute (used in sacking and cords), sisal (used in cords and ropes), hemp (used to make cords), and similar organic materials. Animal fibers include such materials as silk, as well as wool, cashmere, or other types of animal fur. Synthetics may encompass a wide variety of chemically produced materials such as rayon, nylon, polyester, and similar human-made textiles.

In many ways, fibers are a better source of information about a crime scene than hairs belonging to the suspect. Here is why. Fibers are actually more distinguishable than human hair. Microscopic examination can determine the uniformity of thickness of strands, the actual number of microscopic fibers in every strand, color or dye origins, the direction of fiber twist,

Adhesive-tape technique
A method of collecting microscopic evidence in which transparent tape is used to cover an area to which physical evidence such as fibers may have adhered. When the tape is pulled off, the evidence will adhere to the sticky surface of the tape.

The adhesive-tape technique is useful for collecting fibers for microscopic examination.

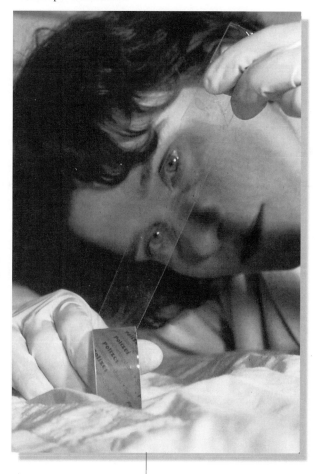

and the thread count. It can even determine whether particular fibers come from a specific garment.

Value in Cases

Fiber evidence can be a corroborative aid in establishing the facts in a number of cases.

Assault   This crime usually involves personal contact of some sort. Clothing fibers may be transferred between victim and suspect. Weapons and fingernail cuttings can also be important sources of fiber evidence.

Burglary   Clothing fibers will almost always be found at the point of entry—a window or other opening. Snags of fibers also may be found on rough surfaces, such as door frames or textured walls.

Death   If entry was gained by climbing through an opening, important fiber evidence may be found.

Rape   The nature of this crime results in the transfer of fibers between the clothing of the victim, the clothing of the suspect, and other articles, such as bedding or automobile seat covers. Weapons and fingernail scrapings may also yield fiber evidence.

Possible Examination Results

From a laboratory examination of fibers, the following questions may be answered:

1. What type of fiber is the sample?
2. Is it the same type of fiber present in samples of the victim's and suspect's clothing?
3. Does the sample exactly match when compared with a standard sample taken from the victim's or the suspect's clothing?
4. Is it the exact shade of color as the standard?
5. Are there any points of similarity?

Glass as Evidence

Glass fragments can be extremely useful as evidence. First of all, there are many different formulas used to manufacture glass. The many variations in density, refractive index, and light dispersion give glass a very high value as evidence. Second, very tiny shards of glass sometimes adhere to a suspect's shoes, clothes, hair, or skin. Criminals frequently are unaware that they are carrying small glass particles or have left glass residue at the crime scene. Furthermore, most criminals do not realize how important even microscopic fragments of glass can be in an investigation. Larger pieces of glass can be examined for fingerprints, or they may be fit back together to indicate how the glass was broken. An investigator may have to decide whether a pane of glass was broken from the inside or the outside, or whether it was struck by a bullet or a rock. Glass from a broken pane can frequently tell an important story.

It is important for criminal investigators to understand the ways in which glass reacts to force. They can then use the patterns in glass fractures to determine facts about the crime scene. Whenever an object is forced through a pane of glass, two types of fractures usually result. Together, these fractures form a pattern that resembles a spider's web. **Radial fractures** are cracks that start at the center of the point where the object struck the glass and radiate outward, creating a slightly star-shaped pattern. **Concentric fractures** form irregular, but concentric, circular crack patterns in the glass around the point of impact. (See Figure 4–3.) It is possible, for example, to tell which of two shots in close proximity occurred first by looking at the radial and concentric fractures to see which stops the fracture lines of the other.

If you look at the edge of a piece of broken glass, you see a series of curved lines that form right angles with one side of the glass and curve obliquely toward the other, forming a shell- or cone-shaped pattern. This is a **conchoidal fracture,** and it can provide information about the direction of the force that broke the glass, because as glass breaks, it breaks first on the side opposite the force applied to it. Thus, when a bullet, for instance, breaks a window, it blasts out a cone-shaped hole on the side of the glass away from the shooter.

Determining the direction of the force that broke the glass involves examining the cone-shaped area created by the conchoidal fracture (see Figure 4–3). Suppose you are on the inside of a house and there are three bullets holes in a window. Two of the holes have the cone-shaped area on the inside of the window, indicating that the shots were fired from the outside. The other hole has the cone-shaped area on the outside of the window, indicating that the shot was fired from the inside of the house.

Radial fractures Cracks that start at the center of the area where the object struck the glass and radiate outward, creating a slightly star-shaped pattern.

Concentric fractures Irregular, but concentric, circular crack patterns in the broken glass around the point of impact.

Conchoidal fracture A series of curved lines along the edge of broken glass that form right angles with one side of the glass, forming a shell- or cone-shaped pattern.

Figure 4–3 Glass fractures from a bullet.

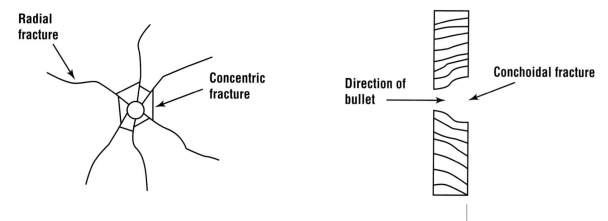

Radial fracture

Concentric fracture

Direction of bullet

Conchoidal fracture

Value in Cases

Physical examination of glass may assist in determining the facts of a case in many different crime situations.

Burglary Burglars often break a window or door to quickly escape the crime scene. Any person standing close to glass when it is broken invariably picks up fragments on his or her clothing. The clothing of burglary suspects, in cases where windows have been broken, will often carry microscopic glass fragments.

Hit-and-Run In a hit-and-run accident, a headlight is often broken. Less common, but also possible, is a broken windshield. The scene of the accident, the vehicle, and the clothing of the victim can all be sources of glass fragments.

Possible Examination Results

From a laboratory examination of glass, the following questions may be answered:

1. If a window was struck by a blunt instrument, such as a rock, stick, or fist, from which side was it struck?
2. If a window was struck by a bullet, from which side was it fired?
3. If two or more bullets were fired, is it possible to determine the sequence of firing?
4. Can the composition of the window glass be compared with and matched to known comparison specimens?
5. Can the refractive index of the glass sample be used to match the sample with known comparison specimens?

Paint as Evidence

Paint can occur as physical evidence in three different forms: (1) chips or flakes, as may be found adhering to clothing; (2) smears, from either fresh paint or old "chalking" paint; (3) intact finishes, on objects such as tools or automobiles at the crime scene.

Value in Cases

Paint evidence may be found in a variety of crimes but is most often present in the following cases.

Burglary Paint fragments, often microscopic, may be found on the clothing of a suspect, on the tools used to commit a burglary, or in a vehicle.

Hit-and-Run The clothing of the victim, upon microscopic examination, will often yield minute paint fragments resulting from the impact of the vehicle. In collisions between vehicles, there will invariably be a considerable amount of paint interchanged.

Possible Examination Results

From a laboratory examination of paint, the following questions may be answered:

1. Can the flakes of paint be fit together along a common fracture to provide a conclusive identification of the paint's source?

2. Can the source of the paint be identified with a high degree of probability if both the sample and the comparison specimen contain identical layers or components?

3. Is it possible to establish the color, year, and make of an American-made or imported vehicle from a paint chip?

Firearms/Ammunition as Evidence

Firearms evidence is common at many crime scenes and can include revolvers, pistols, rifles, shotguns, loaded cartridges, misfired cartridges, casings, bullets, powder residues, shot pellets, and even wads from muzzle-loading black powder weapons and some older shotguns. Many of these objects may offer additional clues to the identity of the shooter, because they may reveal a fingerprint or have blood, hair, or fibers adhering to them.

Investigators should become familiar with different types of firearms. They should develop sufficient familiarity that they can immediately distinguish between a pistol and a revolver or a rifle and a shotgun. They should learn which weapons must be loaded with a single shot, which use a rotating cylinder, which feed cartridges semiautomatically, and which have automatic actions. Investigators should also know how many cartridges different types of firearms can hold and what caliber of cartridge each requires.

An important question that may be asked about crimes involving firearms is "Was this bullet fired from this gun?" Some firearms, such as most shotguns, have a smooth interior the length of the barrel, or **bore,** of the weapon. In contrast, most pistols and rifles have grooves or ridges that run the length of the bore. Bullets typically are softer and just slightly larger than the diameter of the bore. As the bullet speeds through the

Bore   The hollow, cylindrical chamber, or barrel, of a firearm.

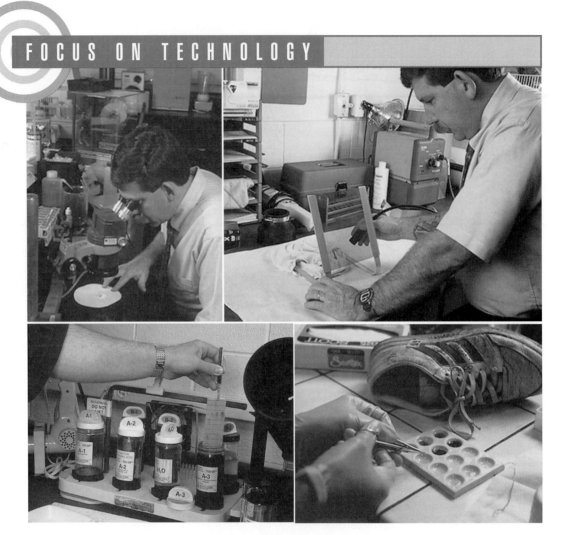

Crime Lab Technologies   TOP LEFT: Microscopic examination of characteristics of vegetation to determine if it is marijuana; TOP RIGHT: Testing for presence of semen on underwear using ultra-violet light and filter; BOTTOM LEFT: Thin-layer chromatography testing to determine the presence of cocaine; BOTTOM RIGHT: Analyzing blood sample from shoe to determine blood type.

Striations Marks, lines, or scratches on the hard surface of an object such as a bullet.

barrel of the gun, it picks up marks, or **striations,** peculiar to that gun. These markings, in turn, enable the lab experts to match a bullet to a particular weapon.

To assess whether a particular weapon has fired a specific bullet, it is necessary to compare the recovered bullet with one test-fired through the weapon. If the recovered bullet is in poor shape or severely fragmented, it will be impossible to make an adequate comparison. Similarly, if the bore has been severely damaged by corrosion, tampering, or mechanical alterations, it may not be possible to positively identify a comparison bullet fired through the weapon.

A physician should remove evidence bullets or pellets from the body of a deceased person. Instruct the doctor to take special care—using rubber-tipped forceps, for example—in recovering the bullet, so as not to damage the delicate markings essential for laboratory identification. Similarly, when pellets are removed, care should be taken to avoid undue damage to them. Never place bullets loose in pockets along with hard metal objects, such as keys or coins.

Value in Cases

Crimes against persons, such as aggravated assaults and homicides, are often sources of firearms evidence. Any stolen, found, or confiscated weapons should be submitted to the laboratory for test-firing and for comparison with evidence in pending cases. Never clean guns before submitting them to the crime lab. Fibers, hairs, or other microscopic evidence may have adhered to the gun and may be matched with similar material in the suspect's pocket.

Possible Examination Results

From a laboratory examination of firearms, the following questions can be answered:

1. From what type or make of firearm was the fatal bullet fired?
2. Was the fatal bullet fired from the suspect's gun?
3. Was the discharged cartridge case fired from the suspect's gun?
4. Were two or more bullets fired from the same gun?
5. Were two or more cartridge cases fired from the same gun?
6. What was the gauge of the shotgun used?
7. What size shot was used?
8. What was the composition of the shot used (lead or steel)?
9. How far from the victim was the gun held?

Investigators should become familiar with the types of firearms so that they can quickly identify them.

10. Is there any foreign material attached to the bullet that would indicate its path or flight?

11. Was this gun carried in the suspect's pocket?

12. What were the serial numbers that might have been ground off this gun?

13. Has the gun ever been used to commit an offense, not yet solved, in which bullets or cartridges were previously submitted?

14. Are there any identifiable fingerprints on either the weapon or the cartridges or shells?

Drugs as Evidence

Criminals are often high on drugs or alcohol when they commit crimes or when they are arrested. Drugs may be found concealed in objects or on individuals, or lying in plain sight. In Chapter 21, we will discuss in greater detail the recognition and investigation of controlled drugs and narcotics.

Value in Cases

Following are some cases in which drugs may be of value as evidence in a case.

Assault   Since assaults generally involve aggressive or violent contact between the victim and the assailant, it is possible that vials or packages of drugs may be lost or dropped during the struggle. Handle any small envelopes, bottles, vials, or plastic bags found at the scene very carefully, as they may contain important evidence and may also hold fingerprint evidence.

Death   As a matter of routine, always look around a homicide crime scene to see if there is any evidence of drugs. Drugs may have been used by either the victim or the suspect or may have been a contributing factor in the homicide—either as the murder weapon or as the subject of the dispute leading to the death.

Illegal Drug Laboratories   Use caution when searching an illegal drug lab, and handle all material found there with care. Until analyzed, all substances found in such crime scenes should be considered highly toxic and dangerous.

Possible Examination Results

From a laboratory examination of drug substances, the following determinations can be made:

1. *Confirm corpus delicti*   Laboratory analysis can establish what the powder or other substance found at the crime scene actually is. In many cases, such analysis is necessary to determine that an illegal act has occurred.

2. *Identify designer drugs*   So-called *designer drugs* involve modifications of controlled substances that alter the chemical structure to the point where it may no longer be identified as an illegal and regulated substance. Nonetheless, the modified drug may still possess all of the original drug's effects on the mind or behavior.

3. *Quantify the amounts of illegal drugs*   Tests can determine the total weight and quantitative analysis of the illegal drugs. The quantity of a particular drug may alter the specific charge brought against a suspect (personal consumption, distribution, or manufacturing).

Documents as Evidence

In considering documents, investigators are generally concerned with comparisons. Handwriting or typefaces may be compared with other written or printed materials to establish their identity. Documents can also be checked for latent fingerprints. Further, documents may contain watermarks or special imprints that can help an investigator identify a distribution or manufacturing source. Always remember to maintain a document, throughout the investigation, in the condition in which it was found. Never handle documents with ungloved hands or subject them to dirt or to unnecessary heat, light, or moisture. Do not fold or tear a document or write directly on it.

Value in Cases

A document is anything on which a mark has been made to convey some message. Any form of document may be useful to investigators in establishing whether or not a crime has been committed.

Suicide   A note or letter left by a suicide, once authenticated, may explain the reason the person took his or her life. If not authenticated, the same document may provide a clue to the person who actually killed the victim and tried to make it look like a suicide.

Forgeries   Copying or simulating a signature on checks or credit card slips is an enormous crime problem. Examination of a document may determine whether the forger simulated the signature, copied it, or had no knowledge of the way the genuine signature looked.

Cases in Which Documents Are Questioned   Documents can play an important part in many types of offenses. An anonymous letter could be important in the investigation of a kidnapping. The handwriting on a hotel registration card might lead to the conclusion that a burglary suspect was in the vicinity on the night of a break-in.

Comparison Specimens of Documents

Document evidence can be useful in answering such crime scene questions as "Is this the deceased's writing on this suicide note?" Therefore, it is important for investigators to know what kinds of documents to examine and how best to obtain comparison specimens. The *Handbook of Forensic Science*[5] lists 14 types of documents and writing implements that might be examined: (1) handwriting (script), (2) hand printing or lettering, (3) forgeries, (4) typewriting, (5) photocopies, (6) mechanical impressions (from printers, check writers, rubber stamps, embossers, and seals), (7) altered or obliterated writing, (8) carbon paper, (9) writing instruments (pencils, pens, crayons, and markers), (10) burned or charred paper, (11) typewriters (brand identification from typewriting), (12) printers (brand identification from printout), (13) facsimile machines (brand identification from sample), and (14) paper (watermark and safety paper identification).

When you have a suspect under investigation and want to collect samples of his or her handwriting to compare with document evidence, use the following technique: If the case involves suspected forged checks, obtain blank check forms of the same size as the checks in question. Then have the suspect write, at your dictation, the material appearing on a worthless check. Do not assist him or her with form, spelling, or punctuation. Also have the suspect use the same type of writing instrument as was used on the fraudulent check. Do not allow the suspect to see the questioned check. Obtain at least six samples—preferably more. Take each specimen from the suspect as he or she completes it. In addition to the writing on the blank checks, try to obtain known genuine standards of the subject's writing from other sources, such as letters, legal documents, or employment records.

If it is impossible to get comparison samples of a suspect's handwriting from other sources, then use this technique. Place the suspect in a writing position comparable to that under which the suspected document was written, if possible. Provide paper similar to that of the questioned document, in texture, size, and format (lined or unlined), as well as a similar writing instrument. Also require the style or method (printing in all capitals, printing in capitals and lowercase letters, or writing in script) used in the questioned document. Then dictate approximately 100 words of text you have created that includes dates, numbers, abbreviations, punctuation, and capitalized proper names. Be sure to include in the dictated text words or phrases similar to those appearing on the document in question. As before, do not assist the writer with spelling or punctuation. Obtain samples with both the right and left hands. As each specimen is completed, remove it from the view of the suspect. Obtain at least three samples of the same material.

If a questioned signature is also involved, obtain 10 or 15 samples of the signature, each written on a different sheet of paper. Remove each signature from the suspect's view as it is completed. Witness each sample on the back, never on the front. If possible, also obtain known genuine standards of the suspect's signature from other sources, such as letters, notes, or legal documents.

Typewriter Comparison Specimens

Type the specimens on paper similar in surface to that in the questioned document. If in doubt, use standard typewriter paper. Type the questioned text word for word three times. If the document is very long, specimens of the first page or two will suffice. On separate sheets of paper, also type some common letter groups, shown in Figure 4–4, as well as three complete impressions of the typewriter typeface, made by striking all the keys in each row. Remove the typewriter ribbon, and submit both the ribbon and the typing specimens to the lab.

Computer Printer Comparison Specimens

Some older printers use daisy-wheel technology, similar to that of a typewriter. The wheel contains metal type that spins and strikes the paper through a ribbon, leaving an impression on the paper. The printed output can look only like the characters that are physically on the mechanical spinning daisy wheel. Other printers use a dot matrix system of printing. Pinlike points press against a ribbon and create letters from several pinpoint marks. This style of printer allows more sizes and shapes

---

Figure 4–4 Common letter groups for typewriter comparison specimens.

```
ing, act, at, ed, it, ar, in, ten, es, ies, eis,
est, art, ord, que, quo, che, chi, men, man, ain,
tion, the, thi, er, ion, ent, ry, pe, pi, pos, poi,
te, ta, po, pie, ew, we, wa, wo, tr, oy, king, rot,
rat, rut, boy, ad, aid, af, go, age, bad, dab,
able, fall, fix, just, sta, sti, gun, ill, igo,
get, gone, hun, hut, hob, had, his, ape, sh, fu,
lu, roc, run, muk, ac, ck, ek, cu, he, bid, bex.
```

of letters to be produced and thus provides a wider variety of fonts. Laser printers, unlike daisy-wheel and dot matrix printers, use no ribbon. Instead, they distribute carbon powder on the page to form letters, lines, and graphics. These printers offer a wide variety of font sizes and styles, and some can print in color.

Regardless of the sort of printer, various characteristics of the printer's letter creation may be observed. In the daisy-wheel style, as with traditional typewriter print, flaws in the characters will be reproduced on the printed piece. Similarly, dot matrix printers sometimes produce identifiable flaws from damaged or misaligned pins. Even with laser printer technology, a microscopic examination may reveal comparable characteristics in letter configurations.

Possible Examination Results

From a laboratory examination of documents, the following determinations can be made:

1. Was a particular document written by a particular individual?
2. Is a particular writing forged?
3. What was the make, model, and approximate age of the typewriter or printer used?
4. Was a particular typewriter used to type a particular document?
5. Was a particular check protector used to make a particular imprint?
6. What was the content of an erased, obliterated, altered, or written-over writing, typing, or printing?
7. What differences, if any, are there between inks in one or several documents?
8. Which stroke was written last, when two strokes of writing cross one another?
9. Did two pieces of paper come from the same source?
10. Do uneven edges of torn paper match, to prove that several pieces originally formed the whole document?
11. Do the perforated edges of a check, receipt, or stamp match the corresponding checkbook, receipt book, or sheet or book of stamps?
12. Will the creases and folds in the document aid in determining where it has been—for example, in a particular billfold?
13. What is the context of writing or printing on burned or charred paper?

Flammables as Evidence

The basic principle of arson evidence collection is to prevent the volatile liquid from evaporating. In some instances, it may be possible to seal the original container, thus avoiding having to pack it in another sealed container.

Value in Cases

When investigating cases in which flammables are involved, the investigator generally wants to determine the source of the flame and what was ignited.

Arson Flammable liquids may be suspected as the cause of fire, either because of the nature of the fire or because of the absence of a natural cause. The most common liquids encountered are gasoline, kerosene, and paint thinner. Less frequently encountered are isopropyl (rubbing) alcohol, charcoal lighter, and a variety of petroleum-based products.

Theft The siphoning of gasoline from automobiles and the theft of petroleum products from storage locations are examples of cases in which flammables may be significant physical evidence.

Possible Examination Results

From a laboratory examination of flammables, the following determinations can be made:

1. *Confirm corpus delicti* The laboratory can isolate the flammable liquid from the fire debris and determine whether it is gasoline, kerosene, or a more exotic flammable. Such examination can furnish evidence from which the jury may infer that the fire was intentionally set.

2. *Connect flammables with a source available to the suspect* If the liquid has not evaporated appreciably (e.g., if it is present in a can left at the scene or is well soaked into an unburned material), the laboratory can compare it with material available to the suspect. The liquid might come from a drum of paint thinner in the suspect's garage or may be gasoline from a service station.

Corrosives as Evidence

Liquids such as acids and alkalies require special handling and containers. Consult and follow the advice of a laboratory expert before handling, preparing, or transporting any such liquids.

Explosives as Evidence

When dangerous explosives are involved, immediately clear the area for a reasonable distance. Notify the crime laboratory. Do not try to disarm, move, or transport explosive materials unless directed to do so by explosives experts.

Evidence Specimen	Identification/Packaging	Notebook Record
Ammunition: Fired bullets	Scratch identifying mark on base of bullet with knife or scriber; otherwise, mark on tip or nose. Wrap each bullet separately in soft tissue or cotton. Pack tightly in small container, seal and label with case identifying data. If more than one bullet, use item number to designate. (If embedded in material such as wood or plaster, cut out and send that portion.) Package and seal in larger, substantial container and transmit to lab.	Record date, time, case number, recovery location, type of identifying mark, location of mark, witness to recovery, and disposition. Sketch recovery area and show relationship to other evidence at scene.
Fired metallic cartridge cases	Scratch mark on inside of open end, or identify on outside near top, with initials and date. Handle evidence and packaging as suggested above for fired bullets.	Same as above.
Loaded metallic cartridges	Scratch identifying mark or initials and date on side of case near top. Note number, location, and manufacturer's designation (e.g., Rem-UMC, .38 S&W). Mark boxes of ammunition on side with ink or indelible marker. Wrap and package as indicated above for cartridge cases, bullets.	Same as above.
Loaded shotgun shells	Place initials and date on side of shell in ink or indelible pencil. Wrap shells separately, and package as noted above for fired bullets.	Same as above.
Fired shotgun shells	Same as above.	Same as above.
Shot pellets	Place collected pellets in cotton or tissue, and package as for fired bullets, above. On outside of container indicate nature of contents, date and place obtained, name of officer, and case identifying data.	Notes should include date, time, location and method of recovery, witness to recovery, method of packaging, and disposition. Make small sketch of recovery area.
Shot wads	Place date and initials on wad with pen or indelible marker. Put in glass vial, small envelope, or pill box. Seal; label with	Notes similar to above.

Evidence Specimen	Identification/Packaging	Notebook Record
	identifying case data. Package and transmit as for fired bullets, above.	
Empty cartridge cases	Scratch mark on *inside* of open end, never on closed end. If found in revolver, note chamber location of each.	Same as for fired bullets.
Blood: Liquid	Have drawn by authorized person, collecting at least 5 cc in a sterile container. Place identifying data on adhesive tape affixed to outside of sterile test tube containing specimen. Seal, and deliver to laboratory as soon as possible. If delay is involved, refrigerate but do not freeze. (Do not use preservative, except when requesting DNA analysis.) Seal and label in more substantial container to submit to lab.	Include date, name of victim or suspect, case identification, identity of doctor who obtained specimen, location where obtained, and disposition.
Liquid recovered at crime scene	Place identifying data on adhesive tape attached to sterile glass test tube containing specimen. Seal and transmit as above.	Record date, time, recovery location, name of victim or suspect, method of collecting and identifying specimen, disposition, and case number. Sketch recovery area, indicating measurements.
Bloodstains: On small objects	Place initials and date on object, away from stain area. Package entire object in appropriate-size container so that stain will not rub against surfaces. Seal package and label it with identifying case data. Forward to lab.	Same as above.
On large, immovable objects	Note size, shape, and location of blood spots. Photograph or videotape. Then cut out portion around stain and remove intact. Place initials and date on material away from stain. Place in container, seal, and label with identifying case data. If stain portion cannot be cut out, scrape or chip each specimen into a clean glass vial,	Same as above.

Evidence Specimen	Identification/Packaging	Notebook Record
	plastic pillbox, or clean sheet of paper. Use a clean instrument for each scraping. Seal and label appropriately. Package in more substantial container to transmit to lab.	
On clothing and other textile materials	Submit the entire article. Mark each item directly on the material, away from stain area. Attach an identifying tag. Never package a wet article; allow it to air dry. Do not fold or crumple garments. Place on clean sheets of paper and wrap separately. Place in larger container, seal, and forward to the lab.	Include date obtained, kind of article, location of recovery, type and place of stain, method of identification, and disposition.
In soil	Place identifying data on adhesive tape affixed to glass jar containing the soil specimen. Seal jar and deliver to laboratory.	Record date, appearance of stain, location, amount, relationship to fixed objects, and disposition. Make sketch, including measurements.
Clothing	Mark identification directly on clothing items in an inconspicuous place. Wrap each item separately, seal, and label with identifying case data. Date and initial.	Record date, case identification, type of article, place of recovery, method of identification, disposition, and case number.
Corrosive materials (acids, alkalies)	Consult crime laboratory for advice.	
Documents: Requiring handwriting examination	Mark on reverse side in lower right or left corner. Place in manila envelope, taking care not to crease. Seal, and label with identifying case data, indicating which writing is in question. In suspected forgeries, submit examples of genuine writing.	Include date and title of case, type of document, identity of person furnishing item or place where obtained, and disposition.
Requiring other examinations (erasures, ink, typewriters, printers)	Same as above.	Same as above.

Evidence Specimen	Identification/Packaging	Notebook Record
Charred or burned paper	Place charred material on top of loose cotton and then in a cardboard container. Seal, mark "Fragile," and deliver to laboratory. Show date, case identification data, and initials of officer.	Same as above.
Drugs: Powders, capsules, pills, tablets, cigarettes	Retain in container or carefully collect loose drugs and place in appropriate container. Place date, initials, and case number on container. Leave drugs in container, and place in special sealing envelope. Identify envelope with pertinent case data.	Record date, place of recovery, suspect's name, method of marking, witness to recovery, and disposition. Make sketch of recovery area. If more than one item, use an item number sequence.
Liquids	Mark and date each bottle. Seal cap tightly, and place in evidence envelope. Label appropriately.	Same as above.
Explosives	Clear the area for a reasonable distance, and notify the crime lab. Do not try to disarm, move, or transport explosive materials.	
Fibers: Visible or firmly attached	Photograph and/or videotape, and draw a diagram of position and amount. Carefully remove and place in small pillbox, glass vial, or other tightly capped container. Label, seal, and transmit to lab. If fibers are small, use adhesive-tape technique. Label, seal, and transmit to the lab.	Record date, place of recovery, suspect's name, method of marking, witness to recovery, and disposition. Make sketch of recovery area. If more than one item, use an item number sequence.
Visible, not firmly attached	Same as above.	Same as above.
Not visible, but suspected	Use adhesive-tape technique, sealing and labeling as above.	Same as above.
Transferred to victim's or suspect's clothing	Keep all items separate when placing in containers. Mark outside stained area with ink or indelible marker. Label as "Fibers possibly transferred to victim/suspect."	Same as above.

Evidence Specimen	Identification/Packaging	Notebook Record
Transferred to other fibrous materials	Same as above.	Same as above.
Fingernail cuttings or scrapings	Cuttings are preferred from both suspect and victim. If scrapings are taken, use a clean instrument for each person. Place cuttings or scrapings from each hand or foot in separate pillbox, glass vial, or other tightly closing container. Label, seal, and transmit as above.	Same as above.
Firearms: Handguns	Scratch identifying mark on frame, side of barrel, cylinder, or other part of gun not readily removed. Attach a reinforced tag to trigger guard. On tag, record make, type, model, case identification data, officer's identity, and date. Place weapon in polyethylene bag, plastic pouch, or manilla evidence envelope. Seal container and label appropriately. If gun is to be unloaded, record the position of the fired and unfired cartridges in the gun's cylinder. Deliver in person. If sent to lab, first unload, then lace with twine into holes punched into box. Place in larger container, wrap, seal, label, and ship.	Include make, type, caliber, barrel length, color, and all numbers showing on weapon. Also record date, time, method of identification, witness to recovery, and disposition of weapon. Draw small sketch of recovery area and relationships to other items of evidence. Include measurements.
Rifles/shotguns	Scratch identifying mark on an inconspicuous part of barrel or other major component of weapon. Attach a reinforced tag to trigger guard, containing identifying data: make, model, caliber, serial number, place of recovery, officer's initials, and date. Package as for handguns. Deliver in person. If gun is to be unloaded, identify position of ammunition in gun and clip, using a numerical figure to represent each round. If sent to lab, follow directions for handguns, above. Dismantle for easier shipment.	Same as above.

Evidence Specimen	Identification/Packaging	Notebook Record
Shot or powder burns	Cautiously remove clothing to avoid dislodging loose particles. Mark outside burn area with ink or indelible marker. Do not fold or cut garment. Place between clean sheets of paper, then between pieces of heavy cardboard, and tape firmly in place. Label, wrap in substantial container, and send to lab. If burn is on unclothed part of body, photograph and videotape before and after cleaning, and forward visuals to lab.	Same as above.
Flammables:		
Liquid in containers	Close top of container and seal with tape, taking care not to destroy fingerprints. Cork uncapped containers, or transfer portion of liquid to clean container. Affix identifying tag, including item number and description of liquid, and transmit to lab. Be sure to request quick analysis.	Record location where liquid was found; date it was obtained; the collector's name, position, and badge or serial number; and case identification.
Distributed at scene	*Soil:* Collect at least 1 gallon of most likely soil in clean 1-gallon paint can or canning jar; seal securely; transmit. *Upholstery:* Collect fabric and stuffing; handle as above. *Flooring/Carpeting:* Cut out section and seal as above, or wrap material in plastic sheeting and deliver to lab. *Rags:* Place in airtight containers as above. Handle as above.	Same as above.
Glass	Preserve as for glass fragments (even though fragments do not retain identifiable traces of liquid) for possible connection to suspect.	Same as above.
Clothing	Quickly obtain samples if suspicious odor is detected on suspect, as flammables quickly dissipate. Handle as above for "Flammables, distributed at scene."	Same as above.

Evidence Specimen	Identification/Packaging	Notebook Record
Comparison specimens	Collect as soon as possible, and seal securely. Do not mix suspected liquids found at the scene. If possible, find out date of delivery. Handle as above for all categories.	Same as above.
Glass fragments: Microscopic	Wrap all articles separately, attaching an identifying tag. Possible sources of fragments should be packed in smallest container possible, to avoid loss. Do not pack with cotton or protective material. May be fastened to bottom of container with cellophane tape. Seal completely so that no particles can escape.	Record date, place of recovery, suspect's name, method of marking, witness to recovery, and disposition. Make sketch of recovery area. If more than one item, use an item number sequence.
Large, visible	If matching of edges is possibility, embed thin, protuding edges in clay, putty, or similar substance. Carefully package in larger, substantial container, and label, seal, and transmit as above. If submitted to determine direction of impact, record which side was on outside and which was on inside.	Same as above.
Comparison specimens	Take samples at least the size of a quarter to accompany other glass evidence submitted. Take from area near point of impact. Keep comparison and evidence samples separate. Package and transmit as above.	Same as above.
Hair: Visible and firmly attached	Leave intact on object. Draw diagram showing position and amount of hair. Label and pack so hairs will not be dislodged. If object is immovable, carefully remove hairs and place in pillbox, glass vial, or clean folded white paper. Label and seal as for fibers, above.	Record date, place of recovery, suspect's name, method of marking, witness to recovery, and disposition. Make sketch of recovery area. If more than one item, use an item number sequence.
Visible, not firmly attached	Collect and handle as above.	Same as above.
Presence suspected	Wrap articles separately in clean paper. Never mix articles from the suspect and	Same as above.

Evidence Specimen	Identification/Packaging	Notebook Record
	the victim. Place wrapped article in larger container, and label, seal, and transmit as for clothing, above.	
Comparison specimens	Pull samples from several areas, obtaining at least several dozen hairs, or run clean comb through hair. Collect and handle as above.	Same as above.
Paint:		
On clothing	Wrap all articles separately, attaching an identifying tag. Mark, label, seal, and transmit as for clothing.	Notes should be similar to those made for glass fragments.
On small, portable objects	Submit entire object, wrapping carefully or placing in clean paper bag, ensuring that area with paint smear is protected. Handle as above.	Notes similar to above.
On large, non-portable objects	Scrape paint fragments off with clean instruments. Record exact location, amount, nature, color, and surface. Keep samples from different locations separate. Handle as for fibers or hair.	Same as above.
As liquid or wet smears	Place liquid samples in widemouthed tins, glass bottles, or jars. Let wet smears air dry completely before preparing for shipment. Handle as for blood.	Same as above.
Comparison specimens	Take samples from area near apparent damage. Put paint samples from each location near point of impact in an individual container. Flake specimen down to the bare surface. Handle as for fibers.	Same as above.
Semen stains:		
On clothing and other textiles	Collect and handle as for bloodstains on clothing.	Record date, time, title of case, type of material, recovery area, and method of collection and identification. Sketch location where obtained.

Evidence Specimen	Identification/Packaging	Notebook Record
On small portable items	Submit all objects, such as paper, wood, and sanitary protection products, with stain intact. Mark, identify, and label completely. Package separately in breathable container such as a paper bag. Ensure that stained areas do not rub against any other surface. Seal and package in a more substantial container, and forward to lab.	Same as above.
On large, immovable objects	Note size, shape, and location of stains. Cut around entire stain and remove it intact, including portion of unstained area. Place specimen in clean box or bag, and handle as above.	Same as above.
On victim or suspect	Have examining professional transfer stain from legs or thighs onto filter paper and clip or pull hairs that may be stained. If applicable, have vaginal smears obtained, and have fluid in vaginal tract preserved. Place soaked-off stains in clean, breathable containers after air drying. Preserve fluid in tightly capped vial. Handle hairs as above. Transport slides in cardboard holders.	Same as above.

NOTE: In each case involving the recovery of evidence, and whenever necessary, obtain adequate standards of material from the crime scene for later comparison with similar materials found on the person, clothing, shoes, car, tools, etc., of a suspect who may be apprehended on the day of the crime or later.

SUMMARY BY LEARNING OBJECTIVES

Learning Objective 1

Scientific examinations conducted in crime laboratories, on specimens collected by criminal investigators, can help determine whether or not a crime has been committed, who may have committed it, and how the crime was committed.

Learning Objective 2

Knowing the correct procedures for collecting, preserving, and transmitting physical evidence is essential to the work of every criminal investigator.

Learning Objective 3

Deoxyribonucleic acid (DNA) is an organic substance found in the molecules of human cells. These molecules carry genetic information and establish each person as separate and distinct. Analysis of DNA from blood, semen, hair, saliva, urine, or tissue can be used to match victims or suspects with a crime scene and to positively identify an individual.

Learning Objective 4

Blood is the most common form of evidence found at crime scenes and may assist in identifying a suspect through blood typing or DNA analysis. How blood evidence is distributed at a crime scene may also help investigators recreate portions of the crime scene. Semen, like blood, may assist in identifying a suspect, through DNA analysis of samples taken from the victim or the crime scene and specimens obtained from a suspect.

Learning Objective 5

Hair is often a valuable means of personal identification. It retains its structural features for a very long time and can be used to identify both the sex and race of a person. Fibers are actually more distinguishable than hair, because microscopic analysis can determine the characteristics of each strand and link it to a specific garment.

Learning Objective 6

Physical examination of glass fragments can help in determining how the glass was broken, what direction the force came from, and whether the glass matches comparison specimens. Paint evidence generally appears in three forms—chips or flakes, smears, and intact finishes on objects—which the crime lab will try to match to known comparison specimens.

Learning Objective 7

Firearm evidence can include a variety of weapons, as well as many types of ammunition. It is important for investigators to be able to distinguish among the various types of firearms and to known the kinds of ammunition each uses. In addition to their value as evidence, firearms may also carry additional physical evidence, such as fingerprints, blood, or hair.

Learning Objective 8

A range of documents and writing instruments can be examined to compare handwriting, typefaces, and other written and printed materials to establish their identity. Samples of a suspect's writing should be obtained from personal and legal documents or in a controlled setting using paper and writing instruments similar to the document in question.

QUESTIONS FOR REVIEW

Learning Objective 1

1. What should an investigator know about collecting, identifying, and managing physical evidence for laboratory examination?
2. What should accompany physical evidence transmitted to the crime lab?

Learning Objective 2

3. Why should an investigator know the correct procedures for collecting, identifying, and transmitting evidence?

Learning Objective 3

4. What is DNA, and why is it important to criminal investigation?

Learning Objective 4

5. How can knowing a suspect's blood type assist in some criminal investigations?
6. What information can a blood spatter tell the investigator?
7. In what types of cases can semen stain evidence be of value?

Learning Objective 5

8. In what types of cases should investigators routinely collect head and body hair samples from victims?
9. Why might finding fibers at a crime scene be a better source of information than finding a suspect's hair?

Learning Objective 6

10. What type of glass fracture appears as a shell or cone? As a series of circular cracks around the point of impact? As cracks that form a star-shaped pattern?
11. What can broken glass suggest about a crime scene?
12. Why must paint samples be chipped from the surface rather than scraped?

13. What is the evidentiary value of glass and paint evidence?

Learning Objective 7

14. Why should investigators develop a familiarity with firearms and ammunition?

Learning Objective 8

15. How might a computer-printed document be matched with the printer that originally produced the document?

CRITICAL THINKING INVESTIGATIVE EXERCISE

Read the following case facts, and write a report in which you answer the questions that follow them. Then participate in a class discussion in which you compare your responses with those of others in the class.

Case Facts

At exactly 9:00 P.M. a man entered a neighborhood grocery store. He grabbed a shopping cart, and the lone store clerk observed him proceeding up and down the store aisles, selecting items. When the man entered, there were three other customers in the store. At one point the man in question was observed at the magazine rack near the front of the store, leisurely flipping through a copy of *Field and Stream.*

A few minutes later, the man approached the checkout counter with several items in his cart. At that point he was the only customer remaining in the store. As the store clerk began to ring up the items from the man's cart, the man drew a blue, short-barrel revolver from beneath his green Miami Hurricanes sweatshirt. He leaned far over the counter and demanded, "Give me all the bills! Make it snappy or I'll blow your head off!"

At first the clerk pretended to comply, but after moving several of the bills from the register into a paper bag, the clerk lunged at the man. There was a scuffle, and the man struck the clerk's head with the barrel of the gun several times, causing a deep, bleeding laceration. The impact of the third blow caused the gun to discharge. A bullet grazed the forehead of the clerk and became embedded in the side wall of the store, just above the milk coolers. The man seemed genuinely surprised by the gun's discharge, and he let it slip from his hand. It fell behind the counter and bounced behind a pile of paper bags on a shelf. The clerk took a solid swing at the man and punched him in the nose. Blood spattered from the man's nose, and he shouted profanities at the clerk as he turned and ran from the store.

As the man fled the store, he ran toward the door with both hands in front of him. He pressed both hands against the glass door and flung it open with such force that it whipped back on its hinges and crashed into the doorstop. By this time, the clerk had come from behind the counter. Though still bleeding himself, he managed to watch through the open doorway as the man ran across the street. The clerk noticed that the man was holding his face with his right hand. In his haste, the man ran into the front corner of a parked car directly across from the store, and barely stopped himself by deflecting the fender with his right hand. He ran up the street about 15 feet farther, jumped into a waiting red Toyota Tercel, and zoomed off. With blood trickling into his eyes, the clerk could make out only that it was a Massachusetts license plate with the first three letters, "TUC-."

When the investigators arrived, they found the clerk and the shopping cart waiting. The cart contained a copy of *Field and Stream,* a can of Edge shaving cream, a loaf of Wonder bread, a flashlight, two D batteries, and a bag of cheese doodles.

The suspect was described to the investigators as a white male in his early twenties, 5′9″–5′10″, who weighed approximately 180 pounds and had short dirty-blond hair. He was wearing white, high-top Nike sneakers, blue jeans, and a green sweatshirt with the Miami Hurricanes logo on it.

1. What areas would you search for evidence?
2. How would you search for the evidence?
3. What types of evidence would you look for?
4. How would you collect the evidence?
5. How would you package, identify, and transport each piece of evidence?
6. What type of analysis would you request from the crime laboratory for each piece of evidence?

INVESTIGATIVE SKILL BUILDERS

Applying Technology to the Task

You have arrived at the scene of a gang-related execution of two teenagers, one male and one female. The female is completely naked and lying on her back. She is about 16 years old, has long brown hair, is about 5′3″ tall, and weighs about 110 pounds.

The male is lying face down about 3 feet from her. His hands and feet have been bound with duct tape. He, too, is about 16 years old. He has short, dark brown hair, is about 5′8″ tall, and weighs about 135 pounds. His head is resting in a small pool of blood that appears to be coming from a wound on his left temple. The female's mouth is filled with what appears to be a pair of panties. There are bruises on the inner portion of her thighs and near her vagina. There is also what may be dried semen on her pubic hair and on her stomach. Like the male, she has what appears to be a single gunshot wound to the left temple.

1. What items of evidence will you collect?
2. What types of tests or analysis will you request from the crime laboratory?
3. Who will you want to interview?

Integrity/Honesty

You are on a drug raid. By the time you and your back-up team enter the home of the known drug dealer, he has already flushed the evidence, about a pound of uncut cocaine, down the toilet. The suspect is laughing at you and your team and saying, "Hey man, look around—you got nothing. You guys are nothing! You can't arrest me. You got nothing." After a thorough search for evidence, you find no drugs.

1. Should you begin carrying small amounts of cocaine or heroin to plant on known drug dealers in the future, in case they also effectively destroy the actual evidence?
2. Should you arrest the suspect and take him to headquarters, just to create an inconvenience for him because he was so arrogant?
3. Could you run cellophane tape over his hands, and have the crime laboratory test for any microscopic evidence of cocaine?

ENDNOTES

1. Bruce L. Berg, *Law Enforcement: An Introduction to Police in Society,* Allyn and Bacon, Boston, 1992.
2. Calvin Goddard, "The Valentine Day Massacre: A Study in Ammunition-Tracing," *American Journal of Police Science,* Vol. 1, 1930, pp. 60–78.
3. Information regarding biological fluids was taken from Maria Josefi (ed.) *Handbook of Forensic Science,* Department of Justice, Federal Bureau of Investigation, Washington, 1995. Additional information was obtained from David Bigbee, *The Examination of Serological Evidence,* Federal Bureau of Investigation Research and Training Center, Quantico, Va., 1989.
4. A. A. Moenssen, F. E. Inbau, and J. E. Starrs, *Scientific Evidence in Criminal Cases,* 3d ed., Foundation Press, New York, 1986.
5. Josefi (ed.), *Handbook of Forensic Science,* pp. 25–28.

CHAPTER 5

Criminal Patterns

CHAPTER OBJECTIVES

After completing this chapter, you will be able to:

1. Discuss the nature and meaning of *modus operandi*.

2. Consider factors influencing *modus operandi*.

3. Discuss how deductions may arise from *modus operandi*.

4. Examine how *modus operandi* can assist in identifying, apprehending, or repressing a suspect.

5. Explore the *modus operandi* parts of a report.

6. Understand how to report *modus operandi* data.

7. Consider psychological profiling and its relationship to *modus operandi*.

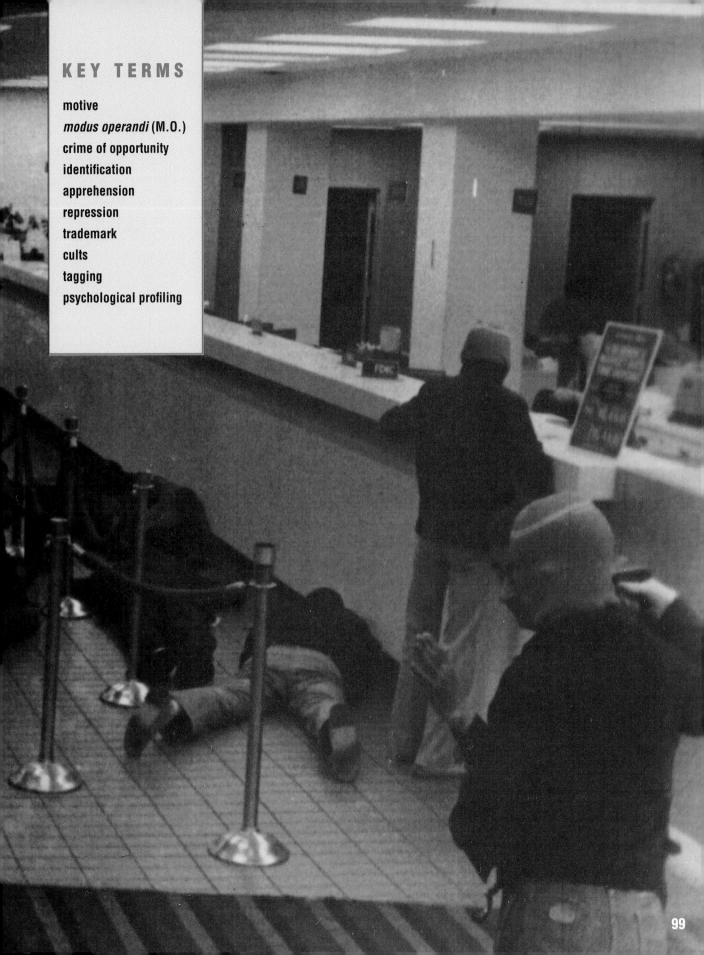

KEY TERMS

motive
modus operandi (M.O.)
crime of opportunity
identification
apprehension
repression
trademark
cults
tagging
psychological profiling

Crime Patterns and Human Behavior

Human beings are largely creatures of habit and, to some extent, predictable in their behavior. If this were not the case, then sociologists, psychologists, and criminologists could never undertake research or suggest any theories or explanations of behavior. This is not to suggest that everything humans do can be predetermined with absolute mathematical accuracy. It does suggest, however, that many criminals commit crimes for specific reasons and take particular repetitive types of actions. In other words, certain types of criminals engage in certain kinds of criminal behavior for similar reasons, or **motives.** Many criminals are consistent in their methods of crime commission. Some actually even have "trademarks" or "signatures" that distinguish them from other perpetrators of the same sorts of crimes. In general, the methods and procedures used by a criminal during the commission of a crime are called the *modus operandi,* or *M.O.* Recognizing an offender's M.O. can assist in identifying a suspect and perhaps even in apprehending him or her.

Motive A wrongdoer's reason for committing the crime.

Modus Operandi

Modus operandi (M.O.) The method of operation that a criminal uses to commit a crime; Latin term for "mode of operation."

Modus operandi is a Latin term for mode, or method, of operation. In police work it describes the activities used by a criminal in committing a crime. It was once believed that every criminal followed a particular M.O. and would rarely, if ever, change the type of crime committed or the method of committing it. For example, in the 1970s it was a relatively simple matter for New York police officers to recognize the work of David Berkowitz, the "Son of Sam," also called the ".44-caliber killer." All of Berkowitz's victims were young females, with the single exception of a long-haired male, whom police believe Berkowitz mistook for a woman. All were shot with the same type of weapon, at close range, and at night. Yet, it was not solely on the basis of his M.O. that Berkowitz was eventually captured. His capture actually resulted from an unpaid parking ticket he received on the night of one of his murders.

Modus operandi data also can assist in more subtle ways. For instance, a neighborhood suffers a wave of burglaries, each committed between 10:00 A.M. and noon and all involving entry through a sliding glass door. It could be inferred that the same people committed all of these burglaries. If only jewelry and stereos are taken in these burglaries, the likelihood that the same party or parties are committing all of these burglaries increases. Now let us say the burglaries suddenly stopped in this community, and burglaries with similar methods of entry, times of

HISTORY

*T*he earliest published material on modus operandi *appeared in 1913, written by Major Sir Llewelyn W. Atcherley, then Chief Constable of the West Riding Constabulary, Yorkshire, England.[1] An American, August Vollmer, former Chief of Police in Berkeley, California, is credited with developing a* modus operandi *index, or compilation of crime scene data, during the early 1900s. Although various refinements have been made to Vollmer's system, it has remained largely intact and is an effective tool for police investigations.*

commission, and items of theft occurred in a nearby neighborhood. One could now infer that the burglar has moved on. The likelihood that these burglaries, in both communities, are unrelated is quite small.

Although the inferences drawn from M.O. are not certainties, they can greatly assist investigators in their pursuit of criminals. In reality, some criminals do commit several different types of crimes and may even intentionally change the type of crime they commit or their methods. Consequently, while a suspect's *modus operandi* may lead an investigator to him or her, it is important never to eliminate a suspect solely because of a different M.O.

Factors Influencing *Modus Operandi*

There are a number of social science explanations for the commission of criminal acts. Relying on the rational-being concept, some suggest that failure to exercise self-control over criminal behavior is an act of free will. Some others support theories that crime is "impulsive" and may occur whenever the opportunity arises. Others claim that some learning or value process has failed. Still others maintain that under certain circumstances most honest, law-abiding individuals might commit a criminal act, a variation of the notion that "locks keep honest people honest." Regardless of what orientation or theory one supports, experience tells us that most crimes are motivated by one or a combination of several specific factors that include the following:

- *Opportunity,* whether accidental or created.
- *Need,* whether real or imagined.

- *Passion,* whether or not the person is mentally stable at the time the crime is committed.

- *Inadequate social skills,* including the inability to be empathic and a lack of belief in conventional values.

Whenever any of the factors (opportunity, need, passion, or inadequate social skills) varies from those of the criminal's previous crimes, the variation may cause a change in the criminal's behavior pattern. For example, suppose a career burglar enters a home and finds a young woman sleeping in the nude. He may decide to rape this woman because he wants personal sexual gratification, because dominating her will make him feel superior to her, and perhaps simply because the opportunity presents itself. To an outside observer, the M.O. appears to have changed, but a trained investigator will look at other elements of the crime to see whether a consistent pattern still exists. Perhaps the burglar always makes a sandwich before leaving the scene, or always breaks into the house in a particular fashion. In other words, the M.O. usually includes a combination of repetitive patterns, not necessarily a single element.

Many crimes can be labeled **crimes of opportunity.** These opportunistic crimes require little or no planning and therefore may have no consistent M.O. For instance, a thief who enters the United States Army and becomes a quartermaster may have no need to steal to support him- or herself. This individual may change his or her M.O. and begin to

Crime of opportunity A crime that is committed, with little or no planning, as the opportunity presents itself.

Crimes of opportunity require little or no planning and, therefore, have no consistent M.O.

embezzle money simply because he or she is in a position to do so. In this case the opportunity to steal may be the key factor that leads to the change in M.O. Often, however, even when the crime is different, there are perceptible similarities in the trademark behavior of the offender.

Conditions during a crime may also create a kind of opportunity and affect the M.O. For example, a warehouse burglar who usually enters through skylights in the roof may find the back door unlocked and use that means to enter instead. Other unexpected occurrences encountered during the course of a crime may likewise alter an offender's M.O. It is important, therefore, that officers understand that they cannot rely solely on a criminal's method of operation to lead to a suspect. The M.O. is only an investigative *aid*. It should be recognized, however, that all acts committed during a crime are important potential clues and possible facets of an M.O. Information obtained through interrogation regarding the suspect's activities (legitimate and illegal), associates, family, personality, intelligence, reputation, and so forth is of tremendous help to an analyst in the identification of criminals.

Deductions From *Modus Operandi* Data

The M.O. file is an orderly method of recording and coding information, designed to reveal habits, traits, or practices of criminal suspects. The trained analyst, as well as the investigator, should be able to see beyond the physical aspects of the way a crime was committed, to determine why it was done in such a manner. Leads regarding M.O. should be weighed according to the degree of probability. Here are some of the deductions that may result from a review of M.O. data:

- A theft by stealth rather than by violence or fraud may indicate either that the criminal is physically nonaggressive and lacks confidence in his or her powers of persuasion or that the theft was more easily accomplished by stealth.

- A theft by stealth may mean the thief is known to the victim or intends to remain in the community and might be recognized later should contact be made with the victim during the crime.

- Well-planned crimes generally eliminate the emotionally unstable as suspects.

- A certain type of premises might be selected, not only because of the type of business conducted, but also because the criminal is familiar with the victim's habits and manner of conducting business.

- A burglary of a residence may suggest a criminal with knowledge of the activities of persons who frequent the area at a certain time (the victim, neighbors, police, and so on) and with an indication of the probable whereabouts of the people living in the residence.

- Crimes committed in areas frequented only by persons working or living in that vicinity usually indicate a local criminal.

- The occupation or previous experience of the criminal may be indicated by the tools selected for the crime, as well as by the skill with which they are employed.

- The point of entry (window, rear door, roof, and so on) may have been chosen because of observation of a burglar alarm system outside the premises.

- Prior "casing" of the victimized premises may have been needed, because of the conditions of the location or precautionary measures taken by the management.

- The selection of a certain victim may be the result of his or her discussing business in public places, keeping large amounts of money at the place of business, hiring transients, employing persons with undesirable associates, and so on.

- A suspect with physical disabilities may be eliminated if the type of crime calls for an agile person, unless evidence of a more physically fit accomplice is developed.

- Burglars known to be adept in the handling of certain tools can be eliminated as suspects where investigation shows that such equipment was used unskillfully.

Uses of *Modus Operandi* Data

One segment of a suspect's M.O. can have greater value than another for purposes of identification, apprehension, or repression. Compiling M.O. information furnished by witnesses in several robberies can aid in the **identification** of a suspect if certain information on physical characteristics—such as facial features, scars, marks, deformities, height, weight, and other data—recurs in descriptions of suspects. Even a nickname or street name (unless used as a decoy) may assist in the identification of a suspect.

The method of operation can assist the police in the **apprehension** of a suspect by pinpointing certain operational patterns. For a check passer, for instance, the type of business establishment victimized, the locality, the time, the day of the week, the type of purchase made, the dress of the check passer, any conversation, and the identification used permit the police to counterattack by alerting merchants in projected areas, placing stops, and using special check bulletins as well as other aids.

Modus operandi data can indicate a likely time and location for future criminal activity. Therefore, steps can be taken in **repression,** or suppression, of criminal activity, given the M.O. data. For example, in a

Identification A process in which physical characteristics and qualities are used to definitely know or recognize a person.

Apprehension The act of seizing or arresting a criminal offender.

Repression The act of suppressing or preventing an action from taking place.

series of prowler complaints, the M.O. data obtained from the reports of several preliminary investigations showed that the incidents occurred generally between 9:30 P.M. and 11:30 P.M. in a certain seven-block area. A concentrated patrol in that area during those times resulted in a sharp drop-off in prowler calls.

In addition to the use of M.O. data for the purposes already set forth, there are other ways in which information obtained in investigative reports is applied. For example, in the interrogation of a suspect, it is possible to clear related cases. Leads are furnished to the investigator to help identify suspects who have used the same M.O. The administrator

National Law Enforcement Telecommunications System The National Law Enforcement Telecommunications System (NLETS) is a computer-controlled message switching network linking local, state, and federal agencies together to exchange information. The law enforcement agencies are linked together by means of computers, terminals, and communication lines. Officers can access the network through mobile data terminals linked to a departmental central computer which is part of a state network tied into NLETS. The system is operational 24 hours per day, 7 days a week.

can use this information in the assignment of personnel and equipment to places where surveillance is needed. Data on M.O. are an excellent means of identifying criminals who move about the state or even the nation.

The *Modus Operandi* Parts of a Report

Much of the *modus operandi* information that investigators work with comes from police crime reports. Crime report forms may vary in format between law enforcement agencies, but the *modus operandi* data are generally broken down into ten categories.

1. Time of Attack, or Date and Time Committed The exact time the offense was committed should be reported if it is known. If the time and date are unknown, then the entire period should be noted in reporting, for example, "May 8 or 9, 7:00 P.M. to 5:00 A.M." Many criminals operate between specific hours, for instance, between 9:00 P.M. and 11:00 P.M. Some commit their crimes only on a particular weekday or only on the weekend. Thus, the time or day can be an identifying trait.

2. Person Attacked (Type of Victim) This subdivision is used because the criminal often picks people of a particular occupation or class as victims. The information wanted here is the type of person attacked, for example, liquor store owner, bank messenger, jewelry seller, high school student, or doctor. The name of the victim is not used.

3. Property Attacked, or Type of Premises Entered The place in which the offense was committed is described in this section. For example, a liquor store robber may rob only those places situated on corners. Therefore, in a report, this type of store location should be listed as "liquor store—corner." Other types of premises attacked should be accurately listed. For example, we might find the descriptions "one-story, six-room, stucco dwelling," "hallway, third floor," "single-family attached corner house," "eight-story office building," or "bank, midblock." For reporting purposes under this section, a street, alley, sidewalk, highway, vacant lot, or field may be considered "property attacked."

4. How Attacked (Point of Entry) This section requires information about how the offense was committed and how it was made possible. The exact type of information is determined by the class of crime committed. For example, in a robbery case, show what induced the victim to hand over the property. The entry for this category might be "beaten," "threatened," "bound and gagged," or something similar. In fraudulent-check cases, the method of attack might be "forged signature," "forged endorsement," "signed fictitious name and address," or "used counterfeit payroll checks." In burglary cases, the method of attack refers to the place of entry and the manner by which entry was effected. If a safe is burglarized, the investigator should also indicate whether the safe was attacked by drilling, explosives, burning, peeling, punching, pulling, hauling away, or some other means. In sex crimes, the method would be what made the victim submit to the offense—promise of marriage, gifts, threat, and others. In a swindle or confidence game, the method might be introducing a companion to the victim as a prominent person in politics, business, entertainment, or other fields.

5. Means of Attack (Tool or Equipment Used in Committing the Crime)

The instrument used to gain entry should be reported, first by size and then by type; for example, in a burglary case "3/4-inch drill," "hook and line," "glass cutter," "1/2-inch jimmy," or ".38-caliber nickel-plated revolver." The means of attack may also be bodily force. In the body of the report, any marks left by the instrument should be described in detail.

6. Objective of Attack (Why the Crime Was Committed or Attempted)

For example, the objective might be to obtain money, jewelry, furs, stamp or coin collections, narcotics, firearms, cigarettes, or other items,

The objective of a crime may be to obtain money, jewelry, weapons, or other items of value.

regardless of value. In crimes against the person, the objective of attack, or reason the crime was committed, may be ransom, revenge, or perpetration of another crime, such as homicide. The objective of attack in a homicide case might be robbery or rape. In other homicide cases, the objective might be to prevent witnesses from testifying, to secure an estate or inheritance, to gratify sexual desires, or another reason. Identifiable property listed in a report as stolen and later found in possession of a suspect tends to connect that person with the crime.

7. Trademark or Peculiarity A **trademark** is a personal habit shown by the criminal. Notes in this section might be "ate food during crime," "wore gloves," "lowered window shades," "left note behind," "malicious damage done to property," or "pretended to be a customer." Some criminals, while committing a robbery, for example, say very little and are cool in their operations; others appear excited and talk more than necessary. Some criminals perform sadistic or perverted acts that establish their trademark. They might, as an example, cut off genitals before killing victims. Generally speaking, the more unusual the trademark is, the greater the value it has in identifying the offender. However, any crime will disclose to the diligent investigator some individual characteristic that will assist in identification of a suspect. The trademark behavior may occur before, during, or after the commission of the crime.

8. What Suspect Said Quote verbatim, if possible. In the investigation and reporting of crimes such as robbery, con games, check forgeries, and others in which the victim conversed with the criminal, pay particular attention to what the suspect said and did, as well as to the physical description. The suspect may mispronounce a particular word or use a peculiar expression, mannerism, or dialect that will assist in identification. Speech habits seldom change over time and may become more pronounced when the individual is under tension. Furthermore, expressions such as "Get your hands up, or I'll blow out your guts," "Reach for God," or "This is a stickup," may unconsciously become a part of the criminal's *modus operandi*.

9. Written Words or Symbols Certain symbols or words are commonly associated with ritualized crimes and those related to cults. Generally speaking, **cults** are groups of people sharing a system of religious or quasi-religious beliefs. Cults both invent their own rituals and use rituals commonly associated with the occult in general. Consequently, many symbols left at a crime scene may offer a potential means of identifying a specific cult. Symbols such as circles, goats' heads, inverted crosses, hexagrams (six-pointed stars), or pentagrams (five-pointed stars) may direct an investigator to a cult (see Figure 5–1).

Trademark A distinctive characteristic by which a criminal becomes known.

Cults Religious or quasi-religious groups sometimes considered extreme, with followers that sometimes act in an unconventional manner.

Figure 5–1 Common occult and satanic symbols.

BEELZEBUB	The Devil; Satan.
MARKOS	Abracadabra.
NATAS	Reversed spelling of Satan.

FFF
666
9 9
6
} Various ways of representing the *Beast* or the *Antichrist*, son of Satan.

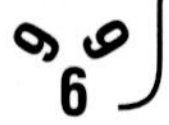

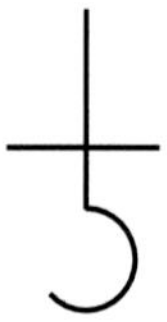

The Cross of Confusion, which questions the existence of Jesus Christ and hence the validity of Christianity.

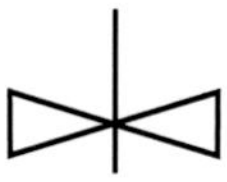

An inverted double-bladed axe, the symbol of antijustice.

Pentagram, representing the four elements of earth controlled by the Spirit.

Inverted pentagram, the symbol of the occult.

Hexagram circle, for protection and control of demons.

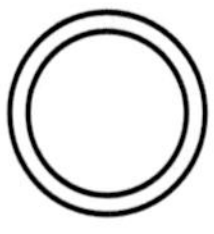

Double circles, representing containment and control over evil power.

Satanic traitor, symbolizing someone who has betrayed the coven. Sometimes used as a warning sign. Sometimes used as a death threat or ritual of revenge.

Tagging Writing a word
or symbol on a wall to
identify a person or a
group such as a gang.

Recently, law enforcement officials have become aware that street gangs have begun using various symbolic codes scrawled on walls to communicate with one another and to issue warnings to rival gangs. Terms and initials once thought to be simply **tagging,** or writing one's street nickname or initials as a form of graffiti, are now believed to be symbolic gang codes.

10. Transportation Used or Observed Include vehicle type, year, make, model, color, license or identification number, and unusual features. Descriptive data, such as type of tires, seat covers, emblems, exhaust pipes, spotlights, antennas, and bumper stickers, are helpful in identifying a car or another vehicle, such as a motorcycle or boat.

How to Report *Modus Operandi* Data

Suppose a series of nighttime burglaries occurred in a certain area. The burglar's M.O. was to enter a medical office building through an open or unlocked window from the fire escape. The burglar gained access to the medical and dental offices by using a 2-inch jimmy bar with a V notched in the blade. Money, narcotics, and prescription forms were taken. The burglar left the premises via the fire escape. The M.O. data from one of these burglaries would be recorded as shown in Figure 5–2.

The body of the report should contain a complete chronological narrative of all the facts obtained during the investigation including an explanation of the M.O. factors. Any details that might be connected with the crime should be set forth. Information that is not strictly part of the suspect's method of operation (a physical description or a description of the property stolen) should also be included. *Modus operandi* factors would include such acts as lying in wait, luring the victim, drugging the victim, detouring a vehicle, casing a target, establishing the confidence of victims, or purchasing or acquiring equipment. Such other procedures as developing contacts, gaining employment with ulterior objectives, procuring accomplices, securing a market for disposal of loot, wiping off fingerprints, wearing a mask, and placing a lookout should also be part of a complete report.

Modus operandi files are typically organized into two major categories of information: (1) information pertaining to crimes committed by unidentified offenders and (2) information concerning crimes committed by identified and apprehended offenders. In many police

FYI

Although many beliefs and practices of cults may appear similar to those of mainstream society, other elements of cult practice do not. Some ritualistic practices of certain cults may be viewed as cruel, violent, evil, deviant, and illegal. Often these sorts of cults are associated with the occult, paganism, witchcraft, demonology, or satanism.

Figure 5–2 *Modus operandi* parts of a report.

MODUS OPERANDI (SEE INSTRUCTIONS)									
39. DESCRIBE CHARACTERISTICS OF PREMISES AND AREA WHERE OFFENSE OCCURRED 5 Klamath, Irvine, CA. Single family attached home – living room/bedroom									
40. DESCRIBE BRIEFLY HOW OFFENSE WAS COMMITTED Window jimmied to gain entrance (front window) Stolen property taken through front door (see attached property list)									
41. DESCRIBE WEAPON, INSTRUMENT, EQUIPMENT, TRICK, DEVICE OR FORCE USED Possible pry marks left on window frame									
42. MOTIVE – TYPE OF PROPERTY TAKEN OR OTHER REASON FOR OFFENSE Color T.V. ; stackable stereo, one gold ring with ruby, one 18k gold 24" necklace									
43. ESTIMATED LOSS VALUE AND/OR EXTENT OF INJURIES – MINOR, MAJOR Total value $1150									
44. WHAT DID SUSPECT/S SAY – NOTE PECULIARITIES Unknown									
45. VICTIM'S ACTIVITY JUST PRIOR TO AND/OR DURING OFFENSE Shopping at local market (appoximately 60 minutes)									
46. TRADEMARK – OTHER DISTINCTIVE ACTION OF SUSPECT/S A pair of victim's panties found on bed – may have semen on them									
47. VEHICLE USED – LICENSE NO. – ID NO. – YEAR – MAKE – MODEL – COLORS (OTHER IDENTIFYING CHARACTERISTICS) Unknown									

48. SUSPECT NO. 1 (LAST, FIRST, MIDDLE) Unknown	49. RACE – SEX -	50. AGE -	51. HT. -	52. WT. -	53. HAIR -	54. EYES -	55. ID NO. OR DOB -	56. ARRESTED YES ☐ NO ☐
57. ADDRESS, CLOTHING AND OTHER IDENTIFYING MARKS OR CHARACTERISTICS Specimen of semen taken in evidence								
58. SUSPECT NO. 2 (LAST, FIRST, MIDDLE) Unknown	59. RACE – SEX -	60. AGE -	61. HT. -	62. WT. -	63. HAIR -	64. EYES -	65. ID NO. OR DOB -	66. ARRESTED YES ☐ NO ☐
67. ADDRESS, CLOTHING AND OTHER IDENTIFYING MARKS OR CHARACTERISTICS N/A								

REPORTING OFFICERS George Billing	RECORDING OFFICER	TYPED BY GB	DATE AND TIME 03-07-98	ROUTED BY ALB

agencies, data that pertain to the *modus operandi* of a reported crime are entered into the department's computer information management system. These M.O. data then are available to investigators to analyze and consider when cases arise with similar characteristics. Often, it is not the unique characteristics of a crime that identify the suspect, but the common elements that reoccur with each criminal incident.

Legally, the *modus operandi* can be used only as an investigative lead. It can be introduced in court only as evidence to show the common purpose and design of the criminal when a series of crimes have been committed and linked to the defendant. Otherwise, enough evidence, direct or circumstantial, must be obtained to prove a specific case against an arrested person.

Psychological Profiling

As we have seen, one of the objectives of a criminal investigation is to identify a suspect in the crime. Comparing the manner in which a crime was committed with available *modus operandi* files is one way of

HISTORY

The process of psychological profiling was developed during World War II by the Office of Strategic Services (OSS), a secret intelligence agency of the United States government that was dissolved after the war ended in 1945. In one of its projects, the agency hired Walter Langer, a psychiatrist, to project a profile of Adolf Hitler. Using all of the information known about Hitler, Langer attempted to predict how Hitler might react to defeat.[2]

Psychological profiling
A method of suspect identification that seeks to identify an individual's mental, emotional, and personality characteristics, as manifested in things done or left behind at the crime scene.

identifying a possible suspect. If the crime has particular abnormalities or suggests a pattern without a reason for the crime, investigators may turn to psychological profiling for help in identifying a suspect.

Psychological profiling is a method of suspect identification that seeks to identify an individual's mental, emotional, and personality characteristics as manifested in things done or left behind at the crime scene. Psychological profiling is typically used in crimes of violence, such as homicides, sex crimes, ritualistic or cult crimes, and arsons in which there is no apparent motive or there is a series of crimes. Profiles provide investigators with corroborative evidence in cases with known suspects or with clues about likely suspects. Profiles do not, however, immediately lead investigators to a given offender. Rather, they point to the type of person most likely to commit the crime under investigation.

The process used to create a psychological profile typically has seven steps:[3]

1. Evaluating the criminal act itself.
2. Analyzing evidence from, and conditions at, the crime scene.
3. Considering characteristics and, when available, statements of the victim.
4. Analyzing all information from the preliminary reports.
5. Evaluating the medical examiner's autopsy protocol or the physician's physical examination report.
6. Developing a profile of the offender's psychological and personality characteristics.
7. Making investigative suggestions to investigators based on the profile.

Psychological profiles sometimes provide the only clues or leads in a case and can be very effective tools. They can help develop suspects or eliminate them, thus saving the investigator time.

Some years ago, a woman in an East Coast city reported that she had been raped. After interviewing the woman, the police compared her statement with a number of similar cases. They determined that hers was the seventh in a string of rapes in which the offender had used the same M.O. Unfortunately, there were neither any promising investigative leads nor any suspects. The victims' interview reports, along with all the incident reports, were sent to the FBI's Behavioral Science Unit. The police asked the Behavioral Science Unit to construct a psychological profile of their suspect. After examining the information received, the members of the unit concluded that the rapes had prob-ably been committed by the same person, whom they described as a white male, aged 25 to 35, divorced or separated, working in a menial job, with no more than a high school education, and with a poor self-image. The unit also suggested that the rapist was likely to be living in the immediate area of the rapes and was likely to be a voyeur—a Peeping Tom.[5]

Within a mere three days of receiving the report, the police had identified 40 possible suspects who met the residence and age requirements of the profile. Using the other information provided in the profile, the police narrowed their investigation to a single suspect. He was arrested within a week.[6]

As in the case above, psychological profiles usually begin with a difficult, bizarre, or persistent wave of crime. A behavioral specialist, often a psychologist or psychiatrist, is asked the basic question, "What sort of person would do a thing like this?" After considering the facts in the case, and frequently after visiting the actual crime scene, the behavioral specialist may be able to suggest a profile of the offender. Typically, psychological profiling is used in extremely serious and brutal criminal cases in which the offender has been especially elusive.

The basic process of psychological profiling is to try to recognize and interpret evidence found at the scene of a crime as indicating certain aspects of the criminal's personality. Profiles are not all-inclusive and do not even always provide the same type of information. They are based on what may or may not have been left at the scene of the crime. Since the amount of physical evidence left at a crime scene varies from one crime to the next, so too will the detail of the psychological assessments that can be made.[7] Typically, psychological profiles try to include the following pieces of information:

- The perpetrator's race.
- His or her sex.
- An age range.
- The likelihood of employment or employability.
- The degree of sexual maturity and ability to function normally.
- Marital status.
- The likelihood that the offender will commit the same crime again.
- The probability that the offender had previously committed a similar crime.
- The possibility of previous arrests.

The physical evidence left at a crime scene often contributes to the development of a psychological profile of the person who committed the crime. Symptoms of various behavioral patterns may be revealed by the way an individual "acts out" and may be observed in the way the crime was committed or in traces of things left behind. Rage or hatred may be revealed by the level of violence or destruction at the crime scene. Sexual dysfunction may be shown by evidence of a postmortem rape in a murder, and so forth. The crime may reflect many of the criminal's personality characteristics, in the same way one's style of dress or choice of car sometimes reflects one's personality.

Sometimes an actual potential suspect will emerge from a consideration of the psychological profile and the offender's M.O. At other times, the profile may cause investigators to eliminate suspects whose past behavior fits the M.O. but not the psychological profile. Profiling is an extremely useful tool, but it is not a panacea. Even in less extreme cases, police officers, calling upon their knowledge and experience, may use their own version of profiling. For example, experienced officers will often draw a mental picture of a burglar or rapist from the crime scene evidence. However, when a crime is bizarre or extremely flamboyant, behavioral scientists can assist police by providing the added dimension of a psychological profile.

STATISTICS

In 1995, 5.8 percent of the population of the United States was arrested for a crime. Here is how those arrests broke down by age groups:[8]

under 15	6.2%
15–19	20.7%
20–24	17.5%
25–29	14.5%
30–34	14.3%
35–39	11.5%
40–44	7.1%
45–49	4.0%
50–54	2.0%
55 and over	2.2%

SUMMARY BY LEARNING OBJECTIVES

Learning Objective 1

Modus operandi (M.O.) is a Latin term for "mode or method of operation." In police work, it describes the activities of criminals in preparing for and committing a crime.

Learning Objective 2

The four factors that influence *modus operandi* are opportunity, need, passion, and inadequate social skills.

Learning Objective 3

The M.O. file is an orderly method of recording and coding information, designed to reveal habits, traits, or practices of criminal suspects. Consideration of these traits and practices allows investigators to make deductions about the crime and possible suspects.

Learning Objective 4

Modus operandi information compiled from several crimes can aid in the identification of a suspect if physical characteristics recur in descriptions of suspects. *Modus operandi* information can aid in the apprehension of a suspect by pinpointing certain operational patterns. It can also aid in the repression of future crimes by indicating where patrols should be increased.

Learning Objective 5

Modus operandi data are generally broken down into major subdivisions that include time and date of crime, person attacked, property attacked, method of attack, means of attack, objective of attack, trademark, words used, symbols, and transportation used.

Learning Objective 6

The body of the report should contain a complete chronological narrative of all the facts obtained during the investigation, including an explanation of the M.O. factors. Information that is not strictly part of the suspect's M.O. should also be included.

Learning Objective 7

The psychological-profiling method of suspect identification seeks to identify an individual's mental, emotional, and personality characteristics as manifested in things done or left behind at the crime scene.

QUESTIONS FOR REVIEW

Learning Objective 1

1. What is meant by *modus operandi?*
2. In what year did the earliest published material on *modus operandi* appear?

CRITICAL THINKING INVESTIGATIVE EXERCISE

Following is a description of a hypothetical case involving the robbery of a motel. After reading the facts of this robbery, decide what data you would include in the *modus operandi* part of a report. Prepare a written report using the subdivisions in the section titled "The *Modus Operandi* Parts of a Report." Then compare your *modus operandi* report with others in the class. Resolve any discrepancies that may have occurred.

Facts

On July 8, 1998, at 12:30 A.M., John Gomer, the night clerk, was working behind the registration desk inside the front entrance of the Shining Star Motel. The motel was located one mile outside town, on State Route 286. A tall man walked in. John noticed that he was rather good-looking except for a small scar over his left eyebrow. The man asked John, "Do you have a room for two, for one night?" John nodded yes and placed a registration card on the counter. As he did so, the man withdrew a black 9-millimeter pistol from his pocket. The man pointed the gun at John and said, "Turn around and don't look at me. If you keep quiet and cooperate, we won't have any trouble." The man reached around to John's eyeglasses and removed them, placing them on the desk. He ordered John to go into a back room, where he bound John's hands and feet with duct tape and covered his eyes with a red bandana. The man also placed a red bandana with a knot in the middle in John's mouth as a gag. The man removed John's watch and wallet and went back into the other room.

John could hear the man moving around in the other room, but could hear no one else. Just as the man opened the door to leave, he called to John, "Hey, you! Don't forget to leave the light on for me now, you hear?" The man laughed and left the motel.

When the day manager arrived in the morning, she freed John, who then telephoned the police. John reported the theft of $1,200 from the cash drawer, $200 from his wallet, and his watch, valued at $198.

Investigating Officer Chuck Waters responded to the call and examined the crime scene. He found the cash drawer open and John's cash-depleted wallet on the desk. All of John's credit cards were still there, as were all of his identification cards. In the back room, Officer Waters collected the pieces of gray duct tape and the bandanas used to blindfold and gag John. One of the bandanas had a small circular price tag on it and the store's name. Officer Waters interviewed several of the motel guests, but no one admitted to hearing or seeing anything. Officer Waters completed his incident report.

INVESTIGATIVE SKILL BUILDERS

Serving Clients

You have just driven into a strip mall parking lot and stopped your car near the grocery store entrance. It is 12:30 P.M. This lot has been the site of a number of reports of items stolen from parked cars. The M.O. report indicated that the thefts occurred between 12:00 P.M. and 2:00 P.M. on weekdays. Although the thefts have been strung out over about four weeks, they have occurred only once or twice a week. The items taken have been only loose things left on the seats of unlocked vehicles. Items have included stuffed animals, toys, and expensive fountain pens. Many of the vehicles have had radios, telephones, and CB radios installed in them, but those items were left untouched.

Your eye catches the image of a small boy moving swiftly between cars. As your eyes meet his, he quickly moves a bag he is holding behind him and starts to move off. You call to him to stop as you get out of your car. The boy is about 7 or 8 years old and is holding his bag behind him to keep it out of your view.

You ask the boy who he is and where his parents are, thinking that a small child such as this should not be in the lot all alone. He tells you his name is Bobby, his father is dead, and his mother is shopping in the grocery store. He also tells you he lives with his mother in the projects and his mother has been unemployed for several months. You ask the boy if you can see what he has in his bag, and he obligingly brings the bag into your view. Inside are several toys and pens and two paperback books. You ask Bobby where he got the items, and he tells you he found them. Bobby is unable to tell you exactly where he found them, and instead simply says "around." You take Bobby by the hand and begin walking back toward your car. As you walk, you notice several parked cars with doors ajar. Again, you ask Bobby where he got the items in his bag. Bobby frowns and begins to cry. He tells you he took the items from the cars, but that he is really sorry. You ask him what he was going to do with the things in the bag. He tells you he just wanted to play with them because his mother cannot afford to buy him things to play with. Just then, a woman exits the grocery store and comes running over, calling Bobby's name. She asks what the problem is and whether Bobby is all right.

1. What can you deduce from the M.O. of the previous thefts about Bobby's possible involvement?
2. What actions should you take?

Integrity/Honesty

You are off duty and shopping with your spouse and teenage daughter in a grocery store. As you walk around, you realize that this is the store you read about during your last shift. The store has been hit recently by a rash of shoplifting. The M.O. report indicated that the thefts have been discovered at various times during the day and on different days of the week. The connecting element has been the finding of empty boxes on shelves from products that have been stolen. Many of these products have been beauty products.

Several of your daughter's friends come over and say hello. Your daughter chats a minute with her friends and then rejoins you and your spouse. As you turn the corner of an aisle a few minutes later, you notice your daughter's friends slipping lipsticks and other small cosmetics into their pockets. As they move away, you see empty packaging from cosmetics on the shelf near where the girls stood. What action will you take?

ENDNOTES

1. *Modus Operandi and Crime Reporting Manual,* State of California, Department of Justice, Division of Criminal Law and Enforcement, Bureau of Criminal Identification and Investigation, Sacramento, 1964.

2. Walter C. Langer, *The Mind of Adolf Hitler,* World Publishing, New York, 1978.

3. John E. Douglas and Alan Burgess, "Criminal Profiling: A Viable Investigative Tool Against Violent Crime," *FBI Law Enforcement Bulletin,* December 1986, pp. 11–12.

4. Thomas Palmer, "A Doctor Smelled Arsenic, Leading to Arrest of a Serial Killer," *Boston Globe,* August 20, 1987, p. 3.

5. Richard L. Ault and James T. Reese, "Profiling: A Psychological Assessment of Crime Profiling," *FBI Law Enforcement Bulletin,* Vol. 49, No. 3, March 1980, pp. 22–25.

6. Ibid.

7. Ault and Reese, loc. cit.

8. Federal Bureau of Investigation, *Crime in the United States,* Government Printing Office, Washington, 1995, pp. 218–19.

CHAPTER 6

Interviews and Interrogations

CHAPTER OBJECTIVES

After completing this chapter, you will be able to:

1. Identify sources of information available to criminal investigators.

2. Explain the difference between *interviews* and *interrogations*.

3. Describe some useful techniques for interviewing witnesses.

4. Discuss the legal aspects of interrogating a person in police custody.

5. Describe some effective interrogation techniques.

6. Discuss special considerations for interrogating juveniles.

7. Distinguish between *confessions* and *admissions*.

KEY TERMS

interview
interrogation
rapport
aware hearing
cognitive interview
complainant
complaint
persuasion
affected words
alibi
third degree
confession
admission
polygraph

Sources of Information

Information is the lifeblood of police work. Without adequate information, a police investigation can very quickly come to a complete standstill. Sometimes information can be obtained from physical evidence and the crime scene itself. Bloodstains, broken glass, footprints, and tire prints tell investigators certain things about the criminal and sometimes about the way the crime was committed. Investigative reports, *modus operandi* files, arrest records, and other reports are also sources of information. In most cases, however, police investigators get the most information and spend most of their time interviewing or interrogating people.

Distinguishing between interviews and interrogations is important. In its most basic form, an **interview** may be defined as "a conversation with a purpose," namely, "to gather information."[1] To accomplish this purpose, police officers must be able to communicate in a self-aware and effective manner with witnesses, victims, informants, and suspects. An **interrogation** may be defined as questioning persons suspected of being directly or indirectly involved in a crime.

There are both legal and practical reasons to make a distinction between interviewing and interrogating. From a practical stance, one typically does not interrogate someone who is not in custody. As we will discuss later in this chapter, once individuals have been taken into custody, information obtained from them cannot be used in court unless they have been advised of their constitutional rights. Interviews, however, do not require that one be either taken into custody or advised of one's rights. Information obtained during the course of an interview and recorded in an officer's field notes is admissible in court if it meets the tests of competency, materiality, and relevancy.

Sometimes a person being interviewed may say something that causes the officer to believe he or she actually should be a suspect. At this juncture the officer may take the person into custody, advise the person of his or her rights, and continue talking. But, technically, the officer is now conducting an interrogation. In other words, what was an interview five minutes ago has now become an interrogation.

In both cases, the officer is seeking information. However, several important changes are likely to have occurred during this shift from interview to interrogation.

During interviewing, officers' attitudes and demeanor are generally open, friendly, informal, and conversational. The direction of the interview is wide open, with the investigator striving to collect as much information as possible about the crime. During interrogation, there is a shift to an adversarial attitude. Officers' attitudes and demeanor become more formal, antagonistic, challenging, and competitive. The direction of an interrogation is narrow, specifically focused on the suspect's direct or

Interview Questioning to obtain information regarding a person's knowledge about a crime, suspect, or event.

Interrogation Questioning to obtain information from persons suspected of being directly or indirectly involved in a crime.

indirect involvement in a crime or in concealing an offense or an offender.

It is important to note that the characterization of interrogations as adversarial does not mean that all interviews are conducted with willing participants. Witnesses and victims may have many reservations about talking with the police or furnishing information. They may withhold information either knowingly or unknowingly. They may consider their information unimportant or insignificant, or they may be fearful of repercussions or retaliation against them or their family members. They may believe that they themselves are involved in some way or may simply feel distrustful of the police or afraid of media publicity. The best results are likely to be obtained if the officer is patient, courteous, open, understanding, and honest with the person being interviewed.

Interviews

Begin by establishing a rapport with the person to be interviewed. **Rapport** is a relationship that develops between an officer and the person being interviewed, in which the interviewee feels that the officer has empathy for him or her or identifies with his or her feelings. Regardless of whether the person being interviewed is a witness, a victim, or a

Rapport A relationship of mutual trust and emotional affinity that develops between an interviewer or interrogator and the person being interviewed or interrogated.

When interviewing victims immediately following a crime, allow them time to compose themselves.

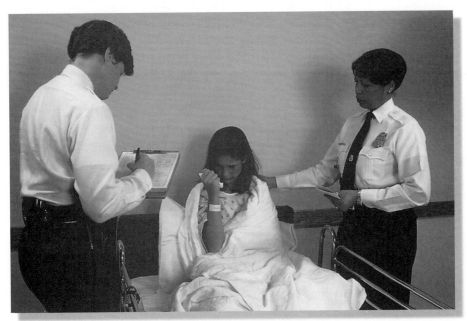

potential suspect, consider for a moment how he or she might be feeling. Showing a little compassion might go a very long way in such a circumstance. If the interview occurs immediately after a crime, allow the person a few minutes to compose him- or herself. If necessary, separate the interviewee from large crowds, family members, the media, darkness, loud noises, or any anxiety-producing situation. Those things may interfere with creating a rapport and a setting conducive to an interview. Always treat the persons you interview with respect, and address them as Mr., Mrs., Miss, Ms., Sir, and so forth. Do not call a witness by his or her first name. It could negatively affect the interview.

Conduct interviews face to face, in a courteous and sincere manner. Learn to listen with **aware hearing,** that is, to focus your listening and hear more than the words being spoken. Also avoid interrupting speakers to interject your own views or comments. Do not interrupt the interviewee by saying such things as "Oh, yeah, I've seen that sort of thing before" or "Gosh, that really was bad, but I know from experience it will be okay" or similar well-intentioned comments. Likewise, learn to distinguish between a pause for breath, a pause for the speaker to recompose him- or herself, and the completion of a statement. Good aware hearing in interviews and interrogations pays off. Experienced investigators know that as many as 95 percent of crimes are cleared through interviews and interrogations.[2]

If time permits, prepare for the interview. In some cases, such as hot crimes or emergencies, there may be no time for preparation. However, in most situations you should know who is being interviewed and who else might be involved in the case, what the crime involved, where the events took place, how the interviewee is involved, and why things may have occurred as they did. The more information you have regarding the case and the people involved, the better you can control the process. Furthermore, sometimes demonstrating that you have some information suggests that you may have more information, and this may encourage the interviewee to open up with additional information.

Separate witnesses, victims, or others who are to be interviewed about a crime. Investigators need to know what each person saw, heard, or knows about the case. Allowing one person to hear what another person has to say contaminates this information. Suggest to the person waiting to be interviewed that he or she mentally review what just happened. The person waiting can then order his or her thoughts before actually being interviewed.

Whenever possible, persons involved in a criminal case should be interviewed in a logical order that provides the investigator with increasing amounts of information. The following order is recommended:

1. Victims or complainants.
2. Eyewitnesses.

Aware hearing A technique of listening and literally hearing what is being said, without interrupting the speaker.

Chapter 6 *Interviews and Interrogations*

3. Informants and others who have relevant information but are not eyewitnesses.

4. Suspects.

A well-conducted interview not only will obtain the desired information but can also serve as an excellent public relations tool. Throughout the interview, the interviewee will be making assessments about the officer, and those assessments, in turn, reflect on the department. A well-handled interview leaves the interviewee feeling confident about the police and their ability to handle the case. A poorly executed interview may leave the interviewee insecure about his or her safety or the ability of the police to solve the crime. It may even make it difficult to gain the continued cooperation of that witness or victim.

It is important to separate witnesses, victims, and others who may be interviewed about a crime.

The Cognitive Interview

Research suggests that interview style is important in determining the amount and type of information subjects provide. The **cognitive interview** is a relatively new technique in law enforcement. This interview technique involves jogging a witness's memory, or doing what social scientists might refer to as triggering memories.[3] A study reported in *Law Enforcement News*[4] reinforced the benefits of this style of interviewing. According to the article, robbery detectives in the study reported that nearly 50 percent more information could be obtained from subjects when the interviewer used cognitive interviewing techniques.

During more traditional interviews, interviewers usually ask witnesses and victims open-ended questions, such as "What happened?" After a 10- or 15-minute narration by the subject, the interviewer then usually asks specific questions to gain additional information on certain points. This passive approach to interviewing fails to aid a witness or victim in remembering details. Many witnesses and victims are in a kind of shock and may have difficulty remembering such obvious details as the color of the criminal's shirt or whether the gun was blue or steel-colored. Cognitive interviewing includes four procedures for triggering these memories.

1. *Reconstruct the circumstances.* Ask the subject to try to reconstruct the incident and focus on it in the mind's eye. Say, "Close your eyes, and try to see yourself back at the scene." Also have the subject try to remember how he or she felt at the time of the event. Ask "How were you feeling just before the robber entered?" or "What were you thinking just after the robber entered?"

Cognitive interview An interviewing technique that helps victims or witnesses mentally put themselves at the crime scene to gather information about the crime.

2. *Report all information.* Have the subject focus on the event and tell all, trying not to edit or omit anything, no matter how trivial it may seem. Then, try not to interrupt the narration.

3. *Recall events in a different order.* Ask the subject to recall the events out of sequence. For example, ask the subject to begin with the most impressive or scariest part of the event. Or simply ask him or her to reverse the order of events.

4. *Change perspectives.* Ask the subject to try to recall the event from the point of view of someone else who was present. Tell the witness to place him- or herself in the person and perspective of some prominent actor in the event (for example, the victim) and imagine what he or she must have seen.[5]

The procedures involved in cognitive interviewing are all designed to draw information along different memory paths.[6] In turn, this allows the investigator to assist the subject in remembering details or triggering memories. For instance, regarding appearance, you might ask "Did the suspect look like anyone you know?" or "Was there anything out of the ordinary about how the suspect looked?" For names, you might ask "Do you recall the sound of the first letter of any of the suspects' names?" or "Did anyone's name have more than one syllable?"

Although a cognitive interview can be very effective for drawing out details of an event, there are also several drawbacks. First, it is much more time-consuming than traditional interviewing strategies. Second, it requires more control over the environment than other interviewing procedures. Finally, it requires that the interviewer be well-practiced in the technique and have more skill than might be required for more traditional sorts of interviews.

Complainants and Complaints

Complainant An individual who seeks satisfaction or action for an injury or for damages sustained. It may be the victim of a crime or someone who acts on behalf of the victim.

A **complainant** is an individual seeking satisfaction or action for an injury or for damages sustained. The complainant may be the victim of a crime or someone who seeks action on behalf of a victim. For example, the parents of a juvenile who has been assaulted may file a complaint with the police. A **complaint,** then, is a formal allegation by which a legal action is commenced against a party. It is a request for police action in some matter. In recent years, some jurisdictions have even provided officers a means of filing a complaint in certain domestic violence situations. In such cases, the officer becomes the complainant.

Complaint A formal allegation by which a legal action is commenced against a party; a request for police action in some matter.

Complainants are especially important during the initial stages of a police investigation. Complainants provide basic information about the crime. They may be able to describe a suspect and the various details, events, and circumstances before and during commission of the crime. Data provided by complainants to an officer may seem trivial at times.

But officers must remember that when a complainant tells the police something, he or she is likely to perceive this information as very important. Once again, then, the way an officer handles the filing of a complaint and the interviewing of the complainant may affect the public image of his or her agency and, indirectly, of the police in general.

All complainants should be taken seriously until their complaints are demonstrated to have no basis in fact or reality. Even mentally deficient and alcohol- or drug-impaired complainants may furnish valuable and necessary information. For example, if an agitated alcoholic street person has just witnessed the mugging of another street person, she may be the only source of information about the crime. In this case, the police will probably hold the complainant and reinterview her after she has sobered up. On the other hand, the complainant may be someone who claims that the silver foil helmet he is wearing protects him from the Martian invaders masquerading as store clerks in the supermarket. In this case, the police may consider referring the man to a psychiatric facility for an intake examination and evaluation. Some police agencies keep a file of repeat complainants who are troubled or psychotic near the complaint or information desk. This provides a reference for officers to check when they suspect a complainant is mentally troubled.

The complaints complainants bring are in two general categories: (1) specific and (2) nonspecific. The classification of a given complaint depends on certain specific facts offered by the complainant. If there is a criminal offense involved and there are supporting data, the matter may be considered a *specific complaint*. If, on the other hand, there is no basis in fact or law to warrant police action, the matter may be considered a *nonspecific complaint*. Sometimes, after taking a nonspecific complaint, the police may refer the complainant to a more appropriate agency or department.

Specific Complaints Whenever a complainant provides information about a possible crime in an initial complaint, a more thorough investigation should be arranged. A detailed interview is the first important step in such an investigation. This interview should be as exhaustive as possible and should obtain the following information: the name, address, telephone numbers, and occupation of the complainant; the time and location of the crime; the nature of the offense; the number of suspects and a description of each; the license number and description of any vehicle involved; the direction of the suspects' flight; the present location of the suspects, if known; a description of property involved; the weapons, if any, that the suspects have; and the identity of any witnesses. The success of most in-vestigations depends on obtaining complete and detailed information during the initial interview with the complainant. If all of the pertinent information is not obtained from a complainant during the initial interview, valuable time may be lost, and the case left unsolved.

Nonspecific Complaints   This type of complaint represents a large proportion of calls to police agencies. Complaints of this kind do not have any basis in fact and are often merely hearsay generalizations. An example of a nonspecific complaint is one in which a caller claims that a person who lives down the block is engaging in criminal activities. The complainant may tell the police that the person down the block has no visible means of support, but drives an expensive car and wears expensive clothes. The complainant may also tell police that the person has no interactions with neighbors and keeps erratic late-night hours. Finally, the complainant may tell police that he or she just has a "gut feeling" about this person. When questioned, the complainant may recall no specific criminal activities committed by the supposed offender, but may state that he is nonetheless "a suspicious character"!

While maintaining a polite demeanor, the officer receiving this complaint should inform the caller that no police action is possible, since no laws have been broken. The caller should be thanked for taking the time to contact the police and encouraged to call again should he or she learn about any specific violations of law by that individual. A brief record should be made of the complainant's information for future reference in the event additional information is received regarding the violation of a specific law.

Witnesses

Investigators solve many cases simply by talking with people and finding out what they may have seen or heard. When preparing to interview a witness, consider the kinds of questions a defense attorney might ask each witness at the trial. Questions by the defense are likely to challenge the credibility of the prosecution's witnesses. The challenge may be directed at such factors as witnesses' physical or mental condition; their emotional state; and their experience, education, and knowledge. Remember that witnesses do not have to be advised of their constitutional rights; however, do not threaten or promise anything to witnesses to obtain statements.

Witnesses are often hastily questioned on the spot, immediately after the reported violation to get quick information that might lead immediately to the apprehension of the perpetrator. Following this preliminary interview at the crime scene, the investigating officer may want to conduct more extensive, formal interviews with witnesses and victims. Be sure to set appointments for interviews at the convenience of the witnesses. It may be necessary to interview them at work or at their homes, rather than at the police station. Also arrange for privacy so that they will be comfortable speaking to you. In addition to the general guidelines we have already discussed, Figure 6–1 lists ten basic

tioning. Do not let a hostile witness know that you resent his or her attitude. Try to determine the reason for the hostility and then try to correct it. It is important to make such individuals feel that their information is greatly appreciated. Appeals to civic duty, personal pride, religion, decency, family, or justice may be helpful. Winning the cooperation of hostile witnesses may ultimately provide the margin of proof necessary to successfully prosecute a suspect.

Timid Witnesses   When witnesses are self-conscious or shy, lack confidence, or have poorly developed language skills, you should make every effort to put them at ease. Conduct all conversations in a relaxed manner and ask questions in a simple, matter-of-fact way.

Deceitful Witnesses   When you encounter such witnesses, listen attentively to their stories, but do not immediately let them know by your conduct or remarks that you do not believe them. Let them recite many falsehoods before confronting them with their questionable remarks. Then inform them of each false statement made, and remind them of the serious consequences of offering perjured testimony before a court of law. Tape-recording and playing back false statements can induce most witnesses to recognize the futility of deception. In some cases, asking the witness if he or she is willing to take a lie-detector test (discussed later in this chapter) may result in a change of attitude.

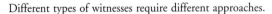

Different types of witnesses require different approaches.

Children Information furnished by children is often unreliable, and corroborative testimony should always be obtained. Children are very imaginative and often confuse fact with fantasy. Judges and juries are therefore hesitant to convict a suspect merely on the testimony of a child. On the other hand, it is very important not to disregard statements by children unless they are shown to be untrue. Always be exceedingly careful about putting words in a child's mouth and avoid asking leading questions.

Young Adults People in this age bracket, whether married or single, are not as reliable or dependable as mature adults. They are usually preoccupied with their own personal affairs or problems.

Mature Adults These individuals have a fuller appreciation of police responsibilities and are generally more dependable witnesses. Their personal adjustments have been made, and their social experiences have been widened. The powers of observation and retention of these adults are usually at their peak, and their opinions are more apt to be reserved.

Taking Notes

When, or if, one should take notes during witness questioning is a controversial issue. It is important for investigating officers to keep field notes; however, whether the records should be handwritten notes or electronic recordings may depend on the witness. Some witnesses are not comfortable having their conversation recorded—no matter how inconspicuous the recording device might be. Others prefer that the interview be taped to ensure that the officer gets all the information accurately and completely.

If you will be using a recording device, inform the witness before the interview begins that a taped record is being made. Explain that the purpose of recording the interview is merely to ensure accuracy in your field notes. If equipment is available, it may also be advisable to videotape the interview. In several jurisdictions, persons suspected of driving under the influence of alcohol (or other substances) are videotaped during their field sobriety test and accompanying interview. Videotaping provides a means of assessing various physical cues during an interrogation as well.

Even when you choose to use only a notebook during the interview, be cautious. Some witnesses may be disturbed or distracted if they see you taking too many or too frequent notes. You need to become sensitive to the verbal and nonverbal clues the witness gives during the interview. If you perceive that note taking is a problem, take very few notes, or no notes, during the interview. Then, at the conclusion of the interview, quickly jot down relevant facts and names the witness has offered.

How and whether to take notes during the interview, then, depends largely on the individual witness. Some people are fearful of any written record. Your main objective is to obtain as much information as possible about the case. Doing so may require a little extra effort on your part.

Interrogations

Interrogating suspects is somewhat more difficult than interviewing witnesses or victims. Once located by the police, a suspect who *is* involved in a crime may or may not be willing to make a statement, an admission of guilt, or a confession. Many investigators believe that the central purpose of an interrogation is to obtain a confession, and the effort to obtain a confession as a means of solving a case is an integral part of police work today. Let us now consider the larger purpose of *interrogation* in modern day police work.

The central purpose of an interrogation is to elicit from a suspect—or from people related to or associated with a suspect—information about a criminal event. An interrogation, in modern police work, *is not* intended to be used as a weapon to get a guilty person to break down and confess. Rather, it is a procedure used to obtain *the truth*. In addition, the interrogation process may accomplish other goals. Possible goals of the interrogation process include the following (no hierarchy or order is intended):

- Learn the truth; possibly establish the innocence of a suspect.
- Obtain an admission of guilt (a confession).
- Ascertain the names of accomplices and accessories.
- Eliminate or incriminate other suspects.
- Gain additional facts and information about the circumstances surrounding the crime.
- Identify new leads, perhaps unwittingly offered or intentionally provided by the suspect.

- Locate or recover stolen property.
- Discover new or additional physical evidence such as weapons, papers, and tools or instruments.
- Obtain additional facts to corroborate or disprove some fact.
- Develop information that might uncover other unlawful activities or resolve other cases.

When suspects under questioning demonstrate that they are innocent, the interrogation has served its professional purpose no less than when a confession is obtained from a guilty party. Many of the techniques used in interviewing are also used in interrogation, but there are some important differences. One of the most important is the manner in which you interrogate suspects to avoid violating their rights and to make sure their statements will be admissible in court.

Legal Aspects of Interrogation

Before being interrogated or questioned while in police custody, an individual must be advised of his or her legal rights. Recall that in Chapter 2, we defined *custody* as detainment by a police officer, that is, a situation in which the person feels he or she is not free to leave. These rights were established in the *Miranda* decision (*Miranda v. Arizona,* 1966).

Ernesto Miranda was a 25-year-old mentally impaired man. He was arrested in Phoenix, Arizona, and charged with kidnapping and rape. After his arrest, Miranda was identified by the complaining victim. Miranda was taken into a small room at the station and interrogated for more than two hours. During this interrogation, Miranda signed a written confession. He was later convicted and sentenced to 20 years in prison. The conviction was affirmed on his appeal to the Arizona Supreme Court. Miranda continued to appeal, eventually being heard by the U.S. Supreme Court. The appeal's argument rested heavily on the facts that Miranda had never been warned that any statement he made could be later used against him and that he had been unaware of his right to have legal counsel present during interrogation.

The *Miranda* case actually was one of four similar cases heard simultaneously by the Supreme Court. Each case dealt with the legality of confessions obtained by the police from suspects being held *incommunicado* and without benefit of knowing their constitutional rights and protections as suspects in a crime. The other cases were *Vignera v. New York* (1966), *Westover v. United States* (1966), and *California v. Stewart* (1966).

The Supreme Court's decision in *Miranda* concerned the Fifth Amendment and the admissibility of statements obtained from suspects questioned while in custody (or when otherwise denied their freedom). Under provisions of the Fifth Amendment, "no person . . . shall be compelled in any criminal case to be a witness against himself." Taken literally, this means that a defendant cannot be required to testify in court. It also means that a suspect cannot be coerced in any manner to confess nor made to confess under fear of duress. According to the Supreme Court, Miranda had confessed as a result of the "third-degree methods" used by the police during their interrogation. Miranda's conviction was overturned, and the Court established a set of guidelines for police to follow prior to interrogating suspects in police custody. Decisions in subsequent cases have refined the rights of suspects set forth in the *Miranda* decision (see Figure 6–2).

FYI

Immediately following the *Miranda* ruling, many police officers believed that cases would be lost as would their ability to obtain confessions. Research during that time, however, demonstrated that few cases were actually lost as a direct result of *Miranda* errors. In fact, the impact on convictions from *Miranda* was largely negligible.[7]

Because of television and the movies, few people have not at least heard of the Miranda warnings. Although there are slight wording variations across the country, all versions share several basic elements. The Miranda warnings inform a suspect who has been arrested or who is to be interrogated that he or she is entitled to certain rights:

1. You have the right to remain silent. You are not required to make any statement or answer any questions. Anything you say will be taken down and can be used against you later in a court of law.

2. You have the right to speak with an attorney. You may consult with an attorney or have one present with you during any questioning.

3. If you cannot afford an attorney, one can be appointed for you. If you want to have an attorney present during questioning, one will be provided by the court at no charge.

4. You retain the right to counsel, even if you speak with the police. If you want to answer questions now, without an attorney present, you will still retain the right to stop answering questions at any time.

Miranda warnings are intended to protect the rights of accused persons held in police custody. However, a suspect can waive his or her rights and answer questions posed by the police. In many jurisdictions, an officer's or investigator's department or the prosecutor's office may require both an oral acknowledgment of one's waiver of rights and a signed statement of waiver. This is because, in court, the burden of proof that *Miranda* has been properly administered is on the shoulders of the prosecutor. Decisions in cases subsequent to the *Miranda* decision have refined the rights of suspects set forth in *Miranda*. See Figure 6–2.

Preparing for Interrogation

In preparing for an interrogation, review all available data concerning the *crime*, the *suspect*, and the *victim*. Review all material in the case

Figure 6–2 Cases affecting interrogation procedures.

Escobedo v. Illinois	1963	A suspect in custody must be advised of the right to silence and the right to advice of an attorney during interrogation.
Miranda v. Arizona	1966	Suspects cannot be questioned without first being advised of certain rights: the right to remain silent, the right to be told that anything said can and will be used in court, and the right to consult with an attorney before questioning and to have the attorney present during interrogation.
Orozco v. Texas	1969	Interrogation does not have to take place in a police station to have a coercive effect, and being in police custody is defined as being deprived of freedom in a significant way.
Harris v. New York	1971	A defendant's statements made in violation of *Miranda* may be used to challenge the defendant's trial testimony.
Michigan v. Tucker	1974	Statements made in violation of *Miranda* may be used to locate prosecution witnesses.
Beckwith v. United States	1976	The application of *Miranda* depends on custodial police interrogation, involving questioning in a coercive, police-dominated atmosphere.
Oregon v. Mathiason	1977	Custodial interrogation is defined as questioning initiated by law enforcement officers after a person has been taken into custody or otherwise deprived of freedom.
Rhode Island v. Innis	1980	Disclosures offered outside the context of interrogation are not violations of *Miranda*.
Harry v. Estelle	1980	*Miranda* applies only in investigative interrogation.
California v. Prysock	1981	Miranda warnings are valid regardless of wording or order given.

file, especially the physical evidence and *modus operandi* information. Check out all available material on the suspect. Such data may include personal property, background, relationship to the victim, motive, alibi, and opportunity to commit the crime. Additionally, review the suspect's identification record, previous employment, occupation, associates, family, hobbies, hangouts, and financial status, as well as the type of automobile he or she drives or has access to. As to the victim, scrutinize such information as marital status, reputation, financial situation, employment, and leisure activities. In addition, look into personal habits, associates, places of amusement frequented, and other activities. This procedure is recommended particularly in those cases where there appear to be

Edwards v. Arizona	1981	Once a suspect in custody states that he or she wants an attorney, police must halt all questioning and may not engage in further questioning unless the suspect requests it.
United States v. Lane	1983	Voluntary statements made without questioning by police may be used against defendants at trial.
United States v. Dockery	1983	This case clarified the meaning of custodial interrogation and the inappropriate use of deception.
California v. Beheler	1983	Miranda warnings are not required when suspects voluntarily go to a police station to make a statement.
New York v. Quarles	1984	The *public-safety* exception to the Miranda warnings exists when a public threat could be removed by the suspect making a statement.0
Minnesota v. Murphy	1984	Probation officers are not required to give Miranda warnings to their clients.
Berkermer v. McMarthy	1984	Miranda warnings are not required for traffic violations.
Lanier v. South Carolina	1986	Illegal arrests invalidate voluntary confessions.
Illinois v. Perkins	1990	Jailed suspects need not be informed of their right to remain silent when they provide information to undercover agents.
New York v. Harris	1990	A suspect's statements made at the police station, after a questionable entrance by the police into the suspect's house, are not barred from being admitted.
McNeil v. Wisconsin	1991	A suspect jailed for one crime can be questioned about a separate crime without the presence of his or her lawyer for the first crime.

discrepancies in the victim's account of the reported incident. Alleged victims in robberies, burglaries, kidnappings, rapes, and arsons have been known to report fictitious crimes. Although this preparation for interrogation appears time-consuming, it actually takes only minutes. In some cases, little information is available. However, experienced investigators seldom conduct an interrogation without first going through as much of this process as time permits.

Interrogation Settings

Because of the slightly adversarial nature of an interrogation, whenever possible it should be conducted in a setting familiar to the investigator. This gives the investigator a psychological advantage, similar to the home-court advantage in a basketball game. As previously mentioned, interviews are often held at the convenience of witnesses or victims, in settings of their choosing (home, office, the station). Interrogations, however, are controlled more firmly by the police. The investigator determines where and when the interrogation will be conducted.

Most interrogations take place at the police station. However, if the suspect refuses to come to the station or if there is insufficient evidence for an arrest, the officer may conduct an on-the-spot interrogation. The suspect may be interrogated in the squad car, at home, or at work. Sometimes, following apprehension at the scene of a crime, a suspect will con-

Sometimes after a crime, suspects are interrogated on the spot.

sent to being interrogated. The suspect may readily waive constitutional rights and attempt to project an aura of innocence. It is somewhat like a poker game in which the suspect tries to bluff the arresting officers with an attitude of cooperation, hoping to convince "the law" that they have the wrong person. In these situations the officer should keep the suspect separate from any family or friends present at the scene. On-the-spot interrogations should be straightforward, and questioning should pertain to the crime and should seek answers about the *who, what, when, where, how,* and *why* of the crime.

Although suspects, in general, should be interrogated as soon as possible after being identified or captured, formal interrogations at headquarters are sometimes more effective than on-the-spot confrontations. The mere fact that a suspect has been brought into the station for questioning can be fairly intimidating. For some people, it may assist in their opening up and admitting involvement in a crime.

As with interviews, interrogation settings should provide some degree of privacy, and distractions should be eliminated before you begin. Interruptions should be limited, whenever possible, to messages or to intentional ploys that are intended to improve the results of the interrogation. Interrogation rooms in police stations should not have telephones, nor should they have windows, pictures on the wall, excessive furnishings, or anything else that might distract a suspect. The interrogation may occur in the presence of the suspect's attorney or, if the suspect waives his or her rights (Figure 6–3), without benefit of counsel.

Customarily, at least two officers are present during the interrogation of a suspect. When the suspect is female, at least one of the officers should also be female. Regardless of the number of officers present, only one officer should ask questions at a time. Other officers may question the suspect regarding a specific point or omission after the original interrogator has exhausted a line of questions. On some occasions, several officers may desire to inject pertinent questions at appropriate times. As long as there is no conflict in the control of the interrogation, and it does not persist throughout, this sometimes works well. The advantage of having several officers present during the interrogation is that it safeguards against unfounded allegations of misconduct, unethical tactics, false charges, or other complaints that a suspect might make. Again, when and where possible, videotaping an interrogation provides a visual record that can easily safeguard against false allegations. It also provides a means of teaching inexperienced interrogators various interviewing and interrogation techniques.

Establishing a Tone

As with interviews, it is important to establish rapport with a suspect before beginning an interrogation. Unlike the interview situation,

Figure 6–3 A *Miranda* warning and waiver used by one police department.

Your Rights
1. You have the right to remain silent.
2. Anything you say can and will be used against you in court.
3. You have a right to talk to a lawyer for advice before we ask you any questions and to have him or her with you during questioning.
4. If you cannot afford to hire a lawyer, one will be appointed to represent you before any questioning, if you wish.
5. If you decide to answer questions now without a lawyer present, you will still have the right to stop answering at any time. You also have the right to stop answering at any time until you talk to a lawyer.

Waiver of Rights
I have read the above statement of my rights, and I understand each of those rights. Having these rights in mind, I waive them and willingly make a statement.

SIGNED:_____ AGE:_____

Address _____

Date _____ Time _____ Location _____

Witness _____ Department _____

Witness _____ Department _____.

however, this is often a more difficult task. If, in fact, the suspect is involved in the crime under investigation, he or she may not be open to friendly conversation. You might instead choose to instill a little fear in the suspect by indicating the very serious consequences that will arise if he or she is not cooperative. Alternatively, you might decide to appeal to the suspect's conscience or sense of guilt. For example, suggest how important it is to get bad things off one's chest and to begin fresh. You might even use information you have about the suspect. For instance, if the suspect has strong family ties, ask how a member of the family, a mother or spouse, might feel about not seeing the suspect for many years should he or she be convicted and sent to prison. Use any approach or tone that results in cooperation rather than resistance to police questions.

Even before beginning the interrogation, you will have to make certain decisions that will affect the tone of procedure. First, decide whether or not to confront the suspect on his or her first apparent lie and on every successive falsehood. If you choose to do so, use the falsehoods as a kind of lever to make the suspect recognize that it is important to offer truthful answers. Second, decide how *persuasive* a stance to take with the suspect. The old saying that one can catch more flies with honey than with vinegar may apply here. An effective interrogator is good at **persuasion,** that is, at motivating and convincing a suspect to be honest and forthcoming. Using persuasive techniques often gets better results than coming on hard and strong.

Persuasion involves tapping into three sources of motivation: emotions, reason, and rationalization. Emotions include beliefs, desires, hopes, and feelings. Reason is more cognitive and includes the ability to understand situations, interpret and anticipate outcomes, appreciate the consequences of one's actions, and solve problems. Rationalization denotes an ability to reason, but one that justifies one's actions and behaviors—whether they are objectively legitimate or not.[8] Interrogators can tap into these three areas to persuade a suspect to talk more openly and completely. An effective and persuasive interrogator should be able to convince a suspect that he or she is sincerely interested in establishing the truth and not merely in obtaining a confession!

During the course of a persuasive interrogation, avoid **affected words** such as *kill, rape, torture,* and other unnecessarily graphic terms. Milder terms will be more useful and persuasive. For example, rather than asking the suspect whether he was alone when he *raped* the girl, substitute the word *attacked*. Although the word *attacked* itself may seem an affected word, it is less severe in this case than the word *raped*.

Additionally, avoid displaying any sign of your own emotions during interrogations. For instance, do not indicate signs of joy, surprise, disdain, or disappointment. The appearance of these emotions may seem judgmental to the suspect and may interfere with his or her willingness to speak freely. Remember, too, as in an interview, to practice aware hearing.

When a suspect has concluded his or her statement, compare the information with statements made by the victim and witnesses and the physical evidence in the case to verify the suspect's story. It is important to remember that things left *unsaid* by a suspect may be just as important to the case as things said in the statement. Also, be sure, throughout the interrogation, to carefully monitor the suspect's nonverbal responses and body language. Emotional outbursts, facial expressions, voice inflection, pauses and delays in response, nervous mannerisms, and indications of surprise, sorrow, regret, remorse, or embarrassment—all may be helpful in unraveling an explanation in the case.

Persuasion Motivating and convincing a person to offer information or to comply with a request.

Affected words Words that have negative connotations in certain contexts in a given culture.

Like interviews, interrogations are a process of questioning, probing, challenging, and gathering information. Interrogators must cast their nets and gather as much information from the suspect as possible while giving out as little of their own information as they can manage.

Interrogation Approaches

Any remark or gesture made to suspects to elicit the truth can be considered an interrogation approach. For example, saying to a suspect "Well, I guess you know why you're here" or "You sure did a foolish thing" could fall into this category. However, there are several ways we might more broadly delineate various approaches to the interrogation process. Before beginning an interrogation, an investigator must assess a suspect's personality and character traits and decide which approach is best. These approaches can also apply to an interview.

The Logical Approach   This approach is based on reason. It assumes that the person being interviewed or interrogated is reasonable and rational and that there is considerable evidence available. The logical approach is often used with suspects who have prior criminal records, with educated people, with mature adults, and with others who have a good rapport with the interrogator.

When using a logical approach, confront the suspect with convincing evidence and overwhelming proof—pointing out all the specific elements that prove the suspect's involvement. Making factual remarks that indicate the suspect's guilt or involvement makes it difficult for him or her to deny involvement with any conviction. However, if firm information or evidence about the suspect's involvement is not available, any reference to such material may expose the weakness of the officer's case. For example, if you remark that a witness took down the suspect's license plate number at the crime scene, when in fact the suspect used a borrowed automobile, the suspect will recognize the bluff. Bluffing is a technique fraught with danger and should be used very cautiously.

Should the suspect offer an **alibi** during the interrogation, have the person repeat the story several times in minute detail. This tactic can uncover discrepancies in "manufactured" statements. A suspect in this situation has two stories to remember—the truth and the fabricated account. Challenge the accused person on each and every inaccuracy, to demonstrate the untenable nature of his or her story.

The Emotional Approach   With this approach, the questioner appeals to a suspect's sense of honor, righteousness, decency, morality, family pride, spiritual beliefs, justice, fair play, restitution, or other such reasons for disclosing the truth. This approach is generally most successful with first-

Alibi   A defense offered by a suspect or defendant that attempts to prove that he or she was elsewhere when the crime in question was committed.

time violators who have committed a careless criminal act because of anger, passion, or other emotions. Calm confidence, understanding, and an interest in knowing the suspect's motivation can help the interrogating officer communicate with the accused. The following are remarks that have been successful in appealing to people's emotions:

- "You're not the first person who has gotten into trouble; however, I see no reason to lie about it."
- "Society can forgive people for their mistakes but will not condone lies, hypocrisy, or cowardice."
- "All of us have made mistakes, but the least a person can do is try to rectify them."
- "It takes courage to tell the truth. Don't compound your crime with lies."
- "The truth is the only thing that all of us want and understand. Why not clear your conscience and have peace of mind?"
- "Is it fair to your family to put them through all of this, when telling the truth could set things right?"
- "Many decent people get into trouble, but they do not lie about it."

FYI

Many television programs and movies about police and crime investigation portray officers threatening suspects with physical harm or actually grabbing or striking suspects. Although such behavior may appeal to some Americans' sense of justice and retribution, it violates the U.S. Constitution. In the real world, upholding the Constitution is among the most important duties of every American law enforcement officer. Flagrant disregard for a suspect's rights jeopardizes the rights of all Americans, guaranteed by the Constitution, and is not tolerated.

Indirect Inquiry Versus Direct Inquiry   An *indirect* approach attempts to draw out information without specifically addressing the actual topic or subject. For example, an indirect approach might be to ask a suspect, "Have you ever been in the vicinity of Market and Gable Streets?" This might be followed by "Have you ever been in the convenience store on the corner of Market and Gable?" And, finally, "Do you have any information regarding a robbery that occurred in that store last Thursday night?" A more *direct* line of questioning might have been phrased, "On Thursday night, September 7, did you rob the convenience store on the corner of Market and Gable Streets?"

An indirect approach may be useful when subjects are being somewhat evasive, or until a stronger rapport is established. Coming on too strong or too directly may close down an otherwise cooperative suspect. On the other hand, following too indirect a line of questioning, or maintaining this style too long, may fail to provide an investigator with necessary information.

Validation Questions   Sometimes, after a suspect has already answered a question, the investigator can attempt a line of questioning to validate the answer or to force the suspect to implicate him- or herself, no matter what answer is given. For example, suppose a suspect has already flatly denied any involvement in the burglary under investigation. Asking him or her "So, what time was it when you got home after breaking into the house?" or "Was it still light outside when you finished up with the house?" forces the suspect to answer with specific information, contradicting his or her denial of involvement in the crime. The only way to consistently maintain one's innocence is to correct the investigator and say, "I told you I never did the burglary!"

Deflating or Inflating Ego   Challenging a suspect's abilities, skills, or intellectual capacity sometimes makes him or her angry enough to admit criminal involvement. For example, an investigator might say, "Look, we know you were involved, but you couldn't possibly have done this alone; you just are not smart enough." Or the investigator might tell a suspect what a rankly amateurish job was done in the crime, in an attempt to challenge his or her sense of pride or professionalism. On the other hand, praising a suspect on pulling off a spectacular crime may also result in an admission of guilt. A suspect may want to take credit for a crime that even the police seem impressed with. In any event, the purpose here is to challenge the suspect in some manner and push the individual into defending his or her criminal prowess in a statement.

Understating or Overstating   Sometimes, it is best to understate the nature or penalties of a crime. If someone stands accused of a multiple murder with special circumstances and may be looking at the death penalty, rather than talking about murder or the electric chair, the interrogator might instead ask about the "accident," the "event," the "thing that happened," or some other understated description. Similarly, saying that cooperation might be viewed positively by the prosecutor may go further than the vague statement "Maybe you can beat the death sentence." Asking someone to admit the truth in a case may be better than asking the person to admit his or her guilt.

Conversely, there may be cases in which overstating the severity of a crime may arouse a response in a suspect. For example, telling the suspect that only a few hundred dollars of the $5,000 stolen has been recovered and asking where the rest is creates a dilemma for the suspect. The suspect, if guilty, knows the truth and may inadvertently correct the officer. Or the suspect may feel he or she is being cheated by an accomplice and may in anger offer up the truth. Furthermore, depending on the amount of the actual and claimed loot, the difference may change the charge from a misdemeanor to a felony. That change may also affect the way the suspect will respond to questions. Hence, overstating crimes or penalties may motivate a suspect to provide information that implicates him or her in the actual crime.

The Third Degree   The **third degree** is the use or threat of physical force, mental or emotional cruelty, or water or food deprivation to obtain information in a police interrogation. At one time in the history of policing, such tactics were used. Third-degree tactics are now completely illegal. Officers cannot hit, punch, strangle, or in any other way cause physical harm to a suspect. They cannot refuse rests, toilet privileges, food, or water to a suspect. Furthermore, police cannot even hold a suspect for more than 48 hours without allowing him or her an opportunity to contact the outside world (a loved one, an attorney, the media, and so on).

Although using the third degree is illegal, it is not illegal to make a suspect feel uneasy about the interrogator's level of actual information or knowledge about the suspect. Asking questions while looking directly into the eyes of the suspect is not unlawful, but it may make the suspect feel uncomfortable. Causing physical harm to the suspect is illegal; however, gently placing a comforting hand on the arm of the suspect is not, and may assist in rapport.

There are many television and movie depictions, and even some literary ones, of the good-cop, bad-cop method of interrogation. In these scenarios, one officer is angry, hostile, violent, and menacing. The other is calm, soft-spoken, and protective of the suspect. However, there is a fine line between the use of this sort of game theory in an interrogation and the violation of a person's rights. Role playing that is too extreme may be considered unethical, even if ruled legal. Always be cautious in using such a tactic.

It is important to remember that suspects being interrogated are *suspects,* and have not been shown to be guilty. They are deserving of all of their constitutional rights and human and social amenities. No explanation, statement, admission, or confession can adequately excuse deliberate violation or debasement of these rights.

Interrogating Juveniles

As the result of the U.S. Supreme Court's decision in *In re Gault* (1967),[9] police officers and probation officers are obligated to advise minors, upon taking them into custody, that they have a right to remain silent, a privilege against self-incrimination, and a right to be represented by private counsel or by counsel appointed by the court. Should the minor, because of youth, be unable to knowingly and intelligently waive these rights, the rights must be explained to the parents or legal guardian before the juvenile is interrogated. The parents or guardian can exercise the waiver on behalf of the child.

Here is how the change in juvenile proceedings came about. In June 1964, in Gila County, Arizona, Gerald Gault, a 15-year-old boy, was taken into custody by a deputy sheriff following a verbal complaint by a female neighbor that he had made obscene telephone calls to her. The youth was placed in a children's detention home. The following day, a petition was filed in juvenile court asking for a hearing regarding the care and custody of Gault. The petition gave no factual basis for the judicial action it initiated, but it recited that Gault was under 18 and needed the protection of the juvenile court. The petition also stated that Gault was a delinquent minor. Gault's parents neither were served with the petition nor saw it. No witnesses were sworn at the hearing or at the second hearing a week later.

The judge declared Gault a juvenile delinquent and committed him to a juvenile correction facility until the age of 21. This meant that Gault was given a sentence of six years for an offense that, if committed by an adult, could be punished by no more than two months in jail and a $50 fine. When Gault's case finally reached the U.S. Supreme Court, the Court held that a juvenile has due-process rights in delinquency hearings when there is the possibility of confinement in a state institution. Specifically, the Court ruled that juveniles have a right against self-incrimination, a right to adequate notice of charges against them, a right to confront and cross-examine their accusers, and a right to assistance of counsel.

In most jurisdictions, a juvenile's parents or guardians must be notified when the child is arrested or taken into custody. Questioning of juveniles usually takes place in the presence of their parents or guardian, or in the presence of an attorney representing the juvenile.

When interrogating juveniles, adjust your usual level of language to ensure that the young witness or suspect clearly understands every question. Adolescents may be physically and mentally more mature than younger children; however, their language skills and vocabulary may not necessarily coincide with their age. Adolescents are likely to respond differently in front of their friends or parents than away from them. Sometimes the same youth putting on a brash, tough-guy image in front of friends will actually speak quite openly when the interview or interrogation is conducted in private. Similarly, some juveniles are resistant when their parents are around, whereas others are more likely to offer admissions when Mom and Dad are in the room.

Juveniles may have very definite images and opinions about the police. Some juveniles have difficulties with adults in general; others are more selective and simply dislike police officers. Like adults, however, many juveniles are cooperative and willing to assist police. Officers, therefore, should not draw conclusions prior to speaking with specific juveniles.

When interrogating juvenile suspects, using profanity, vulgarity, or physical force (real or threatened) is reprehensible. In addition, officers must guard against becoming frustrated or angry with particularly trying or difficult juveniles. Empathizing with the juvenile and exhibiting a little patience may go a long way in getting youthful suspects to answer questions.

Confessions and Admissions

A **confession** is a voluntary statement in which a person charged with the commission of a crime admits participating in or committing the criminal act in question. A confession may be written, oral, or recorded.

An **admission** differs slightly from a confession. An admission is a statement by the accused that contains information and facts about the crime but falls short of a full confession. In connection with proof of other facts, an admission may be used to demonstrate a suspect's guilt. To be received into evidence in court, an admission must relate to relevant and material facts. Admissions, in themselves, do not necessarily incriminate the accused. In an admission, the person is not *confessing* the commission of the crime, only *admitting* certain facts.

Confession A voluntary statement—written, oral, or recorded—by an accused person, admitting participation in or commission of a criminal act.

Admission A voluntary statement by an accused person, containing information and facts about a crime but falling short of a full confession.

An interrogation is an offensive-defensive situation in which investigators try to secure a confession.

For instance, if a suspect were shown a knife, and in turn stated, "Yes, that is my knife—I killed the dirty rat," this would be a confession. If, however, the suspect said, "Yes, that is my knife, but I was not present when the dirty rat was killed," this would be an admission only that the murder weapon was his. That admission, along with evidence demonstrating that the suspect was present at the time of the killing, would go toward proving that the suspect was actually guilty of the murder.

Guidelines for Taking Confessions and Admissions

There are no magic formulas for taking confessions or statements. Officers are more or less on their own and are held strictly accountable by the courts for everything they do. Remember, the courts look at the transaction after it has occurred rather than while it is happening. This puts a large burden on the officer to use great care when obtaining any statements. The following are suggestions for taking statements.

• The form of the confession is immaterial; it may be oral, narrative, question-and-answer, or a combination of the question-and-answer and narrative types.

• The suspect should not be placed under oath; such precautions may reflect a form of compulsion.

• Confessions may be handwritten (in pen, not pencil) by the officer or the suspect. They may be prepared in first person and should be written in the language of the defendant. They may be typewritten, recorded by a stenographer and transcribed into written form for the suspect's signature, tape-recorded, or videotaped. Videotaping the confession in certain cases is of added value. However, the defense may question the failure of the police to use that method in all their cases, contending that such failure implies the possible use of improper methods that they did not want to show on video.

• A tape recorder, if used, should not be turned on until the officer is ready to obtain a concise statement from the suspect.

• When suspects confess orally to a crime, written statements should be immediately prepared for their signatures. Delays or postponements in obtaining a written confession may result in a change of attitude in an otherwise cooperative suspect.

• The basic guidelines, laid down in the *Miranda* decision, of advising the suspect of rights before any questioning or the taking of statements or confessions should be followed. This procedure should be adhered to even if the required warnings were given to the suspect at the time of his or her arrest. If the statement is recorded or videotaped, the *Miranda* warnings should be offered on tape.

- The taking of a statement should begin with the reciting of the suspect's legal rights, followed by questions designed to bring out data related to the identity of the suspect; the type of crime involved; the name of the person being questioned; the date, time, and place the statement is being taken; and the identities of all parties present.

- The number of persons present at the taking of a confession should be kept to a minimum. There may be an implication of coercion or duress if several officers are present, either as interviewers or as interested observers.

- Questions should be asked in the shortest and simplest manner so that they are easily understood by the suspect. This manner of questioning brings out all the facts in the most effective way.

- Clarify all indefinite answers given by a suspect to questions asked during the taking of the statement. This is accomplished by asking specific questions of the suspect about the identity of a particular person, the exact location of a place, the meaning of terminology used, the specific time or date, or other details. For example, such expressions as "hot car" (stolen car), "junkie" (drug addict), and "kibbles and bits" (crack cocaine) should be explained.

- Statements should not include any crime other than that with which the suspect is charged unless it is tied in closely with that particular case. For example, if a suspect burglarized a residence and then raped an occupant at the same location, both the burglary and the rape could be included in the same confession. If the suspect was involved in another burglary a block away prior to the aforementioned burglary-rape offense, then two separate statements would have to be taken.

- In complicated cases, consideration should be given to having the suspect visit the crime scene so that movements before and after the commission of the offense can be clarified. Of course, this assumption hinges on the voluntary cooperation of the suspect.

- Confessions should be as brief as possible while including all the relevant details. There is no minimum length for a statement. The inclusion of details assists the officer in corroborating the statement.

- When alterations, changes, corrections, or erasures are necessary in a statement, they should be made in the subject's own handwriting or made by the officer and initialed by the suspect to show that the suspect is aware of them. This procedure prevents the claim that passages or pages were added to the statement.

- Each page of a statement should be initialed or signed by the subject unless, of course, the subject writes out his or her own confession.

- In the narrative portion of a confession, whether it is a narrative statement or a combination of a question-and-answer and narrative statement, the suspect should be permitted to relate the complete story with a minimum of interruptions, unless clarification is needed.

• The concluding paragraph of a statement should say in the suspect's own handwriting that the suspect has read the statement and acknowledges it to be true. Each officer present should witness the statement with signature, date, and department.

• A confession should appear as a complete unit, independent of any previous questioning and any possible future questioning.

• All statements made by a suspect (entire contents) should be thoroughly checked to determine their accuracy.

• If a confession involves more than one crime, separate statements should be taken for each offense.

• The suspect's identification record should never be included in his or her confession.

• Statements should not be mutilated by holes, staples, stamps, or the addition of case file numbers.

Technology for Seeking the Truth

Throughout history, many cultures have tried to develop a way to prove that a person is telling the truth. In many early cultures, suspected liars were told that if they placed their hands into a cauldron of boiling oil, they could withdraw them uninjured if they were telling the truth. However, if they were lying, their hands would be severely burned. These early truth-seeking ordeals relied heavily on their psychological impact on a guilty person's mind. Lying also has many physiological effects, such as dryness of the mouth, shaking or trembling, perspiration, and increased respiration and heart rate. These were well-known among many cultures. The ancient Chinese, for example, made suspected liars chew a mouth full of uncooked rice. If the rice remained dry after chewing, the person was assumed to have been lying.

We have come a long way from dipping hands in boiling oil or filling people's mouths with dry rice. Today, many agencies commonly use technology and science to try to assess the truthfulness of a suspect's statements.

The Polygraph   The **polygraph** is a mechanical device that permits an assessment of deception associated with stress, as manifested in physiological data. The endocrine system and the nervous system gear up the body to protect it from impending stress or danger. This involves a change in blood volume and pulse rate, along with an increase in respiration. In addition, there is also a change in skin resistance. Each of these changes is

Polygraph   A device that assesses deception by the person responding to questioning by measuring changes in various physiological data, such as respiration, depth of breathing, blood pressure, pulse, and changes in skin's electrical resistance; lie detector.

Computerized Polygraph Testing Replacing mechanical and electronic polygraph systems is computer software that takes the burden of interpretation of results off the examiner. The software measures, records, and analyzes a person's physical reactions to questions. The software then reports the probability that the person has answered the questions truthfully.

recorded by the polygraph.[10] The word *polygraph* actually means "many writings." Typically, a polygraph simultaneously records respiration, blood pressure, heart rate, and even the skin's electrical resistance. Because the polygraph uses physiological data, a subject hooked to the machine does not really need to verbally respond to a question. The polygraph will measure and reflect the somatic and emotional effects of being asked the questions. Two types of questions are traditionally asked during a polygraph examination. The first is *control questions* that will be used as a standard of truthfulness against which the examiner can compare patterns created when the subject is asked questions about the crime, or *investigative questions.* By comparing the patterns produced by the two sorts of questions, the examiner judges whether deception is taking place.[11] Differences in the patterns are believed to be caused by stress and various somatic and emotional protective responses of the nervous system.[12]

More often than not, polygraphs fail to detect lies, rather than verify truths. Nevertheless, they continue to prove beneficial for cross-checking and validating statements. One important reason to use the polygraph, then, is to eliminate suspects or verify a suspect's alibi. Many police departments and prosecutors use the polygraph to see if a

In a recent study of U.S. law enforcement agencies, 93 percent of the responding agencies used polygraphs in their investigations. Of these agencies, nearly three-quarters used sworn personnel as their polygraph examiners.[13] Even among avid polygraph supporters, however, opinion still differs regarding the reliability of the polygraph. Most agree that the technology can detect physiological changes in the subject at least 75 percent of the time, and perhaps as often as 85 or 90 percent of the time. Because variations can occur, polygraph results are not yet accepted in courts as absolute evidence. Thirty states allow polygraph results as evidence if both parties agree, and 13 states allow it even if opposing counsel objects.[14]

suspect is telling the truth and hence can be removed from the primary list of suspects. Many criminals believe that polygraphs are *truth machines.* Consequently, polygraphs sometimes have a significant psychological effect on a suspect. Telling a suspect that you would like to verify his or her statement with a polygraph test sometimes leads to a confession. Although the actual test is not admissible in court, the confession is. It is important to note that witnesses, suspects, and victims cannot be compelled to undergo a polygraph test, because they are protected by the Fifth Amendment against self-incrimination. Subjects can, however, voluntarily submit to a polygraph.

Truth Serums and Hypnosis Using injections of sodium Pentothal, phenobarbital, or other fast-acting drugs that produce a deep-sleep-like condition has not achieved scientific acceptability as a reasonable and accurate means of establishing the truth. The theory in the use of such drugs, often called truth serums, is that the subject is relieved of inhibitions and will make true statements while under the influence of the drug. When a truth-serum test is given, it should always be administered by a physician under controlled conditions. Individuals vary greatly in their reactions to truth serums. Thus, the courts do not officially recognize truth serums or their reliability, nor do they admit the results of such tests as evidence. As to the use of hypnosis, the courts have established guidelines for using testimony from such a procedure. The hypnosis must be performed by a trained professional, independent of either party in the case, after a thorough study of the subject and the case. As when truth serums are used, subjects must be advised of their rights and must give their consent to the procedure.

SUMMARY BY LEARNING OBJECTIVES

Learning Objective 1

To solve a criminal case, investigators rely on physical evidence and the crime scene; information in investigative reports, *modus operandi* files, and other reports; and especially information gathered in interviews and interrogations.

Learning Objective 2

An interview is questioning to gather information from persons who are not suspects but know something about the crime or the persons involved in it. Like an interview, an interrogation seeks information about a crime, but it is more adversarial and is focused on persons suspected of direct or indirect involvement in the crime.

Learning Objective 3

There are several ways to improve communication and obtain useful information from witnesses: prepare in advance; arrange for privacy; establish rapport; practice aware hearing; use cognitive interview techniques; avoid interruptions; and remain adaptable, patient, objective, and sensitive.

Learning Objective 4

Before being questioned in police custody, a suspect must be advised of his or her rights under the *Miranda* decision. These include the right to remain silent, the right to be told that anything said can and will be used in court, the right to consult with an attorney before answering any questions and to have an attorney present during interrogation, and the right to court-appointed counsel if unable to afford an attorney.

Learning Objective 5

Many of the principles that apply to interviews also apply to interrogations. In addition, it is important to conduct the interrogation in a setting chosen by the investigator, use persuasive techniques, avoid affected words, and use a variety of approaches. Approaches include the logical approach, the emotional approach, indirect or direct inquiry, validation questions, deflating or inflating of the suspect's ego, and overstating or understating of the crime or penalty. The third degree is an illegal interrogation technique.

Learning Objective 6

Special conditions must be observed when questioning juveniles. Obtain permission from parents or guardians before interrogating juveniles. Advise juveniles of their rights to remain silent, to avoid self-incrimination, and to have counsel. Generally, question them in the presence of their parents or guardians.

Learning Objective 7

A confession is a voluntary statement—written, oral, or recorded—by a person charged with a crime. The statement must admit participation in or commission of the criminal act in question. An admission differs slightly from a confession. An admission is a statement by the accused that contains information and facts about the crime but falls short of a full confession.

QUESTIONS FOR REVIEW

Learning Objective 1

1. When physical evidence from a crime scene is insufficient to establish a lead in a case, how can an investigator gain more information?

Learning Objective 2

2. How would you distinguish between an interview and an interrogation?

Learning Objective 3

3. How does rapport affect an interview?
4. What is meant by *aware hearing*, and why is it important for a criminal investigator?
5. What are four procedures used in a *cognitive interview?*
6. Why should all complainants be taken seriously?
7. What are some characteristics of an unwilling witness?

Learning Objective 4

8. Does the *Miranda* decision prevent a suspect from answering questions posed by police investigators?

Learning Objective 5

9. What is the central goal of any interrogation?
10. How does the tone of an interrogation affect a suspect's responses?
11. Why should an investigator know as much as possible about the crime, the victim, and the suspect prior to the interrogation?
12. In which interrogation approach do you try to draw out information without specifically addressing the actual topic?
13. How might deflating a suspect's ego bring him or her to admit involvement in a crime?

14. How did the *Gault* decision affect juveniles?

15. How would you distinguish between a *confession* and an *admission?*

16. How accurate are polygraph tests?

CRITICAL THINKING INVESTIGATIVE EXERCISE

Pair up with another member of the class. Each of you will take a turn at practicing interviewing, using the following questions. Make sure to work hard on using aware hearing. Do not interrupt the subject in the middle of a sentence or interject comments or value judgments about the answers. Be sure to thank the subject for taking the time to be interviewed.

1. What is your name?
2. Where do you live?
3. Who else lives with you?
4. Do you have any identification with you that I can look at? (If the subject has no identification with him or her, ask the following.)
   Is there some reason you are not carrying any identification?
5. What were you doing just before we began this interview?
6. Where did you park your car this morning? (If the subject has no car, ask the following.)
   How did you get to school this morning?
7. Where do you usually buy your groceries?
8. Have you ever purchased groceries at (name a different local store)?
9. What did you have for breakfast this morning?
10. What were you doing last night at about 8:00 P.M.?

INVESTIGATIVE SKILL BUILDERS

Acquiring and Evaluating Information

An officer is dispatched to an apartment complex to respond to a call that a young woman has been raped. Upon arriving at the complex, the officer goes directly to the apartment number the dispatcher provided. A woman in a tight-fitting jumpsuit answers the door and tells the officer to come in. She leads the officer into the living room, where a young woman about 16 years old is lying on the couch. The woman who answered the door says that her niece has been raped.

The young woman is dressed in a torn, see-through white blouse, and a pair of light blue short-shorts. She does not appear to be injured physically, but her hair is messed up, and her makeup has run from crying. The living room does not look as if any violence has taken place. A glance into the adjacent bedroom suggests that there may have been some sort of struggle in there. The bed is unmade, blankets and pillows are on the floor, and a lamp is overturned.

The officer begins to interview the girl. "What's your name?" "Olive," the girl replies as she sits up on the couch. The officer asks Olive if she knows who attacked her. She looks toward the other woman and then looks back and stammers, "No, no, no, I never saw him before." When asked if she can describe him, again she looks at her aunt before speaking. "Yes," she says, "I think I can." She gives a description, including a first name of Jimmy. "So you do know him?" the officer asks. Fear crosses the girl's face. "No, . . . yes, well, I've . . . I think I've seen him around." She nervously looks at her aunt, who has now moved closer to the couch. "Jimmy? Did you say Jimmy?" the aunt asks. "Did Jimmy Jacks do this? My Jimmy Jacks?" The girl begins to cry. The aunt slaps her. "You little slut!" the aunt continues. The officer moves between the aunt and Olive saying, "Hey, there will be none of that." "Who is Jimmy Jacks?" the officer asks. The aunt composes herself. "He's a gentleman friend of mine," she says and moves away from the couch. The officer begins to suspect that the aunt is a prostitute and that perhaps Olive is, too. "Exactly what do you do for a living?" the officer asks the aunt. "Me?" she replies. "I'm an escort hostess." When asked if she is in school, Olive shakes her head no and says she works for the same escort service as her aunt. Convinced that both women are prostitutes and that Olive slept with a regular client of her aunt's and didn't get paid, the officer asks Olive, "Are you prepared to press charges against this Jimmy Jacks if I arrest him?" Olive thinks for a minute, glancing first at her aunt, then back at the officer. "I . . . I don't really think so," Olive replies as she looks back at her aunt. "Well, there isn't very much I can do for you then," the officer tells her. Then the officer leaves.

1. Did the officer handle the situation properly?
2. How else might the officer have handled the situation?

Integrity/Honesty

In the preceding scenario, should the officer have arrested the aunt on a domestic violence charge after she struck the niece? Explain your answer.

Responsibility

In the preceding scenario, should the officer have pursued a charge of rape against Jimmy Jacks? A charge of prostitution against Olive?

ENDNOTES

1. Bruce L. Berg, *Qualitative Research for the Social Sciences,* 2d ed., Allyn and Bacon, Boston, 1995, p. 29.

2. Michael J. Palmiotto, *Criminal Investigation,* Nelson-Hall Publishing, Chicago, 1994.

3. Berg, op. cit., p. 109.

4. "Interview Style Pays Off," *Law Enforcement News,* February 14, 1990, pp. 1, 6.

5. J. B. Morgan, *The Police Function and the Investigation of Crime,* Avebury, Brookfield, Vt., 1990.

6. Edward R. Geiselman and Ronald P. Fisher, *Interviewing Victims and Witnesses of Crime,* National Institute of Justice, Washington, 1985, pp. 1–4.

7. Stephen L. Wasby, *The Impact of the United States Court: Some Perspectives,* Dorsey, Homeward, Ill., 1970, pp. 156–57.

8. A. Buckwalter, *Interviews and Interrogations,* Buttworth Publishers, Boston, 1983.

9. *In re Gault,* 875 U.S. 1428 (1967).

10. Harry Hollien, *The Acoustics of Crime: The New Science of Forensic Phonetics,* Plenum Press, New York, 1990.

11. Ray H. Bull, "What Is the Lie-Detection Test?" in Geoffrey Davies (ed.), *The Polygraph: Tests, Lies, Truth and Science,* Sage, Beverly Hills, 1988, pp. 1–10.

12. S. Abrams, "The Directed Lie Control Question," *Polygraph,* Vol. 20, No. 1, 1991, pp. 26–32.

13. Douglas G. McCloud, "A Survey of Polygraph Utilization," *Law and Order,* September 1991, pp. 123–24.

14. D. M. Rafky and R. C. Sussman, "Polygraphic Reliability and Validity: Individual Components and Stress of Issues in Criminal Tests," *Journal of Police Science and Administration,* Vol. 13, No. 4, 1985, pp. 280–96.

CHAPTER 7

Fingerprints

CHAPTER OBJECTIVES

After completing this chapter, you will be able to:

1. Explain the importance of fingerprint identification in criminal investigation.

2. Distinguish among the basic fingerprint patterns.

3. Identify the types of fingerprints that may be found at a crime scene.

4. Describe various methods for developing invisible fingerprints.

5. Tell how computer technology aids in fingerprint identification.

6. Trace the development of the admissibility of fingerprint identification as evidence in court cases.

KEY TERMS

fingerprint
friction ridges
classification
identification
dactylography
bulb
ten-print card
latent print
visible print
invisible print
plastic print
elimination prints
automated fingerprint
  identification system
  (AFIS)

Fingerprint Identification

Fingerprints and palm prints are among the most valuable types of physical evidence found at a crime scene. Prints of bare feet occasionally play an important role as well. These prints are direct evidence of an individual's presence at a crime scene and of his or her identity. Frequently, the principal evidence found at a crime scene is a latent fingerprint that becomes the key to locating and identifying the perpetrator. Of all methods of identification, fingerprint identification has proved the least fallible.

In this chapter, the term **fingerprint** refers to any impression of the friction ridges on a person's hands and feet. **Friction ridges** are minute raised lines on the surface of fingertips, palms, toes, and heels. The prints are caused by grease and perspiration transferred to an object touched by fingertips, palms, toes, or heels. Sometimes prints are created by a substance covering the hand or foot, as when a barefoot killer walks through the spilled blood of his or her victim. Prints may even be formed by the negative impression created when a liquid substance is touched and then allowed to dry. For example, touching wet paint or a freshly plastered wall creates a negative impression of the friction ridges that press against the surface. Upon first examination, it is often difficult to discern whether a print was left by a finger, the palm of a hand, or even the sole of a foot.

Although there are several different systems for filing fingerprints, each is based on a classification of common characteristics. It should be noted that *classification* of fingerprints is not identical to *identification* of fingerprints. **Classification** is a method of organizing fingerprints into certain formula sets based on particular characteristics common to all fingerprints. **Identification,** on the other hand, involves comparing the fingerprints of a suspect with any latent prints found at a crime scene, to determine a possible match. In other words, the fingerprint classification of a suspect is a major point of identification. Since a print of one person's finger has never been known to duplicate exactly that of another person's—not even an identical twin's—fingerprints are important in identifying suspects in criminal investigations.

The study of fingerprints as a means of identification is known as **dactylography.** It has long been regarded as the greatest scientific contribution to law enforcement. Many of the people who contributed to the development of this science are listed in Figure 7–1. The science of fingerprint identification provides an important service in the administration of justice and in many other areas

Fingerprint An impression created by the friction ridges on a person's hands and feet.

Friction ridges Minute, raised lines on the surface of fingertips, palms, toes, and heels.

Classification A method of organizing fingerprints.

Identification The determination of an individual's identity through physical evidence, especially fingerprint evidence.

Dactylography The scientific study of fingerprints as a means of identification.

FYI

The science of fingerprint identification is known as dactylography. The word *dactylography* is a compound word consisting of the prefix *dactylo-*, meaning "finger, toe, or digit" (derived from the Latin *dactylus* and the Greek *daktylos*) and the suffix *-graphy*, meaning "a representation of a specified object" (derived from the Latin *-graphia* and the Greek *graphein*).

Figure 7–1 Precursors of fingerprint identification.

Nehemiah Grew	1684	English physician who first called attention to the system of pores and ridges in hands and feet.
Marcello Malpighi	1686	Italian anatomist who first wrote about elevated ridges of tips of fingers and figures on palms.
Johannes Purkinje	1823	Bohemian anatomist who wrote on the diversity of ridges on fingertips; first outlined broad system of classification.
William Herschel	1858	British administrator in India who was the first government official to use fingerprints for identification.
Henry Faulds	1880	British missionary in Japan who first developed a method for lifting prints, using a thin film of printer's ink as the transfer medium, and who concluded that fingerprint patterns remain unchanged throughout one's life.
Alphonse Bertillon	1883	French police officer who developed the concept of criminal identification, using physical measurements and photographs of criminal suspects.
Francis Galton	1892	British anthropologist who presented statistical proof of the uniqueness of fingerprints and outlined principles of fingerprint identification.
Juan Vucetich	1894	Argentinian police officer who published a book outlining a method of fingerprint classification.
Edward Henry	1897	British police officer in India who developed a method of fingerprint classification that is widely used.

in which positive identification is crucial. Some of the uses of fingerprints include the following:

- Identification of criminals whose fingerprints are found at the scene of a crime.
- Identification of fugitives through comparison with fingerprints in a data bank.
- Exchange of criminal-identification information with identification bureaus of other states or foreign countries in cases of common interest.
- Identification of children kidnapped by family members.
- Identification of bodies, as in the case of homeless persons or persons killed in traffic or airplane accidents.

- Prevention of hospital mistakes in identification of infants.
- Prevention of fraud by people taking specialized examinations, such as the Law School Aptitude Test or police entrance examinations.
- Identification of unconscious people or those suffering from amnesia.
- Identification of missing persons.
- Identification of people found in the aftermath of disasters.
- Identification of participants in sales of gold, silver, or precious stones.
- Identification of applicants for licenses for firearms, aircraft, and other equipment.
- Identification of applicants for certain types of jobs.

The Nature of Fingerprints

Fingerprints are created by the various lines and ridges on the rounded area, or **bulb,** of the end joint of every finger and thumb. These ridges form distinct contours and patterns that distinguish one person from another. These patterns remain unchanged throughout an individual's life.

When crude attempts are made to alter these patterns with abrasives, such as sandpaper, or various chemicals, the ridges eventually

Bulb   The rounded area at the end joint of every finger and thumb.

Fingerprints can sometimes help police identify missing children.

return to their original patterns. Skin conditions such as warts, wounds, blisters, or temporary damage caused by certain occupations have no permanent effect on the pattern. Once the condition changes or the skin heals, the original contours and ridge patterns return.

Fingerprint Patterns

Generally, fingerprints are classified into three main patterns—*arched, looped,* and *whorled.* Further divisions into subgroups result in the basic fingerprint patterns shown in Figure 7–2.

The ridge detail of fingerprints—including the ends of the ridges, the ridge formations, and the relationships between ridges—forms the basis of identification. For instance, look at the two examples of arched prints in Figure 7–2. In a *plain arch,* the ridges enter on one side of the impression and flow, or tend to flow, out the other side with a wave in the center. In a *tented arch,* the ridges enter on one side and flow out the other, as in a plain arch, but the ridge or ridges at the center have a decided upward thrust.

Now look at the two looped patterns. In such patterns, one or more ridges enter from one side, make a hairpin turn, and exit on the side from which they entered. At least one ridge must follow this course and pass between the delta (a triangular area) and the core, or approximate center of the finger. (Note that a loop pattern has only one delta.) In a *radial loop,* the ridges slant toward the thumb, or the radial bone of the forearm. In an *ulnar loop* pattern, they slant toward the little finger, or the ulnar bone of the forearm.

In whorl patterns, at least one ridge must pass completely around the core of the finger. Its path may form a spiral, a circle, an oval, or any

Figure 7–2 The basic fingerprint patterns.

| Plain arch | Ulnar loop | Plain whorl | Central-pocket-loop whorl |

| Tented arch | Radial loop | Double-loop whorl | Accidental whorl |

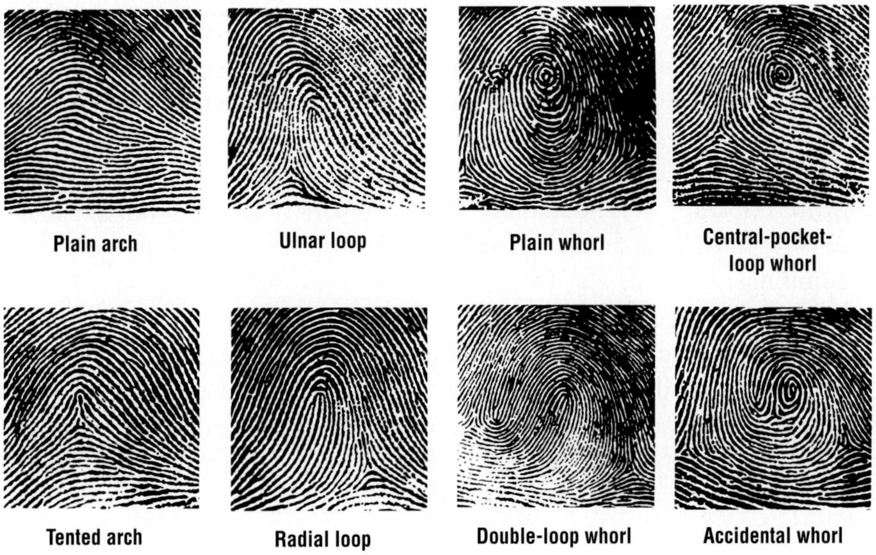

HISTORY

By 1901, England and Wales were officially using fingerprints for criminal identification. The system they used was devised by Edward Henry, then Inspector-General of Police in Bengal, India, and later Commissioner of the Metropolitan Police of London. Henry's system, along with the work of Argentinian Juan Vucetich, forms the basis of all modern ten-print identification. The basic Henry System has been modified and extended. The current system, which incorporates electronic digitization, is used by the FBI and most law enforcement agencies in the United States today.

variant of a circle. It must make at least one recurvature in front of each delta. A whorl has at least two deltas, one at the right side and one at the left side. The *plain whorl* is the simplest and most common of the whorl subdivisions. It has two deltas and at least one ridge that makes a complete circuit about the core of the finger. The *double-loop* type of finger impression consists of two loop formations with two separate and distinct sets of shoulders and deltas. In a *central-pocket loop,* most of the ridges form a loop, with one or more ridges curving completely around the core to form a pocket. An *accidental whorl* is a combination of two or more types of patterns (excepting the plain arch). Look again at Figure 7–2 to see examples of the four types of whorl patterns.

To determine whether two fingerprints are the same, fingerprint analysts compare various characteristics, depending on the types of patterns being examined. These characteristics have to be pointed out as the identifying features to prove that two fingerprint impressions are or are not the same. If the fingerprint exhibits a loop pattern, ridge counting may be used. The analyst counts the ridges that touch or cross an imaginary line drawn between the core and the delta of a loop. Ridge endings —, bifurcations (forks) ⌒, and islands ⌒ are the most common ridge characteristics in such an analysis. See Figure 7–3 for several examples of ridge counting.

If the fingerprint has a whorl pattern, then ridge tracing may be used. Once the deltas are located, the analyst traces the ridge that emanates from the lower side of the left delta toward the right delta until it reaches the point nearest or opposite the extreme right. The ridges between the tracing ridge and the right delta are then counted. Figure 7–3 illustrates this process.

Figure 7–3 Methods of comparing fingerprint impressions.

Ridge counting

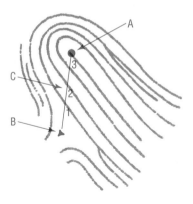

Ridge count three

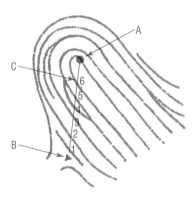

Ridge count six

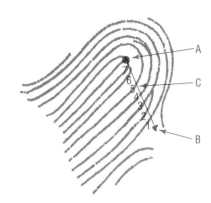

Ridge count seven

A. Core (center)
B. Delta
C. Imaginary line between A and B used to count the total number of ridges touching or crossing it

Ridge tracing

Ridge A is traced from the left delta to the right delta. At a point nearest the right delta, should tracing ridge A pass inside the right delta with three or more ridges intervening between tracing ridge A and the right delta, the tracing is designated as *inner.*

Ridge A is traced from the left delta toward the right delta. At a point nearest the right delta, should tracing ridge A pass outside the right delta with three or more ridges intervening between tracing ridge A and the right delta, it is designated as an *outer.*

Ridge A is traced from the left delta toward the right delta. At a point nearest the right delta, should ridge A pass inside or outside the right delta with less than three intervening ridges between ridge A and the right delta, the tracing is designated as *meet* or *meeting.*

Fingerprinting Procedures

The use of digitized fingerprinting, or the electronic reproduction of fingerprints for computer systems, is growing in the United States. However, inked fingerprints are still a staple in law enforcement.

In ordinary use, the surface of the fingers is inked and the ridges and patterns are transferred to a standard 8- by 8-inch form called a **ten-print card.** This serves as the basic document used in fingerprint files. As will be discussed later, even when fingerprints are digitized for computer record keeping, the format of the ten-print card is used. Although there are variations in the materials used to create fingerprints, there are several basic elements.

A subject's fingers are gently rolled in ink before being printed.

First, one needs a transferring material or medium, such as ink. This may be an inked pad, a tray with ink from a tube of printer's ink, or it may even be an inkless, colorless chemical that will create an impression when contacted by special chemically treated paper. Second, one needs a medium on which the impressions can be made. This may be paper, cardboard, celluloid, or glass. Third, one should have a solid surface to work on. A table or desk serves this purpose. Finally, one should have materials to clean up with, such as denatured alcohol, soap and water, and towels.

The basic method for taking fingerprints is quite simple and usually proceeds as follows:

1. Have the subject stand about an arm's length from the work area.

2. Tell the subject to relax his or her hand and let you do all the work.

3. Take the subject's right hand so that the thumb will be the first to be printed. Press the thumb gently but firmly into the ink medium. Ink the entire *bulb* of the thumb.

4. Next, press the right thumb onto the card or paper intended to receive the impression. Roll the thumb gently from one side to the other to get a complete fingerprint.

5. Repeat the procedure for each of the remaining fingers on the right hand.

6. Repeat the procedure for each finger on the left hand.

7. If using a standard ten-print card, also print the four fingers of each hand together in the space provided and make a second imprint of each thumb.

8. When all the impressions have been taken and the subject has cleaned his or her hands, have the subject sign the fingerprint card. Then you sign as the fingerprint technician.

On occasion, there may be exceptions to these procedures. For example, if a subject has an amputated or missing finger, you will naturally have to leave the appropriate space blank. Similarly, temporary injuries may create problems. For instance, the subject may have a fresh cut, an infection, or a bandaged finger. Indicate these problems in the blank spaces on the card. Expressions such as *amputated, fresh cut,* or *bandaged* inform others why an impression is missing from the records.

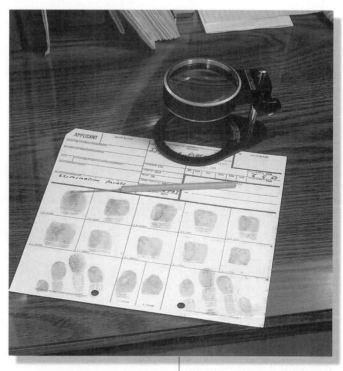

A ten-print card.

Types of Fingerprint Impressions

Several types of fingerprints can be found at crime scenes. These include *latent prints, visible prints, plastic prints,* and *invisible prints.*

Latent Prints   **Latent prints** are impressions transferred to a surface by perspiration or oil from the ridges of fingers, toes, palms, and heels. They also may be created by a residue of mud, blood, paint, or some other sticky substance, such as syrup, adhesive, or lacquer, carried on hands or feet. Latent prints can be visible or invisible. Today, *latent prints* is a generic term applied to almost any sort of print found at a crime scene.

Visible Prints   These are prints made by soiled or stained fingertips or palms. They may include impressions left in dust on solid, nonporous surfaces. **Visible prints** are readily observable on the surfaces of objects that have been touched or carried. Fingerprints of this sort may or may not have identification value, depending on how distinctly friction ridge impressions have been transferred to the object's surface.

Invisible Prints   Such prints are not readily observable, but various powders, chemicals, gases, and lights can make them visible. **Invisible prints** typically are found on nonporous surfaces, such as glass, metal, finished wood, doorknobs, window moldings, telephones, and many other non-absorbent, hard, smooth surfaces.

Plastic Prints   These are a form of visible print created in soft substances. For example, soap, butter, wax, putty, grease, and even paint form a kind of mold of the fingerprint when touched, creating a **plastic print.**

Latent print   An impression transferred to a surface by sweat, oil, dirt, blood, or some other substance on the ridges of the fingers; it may be visible or invisible.

Visible print   A fingerprint, found at a crime scene, that is immediately visible to the naked eye.

Invisible print   A latent print not visible without some form of developing.

Plastic print   A type of visible print formed when substances such as butter, grease, wax, peanut butter, and so forth that have a plasticlike texture are touched.

Elimination Prints When police officers search for latent prints at the scene of a crime, they may find several. Some of the prints may belong to persons who had a legitimate reason for being at the scene. Before checking these latent prints against the fingerprint file, the officer will fingerprint those persons and then will compare the latent prints with these inked prints. The inked prints taken for this purpose are called **elimination prints.**

Elimination prints Fingerprints taken of all persons whose prints are likely to be found at a crime scene, but who have a lawful reason to have been there and are not suspects.

Methods of Developing Invisible Prints

Latent or invisible prints left on surfaces are delicate liquid or semi-solid deposits. They are composed largely of water or other adhering materials, which can bond to various powders to make them visible, or they can be made visible through other print development techniques.

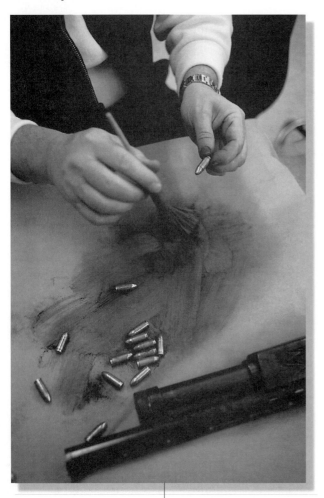

In dusting for latent prints, it is important to use the correct amount of powder.

Powders Traditionally, fingerprint powders were white or black; today, they may also be silver, red, or gray. The color of the background on which the print is made determines the color of powder to use to provide a good contrast: light-colored powders help prints stand out on a dark background; dark powders are more useful on a light background. To develop the print, apply a small amount of fingerprint powder to the area believed to have been touched. Apply the powder with a small brush or a feather, spreading the powder very gently to discover the print without destroying the impression. Never sprinkle the powder directly on the print.

Powders also come in an assortment of fluorescent colors and may be magnetic or nonmagnetic, depending on whether the object or surface to be dusted is a ferrous, or iron-containing, material. By dusting the area with such fluorescent powders and then subjecting the invisible prints to various alternative lights and filters, lasers, or ultraviolet (UV) lights, technicians can cause the prints to fluoresce, or glow, and become visible.[1] Magnetic brushes and powders are particularly useful for dusting overhead, slanting, or vertical surfaces.

Lifting Prints Generally, fingerprints are lifted with a length of clear tape. One end of the tape is usually placed just beyond one end of the print. Then the tape is pressed over the print gently, with an even pressure. Care is taken to avoid or eliminate any air bubbles. Once the tape is in place, the tape may be left on the object to protect the print, and the entire object may be sent to the crime lab. If the object is too large or it is not feasible to send it to the lab, the tape may be lifted from the surface of the object and carefully transferred to a card. The powder that originally adhered to the latent fingerprint on the object will now adhere to the tape in the same pattern. The card with the transferred print should also include all pertinent data—including who found and lifted the print, where it was recovered, and what type and color of powder was used—as well as the officer's or technician's signature.

Rubber fingerprint lifters may also be used to recover fingerprints. They are useful for removing prints from surfaces that are curved or difficult to photograph. The rubber lifter usually consists of a thin black or white flexible material coated on one side with an adhesive. To take a latent print, the officer must first apply print powder to the area. Then, after removing the protective covering from the adhesive, the officer places the adhesive side of the lifter against the print and slowly pulls it away. The covering is replaced on the adhesive, protecting the lifted print.

As a rule of thumb, all invisible prints, once developed, should be photographed with a fixed-focus fingerprint camera before being lifted. It is also important to photograph plastic prints, since they should never be enhanced with powders and may be damaged beyond recognition if lifted. Photographs provide an accurate record of the prints should lifting fail and inadvertently damage or destroy the print.

Fuming In some situations, invisible prints can be made visible by cyanoacrylate vapors that polymerize, or bond, with an invisible print, producing a visible chemical reaction in the form of a white deposit on the print. At one time, this technique involved placing small objects, such as credit cards, soft drink cans, or photographs, in a closed container with superglue and a heat source. The effect was to create a chemical vapor from the cyanoacrylate in the glue, which developed

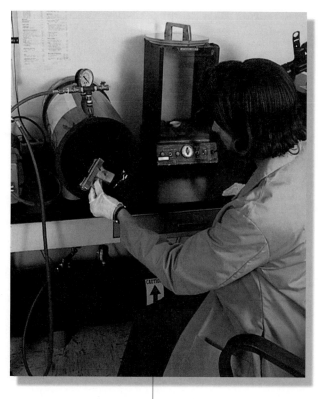

Many of the methods used to develop invisible prints, such as this fuming chamber, require technicians to take safety precautions.

the fingerprint on the small object.[2] Today, many police agencies use commercially developed fuming chambers and fuming wands to develop invisible prints in the laboratory and at the crime scene. Although superglue is no longer used, the process is still sometimes referred to as *superglue fuming*. Safety precautions must be followed with any fuming device, as hydrogen cyanide, a poisonous, highly flammable liquid, can form at higher temperatures.

Chemicals Many chemical methods have been successfully used to develop fingerprints on various surfaces. The following four are the more widely used:

- Iodine method—Fuming with iodine crystals causes latent prints containing fat or oil to develop. The iodine fumes are absorbed and react with perspiration or fatty matter, creating a yellowish or brownish impression. Iodine fuming is effective in developing latent prints on greasy surfaces, paper, cardboard, wood, metal, and other materials. In 1982, iodine fuming was successfully used to develop latent prints on human skin.[3] In this application, the area is fumed with iodine, and a specially treated clear plastic strip is placed over the fumed area. If latent prints are present, they appear in a few seconds as a dark purple positive impression. When using this technique on living victims or suspects, it is important to first establish that they are not allergic to iodine.

- Silver nitrate method—The suspect material is immersed in a silver nitrate solution in a tray. This is called *silvering*. After being taken from the solution, the material is placed between two clean, white photo-blotting papers to remove the excess solution and is allowed to dry. The dry specimen is then exposed to a strong light source, such as a photoflood light, an ultraviolet lamp, a carbon arc, a halogen lamp, or even sunlight. When satisfactorily developed, the print becomes visible as a dark brown outline that can be photographed. This method is sometimes called the *silver chloride method* because the sodium chloride from perspiration that has formed a latent print reacts with the silver nitrate solution to form silver chloride. This method is useful for developing latent fingerprints on paper, unpainted wood, and other porous substances.

- Ninhydrin method—Powdered ninhydrin is suspended in ethyl

FYI

While inkless or colorless chemical processes are cleaner to work with, they do not produce as sharp a fingerprint image as ink. As a result, many police agencies continue to use the messier real-ink version.

alcohol or acetone. The mixture is then applied to the suspect document or surface by spraying, brushing, swabbing, or immersion. Commercially prepared sprays are available that require no mixing or preparation. If the surface is allowed to dry at room temperature, a purple-reddish-brown stain of the ridge pattern in latent prints will develop in about two hours. Applying heat can speed the development process, but may affect the final product. This method is particularly effective on porous materials such as paper and certain types of fabrics. It is especially effective on older prints because it reacts with the amino acids in human perspiration, which remain longer than the salt deposits that the silver nitrate method reveals.

- Chem Print method—Chem Print is a trade name for solution sold in an aerosol container. The suspect specimen is sprayed until moist on all sides and then allowed to air dry. When dry, it is subjected to low heat (about 200 degrees Fahrenheit), and latent prints, if present, will develop. When speed of development is not as important, the material should be warmed at about 75 to 110 degrees Fahrenheit for about 24 hours. Chem Print is particularly effective for developing latent prints on objects made of cardboard, paper, or wood. It also is effective on certain types of fabrics. Latent prints developed by this process remain stable for approximately six months before fading. It is important, therefore, to photograph the prints as soon as possible after developing.

Fingerprint Kits   Because of police shows on television and depictions of police in the movies, the average citizen knows something about *dusting for prints.* Unfortunately, many average citizens expect the police to dust for prints whenever a crime occurs—no matter how small the loss or how futile the dusting might be. A number of police agencies equip their patrol officers with fingerprint kits so that when an officer responds to a simple burglary where there is evidence of forced entry at a window or door, he or she can use the kit to check for latent prints. Often this does more to reassure the victim that something is being done about the case than anything the officer might say. The unfortunate reality is that seven out of every ten burglaries will go unsolved—regardless of dusting for prints.

Even though dusting may not turn up prints or a suspect, it should be taken seriously. Given the advances made in fingerprint identification technology, there is an increasing possibility that dusting in lesser crimes will produce useful evidence. Furthermore, when a burglary suspect or petty thief with a similar M.O. is arrested, these latent prints may allow the police agency to close other cases.

A simple field fingerprint kit might include the following items:

- Flashlight
- Tongs or tweezers
- Latex gloves
- Large and small collection envelopes
- Evidence tags or stickers
- Notebook and pencil
- Transparent lifting tape
- Scissors
- Magnifying glass
- Ruler and measuring tape
- Fingerprint powders (assorted colors and magnetic and nonmagnetic forms)
- Fingerprint brushes (including a magnetic brush)
- Latent-print transfer cards
- Fixed-focus fingerprint camera and film

Fingerprint Files and Searches

At one time, all fingerprint identifications were done by hand. They depended largely on the Henry System of fingerprint identification. After a suspect's fingerprints were received, the first thing done was to search for the suspect's name in the name index file. These manual searches began with a fingerprint classifier determining the primary fingerprint classification in order to assist in distinguishing between people with the same name. If a match was found in the name index file, the case jacket folder number or the master fingerprint classification for that name was noted so that the fingerprint could be checked with the prints on file. Starting with the name of the suspect and consulting the name index file is much faster than completely classifying a set of fingerprints and then searching the main fingerprint files for matches of these classifications.

When efforts to identify a suspect by name failed, fingerprints would then be fully analyzed and classified, and manual searches would be made of the main files. This was a long and laborious task, often requiring many hours of labor. The searching officer would have to visually compare the set of prints in question and the often hundreds of sets on file with similar classifications. See Figure 7–4 for an example of characteristics a fingerprint technician might try to match when comparing file prints with latent prints recovered from a crime scene.

Figure 7–4 Enlarged, inked fingerprint showing the location of twelve ridge characteristics.

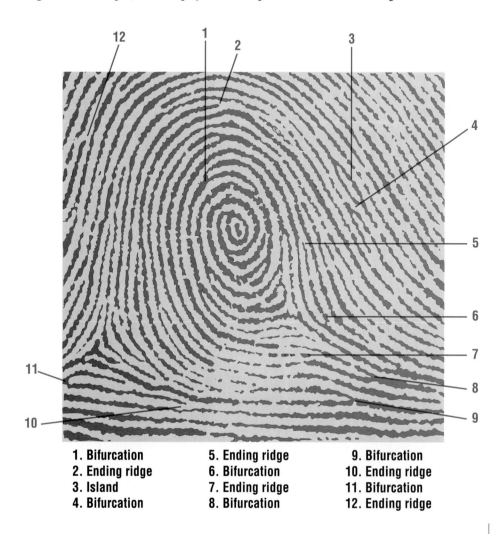

1. Bifurcation	5. Ending ridge	9. Bifurcation
2. Ending ridge	6. Bifurcation	10. Ending ridge
3. Island	7. Ending ridge	11. Bifurcation
4. Bifurcation	8. Bifurcation	12. Ending ridge

Automated Fingerprint Identification Systems

Computer technology has significantly altered and improved many aspects of police work. Among the most important advances is the **automated fingerprint identification system (AFIS)** technology. This computer technology uses a mathematically created image of a fingerprint and identification of up to 250 characteristics for each print.[4] In addition to scanning, storing, searching, and retrieving these images, the computers can reproduce them on a plotter or terminal screen for visual comparison. Standard ten-print cards generally are scanned electronically, digitized, and made readable by the computer system to create the data bank of fingerprint records. Additionally, it is possible with AFIS to

Automated fingerprint
identification system
(AFIS) A computerized
system for scanning, mapping, storing, searching,
and retrieving fingerprints.

create a live digital fingerprint. This process involves placing each finger, in order, on a glass platen, where a laser scans the finger, converting the resulting fingerprint to digital form. Later, images of the fingerprints can be generated for identification.

In many ways, the processes of digital fingerprinting and ink fingerprinting are similar. However, many believe that the digitally produced prints are of a better quality than those produced by ink.[5] Also, AFIS systems allow an agency to compare an applicant's or suspect's fingerprints with thousands or even millions of data bank prints in a matter of minutes. The same search might take weeks or months if done manually.

AFIS rose to national prominence in 1985, when the Los Angeles police department identified and arrested Richard Ramirez as the notorious Night Stalker. The Los Angeles police had used an AFIS built by

FOCUS ON TECHNOLOGY

Automated Fingerprint Identification System (AFIS)   With AFIS, latent prints or prints recovered from a crime scene can be quickly searched against an existing fingerprint database for possible matches. The system is driven by sophisticated image processing procedures that produce a workable list of suspects, often in descending order of probability, for comparison by a fingerprint expert.

Nippon Electronic Company of Japan to sort through 380,000 electronically stored ten-print cards. The computer had identified Richard Ramirez as the most likely match with the latent prints. Ramirez was arrested just two hours after the computer had identified his prints. He was charged with killing fifteen people. Experts have estimated that a comparable search of ten-print cards done manually would have taken a single technician 67 years to complete.[6] By the late 1990s, hundreds of police agencies in the United States had AFIS data banks.

Today, AFIS programs are capable of making extremely fine distinctions between classification points, providing considerable accuracy and reliability. The systems can compare more than 90 minute points along ridges, whorls, bifurcations, islands, and contours on each finger. Although latent prints may not provide 90 points of match, accurate identifications can be made with as few as 12 or 15 matches.

AFIS technology operates with incredible speed and is credited with 98 to 100 percent accuracy. This does not, however, mean the computer makes a match 98 to 100 percent of the time. First, the computer cannot identify a print that is not in the system's data bank. If a suspect's prints have never been taken before, they will not be available to compare with the latent prints. Second, the system does not necessarily identify a single suspect. Rather, the computer generates a list of *candidates* whose prints match at various classification points. Then a qualified fingerprint examiner must determine the best match among the candidates.

The FBI has been working on an integrated automated fingerprint indentification system (IAFIS), scheduled for unveiling in 1998. This system will combine AFIS with other identification and statistical information. Once IAFIS is online, agencies will be able to contact the system, and in addition to running latent prints, they will be able to search the National Crime Information Center (NCIC) databases as well. They will also be able to access an Interstate Identification Index and several other record banks.[8]

STATISTICS

The Identification Division Automated Services (IDAS) system of the FBI maintains a name index and a fingerprint index to the arrest records of 25 million subjects arrested throughout the United States. It processes an average of 35,000 fingerprint identification requests each day.[7]

Admissibility of Fingerprint Evidence

The admissibility of fingerprint evidence can be traced to the case of *People v. Jennings* (1911).[9] This case held that fingerprint evidence was admissible as a means of identification. The court also ruled that people experienced in fingerprint identification may give their opinions about whether the fingerprints found at the scene of a crime belonged to those of an accused individual. The court's conclusions were based on a comparison of the photographs of such prints with the impressions made by the defendant. The court stated that the weight of the testimony of experts in fingerprint identification is a question for the jury to determine.

Cases that followed the *Jennings* decision strengthened the legitimacy of fingerprints as a means of identification. For instance, in 1914 in the case of *New Jersey v. Cerciello,*[10] the trial judge had permitted fingerprint evidence to be introduced. On appeal, the defendant argued that it was an error to allow testimony by fingerprint experts, who had explained the comparison of fingerprints obtained from the defendant voluntarily with fingerprints found on a hatchet near the body of the murder victim. The New Jersey Court of Errors and Appeals disagreed:

> In principle its admission as legal evidence [fingerprint comparisons] is based upon the theory that the evolution in practical affairs of life, whereby the progressive and scientific tendencies of the age are manifest in every other department of human endeavor, cannot be ignored in legal procedure, but that the law in its efforts to enforce justice by demonstrating a fact in issue, will allow evidence of those scientific processes, which are the work of educated and skillful men in their various departments, and apply them to the demonstration of a fact, leaving the weight and effect to be given to the effort and its results entirely to the consideration of the jury.

The U.S. Supreme Court agreed with the New Jersey appellate court and, in two other New Jersey cases several years later, the Court held admissible as evidence a photograph of fingerprints on a balcony post of a house in lieu of producing the actual post and a photograph of the fingerprints on a car door, along with an expert's identification of these prints as belonging to the defendant.[11]

In another case, *Commonwealth v. Albright,* a fingerprint expert had testified in the trial court about a fingerprint on a piece of glass, established to be from a pane in a door of a burglarized house. The expert affirmed that the impression on the glass was the same as that of the defendant's left index finger. The Pennsylvania State Supreme Court confirmed the conviction on the basis of the fingerprint evidence, stating:

> It is well settled that the papillary lines and marks of the fingers of every man, woman, and child possess an individual character different from those of any other person and that the chances that the fingerprints of two different persons may be identical are infinitesimally remote.[12]

A case decided during the civil rights movement of the 1960s established another important principle of admissibility of fingerprint evidence. In *Schmerber v. California*,[13] the U.S. Supreme Court held that the introduction into evidence of fingerprint impressions taken without the consent of the defendant was not an infringement of the constitutional privilege against self-incrimination. The Court ruled that it is constitutional to obtain real or physical evidence even if the suspect is compelled to give blood in a hospital; submit to finger-printing, photographing, or measurements; write or speak for identification; appear in court; or stand or walk. It also held that it is constitutional to compel a suspect to assume a stance or make a particular gesture, put on a blouse to see if it fits, or exhibit his or her body as evidence when it is material. The *Schmerber* case points out that the privilege against self-incrimination is related primarily to "testimonial compulsion."

Numerous U.S. Supreme Court decisions have reinforced the admissibility of fingerprint identification evidence.

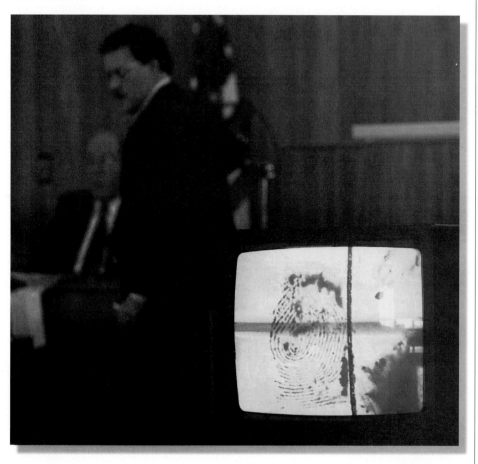

SUMMARY BY LEARNING OBJECTIVES

Learning Objective 1

Fingerprints, palm prints, and sometimes footprints are among the most valuable types of physical evidence found at a crime scene. Fingerprints are created by the various lines and ridges on the end joint, or bulb, of every finger and thumb. These ridges form distinct patterns that are uniquely distinguishable from one person to another. These patterns remain unchanged throughout an individual's life.

Learning Objective 2

Fingerprints are classified into three main groups of patterns: arches, loops, and whorls. There are eight subclassifications of the main groups. Matches of fingerprints are made by comparing numerous characteristics within these classifications.

Learning Objective 3

Several types of fingerprints can be found at crime scenes. They include latent prints, visible prints, plastic prints, and invisible prints.

Learning Objective 4

Invisible prints at a crime scene may be developed using a number of techniques. These include powders, fuming, and chemicals. Many agencies equip their patrol officers with fingerprint kits, enabling them to search for prints as soon as possible after certain types of crimes have been committed.

Learning Objective 5

At one time, fingerprint searches were conducted manually. Today, most fingerprint searches are conducted by computer, often by means of an automated fingerprint identification system, or AFIS.

Learning Objective 6

The admissibility of fingerprint identification as evidence in a criminal court case can be traced to the Illinois case of *People v. Jennings,* upheld by the U.S. Supreme Court in 1911. Subsequent decisions in other cases refined and strengthened the legitimacy of fingerprints as a means of identification.

QUESTIONS FOR REVIEW

Learning Objective 1

1. Define *friction ridges* and *dactylography.*
2. What direct evidence do fingerprints provide about persons and a crime scene?

3. Describe the three main fingerprint patterns.

4. On what portion of the fingertip are friction ridges found?

5. Define *latent prints, visible prints, plastic prints, invisible prints,* and *elimination prints.*

6. Why might an investigator use a particular color of fingerprint powder?

7. How is cyanoacrylate, a chemical used in special glues, useful in developing invisible fingerprints?

8. What is meant by *silvering?*

9. Why do many police agencies rely on computers to electronically search for fingerprints that match specimens recovered at crime scenes?

10. To what U.S. Supreme Court decision can the admissibility of fingerprints as evidence be traced?

CRITICAL THINKING INVESTIGATIVE EXERCISES

You will need a magnifying glass, an ink pad, some blank white paper or cards, and cleanup supplies, such as a towel, soap and water, or denatured alcohol.

1. Divide into small groups. In each group, have each person take the fingerprints of another person in the group, using the steps described in the chapter. Create a ten-print card for each person. Exchange cards. Then, using Figure 7–2 as a guide, determine the fingerprint pattern of each print on the card you have. Return the card to the owner for him or her to verify the classification of the fingerprint patterns.

2. Using the technique described in this chapter, have your instructor fingerprint six members of the class, creating six ten-print cards without the names of the persons fingerprinted. These individuals will be your *suspects*. Next, have your instructor mix up the six ten-print cards, select one, and discard the other five. Then have your instructor reprint each of the six *suspects*. Using these six cards as a data bank, compare them with the one original suspect card. Try to match a suspect print with one of the prints in the data bank, locating a minimum of ten points of match. Refer to Figure 7–4 as an aid in locating points to match.

INVESTIGATIVE SKILL BUILDERS

Applying Technology to Tasks

You are the first to arrive at a home where a bad drug deal resulted in the shooting deaths of three people. In the living room, there is a coffee table with a thin layer of white powder—possibly heroin or cocaine—spread across its surface. A revolver rests on the table as well. With latex gloves on your hands, you carefully lift the gun by placing a pencil in the muzzle. You use the pencil as a lever and handle by which to lift and hold the gun. You can see that five bullets have been fired. You also notice that the powder from the table has adhered to the butt of the gun (its handle). There appear to be fingerprints on the butt, made visible by the powder.

1. How will you lift the prints from the gun?
2. How will you determine whether these prints are from the assailant or one of the victims?

Integrity/Honesty

You are still investigating the crime scene described in the preceding scenario. You notice that sticking out from under the couch is a bundle of $10 bills. You are alone. You count the money and determine that there is a total of $5000. Do you include this money in your evidence list and inventory or say nothing and keep it?

ENDNOTES

1. "Bluemaxx," advertising pamphlet for SIRCHIE fingerprint labs, Inc., Raleigh, N.C., 1994.
2. Joseph Almong and Amnon Gabay, "A Modified Super Glue Technique," *Journal of Forensic Sciences,* Vol. 31, No. 1, 1986, pp. 250–53.
3. M. A. Feldman, C. E. Meloan, and J. L. Lambert, "A New Method for Recovering Latent Fingerprints From Skin," *Journal of Forensic Sciences,* Vol. 27, No. 4, 1982, pp. 806–11.
4. Carroll Buracker and William Stover, "Automated Fingerprint Identification— Regional Application of Technology," *FBI Law Enforcement Bulletin,* Vol. 53, 1984, pp. 1–5.
5. Tod W. Burker, "Laser Fingerprinting: Technology of the 1900s," *Law and Order,* August 1992, pp. 75–76.
6. Phillip Elmer-De Witt, "Take a Byte Out of Crime," *Time,* October 14, 1985, p. 96.
7. Maria Josef (ed.), *Handbook of Forensic Science,* U.S. Department of Justice, FBI, Washington, 1995.

8. Lowell C. Van Duyn, "The FBI's 21st Century Integrated Computer System—'IAFIS'," *Law Enforcement Technology,* April 1993, pp. 40–41.

9. *People v. Jennings,* 252 Ill. 534; 96 N.E. 1077 (1911).

10. *State v. Cerciello,* 86 N.J.L. 309; A. 1112 (1914).

11. *State v. Connors,* 87 N.J.L. 419; 94 A. 812 (1915); *Lamble v. State,* 96 N.J.L. 231; 114 A. 346 (1921).

12. *Commonwealth v. Albright,* 101 Pa. Sup. Ct. 317 (1931).

13. *Schmerber v. California,* 384 U.S. 757, 763–764 (1966).

CHAPTER 8

From Surveillance to Records and Files

CHAPTER OBJECTIVES

After completing this chapter, you will be able to:

1. Explain what is meant by *surveillance*.

2. Discuss the purpose of surveillance and how to prepare for surveillance operations.

3. Describe the various types of surveillance used by police agencies.

4. Provide some tips for surveillance officers and investigators.

5. Discuss the importance of police agency files and records in conducting surveillance.

6. Explain how persons may be connected and traced through public and private records.

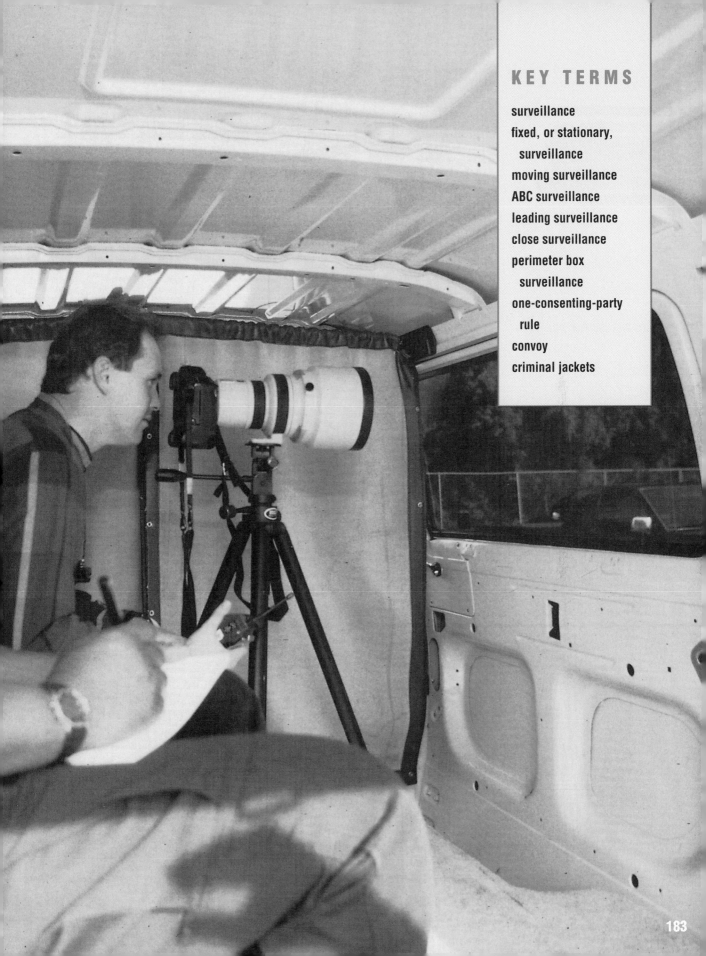

KEY TERMS

surveillance

fixed, or stationary, surveillance

moving surveillance

ABC surveillance

leading surveillance

close surveillance

perimeter box surveillance

one-consenting-party rule

convoy

criminal jackets

Observing the Scene

✗ **Surveillance** The secret observation of people, groups, places, vehicles, and things over a prolonged period to gather information about a crime or criminal.

Surveillance is the secret observation of people, groups, places, vehicles, and things over a prolonged period to obtain information. The word *surveillance* derives from the French word *surveiller,* meaning "to watch over." Surveillance is a valuable investigative tool that can provide information about the activities and identities of individuals. To conduct a successful surveillance, officers must be alert, discreet, and cautious. Surveillance requires great patience, versatility, careful observation skills, and a good memory. The ability to role-play also helps. To better understand surveillance, it is important to understand some of the law enforcement jargon related to it. A number of the more common terms are shown in Figure 8–1.

Figure 8–1 Surveillance terms.

Basic Terms:	
Subject	Person or object being observed.
Surveillance	Careful observation of a person, group, place, vehicle, or thing, undertaken in a secretive manner.
Surveillant	Officer or investigator conducting the surveillance.

Other Terms:	
Aerial surveillance	Use of aircraft to observe and follow a subject or the subject's vehicle.
Being burned	Another term for a surveillant's being recognized by the subject.
Being made	Recognition of a surveillant by the subject.
Blown cover	Synonymous with *being made.*
Bugging	Use of various small electronic listening devices, or *bugs,* located near or on the subject.
Close surveillance	Opposite of loose surveillance; investigators keep the subject under constant surveillance, even at the risk of being identified, or *being made.*
Cover or cover story	A surveillant's use of false identification or a false identity to gain access to or remain undetected in a location or among persons under surveillance.
Covert	Secret, undercover, or unannounced.
Discreet surveillance	Observation at a *discreet,* or cautious, distance from the subject; in such situations, losing sight of the subject may be better than being made.
Electronic surveillance	Use of various cameras and listening and recording devices to monitor a site.

Unlike other aspects of police work, for which the officer can prepare and plan, surveillance depends largely on the actions of the subject. When conducting surveillance without advance knowledge of the subject's plans and activities, officers must simply wait, watch, and respond. In some situations, an investigator may obtain information about a subject's plans from an informant or from a wiretap or other listening device. In these instances, the subject's movements may be anticipated to some degree.

There are no hard-and-fast rules governing how surveillance operates. In fact, actions and activities that work in one situation may prove useless in another. Since surveillance takes time, personnel, and expensive equipment, each case must be carefully considered, and resources allocated accordingly.

Fixed surveillance	Use of a stationary location from which to conduct the surveillance.
Homing device	Small electronic device that emits a radio signal that permits tracking by means of an associated tracking device; also called a *beeper*, a *signal*, a *transponder*, and a *beacon*.
Loose surveillance	Similar to *discreet surveillance;* may involve surveillance of various friends and associates of a suspect, rather than the actual suspect.
Moving surveillance	Following of a subject wherever he or she may go (see *tailing*).
Picking up a tail or growing a tail	Recognition by a subject that he or she is being watched (see *tailing*).
Planted	Intentionally placed in a location, without the knowledge of others at that location, in order to observe.
Shadowing	Closely but secretly following a subject.
Stakeout	Same as a *fixed surveillance.*
Tailing	Following a subject without detection.
Tap or wiretap	Placement of a listening and recording device on the telephone line of a subject; can be undertaken only with a court order.
Tight surveillance	Very close observation of the subject; a minimal distance is permitted between the surveillant and the subject, but secrecy is maintained.
Undercover	Using a *cover* or disguise to gain entry to a location or when *planted* in a location (see *cover* and *planted*).
Visual contact	Ability to see the subject.

The Purpose of Surveillance

In general, surveillance is used to obtain information—about people, their friends and associates, and activities—that may assist in solving a criminal case, protecting a witness, or locating a fugitive. Always keep the purpose of the particular surveillance in mind so that the objectives of the case can be met. Here are some reasons a surveillance is undertaken:

- Gather information to develop a criminal complaint.
- Detect or prevent crime.
- Locate a wanted fugitive.
- Learn about various contacts and associates of a particular suspect or group.
- Gain information sufficient to establish probable cause for issuance of a search warrant or an arrest warrant.
- Discover the activities and movements of suspected individuals.
- Verify statements made by witnesses or informants.
- Observe known members of a terrorist organization.
- Recover stolen property.
- Intercept criminals in the act of committing a crime.
- Prevent a crime from being committed.
- Develop intelligence on criminals and criminal organizations.
- Obtain information to use in interrogations.

Preparing for Surveillance

Although investigators may not be able to anticipate every move of a subject under surveillance, preparations are nonetheless very important. The personnel and equipment needed and the type of surveillance (e.g., loose, tight, stationary, moving) must be considered and determined in advance. The use of code words, methods of summoning aid, methods of entrance and exit from the surveillance location, dress, and safety precautions should also be considered.

Before beginning a surveillance, you should become familiar with all the available facts of the case and the purpose of the surveillance. It is important to know the subject's full name, nicknames, and aliases; residence and business addresses and telephone numbers; known hangouts; and complete physical description. Information on a suspect's habits, mannerisms, friends, and peculiarities may also prove useful.

The type of vehicle the suspect drives, has access to, or prefers driving may be important. Surveillance team members should know the suspect's driver's license number, car tag number, and general driving habits, if available. Whenever possible, team members should become familiar with the streets and neighborhood where the surveillance will take place, and the kind of people living there. To blend in better, officers should dress as people in the neighborhood do. Finally, each team member should have fictitious credentials and a plausible cover story, in case he or she is detected by the subject or the subject's associates.

Types of Surveillance

Although there are a number of different types of surveillance, the two broadest categories are (1) fixed, or stationary, surveillance and (2) moving surveillance.

Fixed Surveillance

Fixed, or **stationary, surveillance** uses a single location from which the surveillants operate and observe the target, or subject, of the surveillance. Fixed surveillance is sometimes also called a *stakeout* or a *plant.* The location may be a room, office, storefront, or surveillance van or truck (see Figure 8–2). During a fixed surveillance, a surveillant may

Fixed, or stationary, surveillance Close watch on a subject or object from a single location, such as a building or vehicle.

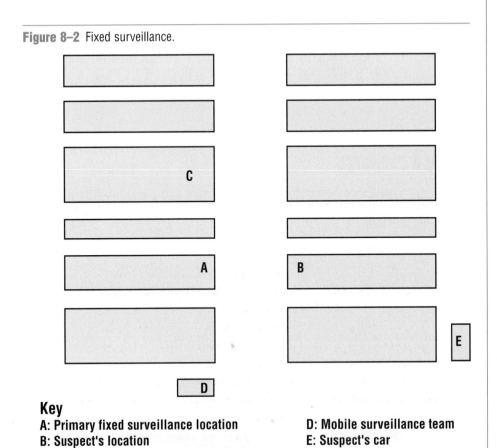

Figure 8–2 Fixed surveillance.

Key
A: Primary fixed surveillance location
B: Suspect's location
C: Secondary fixed surveillance location (rooftop)
D: Mobile surveillance team
E: Suspect's car

assume the guise of a gardener, street repairer, painter, or other laborer. Such covers allow an officer or investigator to move more freely around the area and the subject.

Usually, fixed surveillances, or stakeouts, are limited in their duration. For example, imagine that there had been a series of burglaries in a certain type of business establishment in a particular neighborhood. One strategy the police might employ is a stakeout at a similar establishment in the area.

A stakeout may also be initiated to identify a suspicious individual or vehicle in an area of high crime. Or a fixed surveillance may be ordered because a contemplated robbery, burglary, narcotics operation, or other criminal activity has been reported to the police. Sometimes a stakeout provides a means of identifying a suspect who informants or witnesses have said was involved in a crime. As in any surveillance, the success of a stakeout depends on how well the officers involved have prepared for and understand their assignment.

When establishing a fixed surveillance, the primary requirement is good visibility of the suspect or location being watched. The goal of fixed surveillance is more often to gather information than to arrest or seize a suspect. The quality of the information obtained will be only as good as your ability to see and hear. This means that before starting a fixed surveillance, you must carefully survey the area in question. This survey should take into account such things as your ability to hear and see, the identities of the residents of the immediate area, and their businesses and occupations. It also may include social activities occurring in the area and the trustworthiness of residents in the area.

Moving Surveillance

Moving surveillance
The observation of a subject while moving on foot, in a vehicle, or in an aircraft.

Surveillance becomes increasingly more complex and difficult when an investigator must follow, or tail or shadow, a suspect in a **moving surveillance.** Whether the investigator follows on foot (foot surveillance) or in a car or truck (vehicle, or automobile, surveillance) or even observes from the air (aerial surveillance), the risk of detection increases with movement. More officers and vehicles are required, as well as more extensive planning and communications systems. Complications may include the amount or flow of pedestrian traffic and road congestion caused by accidents or heavy vehicular traffic. Let us consider several variations of mobile surveillance.

Foot Surveillance   In foot surveillance, the number of officers may depend on the amount of pedestrian traffic and the locale of the surveillance. There are three major types of foot surveillance: one-investigator, two-investigator, and three-investigator surveillance.

- **One-investigator surveillance** In a one-person surveillance, a single investigator watches and follows the suspect. There is little margin for error, and there is a fairly high risk of detection if surveillance continues for a long time, since the surveillant must maintain visual contact with the suspect at all times.

- **Two-investigator surveillance** Two-investigator surveillance reduces the threat of detection by providing a degree of flexibility. For example, with two investigators, the position of the investigator directly behind the subject can be changed periodically. Furthermore, the use of two investigators reduces the likelihood of losing the subject in heavy pedestrian traffic. When pedestrian traffic is not too heavy, one investigator may walk behind the subject while the other walks parallel to the subject on the opposite side of the street.

- **Three-investigator surveillance** Three-investigator surveillance is sometimes referred to as **ABC surveillance.** This procedure further reduces the chance of a subject's detecting the surveillance. In ABC surveillance, Officer **A** follows the subject, maintaining visual contact from a reasonable distance. A second investigator, **B,** follows **A.** The distance between **A** and **B** may be somewhat greater than between **A** and the suspect. A third investigator, **C,** participates in the surveillance from across the street (see Figure 8–3). Typically, Officer **C** is approximately where **A** is on the opposite side of the street, or slightly behind **A.** Investigator **C** has to keep both **A** and **B** in sight. A variation

ABC surveillance A three-officer foot surveillance in which Officer **A** follows the suspect and in turn is followed by Officer **B.** The third surveillant, Officer **C,** normally walks on the other side of the street opposite the suspect.

Figure 8–3 ABC foot surveillance method.

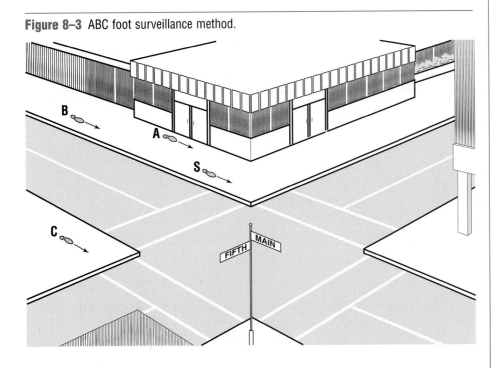

of this technique places one of the officers ahead of the suspect. This procedure, called a **leading surveillance,** is useful when the suspect's route is well established and known to the investigators.

Sometimes officers coordinate their movements in advance and exchange places at designated times or locations to make it more difficult for the subject to notice that he or she is being followed.

Although this three-investigator procedure is very effective, it is sometimes an advantage to have a fourth officer standing by in a car. In addition to providing a measure of safety in an emergency, the fourth officer can be exchanged for one of the others if the suspect begins to act suspicious of being followed.

Vehicle Surveillance   As in foot surveillance, the officer should stay as close to the suspect as possible without becoming conspicuous. Vehicles used for surveillance should be plain and nondescript, to fit into the flow of traffic without being noticed.

Before a vehicle surveillance is begun, the communications equipment should be checked to make sure it is in good working order. However, police radios should not be mounted where they can be seen if someone looks into the driver's compartment. Similarly, no police objects, such as handcuffs, manuals, official papers, or clipboards, should be visible from the outside.

Mobile surveillance may be undertaken with one, two, or several cars. There may be a combination of foot and vehicle surveillance. For example,

Figure 8–4 Perimeter box surveillance method.

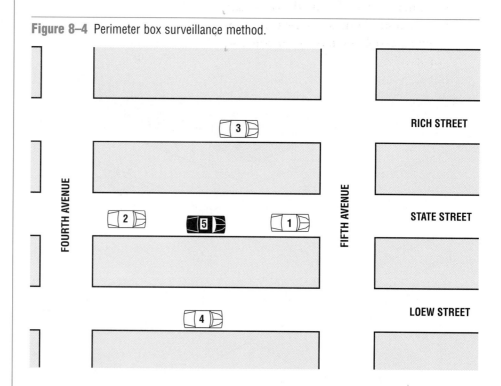

Chapter 8 *From Surveillance to Records and Files*

a subject may be walking, followed by an officer on foot and an officer in a car. Suddenly the subject sees a bus and gets on. The foot officer can continue **close surveillance** by getting on the bus with the subject. The officer in the car can stay with both by following the bus. Similarly, a suspect driving a car may park and enter a shopping mall. An officer in a car may, in this situation, have to leave the car and pursue the subject on foot.

Many police agencies use a strategy called **perimeter box surveillance.** Typically, this procedure involves four cars, with at least two carrying extra foot officers. One car stays ahead of the subject's car, one car follows it, and the other two units maintain positions on streets parallel to that of the subject (see Figure 8–4). This method permits coverage of all turning movements that the subject could make, even if the subject suddenly turns at an intersection when the light is yellow or has just turned red.

Whether following a subject with one, two, or more cars, it is prudent to alter the distance and the location of the cars regularly. An officer driving ahead of a subject should keep in contact with fellow officers by radio and should watch the subject in rearview mirrors. In such situations, it is often convenient to have a second officer in the lead car as an observer.

Aerial Surveillance The use of planes and helicopters for aerial surveillance is becoming more common. Aerial surveillance may be used to obtain information about areas that are not easily accessible by foot or in conventional vehicles. Using communication between aircraft and ground vehicles, investigators can coordinate a more effective surveillance of a subject traveling in a vehicle.

FYI

Aerial surveillance can also be an effective tool for spotting illegal activities. For example, during the early 1980s the Florida Department of Law Enforcement (FDLE), a state-warranted police agency, began to use fixed-wing aircraft to locate crops of marijuana. From a height of about 1000 feet, the FDLE could even find illegal marijuana planted on private property, without violating privacy laws. Other states, including Ohio, use this same aerial surveillance technique to locate illegal drug crops.

Technical Surveillance

A wide variety of sophisticated devices are available to enhance the senses of sight and hearing. Tiny eavesdropping devices, miniature cameras, telescopic lenses, powerful directional microphones, and even compact recording devices are only a few of the items in the investigator's arsenal of technology. The items actually used will depend on the type of surveillance being undertaken, as well as on the financial resources of the agency conducting the surveillance.

Audio Surveillance The use of various audio devices to perform an audio surveillance has become almost commonplace. An investigator may wear

Trap and trace devices can record the telephone number of the sources of all incoming calls to a particular number.

a transmitter both as a safety device to alert his or her partners to trouble and as a means of gathering incriminating evidence during a conversation with a subject. Or a subject's room or vehicle may be bugged, or his or her telephone wiretapped. An important aspect of audio surveillance is the need to make sure it is done legally. Whenever police agencies use electronic listening devices, they must consider the provisions of the Fourth Amendment and various federal and state privacy acts. Many forms of electronic surveillance and wiretapping are considered by the courts to be searches and must follow the same regulations as a physical search would. They require a showing of probable cause and an order from a court.

Current provisions for using electronic listening devices can be traced to the landmark case of *Katz v. United States* (1967). In the *Katz* case, the Supreme Court ruled that the Constitution protects private telephone conversations from unauthorized government intrusions—such as wiretapping or electronic surveillance—even when calls are made from a public telephone booth.[1] According to the *Katz* decision, electronic surveillance and wiretapping are permitted only with probable cause and by court order.

In June 1968, the United States Congress enacted legislation outlawing wiretapping and electronic eavesdropping. However, the act provided for closely supervised, court-approved electronic eavesdropping by federal investigative officers to combat certain serious criminal activity (primarily organized crime). The introduction to Title III of the Omnibus Crime Control and Safe Streets Act of 1968 says:

Organized criminals make extensive use of wire and oral communications in their criminal activities. The interception of such communications to obtain evidence of the commission of crimes or to prevent their commission is an indispensable aid to law enforcement and the administration of justice.[2]

The Crime Control Act of 1968 permitted federal officers to use wiretaps or electronic eavesdropping, provided they first obtained a court order from a federal judge after demonstrating probable cause. Similarly, the act permitted state and local officers to tap wires under similar circumstances, provided the state had a statute authorizing such procedures. In the absence of an authorizing statute or a court order, it is a criminal offense to participate in wiretapping or electronic eavesdropping.

Complicating surveillance legality issues are changes made in a number of state statutes in the past decade. These changes involve what may be called the **one-consenting-party rule.** It is legal to record a two-party conversation if one party consents. This is true even though the other party does not know the conversation is being taped. This rule does not hold, however, for three-party conversations. In other words, it is not a license for law enforcement agents to listen to or record a two-party conversation. Officers should know the law regarding one-person consent in their state. In some states, such as Pennsylvania, it is a felony to record two or more parties in conversation unless all parties have consented.

Video Surveillance   In our technologically advanced society, with its microminiaturization, many law enforcement agencies take advantage of video surveillance equipment that permits them to extend what they see

One-consenting-party rule   A legal principle that permits audio recording of a two-party conversation if one party has consented.

HISTORY

Investigators from the FBI had observed Charles Katz, a racetrack handicapper, for several days. They saw him make calls from a public telephone booth at about the same time each day. Suspecting that he was placing bets, the investigators attached an electronic listening-recording device to the top of the booth and recorded Katz's illegal activities. The recorded evidence was used in obtaining his conviction for violating gambling laws. The U.S. Supreme Court reversed the California conviction on appeal, stating, "[T]he Fourth Amendment protects people not places. . . . Wherever a man may be, he is entitled to know that he will remain free from unreasonable searches and seizures." The investigators had probable cause, but they made the mistake of not presenting their information to a court official to obtain court approval for the electronic surveillance.

and record it for later use. Fiber optics and high-quality reproduction from miniaturized video cameras and recorders allow criminal activities to be viewed and recorded with little danger of discovery by subjects. When played in a courtroom, a videotape of a criminal's activities can be very convincing to a jury.

Video cameras can be placed where the physical surroundings or situations do not permit concealment of officers. For example, they might be used to record a kidnapper picking up a ransom or to identify suspects in an espionage case. Cameras can also be situated to monitor an officer's investigation and ensure safety. This can permit backup officers to step in at the first sign that things are becoming *hinky* (dangerous, problematic, or uncomfortable).

Tips for Surveillance Operations

Officers and investigators on any surveillance operation must maintain constant vigilance. Inattention or unnecessary distraction, even for brief periods, may result in losing the subject or following the wrong vehicle. It is important to be sure during foot surveillance that the surveilling officer is not also being followed. Sometimes a wary criminal will enlist a confederate to intentionally follow him or her to make sure there are no police doing likewise. This is sometimes referred to as a **convoy.** Suspects may try an assortment of techniques to detect a surveillance. Becoming familiar with a suspect's possible countermeasures may help an investigator avoid exposure. Figure 8–5 contains a number of common techniques used to detect surveillance.

Officers on surveillance should try to blend in with other people and activities in the area. Clothing should be appropriate to the locale. Officers should engage in conventional activities, like buying a newspaper from the corner newsstand, a cup of coffee at the luncheonette, and groceries in the local store. In short, the surveillant should do whatever others in the vicinity are doing.

Many officers working under cover carry an assortment of disguises and clothes in their vehicles. This allows them to change disguises very quickly. In some cases, the undercover officer may choose to use a pet, for example, to walk a dog. In other situations, the officer may ride a bicycle, walk along with another officer, make a purchase, and so forth. Inventiveness and originality are important in surveillance.

During any surveillance, the officer must be both stealthful and observant. If the subject stops to make a telephone call, make a purchase, or secure train or airline tickets, an officer should try to stay as close as possible to the subject. It is important that the officer know what goes on during the transaction. Should it prove impossible to remain close, asking for a ticket to the same place or to see "something like that last person bought" might obtain the necessary information. Should the sub-

Convoy The following of a subject by multiple individuals.

Figure 8–5 Countermeasures used to detect surveillance.

During Foot Surveillance:
- Riding backward up an escalator.
- Riding an elevator to the top floor and then back down again.
- Taking an elevator to a floor several floors above or below the desired floor and then using the stairs to get to the desired floor.
- Getting on or off buses or other forms of transit.
- Stopping and talking with a stranger and then watching to see if the person is questioned by anyone.
- Moving quickly around a corner and then waiting to see if anyone hurries around in pursuit.
- Walking through a crowded store, hotel lobby, courtyard, sporting event, or other public place.
- Entering a darkened movie theater and leaving through an emergency exit.
- Feigning a call at a pay telephone to size up people in the vicinity.

During Mobile Surveillance:
- Driving down a dead-end street.
- Speeding up or slowing down.
- Rounding a corner and doubling back.
- Making a sudden U-turn in the middle of the street.
- Running a red light.
- Turning a corner on a red or yellow light.
- Discarding something from a window to see if anyone stops to pick it up.
- Changing lanes frequently.
- Pulling into a parking lot and parking to see if a pursuing vehicle does likewise.
- Stopping at the side of the road to check a rear tire and seeing if anyone else stops.

ject enter a hotel, the desk clerk, manager, and security officer (if trustworthy) can help considerably. With their help, the surveillant can learn about the subject's phone calls and messages, possible contacts, trash, comings and goings, and any other pertinent information.

Sometimes the subject may approach a surveillant. The surveillant should never immediately conclude that he or she has been *made* (identified as an officer). Although the subject may be suspicious, that does not automatically mean he or she has made the officer. The sputterings of an inexperienced surveillance officer are likely to ensure that he or she will be made. An experienced officer knows that subjects look into the eyes of many people around them and may even stop and ask various people questions to test their reactions. A suspect worried about being followed or tailed may walk up to someone and ask directions, request a match, ask the time, or engage in any number of other simple pleasantries. When conducting surveillance, it is always advisable to have a plausible and well-rehearsed story ready in case of a confrontation. If a subject accosts a surveillant and accuses the officer of following him or her, the officer should act surprised. The officer might ask, "Why on earth would I follow you? Do I know you?" Or the officer might act insulted or annoyed to be bothered by this "stranger." In any event, the officer should maintain a consistent role and strongly deny following the subject. Of course, the officer will now need to drop out of the surveillance and be replaced by someone who has not been burned (identified).

Records and Files

An important aid in conducting investigations or surveillance is the department's records and reports. These include preliminary reports of criminal incidents, follow-up reports, offense and arrest records, *modus operandi* files, fingerprint files, missing-person reports, gun registrations, Wanted bulletins and updates, and even various officers' personal information files.

In addition to files housed in the department, there are literally hundreds of persons, places, indexes, directories, file systems, places of business, organizations, newspapers, libraries, and municipal, county, state, and federal sources of records available to an investigator. The more sources an investigator is comfortable accessing, the easier investigations become. The ability to find information may well be as important as or more important than the information itself. By gaining information from various sources, an investigator can shorten an investigation by days or even weeks. Early solutions in an investigation may mean the difference between apprehension and escape or between recovery and loss of property. They may also prevent unnecessary use of expensive equipment and personnel.

Linking People to Records

There are a number of obvious records that contain information about people. These include fingerprint and photograph files and *modus operandi* files. These files can assist an investigator trying to identify a suspect and may complement one another. With the advances in technology and computer databases, fingerprints may soon provide an enormously effective means for identifying criminal suspects on a national level.

Tracing and Locating People

Sometimes the identity of a suspect is known or has been determined by the police, but no records on the suspect are immediately available. When it becomes apparent that this suspect has skipped (fled the area), the police may need to use various techniques to trace him or her. Humans are creatures of comfort and habit. Remembering this can sometimes help an officer locate or trace a person who has left the area. Sometimes a trip to the post office to see if a forwarding address has been supplied is all it takes to locate a suspect. In some cases, a suspect may be located through his or her family. For example, if the suspect has children, the police can ask to be notified if a request for academic transcripts is sent to their old school. Placing known associates, friends, and relatives under surveillance may also lead to the suspect's location.

The suspect's bank may provide an address to which statements are now being forwarded or the name of a bank to which money has been transferred. Utilities often require deposits from customers who have never had a utility account. To avoid paying a deposit to initiate telephone or electric service, a suspect may admit that he or she has previously had an account. When the utility office in the original area has been contacted to verify this information, officials there can inform the police of the new location of the suspect. With a little bit of thought, investigators can find numerous sources of records that can assist them in tracing a missing suspect.

Types and Sources of Recorded Information

Since the quantity and variety of stored information available to investigators is extremely large, an organization scheme or classification system is useful. Let us consider some major categories of sources of information linking people to records.

Law Enforcement Agencies   The first files used to identify or learn more about a suspect are those immediately available to the police, that is, those housed in the police department. These include **criminal jackets,** the files on criminals that list their arrests and convictions. Also included are all arrest and incident files housed at the agency; files on fences (people dealing in stolen property), pawnbrokers, and known or habitual criminals residing in the area; Stop and Wanted bulletins; *modus operandi* files; and other files.

It also may be useful to consult local jail records or prison records if a suspect has been previously incarcerated. Such records may provide investigators with leads regarding the suspect's visitors, cellmates, previous addresses, and places of incarceration.

Investigators should also consider speaking with probation officers and consulting their files. Many probation offices across the country are

Criminal jackets   Official police records of criminals.

Surveillance Technologies   Technical surveillance equipment and techniques extend an investigator's senses of seeing and hearing. TOP LEFT: Wire and recorder used in audio surveillance; TOP RIGHT: Night vision equipment used for video surveillance when there is no light or very poor lighting; BOTTOM: Undercover officer being fitted with hidden recording device.

not computerized. Consequently, it is sometimes easier and faster to talk with the suspect's probation officer than to wade through volumes of written records. The probation officer may give information about the suspect's friends, relatives, and even social haunts.

Federal Agencies   Federal agencies with files of information on people include these major agencies: the Federal Bureau of Investigation (FBI), which has various standard reference files and computerized identification databases; the Drug Enforcement Agency (DEA), which holds records on both individuals and companies that have violated various federal drug laws; the U.S. Marshals Service and the Treasury Department, which includes the Bureau of Alcohol, Tobacco, and Firearms (ATF), the U.S. Customs Service, the Internal Revenue Service (IRS), and the U.S. Secret Service. Each of these agencies has files on suspects and criminals that have been involved with that organization.

As mentioned previously, the U.S. Postal Service can be useful in certain investigations. Similarly, the U.S. State Department may provide information about suspects planning to leave the country and in need of a passport. Finally, the military may be an excellent source of information, especially if a base is in the area. If the suspect is in the military—either active or reserve—it may be rather simple to locate him or her.

State and Local Agencies Most regulatory and licensing powers are in the hands of state agencies. Applying for something as mundane as a fishing license gives information about the applicant to a state agency (the department of fish and wildlife or a similar department). Agencies where information about suspects may be available to investigators include the department of motor vehicles or the motor vehicle registry, the office of employment or unemployment, and various social service agencies. In addition, such local agencies as the county or township clerk's office or various offices typically housed in the local courthouse may offer information.

Public Records Offices and Business Organizations Today it is virtually impossible to live and work in society without taking part in many business transactions. People enter into contracts for housing, credit, various business dealings, and even social or recreational activities. All these activities are likely to put a person's name on some form of record.

Having the water or electricity or gas turned on in one's apartment involves contacting the utility and providing an address and telephone number. If one has even a single gasoline credit card, a credit record exists. In addition to information filed with the company actually distributing the card, *credit reporting agencies* maintain and report information on a customer's credit history—and include a current address.

Many people, including criminals, are concerned about their welfare and that of their family members. Therefore, they may at some point try to obtain some form of insurance. Whether it is automobile, health, or life insurance, there will be an application record.

Miscellaneous Sources and Files The space needed to list all possible miscellaneous sources and files would exceed the limits of this book. However, there are some widely available sources that bear mentioning. These include public libraries, libraries on college and university campuses, auto rental and leasing agencies, city directories, the chamber of commerce, hospitals, hotels, taxi and livery companies, travel agents, and even moving companies.

SUMMARY BY LEARNING OBJECTIVES

Learning Objective 1

Surveillance is the secret observation of people, groups, places, vehicles, and things over a prolonged period to gather information about a crime or criminal.

Learning Objective 2

The purpose of surveillance is to obtain information about people, their friends and associates, and activities that may assist in solving a criminal case, protecting a witness, or locating a fugitive. Considerations of personnel, equipment, and the type of surveillance influence the success of any surveillance operation.

Learning Objective 3

The major categories of surveillance are fixed, or stationary, surveillance; moving surveillance; and technical surveillance. Moving surveillance can include one-, two-, or three-investigator foot surveillance; vehicle surveillance; and aerial surveillance. Technical surveillance can include audio surveillance and video surveillance.

Learning Objective 4

In surveillance operations, officers must maintain constant vigilance, be stealthful and observant, maintain their cover or disguise, be aware of suspect's countermeasures, and try to blend in with other people and activities in the area with their clothing, vehicles, and actions.

Learning Objective 5

An important aid in conducting a surveillance can be the police agency's records, files, and reports. These include preliminary reports of crimes, follow-up reports, offense and arrest records, *modus operandi* files, fingerprint files, and other such records and reports.

Learning Objective 6

Various public and private agencies can provide information about people and assist a surveillance operation. These include federal agencies, state and local agencies, public records offices, and business organizations.

QUESTIONS FOR REVIEW

Learning Objective 1

1. Define *surveillance*.

Learning Objective 2

2. In general, what is the purpose of surveillance?
3. List six reasons a surveillance might be undertaken.
4. Why is preparation for a surveillance important?

Learning Objective 3

5. What are the major categories of surveillance?
6. At what point should a fixed surveillance become a mobile one?
7. What type of surveillance should be used to gather information on a suspected crack house?
8. What might the police do if there were a series of burglaries in a given neighborhood?
9. What are some problems associated with a one-officer moving surveillance?
10. What is meant by an *ABC surveillance* method?
11. How does the strategy of *perimeter box surveillance* work?
12. What case is usually viewed as the landmark case for the legality of police use of listening devices?
13. What is meant by the *one-consenting-party-rule?*

Learning Objective 4

14. What might you suggest that a surveillant do before beginning a surveillance operation?

Learning Objective 5

15. Why is it important to maintain accurate police records and files?

Learning Objective 6

16. How may someone's old mailing address help an investigator locate the person?
17. How might an old credit card bill found in the trash assist the police in locating a missing felon?

CRITICAL THINKING INVESTIGATIVE EXERCISES

1. Along with other members of the class, write your name on a slip of paper. Have your instructor place all these slips in a paper bag and shake

the bag to mix up the slips of paper. Then, when the bag is passed to you, draw out one slip. If you draw your own name, put it back and take another. Do not read aloud the name on the slip you chose or in any other way disclose whose name it is you have drawn. Using the information in the chapter, decide how you will complete the following tasks without directly asking the person named on your slip:

a. Find out his or her home address and telephone number.

b. Find out the home address and telephone number of the person's parents (or nearest relative if both parents are deceased).

c. Determine when the person *usually* goes grocery shopping.

d. During one grocery shopping trip, follow the person, and write a brief field report on what you saw him or her doing, whom he or she spoke with, and what side trips he or she made between home and the store.

2. In a follow-up class session, compare your surveillance results with others in the class. Determine how many surveillants were *made* by their subjects. Break into groups and discuss how you might, as investigators, go about developing information about the manager of the restaurant described in the following scenario:

> The Hot Hot Spot is a restaurant and bar located just outside town in a one-story, wood-frame building. It is adjacent to a small shopping area, a pocket mall, consisting of a grocery store and four other businesses. Directly across from the pocket mall, slightly diagonal to the restaurant, is a paint and wall-paper store. The Hot Hot Spot employs 15 people (7 men and 8 women).
>
> The restaurant's bar has been reported to have sold alcohol to minors, but there has been no investigation of these allegations. Both the bar and the restaurant are frequented by a variety of suspicious characters. The manager is new to the community and claims to have previously owned and managed a restaurant in Boise, Idaho.

Be sure to include in your answer the types of surveillance and tracing techniques you might use in your investigation.

INVESTIGATIVE SKILL BUILDERS

Organizing and Maintaining Information

You receive a bulletin that, en route to the state prison, the prisoner bus has broken down and one of the inmates has escaped. The bulletin includes a description of the fugitive, as well as his last known home address and the address of his parents. What are some of the techniques and sources of information you might use in an effort to locate and apprehend this fugitive?

Integrity/Honesty

An officer arrives at the home of a man believed to be the friend of a fugitive the officer is trying to find. The officer has been tracking this fugitive for nearly two months. The fugitive is wanted for two forcible rapes and a rape-murder. The officer rings the doorbell, but nobody answers. The officer knocks on the door, and it swings open. From the doorway, the officer calls to see if anyone is inside, but there is still no answer. As the officer glances into the living room, he notices a phone bill on the coffee table. The officer thinks, this individual may have made a call to the fugitive, and there may be a record on the phone bill. The officer decides to enter and copy the phone numbers on the bill. When the officer finishes writing down the numbers, he carefully replaces the bill on the coffee table and leaves.

Using the telephone numbers, the police are able to locate and apprehend the fugitive.

1. Given the seriousness of the crimes that the fugitive is believed to have committed, was the officer justified in entering the house and writing down the phone numbers?

2. Since the phone numbers enabled the police to locate and apprehend the fugitive, were the police justified in obtaining the phone information in the manner in which they did?

Creative Thinking

You must locate a father who has taken his two children from their mother. The mother had been granted legal custody after a divorce. You speak with the mother and obtain a list of the man's friends and relatives. You also learn he is a master electrician.

1. What strategies might you try in your effort to locate this man? Be creative in your approach.

2. How might knowing that the man is a master electrician help you in your search?

ENDNOTES

1. *Katz v. United States,* 389 U.S. 347 (1967).
2. Omnibus Crime Control and Safe Streets Act of 1968.

CHAPTER 9

Writing Reports

CHAPTER OBJECTIVES

After completing this chapter you will be able to:

1. Understand the importance of good investigative reports.

2. State the basic questions a good report should answer.

3. Explain some of the uses of police reports.

4. List and describe the characteristics of a good report.

5. List some of the common elements of a police report.

6. Identify the major types of police operations reports.

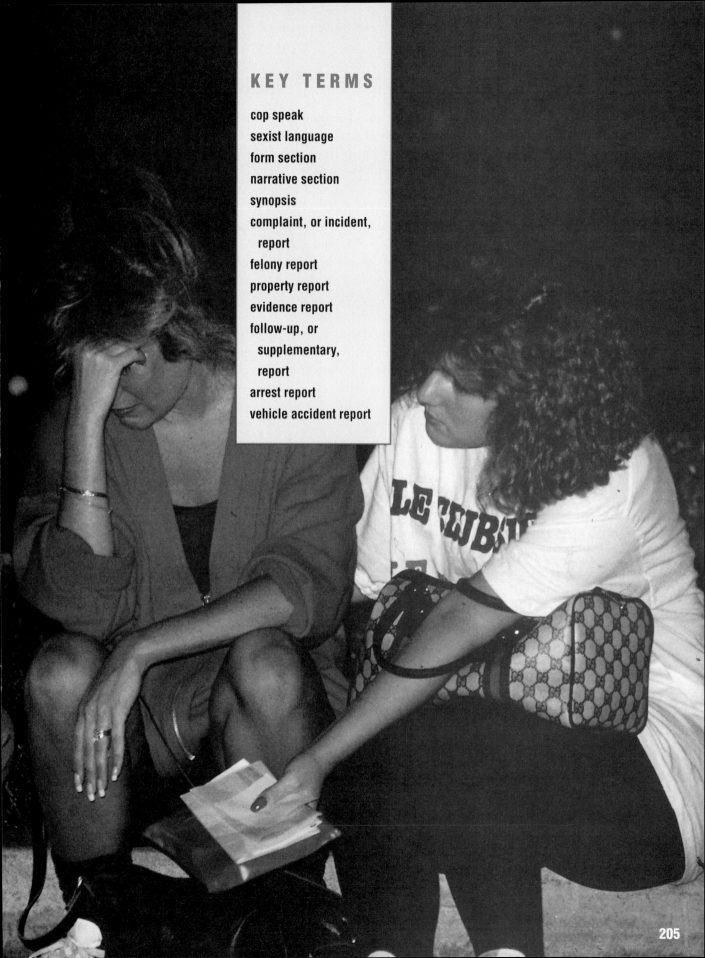

KEY TERMS

cop speak

sexist language

form section

narrative section

synopsis

complaint, or incident,
  report

felony report

property report

evidence report

follow-up, or
  supplementary,
  report

arrest report

vehicle accident report

Communicating Through Reports

ffective communication is essential in all police work, and criminal investigation is no exception. If investigators are to communicate effectively on a witness stand, during interviews and interrogations, and among themselves, they need solid oral and written skills. Their oral skills should include clear enunciation, well-ordered and simple presentation, and suppression of **cop speak,** or police jargon. Written skills such as note taking and report writing are critical tools in the investigation of crimes. Among the more accurate elements of many television and movie versions of police work is the need to write reports. Underplayed in these fictional accounts is the damage that a poorly written report can do to the investigation or prosecution of a criminal case.

Cop speak Specialized vocabulary, or jargon, used by police.

Police reports must set forth information in an accurate, concise, clear, and complete manner. These reports serve as records of the investigative efforts and the criminal incident. Police reports are official records of the activities of a government agency and are used in a variety of ways. Every investigation should be complemented by an accurate report. Report writing is so important that a number of police agencies in the United States have hired technical writers to coach their officers.

Reports provide information to fellow investigators working on a case, to supervisors and administrators who may need to allocate resources for a case, and to the prosecuting attorney who may try the case. Reports may also be used in court to outline a case to the jury. Investigative reports play key roles throughout the criminal justice process. They begin as notes taken during the preliminary investigation, continue as records of the follow-up investigation, and emerge again during the trial and perhaps even during an appeal. Since reports can sometimes create the foundation for a criminal prosecution, it is very important that investigators be mindful about how reports are produced.

In the double-murder trial of O. J. Simpson, the defense initially sought to impugn the police investigation by showing that investigators had botched their reports. The defense team claimed that the investigators had failed to maintain an accurate chronology of events; that specific forms were not always filled out completely; and that in contradiction of department policy, plain sheets of paper had been substituted for certain forms.

Although these concerns regarding report writing may seem to be nit-picking, even such minor flaws could damage an entire prosecution. Reports communicate factual information, descriptions of events and actions, and frequently even motives. If there are errors in police reports, a judge or jury may infer that there are errors in the facts or mistakes in procedures.

Report-Writing Guidelines

There are no magic potions one can take to become a proficient report writer. There are, however, a number of structural elements typically included in a well-written report. These elements are the answers to six basic questions: *who, what, when, where, how,* and *why.* Answering these questions ensures that the necessary elements of the investigation are included in the report and that the report will at least be acceptable. You may recall that these are the same six questions that must be answered when you are taking notes in the field (see Figure 2–2 in Chapter 2).

Who were the people involved?   That is, who are the complainant, the victim, and the witnesses? Are there any suspects? Who are the investigators in the case, and what are the names of the officers who first arrived on the scene and secured it?

What happened?   What was the crime? What events surrounded the criminal event? If there are victims, in what way were they injured or victimized? If property was stolen, a detailed account and description of missing objects should be included. The report should also include such information as the actions of suspects; the evidence located; any special knowledge, skill, or expertise needed to commit the crime; anything reported that is not substantiated by the facts or physical evidence; and, certainly, further actions that may be warranted.

When did the crime occur?   What was the time of day? the day of the week? the month? When was the matter discovered?

Where did the crime occur?   Correct information concerning addresses—including name of street, street number, type of building (house, apartment, store, etc.)—is important in reports. Telling exactly where in a given location a crime or a portion of a criminal event took place is also important. If a criminal matter occurred outdoors, the exact location should be recorded, with stationary objects used as reference points for measurements. For example, a report might say an event occurred "12 feet west of the Oak Park street sign on the west curb."

How was the crime committed?   An investigator should include all information that shows or suggests how the event took place. This may include the *modus operandi,* as well as information about how the suspect or suspects arrived or fled the scene. The report should also contain information, if available, regarding how the suspect may have obtained information necessary to commit the crime (e.g., lock combinations, alarm system details, or floor plans).

Time – Date
Location – Arrived
What – see
who – see
Where
Case number

Why was the crime committed?   Information on motives is usually nothing more than deductions based on experience, evidence, and available facts. Nonetheless, the question why should not be overlooked. Consider such things as the following: How much time elapsed before the crime was reported? Why is a witness so eager to point out a guilty party? Why was the victim so afraid to speak with the police? Why did a particular suspect commit this crime against this particular party? In some cases, such as robbery or burglary, it may be assumed that the crime was committed to obtain possessions, most likely to sell for cash.

It is also worthwhile to consider why a suspect chose a particular victim over another or one set of premises over another. In certain crimes, such as traffic accidents, there seldom are motives. On the other hand, in homicides, the motives may take much investigation to uncover and may not be available for preliminary reports.

Answering these six basic questions (who, what, when, where, how, and why) provides a kind of skeleton on which the reporting officer can hang the facts of the case. Naturally, the order in which these questions are presented and answered will vary with the facts of a case and the reporting officer's own writing style. In some cases, it may not be possible to answer all six questions. Furthermore, these questions should not be literally transcribed in a report. Nowhere in the report does one actually write "Where did the crime occur?" and then the answer to that question. The questions are a guide, especially for inexperienced report writers, to ensure that all necessary information is provided in an investigative report.

In writing reports, as in all other phases of police work, good judgment, a good working knowledge of procedures and department policy, and some practice are necessary for success. As in all writing, consider your *audience*. As an officer or investigator, your audience is likely to include other officers, supervisors, administrators, and prosecuting attorneys. Whenever possible, get advice from more experienced writers about improving your writing skills.

Tests of a Report

For reports to be useful in an investigation, they must have certain basic characteristics. One could easily compile a lengthy checklist of traits of a solid report. It might include clarity, pertinence, brevity, comprehensiveness, accuracy, and a long list of other elements. All the recommendations would be relevant to good report writing. However, all these principles can be inferred from three simple tests of a report:

1. Is the report complete, concise, clear, and accurate?
2. Will an oral explanation be required to explain what is already included in the written report?

Report-Writing Aids Police agencies use a variety of technologies to make report writing much more efficient. TOP: Laptop, or notebook, computers allow officers to input crime scene data, access department arrest records, or search other computerized databases from their patrol vehicles. BOTTOM: Officers can use cellular telephones to dictate their reports from a cruiser to a central processor.

3. Can the statements made in the report be proved, corroborated, or demonstrated by evidence?

If you answer no to the first and third questions and yes to the second, your report is not yet ready for others to see. You want a yes to question 1, a no to question 2, and a yes to question 3.

Communicating Through Reports   **209**

The Value of Reports

Reports provide the data needed to investigate and apprehend criminals and to solve crimes. In some departments, officers come back to the station and type their reports on a typewriter. Others use personal computers and input the information directly to the department's information storage system. Still other departments have their officers telephone from the field and dictate their reports to a clerk at the station, who then inputs the data to the department's information storage system. Some departments even use a digital dictation system, in which officers use a Touch-Tone telephone to reach a special digital computer processor that handles the officer's voice data like data keyed in from a keyboard. (Also see the Focus on Technology feature in this chapter.) However the data are stored, the reports are a valuable asset to the department by performing the following functions:

- Provide a written record and a readily accessible memory bank of police business and information.
- Refresh an officer's memory regarding further investigation and administration.
- Provide a means of controlling communication throughout the police department and its associated agencies.
- Provide a database of information for solving similar crimes, perhaps committed by the same criminals.
- Furnish a base of accurate statistical information on which decisions about resource allocation and policy may be based.
- Aid in identifying criminal patterns, which in turn allows the development of intervention plans.
- Aid in assessing the effectiveness of personnel distribution and analyzing overall agency operations.
- Assist in identifying unusual or periodic intra-agency problems.
- Assist in documenting needs for budget requests and justifications.
- Produce statistical information to be contributed to local, state, or FBI crime databases.
- Provide a vital tool for a department in carrying out its varied objectives.
- Provide a source of accurate, detailed, and succinct information to prosecute a criminal where a law has been violated.

In addition to the benefits just listed, reports permit accountability both inside and outside the agency. Outside the agency, police provide information to their respective communities concerning the local crime rates and efforts planned or undertaken to reduce these rates.

Internally, reports provide supervisors and administrators with information necessary for considering an agency's policies, resources, procedures, and all other matters concerning the work in the organization. Reports also provide means for evaluating the effectiveness of special units or personnel. In all of these situations, reports may serve the additional purpose of interpreting facts, transmitting information, analyzing pro-blems or situations, and educating employees and others about policy and understanding of policy in the agency.

Characteristics of a Good Report

A report may contain all the necessary information, but if it is poorly written, these points may be lost. Some officers dread report writing and find it difficult to master. Others seem to be gifted in this area, and create effective, well-written reports. Police reporting, however, is not an innate trait that some officers are born with and others are not. Similarly, while some officers speak more effectively than others, their ability may not translate into good writing skills. One can learn how to write effective reports by practice and by following some basic rules. Reports should be *complete, concise, clear,* and *accurate.* By directing his or her attention to these characteristics, an officer can make report writing a more positive experience.

Completeness

Completeness means that the report contains all pertinent information. Partial facts may create a false picture of the events. Negative results of investigative leads should be included, along with more successful ones. For example, if an investigator searched a suspect's room and found nothing, this should be included in the report. Having the information in the report will indicate which actions have been taken and which have not. The information, then, can avoid duplication of efforts.

It is a good evaluation technique to have a fellow officer read your report. If the other officer has questions about what you have written, needs certain points clarified, or does not understand the sequence of events, the report needs to be revised. Unanswered questions or confused descriptions create problems for a person who may not have been at the scene. Consider the follow-up investigator or the prosecuting attorney. Will he or she need to call in the morning because information in the report is not complete? Will follow-up investigators or the prosecuting attorney be able to locate witnesses from the information presented in the report? Will follow-up investigators have to duplicate any work that has already been done because it was not mentioned in the report? Ask yourself these kinds of questions before turning in a report as finished.

Conciseness

Reports should be as *concise* as possible while retaining all essential features and details in an understandable manner. Reports should be written as a narrative but should eliminate nonessential modifiers or descriptors. Similarly, technical jargon and unnecessary words should be avoided. Sentences should be kept simple and direct and in active voice rather than passive. Long, convoluted sentences are confusing and sometimes difficult to follow. Do not use meaningless or unnecessary words and phrases. For example, one could write, "I observed a very nice reddish or dark pinkish kind of colored big car pass at a very, very high rate of speed, maybe as fast as 75 mph." A more concise version might be "I observed a red Ford Mustang traveling at an estimated speed of 75 mph."

An inexperienced police report writer might try practicing by writing a composition of at least 75 words on any police topic. The description should then be corrected and condensed to a narrative. After completing this task, the writer should seek advice and suggestions from a more experienced report writer about how to improve the practice report.

Clarity

A report must exhibit *clarity*, that is, it must clearly explain to a reader exactly what the officer saw, heard, and did. Short, active-voice sentences lead to clear meaning and understanding. For example, one might write, "When the officer arrived, the victim was found lying there with the gun next to him having been fired once." A more active and clearer version might be "Officer Thomas Jones arrived to find the victim, Morris Kupnick, lying on the ground. Next to Mr. Kupnick's head, Officer Jones found a blue-barrel revolver with one round discharged." Although brevity is important, it should not be accomplished at the expense of clarity.

Clarity can best be accomplished by the use of standard English, including good sentence structure, correct punctuation, accurate spelling, proper capitalization, and standard paragraphing. The words and phrases selected should enable a reader to easily understand the report. Errors in punctuation, misplaced pronouns, or words used incorrectly detract from the value of a report and could cast doubt on an officer's testimony in a court trial.[1]

Accuracy

Reports must demonstrate *accuracy* to be valuable. Concentrate on specifics and avoid generalities. For example, one might write, "The suspect is big and carried several weapons on his person." A more accurate statement might be "The suspect, Martin Sayre, is approximately 5 feet 9 inches tall and weighs approximately 250 pounds. After being advised of his rights, Sayre was searched by Officer McCarty. Officer McCarty found that Sayre was carrying a .32-caliber derringer, a .38-caliber Smith & Wesson revolver, a folding pocketknife with a single 4-inch blade, and a 6-inch billy club."

It is equally important not to confuse fact with hearsay. Information reported must be only what actually transpired and has been verified by the investigation. Reports should not contain conclusions that the officer has made by supposition or guesswork. Nor should the report contain an officer's personal opinion about the matter. Personal opinions tend to lessen the value of a report. If one is included, it should be labeled: "It is the opinion of the reporting officer. . .," or "It was the opinion of the arresting officer. . . ." It is important to remember that every suspect deserves a fair and unbiased day in court and that in the United States, a person is considered innocent until proven guilty in a court of law. Describing a suspect in an inappropriate manner or giving unsolicited opinions can taint this aspect of due process.

Conscientious efforts also must be made to avoid **sexist language.** A neutral or inclusive wording can usually describe the event or situation without creating a sexist atmosphere. When describing occupations with the ending -*man,* select a more gender-neutral title. For example, instead of using the label *mailman* or *policeman,* substitute *letter carrier* or *police officer.*[2] The use of nonsexist language is further assisted by the use of proper names rather than the pronoun *he* or by the use of the expressions "he or she," "him or her," and so forth. Or completely avoid gender-specific references by writing in the third-person plural and using proper nouns only.[3]

> **Sexist language** Insensitive, politically incorrect language used in reference to gender or gender issues.

Along with avoiding sexist language, also avoid affected words or phrases that suggest judgments and conclusions. For example, do not write about the *criminal,* the *rapist,* or the *felon.* Instead, refer to the person as the *suspect.* After a warrant has been issued, reports may refer to suspects as *defendants.* A person who is a juvenile or is not involved with criminal charges may be referred to as the *subject.*

As a practice, do not use profanity in reports. Some departments do permit the use of profanity if it is an exact quote from a suspect or witness, or it may be kept in the officer's personal notes. In formal police reports, blanks can be used in direct quotes. For instance, one might write, "Yes, I killed the _____ [profanity]." Never use abbreviations for profanity, such as *SOB* or other such epithets. It is nearly always sufficient (with the possible exception of a capital crime) to say, "Barba called Hogan a profane name and was struck in the mouth by Hogan" or "Porter was yelling loudly and profanely at officers." However, the exact words of Barba

STATISTICS

In a recent year, federal, state, and local governments spent a total of $93 billion on direct and intergovernmental expenses to operate and administer their criminal justice systems. Of this total, 43 percent was spent on police protection, 36 percent on corrections, and 21 percent on judicial and legal administration.[4]

or Porter should be recorded in the officer's notes, in the event that a judge in court wants to hear the exact words.

Whether or not to prosecute a case or continue an investigation is frequently decided solely on the basis of a criminal investigation report. Absolute, unbiased accuracy is essential. Care should be taken to report correctly times, dates, names of all parties involved, complete addresses and phone numbers, descriptions of suspects and the crime scene, items of evidence and their security and chain of custody, and proper identification of all investigators and their activities.

Errors or omissions in reports raise doubts about the thoroughness, accuracy, and reliability and, indeed, the truthfulness of the report writer. A suspect's fate often hinges on the accuracy of the information in a police report.

Mechanical Elements Common to Police Reports

The structure and content of a police report may vary. For example, departments may have different policies on report contents, diverse needs or uses of portions of the report information, varying levels of computer-entry sophistication (or none at all), and different statistical or informational requirements. Still, overarching these disparate departmental needs are certain categories of information that are required for the type of report being written.

Names   The names (real names and aliases) of complainants, witnesses, possible suspects, and any parties related to the criminal event should always be obtained. The names of parties involved should be listed first. The sequence should be last name, first name, and middle name, if any. In many departments, the last or family name is written in capital letters—for example, "WILSON, John Edward." In some departments, names are written entirely in capital letters, as follows: "WILSON, JOHN EDWARD." This convention can help a reader find a name in a report.

Be aware that some cultures frequently place the family name first and the given name second. This is common in many Asian cultures and some Middle Eastern and African cultures as well. For example, if a person from mainland China has the name Kim Xin, the family name is actually Kim. But if the person is from Hong Kong, the family name may be Xin. It is important, then, to determine the culture or country of origin of the person whose name is being written in the report.

The designations Mr., Miss, Ms., and Mrs. are not used with names in a report. For instance, it would not be correct to use "*Mr.* John Paul JONES" or "*Mrs.* John Paul JONES." Instead, one would expect to find these names written as "JONES, John Paul" or "JOHN PAUL JONES" and "JONES, Mary Jane (Mrs.)" or "MARY JANE SMITH (Mrs.)." It is preferable to use the full middle name of a person rather than only the middle initial. When a middle name is actually only a single initial, it should be enclosed in quotation marks, as in MOORE,

Alice "P," or ALICE "P" MOORE. If the subject has no middle name, indicate that: MOORE, Alice (NMN) or ALICE (NMN) MOORE.

Race and Sex   Race and ethnicity should always be presented in a proper, nonderogatory manner. Race is ordinarily indicated by abbreviations, such as *W* for Caucasian, *B* for African-American, *H* for Hispanic, *A* for Asian, *I* for American Indian, and *U* for unknown. Sex is always designated by *M* for male and *F* for female. The usual sequence is race first, then sex. A listing of "W/F," then, refers to a Caucasian female.

Age   Age should be based on the person's last birthday. Typically, the first reference to a person's age consists of the date of birth, if known. When such information is not known, as in the case of an unidentified deceased person or an uncooperative suspect, age may be recorded as an approximation or a limited age span—for example, "approximately 40 years old" or "approximately 35–40 years old." Again, age should be handled in a proper and neutral manner, without derogatory or unwarranted reference to senility. Write dates of birth in the sequence month/day/year.

Addresses   Addresses of all crime scenes, victims, suspects, and witnesses should be given if available. Each address, whether residence or business, should include the street number and, if applicable, an apartment, suite, condominium, or room number. If such detail is not available, a general description should be provided so that the location can be later identified.

Telephone Numbers   Always get as many telephone numbers as possible so that it will be easier to contact victims and witnesses. Be sure to include the area code, home and office numbers (including extensions), and cellular phone and pager numbers if available.

Descriptions of People   Whenever there is a witness or a victim of a crime, there is the prospect of obtaining a description of a suspect. Some report forms contain checklists for recording a person's physical description. Try to include the following information in any personal description: height, weight, hair color and general characteristics (e.g., wavy, long, short), eye characteristics and color, build, complexion, facial hair, identifiable marks (e.g., scars, birthmarks, tattoos, a limp, amputations), teeth (color, gaps, shape, etc.), unusual mannerisms or voice, and style and color of dress.

Additionally, in a felony report, under the heading "Details of the Crime," investigators should provide the following information if they are aware of it: education; occupations (present and past); hobbies; parents and siblings; relatives, associates, and friends; military service; social security number; marital status and wife's maiden name, if applicable; and any other pertinent information.

Descriptions of Property   When property is taken, a complete and accurate description may assist in its recovery. If it has been damaged or destroyed, a thorough description may be required by an insurance agency.

Whenever property is involved in the crime, the minimum description should include: quantity; kind; physical description, including model, style, design, shape, and size; material; color; condition, including age and apparent wear; approximate value (indicate method of determining value, e.g., "owner's estimate," "receipts," "written appraisal"); trade name; and serial or identification numbers, initials, marks, or unique markings.

Stolen property should be listed in orderly groups. Property that can be distinguished by identification or serial numbers should be grouped together. Items that are listed by brand or trade names should be in a separate group. Articles that have neither identification numbers nor trade names can be placed in yet another group. When recording the information on the crime report, give every item on each list a unique number. In a separate column, describe each item, and in a third column, show the value of each item.

All articles should be described as completely as possible, with emphasis on special features of identification—even when the manufacturer's name is not known and the item bears no identification marks or numbers. For instance, an important identifying piece of information about a stolen gold necklace is that the barrel catch has been resoldered. Or knowing that a man's gold wedding ring has the words "Love Forever, Grace" engraved on the inside can help identify the article when it is recovered.

Descriptions of Vehicles   Whenever a vehicle is involved in a crime, a description of it should be carefully worked out. In addition to a general description of the vehicle's condition, the report should contain the following basic information: year and make; model and body type (e.g., coupe, sedan, two-door, convertible); color; license number; motor number or vehicle identification number (VIN); accessories, distinguishing marks, or characteristics, including upholstery, interior of vehicle, dashboard, paneling, seat covers, ornamentation; registration information; and owner's name, address, and telephone numbers.

Descriptions of Physical Areas   All pertinent information regarding an area should be included in a description entered in the crime report. The data should include various dimensions, topography, vegetation, access, types of buildings or structures, and even the size and height of various buildings or structures.

Dates   Write dates as month/day/year, using two digits for each. For instance, write September 7, 1998, as 09/07/98. Be careful when recording dates. Errors in dates can create havoc when discovered during a trial and can draw into question the reliability of other aspects of the report.

Time   Most police agencies use the military system of hundred hours in their reports. See Figure 9–1. The only exception is when reporting the exact words of a witness or subject regarding time.

Figure 9–1 Military system of 100 hours.

Clock Time	100-Hour Time
12:01–12:59 PM	0001–0059
1:00–1:59 AM	0100–0159
2:00–2:59 AM	0200–0259
3:00–3:59 AM	0300–0359
4:00–4:59 AM	0400–0459
5:00–5:59 AM	0500–0559
6:00–6:59 AM	0600–0659
7:00–7:59 AM	0700–0759
8:00–8:59 AM	0800–0859
9:00–9:59 AM	0900–0959
10:00–10:59 AM	1000–1059
11:00–11:59 AM	1100–1159
12:00 NOON	1200
12:01–12:59 PM	1201–1259
1:00–1:59 PM	1300–1359
2:00–2:59 PM	1400–1459
3:00–3:59 PM	1500–1559
4:00–4:59 PM	1600–1659
5:00–5:59 PM	1700–1759
6:00–6:59 PM	1800–1859
7:00–7:59 PM	1900–1959
8:00–8:59 PM	2000–2059
9:00–9:59 PM	2100–2159
10:00–10:59 PM	2200–2259
11:00–11:59 PM	2300–2359
12:00 MIDNIGHT	2400

Format of a Report

Reports and reporting forms used by police agencies vary considerably. Differences in reporting forms are the result of department needs, requirements, policies, and preferences. In spite of the variations in reporting forms, the information sought by officers regarding crime detection, apprehension of criminals, solving of crimes, and rendering of police services is essentially the same. Many report forms used by police agencies contain two parts (see Figure 9–2).

The first section of most police reports is a printed **form section** that can vary in length and content. Typically, it consists of labeled fill-in blocks and blanks that call for specific responses by the officer. Whether it is a paper form or an electronic form on the computer, the spaces and blocks guide an officer through important information that should not be omitted from the report.

The types of information required in the form section of the report generally include the case or file number; the date and time of the report; the type of offense and the classification if applicable; the date and time the incident was reported; the victim, complainant, or source of the complaint; addresses; telephone numbers; the officers involved; and descriptions of suspects and vehicles. It is very important that all the labeled spaces provided on the form section of the report be filled in. When information requested on a form blank is not known,

Form section A boxed section of a police report form, designed for fill-in and checkoff of information.

Figure 9–2 Major parts of police reports.

Reports

DETAILS OF COMPLAINT, OR INCIDENT

Part I
Information required:
In crime reports, this section provides statistical data for local, state, and federal computer analysis.

Part II
Narrative portion:
This section states all the facts, establishes the crime, identifies the suspect, and aids in prosecution.

unknown should be written in the space. This assures a reader that the information was not overlooked, but was not known by the reporting officer. In most agencies, separate forms are used for a felony and a misdemeanor. A felony crime report format is typically longer and has a more detailed form section than misdemeanor or other nonfelony report forms.

The second portion of the form is the **narrative section,** or body of the report. This section sets forth the details of the matter being reported. There are no hard-and-fast rules about how to begin the narrative. Many officers prefer to begin with the suspect's first known act and to record successive acts in the sequence in which they occurred. It is important throughout the narrative to describe exactly what the witnesses saw, heard, or did. In the narrative portion of the report, officers must be mindful to refer to individuals as suspects, witnesses, and victims. Reference, for example, may be made to witness KAZINSKI, suspect BOURNE, defendant NOOJIN, or victim MYERS.

The narration should be direct and clear, without tangents. Details of the incident, descriptions of evidence, explanations of who found what and where it was found, descriptions of suspects, and the disposition of the case should all be carefully spelled out in the narrative section of the form. All details connected with the incident should be set forth. Stolen property should be itemized and described completely and accurately, and its value should be listed (according to the owner's estimates) or approximated.

Some agencies require a summary, or **synopsis,** of the full report as the first item in the narrative section. Statements made in the synopsis must be substantiated by information set forth in the full report.

FYI

A synopsis that answers the questions *who, what, when, where, how,* and *why* serves as the completed report for 80 percent of misdemeanor crimes reported.

Types of Reports

Reports and reporting forms vary considerably in local, state, and federal agencies. Variations occur because of such factors as the responsibility and jurisdiction of an individual department or agency, the nature of the subject matter, and agency preferences and particular needs. Regardless of the variations and differences, police agencies tend to concern themselves with four basic categories of forms and reports: internal business-related reports, technical and specialized-equipment reports, intelligence reports, and day-to-day operations reports. The operations reports are the type most often prepared by officers. Operations reports include misdemeanor and/or miscellaneous reports, felony reports, follow-up reports, arrest reports, and vehicle accident reports. We will next take a closer look at each of these types of reports. The reports depicted are only samples of reports that a law enforcement agency might use.

Misdemeanor and/or Miscellaneous Reports

Misdemeanor reports record all lesser crimes and miscellaneous incidents. Sometimes such a report is called a **complaint report** or an **incident report.** The completed report contains such identifying data as the nature of the complaint; the code violation, if any; the file number; the date and time the complaint was received; the location of the incident; names of the victim, witnesses, and subjects; addresses and telephone numbers of all persons involved; and descriptions of suspects.

You may occasionally encounter some obstacles in completing a report. Frequently, victims of minor crimes do not want a report made and indicate that even if one were drawn up, they would not sign it. Often, victims are unwilling to sign a complaint on a misdemeanor because they "do not want to cause any trouble." It is important, though, to record the information concerning the misdemeanor for the following reasons:

- It provides intelligence for detectives and uniformed officers about the types of crimes being committed in the area and can serve as a database from which to establish a crime pattern.

- Victims may change their minds later, or may discover additional loss or damage.

- Most insurance claims cannot be made unless a police report has been filed.

- Known suspects for unreported crimes may be sought for similar crimes in reported cases.

A sample completed misdemeanor and/or miscellaneous report involving a prowler complaint appears in Figure 9–3.

Sometimes, after completing a misdemeanor or miscellaneous report, an investigator may determine that the incident is actually a felony, an attempted felony, or a crime that requires the filing of a felony report. Under such circumstances, the report writer should find the heading of the narrative section of the misdemeanor report, often called "Details of Incident." In this space, the reporting officer should write, "See crime report." The crime report or felony report should then be produced, together with any follow-up reports. These various report forms would together make up the case file on that offense and would become part of the record in court.

Complaint report (incident report) A police report written to document events surrounding misdemeanors and miscellaneous incidents.

Figure 9–3 Misdemeanor and/or miscellaneous report.

MISDEMEANOR and/or MISCELLANEOUS REPORT   ORIGINAL

CRIME OR INCIDENT: 647g PC PROWLER   FILE NO. 98-224

STATION Central   DATE RECEIVED 2-6-98   TIME 2215   RECEIVED BY Sgt. J.R. Brown

                    LAST   FIRST   MIDDLE

INFORMANT'S NAME PALMA, Helen   Marie (Mrs.)   TELEPHONE 555-5441

                STREET   CITY

ADDRESS 567 Maple St. , Apt. "C"   Chico, California   95926

                LAST   FIRST   MIDDLE

VICTIM'S NAME Same as above   TELEPHONE

(IF DIFFERENT
FROM INFORMANT)

ADDRESS   Same as above

LOCATION 567 Maple St., Apt. "C"   DATE OCCURRED 2-6-98   TIME 2210

SUSPECT Unknown Suspect

ADDRESS   TELEPHONE

	SEX	RACE	AGE	HEIGHT	WEIGHT	HAIR	EYES	DIST. MARKS
DESCRIPTION	M	W	17-19	5'10-0'	150-100	Dk.Brn	Unk	High cheek bones/ large eyes

OTHER DESCRIPTION Long Dk. Brn.Hair, shoulder length, parted in center; small frame silver rimmed glasses; lt. tan windbreaker jacket; yellow sport shirt, blue jeans

VEHICLE (none seen)   LICENSE NO.

DETAILS OF CRIME OR INCIDENT:

Advised by radio, 2217 hours this date to contact female victim of a Peeping Tom, at Apt. "C", 567 Maple St.; suspect scared away. Last observed fleeing north on Maple St.

Apt. located mid-block on W side of Maple; 3-story white stucco; Caucasian middle class neighborhood. Apt. set back about 30' W of sidewalk line. A 6' wood fence borders property on both sides and rear. Victim, WFA, age 42, resides on first floor.

Victim advised that she was sitting alone in her living room which fronts on Maple St., watching TV at 10:10 p.m. 2/6/98, when she heard a noise outside ground floor window on E side of her apartment. She stated that she looked out her apartment window but saw no one. Victim said that 10 minutes later she again heard noises outside the same window and proceeded to the window to draw the shade. On approaching this window victim observed above-described young man peering into her window. She stated that suspect fled as soon as he realized he had been seen; running north on Maple St.

Victim stated that she resides alone and has been bothered on three previous occasions by a suspect of similar description. Mrs. Palma mentioned that due to the poor lighting in her room her description of the suspect is not too accurate.

Several overlapping footprints noted outside victim's front window; one clear shoeprint located; cast made. Neighbors contacted and area cruised with negative results. Shoe design set forth -

Follow-up investigation to be conducted.

INVESTIGATING OFFICERS Wilson #34/Brown #8 SUPERVISOR Lt. Moore

Felony Reports

The information required in a **felony report** is much more detailed than that required in a misdemeanor report. Many police agencies have specially printed felony crime report forms that contain the reporting requirements of that particular agency. It is beyond the scope of this book to comprehensively outline all of the different police report forms and reporting procedures used by law enforcement agencies across the United States. Nonetheless, it is possible to emphasize a virtually universal requirement of all felony crime reports—a description of the *modus operandi* (M.O.) of a suspect.

When describing the *modus operandi* in a felony crime report, be sure to report the following information: the time the incident occurred, the type of premises where the incident occurred, the victims involved, the method of the crime, methods of access or entry and withdrawal or escape, characteristics and peculiarities of the perpetrator, and any transportation used. For example, whether or not a burglar could see an alarm from outside the premises might be a key factor in determining whether the point of entry was through a window, a door, or a skylight. The types of objects taken and the condition of the premises after a break-in might even suggest the age and interests of the perpetrators. For example, juvenile perpetrators typically leave more of a mess than professional burglars. Figure 9–4 illustrates a report on an armed robbery. This sample felony crime report illustrates the proper recording of *modus operandi* details of a crime. Recording *modus operandi* details of a crime is one of the most important elements of a crime report.

The crime report shown in Figure 9–4 includes the information that an officer should obtain to allow the report to be properly classified, searched, filed, and retrieved. In addition to reporting the method of operation of the criminal, the report would include an accurate and detailed description of the suspects and the stolen property. Attached to the felony crime report or submitted separately could be a **property report** and an **evidence report.** The property report shown in Figure 9–4a and the evidence report shown in Figure 9–4b are a continuation of the crime report depicted in Figure 9–4.

Insofar as is possible, each felony crime report should describe only one offense. However, when multiple crimes, such as robbery, rape, and kidnapping, are committed against the same victim and constitute what might be considered one continuous action, then one report can be used to cover the events. It should be recognized, however, that robbery, rape, and kidnapping are separate and distinct offenses. When two or more offenses arising from the same incident are described in a single crime report, the most serious is reported first.

In offenses with separate victims—as when an incident involves the rape of one person, aggravated assault against another, and the homicide of a third—a separate crime report is generally prepared for each victim

> **Felony report** A police record created to document the events surrounding a felony.

> **Property report** A specific report directed toward documenting property taken or damaged in a crime.

> **Evidence report** A report written about the evidence found at a crime scene; usually an evidence inventory is attached as part of the report.

Figure 9–4 Felony crime report.

Robbery

Felony Crime Report
San Bernardino Police Department
San Bernardino, California 92410

1. CASE NO.
98-1024

2. CODE SECTION	3. CRIME	4. CLASSIFICATION	5. REPORT AREA
211a PC	Armed Robbery	Market w/revolver	5

6. DATE AND TIME OCCURRED - DAY	7. DATE AND TIME REPORTED	8. LOCATION OF OCCURRENCE	
12/29/98 0700 Friday	12/29/98	100 North "C" St., San Bernardino	92410

9. VICTIM'S NAME LAST, FIRST, MIDDLE (FIRM IF BUSINESS)	10. RESIDENCE ADDRESS	11. RES. PHONE
McDaniel's Market		

12. OCCUPATION	13. RACE-SEX	14. AGE	15. DOB	16. BUSINESS ADDRESS (SCHOOL IF JUVENILE)	17. BUS. PHONE
Grocery Store				Same as 8	555-1505

CODES FOR V = VICTIM W = WITNESS P = PARENT RP = REPORTING PARTY DC = DISCOVERED CRIME	18. CHECK IF MORE NAMES IN CONTINUATION X
BOXES 20 AND 30	

19. NAME - LAST, FIRST, MIDDLE	20. CODE	21. RESIDENCE ADDRESS	22. RESIDENCE PHONE
McDaniel, John Joseph	RP	1234 Elm Avenue	555-3210

23. OCCUPATION	24. RACE -SEX	25. AGE	26. DOB	27. BUSINESS ADDRESS (SCHOOL IF JUVENILE)	28. BUSINESS PHONE
Owner	MWA	54	9/9/44	Same as 8	555-1505

29. NAME - LAST, FIRST, MIDDLE	30. CODE	31. RESIDENCE ADDRESS	32. RESIDENCE PHONE
Johnson, Mary Lois	W	955 North "C" San Bernardino	555-1433

33. OCCUPATION	34. RACE-SEX	35. AGE	36. DOB	37. BUSINESS ADDRESS (SCHOOL IF JUVENILE)	38. BUSINESS PHONE
Housewife	WFA	48	12/12/50	None	

MODUS OPERANDI (SEE INSTRUCTIONS)

39. DESCRIBE CHARACTERISTICS OF PREMISE AND AREA WHERE OFFENSE OCCURRED
Large groc. mkt. in downtown area next to hotels. Alley in rear, Pkg. lot on E. side

40. DESCRIBE BRIEFLY HOW OFFENSE WAS COMMITTED
Climbs fire escape on adjoining hotel, jumps to roof of mkt., drills out 20" hole in roof, lowers self
via rope to floor of store, waits till opening, forces mgr., to open safe, locks victims in walk-in
cooler, leaves through rear alley exit.

41. DESCRIBE WEAPON, INSTRUMENT, EQUIPMENT, TRICK , DEVICE OR FORCE USED
2" B/S Rev. 1-1/4" drill, chisel, hammer, rope

42. MOTIVE - TYPE OF PROPERTY TAKEN OR OTHER REASON FOR OFFENSE
Money & Checks

43. ESTIMATED LOSS VALUE AND/OR EXTENT OF INJURIES - MINOR, MAJOR
$8,110.

44. WHAT DID SUSPECT/ S SAY - NOTE PECULIARITIES
"This is a robbery, behave and you won't get hurt. Get over here 'fass'."

45. VICTIM'S ACTIVITY JUST PRIOR TO AND/OR DURING OFFENSE
Opening Store

46. TRADEMARK - OTHER DISTINCTIVE ACTIVE OF SUSPECT/S
Ate on premises, drank Vodka

47. VEHICLE USED - LICENSE NO. - YEAR - MAKE - MODEL - COLORS (OTHER IDENTIFYING CHARACTERISTICS)
None seen

48. SUSPECT NO. I (LAST, FIRST, MIDDLE)	49. RACE- SEX	50. AGE	51. HT.	52. WT.	53. HAIR	54. EYES	55. ID. NO. OR DOB	56. ARRESTED
S-1 Name Unknown	WMA	30-35	6'	200	blk	brn		☐ X

57. ADDRESS, CLOTHING AND OTHER IDENTIFYING MARKS OR CHARACTERISTICS
Work clothes, wore flashy ring with large brilliant stone

58. SUSPECT NO. 2 (LAST, FIRST, MIDDLE)	59. RACE- SEX	60. AGE	61. HT.	62. WT.	63. HAIR	64. EYES	65. ID. NO. OR DOB	66. ARRESTED
S-2 Name Unknown	WMA	30-35	5'8	180	blk	brn		☐ X

67. ADDRESS, CLOTHING AND OTHER IDENTIFYING MARKS OR CHARACTERISTICS
Work clothes, Army type boots, small blue dot left cheek under eye

68. CHECK IF MORE NAMES IN CONTINUATION

REPORTING OFFICERS	RECORDING OFFICER	TYPED BY	DATE AND TIME	ROUTED BY
Samons #18 / Jacobs #35	Jacobs	mmk	12/29/98 1300	Owens

FURTHER ACTION	X YES	X DETECTIVE	X C11		
	☐ NO	☐ JUVENILE	☐ PATROL		
		X DIST. ATTNY	☐ OTHER		
		X SQ./ P.D.	☐ OTHER	REVIEWED BY Moore, R.L. Lt.	DATE 12/29/98

Figure 9–4 Felony crime report. (continued)

Robbery

69. CASE NO.
98-1024

(2)
San Bernardino Police Department
San Bernardino, California 92410

70. CODE SECTION	71. CRIME	72. CLASSIFICATION
211a PC	Armed Robbery	Market w/revolver

73. VICTIM'S LAST, FIRST, MIDDLE (FIRM IF BUS.)
McDaniel's Market

74. ADDRESS RESIDENCE [ ] BUSINESS [X]
100 North "C" St.

75. PHONE
555-1505

W 2 RENTS FROM, Josephine Mary, Rm 410 Shasta Hotel, 555-1349
    Beauty Operator, WFA, 52, 2/18/45, Classic Beauty Salon, 10th and K Sts.
    Phone 555-1010

12/29/98 0700 RP after unlocking front door of store, proceeded to the back
storeroom where he was confronted by two unknown suspects. S-1, the taller
of the two, pointed a 2" B/S revolver at RP stating –"This is a robbery, behave
and you won't get hurt, get over here fast (the word fast slurred to sound like 'fass')."
S-2, an African American, short and stocky, did not speak. At that time W-1
entered the market at which time S-2 escorted her to the rear of the store where
RP and S-1 were standing.

S-1 then ordered RP into rear office where he commanded RP to open the floor safe
(combination Mosler) and get the money. $8,110 in used currency and checks given
to S-1. (Three $100 bills, two $50 bills and about 20 checks were included).

Thereafter, S -1 ordered RP and W-1 into the walk-in refrigerator
at which time the door was closed, the outside strap latch locked,
and a stick of wood put in the hasp to secure the lock. After
about 24 minutes, RP succeeded in opening the door.

Entrance to the market was determined to have been gained by cutting a 20" square
hole through the roof. A series of holes were cut through the tar paper and wood with
a $1\frac{1}{2}$" bit. Some holes overlapped. Where they did not, the wood between the
holes appeared to have been cut with a chisel. Two sets of shoeprints were
observed to lead from the edge of the roof to the hole, but did not return. It was
noted that the Shasta Hotel is located adjacent to this market, which hotel has
a fire escape opposite the edge of the roof where the shoeprints start. In the market
attic, trails in the dust led from a point just below the hole in the roof to a trap door
in the store ceiling. The trap door, which had been closed at the end of the previous
business day, was open. From this point there was noted to be a 12' drop to the
open storeroom floor below. Dust, scuff marks, and partial shoeprints of the same
pattern which appeared on the roof, were observed on the linoleum floor just
below the trap door.

Two $\frac{1}{2}$" holes, $4'8\frac{1}{2}$", and the other 5'2" above floor level had been drilled
through the storeroom wall which faces the front of the store.

REPORTING OFFICERS	RECORDING OFFICER	TYPED BY	DATE AND TIME	ROUTED BY
Samons #18/ Jacobs #35	Jacobs	mmk	12/29/98	Owens

FURTHER ACTION [X] YES [ ] NO

COPIES TO:
[X] DETECTIVE   [X] C11
[ ] JUVENILE   [ ] PATROL
[X] DIST. ATTNY   [ ] OTHER _____
[ ] SQ./P.D.   [ ] OTHER _____

REVIEWED BY
Moore, R. L. Lt.

DATE
12/29/98

Figure 9–4 Felony crime report. (continued)

Robbery		**69.CASE NO.** 98-1024
(3) **San Bernardino Police Department** **San Bernardino, California 92410**		

70.CODE SECTION 211a PC	**71. CRIME** Armed Robbery	**72. CLASSIFICATION** Market w/revolver
73.VICTIM'S NAME LAST, FIRST, MIDDLE (FIRM IF BUS.) McDaniel's Market	**74. ADDRESS** RESIDENCE X BUSINESS 100 North "C" St.	**75. PHONE** 555-1505

Fresh sawdust and plaster was found on the floor on both sides of the wall just below the holes. Remnants of three packages of Gallo salami, three empty milk cartons, a half-pint of Samarov Vodka and a brown plastic satchel were found in the storeroom. The satchel had a 16" length of 1/2" hemp rope tied to its handles and contained the following tools: wood brace, four wood bits, a carpenter's hammer, wood chisel, linoleum knife, 12" crow bar, pair of side cutters, and a keyhole saw. The tools, satchel, and rope were foreign to the crime scene and were not recognized by anyone who had legal access to the property.

W-2   a guest of the Shasta Hotel reported that about 0200 hours she got up to take an Alka-Seltzer and saw a black man and a white man ascending the fire escape of the hotel. She stated that she returned to bed and did not notify anyone. W-2 advised that she did not believe she could identify either of these suspects.

PROPERTY REPORT ATTACHED.

Investigation continuing.

REPORTING OFFICERS Samons #18/ Jacobs #35	**RECORDING OFFICER** Jacobs	**TYPED BY** mmk	**DATE AND TIME** 12/29/98 1300	**ROUTED BY** Owens

FURTHER ACTION	X YES	X **DETECTIVE**	X **C11**		
	NO	**JUVENILE**	**PATROL**		
		X **DIST. ATTNY**	**OTHER** _____		
		SQ./P.D.	**OTHER** _____	**REVIEWED BY** Moore, R.L., Lt.	**DATE** 12/29/98

Figure 9–4a Property report.

Robbery				69.CASE NO. 98-1024
	San Bernardino Police Department **San Bernardino, California 92410**			

70.CODE SECTION 211a PC	71. CRIME Armed Robbery		72. CLASSIFICATION Market w/revolver	
73.VICTIM'S LAST, FIRST, MIDDLE (FIRM IF BUS.) McDaniel' s Market		74. ADDRESS RESIDENCE [X] BUSINESS 100 North "C" St.	75. PHONE 555-1505

<u>PROPERTY REPORT</u>

ITEM	DESCRIPTION	VALUE
1.	Currency in denominations of $1, 5, 10 20's; 3 - $100's; 2 - $50's and approximately 20 checks. (Owner's estimate.) Checks taken were personal type checks under $50 and drawn on the Bank of America or Wells – Fargo National Bank.	$8,110.00

REPORTING OFFICERS Samons #18/ Jacobs #35	RECORDING OFFICER Jacobs	TYPED BY mmk	DATE AND TIME 12/29/98 1300	ROUTED BY Owens

FURTHER ACTION	[X] YES [ ] NO	COPIES TO	[X] DETECTIVE [ ] JUVENILE [X] DIST. ATTNY [ ] SQ./P.D.	[X] C11 [ ] PATROL [ ] OTHER [ ] OTHER		

REVIEWED BY Moore, R. L., Lt.	DATE 12/29/98

Figure 9–4b Evidence report.

Robbery

69.CASE NO.
98-1024

San Bernardino Police Department
San Bernardino, California 92410

70.CODE SECTION 211a PC	71. CRIME Armed Robbery	72. CLASSIFICATION Market w/revolver		
73.VICTIM'S NAME LAST, FIRST, MIDDLE (FIRM IF BUS.) McDaniel's Market		**74. ADDRESS** ☐ RESIDENCE ☒ BUSINESS 100 North "C" St.		**75. PHONE** 555-1505

EVIDENCE REPORT

ITEM   DESCRIPTION

1.   One brown satchel (plastic material), 18" x 14" x 8",
        with a 16' length of 1/2" hemp rope tied to its
        handles. Contents of bag included: 1- wood brace (red
        in color), 4- $1\frac{1}{4}$" bits, carpenter's hammer, wood chisel,
        linoleum knife, 12" crowbar, side cutters, keyhole saw.

2.   3 empty pint milk cartons (Arden Farms Dairy).

3.   Remnants of 3 packages of salami (Gallo brand).

4.   One-half pint empty bottle of vodka (Samarov label).

   The above items were collected and marked for identification
by Officer JACOBS #35, with the initials "L.J."and maintained
by him until delivered to Lt. JOHN WILSON, Police Crime Laboratory
on 12/29/98. Specimens of tar paper, insulation material,
wood chips, and ceiling plaster were obtained by Officer
JACOBS from area of roof breakthrough, for possible future
comparison purposes. Ten photographs of shoeprints taken from
the surface of the market roof, the attic, and from the area
below the trap door of the market ceiling were also obtained
by Officer JACOBS for comparison with the footwear of suspects
developed in this investigation.

REPORTING OFFICERS Samons #18 / Jacobs #35	RECORDING OFFICER Jacobs	TYPED BY mmk	DATE AND TIME 12/29/98 1300	ROUTED BY Owens

FURTHER ACTION	☒ YES ☐ NO	☒ DETECTIVE ☐ JUVENILE ☒ DIST. ATTNY ☐ SQ./P.D.	☒ C11 ☐ PATROL ☐ OTHER ☐ OTHER	

REVIEWED BY   DATE
                              Moore, R.L., Lt.   12/29/98

against whom a crime was committed or attempted. In thefts, a report is made for each distinct operation undertaken or attempted. A robbery report is prepared for each separate robbery. Each offense or attempt is considered only one case, even if there are two or more victims. In burglaries of hotels, hospitals, nursing homes, or other boarding residences, any single burglary event, regardless of how many rooms are involved, is considered a case. In burglaries of separate apartments or separate dwellings in close proximity, a report must be filled out for each dwelling entered during the commission of the crime. Crime reports are recorded in all felony cases, regardless of whether the victims are willing to file a report or sign a complaint.

Follow-Up, Continuation, and Supplementary Reports

A **follow-up report** or a **supplementary report,** as it is sometimes called, is made after the initial report. It is made by an officer who obtains additional information on a case under investigation. The label *continuation report* or *supplemental report* is sometimes used on reports describing crimes incidental or secondary to the primary felony. For example, a suspect might carjack a vehicle to make his or her escape after killing a person. The suspect may even injure the driver of the carjacked car. The homicide will be written up on an initial felony crime report, but the carjacking and the possible aggravated assault on the driver will be recorded in a continuation or supplementary report that also becomes part of the case file of the offense.

Follow-up report (supplementary report) A report written during the secondary level of a criminal investigation.

In many felony cases, the investigation spans several days or weeks. Whenever an officer rechecks any offense previously reported, he or she must fill out a supplementary report describing what was discovered or what additional property was recovered. The value of such a report depends on the thoroughness of the investigating officer.

In most instances, the follow-up reports are made by the officer assigned to the case. However, if other officers receive information regarding the case, they, too, should complete follow-up reports. For example, during a routine drug bust, a uniformed officer discovers that a drug dealer is wearing an unusual ring. The officer recalls that the ring was described in a recent burglary report. After discussing this with the dealer, the officer learns the name of the person who sold the dealer the ring. All of this information should be submitted in a follow-up report, filed with the initial burglary report. The information can help to establish or verify a *modus operandi*.

Follow-up reports always carry the same case number as the original case, regardless of the number of supplemental reports. Figure 9–5 is an example of a supplemental report in a burglary investigation. The report covers an interview with a witness two days after the actual burglary and the subsequent arrest of a suspect.

Figure 9–5 Follow-up report.

Burglary		**69.CASE NO.** 98-313

San Bernardino Police Department
San Bernardino, California   92410

70.CODE SECTION 459 PC	**71. CRIME** Burglary	**72. CLASSIFICATION** Commercial - Jewelry Store	
73.VICTIM'S NAME LAST, FIRST, MIDDLE (FIRM IF BUS.) Leighton's Jewelry Store		**74. ADDRESS** ☐ RESIDENCE ☒ BUSINESS	**75. PHONE** 555-5643

FOLLOW-UP REPORT

On 2/27/98, 1030 hours, WALTER J. SAUGER, Mgr., Fidelity Loan Co., 208 S. Spring Street, telephoned and advised the writer that an unknown individual had tried to pawn a lady's W/G diamond ring, set with a 1/2 karat diamond in a basket setting, engraved "J.A.". Mr. SAUGER stated that he did not like the looks of this suspect and refused to take the items. The unknown person left the store and walked south on Spring St., according to SAUGER. Suspect was described as M/W/A, 35- 38 yrs, 5'7-9", 160-170, wearing dark trousers, faded blue shirt with white square-shaped buttons; dk. brn.hair—neck length; dk. sunglasses.

Since the above jewelry fit the description of some of the property taken in the burglary of the LEIGHTON'S JEWELRY STORE on 2/25/98, reporting officer proceeded to S. Spring St., where an individual similar to the person described by Mr. SAUGER, was observed walking south on the east side of Spring St. Suspect was placed under arrest by reporting officer at 1040 hours. At this time Officer Tuscillo informed suspect that he had a right to remain silent and that any statement he did make could be used against him as evidence in a court of law. He was advised that he had the right to speak with an Attorney of his own choice and to have the attorney present during questioning; that if he so desired and could not afford one, an attorney would be appointed for him without charge. At this time suspect stated that he understood his rights but was willing to make a statement.

A search of suspect's person disclosed several articles of jewelry similar to the items taken in the LEIGHTON store burglary as well as an eight-inch screw driver. The screw driver tip appears similar to the tool impression left on the window ledge of victim jewelry store.

Suspect was identified as HARRY AMES, 405 Maple St., San Francisco, California 94118, and claimed he had just been released from Soledad Prison on 2/22/98, where he had served four years on a burglary conviction. He was booked at Central Jail on suspicion of Burglary, Booking #6345k.

ROBERT B. LEIGHTON, owner, Leighton's Jewelry Store, identified the three rings found on suspect's person, and the lady's Bulova watch, as being part of the stolen jewelry taken in instant case on 2/25/98.
(Include in report)
SUSPECT: (description)
PROPERTY: (list of items, description, value)
ARREST REPORT: (attach copy of arrest report)

REPORTING OFFICERS Tuscillo, Michele. #436	**RECORDING OFFICER** Tuscillo	**TYPED BY** mmk	**DATE AND TIME** 2/27/98 1030	**ROUTED BY** Miller

FURTHER ACTION ☒ YES ☐ NO	☒ DETECTIVE ☒ C11 ☐ JUVENILE ☐ PATROL ☒ DIST. ATTNY ☐ OTHER ☐ SQ./ P.D. ☐ OTHER	
	REVIEWED BY George Aplin, Capt.	**DATE** 2/27/98

Arrest Reports

An **arrest report** documents the circumstances of the arrest or detention of individuals by the police. Its purpose is to serve as a basis for prosecution. To accomplish its purpose, the report must meet two qualifications: (1) it must demonstrate a legal, proper arrest for which there was probable cause; and (2) it must be complete and correct to serve as an adequate guide for follow-up investigation.

The effectiveness of the prosecution is generally equal to the effectiveness of the arrest report. Evidence located by follow-up investigation does not carry the same weight as facts and evidence discovered at the time of arrest. The defense attorney may try to rebut follow-up evidence by asking the court or jury, "Why didn't the officer who made the arrest find this damaging bit of evidence?" Many cases are lost in court because of poor investigations, but more are lost because evidence was not properly reported. An officer who demonstrates the most commendable initiative and intelligence in making an arrest will fail to bring about a conviction in court if the arrest report is not correct and as complete as possible.

Arrest reports are generally completed by officers immediately upon making an arrest, with or without a warrant. A report must be submitted for an arrest in any of the following situations:

- Misdemeanor or felony.
- Commitment to a mental institution.
- Service of an arrest warrant.
- Desertion or other crime by military personnel.
- Transfer of custody of a suspect arrested by another agency.

The arrest report form, like most other reports, has a form section and a narrative section. Generally, the arrest report is typed, but when the arresting officer does not have the opportunity to type the report, it may be hand-printed or handwritten. In many agencies today, officers type their reports directly into a computer and print them out as a prestructured form. Figure 9–6 shows an example of a completed arrest report. This specimen report demonstrates facts sufficient to establish the basis for the arrest of a robbery suspect.

The circumstances of the arrest and the *corpus delicti* of the crime should be set forth. The report should describe what happened in chronological order, beginning with the first act of the suspect. It should include what was said to whom and all statements made by witnesses and victims as well as the suspect. Statements made by the suspect should be recorded as accurately as possible. If there is any physical evidence associated with the arrest, such evidence should be itemized with where it was found, the person who found it, and the date, and the final disposition should be indicated.

For arrests in which large amounts of property are recovered, there may not be room on the arrest report to itemize such property. In such

Figure 9–6 Arrest report.

<table>
<tr><td colspan="2">SHERIFF'S DEPARTMENT</td><td></td></tr>
</table>

Sherriff Station/Div. ☐ Central

Other Agency ☐ _____

SHERIFF'S DEPARTMENT

65432k

98-305

555-44-3210

Y-12992

ARREST INFORMATION

Defendant

Last	First	Middle
DAWSON,	Richard	Joseph

Date of Report 2/11/98

Crime 211 PC, Robbery; 12025PC Carrying Concealed Weapon;

Warrant # _____

	Race	Sex	Age	DOB	Ht.	Wt.	Hair	Eyes
Description:	Cauc.	M	36	1/25/63	5'10	165	Brn.	Brn.

Address: 1331 Taylor St., Rm. 15, (Apache Motel)   **Phone** 555-3042

Time at Above Address 1 day   **Time in State** 1 month   **Martial Status** Single

Dependents No. 0 / Ages   **Employment** Unemployed   **How Long** -

Place of Arrest Alley, (across street from 4489 Fairview)   **Court** _____

Arrested by Tansky #109/Roberts #155   **Date** 2/11/98   **Time** 1420

No. Prior Arrests 3   **No. Misc. Convictions** 1   **No. Felony Covictions** 1   **X-Con** Yes

Is Defendant Currently On: No   **Parole** No   **Probation** _____   **Bail** _____   **O.R. Release** _____

Holds: None   **Locaton of Vehicle** Wilson's Garage

On 2/11/98, 1345 hours, Officers TANSKY and ROBERTS were S/B on Fairview Ave. when they observed an unknown person seated in a 1995 Ford 2–Dr Lt. Blue/White, Colorado Lic. SUZO38 which was parked in a no parking area in the alley across the street from HENRY'S LIQUOR STORE, 4489 Fairview. The car was facing the liquor store headed east. Officers had been advised at roll call on 2/10/98 that a Lt. Blue/White Ford with a partial license S----8, possibly Colorado, had been used in a robbery of the ACME LIQUOR AND DELICATESSEN STORE (File 98-297) on 2/9/98. Above Colorado Licence SUZO38 was checked through NCIC with negative results.

Because of several recent liquor store robberies in this section of the city between 1300 and 1400 hours, and the similarity of the above Lt. Blue/White Ford with that of the car used in the ACME LIQUOR STORE robbery on 2/9/98, officers drove around the block and parked where they could observe the defendant and vehicle. During this observation suspect was noted to glance furtively all around and to be particularly watching HENRY'S LIQUOR STORE. On two separate occasions during this surveillance, suspect leaned forward in the front seat of his vehicle (below the window ledge of the door), to apparently avoid being observed by pedestrians who passed close to his car.

At approximately 1420 hours, both the undersigned officers approached the suspect and requested him to get out of his vehicle. Officers noted that suspect was extremely

Signature of Arresting (or Transporting) Officers /s/ M. R. Tansky #109; J.J. Roberts #155

15–6554–401 Rev. 11/95   **Approved by** /s/ Lt. R. L. Hogan

Figure 9–6 Arrest report. (continued)

Page 2

ARREST REPORT   Booking No. 65432k
DAWSON, Richard Joseph   DR No. 98-305

nervous and closely resembled the description of the suspect involved in recent
liquor store robberies. A quick search of suspect's person was made by Officer
ROBERTS but no weapons were found.

Suspect was asked what he was doing in the area. He replied,"I'm just waiting for a
friend who lives near Fairview Ave. and Taylor St." He refused to disclose the name
or specific address of the "friend" for whom he was waiting. Suspect also was
unable to explain why he was at this location when his alleged friend lived several
blocks south of this address.

When officers asked if they could search his vehicle, the suspect consented but was
noticeably nervous. Officer TANSKY searched the vehicle and found a .38 cal. B/S
automatic, serial #123561, under the front seat on the driver's side, which gun was
fully loaded (including one round in the chamber). On noting the found gun, subject
remarked –"I keep it there for protection." He was advised by Officer TANSKY that
he was under arrest.

At this time the following statement was read to the arrestee by Officer TANSKY -
"You have the right to remain silent. If you give up the right to remain silent,
anything you say can be used against you in a court of law. You have the right to
speak with an attorney and to have the attorney present during questioning. If you
so desire and cannot afford one, an attorney will be appointed for you without charge
before questioning."

Following the reading of the above admonition to suspect, he was then asked by
TANSKY whether he understood these rights. To this question suspect replied- "I am
well aware of my rights, I don't want an attorney, I'll tell you guys what you want to
know." Officer TANSKY then asked the suspect - What do we want to know? Suspect
replied - "About that ACME LIQUOR STORE job the other day, it's the only place I've
hit."

Suspect was transported to headquarters where he was booked by Officers TANSKY
and ROBERTS on the above charges, per Desk Sergeant HUNT #305.

The .38 cal. automatic (Colt) and cartridges (9), were identified by Officer TANSKY
with the initials "J-R," and booked by Officer TANSKY at headquarters crime lab.,
property tag No. 6642L. Suspect's vehicle was impounded at WILSON's GARAGE -
"Hold for Detectives."

instances, it is customary to create a full description on a separate continuation sheet entitled *Evidence Report*. This report should carry the name of the person arrested, the crime for which he or she was arrested, the booking number, and the case number. This evidence report should be attached to the arrest report. The arrest report should include the statement "See attached evidence report."

Injuries Associated With an Arrest   Persons arrested are sometimes injured during the arrest or have been injured in fights or accidents before the arrest. As a result, special attention is required to protect both the prisoner and the police agency. The injury or any illness noted should be described in the arrest report, and the medical or first-aid treatment administered at the scene should be listed. If the injury was the result of force used to overcome resistance to the arrest, outline the details of the force and the resulting injury in the narrative part of the arrest report. As soon as possible after the injury is discovered, if it is not minor, the prisoner should be examined by a licensed physician, since officers are not capable of determining the seriousness of illness or injury. Obtain photographs of any visible marks or bruises. Some departments have special forms for reporting injuries during an arrest. Recording injuries during an arrest serves two purposes: it protects prisoners, as it assures them of adequate medical examination; and it protects the police agency by recording approval by a competent medical authority of the prisoner's incarceration.

Property or Evidence Held in an Arrest   When evidence is held or property is impounded as part of an arrest, all items should be accurately identified and described so that they can be released to a suspect or victim when no longer needed. Property receipts should be issued whenever possible. If property taken from an arrestee is identifiable by number or inscription, it should be checked against the stolen-property file of the arresting agency or of other state and federal agencies when warranted. A list of property taken from a prisoner may serve to connect the prisoner with unsolved or uncleared crimes. When the suspect arrested has a vehicle, the disposition of the vehicle should be shown in the report—for example, "released to witness LOPEZ," "left at scene," "released to Boatman Towing," or "held for processing." Impound reports are prepared by many agencies to show the condition of vehicles when impounded.

Vehicle Accident Reports

Vehicle accident reports are an important source of information in a number of areas. First, in a traffic fatality, the vehicle accident report is part of a homicide investigation. As a result of such an investigation, a surviving driver may face aggravated vehicular homicide or vehicular homicide charges. Also, the families of the victims deserve a thorough investigation of the victims' deaths. Second, information from vehicle accident reports can help courts assess liability in personal-injury or property-damage cases. Third, enactment of traffic and vehicle safety laws often results from information gathered from accident reports. And fourth, many safety advances in vehicles, such as hydraulic brakes, safety glass, shock-absorbing bumpers, and air bags, as well as accident reduction techniques, result from accident investigation reporting and crash research.

Policies, laws, and ordinances dictate whether a written report must be made for every traffic accident that comes to a police department's attention. Most police agencies require a written report in accidents involving appreciable property damage, but do not require a report covering minor damage, such as a slightly dented fender. However, damage does not have to exceed a specified amount for an accident to constitute a traffic accident. The investigation and reporting of all known vehicle accidents in public places is suggested, since the only difference between a fatal accident and one involving only property damage is a matter of chance, a small difference in position or time, or a slight variation in speed. Information in a vehicle accident report must be written in such a way that anyone who refers to the report will have as much knowledge of the circumstances as the investigator does. The report must contain all facts about the accident.

A **vehicle accident report** is generally a form that supplies a detailed framework. The officer completes the form by filling in the blanks with the requested information and placing Xs in the appropriate boxes. Additional information about details or a summary is recorded on supplementary sheets, which are attached to the face sheet (front page). Figure 9–7 shows the first page of a sample vehicle accident report.

Vehicle accident report A police record created to document the events surrounding a vehicular accident.

The Completed Report

When a written report is completed, it is reviewed by the officer's immediate superior. In addition, it may be read by a number of others inside and outside the department. These persons may include the following:

- Department administrators
- The chief or sheriff
- Records clerks
- The court administrator
- Other law enforcement agencies
- Various assistant district attorneys
- The district attorney
- The grand jury (in jurisdictions where they apply)
- The defendant
- Defense counsel
- The trial judge
- Various court officials

Figure 9–7 Traffic accident report.

TRAFFIC COLLISION REPORT

SPECIAL CONDITIONS	NO. INJ. 1	H & R FELONY ☐	CITY Upland, Ca. 91786				JUDICAL DISTRICT		NO. 98-233T	
	NO. KILLED 0	H & R MISD. ☐	San Bernardino 92410	REPORTING DISTRICT		BEAT 5				

LOCATION

COLLISION OCCURED ON					MO. 1	DATE 24	YR. 98	TIME(2400) 0800		OFFICER I.D. 1408
☐ AT INTERSECTION WITH ☐ OR 40 FEET /MILES	S	OF	"A " Street				INJURY, FATAL OR TOW AWAY ☒ YES ☐ NO		STATE HWY ☐ YES ☒ NO	

PARTY 1	NAME (FIRST, MIDDLE, LAST) Robert Edward Young								STREET ADDRESS 845 Taylor St.		

DRIVER ☒	DRIVERS LICENSE D543104	Ca.	MO. 4	BIRTHDATE DAY 8	YR. 42	SEX M	RACE C	CITY Ontario,	STATE Ca. 91761	PHONE 555-4543
PEDES- TRAIN ☐	VEHICLE YR. 1992	MAKE Chev.	LICENSE NO. 129 SUZ					OWNER'S NAME	☒ SAME AS DRIVER	
PARKED VEH. ☐	DIRECTION OF TRAVEL N	ON/ACROSS (STREET OR HIGHWAY) 2nd Street						OWNER'S ADDRESS	☒ SAME AS DRIVER	
BI- CYCLIST ☐ OTHER ☐	SPEED LIMIT 35	DISPOSITION OF VEHICLE Towed to Wise's Garage	☐ BY DRIVER	ON ORDERS OF Driver		VEHICLE DAMAGE ☐ M INOR ☒ MOD. ☐ MAJOR ☐ TOTAL R. F. Fender			VIOLATION CHARGES 1_____ 2_____	

PARTY 2	NAME (FIRST, MIDDLE, LAST) Walter Joseph Murray								STREET ADDRESS 643 Broadway		

DRIVER ☒	DRIVERS LICENSE W533421	Ca.	MO. 9	DAY 15	YR. 70	SEX M	RACE C	CITY Ontario,	STATE Ca.	PHONE 555-4321
PEDES- TRAIN ☐	VEHICLE YR. 1992	MAKE Ford	LICENSE NO. 155 OLC	Ca.				OWNER'S NAME	☒ SAME AS DRIVER	
PARKED VEH. ☐	DIRECTION OF TRAVEL W	ON/ACROSS (STREET OR HIGHWAY) Private Drive to 2nd St.						OWNER'S ADDRESS	☒ SAME AS DRIVER	
BI- CYCLIST ☐ OTHER ☐	SPEED LIMIT	DISPOSITION OF VEHICLE Cared for	☒ BY DRIVER	ON ORDERS OF		EXTENT VEHICLE DAMAGE ☐ M INOR ☒ MOD. ☐ MAJOR ☐ TOTAL	LOCATION L.F. Fender		VIOLATION CHARGES 21804a VC 268483 VC	

PROPERTY

DESCRIPTION OF DAMAGE		
OWNER'S NAME	ADDRESS	NOTIFIED ☐ YES ☐ NO

INJURED/WITNESS

WITNESS ONLY	AGE	SEX	EXTENT OF INJURY				INJURED WAS (check one)					IN VEH. NUMBER
			FATAL INJURY	SEVERE WOUND DISTORTED MEMBER	OTHER VISIBLE INJURIES	COMPLAINT OF PAIN	DRIVER	PASS.	PED.	BI- CYCLIST	OTHER	
☐			☐	☐	☐	☒	☒	☐	☐	☐	☐	2

NAME Walter Joseph Murray   PHONE 555-4321
ADDRESS 643 Broadway, Ontario, Ca.   TAKEN TO (INJURED ONLY) Refused medical care

☐	☐	☐	☐	☐	☐	☐	☐	☐

NAME   PHONE 555-4321
ADDRESS   TAKEN TO (INJURED ONLY)

☐	☐	☐	☐	☐	☐	☐	☐	☐

NAME   PHONE
ADDRESS   TAKEN TO (INJURED ONLY)

SKETCH

(see page 3)

INDICATE NORTH

MISCELLANEOUS

Suggested:

Vehicle Description

and

Driver Description

(put in this

section)

VEHICLE TYPE			
PARTY 1	01	PARTY 2	01
ROAD TYPE			
A CONVENTIONAL, ONE WAY			
X B CONVENTIONAL, TWO WAY			
C EXPRESSSWAY			
D FREEWAY			
E OTHER (EXPLAIN IN NARRATIVE)			

555 (REV 11-93)

57698- 456 555 REV 11-93 500M OSP

Police reports carry information needed for making a wide variety of important decisions about the liberty of a suspect in a crime or the role of parties involved in an incident. Therefore, it is critical that they be forthright and accurate enough to withstand attacks from any quarter. Reports are the professional tool of law enforcement used in the administration of justice.

SUMMARY BY LEARNING OBJECTIVES

Learning Objective 1

Effective communication is essential in all police work. Written skills, as evidenced in good report writing, are among the most important tools in the investigation of crimes, apprehension of criminals, and prosecution of crimes.

Learning Objective 2

A well-structured police report contains all the essential information to answer the questions *who, what, when, where, how,* and *why* about a crime that has been committed.

Learning Objective 3

In addition to serving as a record of an investigation, a basis for prosecution, and an aid in developing a database of crime statistics, written reports can also help in making departmental decisions regarding resource and personnel allocation, as well as in assessing accountability within and outside the agency.

Learning Objective 4

A good police report has four characteristics: it is complete, containing all pertinent information; it is concise, presenting all essential features while eliminating nonessential details; it is clear, relating exactly what an officer saw, heard, and did; and it is accurate, concentrating on specifics and avoiding generalities.

Learning Objective 5

The structure and the content of police reports vary by department and agency, but most contain a number of common elements, including the following: names; race; sex; age; addresses; telephone numbers; descriptions of people, property, vehicles, and physical areas; dates; and times.

Police agencies tend to concern themselves with four basic categories of reports: internal reports, technical and specialized-equipment reports, intelligence reports, and operations reports. Operations reports are the type most often prepared by officers. They fall into these four categories: misdemeanor and/or miscellaneous reports, felony reports, arrest reports, and vehicle accident reports.

QUESTIONS FOR REVIEW

Learning Objective 1

1. How may poor oral or written skills adversely affect a criminal investigation?
2. Why might a prosecutor be concerned about how well police officers communicate in writing?

Learning Objective 2

3. What are the six basic elements of a well-written report?

Learning Objective 3

4. How could an investigative report help an officer testifying in court?

Learning Objective 4

5. What are the characteristics of a good report?
6. Why must a police report be concise?
7. Why must a police report be accurate?
8. What should officers be aware of concerning different cultures when writing names in their reports?
9. How should affected words be handled in reports?
10. What time is it in military time at three o'clock in the afternoon?

Learning Objective 5

11. Why is it important to include distinguishing characteristics of stolen property?
12. How much detail is enough when trying to identify a suspect?

Learning Objective 6

13. What is the difference between a felony report and a misdemeanor report?
14. When are vehicle accident reports written?
15. What are some of the purposes of vehicle accident reporting?

CRITICAL THINKING INVESTIGATIVE EXERCISES

1. Drop a small item of personal property (e.g., a ring, watch, pen, necklace, broach, or pin) into a large box that your instructor will provide. Then write a lost-property description of the "missing property." Be sure to include a value for each item. Read your property description aloud and see if your instructor or a fellow student can retrieve your "missing item" from the box.

2. The following is a narrative of a homicide written in an unacceptable manner. The report contains many unnecessary words and sentences. It contains accurate facts, but they are presented in an awkward fashion. Rewrite this report, correcting the various errors. Be certain to use good sentence structure, punctuation, and proper paragraphing and organization.

Narrative

On December 21, 1998 at four thirty in the afternoon, just before the sun began to set, officer Jack Jones was notified by Mrs. Janet Parson, the department dispatcher, that someone had been shot at the Giant Eagle supermarket, down the road from the Pressly Dry Cleaning store, in Indiana, Pa. The Giant Eagle is located on the West side of Wayne Avenue, and faces Getty street on the corner. Its address is 678 GETTY STREET. A white man was shot by another white man, according to several people who may have seen the crime, including Mark LaPage, who lives at 242 Sycamore Street, in the borough of Indiana, about 60 miles from Pittsburgh.

After having a cup of coffee, Officer Jack Jones, the reporting officer, got to the scene of the crime. He spoke with another witness, JUDY Wilson who said she could recognize the man who was shooting Mr. Peitry the Giant Eagle manager. The shooter was described as having a baseball cap on, so Judy couldn't see his hair color. He had on blue jeans, with the left back pocket torn off. A light brown colored jacket over a beige colored shirt that also had dark brown stripes on it. Judy told me that things happened to fast to get any more information or details about the murderer, but that she could recognize him if she saw him again, even thought she doesn't thing she has ever seen him before.

Mr. Gary Peitry was laying on the ground when Officer Jack Jones arrived. There was a lot of blood pooling around his head and several of the onlookers were turning kind of green. There was a star shaped entry wound by the neck and base of Mr. Peitry's head on the left side, just below his ear. There was an earing in Mr. Peitry's left ear, kind of a bluish or greenish stone. Mr. Peitry wasn't breathing, and Officer Jones could find no kind of a pulse, even though he looked for a few minutes. Mr. Peitry's body was laying on the East side of the parking lot, with his head facing Wayne avenue.

INVESTIGATIVE SKILL BUILDERS

Acquiring and Evaluating Information

You have been working as a small-town police officer for five years. You work in a college town, where the campus police number about 16. You have been working as one of the town police department's three investigators, a rotating position that each officer holds for 90 days at a time. During the current period, you have investigated several rapes, robberies, burglaries, and assaults. You have recently been asked to assist in the investigation of several rapes of young women attending the college. Two of these rapes actually occurred in dormitories on the campus, and two in your jurisdiction, in apartments.

The college is a medium-sized, four-year residential college. Approximately 12,000 students attend the school. The campus police serve largely as security guards and lack the capacity to conduct a criminal investigation.

You receive copies of the incident reports completed by the campus police and compare them with those you have completed. All the rapes have occurred at night. The assailant seems to choose women who are walking home alone from a night class. All of the rapes occurred as soon as the women had unlocked their doors. Each woman was rushed by someone who forced her into the dorm room or apartment, slapped her, brandished a knife, and then raped her.

The description of the attacker is sketchy, but all of the victims agree that the man was white, 20–25 years old, and five feet eight to five feet ten inches tall and that he wore an unusual, overpowering aftershave or cologne.

One morning as you sip your coffee and review the criminal reports, you receive a call from the campus police. They tell you that they think they have captured the rapist. You rush to the campus police office and are met by Officer Dave Martin. Officer Martin tells you, "It's the wildest thing I have ever seen. This guy came in this morning and told us he did it. That he was the rapist. We read him his rights, and he has already given us a statement." Martin hands you a written statement.

When you meet the man, you introduce yourself as a police officer and ask him his name. He tells you it is Jason Gibbson. Next you repeat his Miranda warnings and ask him if he is willing to talk with you. He tells you he is. You look over his statement and ask if he wrote it. He nods. The statement contains superficial information, the type anyone might have obtained from reading accounts in the campus or local newspaper. You ask him to tell you some details that were not in the papers. He becomes agitated and angry.

You take out the case reports and look through the evidence reports. You see that there is little physical evidence to connect anyone to the crime. There were no semen stains or samples, since the rapist wore a condom. Although the rapist slapped the victims, there were no real struggles, scratches, or blood samples. You ask Officer Martin whether Gibbson had any weapons on him when he came in. Officer Martin says he was carrying a knife. You ask to see it. The reports indicate that the rapist carried a folding pocketknife, but such knives are fairly common. Gibbson's knife is such a folding pocketknife. You sniff the air and notice that Gibbson has no particular scent. Yet all the victims agreed that the attacker was wearing an overpowering cologne or aftershave. You are not comfortable that this is your man.

1. Should you keep this man in custody?
2. What actions might you take to check whether Gibbson is the right suspect?
3. What sort of defense might Gibbson mount in court?

Decision Making

Using the information in the preceding story, answer the questions below:

1. Should you pursue the case, since Gibbson has already confessed?
2. What should you tell the victims, if anything?

Integrity/Honesty

Using the information in the preceding story, consider the questions below:

1. Should you mention to anyone else that Gibbson does not have the cologne smell, or should you wait to see if others notice that missing element on their own?
2. Since your evidence is largely circumstantial, and you are not really comfortable with Gibbson as a suspect, will you try to find another suspect?

ENDNOTES

1. Paul A. Godwin, "Painless Report Writing," *Law and Order,* Vol. 41, no. 2, 1993, pp. 38–42.
2. Maxine C. Hairston, *Successful Writing—Rhetoric for Advanced Composition,* W. W. Norton, New York, 1981.
3. Hans P. Guth, *New English Handbook,* 3rd ed., Wadsworth, Belmont, Calif., 1990.
4. U.S. Bureau of Justice Statistics, *Sourcebook of Criminal Justice Statistics,* 1994.

CHAPTER 10

Robbery

CHAPTER OBJECTIVES

After completing this chapter, you will be able to:

1. Provide an overview of the crime of robbery in the United States.

2. Explain the legal elements of the crime of robbery.

3. List and describe the main categories of robberies.

4. Name and describe the principal classes of robbers.

5. Enumerate basic procedures used in robbery investigations.

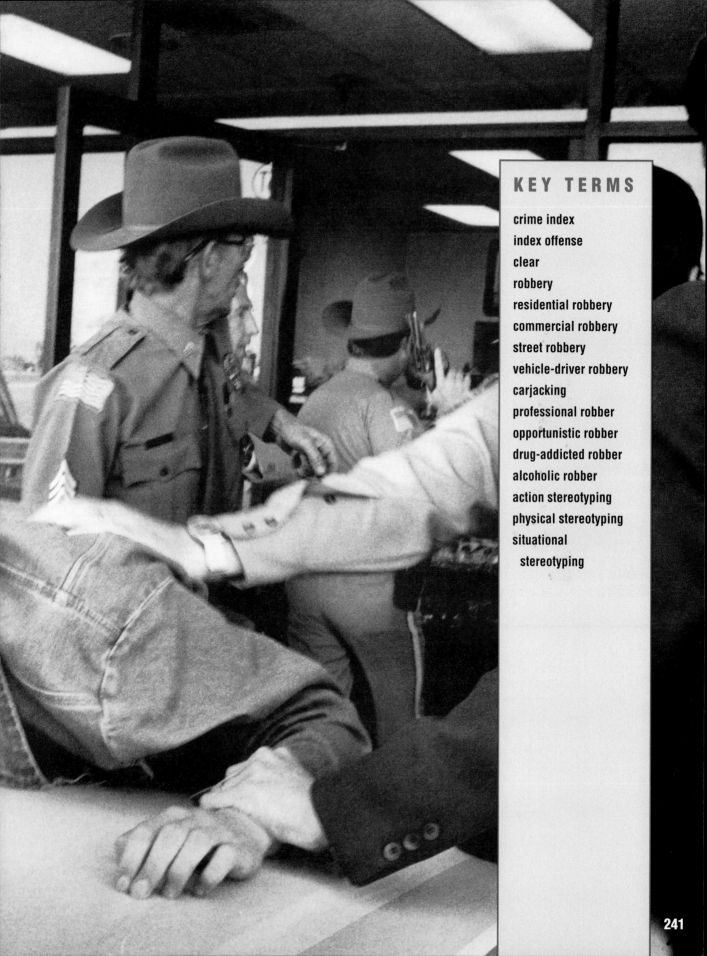

Overview of Robbery

Television and movies have created an image of robbers from yesteryear as romantic and colorful characters. Bonnie Parker and Clyde Barrow, John Dillinger, Baby Face Nelson, Bugsy Malone, Al Capone, to name but a few, all conjure up images of exciting and adventurous desperados. But these poorly cast folk heroes killed many people, exhibiting the violence of many robberies.

Robbery is a very serious crime that costs citizens and the government millions of dollars each year. The FBI has identified it as one of the eight most serious crimes in our society and reports yearly statistics on robbery in its Uniform Crime Reports (UCR). These reports track the fluctuations in the overall volume and rate for murder, rape, robbery, assault, burglary, larceny-theft, motor vehicle theft, and arson. The reported incidence of these crimes is combined to create the **crime index** (see Figure 10–1). Each of these offenses (except arson, because of problems with accurate reporting), because it is part of the crime index and because it is believed to be an important crime to track, is also referred to as an **index offense.** As Figure 10–2 shows, most index crimes are property crimes, not violent crimes.

Robbery is among the leading criminal problems facing law enforcement officers in America today. Perpetrators include people of every age group, occupation, social stratum, gender, and race. Perhaps the single characteristic linking persons who engage in robbery is the desire to obtain money or property without working or paying for it.

Robbery does not always involve only loss of money or property. Violence or the threat of violence often accompanies the commission of a robbery. In 1995, the UCR indicated that firearms were used in 41 percent of robberies, strong-arm tactics in another 41 percent, knives or cutting instruments in 9 percent, and other weapons in the remainder. Robberies are of major concern to law enforcement officials because of their economic effects; the fear, injury, and death they cause; and the difficulty of investigating and clearing them. For UCR purposes, law enforcement agencies

Crime index A collection of statistics in the FBI's Uniform Crime Reports on the numbers of murder, rape, robbery, assault, burglary, larceny-theft, motor vehicle theft, and arson crimes reported in a calendar year.

Index offense One of the eight crimes (murder, rape, assault, robbery, burglary, larceny-theft, motor vehicle theft, and arson) that the FBI considers the most serious which are combined to create the crime index.

Figure 10–1 The FBI Crime Index.

Crime Index	
Violent Crime	**Property Crime**
Murder and nonnegligent manslaughter Forcible rape Robbery Aggravated assault	Burglary Larceny-theft Motor vehicle theft Arson

Figure 10–2 Percentage distribution of crime index offenses.

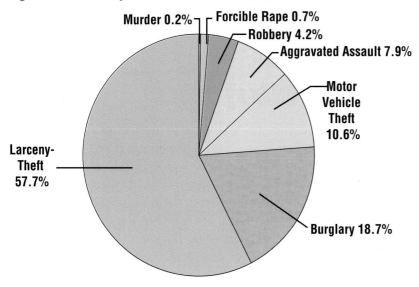

Murder 0.2%
Forcible Rape 0.7%
Robbery 4.2%
Aggravated Assault 7.9%
Motor Vehicle Theft 10.6%
Larceny-Theft 57.7%
Burglary 18.7%

Source: Federal Bureau of Investigation, *Crime in the United States,* Government Printing Office, Washington, 1995.

clear, or solve, a criminal offense when at least one person is arrested, charged with the crime, and turned over to the courts for prosecution.

Figure 10–3 provides a 16-year summary of robbery crime index totals reported by the FBI. It shows fluctuation in the number of rob-

Figure 10–3 Robbery crime index totals.

Year	Population	Crime Index Total	Number of Robbery Offenses
1980	225,349,264	13,408,300	565,840
1981	229,146,000	13,423,800	592,910
1982	231,534,000	12,974,400	553,130
1983	233,981,000	12,108,600	506,570
1984	236,158,000	11,881,800	485,010
1985	238,740,000	12,431,400	497,870
1986	241,077,000	13,211,900	542,780
1987	243,400,000	13,508,700	517,700
1988	245,807,000	13,923,100	542,970
1989	248,239,000	14,251,400	578,330
1990	248,709,873	14,475,600	639,270
1991	252,177,000	14,872,900	687,730
1992	255,082,000	14,438,200	672,480
1993	257,908,000	14,144,800	659,870
1994	260,341,000	13,989,500	618,950
1995	262,755,000	13,867,100	580,550

Source: Federal Bureau of Investigation, *Crime in the United States,* Government Printing Office, Washington, 1995.

beries reported. Although the number of reported robberies has decreased recently, robbery, because of its personal and often violent nature, remains one of the crimes the public most fears.

Legal Elements of Robbery

✗ **Robbery** The unlawful taking or attempted taking of another's personal property in his or her immediate possession and against his or her will by force or the threat of force.

Robbery is the unlawful taking or attempted taking of another's personal property in his or her immediate possession and against his or her will by force or threat of force. To legally qualify as robbery, *force* must be more than merely enough to remove the property. For robbery, force must be sufficient to overcome even slight resistance. *Fear* must be present. It may be (1) fear of threatened injury to the victim, the victim's property, or a relative of the victim; or (2) fear of immediate injury to the victim or the victim's property or to anyone in the immediate company of the victim at the time of the offense.

State statutes precisely define the crime of robbery. Some states have only one degree of robbery, while others have simple and aggravated. Some states even have first-, second-, and third-degree robbery. As an investigator, you should be familiar with the criminal definitions of robbery in your state and be able to recognize the *corpus delicti* of the crime. Generally, robbery is distinguished from theft or burglary in that it (1) involves the wrongful taking of personal property, (2) in the presence of or from the owner or person in control of the property, and (3) against the person's will, by force or the threat of force.

Categories of Robberies

In addition to knowing the elements of the crime of robbery, an investigator also should be familiar with the kinds of robberies. Robberies can be divided into four categories, depending on the *modus operandi* of the perpetrator. These categories include *residential robberies, commercial robberies, street robberies,* and *vehicle-driver robberies* or *carjackings.*

Residential Robberies

Residential robbery A robbery in which the target is a person in a private residence, hotel or motel room, trailer or mobile home, or other attached areas of a residence.

Residential robberies include those in which a perpetrator enters a home or a hotel or motel room and uses force against the occupant to steal money or valuables. In addition, such crimes include robberies committed in garages, trailers, mobile homes, and even elevators. Residential robberies are less frequent than other types of robberies. In 1995, they represented about 11 percent of all robberies in the UCR. It is not unusual for robber and victim to be at least acquainted and for the robber to have selected the victim because the robber believed there was money or valuables in the home. Even when victim and robber are not acquainted, the victim is likely to have been selected because of the robber's belief that valuables were kept at the home. In hotel or motel robberies, the robbers may gain their information from an employee who believes valuables may be found in the victim's room.

Perpetrators of residential robberies are typically armed with firearms, knives, or other weapons. In hotel, motel, garage, or elevator robberies, the crimes are swift and frequently involve violence.

Neither gang violence or residential robberies are new in the United States. However, one of the more recent incarnations of residential robbery—home invasion—presents law enforcement with a new twist. Beginning in 1990, there were reports that groups of young men were traveling around the country terrorizing selected community members. In Fairfax County, Virginia, police reported seven such home invasions during the first six months of 1990 alone. The interesting twist in these recent cases is that the *invaders* were young Asian men (largely in their twenties) who robbed Asian families. Their rationale for targeting such families was that Asians often distrust banks and therefore were likely to have large sums of money and jewelry in their homes.

These Asian home invaders operated in a very organized manner and usually worked in groups of two to nine people. Entrance into the victim's home varied. In some cases, entry was through an open door or window. In other cases, brute force was used to gain entry through the front door.

Home invaders are terroristic, using violence or threats of violence to intimidate the victims into submission. Their actions might include aiming guns at children and threatening to shoot or even firing warning rounds. Furthermore, invaders threaten to return and retaliate should the crime be reported.

Not all jurisdictions have had identical types of invaders recently. For example, in Florida, where home invasions have been increasingly common, the perpetrators are more often young African-Americans between the ages of 18 and 30. Although the general means of entry and intimidation are similar to those used by the roaming Asian gangs, the target families are more racially varied. Police in Florida report that much of the home invasion there is drug-related. Most of the gangs involved seek money to support the gang members' drug habits.

Thus, there is no reason to expect home invasion to be restricted to certain ethnic or cultural groups. Police agencies in many areas are working with community members to increase awareness of this growing problem.

Commercial Robberies

* **Commercial robbery** Robbery of a commercial location such as a bank, service station, restaurant, or convenience store.

Perhaps the most obvious **commercial robbery** is that of a bank. However, small businesses, service stations, convenience stores, bars, fast-food establishments, or any commercial houses or businesses open late at night or all night may be targets of commercial robbery. Commercial robbers may also invade restaurants or markets and rob patrons of their cash, jewelry, and other valuables.

With the exception of banks, commercial robberies usually occur toward the end of the week and in the twilight to early-morning hours, from around 6:00 P.M. to around 4:00 A.M. Stores where visibility from the street or lighting conditions are poor make good targets for robbery. Similarly, businesses near on and off ramps of highways are likely targets.

In an attempt to deter robbers, many small businesses use video cameras, armed guards, guard dogs, and alarm systems. Some have conspicuous signs indicating that all money is kept in a safe and that the employees do not have the combination or key.

With the exception of bank robbers, who may be either professional or amateur, a great many commercial robbers are experienced criminals. This means they are more likely to have previous police records and to be following an identifiable *modus operandi*.

> # FYI
>
> **B**ank robbery is both a federal and a state offense. United States Code Title 18, Section 2113, defines the elements of the federal crime of bank robbery. Thus, bank robberies are within the jurisdictions of the FBI and the state and the community where the crime occurred and are jointly investigated.

Street Robberies

* **Street robbery** Any of an assortment of robberies that occur in street settings.

Street robberies are likely to occur on public streets and sidewalks or in alleys and parking lots. Street robberies are generally fast and opportunistic. Often they occur so fast that the victim is unable to offer police anything but a vague general description of the offender. Many jurisdictions classify purse-snatching as robbery. A purse snatcher can run past the victim and grab her purse so quickly that she may never have an opportunity to clearly see her attacker.

In a street robbery, the victim may be injured when pushed to the ground or when struck as the robber flees. Street robbers may use weapons or rely on speed, a punch or shove, and the element of surprise to accomplish their robberies.

Elderly people are often the victims of street robberies because they are perceived as likely to offer little resistance. However, since street robberies are opportunistic, younger victims are also common.

In larger cities, where there are diverse immigrant groups, special problems arise, particularly among those illegally in the country. Persons who are in the country illegally are less likely to report being the victims of a robbery. A further complication may be fear or mistrust of the police left over from negative experiences in their native countries.

Vehicle-Driver Robberies

Vehicle-driver robberies may be committed against drivers of commercial vehicles, such as taxicabs, buses, long-haul trucks, delivery vans, armored trucks, and even package or messenger service trucks. With the exception of armored trucks and perhaps delivery vans, vehicles are typically robbed in the evening or at night.

Taxicab drivers are a likely robbery target because they can easily be lured to a location with a simple telephone call. Once the passenger enters the cab, he or she can direct the driver to a secluded spot and carry out the robbery. Many cab services have placed bulletproof barriers between the passenger and the driver. However, such a separation fails to accomplish anything if a single rider is permitted to sit in the front seat next to the driver!

Drivers of personal cars are also potential victims of vehicle robberies. When stopped at a light or a stop sign, a driver may be approached and robbed at gunpoint. In some cases, the robber may come from the passenger side of the car, smash the window and grab a purse carelessly left on the seat. Whenever a driver picks up a hitchhiker, the driver is inviting a robbery—if not a more serious assault or homicide. Sometimes robbers feign car trouble or an accident in order to lure a Good Samaritan to stop and assist. Once stopped, the motorist is robbed.

Armored-Car Robberies Armored-car robberies are in a slightly different class from other vehicle robberies. Usually, armored-car robberies are undertaken by professional criminals, are well-planned, and are accomplished with considerable speed and precision. By comparison, the robbery of most commercial vehicles is crude and more terroristic.

Carjacking In the early 1990s, the news media began reporting stories about a category of violent crime called carjacking. **Carjacking** involves the theft of an automobile from a driver, with the driver still in the car. This crime is similar to the hijacking of long-haul trucks or airplanes. The Pamela Basu case made *carjacking* a household word.

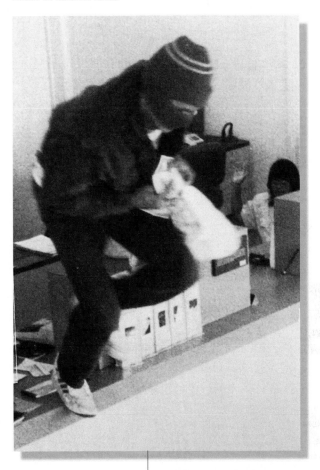

Bank robbers often use disguises to make it difficult for witnesses to describe them.

Vehicle-driver robbery Robbery of an object of value in or attached to a vehicle or from the driver of the vehicle.

Carjacking Robbery of a car with the driver and/or occupants still in it.

On Tuesday, September 8, 1992, two men hijacked Pamela Basu's car by pushing Mrs. Basu out of the vehicle at a stop sign. Entangled in her seat belt, Mrs. Basu was dragged for almost two miles after her vehicle was commandeered. Her 22-month-old daughter, who was strapped in a car seat, was tossed into the roadway a few blocks after the vehicle was seized. Mrs. Basu was killed, but her daughter survived the attack.

Another case that received national coverage was that of Sherri Foreman, a pregnant 29-year-old beautician who was stabbed by a carjacker while sitting in her 1984 BMW at an automated teller machine in Los Angeles, California. By the time she reached the hospital, her 12-week-old fetus was dead. A day later, so was Sherri Foreman.

In still other cases with wide media coverage, the public has heard about teenagers whose cars were taken at gunpoint and who were placed in their own car trunks until they were nearly dead. Carjackers have sometimes shot their victims even when the victims offered no resistance. Many Americans fear being victims of carjacking, because of the violence often associated with this crime.

Taxicab drivers are frequent targets of robberies because they can be lured to remote locations with a simple telephone call.

Carjackers use surprise and weapons to carry out their robberies. Sometimes they choose victims who are waiting for a light to change or who have stopped at a stop sign. Frequently, they strike in supermarket or shopping mall parking lots. What is even more frightening to potential victims is that carjackings occur randomly, at night or in the daytime. The violence now commonly associated with this crime is so widespread that extra guards, roaming patrols, and escort services have been added at many shopping malls.

In a further variation on carjacking, in April 1993, a series of unrelated *bump-and-stop* carjackings began in Florida. The initial targets were tourists driving rental vehicles. In the first of these crimes, Barbara Meller-Jensen, a German visitor, was driving from the airport in a rental car with her six-year-old son. Suddenly she felt her car being struck from behind. She pulled over to check things out and was grabbed by the drivers of the vehicle that had struck her. She was beaten to death and robbed as her son watched helplessly from the car.

Almost immediately, car rental agencies removed all telltale signs that vehicles were in a rental fleet. Also, the Florida legislature outlawed special license plates for rental and leased cars. In spite of all these efforts, and even of safety pamphlets telling tourists not to stop on lonely roads when they were bumped, the carjackings in Florida persisted.

The violence of carjacking has even struck police officers, suggesting that no one is safe from attack. As Randy Ballin, head of the California Highway Patrol's Los Angeles auto-theft unit has stated, "These people don't care who you are. They don't care that you are a cop and may be armed. They have nothing to lose. The criminal justice system is not a deterrent. It's a minor inconvenience."[1]

Carjacking is actually not a new crime. Bonnie and Clyde were carjackers. However, there have been several new twists. At one time, expensive cars were the usual targets of carjacking, which was a variation on car theft. However, recently the driver's cash and valuables have become the target in the crime. As a result, the actual make, model, and year of the car have less and less to do with the choice of a victim.

Carjacking has become a serious problem for law enforcement officers. It is investigated and treated as any other armed robbery would be. Many police agencies have worked with local chambers of commerce to produce pamphlets on techniques for guarding against carjacking. In October 1992, Congress passed the Anti-Car Theft Act. This legislation made carjacking a federal crime carrying a minimum 15-year sentence upon conviction and made it a crime for which the death penalty may be imposed if a victim is killed.

FYI

A carjacking takes only about 15 seconds. Nearly 70 carjackings occur each day in the United States.

Classification of Robbers

Recognizing the type of person who committed a robbery can help an investigator build a case. Robbers can be classified by their techniques, their motives, and even their worldview or outlook on life. Borrowing from a typology suggested by John Conklin we will classify robbers into these four groups: professional, opportunistic, drug-addicted, and alcoholic.[2]

Professional Robbers

Professional robbers have incorporated robbery into their lifestyles and have committed themselves to this crime form as a means of economic support. Professional robbers tend to plan and organize their crimes before committing them. Because professionals are well organized, they may divide up the tasks related to a robbery and may sub-

Professional robber A person who has incorporated robbery into a lifestyle and who robs as a means of economic support.

contract some of them to other professionals. For example, a driver for the getaway car may be engaged, as may an alarm specialist.

Professionals see robbery as their job, and they treat their criminal activities as others treat going to work. Many professionals are exclusively robbers, while others engage in various criminal endeavors. However, they take all their criminal involvements seriously. Typically, professional robbers are highly skilled at their chosen work and frequently carry weapons, which they are likewise skilled with. Professionals are likely to target large commercial establishments rather than mom-and-pop businesses.

Opportunistic Robbers

Opportunistic robber A person who steals small amounts of property or cash whenever the opportunity presents itself.

Opportunistic robbers are the most common. Opportunists typically steal small amounts of money whenever a likely target presents itself. Opportunists are likely to engage in a variety of other crimes of opportunity, such as shoplifting, petty theft, and larceny. Hence, opportunistic robbers are seldom committed to robbery as a career in the way professionals are. Opportunists tend to be young minority-group members, frequently gang-involved and seldom well organized or highly skilled. They spend little time organizing or planning a robbery and generally do not use weapons.

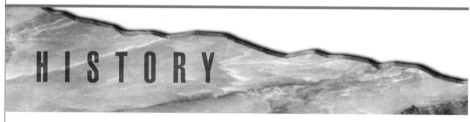

The FBI began collecting and dispensing the Uniform Crime Reports (UCR) in 1930. In that year, 400 cities, representing 20 million inhabitants, participated. In 1995, reporting agencies representing 251 million inhabitants, or 95 percent of the population, provided crime data to the FBI.

Drug-Addicted Robbers

Drug-addicted robber A person who robs to sustain an addiction to some type of illegal drug.

Another large category of robbers is made up of drug addicts. **Drug-addicted robbers** typically rob to support their drug habits. Addicted robbers have a relatively low commitment to robbery per se. They see it simply as a means of getting money to buy drugs. Because robbery is more dangerous than other forms of crime, addicts resort to it less often than other forms of criminal activity, such as theft or burglary. Addicted robbers tend to be desperate and careless in their handling of a robbery and may choose their targets poorly. They are seldom interested in a planned or organized *big score* and usually seek only enough money to purchase their next drug fix.

Alcoholic Robbers

Like addicted robbers, **alcoholic robbers** tend to be disorganized and opportunistic. Some alcoholic robbers attribute their crimes to a state of alcohol-induced disorientation. Others may simply engage in robbery as a method of obtaining money for alcohol, much as addicts seek funds for drugs. In some cases, alcoholics whose condition has caused them to lose their jobs, may engage in robbery as a method of economic support. More commonly, however, alcoholic robbers are not committed to robbery, are not very skilled at it, seldom plan their crimes in advance, and haphazardly choose their victims. Alcoholic robbers are among the most likely to be apprehended, owing to their generally disorganized and haphazard attitudes toward the robberies. Some alcoholic robbers may be impelled to rob by forces similar to those that impel them to drink alcohol abusively.

Alcoholic robber A person who robs to sustain an addiction to alcohol or who attributes criminal actions to the influence of alcohol.

Investigation of Robberies

Robbery has a comparatively low rate of clearance by arrest. The UCR indicates that the 1995 clearance rate for robbery was 25 percent nationally. A number of things hamper the investigation of robberies and contribute to this low rate of clearance. For instance, physical evidence may not be found, the crimes are often committed swiftly, and victims and witnesses are frequently so terrified that they cannot provide much of a description or other information.

When the police are informed of a robbery, the robber has usually left. In some situations, however, as in the case of silent alarms, the police are informed while the robbery is in progress. In either case, once the police are aware that a robbery has occurred, *time* becomes a critical factor. The lag between a robbery's commission and its being reported to the police, the response time of the police, and the number of personnel devoted to a particular robbery—all affect the potential for successfully solving the crime.

Response and Approach to the Robbery Scene

Because circumstances vary, procedures or strategies for investigating robberies must be flexible. An in-progress robbery reported through a silent alarm justifies an "all-units" emergency response. All-units broadcasts are justified by police incidents that involve violence, physical danger, or the presence of a felony suspect at the scene. The obvious reason for an all-units call is to ensure that police units arrive at the scene as quickly as possible. It is the radio dispatcher's job to direct enough units to the scene and to identify the unit closest to the location.

En route to the crime scene, officers should make sure that all available information has been received accurately from the dispatcher. Such information should include the address of the location and, if known, whether the robbery is still in progress, how many suspects there are, what sort of weapon was shown or used, and whether there is any description of the suspect or suspects.

As an officer approaches the scene, he or she must be alert for a number of possibilities:

The primary objectives of an officer arriving on the scene of a robbery are to ensure the public's safety, protect all police officers involved, and control the scene of the crime.

- A fleeing suspect may be lurking in a doorway, walking on the sidewalk, or feigning interest in the activities of the police.

- A fleeing suspect may open fire on approaching officers.

- The dispatcher may provide information on the direction in which a suspect fled or the type of vehicle the suspect used to escape.

- The officer may notice evasive actions by another driver or by pedestrians, suggesting implication in the robbery.

In addition, it is a good practice to shut off the siren and red lights when in the vicinity of the robbery, to avoid warning the suspects. An exception is when the dispatcher has indicated *an officer in need of assistance* or *an officer down.*

An officer arriving on the scene of a robbery has three primary objectives: public safety, officer protection, and control over the scene. Investigating officers should be alert, curious, and identification-conscious. Officers should proceed cautiously until the true situation is known and should avoid action stereotyping, physical stereotyping, and situational stereotyping.[3]

Action stereotyping occurs when an officer misreads common or stereotypic behaviors of people at or near a crime scene. For example, a person may call out to the officer, saying, "Everything is OK," but may not be telling the truth. The apparently helpful person may actually be the robber. Or, perhaps the bandit has forced an employee to make the statement in an attempt to fool the police. It may be wise and cautious to call people from where they are and talk with them alone. This can help ensure that the person talking is not literally under the gun of the bandit. Any strange actions on the part of employees at a robbery scene should be cause for suspicion and should be investigated.

In the absence of a physical description of a suspect, officers must avoid possible **physical stereotyping,** that is, expecting that a robber is a certain type of person. The expectation that a convenience store robber is a young male member of a minority group may allow the middle-aged, white, female robber to escape unnoticed.

In a similar manner, **situational stereotyping,** or mistaken conclusions from the appearance of a situation, can create serious problems in a robbery investigation. Even if a jewelry store owner is a nervous person who has previously triggered several false silent alarms, this time it may be the Real McCoy. The misuse of silent alarms in many jurisdictions is handled by fines and sometimes by suspension of privileges. However, whenever a silent alarm is received, it must be handled diligently and with all necessary precautions. In some jurisdictions, a silent alarm results in a telephone call to the store for a predetermined false alarm code. If the code cannot be given or is given incorrectly, police are dispatched.

Action stereotyping
Misreading of common or stereotypic behaviors of people at or near a crime scene who may actually be the offenders.

Physical stereotyping A misconception that a criminal is a certain type of person.

Situational stereotyping
False or mistaken conclusions from the appearance of certain situations.

Duties at the Scene

The order of investigative activities in robbery cases is dictated by the facts of each situation. In all crimes, however, patrol officers typically are the first to arrive at the scene, and they have certain responsibilities. These responsibilities include apprehending the suspect, if possible; securing the names, addresses, and telephone numbers of all witnesses and victims as soon as possible; and safeguarding any evidence.

The first officers to arrive at the scene should conduct brief interviews with all parties concerned. Using this information, they should transmit the initial broadcast data as quickly as possible. As previously mentioned, time is the enemy of the investigator in a robbery case. The sooner robbery information is broadcast, the greater the likelihood of other officers' spotting a fleeing robber. The information needed for the initial broadcast includes the following:

- Type of robbery.
- Type of premises.
- Location of occurrence.
- Time of occurrence.
- Number of suspects.
- Gender of suspects.
- Race of suspects.
- Direction suspects are believed to be heading.
- How suspects left the scene (on foot, by car, by bicycle, etc.).
- Description of the escape vehicle.
- Type of weapon used, if any.

As soon as possible, a supplemental broadcast should be made. The supplemental broadcast should contain a detailed description of the suspects, including clothing worn, any visible characteristics, and any special equipment that might have been carried. The vehicle used in the escape should be described as completely as possible, including color, make and model, and any noticeable damage (e.g., crushed fenders, broken lights, or rusted areas). A supplemental broadcast should also be issued to advise other officers if a previous robbery call was a false alarm.

Witness Descriptions and Identification of the Suspect

The various strategies discussed in Chapter 2 regarding identification of a suspect are relevant here. If a suspect can be located and apprehended in a short time (perhaps 15 or 20 minutes), he or she may be immediately taken back to the crime scene for identification. Alternatively, victims and witnesses may be transported to where the suspect is

Computer Imaging System Sophisticated software makes it possible to generate a likeness of a suspect from a victim's or a witness's description. A sketch is automatically assembled from a stored library of thousands of features on the basis of the description given. The initial sketch can then be modified to portray unique characteristics.

being held. If a suspect is not found for several hours, a photo lineup may be used to secure a positive identification.

To expedite obtaining information from witnesses at the scene of a robbery, some police agencies use a standardized form to record witness data. A form, however, is not intended to replace a face-to-face interview. Rather, it is a means for quickly obtaining some basic information. Forms can be especially useful when police personnel are in short supply and there are many witnesses or victims.

Preserving the Crime Scene

Preserving the crime scene, as described in Chapter 3, is the responsibility of the first officer who arrives. All available evidence must be safeguarded if it is to be useful in the investigation. Only those officers whose presence is necessary should enter the immediate crime scene area. Officers involved in collecting evidence should not move any items until notes are made, photographs are taken, sketches are drawn, and measurements are recorded.

Often robberies leave little physical evidence for the police to use. However, in some cases, investigators may find useful footprints, fingerprints, or discarded articles belonging to the robber. Since, however, eyewitnesses may change their testimonies, a search for physical evidence should be undertaken at any robbery scene. The actual nature and extent of a search for evidence depends on the type of property taken, the location of the robbery, and the kind of articles or materials involved. In a bar or restaurant, for example, investigators might ask whether the robber sat down and, if so, where? The counter or tabletop could produce useful fingerprints, as could the menu or the salt and pepper shakers or the glass of water he or she may have drunk from. In a convenience store robbery, one might examine the front doors to see if the subject has left prints on the glass or handle. All physical evidence must be collected in accordance with department policy and recorded and transferred according to strict guidelines for chain of possession.

Surveillance Cameras and Robbery Investigations

As already suggested, physical evidence in robberies is often scant. Sometimes, however, an establishment that has been robbed has a surveillance camera that was operating during the robbery. The tape from such a camera can be an important tool for identifying the suspects and can serve as evidence in court after their apprehension.

Hidden surveillance cameras have been used successfully in banks, large department stores, and even small convenience stores. Provided they have been installed and positioned properly and the lighting is adequate, surveillance cameras can provide investigators with particularly useful information.

SUMMARY BY LEARNING OBJECTIVES

Learning Objective 1

Robbery is a very serious crime that costs citizens and the government millions of dollars each year. Robbery is one of eight crimes that the FBI considers the most serious crimes in American society. The FBI reports yearly statistics on robbery in its Uniform Crime Reports (UCR). In 1995, robbery made up 4.2 percent of the crimes reported in the UCR. Although the percentage of robbery crimes is low, robbery is a crime feared by many people because of its potential for violence.

Learning Objective 2

State statutes precisely define what constitutes the crime of robbery in each state. Generally, these statutes have the following elements in common: Robbery (1) is the wrongful taking of personal property (2) in the presence of or from the owner or person in control of the property and (3) against the person's will by use of force or the threat of force.

Learning Objective 3

Robberies can be divided into four categories: residential, commercial, street, and vehicle-driver.

Learning Objective 4

Robbers can be divided into four types: professional, opportunistic, drug-addicted, and alcoholic.

Learning Objective 5

Because the circumstances of the crime vary, any procedures or strategies used in investigating a robbery must be flexible. En route to the crime scene, officers should make sure all information available has been received accurately from the dispatcher. The responding officer should check the address of the location and, if known, whether the robbery is still in progress, how many suspects there are, what sort of weapon was shown or used, and whether there is any description of the suspects. The three primary objectives of an officer arriving on the scene of a robbery are (1) public safety, (2) officer protection, and (3) control over the crime scene.

QUESTIONS FOR REVIEW

Learning Objective 1

1. Why do many Americans especially fear being robbed?
2. Robbery is considered an *index offense*. What does that mean?

Learning Objective 2

3. What are two key elements that distinguish *robbery* from *theft?*
4. How much force must be used to qualify as an element of robbery?
5. What kind of fear is necessary for the crime of robbery?
6. What are the legal elements necessary for a crime to be classified as a *robbery?*

7. How would you classify the robbery of someone living in a trailer?

8. If the patrons of a doughnut shop are robbed during broad daylight, how would you classify this crime?

9. Why do some jurisdictions classify purse snatching as a street robbery?

10. Why do street robbery victims sometimes offer little information about their attackers?

11. Why are taxicabs frequent targets of vehicle robberies?

12. How is a carjacking different from a car theft?

Learning Objective 4

13. What may motivate an alcoholic robber to commit robbery?

14. Describe some characteristics of a professional robber.

Learning Objective 5

15. What is meant by *action stereotyping?*

16. When is a supplemental broadcast sent?

17. How might a surveillance camera aid in the investigation of a bank robbery?

CRITICAL THINKING INVESTIGATIVE EXERCISE

Divide into several small groups of no more than five or six persons. Read the scenario that follows, and devise a group response to the question. Compare your group's response with that of other groups.

You and your fellow officer have just responded to a robbery call at a supermarket. Upon arriving at the scene, the two of you split up. While conducting an immediate investigation, you are confronted by a robbery suspect, who has surprised and disarmed your partner. The suspect shouts angrily for you to drop your gun and threatens to kill your partner if you do not comply. What will you do?

INVESTIGATIVE SKILL BUILDERS

Problem Solving

You answer a robbery-in-progress call at a drugstore. When you arrive, a middle-aged man wearing a white lab coat is behind the counter. He assures you that the call must have been a prank or a false alarm and that everything is fine. What should you do before leaving?

Integrity and Honesty

You have been working a foot-patrol beat for several months. During that time you have regularly eaten your lunch at Big John's Diner. Normally, when you eat at the diner, you receive your bill and pay it like any other customer. However, last week you foiled an armed robbery at the diner. To show his appreciation, Big John has told you that he really does not want you to pay for your meals there. Today, when you leave the money for your lunch, Big John comes running after you with the money. He pushes it back at you and says, "If you keep paying for your meals, I am going to be insulted." How should you handle this situation?

ENDNOTES

1. Kevin Fedarko, "Miami's Tourist Trap," *Time,* September 20, 1993, p. 71.

2. John Conklin, *Robbery and the Criminal Justice System,* Lippincott, New York, 1972.

3. Jerry W. Baker and Carl P. Florez, "Robbery Response," *The Police Chief,* Vol. 47, no. 10, 1980, pp. 46–47.

CHAPTER 11

Assault

CHAPTER OBJECTIVES

After completing this chapter, you will be able to:

1. Provide an overview of the crime of assault.

2. Explain the legal elements of the crime of assault.

3. Enumerate basic procedures used in assault investigations.

4. List and describe forms of domestic assault.

KEY TERMS

assault
battery
simple assault
aggravated (felonious)
  assault
stalking
restraining order
domestic assault
complacency
citizen's arrest
intrafamily violence
domestic violence
  statute
child abuse
battered child
  syndrome

Overview of Assault

An assault is an unlawful attempt or threat to commit a physical injury to another through use of force. In 1995, the FBI reported nearly 1.1 million assaults, indicating a decrease of approximately 1 percent from the preceding year. As Figure 11–1 shows, the number of aggravated assaults decreased for the second consecutive year. Also showing a decrease in 1995 were three of the four categories of weapons. Personal weapons (hands, fists, feet) showed the only increase. In 1995, firearms were the weapon of choice in 22.9 percent of all aggravated assaults, knives or cutting instruments in 18.3 percent, and personal weapons in 25.9 percent. The remaining 32.9 percent involved other weapons, such as clubs and blunt objects. Figure 10–2, in the preceding chapter, shows that aggravated assault made up 7.9 percent of crimes reported in the Uniform Crime Reports (UCR) in 1995, making it the most frequent of the crimes against people.

Figure 11–1 Aggravated assault crime index totals.

Year	Population	Crime Index Total	Number of Aggravated Assault Offenses
1980	225,349,264	13,408,300	672,650
1981	229,146,000	13,423,800	663,900
1982	231,534,000	12,974,400	669,480
1983	233,981,000	12,108,600	653,290
1984	236,158,000	11,881,800	685,350
1985	238,740,000	12,431,400	723,250
1986	241,077,000	13,211,900	834,320
1987	243,400,000	13,508,700	855,090
1988	245,807,000	13,923,100	910,090
1989	248,239,000	14,251,400	951,710
1990	248,709,873	14,475,600	1,054,860
1991	252,177,000	14,872,900	1,092,740
1992	255,082,000	14,438,200	1,126,970
1993	257,908,000	14,144,800	1,135,610
1994	260,341,000	13,989,500	1,113,180
1995	262,755,000	13,867,100	1,099,180

Source: Federal Bureau of Investigation, *Crime in the United States,* Government Printing Office, Washington, 1995.

Legal Elements of the Crime of Assault

At one time, in many states, the term **assault** referred to threats of or attempts to cause bodily harm. The term **battery** referred to the actual carrying out of these threats of physical harm. Actual physical contact is not required for an assault to have taken place. The mere threat or fear of an attack coupled with the ability to carry it out is sufficient.

Today, most states have revised their statutes, and the term *assault* is used synonymously with *battery,* or the once separate crimes have been combined in a single crime called *assault.* Some states do, however, still have separate statutes for assault and battery. You should, therefore, be aware of your state's particular statutes. In this chapter, we use the term *assault* to include the more serious crime of battery.

Classification of Assaults

Assaults are frequently divided into two general categories: *simple assault* and *aggravated assault* (or *felonious assault*).

Simple Assault   **Simple assault** can be defined as the intentional causing of fear, in another person, of immediate bodily harm or death. It also may include intentionally inflicting or attempting to inflict bodily harm on another person. Simple assault is usually a misdemeanor. Although different jurisdictions may have slightly varying statutes, most share several common elements:

1. Intent to do bodily harm to another individual.
2. Actual and present ability to do bodily harm.
3. Commission of some overt act demonstrating intent to carry out the assault.

The basic purpose of the first element is to assure that an *accident* did not cause the injury and that the person acted intentionally. For instance, while a person is trying on a pair of tight-fitting driving gloves in a department store, his or her hand slips and strikes another person who is trying on gloves. The striking is an accident and therefore not legally an assault.

The second element assures that the accused person was physically capable of committing the act at the time. For example, someone throwing a baseball at the head of a person 800 yards away does not really have the ability to hit his or her victim.

The third element assures that more than an empty threat or meaningless gesture occurred or was perceived. If a subject was in range of striking another, and took a menacing step in the direction of the would-be victim with his or her fists clenched, an assault can be proved—even if a third party interrupted the act by stepping between the other two.

Assault   An unlawful attempt or threat to commit a physical injury to another through use of force.

Battery   Once, used to refer to the actual carrying out of the threat of physical harm in an assault; today, in most jurisdictions, the term is synonymous with *assault.*

Simple assault   The intentional causing of fear in a person of immediate bodily harm or death.

Aggravated (felonious) assault An unlawful attack on another person with the intention of causing severe bodily harm.

Aggravated Assault In an **aggravated assault,** an individual unlawfully attacks another person with the intention of causing severe bodily harm. Aggravated assaults are considered felonies. An aggravated assault must include all three elements of a simple assault, with a fourth additional element:

4. Intentional infliction of bodily harm that has resulted in one or more of the following:

   a. Sufficient injury to cause a high probability of death.

   b. Severe physical disfigurement.

   c. Permanent loss or prolonged impairment of the use or function of any body part or organ, or any severe injury to the body.

Aggravated assaults are usually committed with a weapon that is likely to produce serious injury or a potentially fatal wound. Thus, if a blow to the head with a golf club is sufficient to cause unconsciousness, the blow is classified as an aggravated assault. A knife or gunshot that causes massive bleeding is likewise considered an aggravated assault. The loss of an eye after a severe trauma, such as being struck by a fist or club, makes the striking an aggravated assault. Finally, maiming, such as inflicting a wound that results in the loss of an arm or a leg, is also considered aggravated assault.

Any one of these additional elements changes the assault from simple to aggravated. In some jurisdictions, the statutes do not require actual damage to the body to shift from simple to aggravated assault. In these states, it is sufficient that the attacker employed a weapon that caused another to fear or expect immediate harm or death.

STATISTICS

The FBI's UCR for 1995 showed that 7 of every 10 violent-crime arrests were for aggravated assault. Of more than 437,000 arrestees, whites made up 60 percent, blacks 38 percent, and all other races the remainder. Eighty-two percent of the arrestees were male, and 85 percent adults. Nationwide, during 1995, law enforcement agencies recorded a 56 percent clearance rate for aggravated assaults.

Stalking: A New Assault Technique

Stalking Intentionally and repeatedly following, attempting to contact, harassing, or intimidating another person.

Stalking is behavior in which a person "intentionally and repeatedly follows, attempts to contact, harasses, and/or intimidates another person."[1] Although some stalkers are enamored with famous people, the majority are estranged husbands or boyfriends. In the United States, 90 percent of the women murdered by their boyfriends or husbands were first stalked by them.

Restraining order Court order requiring a person to do or refrain from doing a particular thing.

Traditionally, most police agencies have responded to stalking by recommending that the victim seek a **restraining order.** Until recently, however, restraining orders were really not worth the ink they were printed with. In 1994, Colorado led the way by passing a domestic violence act that includes arrest for violating a restraining order. Also, a number of states have established specific stalking laws, which make it a crime to persistently follow or annoy another person.

Investigators should be aware of the appropriate statutes in their jurisdictions pertaining to stalking, intimidation, threats, and domestic assault. When dealing with stalkers or domestic violence, investigators should encourage victims to make police reports of assaults or harassment. Officers may also want to provide victims with local telephone numbers for counseling and battered women's shelters.

Investigating Assaults

In many assault cases, the assailant and the victim know each other well or are at least acquainted with one another. Every year, the Bureau of Justice Statistics conducts a national survey of the victim-offender relationship in crimes of violence. Information from the 1994 survey indicates that 7 percent of the aggravated assaults were between relatives, 21 percent involved victims and assailants who knew each other well, and 12 percent involved casual acquaintances. These three categories made up 40 percent of the aggravated assaults reported in 1994.

Domestic assault Any type of battery that occurs between individuals who are related or between individuals and their significant others.

The relationship between parties in an assault can create certain investigative problems. Friends or relatives may be unwilling to file a complaint against an assailant. In addition, it is difficult to tell who is the victim in some assaults. This is particularly true when a fight has occurred. Furthermore, responding to an assault call—especially between family members—can be particularly dangerous for the officers.

Usually, patrol officers make the initial response to an assault call. According to the UCR, each year more officers are injured and killed answering assault and **domestic assault** (assault between family members) calls than calls for almost any other category of crime. Officers must use extreme caution when answering assault calls.

Investigating assault cases has a number of dangers. For example, officers frequently arrive on the scene when the parties are in heated emotional states or in the middle of a fight. The officer's immediate task is to take control of the situation, separate the parties, and check for injuries. If injuries are found, they should be treated with first aid, and if needed, appropriate medical personnel should be summoned.

Next, the officer should find out what happened and try to determine who is an assailant

Pro football running back Lawrence Phillips appears with his attorney after his release from jail for violating his probation from the 1995 assault on Nebraska basketball player Kate McEwen.

and who is a victim. It is important that the officer remain emotionally detached and not take sides in a dispute. Arguments and problems arising from simple assaults are not always all that simple. The assault may be the culmination of a long history of complicated disagreements. Moreover, what an officer sees immediately upon arriving is not always what it seems. A wounded or unconscious person lying on the couch may not be the victim. It may be the assailant, overcome by the victim.

Complacency Unconcern resulting from having grown accustomed to a given pattern of events or behavior.

A second danger to officers investigating assaults is **complacency,** or taking things for granted. Officers on patrol sometimes grow accustomed to being sent to a particular address for a domestic violence call. Because they have been there before and feel they know the parties involved, they become careless. Officers must stay guarded and alert whenever answering assault calls. The victim of domestic violence can quickly shift gears and become an ally to the attacker when the police arrive. Suddenly, both parties may be attacking the officer.

After carefully separating, interviewing, and checking the suspect and the victim, the officer should determine whether a crime has occurred and whether the assault is simple or aggravated. Next, the officer must determine whether an arrest is warranted. A simple assault committed outside the officer's presence is a misdemeanor, and the victim must file a complaint for action to be taken. The officer should advise the victim that he or she can file a complaint against the assailant, and the officer should explain how to file one. In some jurisdictions, the victim can even make a private person's arrest—often called a **citizen's arrest.** Officers can assist the victim in making such an arrest, if that is the victim's desire. If necessary, refer the victim to appropriate social service agencies for follow-up counseling or assistance.

Citizen's arrest An arrest by a private citizen, as contrasted with a police officer, permitted under certain circumstances, generally for a felony or for a misdemeanor amounting to a breach of the peace.

When investigating an aggravated assault, investigators must be sure to obtain all facts relative to a complaint. As in other criminal investigations, a series of ordered steps can be suggested for investigating aggravated assaults:

- Render first aid if needed and determine the need for additional medical support.

- Determine whether a crime has been committed. If so, what specific crime or crimes?

- Protect the crime scene. Follow the usual procedures for finding and securing evidence. Two important pieces of evidence are photographs of the injuries and the weapon used in the assault.

- Identify and locate witnesses, victims, and suspects. Keep all parties separated so that in interviews, they will state their own observations and accounts.

- Identify and arrest the assailant, if possible. Or determine whether a fresh pursuit would be of value and whether the suspect is even in the vicinity.

- Initiate a radio broadcast of the suspect's description, including any other pertinent information.

Domestic Assault

Many of the nation's assaults occur between family members. **Intrafamily violence,** as many sociologists now call this phenomenon, has become a serious and perplexing problem in the United States in recent years. Assaults by strangers often occur in public places, such as the street, a store, a park, or a parking lot. Such crimes are preventable through police patrols or other police intervention strategies. Domestic assaults usually occur in private residences and were believed to be largely inaccessible to police. As a result, the police were thought to be unable to do anything to prevent them, unless summoned by one of the parties.

In a study published in 1977, the Police Foundation examined domestic assaults and domestic homicides that occurred in Kansas City, Missouri, during a two-year period. It discovered that in the two years preceding a reported domestic assault or homicide, the police had been called to the address of the incident five or more times in half of the cases.[2] In short, in a number of instances, police intervention may reduce or prevent intrafamily violence. Failure to take more serious action than arriving on the scene has caused many states to adopt laws that mandate an arrest in apparent domestic assault cases.

In another study, the researchers found that when police made an arrest, the suspect was less likely to assault his spouse or girlfriend again than if the police merely gave advice or ordered him to leave the premises.[3] The study concluded that in cases of domestic assault, whenever possible, officers should make an arrest unless there is a clear reason to believe an arrest would be counterproductive.

A third study, which examined whether calling the police had any impact on subsequent violence in domestic assault cases, found that it did.[4] Calling the police was associated with lower rates of subsequent violence. Moreover, even when violence *did* occur after a call to the police, it was no more serious than violence against women who had not called the police.

Taken together, these studies strongly suggest that police can reduce intrafamily violence. It is important that officers consider carefully whether they should or should not make an arrest on a domestic assault call. As will be discussed, in some jurisdictions, this decision is backed by statutes.

Assaults Against Spouses

The shadowy figures of death and mayhem related to domestic assaults and homicides have always been with us. They came to the fore-

Intrafamily violence Any type of violent behavior that occurs within a family.

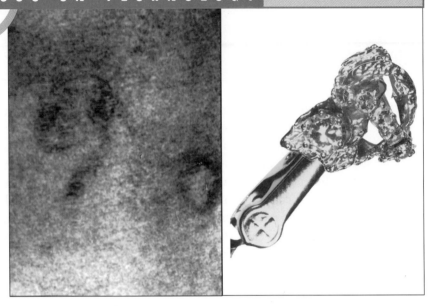

Reflective Ultraviolet Photography   A photographic technique can record visibly healed injuries to flesh and bring more definition to a visibly mottled area of irritation on the skin. The technique is useful in documenting pattern injuries in child abuse and assault cases where there has been a delay in reporting the crime, evidence of injury has faded or disappeared visibly, or to document prior abuse. Using a Kodak 18A filter, film is exposed to ultraviolet light allowing the photographic image to reveal seemingly invisible injuries.

Reflective ultraviolet photography can document two identifiable conditions. Melanocytes, the cells that produce pigment or melanin, are located in the base layer of the epidermis which is the outer layer of skin. When the skin is irritated, these cells produce excess melanin, causing hyperpigmentation, or abnormally increased coloration. This condition appears as darker areas than the surrounding flesh on photographic prints. A traumatic injury causes the melanocytes to reduce or stop producing melanin for a period of time. The result is hypopigmentation, or abnormally decreased coloration. This condition appears lighter than the surrounding flesh on photographs. This technology has been used to document bite marks up to nine months after healing.

LEFT: Invisible pattern injury on two-year-old boy; RIGHT: Reversed image of a unique ring matched to victim's injury.

front in 1994 with the enormous media coverage of the O. J. Simpson murder trial and allegations of Simpson's spousal abuse throughout his marriage to Nicole Brown Simpson. The Simpson case showed many American women that clinging to destructive relationships can place them in dire jeopardy.

In New York, only weeks after the murder of Nicole Simpson, the state legislature unanimously passed a sweeping bill that mandates arrest for any person who commits a domestic assault. In 1994, Colorado put into operation one of the toughest anti-domestic-violence laws in the country. Not only are police officers required to take assailants in domestic assaults into custody at the scene of violence, but they are also required to arrest a subject for a first-time violation of a restraining order! Subsequent violations of the restraining order carry mandatory jail time. In many ways, domestic violence coalitions across the country used the media coverage of the O. J. Simpson trial to educate the public on domestic assault and homicides.[5]

Slightly more than a third of all visits to emergency rooms by women are for injuries that occur during a domestic assault. Although some studies have found that some women are just as likely to start a fight as men, many other studies indicate that women are six times as likely to be seriously injured in a fight. In 1992, the American Medical Association, along with the Surgeon General, declared that violent men constitute a major threat to women's health. The National League of Cities has estimated that as many as half of all American women will experience violence from their spouses or boyfriends at some time during their relationships.[6]

Slightly more than a third of all visits to emergency rooms by women are for injuries from domestic assault.

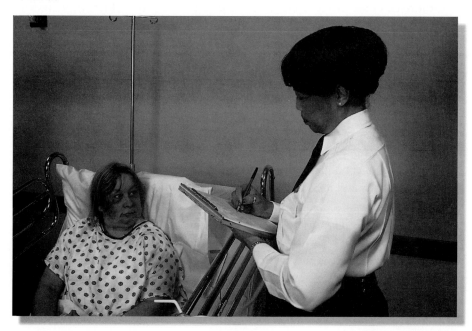

Perhaps most gruesome is a report by the March of Dimes that concluded that the battering of women during *pregnancy* caused more birth defects than all the diseases for which children are usually immunized combined.[7]

It has been estimated that 6 million women and men are battered by spouses each year. Because of the enormity of violent assaults between spouses, many jurisdictions have developed domestic violence statutes. **Domestic violence statutes** require officers to make arrests even without a signed complaint.[8] In effect, the officer becomes the complainant. Under these statutes, a responding officer must make an arrest even if the victim does not wish to file a complaint and the officer was not present during the attack. Typically, these statutes require that the officer have probable cause to believe that there has been some form of physical violence. This might be fresh scratches or bruises on the arms or face of the victim, or trickles of blood from a small cut on a victim's lip or nose.

FYI

A federal law designed to get tough on those convicted of assaulting spouses and other loved ones went into effect on September 30, 1996. The law prohibits the possession of a gun by anyone convicted of domestic violence or other misdemeanors where force or attempted force is used. The Bureau of Alcohol, Tobacco, and Firearms is in charge of enforcement and has put the burden on police agencies to determine whether any of their officers are affected.

Assaults Against Children

Child abuse Physical harm, including sexual abuse, or emotional harm to children.

No one knows for sure how many children are assaulted in families. The statistics represent only reported cases, and it is likely that many more cases are unreported. **Child abuse** can be physical harm, including sexual abuse, as well as emotional harm. Generally, the abusers are parents or close relatives, and the incidents happen repeatedly. In many cases, parents and other relatives who assault children were themselves abused children.

Battered child syndrome
The group of injuries suffered by physically abused children.

The clinical term for the injuries suffered by physically abused children is **battered child syndrome.** The physical abuse of children takes many forms, from minor assaults to outright physical torture. Children may be beaten with a belt or cord; burned with cigarettes, flames, or hot liquids; or slapped, punched, thrown, or knocked down. Abusive parents are generally isolated. They may have no one to turn to for relief from everyday frustrations. In many cases, such parents lack information about child development. They do not know what a child can reasonably be expected to do or how a child may act at certain ages. The tendency to abuse children is increased by such problems as unemployment, low self-esteem, poor stress management skills, marital conflicts, and drug and alcohol use.

Parents or caregivers may give various reasons for injuries to their children. They may blame an injury on an accident or the actions of a sibling. Investigators should always be suspicious of explanations that seem inconsistent with the injuries received. Intentional injuries to children generally occur on the face, back, ribs, buttocks, genitals, palms, or soles of the feet.

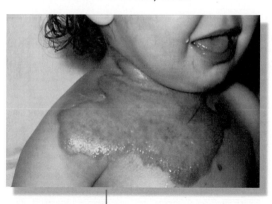

Assaults against children have increased dramatically. The abuse of children takes many forms.

One form of child abuse that police have recently encountered is Munchausen Syndrome by Proxy (MSBP). The parent or caregiver may feign or create illness in a child. For example, the subject may report finding blood in the child's urine when, in reality, the subject has pricked his or her own finger and introduced the blood into the urine sample. Repeated retesting of new samples of urine, taken when the offender is not present, will fail to uncover blood. In some instances, the offender will tamper with a medical chart once the child is hospitalized, indicating fevers or other symptoms that were never actually detected. In other cases, the offender will induce illness in the child. Some offenders have actually suffocated children to cause respiratory distress or injected feces diluted with water or household chemicals into a child to create a toxic reaction. Many times these events become life-threatening emergencies.[9]

The motivation behind MSBP is believed to be an attempt to elicit the attention, sympathy, or adoration of family, friends, and others. Munchausen syndrome was first diagnosed in individuals who inflicted serious wounds on themselves or ingested various toxins to induce symptoms of illness. They then arrived at emergency rooms and were admitted to hospitals, where suddenly their symptoms of illness began to wane.[10] When police are contacted about a possible case of MSBP, it is usually because of the suspicions of a health professional. Investigators should make use of this medical contact and any other relevant contacts with social services or social welfare agencies, as well as the prosecutor's office.[11]

As in any assault case, evidence is an important investigative goal. Among the most common procedures for securing evidence in a MSBP case is separation of the suspect and the victim. If, when the two are kept separated for a period, the symptoms of illness cease or dissipate, and if the symptoms reappear shortly after the two are reunited, the inference of MSBP is quite strong.

Hidden cameras are also effective in investigating MSBP cases. Video surveillance can be particularly effective for confronting the offenders, who frequently lie pathologically about their involvement. Extreme care must be taken when surveillance is used, since the suspect has access to the victim and may cause further harm.

Assaults Against Elders

Elderly family members may also be the objects of physical violence. A family member may take out his or her frustration on elderly parents or aunts or uncles who cannot defend themselves. Such abuse may also take place in rest homes and nursing facilities. As in child abuse cases, investigators should look for an injury that does not fit the explanation for the injury. Common injuries inflicted on elders include burns, cuts, pinches, bruises and welts, dehydration or malnourishment, soiled clothing or bedding, and injuries to parts of the body normally hidden by clothing.

SUMMARY BY LEARNING OBJECTIVES

Learning Objective 1

Assault is an unlawful attempt or threat to commit a physical injury to another through the use of force. Aggravated assault is one of the eight crimes that the FBI considers the most serious. The FBI reports yearly statistics on aggravated assault in its Uniform Crime Reports (UCR). In 1995, the total number of aggravated assaults declined for the second consecutive year, but the use of personal weapons, such as hands, fists, and feet, showed an increase. Aggravated assault made up 7.9 percent of all index offenses in 1995.

Learning Objective 2

Assaults are classified as *simple assaults* and *aggravated (felonious) assaults,* which are defined by state statutes. Generally, simple assaults have these elements: intent to do bodily harm to another individual, actual present ability to do bodily harm, and commission of an overt act demonstrating intent to carry out the assault. An aggravated assault has these three elements plus an intentional infliction of bodily harm that results in (a) injury sufficient to cause a high probability of death; (b) severe physical disfigurement; or (c) permanent loss or prolonged impairment of the use or function of any body part or organ, or any severe injury to the body.

Learning Objective 3

The responding officer's immediate task is to take control of the situation, separate the parties involved, and check for injuries. Next, the officer should find out what happened and try to determine who is an assailant and who is a victim. After separating, interviewing, and checking the suspect and the victim, the officer should determine whether a crime has occurred and whether the situation is a simple or aggravated assault. The crime scene should then be preserved, and evidence should be collected. Investigating an assault requires extreme care because the responding officer frequently enters an emotionally charged situation that can change quickly.

Learning Objective 4

Assaults among family members are a serious and growing problem. Intrafamily violence can take the form of spousal abuse, child abuse, or elder abuse. Many police agencies are taking a proactive approach to domestic violence and are using intervention strategies to reduce or prevent intrafamily violence. Some states have passed domestic violence statutes under which the responding officer can serve as the complainant in a domestic violence situation under certain circumstances.

QUESTIONS FOR REVIEW

Learning Objective 1

1. What are the essential elements *(corpus delicti)* of a simple assault?

Learning Objective 2

2. What element distinguishes an *aggravated assault* from a *simple assault?*
3. If a victim lost an eye after being intentionally punched, how would you classify the assault?
4. If a victim lost an eye after being accidentally punched, how would you classify the assault?
5. What is *stalking,* and how is it related to assault?

Learning Objective 3

6. Why is an immediate police response to assault calls usually recommended?
7. Why is the relationship between parties in an assault case important to consider?

Learning Objective 4

8. Why might it be better to arrest an assailant in a domestic assault than just to advise him at the scene?
9. What is meant by *intrafamily violence?*
10. Why should an officer never take a domestic violence call for granted?

11. How can *complacency* become a serious risk to an officer's safety on a domestic assault call?

12. What is meant by Munchausen Syndrome by Proxy?

CRITICAL THINKING INVESTIGATIVE EXERCISES

1. Consult your state's criminal statutes and locate the definitions of all the classes of the crime of assault in your state. Using these definitions, create a list of possible misdemeanor and felony assaults that would fit into the classes. Share your list with others in the class, and resolve any disagreements about classification.

2. In your local newspaper, find a recent article that describes a domestic assault or homicide. Discuss the facts of the case in class, and consider what the police might have been able to do to prevent the assault or homicide.

INVESTIGATIVE SKILL BUILDERS

Acquiring and Evaluating Information

You arrive at the scene of a domestic violence call. After you and your partner have separated the husband from the wife, you interview the husband. He tells you that he is tired of seeing his kid sick all the time. Every time the man goes on a business trip, he comes home to find that his son, Gerald, has gone to the emergency room. You learn that this seems to have started about three years ago, about the time the man began a job that takes him out of town twice a month. You ask what types of problems Gerald has been having, and he tells you, "That's the funny thing, Officer. He seems to keep getting these strange infections. Sometimes he has violent vomiting that the doctors just can't figure out a cause for." You ask if Gerald has seen a regular doctor to monitor any of these mysterious illnesses. He tells you that his wife has trouble keeping doctors, since they can never determine the cause of Gerald's illnesses.

1. Should you investigate anything more than what actually caused the domestic disturbance?

2. Do you have any suspicions about what may be happening?

3. Should any follow-up investigation occur? If so, what should be investigated?

Integrity/Honesty

You and your partner receive a call that a fight has broken out at a local neighborhood bar. When you arrive, you realize that one of the two men fighting is a good friend of yours. When you separate the two, you take your friend aside and have your partner take the other man to find out what happened. From your friend, you learn that both men had been drinking and that they had gotten into an argument over a football game bet. Your friend also admits to you that he threw the first punch—and maybe even the second punch. The other man is bleeding from his mouth and lip and is insisting on filing charges of assault.

1. What type of assault has taken place?

2. Should you arrest your friend or try to talk the other man out of filing charges?

ENDNOTES

1. Vernon J. Geberth, "Stalkers," *Law and Order,* October 1992, pp. 138–143.

2. Police Foundation, *Domestic Violence and the Police: Studies in Detroit and Kansas City,* Police Foundation, Washington, 1977.

3. Lawrence W. Sherman and Richard A. Berk, "The Specific Deterrent Effects of Arrest for Domestic Assault," *American Sociological Review,* Vol. 49, No. 4, 1984, pp. 261–272.

4. Patrick A. Langan and Christopher A. Innes, "Preventing Domestic Violence Against Women," Bureau of Justice Statistics Special Report, Department of Justice, Washington, 1986.

5. Ann Blackman, Wendy Coe, Scott Norvell, Elizabeth Rudulph, Andrea Sachs, and Richard Woodbury, "When Violence Hits Home," *Time,* July 4, 1994, pp. 18–25.

6. Cathy Booth, Jeanne McDowell, and Janice C. Simpson, "Till Death Do Us Part," *Time,* January 18, 1993, pp. 38–45.

7. Ibid.

8. Greg Connor, "Domestic Disputes: A Model Pro-Arrest Policy," *Law and Order,* February 1990, pp. 66–67.

9. Vernon J. Geberth, "Munchausen Syndrome by Proxy (MSBP)," *Law and Order,* August 1994, pp. 95–97.

10. Peter Divasto and Gina Saxton, "Munchausen's Syndrome in Law Enforcement," *FBI Law Enforcement Bulletin,* Vol. 61, No. 4, April 1992, pp. 11–14.

11. K. Hanon, "Child Abuse: Munchausen's Syndrome by Proxy," *FBI Law Enforcement Bulletin,* December 1991, pp. 8–11.

CHAPTER 12

Sexual Assault and Rape

CHAPTER OBJECTIVES

After completing this chapter you will be able to:

1. Provide an overview of sex crimes in the United States.

2. Identify six categories of sex offenses.

3. Explain the legal elements of the crime of rape.

4. Distinguish between *forcible rape* and *statutory rape.*

5. Discuss the special circumstances of rape and sexual assault investigations.

6. List the categories of sex crimes against children.

7. Describe the special demands of investigating sex crimes against children.

8. Specify the five basic stages of child development and tell how knowledge of these stages can assist an investigator.

KEY TERMS

sex crime
mutual consent
forcible rape
statutory rape
rape
date rape
rape kit
child molesting
sexual seduction
lewd and lascivious
 behavior with a child
indecent exposure
contributing to the
 delinquency of a
 minor
incest
pedophile
anatomical dolls

Overview of Sex Crimes

Sex crimes represent a broad classification of illegal behavior. They range from nuisance crimes, such as voyeurism and exhibitionism, to offenses such as forcible rape and lust crimes, which are a significant threat to society. Investigating sex crimes is a challenge for criminal investigators. As in other crimes, the quality of the investigation will significantly affect the outcome in a court case. However, in serious sex crimes, the manner in which the investigation is conducted will also have an effect on the victim's psychological well-being.

Forcible rape is the only sex offense that is an index crime. By Uniform Crime Reports (UCR) definition, the victims of forcible rape are always female. As Figure 12–1 shows, the number of reported forcible rapes declined in 1995 for the third consecutive year. Rape is known to be the least reported of the index offenses. If you look again at Figure 10–2 in Chapter 10, you will see that in 1995, forcible rape comprised

Figure 12–1 Forcible rape crime index totals.

Year	Population	Crime Index Totals	Number of Forcible Rape Offenses
1980	225,349,264	13,408,300	82,990
1981	229,146,000	13,423,800	82,500
1982	231,534,000	12,974,400	78,770
1983	233,981,000	12,108,600	78,920
1984	236,158,000	11,881,800	84,230
1985	238,740,000	12,431,400	88,670
1986	241,077,000	13,211,900	91,460
1987	243,400,000	13,508,700	91,110
1988	245,807,000	13,923,100	92,490
1989	248,239,000	14,251,400	94,500
1990	248,709,873	14,475,600	102,560
1991	252,177,000	14,872,900	106,590
1992	255,082,000	14,438,200	109,060
1993	257,908,000	14,144,800	106,010
1994	260,341,000	13,989,500	102,220
1995	262,755,000	13,867,100	97,460

Source: Federal Bureau of Investigation, *Crime in the United States,* Government Printing Office, Washington, 1995.

less than 1 percent of the offenses reported. The low rate of forcible rape in comparison with other index offenses does not diminish the violence of the crime. Except for murder, no other crime generates more public concern and causes more personal devastation than forcible rape.

This chapter is not designed to teach what prompts a person to commit sex crimes, what course of therapeutic treatment may be appropriate, or even whether criminals who commit sex crimes can be rehabilitated. The evaluation, diagnosis, treatment, and possible rehabilitation of such criminals are within the scope of the courts and in the hands of psychological and correctional professionals. The purpose of the material set forth in this chapter is to help the reader gain a better understanding, in general, of sex offenses. It is further intended to provide the reader with a working vocabulary of relevant terms and knowledge of the ramifications of specific violations. The sex crimes discussed in this chapter are some of the more common offenses that an investigator might encounter. That does not mean that more exotic, perverse, and bizarre crimes do not occur with some regularity.

Classification of Sex Crimes

The term **sex crime** covers a multitude of offenses ranging from indecent exposure to forcible rape. Some people try to classify sex crimes on the basis of consent, or more precisely, mutual consent. However, the exact definition of **mutual consent** can be quite elusive. It is not clearly defined in law and is often misinterpreted by defendants who look to it as a defense. A person under the temporary influence of alcohol or drugs, for example, may not be able to actually or legally consent to a sexual act. A wife who is unwilling to have intercourse with her husband does not consent to sex merely by virtue of marriage vows. Similarly, a prostitute who decides she is not interested in a particular customer can decline sex. Minor children cannot legally consent to sex even if they do so verbally and without duress or coercion.

Even when there is mutual consent, there are a number of acts that remain illegal. For instance, in most jurisdictions, prostitution is illegal regardless of whether both parties consent or not. Homosexual behaviors and even certain nontraditional sexual acts between heterosexuals, such as anal intercourse, are illegal in some jurisdictions.

Classification of each of these categories of crimes separately, or on the basis of mutual consent, is not necessary. Instead, we suggest a classification scheme that encompasses six categories. This proposed typology is shown in Figure 12–2. From the perspective of the general public, the most serious offense is probably forcible rape, or forcible rape and murder. Rape can be difficult to prove in a court of law. It is up to the investigator to obtain sufficient evidence to make a solid case against a rapist or rapist-murderer.

Sex crime Any of an assortment of criminal violations related to sexual conduct.

Mutual consent Willing participation by both parties in sexual acts.

Figure 12–2 Typology of sex offenses.

Voluntary (but between inappropriate partners):	Lewd and lascivious behavior with a child
Fornication	**Nuisance:**
Adultery	Voyeurism
Incest	Indecent exposure (exhibitionsm)
Bigamy	Frottage
Lewd and illegal cohabitation	Transvestism
Involuntary:	Fetishism
Forcible rape	Obscenity by phone, letter, or literature
Seduction	Public obscenity by gesture or statement
Abduction	
Commercial:	**Dangerous:**
Prostitution	Sexual asphyxiation
Pimping and pandering	Flagellation (sadism, masochism)
Indecent publication	Anthropophagy (cannibalism)
Obscene pornography	Sex pyromania
Abnormal:	Piquerism
Sodomy	Pedophilia
Bestiality	Lust murders
Sexual perversion	Rough sex

Legal Elements of the Crime of Rape

Rape is usually classified as either forcible or statutory. **Forcible rape** is sexual intercourse against a person's will by the use or threat of force. **Statutory rape** is sexual intercourse with a minor, with or without the minor's consent. The definition of a *minor* varies from state to state. Some states define a minor as someone under the age of 18. Others have more complex definitions, which may distinguish victims under 13 from those between 13 and 18 or may make a similar distinction between different ages. In states making these distinctions, the younger the victim, the more serious the offense and the more severe the penalty. See Figure 12–3 for one state's definitions of sex offenses.

Although each state has its own statutes defining **rape**, all definitions share certain *corpus delicti* elements:

- An act of sexual intercourse or penetration of the victim's vagina
- Without consent from the victim
- Against the victim's will and by force, coercion, or duress

To create more flexible sexual offense laws, a number of states have substituted the words *sexual assault* for the word *rape* in their statutes. In

Forcible rape Sexual intercourse against a person's will by the use or threat of force.

Statutory rape Sexual intercourse with a minor, with or without the minor's consent.

Rape An act of sexual intercourse, or penetration of the victim's vagina, without consent from the victim and against the victim's will by force, coercion, or duress.

some states, if the suspect is prevented from completing the act, it is classified as *assault with intent to commit rape* or *attempted rape.* Recently, attention has been focused on sexual offenses that occur between friends or while a couple is on a date. Such crimes are usually labeled **date rape** or *acquaintance rape.* In addition, in keeping with the changing values of society, several states now provide that the victim and the assailant may be of either sex.

When you investigate sexual assault crimes, be aware of several common reactions of the victims of such crimes. Many victims develop an overwhelming feeling of guilt, shame, and worthlessness after a sexual assault. Some fear that their friends and relatives will blame them for the attack and will react differently to them. Others had a close relationship with their attacker, or may even be related, and fear that a charge of rape will create family problems. Some victims fear having to go to court and relive their sexual assaults.

Date rape Forced sexual intercourse that occurs between friends or acquaintances or while a couple is on a date; also called *acquaintance rape.*

Figure 12–3 Definitions of sex offenses in Ohio.

■ **RAPE***

Purposely compelling another to engage in sexual conduct by force or threat of force; inserting any part of the body, instrument or object into the victim without privilege to do so.

Maximum penalty: 10 years, $20,000 fine. An additional 10-year sentence is possible for repeat violent offenders. If victim is younger than 13 and force is used, the maximum is life in prison.

■ **SEXUAL BATTERY**

Engaging in or knowingly coercing sexual conduct with someone other than spouse who is substantially impaired, or is a child, stepchild or student.

Maximum penalty: 5 years, $10,000 fine

■ **GROSS SEXUAL IMPOSITION**

Having sexual contact with someone other than the spouse or causing someone else to have sexual contact with another; or contact with someone who is substantially impaired by drugs, alcohol or mental and physical condition.

Maximum penalty: 5 years, $10,000 fine

■ **SEXUAL IMPOSITION**

Sexual contact that is offensive to the other person or is reckless; or victim submits because of being unaware of the nature of the contact; victim is 13 to 16 and the offender is at least 18.

Maximum penalty: 60 days, $500 fine

*A victim need not prove physical resistance.
Source: Ohio Revised Code.

Investigating Sex Offenses

There are two tasks that an investigator should attend to right away in a sex crime investigation. First, he or she should make sure that the victim receives any medical attention needed and that a physical examination is done to establish that a rape or sexual assault has occurred. Second, the investigator must protect and preserve the crime scene and any evidence therein. If a suspect is identified incident to or soon after an assault, the suspect's clothing and other physical evidence should also be secured.

An appropriate, understanding, and sensitive attitude is essential in sexual assault cases. As previously mentioned, victims of sexual assault are often on tenuous psychological ground. They are likely to feel frightened, insecure, and sometimes desperate. Some large departments have special sex crime units whose sole task is to investigate sexual offenses. In these situations, the investigators are likely to have developed relationships with medical professionals in the local hospitals. Investigators may even have fostered alliances with hospital social workers, who can assist in calming and communicating with victims.

During the past decade, many police departments have developed **rape kits,** which are usually housed in the emergency room of the local hospital. A typical kit contains tags and containers for specimens taken from a victim of sexual assault. There may be no evidence at the scene and no witnesses in a sexual assault case. It is therefore crucial to collect and properly label any evidence found on the clothing or person of the victim.

After a victim has received medical attention and any evidence has been collected, a follow-up interview should be conducted. In a further effort to consider the feelings of the victim, many departments assign a female officer to interview the victim or to investigate sexual assaults on women and children.

As a matter of practice, the preliminary interview is usually undertaken by a responding officer. While the responding officer may not be female, the officer should be trained to handle preliminary interviews with victims of sexual assault. Many police academies are now including such training in their curriculum.

Preliminary interviews with victims should seek information about the attacker, where the assault occurred, and any relevant circumstances surrounding the offense. The preliminary interview should be conducted in a manner that protects the modesty of the victim. If a female officer is not available, the assistance of a female nurse, social worker, or doctor should be requested. Having another woman present during the interview often helps to reassure the victim.

Frequently, preliminary interviews take place shortly after the actual assault. This means that the trauma and the feelings surrounding the attack are still very intense. Investigators should not focus too much on

Rape kit An evidence kit used in many hospital emergency rooms to secure physical evidence specimens in rape cases.

Rape kits are commonly housed in emergency rooms of hospitals.

the specific details of the assault. If the victim claims she has been raped, the officer should assume that this is accurate and should proceed. If the victim is talking and describing the assault, it is advisable not to interrupt, but to allow the story to flow at the victim's own pace. Good investigative technique in sexual assault cases includes careful word choices and questions. Avoid accusatory questions, such as "Why did you go back to his apartment?" or "Why were you drinking so heavily?" Such questions have little investigative value and are likely to close down the subject.[1] Figure 12–4 shows a national survey of characteristics of rape/assault incidents.

Figure 12–4 Characteristics of rape/sexual assault incidents.

Characteristics of Incident	Rape/Sexual Assault %
Victim/offender relationship:	
Relative	11
Well-known	35
Casual acquaintance	21
Stranger	33
Time of day:	
6 A.M. to 6 P.M.	31
6 P.M. to midnight	37
Midnight to 6 A.M.	32
Location of crime:	
At or near victim's home or lodging	37
Friend's/relative's/neighbor's home	21
Commercial places	7
Parking lots/garages	6
Schools	3
Streets other than near victim's home	8
Other	17
Victim's activity:	
At work or traveling to or from work	8
At school	5
Activities at home	38
Shopping/errands	2
Leisure activities away from home	32
Traveling	6
Other	8
Distance from victim's home:	
Inside home or lodging	34
Near victim's home	10
1 mile or less	12
5 miles or less	14
50 miles or less	23
More than 50 miles	6
Weapons:	
No weapons present	84
Weapons present	16

Source: Bureau of Justice Statistics, *Criminal Victimization 1994,* April 1996.

Certain essential pieces of information should be gathered during sex crime investigations.

- Date and time of the offense.
- Type of assault.
- Age of the victim.
- Physical description of the attacker.
- Location of the assault, including a description of the room, alley, park, car, and so on.
- Description of weather conditions, lighting, visibility, or other environmental factors.
- General condition of the victim: emotional state, presence of drugs or alcohol, physical condition (bruises, scratches, cuts, bleeding), medical examination findings, and any indication of pregnancy.
- General condition of the attacker: torn clothes or scratches or wounds inflicted by the victim.
- Identity of any possible witnesses, either witnesses to the crime or persons who saw the subject with the victim shortly before the crime.
- Any special features, mannerisms, or statements of the suspect or any unusual occurrences recalled by the victim.
- Description of the circumstances leading to the attack, according to the victim: the establishment of the *modus operandi.*
- Description of any weapon shown or used in the assault.
- Any information about how the attacker fled: description of car or other vehicles, direction, and so on.
- All physical evidence collected from the person and clothing of the victim that might show that a sexual act took place or that might link the act with the suspect.
- All physical evidence found at the scene of the crime that might connect the suspect with the crime.

Sex Crimes Against Children

Perhaps more heinous than the crime of rape is the crime of sexual assault against a child. Even violent inmates in prisons place child molesters (*short-eyes* in prison slang) at the bottom of the pecking order. Child molesters in prisons are sometimes found beaten or killed simply because others have learned that their crimes include the rape of a small child or infant.

Categories of Sexual Assaults Against Children

Sexual assaults on children include child molesting, sexual seduction, lewd and lascivious behavior, indecent exposure, contributing to the delinquency of a minor, incest, and several other statutory offenses.

Child Molesting **Child molesting** is a broad category that includes any behavior motivated by an unnatural or abnormal sexual interest in children. Typically, the behaviors are ones the victim finds emotionally upsetting, physically harmful, and inappropriate. The behaviors range from fondling and exhibitionism to rape, mutilation, and murder. Many states have specific statutes defining this type of sexual offender. Several states have broadened penalties to allow them to fit the severity of the crime, especially when the victim is very young or an infant.

Sexual Seduction Like statutory rape, **sexual seduction** involves sexual intercourse by an adult with a consenting minor. It may additionally represent various forms of sodomy, anal intercourse, cunnilingus, or fellatio committed by an adult with a willing child.

Lewd and Lascivious Behavior With a Child The elements of **lewd and lascivious behavior with a child** include touching any part of a child to arouse, appeal to, or gratify the sexual desires of either the child or the perpetrator. Laws against such behavior generally apply to any gender combination of perpetrator and victim. If elements of the crime are present, and the suspect is positively identified, a private person can arrest the victim as a public nuisance at the scene. If the act is observed by an officer, he or she can make the arrest.

Indecent Exposure The crime of **indecent exposure** is among the most common of the standard sex offenses. It involves publicly exhibiting one's genitals. Victims can be either children or adults. The exhibition may occur in any public location, such as in a street or park or from an automobile. The reaction to the offense is a source of sexual pleasure for the offender.

Contributing to the Delinquency of a Minor Statutes pertaining to **contributing to the delinquency of a minor** impose a duty on parents, caregivers, or other adults to refrain from committing any act or omitting the performance of any duty if the act or omission causes or tends to cause or encourage a minor to violate any law or might lead the minor to lead a dissolute, lewd, immoral, or criminal life. It is often a lesser crime included in other offenses, such as statutory rape, procuring alcohol for a minor, or other felonies in which a minor is a principal in a crime committed by an accompanying adult.

Child molesting Broad term encompassing any behavior motivated by an unnatural sexual interest in minor children.

Sexual seduction Sexual intercourse between an adult and a willing minor.

Lewd and lascivious behavior with a child Touching any part of a child to arousal; appealing to, or gratifying the sexual desires of either the child or the perpetrating adult.

Indecent exposure Exhibiting the private parts of one's body in a lewd or indecent manner to the sight of others in a public place.

Contributing to the delinquency of a minor An act or omission that contributes to making or tends to make a child delinquent.

Incest Sexual intercourse between persons who are so closely related that their marriage is illegal or forbidden by custom.

Incest   The laws surrounding the offense of **incest** vary from state to state. Most focus on the general prohibition of sexual intercourse between biological relatives. These usually include mother and son, father and daughter, and siblings. However, some state statutes merely prohibit marriage between biological relatives through first cousins, with no specific mention of sexual behavior or regard for the ages of parties involved.

It is commonly thought that incest taboos, which are nearly universal, originated as a means of avoiding the disastrous results of genetic inbreeding. This logic, however, is faulty because many societies in the world do not understand biology or paternity, let alone genetics. More likely, this *natural law* evolved to promote harmony within the family and the society. If a father and a son competed for the sexual and romantic attentions of the father's daughter, the unity of the family would be seriously disrupted. Furthermore, there would be serious role confusion for all members of the family.

In spite of existing laws and the social taboo against incest, it continues to occur at alarming rates. Perpetrators of incestuous assaults on children come from all walks of life and all educational levels. Because usually an older relative perpetrates the sexual assault, it is difficult for a child to come forward, or to admit such behavior has occurred. The most frequently reported form of incest is between fathers and daughters.

Statutes relating to child sexual assault may define various other crimes that sexually exploit children. These may include the visual or commercial exploitation of children through pornography or pandering (catering to the lower tastes and desires of others). In 1984, Congress passed the Child Protection Act, designed to protect children from exploitation. The act specifically prohibits child pornography and significantly increases the penalties for it.

Characteristics of Child Molesters

Pedophile An adult who is sexually attracted to children or performs sexual acts with children.

Pedophiles, or adults who are sexually attracted to children, prey on the vulnerability of children. These child molesters may befriend lonely children or children whose parents are not providing sufficient emotional support. Investigators should be aware of a number of false stereotypes commonly associated with pedophiles. First, pedophiles are not miserable "dirty old men."[2] The majority of offenders are under the age of 35 at the time of their first arrest. Many begin illegal sexual activity as teenagers.

A second false stereotype is that pedophiles are strangers to their victims. In most cases, the victim knows his or her attacker, at least casually. In many cases, it is a relative, stepparent, or caregiver.

Another common misconception is that child molesters are incapable of normal sexual relations with an adult partner. This, too, is usually not accurate. According to Nicholas Groth and his associates, many child molesters are married, and their sexual interest in children coexists with their sexual contacts with adults.[3] Incestuous fathers, however, have been found to have social skill deficits and relatively weak masculine identification.[4] Yet family disorganization seems a more serious problem for these men than marital dissatisfaction. Many incestuous fathers maintain sexual relations with their spouses during the time they are incestuously assaulting their children.

Like rape, child molestation is not primarily motivated by sexual gratification. Rather, a distorted kind of identification with the victim and a desire to maintain control and power over a situation seem to propel offenders. We know that most pedophiles are not retarded or insane. The proportion that are homosexual is about the same as in the general population. Pedophiles' behavior is fairly predictable, since it tends to be compulsive and repetitive.

Investigating Sex Crimes Against Children

Newspapers, magazines, and even the television news constantly bombard the public with stories of children who have been molested or sexually abused. There have been cases of mothers having their 11-year-old daughters perform sexual favors for men in exchange for crack cocaine, children being held in basements by foster parents and made to perform sexual acts for friends and the foster parents, even social and religious organizations whose members have engaged in sexual misconduct with children. Many people do not believe that such incidents have radically increased in number in recent years. Rather, they suggest that parents and children are more aware and better educated and that reporting techniques have become more effective. Yet, some perpetrators of child sexual abuse will never be prosecuted. Some remain secretly in the same community, while others move from one community to another to avoid detection. However, relocating may no longer be a solution, because in May 1996, Megan's Law was signed by President Clinton. It was named after a child who was raped and killed in 1994. That law requires convicted rapists to register with the police when they move into a new community. The police in turn notify schools, daycares, and so on.

A number of federal and state regulations require teachers, doctors, and child care workers to report to the police any suspicion of child abuse. Frequently, concerned neighbors contact the police with allega-

STATISTICS

In 1995, the UCR indicated that more than half the rapes reported to law enforcement agencies nationwide were cleared by arrest or exceptional means. Rural and suburban clearance rates, both 52 percent, were slightly higher than the rate in cities, 51 percent. Of forcible rape arrestees, 41 percent were under 25, 28 percent were under 21, 15 percent were under 18, and 5 percent were under 15. More than half of those arrested were white.

Combined DNA Index System   The FBI is developing CODIS (Combined DNA Index System) as a national DNA database to allow state and local law enforcement agencies to link serial violent crimes, especially rapes, to each other, and to identify suspects by matching DNA from crime scenes with state databases of convicted sex offenders. As of May 1997, 45 states have passed legislation requiring convicted sex offenders to provide biological samples for DNA databasing.

tions or fears of a child's abuse, neglect, or sexual assault. When such a report reaches the police, they sometimes investigate the allegations on their own. In other cases, police agencies cooperate with the local social service agencies to investigate potential crimes against children.

Under welfare regulations and codes, an investigating officer or welfare agent is empowered to place a child in temporary custody—even without a court order—if there is an apparent emergency or if the officer believes the child would be in imminent danger if left in the situation. This power is provided for in the law for the protection and welfare of children at risk.

Multidisciplinary Approach   For a number of reasons, child sexual abuse is difficult to investigate and even more difficult to prosecute. First, in small communities, no one wants to believe such crimes could occur. This sort of denial is more acute when it appears the offender is a friend or relative. Evidence in these cases is often difficult to obtain, and there is a shifting of blame from one child protection agency to another for mishandled cases.[5] Similarly, local community members and child protection agency workers tend to blame the prosecutor's office when child molesters escape justice.

The explanation for these problems rests in part on the way we have historically approached child sexual abuse—namely, as a *family problem* rather than as a *criminal offense*. As a family problem, it has traditionally been handled by child protection agencies. For a very long time, it was handled discretely by counselors and social service agency personnel.

During the past two decades, however, police have become more inclined to respond to child sexual abuse as a serious and insidious crime. Today, most child sexual abuse cases are referred to the criminal justice system and not simply a child welfare agency.[6]

Police agencies have also recognized that child sexual abuse cases require investigators with special training and skill. Yet, most police academies in our nation offer only minimal training in child molestation and sexual abuse cases. Consequently, many—perhaps most—police agencies do not have personnel with the skills needed to effectively investigate such cases.

FYI

The presence of semen is not evidence of rape, nor does its absence mean that a rape has not occurred. Some rapists experience sexual dysfunction. The rapist may be unable to achieve an orgasm, may have difficulty in achieving and sustaining an erection, or may experience premature ejaculation.

Therefore, police agencies and social service agencies need to work in concert, to form *multidisciplinary teams*. In effect, these investigations require the combined talents of police departments, social welfare agencies, and the prosecutor's office. Police personnel process the evidentiary elements of the case, social welfare agency personnel provide therapeutic input, and assistant prosecutors ensure that the rights of both victims and defendants are protected. All these elements are needed to effectively handle the victim and the perpetrator in a child sexual abuse prosecution.

Multidisciplinary teams provide several distinct advantages over more traditional practices, which were nearly adversarial. First, procedural policies and planned activities can be established, minimizing the number of times the same ground must be covered with victims in interviews. Second, team members can be trained to work together to conduct more effective and therapeutic interviews that yield prosecutable findings. Finally, a team that has worked together on similar cases for a long time increases its shared sensitivity to various issues. For example, team members become more adept at recognizing whether child victims are hiding facts, lying, or telling the truth. Often, these cases consist mainly of the child's claim of abuse against the denial of an adult. If there is any question about the truthfulness of the child's testimony, it may be very difficult to obtain a conviction.

The multidisciplinary approach to investigating child sexual abuse cases offers a way to streamline and coordinate prosecution. Furthermore, it tends to reduce the secondary harm and anguish caused by the prosecution of such cases.

Interviewing Child Victims   Although interviewing any victim of a sexual assault requires care and concern, interviewing a child victim requires even greater sensitivity. Unless there is a reason for urgency, investigators should interview child victims of sexual assault with the assistance of a qualified professional. Investigators should assess the situation and consider the extent of the child's physical injuries as well as his or her emotional condition.

Children who have been severely brutalized may not be able to provide much information. Yet, it is difficult to predict the quantity or quality of information that may be offered by very young children. It is important, therefore, that the investigator carefully consider when and how to interview the child.

Although interviewing any victim of sexual abuse requires care and concern, interviewing child victims requires even greater sensitivity.

It is also important for investigators to have some understanding of child development. That will allow them to choose appropriate methods and language to gain information and assess a child victim's responses. There are five basic stages in a child's development: infancy, early childhood, preschool age, school age, and adolescence.[7] Investigators familiar with these developmental stages can better determine how likely a victim of a certain age is to understand the events that occurred and what kinds of questions would be most appropriate to ask. Successful communication with the victim is the key to a favorable outcome in a prosecution.

For example, if an investigator knows that children aged 4 to 6 do not generally understand concepts of relative time, physical space, and distance, he or she can avoid asking such questions as "What time was it when Uncle Dan touched your private place?" or "How long was Uncle Dan in the bed with you?" Instead, a time frame relevant to the child might be used. For example, the question might be "Was it before supper or after supper that Uncle Dan touched you?" or "Would you say Uncle Dan was in your room for about the same time as one whole cartoon show?" It is important for investigators to know that children develop at varying rates. The different levels of maturation are discussed in Figure 12–5.[8]

A number of police agencies and courts have made active use of anatomical dolls in interviews with child sexual abuse victims. **Anatomical dolls** are male and female dolls with gender-appropriate genitalia. Research has shown that children who have been subjected to sexual abuse react differently to anatomical dolls than children who have not.[9] Typically, sexually abused children bring sexual behavior into their play with anatomical dolls, while children who have not been sexually abused do not.

As abhorrent to society as child sexual abuse is, investigators must be cautious to protect the innocent. Anyone who has worked with children for long periods knows they can have vivid imaginations and will often lie to avoid getting into trouble. Although most child abuse reports are accurate, investigators should be mindful that some reporters of child sexual abuse may be liars or may have other axes to grind with the adult alleged to have committed the crime. Some children may also lie as a form of revenge or to avoid unpleasant situations, such as the disapproval of a parent or the admission of some misdeed. For example, a mother who discovers that her 13-year-old daughter is pregnant may jump to the conclusion that her daughter has been molested. The daughter, who was actually a consenting participant in a sexual relationship, may lie and claim that someone—perhaps the bus driver or a teacher—molested her.

Another problem investigators face when interviewing child victims is that young children tend to

Anatomical dolls Dolls or puppets with sex-appropriate genitalia, used in interviews with suspected child victims of sexual abuse or assault.

A variety of techniques are used to help children explain what happened to them during a sexual assault.

Figure 12–5 Stages of child development.

Infancy (birth to 2 years old)

Infants rely on *sameness* and continuity of caregivers. They are dependent on their caregivers and begin to develop *basic trust* or *mistrust*. Infants have limited cognitive abilities, are unable to form complex concepts, and have little language ability.

Early childhood (2 to 4 years old)

For the first two years, children try to make their bodies do what they want. By age 3, they have gained sufficient muscle control to walk, grasp, control their bowels, and use language. They experiment with *autonomy* and develop a sense of control over their environment. They also begin to develop *preconcepts*. This means that the child is able to respond to symbols and signs but still lacks the capacity to understand most common concepts.

Preschool age (4 to 6 years old)

The child develops *initiative*, which adds to the already developing autonomy. The child uses free choice and begins to manipulate and control his or her environment. This period is sometimes referred to as the *play stage.* Children begin to act out adult roles and, importantly, begin to initiate purposeful activities on their own. They still have limited abilities to understand abstract concepts. Their verbal skills, however, may imply greater understanding than they actually possess. Children in this stage frequently begin to read words, but

have very short attention spans.[10] It is best to keep interviews with young children brief, perhaps only 15 to 20 minutes long. It is also important when investigating sexual abuse of children that investigators understand what the child means when he or she describes behaviors. To a 5-year-old, *sex* may mean kissing someone on the lips or taking a nap on someone's lap. It is important to be sure both the child and the investigator understand *what the child means.* Toward this end, investigators should refrain from defining words for the child and, instead, should ask the child to explain what he or she means.

Investigating a child sexual abuse or molestation case should include obtaining all the kinds of essential information we have already discussed. However, when investigating child victims, there are several things investigators must bear in mind, because those things will affect the information provided by children:

- The closeness of the child's relationship with the offender.
- The duration of the sexual abuse (whether it went on for a long period or was a sudden attack).

they have only limited comprehension of meanings. Memory may be spotty, and some may have difficulty distinguishing fantasy from reality. Children at this development stage are fully capable of lying and do so frequently to avoid punishment or difficult situations.

School age (6 to 11 years old)

The social arena shifts from the home and family to school and peers. Language skills increase, and children begin to understand technology around them. As children begin to master skills, they also begin to take pride in being industrious. This period of *industry* is also characterized by chumming with members of the same gender and a general tendency toward truthfulness on most important issues.

Adolescence (12 to 18 years old)

Adolescence is a difficult time for young people. The child stands on the threshold of adult emotional feelings and physiology, yet is still drawn to childish ways of play. Rapport with adults may be strained or difficult. It is a period of searching, testing, and experimentation and a time of *identity* development. Interest in intimate relationships begins to emerge. Some adolescents may be shy and reserved in discussions of intimate matters. Others may be outgoing and boisterous about intimate issues. Adolescents are fully capable of fabricating elaborate lies to protect themselves or friends they think need protection. They have a full understanding of abstract concepts and considerable mastery of language, reading, and writing.

- The amount of violence or threat of violence associated with the assault or assaults.
- The age and understanding (general developmental level) of the child.
- The child's ability to read, write, count, and tell a story.
- Knowledge and understanding of names for body parts.
- Knowledge and understanding of sexual behaviors.
- The child's recent sleep and behavior patterns (moodiness, fighting, night frights, and so on).

It is advisable for investigators to consult the child's parents regarding many of these issues before interviewing the child victim. Having this background information about the child will help the investigators know what to expect and how best to phrase questions to the child.

Learning Objective 1

Sex crimes represent a broad classification of illegal behavior. They range from nuisance crimes, such as voyeurism, to offenses that are a significant threat to society, such as rape. Forcible rape is one of eight crimes that the FBI considers the most serious in American society. The FBI reports yearly statistics on forcible rape in its Uniform Crime Reports (UCR). In 1995, the total number of reported forcible rapes declined for the second consecutive year. Forcible rape made up 0.7 percent of all index offenses in 1995.

Learning Objective 2

Sex offenses can be put into these six categories: voluntary, involuntary, commercial, abnormal, nuisance, and dangerous.

Learning Objective 3

Rape is a crime of violence and control, not sexual satisfaction. Although each state has its own statutes defining the crime of rape, all the definitions share certain elements: (1) an act of sexual intercourse, or penetration of the victim's vagina, (2) without consent from the victim, (3) against the victim's will, by force, coercion, or duress. Additionally, some states may define other classes of crimes, such as *attempted rape* or *date rape*.

Learning Objective 4

Rape is usually classified as either *forcible rape* or *statutory rape*. Forcible rape is sexual intercourse against a person's will by the use or threat of force. Statutory rape is sexual intercourse with a minor with or without the minor's consent. The definition of a *minor* varies from state to state.

Learning Objective 5

Special circumstances of rape and sexual assault investigations include the sensitive nature of the offense, society's attitudes toward it, and the victim's embarrassment and possible reluctance to discuss the crime. Investigating a rape requires tact and understanding on the part of the investigator. Important information to obtain about a sex offense includes date and time of offense, type of assault, age of victim, physical description of attacker, location of assault, weather conditions, general condition of victim and attacker, words spoken, weapon used, method of attack, witnesses, and any physical evidence that can connect the attacker to the victim and establish that a crime was committed. Investigating rape and sexual assault often requires cooperation among many different agencies and organizations.

Learning Objective 6

Sex crimes against children include child molestation, sexual seduction, lewd and lascivious behavior, indecent exposure, contributing to the delinquency of a minor, incest, and several other statutory offenses. Child molesters generally are under age 35 at the time of their first arrest, know their victims at least casually, and may maintain their sexual interest in children while also performing sex normally with an adult partner.

Learning Objective 7

Sexual abuse of children is difficult to investigate and even more difficult to prosecute. Interviewing child victims requires extreme sensitivity to the child's emotional and physical welfare. In recent years, police have come to recognize child sexual abuse as a criminal offense, not a family problem. Police, social service agencies, and prosecutors often cooperate in multidisciplinary teams to effectively deal with the victim and the perpetrator in child sexual abuse cases.

Learning Objective 8

The five basic stages of child development are infancy, early childhood, preschool age, school age, and adolescence. Knowing the characteristics of children at these various stages can help investigators know better how to interview children who are victims or witnesses of a crime.

QUESTIONS FOR REVIEW

Learning Objective 1

1. Why is the investigation of sex crimes a challenge for investigators?

Learning Objective 2

2. What is meant by *mutual consent?*
3. When might sex between a husband and wife be classified as rape?

Learning Objective 3

4. What are the three basic elements of forcible rape?

Learning Objective 4

5. Why is sex between a 12-year-old girl and a 20-year-old man illegal?
6. How does *statutory rape* differ from *forcible rape?*

Learning Objective 5

7. What are some pieces of information necessary to a sex crime investigation?

CRITICAL THINKING INVESTIGATIVE EXERCISE

A 14-year-old girl is brought to the police department by her mother. The mother has just learned that her daughter is pregnant. The girl now claims that she was seduced by her 25-year-old gym teacher. Divide into three groups. In each group, as assigned by your instructor, have a team leader write separate series of questions that might be used in an interview with (1) the girl, (2) the gym teacher, and (3) the mother. Share your group's questions with the class, and determine from their reaction whether any questions should be amended, deleted, or expanded.

INVESTIGATIVE SKILL BUILDERS

Negotiating to Arrive at a Decision

You arrive at the home of Gary Epstein, a prominent businessman in the community. He informs you that he has just caught an 18-year-old boy having intercourse with his 16-year-old daughter in the basement of his home. He tells you that he wants the boy arrested for statutory rape. You ask where the boy is now and are directed to the living room. The youth is sitting on the sofa next to a young girl. She is pressing a cloth to his mouth. The cloth has blood on it. The boy stands as you enter. You see that his lip is bleeding and a bruise is forming on his left cheek. You ask, "What happened to the boy?" The boy sheepishly says, "Mr. Epstein hit me." Mr. Epstein jumps into the conversation, saying, "It was just a slap." The daughter then says, "No, Dad, you punched him in the face, and he wants you charged with assault."

1. Should you try to negotiate things between the boy and the father? Explain your answer.

2. Should you make any arrests? Explain.

Integrity/Honesty

A man suspected in a series of rapes in the neighborhood has just been arrested. The suspect has been given his Miranda warnings and is sitting in an interrogation room. The investigator tells the suspect that if he does not come clean and tell the truth about his involvement, it will be necessary to involve his family—including his wife and children—and his employer. The suspect then offers a full confession.

1. Would this confession be admissible in court? Explain.

2. How would you have handled the situation?

ENDNOTES

1. Art Buckwalter, *Interviews and Interrogations,* Butterworth, Boston, 1983.

2. Nicholas A. Groth, Ann W. Burgess, H. J. Birmbaum, and Thomas S. Gary, "A Study of the Child Molester: Myths and Realities," *LAE Journal of American Criminal Justice Association,* Vol. 41, No. 1, 1978, pp. 17–73.

3. Groth, op. cit.

4. L. M. Williams and D. Finkelhor, "The Characteristics of Incestuous Fathers: A Review of Recent Studies," in W. L. Marshall, D. R. Laws, and H. E. Barbaree (eds.), *Handbook of Sexual Assault: Issues, Theories, and Treatment of the Offender,* Plenum, New York, 1990.

5. W. C. Overton, D. Burns, and J. Atkins, "Child Sexual Abuse Investigation," *Law and Order,* July 1994, pp. 97–100.

6. Ibid.

7. David Gullo, "Child Abuse: Interviewing Possible Victims," *FBI Law Enforcement Bulletin,* Vol. 63, No. 1, January 1994, pp. 19–22.

8. Erik Erikson, *Childhood and Society,* 2d ed., Norton, New York, 1963; Robert A. Stebbins, *Sociology: The Study of Society,* 2d ed., Harper & Row, New York, 1990; Gullo, op. cit.

9. Lois Jampole and Kathie M. Weber, "An Assessment of the Behavior of Sexually Abused and Nonsexually Abused Children With Anatomically Correct Dolls," *Child Abuse and Neglect,* Vol. 11, No. 2, 1987.

10. Raymond Lynch and Michael Bussiculo, "A Law Enforcement Officer's Guide to Interviewing Child Sex Abuse Victims," *Law and Order,* May 1991, pp. 90–94.

CHAPTER 13

Kidnapping and Extortion

CHAPTER OBJECTIVES

After completing this chapter, you will be able to:

1. Explain the nature of kidnapping.

2. Discuss the effect of the Lindbergh kidnapping on federal law.

3. Outline the legal aspects of the crime of kidnapping.

4. Describe procedures used in kidnapping investigations.

5. List three rules for dealing with hostage situations.

6. Discuss child stealing as a form of kidnapping.

7. Describe the nature of extortion and explain how it differs from blackmail.

KEY TERMS

kidnapping
ransom
Lindbergh law
hostage
hostage negotiator
line of communication
extortion
blackmail

Kidnapping

Kidnapping Taking another person from one location to another against that person's will, by using force or coercion.

Ransom Money, property, or other consideration paid or demanded in exchange for the release of a kidnapped person.

As we have seen, crimes against people encompass a range of conduct that injures, inflicts property losses, invades personal sexual integrity, and exploits children. Also among these crimes against people are the crimes of kidnapping and extortion. Kidnapping, extortion, and the threat of violence associated with them have increased in recent years. **Kidnapping** is taking someone away by force, often for **ransom,** or some form of payment.

In many recent kidnappings, the victims have been relatives of the kidnapper. A divorced mother, fearing for the safety of her children when they are in the custody of their father, may take the children and leave the state, committing a kidnapping. In other kidnappings, the perpetrators demand hundreds of thousands of dollars in ransom from wealthy people or civic leaders. Or the ransom demand may be made against a corporate or industrial enterprise with which the victim is associated. Terrorists (discussed in detail in Chapter 22) have for years used kidnapping to coerce governments into changing policies or releasing prisoners. In one highly publicized case in 1988, 11-year-old Jacob Wetterling was taken at gunpoint from near his home by a masked man. No ransom was demanded, and, despite national publicity and a nationwide search, Jacob remains missing.

Kidnapping and similar crimes are among the most reprehensible encountered by law enforcement agencies. Also, kidnappings are often among the most difficult crimes to investigate. Although apprehending the perpetrator is important in every kidnapping case, the safety and welfare of the victims often become the primary concern of investigators.

People take a keen interest in kidnapping cases. In no other crime does public sympathy extend so thoroughly to the victim and the victim's family. In cases of kidnapping, people are usually quite cooperative with law enforcement efforts to locate and free the victims. Unfortunately, some cases of kidnapping turn out to be hoaxes. When the hoax is discovered, the public feels betrayed. An example of this occurred in a small town in South Carolina in October 1994. For nearly two weeks, Susan Smith made tearful pleas on national television to the alleged kidnapper of her two small sons. Then she broke down and confessed to having drowned the two boys herself.

In kidnapping cases, particularly when the fate of the victims remains uncertain, the media tend to show considerable interest. Yet, the media must exercise restraint to ensure the safety of the victims. Kidnapping for ransom, and other variations on this crime, are typically investigated in two phases. The first occurs while the victim's fate remains in question, and the second occurs after the victim has been released or is found.

The Lindbergh Case

Federal kidnapping legislation was a response to a series of kidnappings for ransom in the 1920s and 1930s. Rival gangs seized each other's members and held them for ransom. In many of these seizures, victims were snatched in one state and held in another. These seizures were followed by similar kidnappings of members of wealthy families. Each time, ransom demands went up.

The most notorious of these seizures was the kidnapping and murder of the son of Charles Lindbergh, a hero because of his trans-Atlantic flight, and Anne Morrow Lindbergh. On March 1, 1932, the couple's 20-month-old son was kidnapped from their home in New Jersey. Although the child was seized in New Jersey, most of the ransom negotiations were conducted in other states. About 10 weeks after the kidnapping, the child's badly decomposed body was found partially buried near the Lindbergh estate. Although the Lindberghs had paid the ransom, their child had been murdered by a blow to the head, and the body had been partially dismembered. Two years later, police arrested Bruno Hauptmann, a carpenter, after he bought gas with a $10 bill from the ransom money and a search of his garage yielded more than $13,000 of the ransom money. In spite of inconsistencies in police reports and testimony in court and Hauptmann's claim of innocence, he was convicted and executed.

The Lindbergh case led to the passage of a federal kidnapping statute. The federal kidnapping statute, sometimes referred to as the **Lindbergh law,** was passed on June 22, 1932. This law made it a federal offense to transport in interstate or foreign commerce a kidnapped

Lindbergh law Federal antikidnapping legislation passed in 1932.

HISTORY

*O*n *March 10, 1932, Al Capone, who had recently been sentenced to prison on a tax evasion charge, sent word to Charles Lindbergh through Arthur Brisbane, a writer and spokesperson for the William Randolph Hearst newspaper empire. If Lindbergh could arrange Capone's release from prison, Capone would personally try to find the kidnapped Lindbergh baby through his connections to the underworld. Initially, the kidnapping was thought to be connected to the underworld, since many such kidnappings had taken place as rival gangs competed for power. Capone's offer was declined.[1]*

person for purposes of ransom, reward, "or otherwise" (see Figure 13–1). Included in the "or otherwise" clause of the kidnapping statute are such offenses as sexual assault, bank robbery, and the taking of a child by a parent without legal custody. State legislatures followed the federal model in their kidnapping statutes, which were often nicknamed "little Lindbergh laws."

Legal Aspects of the Crime of Kidnapping

By modern statutes, kidnapping is the unlawful taking of an individual against his or her will. Many states have separate statutes to prohibit the unlawful taking of a person against his or her will for ransom and have harsher penalties for such a crime. State statutes vary with regard to whether kidnapping is a felony.[2] In some states, simple kidnapping is a felony, while in others, only more serious forms of kidnapping, such as those for ransom, rape, or revenge, are felonies. Some states define more than one degree of kidnapping, requiring aggravating circumstances for the more serious offense of first-degree kidnapping. For the more serious forms of kidnapping, a number of states impose the death penalty or life imprisonment. Since statutes vary, investigators must know what constitutes the crime of kidnapping in their respective

---

Figure 13–1 Title 18, U.S. Code, Section 1201.

(a) Whoever knowingly transports in interstate or foreign commerce, any person who has been unlawfully seized, confined, inveigled, decoyed, kidnapped, abducted, or carried away and held for ransom or reward or otherwise, except, in the case of a minor, by a parent thereof, shall be punished (1) by death if the kidnapped person has not been liberated unharmed, and if the verdict of the jury shall so recommend, or (2) by imprisonment for any term of years or for life, if the death penalty is not imposed.

(b) The failure to release the victim within twenty-four hours, after he shall have been unlawfully seized, confined, inveigled, decoyed, kidnapped, abducted, or carried away shall create a rebuttable presumption that such person has been transported in interstate or foreign commerce.

(c) If two or more persons conspire to violate this section and one or more of such persons do any overt act to effect the object of the conspiracy, each shall be punishable as provided in subsection (a).

jurisdictions. Although state statutes define kidnapping differently, the definitions have certain key elements in common:

1. Unlawful taking or seizing of a person without his or her consent.
2. Carrying away or transportation of the victim.
3. Unlawful confinement of the victim.

Kidnapping Investigations

The investigator must try to learn the *who, what, when, where, why,* and *how* of the situation. Some people tend to label every disappearance a kidnapping. Police must distinguish between legitimate cases and hoaxes. Alleged kidnappings may actually be attempts to cover up murders. Disappearances may involve youngsters who have run away from home, spouses who have fled their partners, or parents who have taken children not legally in their custody. As the investigator determines the likelihood that the disappearance is a genuine kidnapping, he or she also needs to determine the specific type of kidnapping it is. Is it a kidnapping in connection with another crime, such as a robbery? Is it a kidnapping for sexual assault? Is it a kidnapping motivated by politics or business? Gathering information to establish that a kidnapping has taken place should be an investigator's first consideration.

If the information gathered establishes that a kidnapping has occurred, a broadcast should be made, the watch commander notified, and an immediate investigation begun. The investigation should include a thorough interview with the victim, if available, or with the complainant or family members, as soon as possible. Investigators should search the crime scene, interview any witnesses, and broadcast follow-up information. Additionally, information should be updated in the national missing persons computer network that the department uses. Investigators should also have witnesses try to identify suspects through mug books—whether traditional or electronic—and should examine cases with similar M.O.s.

Kidnapping With Ransom Demand

The first concern of law enforcement personnel during the primary stages of a kidnapping involving ransom is

FYI

A change in U.S. monetary policy had a significant effect on the investigation of the Lindbergh kidnapping case. In April 1933, President Roosevelt ordered the recall of all gold and gold certificates to the U.S. Treasury. From August 20, 1934, to September 1934, 16 gold certificates turned up in the metropolitan New York area. Investigators were extremely interested in the source of these bills, as $40,000 of the ransom for the Lindbergh child had been paid in gold certificates. Several more gold certificates appeared, including one at a gas station. The description the suspicious attendant gave of the driver matched descriptions others had given of a man who also paid them in gold certificates. The license plate number copied down by the attendant led to Bruno Hauptmann, who lived in the Bronx.

the life of the victim, and it involves two major objectives: (1) the safe return of the victim and (2) identification and apprehension of the responsible party or parties.

When a call is received indicating a kidnapping in which a ransom demand has been made, the officer or 911 operator should obtain the basic information already outlined and forward the call to the proper authority. In larger agencies, a particular unit or division may handle such cases; in smaller agencies, the operator or officer may gather the preliminary information and advise the complainant or caller about specific actions to take.

It is important to obtain the exact wording of the ransom note, letter, or telephone call. Ask the complainant to avoid handling the note or letter and to see that no one else handles it. Determine whether anyone else knows the contents of the ransom note, letter, or telephone call; if so, find out who. Furthermore, the officer should advise the caller not to discuss or divulge the contents of the note, letter, or telephone call to anyone except police officials and to treat everything concerning the note, letter, or telephone call with the utmost secrecy. Emphasis should be placed on the importance of silence to protect the safety of the kidnapping victim. Also, the complainant should be advised not to disturb anything at the kidnapping scene and to try to keep others away from the area as well.

The officer assigned to the investigation should immediately start a log and begin chronologically recording the facts of the case, procedures undertaken, and assignment of personnel. Most important to the preliminary investigation is arranging an interview with the complainant and any other witnesses to obtain firsthand information about the crime. After compiling the information necessary to determine that a kidnapping with ransom demand has occurred, the investigator should broadcast a general alert concerning the kidnapping and ransom demand. To aid the investigation, the officer should contact the local office of the FBI and notify it of the status of the kidnapping.

All activity around the victim's residence should be kept at a low profile to avoid arousing the suspicion of the kidnapper, the neighbors, or the public. The investigator's interview with the victim's family should include an explanation of police procedures in kidnapping cases and the assurance that everything humanly possible is being done to effect the safe return of their loved one. The cooperation and confidence of the family should be sought and as much information as possible obtained from them.

If the media do learn of the kidnapping, the officer in charge should solicit their cooperation to help bring about the safe return of the victim. All press inquiries should be handled by the ranking officer or by a public relations officer if the department has one. Members of the media can unwittingly destroy evidence, frighten or alarm the kidnapper, and block efforts to return the victim or complete ransom negotiations.

Kidnappings attract media attention. The officer in charge of a kidnapping must use caution when releasing information to the media.

Withholding information from the media is temporary and does not infringe on the "people's right to know," because the information will be published when the immediate danger to the victim has passed. If kidnappers are kept in the dark, they can only guess whether the family has contacted the authorities, what investigative measures have been taken, what evidence has been located, and so on.

The following procedures are often helpful in investigating a kidnapping with ransom demand:

- Determine the method of entry used so that the area can be processed for possible evidence.
- Obtain and preserve the ransom note for laboratory processing.
- Furnish the family with an exact copy of the note in case they need it for negotiations.
- Review the ransom note, letter, or telephone instructions with the family to make sure that they understand the contents.
- Make sure that the person answering the suspect's telephone call follows the instructions of the officer in charge.
- Determine the financial status of the family.
- Determine if the family intends to pay the ransom; avoid giving any opinion about the ransom.
- Find out how the members of the family can raise the ransom money and have it available if they decide to meet the demand.

- Help family members decide who should make the payoff.
- Obtain information about all cars that might be used in payoff negotiations—complete descriptions and license plate numbers.
- Discuss with family members ways in which they can verify that the victim is still alive.
- Obtain permission for officers to stay in the home of the family during the crisis.
- Arrange for a private telephone line and the tapping and tracing of all incoming calls.
- Obtain permission from the family to intercept any mail and telegrams.
- Obtain a complete description of the victim (including clothing worn) and the best available photograph of the victim.
- Obtain a family history, particularly pertaining to the victim.
- Request permission from the family to examine personal possessions of the victim for possible leads.
- Ask whether the victim's fingerprints are available.
- Arrange to record all calls.
- Obtain specimens of the victim's handwriting.
- Ascertain the identity of local tradespeople and delivery people with whom family members may have had disagreements or arguments.
- Obtain information about the victim's place of employment.
- Determine what each family member was doing for an appropriate period before and on the day of the kidnapping.
- Assign unmarked police cars to strategic areas for surveillance and for backup if needed.
- Depending on the facts and circumstances, conduct any other appropriate investigation that can be accomplished without endangering the life of the victim.

Return or Discovery of Victim   The secondary stage of a kidnapping investigation is the period after the victim has been returned or the victim's body has been found. When a victim is returned, the first thing to do is notify family members that their loved one has been found alive and well. This is especially important when the victim is a child. Once this task is accomplished, the investigation changes. An all-out, no-holds-barred investigation is conducted to meet the second objective—namely, to identify and apprehend the person or persons responsible for the kidnapping.

Since the life of the victim is no longer at risk, the media can be kept apprised of the situation. In fact, the media may be of great help in this phase. Broadcasting or publishing descriptions or pictures of the suspected kidnapper, information concerning the kidnapper's vehicle or the ransom, or other pertinent facts may bring in new leads.

There are, however, some facts of a kidnapping case that *should not be given to the media.* These include confidential investigative techniques, current plans for the investigation, investigative steps being taken, identities of witnesses, details of the ransom note, information about the payoff spot, or any other confidential information. There may also be information that should be withheld to ensure that the defendant will ultimately receive a fair trial. Some other information about the crime, such as the type of bindings used on the victim's hands or the type of weapon used to force the victim into the car, may be intentionally withheld. This assures that a suspect has direct knowledge of the crime, not merely information published in the newspaper or reported on the evening news. Kidnappings, like many other crimes that attract media attention, sometimes draw out celebrity wanna-bes who crave attention so much that they claim responsibility for crimes they did not commit.

During this secondary phase of the kidnapping investigation, the officer in charge should conduct regular briefings to keep all the investigative personnel who are working on the case informed of developments. An investigation should be conducted in every aspect of the case suggested by the information received. Activities and procedures during this phase of the investigation should include the following:

- Thoroughly interview the victim, obtaining every minute detail.
- Obtain victim's clothing for laboratory examination for possible transfer evidence, such as hair or fiber.
- Thoroughly search the crime scene for physical evidence, including in the search the sites where the victim was kidnapped, where he or she was held (if known), and where the ransom was dropped off or paid.
- Take soil samples from the crime scene and from locations in the immediate vicinity (distances of approximately 10, 50, and 100 feet from the immediate crime scene).
- Carefully process all fingerprints found at the crime scene and compare them with those of possible suspects.
- Reinterview witnesses when necessary.

FYI

There is a difference between abduction and kidnapping. Abduction can be committed only against females. An abductor takes a female either for illicit sex or for marriage. A kidnapper may take a person for any reason, from monetary gain to revenge, and the victim's sex makes no difference. Because the intent in each crime is different, it is possible for someone to be guilty of both kidnapping and abduction.

- Place stop and question notices against suspects and their vehicles.
- Have drawings or computer-generated pictures created, with the assistance of the victim, to aid in identifying the suspect.
- Consult usual informants on the street for possible leads.
- Undertake surveillance of possible suspects or their associates as needed.
- Try to determine why this particular victim was kidnapped.
- Determine whether the kidnapper is familiar with the victim's neighborhood, habits, financial status, and so forth.
- Obtain handwriting, fingerprints, and palm prints from all members of the victim's family and household and from all the victim's associates.
- Canvass pertinent neighborhoods for possible leads or suspects and interview neighbors, local storekeepers, and delivery persons.
- Maintain liaison with other law enforcement agencies for possible suspects and coverage of leads.
- Maintain a chronological log of all investigative attempts and findings.

It is important not to immediately rule out family members or trusted friends of the family in kidnappings. As the case of Susan Smith discussed earlier in the chapter illustrates, kidnappers are not always strangers. Be tactful but thorough in considering the involvement of a family member or close friend in the kidnapping. Since a kidnapping victim's life may depend on determining who is involved, it is better to err on the side of rudeness than to overlook a relative or friend of the family who is actually the culprit.

Hostage Taking

The taking of hostages by a career criminal, a psychopath, or a would-be robber presents a highly sensitive situation for police personnel. Hostage takers are usually criminals whose escape from a crime scene has been interrupted, either by the police or by another individual. Realizing their dilemma, they take hostages to bargain for freedom, money, or means of escape. Resolving a hostage situation requires careful application of proper police response tactics.

Many large municipal police departments, the FBI, and a number of other federal agencies now have hostage negotiators ready to deal with cases involving **hostages,** or people being held against their wills for various reasons. **Hostage negotiators** are usually people specially trained to communicate with felons holding hostages, with the inten-

Hostage An innocent person held captive by one who threatens to kill or harm the person if his or her demands are not met and who uses the person's safety to negotiate for money, property, or escape.

Hostage negotiator An individual specially trained to deal with persons holding hostages.

tion of obtaining the release of these hostages. Smaller departments frequently have arrangements with local clinicians skilled in negotiating with troubled people. The idea behind negotiating is to resolve hostage incidents without bloodshed—to defuse potentially lethal situations by talking with the suspect before deaths occur. Hostage negotiation was pioneered by a volunteer team of three New York City detectives. The FBI now has trained hostage negotiators in each of its field offices. A number of larger departments also have highly trained SWAT (special weapons and tactics) units capable of containing a suspect or handling barricaded suspects and other hostage situations.

When people are taken as hostages, the last thing their captors want is to have to kill them. Once the hostage is killed, the captor no longer has bargaining power. Hostages may not be part of a criminal's original plan. For example, when a bank robbery is interrupted by a passing police car, the robber may take bank clients and workers hostage. In such a situation, a hostage negotiator might have to work with the personality of the robber and the specific circumstances of the situation. No hard-and-fast rules can be laid down to cover all hostage situations. Nonetheless, we can suggest some general principles concerning hostage or kidnapping situations.

The first general rule is *Give the culprit a chance to save face.* Orders for unconditional surrender place the hostage in needless peril. It has been said that strategy takes place in the area of ego. To be sure, the kidnapper has an ego, the investigator in charge of the scene has an ego, and all the back-up officers have egos. Law enforcement personnel working in these situations must remain flexible. Efforts must be made to let suspects feel that they can walk out and still be human beings. Law enforcement officers should use toughness only as a last resort. In rare cases, when a culprit is bent on wanton killing or self-destruction, negotiation techniques may be ineffective. In such cases, an armed assault may be in order. Negotiating is not the solution to every situation. There are times when words have to be replaced with stronger tools, such as weapons. However, hostage negotiations give the police an important tool with which to do their job.

Hostage negotiators are usually persons specially trained to communicate with individuals who are holding hostages.

FYI

The negotiator in a hostage situation must be mentally, physically, and emotionally prepared for a long ordeal. Hostage situations may last less than an hour or more than 40 hours. The average length is about 12 hours.

The second general principle or rule is *Always tell the truth*. Lying weakens the function of the negotiator. Negotiators must establish credibility; getting caught in a lie destroys any possibility of being viewed as credible. It is much better to honestly tell the captor that his or her demand is impossible to meet than to make a promise that cannot be kept.

The third rule is *Be patient*. No effort should be made to force the situation. Time is the ally of the police in a hostage situation. One basic concept to follow in critical situations is that good decisions are based on complete and accurate facts. The fundamental goal should be that no one gets hurt. Kidnappers can be caught and property replaced, but human life can never be restored.

Hostage takers may be categorized as follows: (1) the ordinary or professional criminal, (2) the mentally unbalanced or psychotic captor, (3) the political terrorist, and (4) the hijacker or carjacker. Hostage takers in the first category are the most predictable. They usually do not intend to take hostages, but when they are trapped, they use their victims to bargain for escape. Even when hostages are intentionally taken by professional criminals, it is unusual for the plan to include intentionally killing them. Sometimes a criminal will take hostage the family of a bank manager or supermarket manager. In these cases, the criminal uses the hostages as leverage to get money from the bank or market manager.

Mentally unbalanced or psychotic hostage takers are usually looking for a forum to make a statement or to get some message out. They regard themselves as trapped by society or some other imagined constraints or unknown force. They often have a wish for someone to take control and talk them out of dying—and killing. This is one of the areas where negotiators can best function. It is not uncommon for those who harbor strong feelings of frustration to commit suicide.

Hostage taking in category three is extremely dangerous and somewhat unpredictable. Terrorists (discussed in greater detail in Chapter 22) seldom agree to negotiate and are usually acting in accordance with their ideals or a cause. Because they may be religious or political zealots, reason is not always an avenue that works. Nonetheless, negotiators must attempt to channel the hostage taker's thinking toward more realistic terms.

The final category, hijackers and carjackers, is sometimes related to terrorist behavior. Terrorists may undertake a mass kidnapping, such as the commandeering of an airplane, a situation in which immobilizing them may cause a catastrophe. Airplane hijacking requires a friendly power that will allow the kidnappers to land and receive sanctuary. Thus, most hijackers are politically motivated. Carjackings, on the other hand, are generally crimes for profit (see Chapter 10). Carjackings are perilous situations because the victim is frequently beaten, shot, or stabbed. If cornered, however, the carjacker will use the victim as a hostage to try and engineer an escape.

In any hostage situation, one of the initial steps is to establish a line of communication with the captor. A **line of communication** may involve direct, face-to-face conversation with the captor or the use of a telephone. Using the telephone allows the negotiator to develop a one-to-one relationship with the hostage taker. Negotiators can also be valuable in a hijacking in which hostages are being held aboard a grounded airplane or in instances in which a criminal is trapped with hostages in a bank or store. Negotiators try to formulate a psychological profile of the suspect after the first contact. Friends, neighbors, associates, and relatives are quickly contacted and interviewed regarding various aspects of the captor's life and personality. Having an idea about how the hostage taker acts in various circumstances allows the negotiator to tailor police tactics and strategies specifically to the situation and the suspect.

> **Line of communication**
> A channel for communicating with another party.

Throughout all negotiations, the hostage taker and the victims should be contained within a confined area. In addition, an outer perimeter should be established to keep out traffic and curious people who might interfere with police operations.

STATISTICS

According to the Bureau of Justice Statistics, of the 62 defendants convicted of kidnapping/hostage taking in U.S. district courts in 1995, 59 were male, and 3 were female; 21 were white, 17 black, 13 Hispanic, and 11 other races.

Child Stealing

Recently, a new form of kidnapping has become prominent. This offense is committed against the parent or other legal guardian and not against the child. Increasing numbers of noncustodial parents are no longer willing to endure long periods without seeing their children. In many cases, the parent simply refuses to accept the noncustodial role. Instead, he or she takes desperate action and steals the children from the custodial parent or guardian. The taking of a child must only be against the will or without the consent of the parent, guardian, or person with legal custody for it to be classified as child stealing. If no judicial decree grants the custody of the child to one spouse, however, the other spouse is not guilty of child stealing if he or she takes the child away against the other's will. In the statutes on child stealing, the consent of the child under the age specified is no defense to a charge of the crime, because the child is considered incapable of giving legal consent.

In one case, a woman stole her 4-year-old son during a visit with him, arranged through the county welfare department adoption agency at an agency office. The boy was a ward of the court at the time. He was

Age Progression Technology   Computer technology to age enhance photographs has become an important tool in searching for children who have been missing for a long time. From photographs and videotapes of the child and the child's family as well as descriptive information about the child, the imaging technology produces an image of the child as he or she might currently appear.

in the custody and care of foster parents, who were in the process of adopting him. When he disappeared, the foster parents were waiting for him in a car parked outside the adoption agency. In this case, the mother was prosecuted for child stealing. In another case, a divorced mother in Nevada hired a security professional and convinced him, on the pretext of fighting conflicting custody decrees, to help her take her children from their father, who had moved with the children to Arizona. The plan failed, but the security professional was convicted of kidnapping, and his conviction was upheld on appeal.

Extortion

Like a kidnapping with ransom demand, extortion is a hybrid crime, against the person and against property. **Extortion** is the obtaining of money, property, or other consideration by one party from another with the appearance of consent. However, the consent has actually

> **Extortion** The obtaining of money or property from another by wrongful use of actual or threatened force, violence, or fear, or under color of official right; refers to such acts by public officials.

been induced by force, fear, or coercion. Extortion is also the use of threats to force or manipulate a public officer to take some official action. A public officer is one who works for a government or holds elective office. This includes municipal, county, state, and federal officials.

Legal Aspects of the Crime of Extortion

To constitute extortion, the wrongful use of force or fear must produce consent. Although most states have separate criminal extortion statutes, extortion can also be found in the bribery or theft statutes of some states. The definition of extortion found in the Model Penal Code (see Figure 13–2) provides an expanded definition of this crime.

More typical today are ordinary cases of blackmail. In fact, in some jurisdictions, *extortion* is simply referred to as *blackmail*. However, one can differentiate between extortion and blackmail as follows: Demands made by public officials in their official roles for illegal payments or presents are extortion. Illegal payments or demands for property made by private citizens are better known as **blackmail.** Blackmail is typically classified as a person's use of written or oral threats of force or terror to demand money or property to which he or she is not actually entitled.[3] Extortion can also be distinguished from robbery in that a kind of choice is given to the victim of extortion. In robbery, the intimidation is so extreme as to overpower the will of the victim and coerce him or her to give up money or property without consent.

Blackmail The unlawful demand of money or property under threat to do bodily harm, to injure property, to accuse of crime, or to expose disgraceful defects; commonly included under extortion statutes.

Figure 13–2 Model Penal Code, Section 223.4.

A person is guilty of theft by extortion if he purposely obtains property of another by threatening to:
(1) inflict bodily injury on anyone or commit any other criminal offense; or
(2) accuse anyone of a criminal offense; or
(3) expose any secret tending to subject any person to hatred, contempt or ridicule, or to impair his credit or business repute; or
(4) take or withhold action as an official or cause an official to take or withhold action; or
(5) bring about or continue a strike, boycott or other collective unofficial action, if the property is not demanded or received for the benefit of the group in whose interest the actor purports to act; or
(6) testify or provide information or withhold testimony or information with respect to another's legal claim or defense; or
(7) inflict any other harm which would not benefit the actor.

Victims of extortion may include railroads, airlines, banks, amusement parks, utility companies, sports stadiums, celebrities, politicians, corporate executives, and even ordinary people. Extortionists have been known to select names at random from newspaper articles, telephone directories, or organization membership lists.

Threats to kill, kidnap, or injure a person; ransom demands for the release of a kidnapped person; and threats to destroy private or public property are investigated by the FBI under the Federal Extortion Statute.[4] The FBI can investigate these threats if they are transmitted in interstate commerce or sent through the U.S. Postal Service. If letters accusing a person of a crime or injuring his or her reputation are sent through the mails, they are investigated by postal inspectors. Federal prosecution under the Hobbs Act is often used against extortionists who attempt to obtain money from federally insured banks or loan companies by threats against employees and their families. This act prohibits interfering with commerce by robbery or extortion or attempting or conspiring to do so.

Extortionists deliver their threats by various means, including telephone, electronic computer communications networks or bulletin boards, and letter. Threats may be of personal injury, mutilation, kidnapping, or killing. Or they may involve burning, blowing up, or in other ways damaging or destroying property. In some cases, threats are used merely to antagonize or frighten a victim or to cause mental anguish. An extortionist often sends letters to families of kidnap victims, demanding money for the return of the victim, thereby taking advantage of the family's predicament. Invariably the threats indicate that harm or injury will befall the loved one should the police be notified. The extortionist usually works alone, although the messages may carry the pronoun *we*. Threats are seldom actually carried out. However, threats against life or property cannot be ignored. Appropriate and timely police action must be taken.

The payoff location chosen by an extortionist may be any place that suits the culprit's purpose. It may be a church, a trash barrel in a park, an alley, a telephone booth in front of a police station (for an ironic twist), a cemetery, and so forth. Would-be extortionists have been known to send victims on wild-goose chases during payoff runs, to make sure police are not following or watching a payoff area. Sometimes a suspect will ride a bus or drive a car past the location, hoping to spot police surveillance activities. The extortionist may even call the victim and accuse him or her of contacting the police, hoping to further intimidate the victim into full cooperation.

Extortion Investigations

Often, solving an extortion case requires the complete cooperation of the victim. In extortion cases, the first concern of the police is the safety of victims. The recovery of extorted money or property and the apprehension of the suspect are a secondary concern. If a letter is involved, both the letter and the envelope may furnish valuable evidence about the educational background of the writer. Spelling, word choice, punctuation, and other writing elements can be studied and may offer insight. A thorough interview with the victim often results in the description of a logical suspect. The suspect may be a discharged or disgruntled employee, a business competitor, or a jealous suitor. She or he may be someone seeking revenge for some past incident, someone with a long-standing hatred or jealousy of the victim, or a vindictive neighbor. Seemingly irrelevant information that does not mean much to the complainant during an interview may become valuable to the investigator in identifying a suspect.

Extortion letters can sometimes reveal important information about their authors.

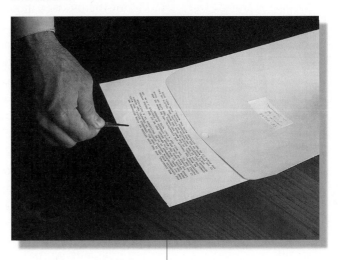

When covering an extortion payoff there are many things that the investigator must take into account. These include coordination, the number of surveillants needed, communications equipment, photographic and video equipment, and the type and number of surveillance vehicles. Specific considerations vary, of course, depending on the facts of the case, the location and terrain of the payoff area, and various unique circumstances in each case.

In many respects, extortion investigations are similar to kidnapping investigations. Investigations are governed by the identity and lifestyle of the victim, the location of the occurrence, and other routines and activities of the victim—employment, recreation, health needs, social practices, and so forth.

Extortion Threat by Telephone

The following procedures are in order when investigating telephone extortion threats:

- Ascertain the date and exact time the call was received.
- Determine what was said and by whom.
- Find out what threats were made and what instructions were given.
- Ask whether any background noises were heard, such as music, traffic, bells, or train or boat whistles.
- Ask whether the suspect said that he or she would call again and, if so, when.
- Determine whether any regional or foreign accent was detected in the suspect's voice; similarly, ask about speech impediments.

The victim should be advised that if any additional calls are received, he or she should cooperate with the caller, take detailed notes of the message, note the exact date and time of the call, and write down any directions for a payoff. As soon as possible, arrange to monitor and record calls at the victim's home or place of work or both. Instruct the victim to have the caller repeat instructions, even if he or she understands them, to ensure that they are clear. Endeavor to have calls traced by keeping the caller on the line as long as possible. The victim should ask such questions as, "With whom am I speaking?" "How do I know you're not joking?" "Why did you pick me?" "What denominations of money do you want?" "Where is the money to be delivered?" "When will I get additional instructions?" "How will I know when I have reached the location?" "What guarantees do I have that you will keep your word?" It is useful to have the victim ask as many of these types of questions as possible, to get all the necessary information and to try to determine who the extortionist is or where he or she may be.

In one attempted extortion case, the manager of a supermarket received a telephone call from an unknown person, who stated that he was holding the manager's wife and children hostage in his car. He advised the manager to meet him at a designated spot and to bring all the money in the store to secure their safe return. The manager immediately telephoned his home, knowing that his wife had not planned to leave the house that afternoon. The manager received no answer at his home. Next, he called the police, who sent a unit to the manager's residence. The officers determined that the wife and child were at home unharmed. The arranged payoff spot was covered by police, but the extortionist failed to appear.

When asked why she had not answered the telephone when her husband called, the wife replied that she had received a call shortly before her husband telephoned. The caller had identified himself as a telephone company employee. He told her that the phone line was being worked on, and that though the phone might ring, she should not answer it for at least one hour.

Later that same day, the manager of a supermarket in a city 70 miles away from the original store received a similar extortion call. This manager, like the other, called his home, and when he received no answer, he notified the police. The same M.O. had been used, but in this case, the extortionist showed up at the payoff location, where he was arrested by waiting police and charged with extortion. When arrested, the extortionist was carrying a loaded automatic pistol and a loaded revolver.

Extortion Threat by Letter

The following procedures are useful when investigating extortion threats involving letters:

- Ask when the letter was received.
- Find out how it was delivered.
- Get the postmark and date of the letter.
- Determine whether the letter was handwritten, hand-printed, typed, or computer-printed.
- Note the signature on the letter.
- Ask the recipient to maintain absolute secrecy and not to handle the letter or envelope or permit anyone else to touch them; instruct the complainant not to reveal the contents to anyone except law enforcement authorities.
- Instruct the complainant to maintain a normal routine around the house and place of employment.
- Ask the complainant if he or she suspects anyone of sending the letter.
- Find out if any prior communication had been received.
- Obtain and preserve the extortion letter for laboratory examination.
- Obtain permission to tape-record all telephone calls to the complainant's home and place of employment.
- Arrange for the tapping and tracing of all telephone calls to the victim's home and place of employment.
- Brief all personnel involved with the case.
- Make certain that the victim's movements are coordinated with police instructions at all times during the crisis.
- Arrange personnel, vehicles, and equipment for any required surveillance.
- Obtain fingerprints and palm prints of the victim and others known to have handled the letter or envelope.
- Investigate the area of the victim's residence if it is relevant to the facts, circumstances, location, or other elements of the case. Extortionists have been known to observe their intended victims before and during the period of the extortion demands.
- Oversee the preparation of the payoff package.
- Alert all personnel and the victim to the danger of the suspect's stopping or intercepting the victim at any point along the payoff route.

FBI special agents investigate violations of federal law. Violations may include such crimes as kidnapping, extortion, bank robbery, fraud and theft against the federal government, espionage, interstate transportation of stolen property, mail fraud, and sabotage. Agents may be required to do sophisticated surveillance, monitor court-authorized wiretaps, examine business records, collect evidence, interview and interrogate witnesses, or be assigned to sensitive undercover operations.

U.S. citizenship, availability for assignments anywhere in the Federal Bureau of Investigation's jurisdiction, and being between the ages of 23 and 37 are the initial requirements. All applicants must also pass vision and hearing tests. Finally, applicants must have a valid driver's license and be in excellent physical condition with no physical defects that would interfere in firearm use, raids, or defensive tactics.

If candidates meet all of the general requirements, there are five special agent entry programs for which applicants must meet specific requirements: law, accounting, language, engineering/science, and diversified. Those qualifying for appointment as special agents must pass a written examination and undergo a thorough background check. New agents receive intensive training in federal criminal law and procedures, investigative techniques, physical fitness, and firearm use.

The pay scale for jobs with the federal government is a graded scale, from GS-1 (lowest) to GS-18 (highest). An entry level special agent is a grade 10 job. In 1995, the salary for a special agent ranged from $32,290 to $60,925. Under certain conditions, special agents can earn overtime pay.

- Check the anonymous-letter file of the local and state police and the FBI for similar letters.
- Record the license plate numbers of all cars that pass a payoff location; a video camera or a still camera with a telephoto lens can assist in this surveillance.

If a suspect is taken into custody, fingerprints and palm prints should be taken for comparison with the unidentified prints obtained during the course of the investigation. Handwriting or hand-printing specimens should also be obtained from the suspect, depending on whether the letter was written or printed. Voiceprint samples may also be taken for comparison with tape recordings made during extortion calls. It should also be determined whether the suspect has access to the particular make of typewriter or computer printer used to prepare any extortion notes (if the extortion note was printed or typed).

SUMMARY BY LEARNING OBJECTIVES

Learning Objective 1

Kidnapping is taking someone away by force, often for ransom or some form of payment. In many cases of kidnapping, the perpetrators demand large sums of money from wealthy people or civic leaders, or from a corporation or industrial enterprise. Terrorists have used kidnapping as a means of coercing governments into changing policies or releasing prisoners.

Learning Objective 2

The Lindbergh kidnapping case in the early 1930s received worldwide attention and led to the passage of federal antikidnapping legislation. The "Lindbergh law," as it came to be known, made it a federal offense to transport a kidnapped person in interstate or foreign commerce for purposes of ransom, reward, or otherwise.

Learning Objective 3

State statutes define what constitutes the crime of kidnapping in each state. Despite variation among the states, state kidnapping statutes have certain key elements in common. Kidnapping is (1) the unlawful taking or seizing of a person without his or her consent; (2) the carrying away or transportation of the victim; and (3) the unlawful confinement of the victim.

Learning Objective 4

As in any criminal investigation, it is important to ascertain the *who, what, where, when,* and *why* to establish that a kidnapping has indeed taken place. In addition, extreme tact, care, and control of dissemination of information regarding the kidnapping must accompany the investigation to ensure the safe return of the victim and to avoid tipping off the kidnapper as to what measures have been taken or what evidence has been located.

Learning Objective 5

A hostage taking is a highly tense and extremely sensitive situation for police personnel to resolve. Three general rules are helpful in dealing with such a situation: Give the culprit a chance to save face. Always tell the truth. Be patient.

Learning Objective 6

Recently a new form of kidnapping—child stealing—has become prominent. This is an offense against the parent or other legal guardian of a child and not against the child. In many cases, the noncustodial parent refuses to accept the noncustodial role and takes desperate action to steal his or her own child from the custodial parent or guardian.

Learning Objective 7

Extortion is the obtaining of money, property, or consideration by one party from another with the appearance of consent. However, the consent has actually been induced by force, fear, or coercion. Generally, extortion refers to such criminal acts by municipal, county, state, or federal officials. Illegal payments or demands for money, property, or special consideration made by private citizens are better known as blackmail. State statutes define what constitutes extortion or blackmail and may include such definitions in bribery or theft statutes.

QUESTIONS FOR REVIEW

Learning Objective 1

1. Define *kidnapping, ransom.*
2. Name some possible reasons for a kidnapping.

Learning Objective 2

3. What is the popular name for the Federal Kidnapping Statute?
4. What was the big break in the Lindbergh kidnapping investigation?

Learning Objective 3

5. What elements do most state statutes have in common in defining the crime of kidnapping?

6. What is the primary objective of a kidnapping investigation?

7. What kind of information is important to obtain during a kidnapping investigation?

8. Why should investigating officers not offer advice about whether family members should pay a ransom?

9. When investigators learn that a victim has received a ransom note, what should they tell the victim to do?

10. Who should conduct the interview with a kidnapping complainant?

11. When a kidnapping victim has been released and the kidnapper is still at large, should the media be given the full story? Explain.

12. Should a hostage negotiator ever lie to the hostage taker?

13. One of the three basic rules of hostage negotiation is *Be patient.* What are the other two?

14. Under what circumstances would child stealing not be considered illegal?

15. Against whom is the crime of child stealing directed?

16. What are some of the questions an investigator should ask the victim of an extortion call?

17. How would you differentiate between extortion and robbery?

CRITICAL THINKING INVESTIGATIVE EXERCISE

You are the desk sergeant in a small-town police department. A young woman runs into the station with tears streaming down her cheeks. "He's taken my children, he's taken my children," she screams. After she calms down, she offers the following account:

> I was getting into my car after shopping down at the Winn Dixie. I had just put the baby into his car seat and checked on my big boy's seat belt, when a man wearing a ski mask rushed over to the car. He had a gun and ordered me out of the car. He jumped in and would not even let me get my kids out of the back seat. He promised that he would not hurt my boys but said that it would cost me money to get them back. He took my wallet and said he'd be in touch about the ransom.

1. What questions would you ask the victim?

2. What actions and activities would you suggest the police take to secure the release of the children and the apprehension of the carjacker-kidnapper?

3. What information should be released to the media?

INVESTIGATIVE SKILL BUILDERS

Participating as a Member of a Team

You are a member of a hostage negotiation team. You have been called to the scene of a carjacking standoff between local police and two would-be carjackers. They have a woman and two children hostage in the woman's car. One of the men has a handgun and the other a hunting knife. After nearly an hour of coaxing, your team leader has opened a line of communication with the carjackers. During his conversation with these men, he has learned the following:

Both men are two-time losers for armed robbery.

Their names are Darryl and Wayne.

They might be willing to give up one of the hostages for some food and water.

The woman has a superficial knife wound on her left arm from the carjackers' first effort to take control.

The two men are demanding to be allowed to drive away with one hostage. They claim that they will release the others as a sign of good faith. They say that they will release the last hostage after getting some distance away—if they are not followed.

They threaten that if the police try to move in on them, they will kill the children first and then the woman.

They say they want an answer in 15 minutes.

Your team has now assembled to discuss possible actions.

1. What actions would you suggest?

2. Should the negotiating team capitulate on *any* of the demands?

3. What other information might the team leader try to solicit from these men?

Integrity/Honesty

You are working on a kidnapping case involving a divorced couple. The father had been granted legal custody of the child, a 7-year-old girl. Yesterday, the girl was picked up from school by a woman and has not been seen or heard from since. At the time of the incident, the girl's mother claims to have been working, but she cannot account for her whereabouts or provide any witnesses. The father maintains that they had gone through a terrible divorce and custody battle and says that he believes his wife is responsible for the kidnapping.

The mother of the girl maintains her innocence and suggests that her ex-husband has contrived this situation to make her look bad. She suggests that one of her ex-husband's girlfriends might have taken the girl at his request. During the interview with the mother at her home, your partner finds himself extremely attracted to her. They get to talking and you overhear that he has made a date to see her socially later that evening. As you leave with your partner, he begins to suggest following up on the woman's suggestion that the ex-husband may have had something to do with the crime. He also suggests that you and he should drop the woman as a suspect.

1. How will you respond to your partner's suggestion?
2. Should you report his activities to your superior?

ENDNOTES

1. Hank Messick and Burt Goldblatt, *Kidnapping: The Illustrated History*, Dial, New York, 1974.
2. Neil C. Chamelin and Kenneth R. Evans, *Criminal Law for Police Officers*, 5th ed., Prentice Hall, Englewood Cliffs, N.J., 1991.
3. Messick and Goldblatt, op. cit.
4. United States Code, Title 18, Secs. 873, 875–877 (1970).

CHAPTER 14

Homicide

CHAPTER OBJECTIVES

After completing this chapter, you will be able to:

1. List the four general categories of death and explain the goal of classifying a death into one of these categories.

2. Explain the legal aspects of homicide.

3. Specify various motives for homicide.

4. Describe the role of forensic pathology in homicide investigations.

5. Tell how to determine if a person is dead.

6. Indicate ways in which homicide victims may be identified.

7. Identify factors used to estimate time of death.

8. Name and describe the types of deaths investigated and the weapons used.

homicide
justifiable homicide
excusable homicide
criminal homicide
  (felonious homicide)
murder
felony murder
manslaughter
forensic pathology
rigor mortis
cadaveric spasm
livor mortis
adipocere
forensic
  entomologist
toxicological screening
defense wound
wipe ring (smudging)
tattooing
contact wound
asphyxiation
autoerotic asphyxiation

Homicide and the Law

O f all the serious crimes committed, homicide is the one whose investigation demands the greatest effort by the police. Human life, in our society, simply has no price; it is an incalculable and irreplaceable commodity. The seriousness of homicide is reflected in the penalties for its commission, which include lengthy prison sentences and sometimes even death. The types of deaths that confront the police can be divided into four major categories: homicide, natural causes, suicide, and accidental causes. The goal of classifying a death in one of these categories is to assign *responsibility* in both a moral sense and a legal sense. Let us now consider some of the legal implications.

Homicide is the killing of one person by another. It is important to note, however, that not all homicides are criminal. Some homicides may occur because of an accident, owing to negligence, in self-defense or in the defense of another, or as the only way of apprehending a dangerous fleeing felon. Even self-inflicted deaths are generally treated as homicides until the police can establish them as suicides. **Justifiable homicide** is the intentional killing of another person in the performance of a legal duty or the exercise of a legal right. An example is the shooting death of an armed robber by a police officer who has arrived on the scene only to be met by the robber's gunfire. **Excusable homicides** are accidental killings where there is no gross negligence. For instance, every year there are hundreds of accidental, but fatal, shooting accidents when one hunter mistakes another hunter for quarry. Although the question of gross negligence may be raised in a hunting incident, the death is usually considered accidental. Generally, all these homicides are considered nonfelonious because they are justifiable or excusable.

A **criminal homicide,** on the other hand, is the unlawful taking of another person's life. Criminal homicides are sometimes referred to as **felonious homicides** and are further divided into murder and manslaughter. **Murder** is the unlawful taking of human life with *malice aforethought,* meaning premeditation. In many jurisdictions, the killing of a person during the commission of a felony is also murder. Thus, an armed robber who shoots and kills a storekeeper who has grabbed for the robber's gun will be charged with murder. In fact, a number of jurisdictions would charge the robber's partner with murder, too, even if the accomplice was waiting outside in the getaway car during the shooting. A killing, incident to the commission of a felony, is commonly referred to as **felony murder.**

Sometimes a criminal homicide occurs under circumstances that are not severe enough to constitute a murder, but the homicide cannot be classified as excusable or justifiable. This is the crime of **manslaughter,** and it can be voluntary or involuntary. *Voluntary manslaughter* is the intentional killing of another in the sudden heat of passion caused by words or actions that provide a provocation. *Involuntary manslaughter* is the accidental killing of another as a result of an act of extreme and cul-

---

Homicide The killing of one human being by another.

Justifiable homicide The killing of another in self-defense or defense of others when danger of death or serious bodily injury exists.

Excusable homicide The killing of a human being without intention and where there is no gross negligence.

Criminal homicide (felonious homicide) The wrongful killing of a human being without justification or excuse in the law. There are two degrees of the offense—murder and manslaughter.

Murder The unlawful killing of a human being by another with malice aforethought.

Felony murder The killing of a person during the commission or attempted commission of a felony other than murder.

Manslaughter The unlawful killing of another without malice. It may be voluntary—upon sudden heat of passion—or involuntary—in the commission of an unlawful act.

pable negligence. Suppose a motorist skids on an icy road and careens into another automobile, killing the other driver. Provided that the surviving driver was sober and had not violated any traffic laws, the incident would probably be ruled accidental manslaughter or involuntary manslaughter. On the other hand, if police learn that the surviving driver was intoxicated, he or she may be charged with vehicular manslaughter, a felony murder in most jurisdictions.

ƛ Most state statutes provide for varying degrees of murder, such as *first-degree* and *second-degree murder* or *murder one* and *murder two,* as television prosecutors seem so fond of labeling them. In some states, *heat-of-passion murder,* or killing motivated by some strong emotion, may also be defined in certain circumstances. The prosecuting attorney decides what charge to bring, based on available evidence. Most state statutes have common elements in their definitions of murder. These include purposely, knowingly, recklessly, or negligently causing the death of another human being.

In 1995, the FBI reported 21,600 incidents of murder and nonnegligent manslaughter (see Figure 14–1). This was a decrease of 7

Figure 14–1 Murder and nonnegligent manslaughter crime index totals.

Year	Population	Crime Index Total	Number of Murder and Nonnegligent Manslaughter Offenses
1980	225,349,264	13,408,300	23,040
1981	229,146,000	13,423,800	22,520
1982	231,534,000	12,974,400	21,010
1983	233,981,000	12,108,600	19,310
1984	236,158,000	11,881,800	18,690
1985	238,740,000	12,431,400	18,980
1986	241,077,000	13,211,900	20,610
1987	243,400,000	13,508,700	20,100
1988	245,807,000	13,923,100	20,680
1989	248,239,000	14,251,400	21,500
1990	248,709,873	14,475,600	23,440
1991	252,177,000	14,872,900	24,700
1992	255,082,000	14,438,200	23,760
1993	257,908,000	14,144,800	24,530
1994	260,341,000	13,989,500	23,330
1995	262,755,000	13,867,100	21,600

Source: Federal Bureau of Investigation, *Crime in the United States,* Government Printing Office, Washington, 1995.

percent from the previous year. Not included in the total count for this classification are deaths caused by negligence, suicide, or accident; justifiable homicides; and attempts to murder or assaults resulting in death, which are counted as aggravated assaults. As in previous years, firearms were the weapon of choice in more than 70 percent of murders committed nationally; 59 percent of murders were by handguns, 5 percent by shotguns, 3 percent by rifles, and 5 percent by other types or unknown types. Among the other weapons used, knives or cutting instruments were used in 13 percent of murders, personal weapons (hands, fists, feet, etc.) in 6 percent, blunt objects (clubs, hammers, etc.) in 5 percent, and other dangerous weapons (poison, explosives, etc.) in the remainder. If you look again at Figure 10–2 in Chapter 10, you will see that murder is the least frequent of the index offenses. Despite its low significance statistically, murder receives the most attention from police. It is the most serious crime and is often very difficult to investigate. Murders also draw media attention, and this attention can affect what the police can and cannot do within their jurisdiction.

Motives for Homicide

Motive is important in the investigation of a homicide. If an underlying motive for the homicide can be determined, a suspect may be identified. Because motive also allows an investigator to better understand why a homicide has occurred, it gives the investigation a kind of focus. Now let us consider some of the more common motives for homicide.

Unplanned or Spontaneous Murders

Unplanned or spontaneous murders occur quite frequently and are likely to be motivated by one or more of a variety of causes:

- Use of drugs or alcohol, resulting in a fight that turns lethal.
- Reaching for a handgun or rifle during the heat of an argument.
- Dispute between a boyfriend and girlfriend.
- Dispute between friends over a boyfriend or girlfriend.
- Disagreement over money or a business transaction.
- Heat of passion when a spouse discovers his or her partner is cheating on the relationship with another.

- Unintentional killing during the commission of another crime, such as robbery or burglary.

As each example suggests, spontaneous murders lack planning and premeditation, but are highly related to opportunity. They spring from an emotional base and occur swiftly, seemingly without reason. Jealousy or emotionally charged disputes are typically at the root of spontaneous murders. Spontaneous murders usually have a high clearance rate since frequently there are witnesses and evidence available to the investigator. The perpetrator may even be arrested at or near the scene of the murder.

Murder for Financial Gain

Murders for financial gain often occur between individuals who have a professional or contractual relationship or are linked as beneficiaries of a will or insurance policy. The financial gain may be in real wealth or in property or business holdings. For example, many small businesses have partner's wills, by which the death of one partner transfers sole ownership of the business to the surviving partner. In other financially motivated homicides, a person may stand to collect a sizable inheritance upon the death of another person. A common question for an investigator to ask when considering the motive in a homicide is "Who had something to gain from this death?"

It is also important to consider that a murderer motivated by a significant amount of wealth may hire a third party to actually commit the crime. Frequently, the truth in such murders will be brought to light only if the actual killer is apprehended and turns on his or her employer.

Unlike spontaneous homicides, murders for financial gain are carefully planned and generally meticulously carried out. The killer may go to elaborate and sometimes expensive lengths to make the murder appear accidental or to arrange a viable alibi.

Sexually Motivated Murders

Sexually motivated murders, also sometimes called lust murders, may be planned and intentional or may occur spontaneously as a secondary aspect of a rape or another sex crime. The actual murder may occur before, during, or after the sexual assault. In some cases, the murder is connected to the psychological problems that motivate the person to commit the sex crime. In other cases, the murder is a way of eliminating a possible witness, or it occurs while the assailant is trying to subdue a struggling victim.

Another type of sexually motivated murder is the killing of a spouse to make way for another mate. This is more likely when a large estate is under the control of the murdered spouse or when a divorce might result in the loss of large amounts of money or property.

In some cases of sexually motivated murder, particularly those involving homosexuals, friends of the victim may provide important clues to the identity of the killer. The victim's neighborhood should be canvassed, as well as places the victim might have spent time (local bars, gyms, and so on). Interviews with people in these locations may provide significant information regarding who a suspect might be and where he or she might be found.

Murder for Revenge

On television detective shows, a question frequently asked by the investigator is "Did the deceased have any enemies?" Answering this question may lead to information about the murderer in a murder for revenge. Many public figures, such as judges, prosecuting attorneys, politicians, and prominent businesspeople, knowingly and unknowingly make enemies. In addition, drug dealers and other criminals may cross one another and thus create enemies—sometimes numerous ones, each with a motive to murder. In some cases, the actual victim of murder may not even have been the true target of the revenge. For example, a felon angry with a judge who sent him to prison might rape and murder the judge's young daughter as a means of hurting the judge in revenge. Because the victim is not always the actual target, revenge murders are sometimes difficult to investigate.

Elimination Murders

Elimination murders are committed to remove some obstacle to a desired goal. The obstacle may be an eyewitness to another crime, or a business rival, or even an opposing criminal boss. Checking on the background of the victim may provide clues to the reason for the murder. In some cases, the victim may have been eliminated because he or she was an informant or potential informant for police authorities. In such a case, how apparent the likely murderer is may depend on whether the authorities have already received information about someone from the murdered informant. However, the victim may have been providing information on a number of individuals, giving each a potential motive for murder. Although the playing field may be thus reduced, it will still require considerable investigation to identify which of the possible suspects is responsible.

Motiveless Murders

There are at least two forms of what might be called motiveless murders. These include stranger-to-stranger murders and mistaken-identity murders. Stranger-to-stranger murders have been on the increase during the past decade. Often these deaths are of bystanders killed by gang members in drive-by shootings. In some cases, the killing is a *hate crime,* in which an individual is killed because of some physical or personal characteristic. For example, a homosexual man may be beaten to death by someone he meets in a bar; a Hasidic Jew may be shot by a neo-Nazi skinhead; or an African-American woman may be murdered simply because she walked into a neighborhood where a Ku Klux Klan meeting was going on. Alcohol and drugs sometimes play a role in such stranger-to-stranger murders. The initiation rituals of some gangs may also contribute to these kinds of murders. Some gangs require new members to *make their bones*— or murder someone to prove their worth.

Mistaken-identity murders are not especially common. However, occasionally an investigator will confront a murder that seems both senseless and without motive. A thorough examination of the victim's background may indicate that he or she had no enemies and was not worth killing for financial gain. In fact, no reason for the murder can be found. For example, a blond-haired woman is shot in the back of the head while sitting in a blue Volvo parked in the lot of a local supermarket. A background investigation reveals that the woman was happily married, had two small children, was active in civic projects, and had no apparent enemies. The case seemingly comes to a standstill. However, several weeks later, another blond-haired woman is found shot in the head in a blue Volvo outside the same supermarket. This time, however, the assailant has been seen and recognized by a supermarket employee. The police arrest the woman identified by the supermarket worker and recover the murder weapon. When arrested, the woman bursts out, "I don't care if I go to jail, as long as that bitch doesn't get my man." By interrogating the suspect, the police learn that she shot the first woman by mistake; she had not previously seen the woman she meant to kill, but she had a description of her and her car. The first murder, then, was a case of mistaken identity.

STATISTICS

According to the Uniform Crime Reports, 77 percent of murder victims in 1995 were males, and 88 percent were persons 18 years of age and older; 45 percent were aged 20–34. Of victims whose race was known, 49 percent were black, 48 percent were white, and the remainder were of other races.

HISTORY

Historically, statistics on relationships of victims to offenders have shown that the majority of victims knew their killers. During the 1990s, however, the relationship percentages have changed. According to the Uniform Crime Reports, in 1995, 16 percent of victims were killed by strangers, and 39 percent of victims were killed by persons whose relationships with them were unknown, for a total of 55 percent unknown; 34 percent of victims were acquainted with their assailants, and only 11 percent were related, for a total of 45 percent known.

The Homicide Investigation

Although detectives handle the majority of dead-body calls, patrol officers are often called on to conduct or assist in an investigation involving a death. Therefore, all officers need at least a working knowledge of the problems and procedures involved in a death investigation.

The responding officer's first priority is to give emergency aid to the victim, if he or she is still alive, or to determine that a death has occurred. A person who is near death may appear dead to the untrained observer. Consequently, officers responding to dead-body calls should, upon arrival at the scene, examine the body. While the investigator must be careful not to destroy evidence, it is equally important to be sure that the person is dead, rather than in need of immediate medical help. It is not advisable to rely on the opinion of a witness or bystander, unless he or she happens to be a doctor, coroner, or similarly trained clinical specialist. If there is the possibility, regardless of how remote, that the victim may still be alive, an ambulance should be summoned. First aid should be administered by the officer until the ambulance arrives. There are a number of ways to determine whether a person is dead:

- **Appearance**   In death, the face becomes pale or ashen and waxy, the lower jaw drops a bit, and the mouth may sag open. The eyes become soft to the touch, and the eyelids may be open slightly but will show no sign of movement or reflex action when touched.

- **Pupillary reaction**   The pupils of a living person's eyes contract when a bright light, such as a flashlight beam, is shined into the eyes.

- **Pulse**   A check for a pulse may be made on the wrist, inside the upper arm at the elbow, or under the chin at the neck.
- **Visible breathing**   Note the movement of the chest or abdominal area.
- **Nose**   Listen or place hand at nostrils to hear or feel breathing.
- **Muscle resistance or muscle reflex**   Muscle resistance and reflex are present in the body to some degree until death. Note whether limbs can be moved without resistance.
- **Cyanosis**   In death, the lips become cyanotic, or bluish, as do the nail beds.

The type of investigation conducted at the scene is determined by the category of the death being investigated. The first officer responding to the death call must come to a general conclusion about the cause of death. This is important, since it will dictate the type and degree of the investigation that will follow. Things that influence an officer's decision about whether a homicide has occurred include the type and amount of information furnished by the complainant and witnesses and an examination of the body. Close observation of the crime scene and body for marks of violence and other indicators, such as signs of struggle, cuts, wounds, weapons, poison, pills, blood, bruising on the body, or bullet holes may assist the officer in drawing a conclusion. Information furnished by relatives, friends, and neighbors may permit early conclusions about the noncriminal nature of a case. For example, the person's past history of illness and absence of any signs or evidence of violence may suggest that the death was by natural causes.

Procedures in the Preliminary Investigation

The first officers arriving at the scene should observe the following priorities:
- Record the time they were notified of the death complaint.
- Record the identification information about the complainant. Include the date and the location from which the complainant called.
- En route to the scene (depending on the elapsed time between the call and the alleged death) be alert for possible fleeing suspects—people with fresh wounds, torn or bloody clothing, or any sort of furtive or evasive actions.
- Record the time of arrival at the scene and the exact location.
- Determine whether the victim is dead or severely injured. Request medical assistance if necessary. Use caution when approaching the victim, to avoid disrupting or destroying

possible evidence and to protect your safety in case the victim is armed.

- Determine and verify the identities of those present at the scene and anyone who left before the officers' arrival.
- Record the license plate numbers of vehicles parked near the scene, so that their owners may be contacted if necessary.
- Begin brief and informal interviews of witnesses; be sure to obtain their home and business addresses and telephone numbers.
- Take immediate action to block off the crime scene to prevent contamination or destruction of evidence.

After these preliminary matters have been taken care of, the homicide investigation generally shifts its focus to other high-priority matters, which include identifying the victim, establishing the cause of death, determining the time of death, and developing a suspect.

Arrival of Investigators and Medical Examiner

When the investigators arrive at the scene, one of them will take charge of all aspects of the case. The lead investigator will coordinate and direct all investigative assignments. The head investigator should immediately take inventory of all personnel at the scene. A recap of all the information already gathered should be requested from the responding officers, and everyone at the scene should be brought up to date before continuing the investigation.

As in any other criminal investigation, the homicide scene must be secured and protected, photographed, and sketched, and all evidence must be carefully gathered, identified, preserved, and forwarded to the lab. An accurate description of the body and all clothing worn by the victim should be recorded. (When describing a body, proceed from the head to the feet.) Observe the victim's face for injuries, blood, dirt, extraneous matter, or marks. Take color photographs of bruises or other marks on the victim's body. Note the eyes, mouth, and facial expression. Examine the victim's hands, noting whether they are clean, dirty, open, clenched, holding anything, or wearing any articles of jewelry. If the victim has been sexually molested, the medical examiner should check for pubic hairs or semen stains. Also carefully package and label the contents of wastebaskets, glasses, cups, bottles, ashtrays, and any other containers at the scene.

STATISTICS

Homicides have the highest clearance rate of any index offense. According to the FBI's Uniform Crime Reports, the 1995 clearance rate for murder was 65 percent for law enforcement agencies nationwide.

In addition to securing and preserving physical evidence, investigators should identify and interview possible witnesses and suspects, as well as relatives and friends of the deceased. All persons with any connection to the deceased should be asked to describe exactly what they were doing when they learned of the death. Canvassing the neighborhood may also lead to direct or hearsay information about the time of the homicide.

All violent or suspicious deaths require the coroner or medical examiner to determine the time and precise cause of death. The determination of criminal responsibility in a death has evolved into a highly specialized field of medical science called **forensic pathology.** Most large departments have medical examiners and forensic pathologists on staff or available to assist in investigation at a death scene or death discovery scene. In other situations, the on-the-scene investigation is conducted by police investigators, who then forward all evidence with the body to the coroner's office. There an autopsy is done to establish the cause and time of death and, in some instances, to identify the victim.

Forensic pathology A specialized field of medicine that studies and interprets, in relation to crime investigation, changes in body tissues and fluids.

If possible, the homicide investigator should be present during the autopsy, to observe firsthand and ask questions about the case. The pathologist or medical examiner can explain the autopsy findings as they progress. The firsthand results can then be passed on directly to others working on the case. Should the investigator have a suspected murder weapon, that weapon can be compared with wounds on the body. The officer present at an autopsy can also testify about the autopsy at a coroner's inquest, should one be conducted.

Identifying the Victim

Knowing who the victim is and how the victim was killed may provide clues about motive or the suspect's identity. The inability to identify a dead body greatly complicates the investigation. When investigators do not know who the victim is, it is difficult to delve into his or her background. Different types of evidence can contribute to ascertaining a deceased person's identity.

Fingerprints   Fingerprint identification is the most efficient way to identify the body of a murder victim. However, this technique is effective only if the victim's prints are on file and if prints can be obtained from the corpse. If the hands or fingers have been mutilated or in other ways destroyed, investigators may not be able to use fingerprints to identify the body.

Skeletal Studies   Examination of the skeleton may provide a basis for identification. This is especially true if the body has any skeletal peculiarities, such as old fractures, metal plates or pins, or evidence of certain bone diseases. Also, bones may provide clues about the victim's age, gender, and race.

Visual Inspection   The victim may be recognized by someone who knows him or her, for example, a friend, relative, or coworker. However, severe trauma, incineration, or decomposition may make it impossible even for a mother to identify her own child. Visual inspection without verification has a risk of subjective error. This may occur because the person making the identification is psychologically unable to accept the death of a close friend or relative. The misidentification may occur by accident, or it may be deliberate. Visual identification combined with another method, such as fingerprint matching, is a favored method for reliable identification.

Personal Effects   Sometimes a victim may be identified through his or her personal effects, such as jewelry, identification cards, or letters in pockets, a wallet, or a purse. Personal effects, however, may prove unreliable, given the easy transferability of such items. Despite their possible lack of reliability, personal effects often do provide leads to the actual identity of the victim.

Tattoos and Scars   Tattoos, scars, pockmarks, birthmarks, moles, and other such skin markings may be helpful in establishing a victim's identity. Alone, these markings provide only tentative or somewhat unreliable identification, but in conjunction with other, more reliable forms of identification, skin markings can lead to a positive identification.

Odontology (Dental Evidence)   Identification based on the examination of teeth, fillings, inlays, bridges, crowns, and so forth is valuable because teeth are among the most durable parts of the human body. When incineration, animals, trauma, decomposition, and insects have destroyed virtually everything else, the teeth often remain undamaged. It is unlikely that two people have identical sets of teeth. Dental evidence is legally recognized and accepted when properly presented in court.

Clothing   Articles of clothing frequently contain identification clues such as cleaner's marks, labels, initials, and similar information. Identification by clothing alone, of course, is inexact, since clothing may be easily loaned, sold secondhand, or stolen. Furthermore, articles of clothing, in themselves, are seldom unique enough to provide a reliable basis for identification. They are useful, on occasion, when searching for a missing person who is reported as wearing certain clothing.

Photographs   It is not uncommon, when other methods fail, to ask the public for help in identifying a murder victim. Photos of the victim are sometimes published in local papers or shown on local news programs.

When photos are not appropriate, as in the case of disfigurement or mutilation, an artist's rendering may be substituted. Sometimes, information about the identity of the victim and about the murder itself results from such public showing of the victim.

Estimating the Time of Death

It is important to establish the time of death as precisely as possible. If the time of death is too vague, it could provide enough time for the murderer to have an alibi. In some suicides, the time of death may determine whether an exclusion clause in an insurance policy can be enforced. In traffic accidents, double murders, murder-suicides, or suicide pacts, it is also important to determine the order of the deaths.

Typically, both the investigator and the medical examiner are responsible for estimating the time of death. Understanding how medical examiners estimate time of death allows the investigator to better consider the elements at the crime scene that will be relevant.

Only when a murder has witnesses can investigators pinpoint the time of death with absolute precision. In the absence of witnesses, the time of death can be estimated fairly accurately. Usually, if the death occurred within the past four days, the time of death can be placed within four hours of its actual occurrence. Naturally, this may vary with the factors an examiner uses and the factors available. A number of factors can be used to estimate time of death.

Rigor Mortis Although limp immediately after death, a body stiffens as substances (mainly lactic acid) accumulate in the muscles. This stiffening is known as **rigor mortis.** Warm temperatures accelerate its appearance and disappearance, and cold slows them down. *Rigor mortis* usually begins 2 to 4 hours after death and affects the entire body in approximately 6 to 12 hours. *Rigor mortis* will frequently disappear in 24 to 36 hours. It disappears in about the same sequence as it appears. The early stages of *rigor mortis* can be noted in the jaw and the back of the neck, with stiffening of other muscles proceeding down the body.

Closely associated with *rigor mortis* is a condition called **cadaveric spasm.** This condition is sometimes referred to as *instantaneous rigor.* This rigidity of specific muscle groups cannot be fully explained. It typically occurs after a sudden injury to the central nervous system, but it should not be confused with *rigor mortis.* It manifests itself as a death grip, usually on a weapon, and is generally most evident in suicides. It does not disappear, as *rigor mortis* does.

Livor Mortis (Postmortem Lividity) *Livor mortis,* also often called *postmortem lividity,* is a dark discoloration (usually dark blue or purplish) under the skin. It is caused by the draining of blood to the parts of the

Rigor mortis A stiffening of the body after death that disappears over time.

Cadaveric spasm A rigidity of certain muscles that usually occurs when the victim is holding something at the time of death and the hand closes tightly around the object; sometimes a sign of suicide.

Livor mortis A dark discoloration of the body where blood has pooled or drained to the lowest level; also called *postmortem lividity.*

body nearest the ground when the heart stops beating and circulating the blood. It is especially useful to consider when trying to determine if a body may have been moved after death. Particularly when the body has lain in the original position for several hours before being moved, *livor mortis* may be pronounced. Investigators should be careful not to confuse lividity with discoloration caused by bruises on the body. *Livor mortis* can also be useful in indicating the cause of death. For instance, in carbon monoxide poisoning, some forms of cyanide poisoning, or extremely cold conditions, *livor mortis* is not dark purple but cherry red.[1] In potassium chlorate poisoning, lividity is light brown. Lividity usually begins within 1 hour after death, congeals after 3 or 4 hours, and reaches a maximum in 10 to 12 hours.

Body Temperature   Body temperature, though not entirely accurate alone for determining time of death, can assist in its estimation. After death, the body tends to lose heat at about 1 to 1.5 degrees per hour until it reaches room temperature. Although heat loss may be rather rapid during the first 3 hours after death, it levels off then, occurring more slowly until the body reaches room temperature, or the temperature of its environment. Factors influencing the time required to cool the body include the difference in temperature between the body and the medium in which it is found (e.g., water, air, soil). In addition, clothing, the victim's physical size and weight, and the weather may all affect the cooling rate.

Livor mortis, or discoloration of the body where the blood has pooled internally, may be pronounced, especially if the body has lain for several hours before being moved.

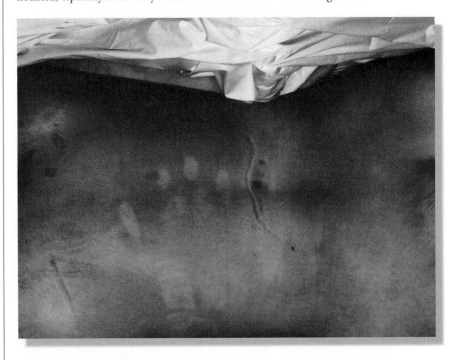

Body Decomposition   Decomposition is the breaking down of a human body, due to the effects of temperature, animal and insect attack, and general putrefaction through the softening and liquefaction of tissue and the conversion of soft tissues to liquids and gases.

The actual rate at which the human body decomposes depends on a number of factors. These include air temperature, levels of moisture, the body's own bacteria and enzyme levels, and assaults by animals or insects. Early signs of putrefaction, noticeable after about 24 hours, are a greenish-red or blue-green coloration of the abdomen or groin. Darkening continues until the tissue color of the entire body is completely brown or black.

The rate of decomposition is influenced by the environment and the weather. The colder the temperature, the slower the decomposition, whereas warmer temperatures increase decomposition speed. Similarly, bodies tend to decompose more rapidly in water, owing to large amounts of bacteria in the water and attacks by fish and other aquatic life forms.

Since the human body has a greater specific gravity than water, a corpse may sink initially when placed in water. However, within three days to a week (depending on water temperature) the body will surface because of the formation of gases. Prolonged submersion in water causes the skin to wrinkle, and as liquids and gases move beneath the skin, the body will bloat and sometimes even burst.

Adipocere is a whitish gray, soapy or waxy substance that forms on the surface of the body after about six weeks. It is caused by changes in the fatty tissue and may not be seen unless there is fat in the tissue beneath the skin. When a body has been buried in damp ground or submerged in water, adipocere usually forms.

Adipocere A whitish gray, soapy or waxy substance that forms on the surface of a body left for weeks in a damp location.

Carrion Insects   During the past several years, the role of the **forensic entomologist** has expanded, and such scientists now assist in estimating the time of death of decomposed bodies by examining the attack of the body by certain insects.[2] Several guidelines should be followed to assist the work of the forensic entomologist. First, do not move or in other ways disturb the body. As in other crime scene investigations, take photographs of the body, including close-up photographs of the areas where insect activity is detected. The investigator should carefully describe in his or her notes the environment where the body was found (forest, bedroom, dark shed, etc.). Also, the investigator should record the temperature at the time of investigation, the relative humidity, and the general weather conditions, if the body was found in an open or exposed area.

Forensic entomologist A person who specializes in the study of insects in relation to determining the location, time, and cause of death.

Insects must be collected from the body as soon as possible, beginning with areas of greatest decomposition, usually the face or an open wound. The goal is to collect as many different insects as possible, and at all stages of the insect's life cycle (adults, pupae, larvae, eggs). Flies typically are the first insects to attack a decomposing body. A search for fly larvae, even in the absence of other insects, may assist the investigation. Folds in the deceased's clothing and the soil directly beneath the body should be carefully examined, as they frequently conceal insect larvae. If the search does not locate any evidence of hatched fly pupa cases, one may assume that the fly larvae collected represent the first cycle of an insect attack.

Other Indicators   In addition to the factors already suggested, medical examiners can draw conclusions regarding the time of death by considering the contents of the stomach. The investigator can assist the medical examiner's estimate by trying to learn what time the victim last ate. Food digestion is affected by a number of factors, and investigators should note, for example, whether vomit is found near the victim. During an autopsy, the medical examiner can ascertain to what extent items in the stomach have been digested and can infer from that about how long after a meal the death occurred.

Watches and other timepieces found near the victim of a murder may also assist the investigator in approximating the time of death. A watch or a clock in a room may be broken during a scuffle or by a stray bullet in the course of the murder. This may give an indication of the time of death. Old watches and many inexpensive timepieces will stop almost immediately when submerged in water. This too may offer some indication of when the body was placed in the water or killed.

When a body is found outdoors, time of death may be inferred roughly by the vegetation under and around it. If a body has remained on the ground for a long period, the decaying of vegetation underneath the body may also help in determining the time of death.

Developing a Suspect

Should a suspect be apprehended at the scene, follow procedures outlined in Chapter 2 for arresting suspects and giving *Miranda* warnings. If witnesses at the scene have provided descriptions of a suspect, interview that suspect, following the procedures set forth in Chapter 6. If a suspect has not been identified, it is important to try to determine a motive for the murder (see "Motives for Homicide," earlier in this chapter) to point the way to a possible suspect. Here are some suggested investigative procedures for developing a case against a suspect who is in custody:

- Administer a polygraph examination if the suspect is willing and signs a waiver of legal rights.
- Have the suspect reenact the crime, and make a videotape of this reenactment.
- Take photographs of the suspect.
- Take into custody the clothing the suspect wore at the time of the homicide, and have it processed by the crime lab.
- Conduct a sobriety test, and take specimens of saliva, urine, and blood.
- Collect fingernail clippings and hair samples from the suspect.

- Examine the suspect for wounds, bite marks, or scratches.
- Take fingerprints of the suspect, and check them against available files.
- Check all telephone calls made by the suspect during the recent past, and verify the identities of people called.
- Verify all statements made by the suspect to either corroborate or disprove information given by witnesses or other sources.

Types of Deaths Investigated and Weapons Used

Knowing about the most common kinds of deaths and their characteristics can greatly assist homicide investigators. Being able to recognize types of wounds and knowing what kinds of evidence to look for in certain situations can improve the chances of a successful homicide investigation. Figure 14–2 shows the various types of weapons used to commit murder in one recent year.

Natural Death

The true disposition of a dead-body call is generally not known until after a preliminary investigation has been conducted. The officers

Figure 14–2 Murder circumstances by weapon.

Firearms (handguns, rifles, shotguns, others)	13,673
Knives or cutting instruments	2,538
Personal weapons (hands, fists, feet, etc.)	1,178
Blunt objects (clubs, hammers, etc.)	904
Strangulation	232
Explosives	190
Asphyxiation	135
Fire	166
Drowning	29
Narcotics	22
Poison	12
Pushed/thrown out window	4
Other	960
TOTAL MURDERS	20,043

Source: Federal Bureau of Investigation, *Crime in the United States,* Government Printing Office, Washington, 1995.

receiving the call have many investigative responsibilities, particularly in unattended deaths and other types that fall under the purview of the coroner or the medical examiner's office. Teamwork with the coroner or the medical examiner's investigator at the scene of death is essential to the determination of the cause of death. Most state laws require that the death certificate include a statement, not only of the cause of death, but also of the mode—that is, whether the death was by natural causes, accident, suicide, or homicide. In natural deaths, the coroner or the medical examiner's office is primarily interested in establishing a cause to (1) rule out unnatural causes, (2) determine whether the death was an accident, a suicide, or a homicide, (3) eliminate dangerous conditions, and (4) determine liability.

When approaching the location of a death call and after arriving at the scene, responding officers should be particularly alert for any unusual conditions or suspicious activities. Immediate steps must be taken to protect the scene and the property of the deceased. Nearly always, the scene of death has been disturbed, making it difficult at times to reach an early conclusion. The disturbance may have occurred in several ways. The injured victim may have been thought alive at the time of the discovery, and the scene may have been disturbed by attempts to revive or save the life of the victim. The assailant or a bystander may have moved the body for some reason. Another possibility is disturbance by early arrivals, sometimes even inexperienced police officers.

Once the officers are satisfied that the death was the result of natural causes, the following investigative duties remain:

- Notify the desk sergeant as soon as possible after verifying the validity of the complaint. Request any needed assistance and the coroner.

- Determine who discovered the body.

- Determine the deceased's name, race, gender, age, and marital status; the name and relationship of the next of kin; and the preference of mortuary.

- Find out who was the last person to see the deceased alive. Note when and where that happened, who else was there, and what activities occurred.

- Obtain short statements from people who witnessed the death or found the body. Establish the time of death.

- Inquire about the health history of the deceased. Also find out the actions and remarks of the deceased prior to death.

- Contact the victim's doctor if the victim was receiving treatment. Determine whether a doctor or another legally authorized health professional had attended the victim in the previous 48 hours.

- Check for additional injuries or other possible causes of death, even if the cause of death seems obvious.

Computerized Photographic Lineup To aid in suspect identification, computerized photographic lineups can now be quickly assembled. The technician keys in the physical characteristics (reported by the victim or witnesses) that he or she wants displayed in each of several panels of composite photographs that the system will assemble. The remaining panel is a photograph of the suspect.

Suicide

Suicide is intentionally killing oneself. People choose a variety of ways to end their lives, but the ten most common are hanging, taking overdoses of pharmaceutical or illegal drugs, drowning, taking poison, inhaling gases, jumping from high places, self-inflicted gunshot wounds, self-inflicted cuts or stabs, electrocution, and intentional crashes of aircraft or automobiles. The reasons, motives, and psychological intentions of suicidal people are quite complex. Self-destructive ideas or impulses that ordinarily are well controlled or mostly unconscious can be activated or released by emotional stress, physical or mental exhaustion, or alcohol- or drug-induced conditions. All of these situations intensify suicidal behavior.

Suicide is not a criminal offense, but in some jurisdictions, attempted suicide is. Some jurisdictions hold an attempted suicide that kills an innocent bystander or a would-be rescuer to be murder; others, manslaughter; and still others, no crime. Some jurisdictions hold it to be murder for one person to persuade or help another to commit suicide; others make it manslaughter or a separate crime.

It is sometimes difficult to distinguish between homicide and suicide (or accidental death) by a quick examination of the crime scene. Many deaths by suicide have all the outward appearances of murder to an untrained eye. This is an important question to be answered by the responding officers. As a rule, however, self-inflicted injuries have certain fairly predictable physical features. Although the location of a wound and the manner of its occurrence are not always conclusive, they do provide a degree of probability of suicide versus homicide. For this reason, investigating officers should examine the injury and consider its manner and direction, the nature of the weapon, the presence or absence of a note, and information from any witnesses.

Suicide occurs at all socioeconomic levels; cuts across religious, racial, and political lines; and can occur among very young children and the aged. During the investigation of suicides, the officer may encounter evasion, denial, concealment, and even direct suppression of evidence. The investigator should try to reconstruct the true conditions of the crime scene at the time of the discovery of the body, to avoid false conclusions. Some of the questions an investigator should try to answer during the investigation of an apparent suicide include the following: Has anyone touched or moved the body or removed any property before the arrival of the police? If *livor mortis* has set in and the officer knows how to interpret it, does it indicate that the body has been moved? What is the temperature of the room? Has it been changed since the time of discovery? Have heaters been turned on or off? Were windows found open or closed, doors locked or unlocked? Were lights turned on or off when the discovery was made? Who turned off the automobile ignition in a carbon monoxide poisoning? Who shut off the gas on the stove (or other source) in a home gas-inhalation poisoning? What are the identities of the people present and any who left before the officers arrived?

Investigators should be cautious when investigating suspected suicide cases. Hanging victims are sometimes cut down and the knot untied (see Figure 14–3), plastic bags are removed from suffocated victims, drowning victims are pulled from swimming pools, and instruments and suicide notes are sometimes removed to cover up a suicide. Such a cover-up may be fabricated by well-meaning family members because of religious beliefs or to protect the public image of their loved one. It may also be an effort to defraud an insurance company that has a nonpayment-for-suicide clause.

Some people leave notes indicating why they killed themselves. Not all suicides, however, leave notes, letters, or even clues to their reasons for killing themselves. Only about 25 percent of all people who commit suicide leave notes. Even when notes are found, they may not conclusively show that a suicide, rather than a murder, has been committed. Nor is the absence of a note an indication that there is no suicide.

If a note is found, investigators should be careful not to handle it and should learn if other members of the family or witnesses have

Figure 14–3 Characteristic bruise patterns in homicide and suicide strangulation.

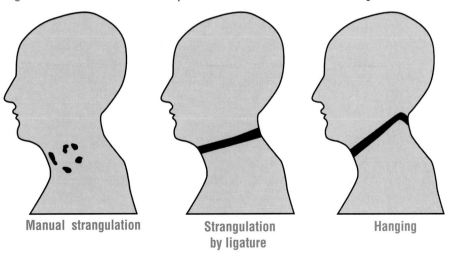

Manual strangulation

Strangulation by ligature

Hanging

already handled it. A suicide note should be handled like any other piece of physical evidence. It should be photographed and then carefully packaged in an evidence envelope bag and identified. If available, a sample of the deceased's writing should be obtained. In addition to traditional written notes, in today's technologically advanced age, investigators should not overlook the possibility of a recorded or videotaped suicide message.

Procedures in Suicide Investigations The investigation of a suicide is not nearly as complex or lengthy as the investigation of a homicide. It is recommended, however, that the following procedures be taken:

- Examine the victim. If doubt exists about the victim's being dead, call for an ambulance. Administer first aid while awaiting the ambulance.
- If the victim is obviously dead, observe the scene carefully for indications of a struggle, the locations of objects in the room, the positions of chairs, the contents of ashtrays, and any weapons, pills, prescription bottles, glasses, suicide notes, and so on.
- Notify headquarters of findings at the scene and request the coroner.
- Be alert for efforts to make the victim's death appear accidental.
- Ask about the medical history, ailments, medications taken, and prescriptions (type, when filled, amount remaining, etc.).
- Examine any containers of prescription drugs and the accompanying labels. A prescription drug label should have the name of the drug and the name of the physician who issued the prescription. Generally, the name of the pharmacy is also

on the label. The label should also indicate the date the prescription was filled, the number of tablets or capsules originally in the container, and the recommended dosage.

- Note the location of the medication and any indication of overdose or recent use. Also note any containers (glasses or cups) or loose tablets or capsules near the body.
- Check with relatives, friends, and neighbors. Before committing suicide, a person may make suicidal statements, give away personal items, or engage in certain other behaviors.
- Check for suicide notes (usually found quite close to the body). With handwritten notes, compare the handwriting on the note with known samples of the victim's writing. Preserve the note and turn it over to the coroner.

Poisoning

Poisoning is among the oldest methods of murder. It can be accomplished with a single lethal dose or by the accumulation of many small doses given to a victim over time. Some poisons can be administered by contact with the skin, while others need to be ingested. Still others can be injected into the muscle or blood of a victim, and some may be lethal if inhaled. There are even some versatile poisons that are lethal whether ingested, absorbed through the skin, or inhaled. Brucine, for example, is an extremely toxic chemical commonly found in pharmaceutical laboratories, as well as in many college chemistry classes. Even a very small amount, perhaps enough to cover the head of a pin, can kill a man of average height and weight.

Whenever a death is suspected to be the result of poisoning, a **toxicological screening** (an examination of tissue and body fluids for poisons) should be requested by the investigator. This will involve the collection of tissue and body fluid samples by the coroner or medical examiner's investigator, or some other authorized person. The contents of the stomach may also assist in the investigation of a suspected poisoning. It is important for the investigator to collect for analysis any drugs or drug containers that may have been used by the decedent.

A toxicological screening can sometimes reveal the presence of a toxic substance in a victim. Some drugs and poisons can be detected easily in blood, urine, or other body fluids. Others are detected only in tissue samples from the liver, kidney, or brain. Some poisons, however, such

> ## FYI
>
> Many poisoning attempts are thwarted because the assailant uses too much poison. As a result, the victim vomits up most of the toxin before it can cause lethal damage.

Toxicological screening An examination of body tissue or fluids for poisons or other toxins.

as brucine, may be missed by even highly skilled toxicologists if they are not looking specifically for that substance. Gaseous poisons and some harsh astringent fumes may be detected by an examination of lung tissue, as well as by their presence in the blood.

A point to be mindful of is that many symptoms of poisoning also appear in certain diseases; however, symptoms of poisoning typically occur suddenly to a person who was previously in good health. The disease process is usually more gradual, proceeding over a period of many hours, days, or even weeks. A specific poison must be isolated and identified from tissue or body fluids before investigators can assume that the poison was taken or administered with the intention of killing the victim.

Stabbing and Cutting Wounds

Stabbing and cutting wounds differ in depth, shape, and size. Cutting, or incision, wounds are typically inflicted with a sharp edge, such as a razor or knife blade. However, any sharp flat instrument, such as the edge of a credit card, a piece of metal, or a shard of glass can produce a serious incision wound. Cutting wounds usually have even edges where the tissue has been cut. When the incision is parallel to the tissue fibers, the wound's edges lie close against one another. On the other hand, when the incision cuts across the fibers, the wound typically gapes open.

Since incisions are made quickly by the sharp edge of an instrument, bruises are usually not present. As a result, it is often difficult to tell whether they were made before or after death. As a general rule, incisions are deepest at the point where the cutting edge of the instrument first cut the skin. Thus, the direction of the wound can be determined by examining the cut from its deepest to shallowest points.

Stabbing wounds may be produced by a knife, a knitting needle, a screwdriver, scissors, an ice pick, or any other tipped or pointed instrument. If a stab wound was produced by a sharp, flat instrument, such as a knife, it may not be possible to determine the width of the blade or instrument from the size of the external wound. This is because the wound channel may be larger than the instrument that inflicted the damage. This is especially true for two-edged instruments, such as some throwing daggers and knives. This difference in size is due to the cutting action of the blade when it strikes the body and creates the entrance wound, as well as the cutting action when the weapon is withdrawn. If the knife is moved or turned while being withdrawn, the wound may further increase in size and develop a curved or angular surface. The wound may also exhibit characteristics related to the shape of the cutting instrument. For instance, a thick blade may produce a wedged-shaped wound, round weapons produce

TOP LEFT: Cutting wounds produced by a single-edge blade; TOP RIGHT: Penetrating stab wound caused by a sharp object; BOTTOM LEFT: Lacerations on head from tire iron; BOTTOM RIGHT: Defense stab wound on inside of arm.

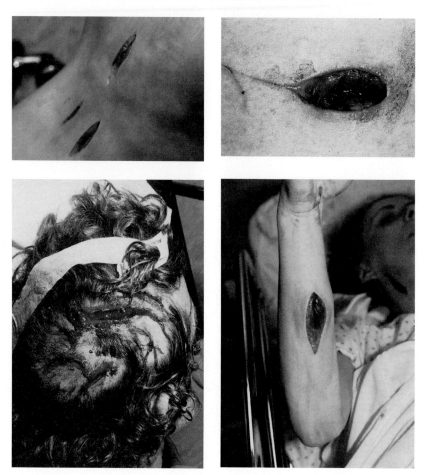

puncture wounds, serrated edges may produce slightly jagged edges on the surface wound, and so forth. The depth of a stab wound's channel may assist the medical examiner in determining the length of the weapon used.

Cutting wounds along the insides of a person's wrists, if deep enough to sever arteries, may result in death from loss of blood. Similarly, incisions that sever arteries in the neck of a victim will likewise cause death. Stabbing wounds typically result in death when vital organs are irreparably damaged or when arteries are severed.

Defense wounds result when a victim tries to ward off an attack. They may appear as stabs through the hand or cuts on the hands, fingers, or arms. Cuts on the palm or fingers may indicate that the victim sought to grab the weapon, while slashes on the arm or shoulder suggest an attempt by the victim to block or shield him- or herself from a cut or stab. Investigators should carefully examine the hands, arms, and shoulders of victims to identify possible defense wounds. Bruises on the

Defense wound A wound on the hand or forearm of a victim who has attempted to fend off an attack.

knuckles of a victim should also be noted, since they may indicate that the victim struck his or her assailant.

Gunshot Wounds

Injuries and deaths resulting from gunshots are a special category of injury. The wound may result from a handgun, rifle, or shotgun. When a gun is fired, a number of things may affect the wound that results. These include the caliber of the weapon, the distance at which the weapon was fired, any materials the bullet traveled through before striking the victim (e.g., a wooden door or a plasterboard wall), the shape and nature of the bullet (e.g., jacketed, pellet, hollow, flat-tipped), and whether the bullet was shot directly into the victim or ricocheted off some object.

Investigators should note both the entry and exit wounds of a gunshot. This is particularly important for determining whether the gunshot was intentional, accidental, or self-inflicted. Although the medical examiner will make the final determination during an autopsy, the investigator should be aware of wound characteristics to be able to determine the type of investigation to pursue.

Gunshot wounds may exhibit certain characteristic entry patterns. The size of the wound depends on the caliber of the weapon firing the bullet, although the entry wound may be somewhat smaller than the bullet because the elasticity of the skin closes the entry point slightly. Frequently, there is a gray ring around the wound. This ring may be more pronounced when the gun is fired at very close range. The discoloring results from the deposit of gunpowder on the skin and is sometimes called a **wipe ring** or **smudging.** When a gun is fired at extremely close range, the skin around the wound may even be burned by the muzzle flash and hot gunpowder. The burn is sometimes referred to as **tattooing.**

When a gun is fired while being held against the skin of the victim, a **contact wound** results. Contact wounds generally are larger than wounds inflicted at a distance because gases discharged when the gun is fired enter the wound with the bullet. (These gases dissipate

Wipe ring (smudging) A gray ring around a gunshot wound, resulting from the deposit of gunpowder by a gun blast at close range.

Tattooing The burned skin around a gunshot wound, resulting from hot gunpowder from a gun blast at very close range.

Contact wound A wound created when a gun is fired while being held against the skin of the victim; typically found in self-inflicted wounds and execution-type murders.

Gunshot contact wounds with muzzle imprint.

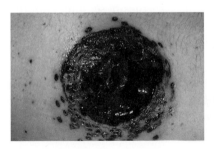 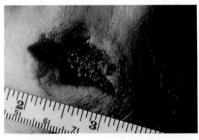

into the air when a gun is fired at a distance from the victim.) Having no place else to go but into the wound when the gun is placed against the skin, these gases burst the tissue, causing a larger entry wound. Contact wounds are typically found in suicides and in execution-type murders.

The difference between entry and exit wounds is observable. Exit wounds are generally larger than entry wounds, are likely to bleed more profusely than entry wounds, and are often irregularly shaped. The shape of the exit wound depends on the path and condition of the bullet as it passes through the victim. If the bullet has struck bone, mushroomed, or fragmented, the wound's shape will vary.

When weapons are found at the scene, they should be photographed, sketched, measured, identified, and handled only with gloved hands (see Chapter 4). Notes should be made to support the officer's actions, and the weapon should be submitted to the laboratory for examination. The trial of a homicide case often hinges on information about the weapon and the positions and types of wounds inflicted on the victim. Investigators should use extreme care when writing notes regarding these elements of a case.

Asphyxia

Asphyxiation Death due to a lack of oxygen and an excess of carbon dioxide in the blood.

Death from **asphyxiation** is an extreme condition caused by a lack of oxygen and an excess of carbon dioxide in the blood. It can result from choking, suffocating, smothering, drowning, or electrocution. As previously mentioned, body discoloration occurs in all deaths. In cases of asphyxia, it is usually quite pronounced and is characteristically blue. It is particularly noticeable around the mouth and lips and finger- and toe-nails. In cases of asphyxiation from strangulation, one frequently finds hemorrhaging in the eyes (broken blood vessels in the white portion, which appear as red blotches). This bleeding results from increased blood pressure brought on by compression of the throat or neck.

Strangulation In death by strangulation, external pressure closes the airway or compresses the main arteries in the neck. Oxygen is withheld from the lungs, and the blood supply to the brain is drastically curtailed, resulting in death. When investigating a suspected strangulation, look for bloody fluids at the nose and mouth, tongue displacement, and marks on the neck indicating hands, fingers, or a ligature that may have been used to compress the throat. Also, note the scene for disturbances or signs of a struggle, and note the condition of the ground or floor beneath the body. Likewise, check the victim's fin-

FYI

In some cases of strangulation, skin is removed from the neck area to recover the killer's fingerprints.

gernails for signs of skin tissue or hair or other trace evidence of the assailant. A ligature, such as a rope, strap, wire, scarf, or other pliable material, will leave horizontal marks low on the neck and show equal pressure around the neck. Manual strangulation leaves a different pattern of soft tissue damage and may occur higher on the neck. (See Figure 14–3.) Most strangulations are murders.

Hanging   Most hangings are suicides, but some are accidental. Victims are found in sitting, standing, and lying positions. Belts, towels, bandages, wire, fabric strips, rope, and assorted other tying materials are used. Hanging does not require that the body drop or swing freely, since only pressure is required to cause death. As in strangulation, air and blood flow are restricted. In hangings, ligature marks typically start below the chin and travel up diagonally toward the ears or the top of the head. The entire noose should be removed from a hanging victim without disturbing the knot. This can be accomplished by cutting the noose and securing the ends with a cord. If the noose consists of a slipping sort of knot, the knot should be secured with a cord before the noose is cut and then secured.

Some points to consider when investigating a hanging include the following: Did the victim die as the result of the hanging, or was he or she unconscious before being placed in a hanging position? Where and how was the ligature tied? With what type of knot? Could the victim have tied the knots him- or herself? Was there a disturbance of any kind in the area? Evidence of a struggle? What paraphernalia, including the source of the ligature material, are present? Is there a suicide note and a sample of the decedent's handwriting? Did family members or someone else find a note? Did the victim provide for the possibility of "stepping back" should he or she have a change of mind or hope to be discovered? Were there any previous suicide attempts? Were there any recent changes in the behavior of the deceased? Did the deceased have any organic or terminal diseases that might have led him or her to consider suicide? Did he or she have financial problems or concerns? Did the deceased recently lose a loved one? Was the deceased trying to punish someone? Who did the victim contact just prior to death? Can it be established from *rigor* and *livor mortis* that the victim was the sole active agent of his or her own death?

Smothering   Although many movies and television shows dramatically show murderers smothering their victims with pillows, smothering is actually a fairly uncommon mode of murder. People under the influence of drugs and alcohol, invalids, the aged, and infants are much more likely victims of accidental smotherings. In each of these cases, the victim is likely to turn face down onto a pillow, or to become tangled in blankets, and, owing to an intoxicated or weakened condition, accidentally smother to death.

Smothering has murder implications when it becomes a form of infanticide. The assailant may place a hand over the mouth and nose of the child until he or she suffocates. In some cases of adult smothering, the assailant may use a plastic bag or a sheet of plastic pulled tight around the face of the victim. In such cases with adults, considerable force must be used and is likely to result in signs of a struggle, indicating that the death was not an accident.

Choking   Choking involves a foreign substance or object blocking the throat and airway and generally is accidental. Small children are notorious for placing in their mouths anything that will fit. If an object is swallowed, it may tragically result in an accidental choking. In some instances, choking occurs because a person has tried to swallow too large a piece of food, has swallowed a bone, or has gasped or otherwise inhaled while swallowing.

Carbon Monoxide Poisoning   Death from carbon monoxide may be an accident, a suicide, or occasionally a homicide. Carbon monoxide is an odorless, colorless gas. Sources include unvented or poorly vented gas heaters and automobile exhaust from defective muffler systems. Perhaps the most frequent source of carbon monoxide poisoning is the exhaust of a car. In a suicide, the decedent may have intentionally closed the air escapes in a garage or may have run a garden hose from the exhaust pipe into the car cabin. Carbon monoxide causes death because it combines with the hemoglobin in the blood, making it impossible for the hemoglobin to combine with life-giving oxygen. Accidental carbon monoxide poisonings have occurred when someone sat in a car in the garage while warming the engine on a cold winter morning. Also, during the past several years, homeowners have become more aware of the dangers of accidental carbon monoxide poisoning from faulty or inadequately vented heating systems. Several companies now produce carbon monoxide alarms that sound if the concentration of the gas becomes too high in a home.

Volatile Intoxicant Sniffing   Volatile intoxicants include all substances that when inhaled produce altered states of consciousness (e.g., ether, nitrous oxide, paint thinner, some glues, and gasoline). Model airplane glue (with toluene or benzene as a solvent), for example, produces a form of intoxication often accompanied by hallucinations. The glue is usually applied to a handkerchief or a piece of cloth, and the treated material is inserted in a paper bag. The bag is then placed over the mouth and nose, and the person breathes deeply of the fumes trapped in the bag. A similar procedure is used with several other substances, including gasoline. Sniffing volatile intoxicants causes serious liver damage and can result in death after only a short period of repeated use. There are also cases of accidental death from suffocation when sniffers use plastic bags to inhale fumes and continue inhaling even after the oxygen is gone from the bag.

Another method of intoxicant sniffing includes sitting near air-conditioning units to sniff Freon. Freon, however, is extremely toxic, and sniffing it is often fatal.

Drug Overdoses   The respiratory center of the central nervous system is depressed by certain drugs. Muscle paralysis, including paralysis of the muscles of respiration, can also occur. Narcotics and barbiturates, their effects sometimes exacerbated by alcohol, are the principal groups of drugs encountered. Other central nervous system depressants, however, may also be responsible for death by asphyxia. In general, a complete autopsy must be done in cases of suspected drug overdoses.

Autoerotic Asphyxiation   In **autoerotic asphyxia,** sexual gratification is sought by near asphyxia. A rope or other ligature around the neck reduces the flow of air and oxygen to the brain, and at the same time, the individual may masturbate. Unfortunately, in some cases, unconsciousness results, and eventually total asphyxia and death. A variation of autoerotic asphyxia—or *gasping,* as it is sometimes called—may be undertaken by partners, with one partner restricting the air in the other and, theoretically, monitoring the level of consciousness.

Autoerotic asphyxia is not the most common form of death by asphyxia. However, investigators should be aware of its possibility and recognize certain of its attributes. Typically, the body of the victim is found nude or with genitalia exposed. In some cases, men are found dressed in women's underwear or clothing. There is often evidence of masturbation. There may be sexually stimulating paraphernalia, such as vibrators, sexual aids, or pornographic photos or magazines. Protective measures may have been taken, such as placing padding between the ligature and the neck to prevent marking. Sometimes, mirrors are found near the body, intended to allow the victim to observe the ritual.[3]

Autoerotic asphyxiation
The seeking of sexual gratification by near asphyxia.

Drowning   Death by drowning is the result of any liquid's entering the breathing passages and preventing the access of air to the lungs. The liquid need not be water; it can be any fluid, mud, or other flowing substance. Nor is it necessary for the entire body to be immersed in the liquid. A person can drown when only the mouth and nose are under the surface. Most drownings are accidents. Simulation of drowning has to be ruled out by a medical examiner to assure that a homicide has not been masked as a drowning after the actual murder was committed. A death by natural causes that occurs in the water must likewise be determined by an autopsy.

Vehicular Manslaughter

Many states have a statutory classification of manslaughter. In some states, special statutory rules are applied where death results from the negligent operation of a motor vehicle. Concerns about drunken and reckless driving and homicides caused by these activities have placed considerable pressure on the criminal justice system to provide harsher penalties. Since about 1983, prosecutors in most of the United States have begun prosecuting killing caused by drunken or reckless driving as an offense greater than simple vehicular homicide. Many jurisdictions now employ the same statutes as for general murder and manslaughter.[4] Investigators, therefore, should be aware of the statutes for vehicular homicides, murder, and manslaughter in their jurisdictions.

Vehicular manslaughter may involve one or more cars, a collision with a pedestrian, or the death of one or more passengers. It may result from gross negligent behavior, reckless driving, or driving while under the influence of alcohol or other mind-altering substances. In addition to the activities and duties set forth earlier in this chapter for homicide investigations in general, the following should be undertaken in investigations of vehicular manslaughter cases:

- Note whether traffic control devices are present and are function-ing properly. Note also whether these devices are clearly visible.
- Make notes about the weather, visibility, lighting, road conditions, obstructions, signs, signals, and markings.
- Identify the driver of the vehicle causing the fatality, and make an arrest if he or she is present.
- Note all injuries, any statements or admissions, and possible indications of intoxication or other impairment.
- Examine the suspect's car for physical evidence (e.g., fabric marks, shreds or fibers from the victim's clothing, blood, paint transfers, broken glass or lights, missing trim, or the presence of skin, hair, or stains made by the property of the victim).
- If the suspect has fled the scene, as in the case of a hit-and-run, contact the dispatcher with all available information for a local and regional broadcast.
- If a suspect has been apprehended, provide *Miranda* warnings, and interview him or her if rights are waived.
- Check all information and defenses offered by the suspect to verify whether they are true.
- Conduct a field sobriety test if it appears warranted. Depending on state statutes, a blood test may also be called for.
- Locate and interview any witnesses to the incident; obtain signed statements.

Vehicular manslaughter generally involves some type of negligent behavior.

- Photograph the scene as it is, before anything is touched or moved. Take pictures from different distances and angles to show intersection, streetlights, crosswalks, traffic devices, signs, skid marks, or whatever conditions exist at the scene of the incident.

- Determine the *point of impact* (POI) of the collision. This can be ascertained from debris at the location, such as broken glass and radiator water, and from skid marks and other evidence.

- Determine the *point of rest* (POR), where each vehicle came to rest after the accident, and anything to show the positions of the vehicles in the road before the collision.

- Accurately measure skid marks and their positions relative to fixed objects, measuring each skid mark separately. Link skid marks to the vehicles.

- Check conditions of the suspect's vehicle: tires (e.g., condition and wear of treads), brakes, steering, position of gearshift, emergency brake, windshield, wipers, headlights and taillights, rearview mirrors, mileage, and so on.

- Ask that the autopsy be conducted with special attention to impact patterns. This is important in reconstructing the fatal accident. Documentation of the wound pattern is likewise critical.

- Obtain a traffic accident report, and try to reconstruct the impact patterns in light of the autopsy findings, with special attention to the direction of the suspect's car and the positions of the victims.

- Conduct any other investigation deemed necessary because of the specific facts of the case.

- Complete all reports, and discuss them with the district attorney for trial purposes.

Suspicious Circumstances

The criminal codes of many states provide for various circumstances in which a physician, funeral director, or other person shall notify the coroner's office of a death that may have occurred under suspicious circumstances. The code generally directs the coroner's office to inquire into and determine the circumstances, manner, and cause of death in the following circumstances: violent, sudden, or unusual deaths; unattended deaths; deaths in which the deceased has not been attended by a physician in the past week (or some other specified time); deaths related to or following known or suspected self-induced or criminal abortions; deaths related to known or suspected homicide, suicide, or accidental poisoning; deaths known or suspected to have resulted from or to be related to an accident or injury, either old or recent; deaths due to drowning, fire, hanging, gunshot, stabbing, cutting, exposure, starvation, alcoholism, drug addiction, or asphyxiation; deaths incident, in whole or in part, to criminal activity; deaths associated with a known or alleged rape, aggravated assault, or sodomy; deaths while in the custody of law enforcement or correctional agents; deaths known or suspected to be the result of a contagious disease that constitutes a possible health hazard to the public; deaths from occupational accidents; deaths from occupational disease or occupational safety hazards; and deaths that afford reasonable ground to suspect that they were caused by the criminal behavior of another.

As with other deaths, the primary duty of the coroner or medical examiner is to determine the cause of death. The coroner conducts a separate investigation, usually including an autopsy performed by a qualified pathologist (a medical doctor). For the criminal investigator, the procedure for investigating these cases is substantially the same as for other types of homicides.

SUMMARY BY LEARNING OBJECTIVES

Learning Objective 1

Investigation of deaths requires skill, care, and sensitivity. In general, deaths can be divided into four categories—natural, suicide, accidental, and homicide. The goal of classifying a death into one of these categories is to assign responsibility in both a moral sense and a legal sense.

Learning Objective 2

Homicide is the killing of one human being by another. Some homicides are premeditated; others may occur because of an accident, owing to negligence, in self-defense or in the defense of another, or as the only recourse of apprehending a dangerous fleeing felon. Even self-inflicted deaths are typically treated as homicides until the police can establish them as suicides. Homicide can be classified legally as justifiable homicide, excusable homicide, or criminal homicide, which is further divided into murder and manslaughter. State statutes further define murder and manslaughter by degrees or specific crimes.

Learning Objective 3

Some of the more common motives for homicide include unplanned or spontaneous murders, murders for financial gain, lust murders, murders for revenge, elimination murders, and motiveless murders, including stranger-to-stranger murders and cases of mistaken identity.

Learning Objective 4

When investigating a homicide, police and investigators should follow established procedures for responding to a call; protecting and preserving the crime scene; collecting, identifying, and managing evidence; interviewing and interrogating witnesses and suspects; and writing reports. Determination of criminal responsibility in a homicide has evolved into a highly specialized field of medical science known as forensic pathology. Forensic pathologists study and interpret changes in body tissues and fluids to determine such factors as time of death, circumstances of death, and scene of death.

Learning Objective 5

There are a number of ways one can determine whether a person is dead, including appearance, pupillary reaction, pulse, visible breathing, solar plexus movement, muscle resistance or muscle reflex, and cyanosis (blue color of lips and nail beds).

Learning Objective 6

A number of practices can aid in identifying a dead person, including matching fingerprints, conducting skeletal studies, making a visual inspection, searching personal effects and clothing, noting tattoos and scars, examining dental evidence, and disseminating photographs and sketches.

Learning Objective 7

Factors used to estimate time of death include postmortem changes in the body, changes in temperature, *rigor mortis* and *livor mortis,* decomposition of the body, insect infestations, and witness information, including when the victim was last seen alive. In addition, the contents of the victim's stomach and the degree of digestion of this food may assist in estimating time of death.

Learning Objective 8

Homicide investigators are called on to investigate many different types of deaths, including natural deaths, suicides, poisonings, stabbings and cuttings, gunshot wounds, asphyxia, vehicular homicides, and deaths under suspicious circumstances. Each of these types of deaths has characteristics that investigators should be trained to recognize to determine what type of weapon to seek and how to focus the investigation.

QUESTIONS FOR REVIEW

Learning Objective 1

1. Why are deaths classified into categories?

Learning Objective 2

2. Define *homicide, justifiable homicide, excusable homicide, criminal homicide, murder,* and *manslaughter.*

3. What is the major difference between felonious and nonfelonious homicide?

4. How would you distinguish between murder and excusable homicide?

Learning Objective 3

5. Why is it important to try to establish a motive for a homicide?

6. Why is a murder for revenge often difficult to investigate?

Learning Objective 4

7. What things should an officer be alert to when en route to a possible homicide crime scene?

8. What is the first thing an officer should do upon receipt of a call to a death scene or a possible homicide crime scene?

9. What is *forensic pathology?*

Learning Objective 5

10. How can the appearance and color of a victim assist in determining if the victim is dead?

11. What is *cyanosis?*

Learning Objective 6

12. How might dental records assist in identifying a victim?

13. How might photographs or drawings of the victim assist in determining his or her identity?

Learning Objective 7

14. How might vegetation assist in estimating time of death?

15. How might stomach contents assist in estimating time of death?

16. How might *rigor mortis* assist in estimating time of death?

Learning Objective 8

17. How are poisons detected in a victim?

18. Briefly describe the differences between cuts (or incisions) and stab wounds.

19. What are defense wounds, and where can they be located?

20. Briefly describe the appearance of an entry wound and an exit wound caused by a bullet.

21. What are some characteristics of a contact wound?

22. What are the ten most common forms of suicide?

23. What causes death in asphyxia?

24. How is negligence involved in the charge of automobile manslaughter?

CRITICAL THINKING INVESTIGATIVE EXERCISES

1. When you arrive home today, assume you are the investigating officer arriving at a death scene outside your house or apartment building. What are the first things you will do? Be sure to consider where you might locate witnesses, how you would observe and protect the scene and possible evidence, who you would notify, how identification of the victim might be made, and so forth. Write a brief paragraph recording your response. Then compare your response with others in the class. Discuss and resolve any variances.

2. Judy Jones, 14 years old, was babysitting her 10-year-old brother, Tom. They were both sitting in front of their home when a car pulled up. A man called to Judy by name and beckoned her to come over. As Judy moved toward the vehicle, the passenger door swung open. From his vantage point, Tom saw a man pointing a gun at Judy and ordering her into the car. Judy hesitated a moment, then started to move away from the car. The man fired the gun. Tom could see sparks as the bullet struck the ground near Judy's foot. Judy stopped in her tracks and

moved back toward the car, crying. Tom ran into the house as the car sped off. Tom called 911 and reported what had just happened. The police arrived a few minutes later to take Tom's statement and investigate the scene. While the officers were still present, a report came in that Judy's body had been found in a nearby alley. She was naked from the waist down and had been shot once in the chest.

a. What are the next steps that the police should take?

b. Where would one expect to find clues or leads in this case?

c. What physical evidence should be sought?

d. What forensic evidence should be sought?

e. How would you investigate this case?

INVESTIGATIVE SKILL BUILDERS

Acquiring and Evaluating Information

You have arrived at the scene of a dead-body call. The location is an old, dilapidated shed behind a house in a rural area. There is no glass in the windows, and the wooden floor is rotted. In the middle of the floor is the body of a man. The victim is wearing a nice suit of clothes, but the body is badly decomposed, and there is no wallet or other identification in any of the pockets. The man is wearing an expensive-looking heavy gold chain around his neck.

1. How might you estimate time of death?

2. How might you determine the identity of this victim?

3. What questions would you ask while canvassing the area?

Integrity/Honesty

You are investigating the death of a fellow officer in a freak automobile accident. The car apparently went out of control for no apparent reason and crashed into a wall, killing the officer instantly. During the course of the investigation, you learn that the officer had recently taken out a $1 million life insurance policy with double indemnity (double payment) in the case of accidental death. The policy also has a two-year suicide clause, whereby it pays nothing if death occurs by suicide in the first two years the policy is in effect. The beneficiary is his 12-year-old daughter. You also discover that the officer recently learned that his wife has had affairs with several men in the last several years and was planning to leave him. From what you have learned in your investigation, you suspect that the officer killed himself.

1. Do you file a report of suicide, knowing that this will void the officer's insurance policy?

2. Do you tell the wife what you suspect—whether or not you file a report of suicide?

ENDNOTES

1. Frances E. Camps, ed., *Grandwohl's Legal Medicine,* 3d ed., John Wright and Sons, Bristol, England, 1976.

2. W. C. Rodriguez and C. Bass, "Determination of Time of Death by Means of Carrion Insects," paper presented at the annual meeting of the American Academy of Forensic Sciences, February 15–19, 1983, Cincinnati, Oh. See also N. H. Haskell, David G. McShaffrey, D. A. Hawley, R. E. Williams, and J. E. Pless, "Use of Aquatic Insects in Determining Submersion Interval," *Journal of Forensic Sciences,* Vol. 34, No. 3, May 1989, pp. 622–23.

3. Vernon J. Gebreth, *Practical Homicide Investigations: Tactics, Procedures and Forensic Techniques,* 2d ed., Elsevier Science Publishing, New York, 1990.

4. Neil C. Chamelin and Kenneth R. Evans, *Criminal Law for Police Officers,* 5th ed., Prentice Hall, Englewood Cliffs, N.J., 1991.

CHAPTER 15

Burglary

CHAPTER OBJECTIVES

After completing this chapter, you will be able to:

1. Provide an overview of the crime of burglary in the United States.

2. Explain the legal elements of the crime of burglary.

3. Distinguish among the main types of burglaries.

4. Describe the trade and tools of burglars.

5. Enumerate basic procedures used in burglary investigations.

6. Discuss the special concerns of investigating safe burglaries.

KEY TERMS

burglary
residential burglary
commercial burglary
jimmy
burglary tools
alarm call
nonalarm call
diagonal deployment

The Nature of Burglary

Burglary is the first of the four property-crime index offenses we will consider. (The other property-crime index offenses are larceny-theft, motor vehicle theft, and arson.) According to the FBI's Uniform Crime Reports (UCR), an estimated 2.6 million burglaries were reported in 1995, the lowest total in 16 years (see Figure 15–1). Burglaries made up 21.5 percent of property crimes (not including arson) in 1995, considerably less than the total of larceny-theft offenses, but more than the total of vehicle theft offenses (see Figure 15–2). Almost 67 percent of all burglaries in 1995 were residential in nature, and more of them (59 percent) occurred during the daytime; in contrast, 61 percent of nonresidential burglaries occurred during nighttime hours.[1]

Burglaries are among the most difficult crimes to solve. Contact between burglars and victims is infrequent, and burglaries may not be

---

Figure 15–1 Burglary crime index totals.

Year	Population	Crime Index Total	Number of Burglary Offenses
1980	225,349,264	13,408,300	3,795,200
1981	229,146,000	13,423,800	3,779,700
1982	231,534,000	12,974,400	3,447,100
1983	233,981,000	12,108,600	3,129,900
1984	236,158,000	11,881,800	2,984,400
1985	238,740,000	12,431,400	3,073,300
1986	241,077,000	13,211,900	3,241,400
1987	243,400,000	13,508,700	3,236,200
1988	245,807,000	13,923,100	3,218,100
1989	248,239,000	14,251,400	3,168,200
1990	248,709,873	14,475,600	3,073,900
1991	252,177,000	14,872,900	3,157,200
1992	255,082,000	14,438,200	2,979,900
1993	257,908,000	14,144,800	2,834,800
1994	260,341,000	13,989,500	2,712,800
1995	262,755,000	13,867,100	2,595,000

Source: Federal Bureau of Investigation, *Crime in the United States,* Government Printing Office, Washington, 1995.

immediately discovered. Since victims seldom see the burglar and a time lag may interfere, investigators must identify the *corpus delicti* (essential elements) of the crime through largely circumstantial evidence. To conduct an efficient investigation, therefore, investigators should have a solid knowledge of the legal aspects of burglary.

Legal Aspects of the Crime of Burglary

In common law, the offense of burglary was defined as the breaking and entering of the dwelling house of another in the nighttime, with intent to commit a felony therein. The common law sought to protect a person's habitation, and the definition of burglary therefore was confined to dwelling houses and any buildings connected to them or included within their enclosures.

Although most state burglary statutes retain elements of the common law definition of the crime, they are less restrictive. They commonly encompass entry at all times into all kinds of structures. The element of breaking originally conveyed the notion that there had to be some form of forcible entry, regardless of how slight the force. Modern-day courts have extended this interpretation. For example, if an accused broke a pane of glass to unlock a window or door, such an action would satisfy the definition of the use of some type of *force,* as would the force required to turn the handle of an unlocked door.

Entry into the dwelling has been interpreted as the insertion of any or all of the accused's body into the dwelling. Thus, the element of entry would be satisfied if an accused extended his or her arm through a window, using a pole or stick to reach property inside a room. State burglary statutes generally hold that the crime of **burglary** consists of (1) entering a building or occupied structure (2) without the consent of the person in possession (3) to commit a crime therein. In addition, certain state statutes classify it into first-, second-, and even third-degree burglary.

As we have previously indicated, most states have enacted statutes that expand the common law definition of burglary. These statutes provide criminal penalties for such behaviors as entering a dwelling without breaking, breaking and entering the dwelling house of another in the daytime (instead of at night), breaking and entering a building other than a dwelling house, and breaking and entering with intent to commit a misdemeanor.[2] Crimes may be classified as *breaking and entering* rather than *burglary* to further distinguish the criminal act. Since many people use the terms *burglary* and *breaking and entering* as

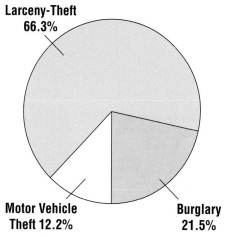

Figure 15–2 Percentage distribution of property-crime index offenses.*

Larceny-Theft 66.3%

Motor Vehicle Theft 12.2%

Burglary 21.5%

*Sufficient data are not available to estimate totals or distribution for arson.
Source: Federal Bureau of Investigation, *Crime in the United States,* Government Printing Office, Washington, 1995.

Burglary Entering a building or occupied structure, without the consent of the person in possession, to commit a crime therein.

synonyms when referring to any one of these offenses, it is important for investigators to know the elements of the crime of burglary as defined in their respective jurisdictions.

Types of Burglaries

Burglaries are generally classified as residential or commercial. **Residential burglaries** are those that occur in buildings that are commonly used or are suitable for habitation, or in attached structures. For a crime to be a residential burglary, the building does not have to be inhabited at the time of the crime. Rental property, mobile homes, dormitory rooms, cabins, rooms rented within a house, houseboats, or any other suitable dwelling places may be burglarized. More than two-thirds of all burglaries are residential.

Most residential burglars target items of moderate value, such as televisions, stereo equipment, and jewelry, that are easily transported and fenced (sold for cash or drugs). Most residential burglars are not interested in confronting home dwellers. Selecting a burglary target, then, involves locating dwellings where no one seems to be home.

Commercial burglaries are those that occur in nonresidential buildings or structures where some form of commerce takes place. Schools, churches, ships, stores, offices, factories, warehouses, trucks, hospitals, public buildings, and so forth are all potential targets of commercial burglars. Commercial buildings in secluded or poorly lighted areas are particularly likely candidates for burglary. Frequently, commercial burglars specialize in one type of target.

In many cases, commercial burglaries are better planned than residential ones. Targets may be cased by burglars in disguise to detect security devices, learn delivery dates of cash or merchandise, or gain operational information from employees. Yields in commercial burglaries usually are larger than in most residential burglaries. They are also more likely to be undertaken by professionals than are most residential burglaries.

> # FYI
>
> According to the FBI's Crime Clock, which shows the relative frequency of occurrence of index offenses, a burglary was committed every 12 seconds in 1995.

The Burglar—Trade and Tools

We may have a stereotype of a burglar as a person dressed in black who silently scales the outside of a building, deftly opens a window, and glides into a room to secretly gather valuable loot. While some cat burglars may fit this image, burglars use a variety of methods of operation and come from many socioeconomic levels.

Methods of Operation

The ways in which burglars operate are quite varied. Being familiar with some of the more common types of burglary operations can help in a burglary investigation. You may also be able to help a victim take precautions to prevent a reoccurrence of the crime.

During a Party   The burglar loots bedrooms or other household areas where guests leave their valuables; he or she may be an actual guest or a person who crashed the party.

Following a Telephone Call   The burglar telephones a residence and, if no one answers, proceeds to the residence and knocks or rings the front doorbell. If someone answers the door, the burglar hands the resident a household sample or handbill and leaves. If no one answers, the burglar picks the lock or calls an accomplice and burglarizes the residence. Often, if a dog barks from within the residence when the burglar knocks, or rings the bell, the burglar leaves.

Package Delivery   The burglar feigns a package delivery. If no one answers the door, he or she picks the lock and burglarizes the premises. If someone does answer the door, the culprit asks for the addressee on the package and leaves.

Careless Residents   Many burglars take advantage of the carelessness of occupants who leave doors or windows unlocked or spare keys in obvious places (e.g., under mats, over door frames, or in flowerpots). Some burglars use accomplices to watch for the occupant returning home unexpectedly. When this occurs, the accomplice signals the inside burglar with a blast of a car horn or even with a beeper signal.

Tunnel or Cut-In   The burglar tunnels or cuts through the roof, the ceiling, a wall, or the basement. Entry may be from above or below the premises. This method is used mostly in apartments or commercial locations.

Cat or Human Fly   This burglar is an aerialist, climbing up or down the side of a building to gain entry through a window or balcony door. In some instances, the burglar will enter a target apartment or office by "stepping over" from one balcony to another.

Jimmy A prying tool of
any sort, used to force
open a door, window, or
lock.

Jimmy or Celluloid The burglar forces open doors or windows by using a metal tool, or **jimmy**, such as a tire iron, crowbar, heavy-duty screwdriver, or similar implement. Jimmying is the most common method of entry to commit a burglary. Some burglars use a small piece of celluloid plastic, such as a credit or ATM card, to open some doors by forcing the card between the doorjamb and the lock's spring bolt. Dead-bolt locks eliminate this sort of entry.

Hiding Out The burglar enters a commercial establishment during regular business hours and then conceals him- or herself, remaining hidden until the business has closed and all employees have left. The perpetrator then steals items from the premises.

Opportunistic The burglar drives around residential communities, looking for a good target. A good target is a darkened home or a house where the intended victims seem to be away, as indicated by a pileup of newspapers or by mail in the mailbox. The burglars may even check to see if air conditioners are not running during hot weather.

Smash and Grab While an accomplice sits at the wheel of a waiting getaway car, the burglar smashes a store window, grabs jewelry or other display merchandise, and flees. Generally, this sort of burglar is a young person in need of fast cash. Recently, some gangs have developed a variation of this style of burglary. A bunch of gang members smash the glass out of a store's window or front door and then swiftly run through the store, grabbing expensive items. As much as $150,000 in wares has been stolen during such hit-and-run burglaries. The entire crime takes only a few minutes.

Research Before Burglary The burglar researches a potential target before striking. The burglar may read the newspaper to determine which prominent people are taking trips abroad or attending social functions. The burglar may even read obituaries to find out which prominent people have died, when their funerals are being held, and, thus, when family members will be out of the house. Some burglars have accomplices in hotels, such as bellhops, clerks, or maids, who provide information about the comings and goings of wealthy guests.

Dishonest Workers With access to keys and knowledge of intimate details of business and financial operations, many workers may commit burglaries themselves. Or they may provide information or keys to accomplices, who actually commit the burglaries.

False Report It is not uncommon for someone, trying to conceal some financial loss, to report a burglary that never happened. Generally, in these cases, a careful investigation will reveal inaccuracies in the complainant's account of the theft, particularly in the method of operation, which is likely to be unlike that of actual burglars.

Tools of the Trade

The tools chosen by burglars usually depend on the method of entry and the type of burglary planned—a residence, a commercial enterprise, a vault, or a safe, for example. In most jurisdictions, possession of **burglary tools,** or implements obviously used to pick locks or jimmy doors or windows, is considered a separate felony offense.

Burglary tools may consist of specialized tools used by locksmiths and having little other use. These might include various picks, master keys, and tools similar to jewelers' tools. On the other hand, burglary tools may consist of a wide variety of run-of-the-mill household tools such as screwdrivers, hammers, hacksaws, crowbars, power drills with various bits, tin snips, stiff wire, pieces of plastic, glass cutters, and flashlights. Other common items found on burglars include adhesive tape, rope, pipe wrenches, water pistols filled with noxious fluids to ward off watchdogs, chisels, punches, and even suction cups to hold and remove glass when it is cut. Many of these tools may be easily concealed and carried in briefcases, sports bags, overnight suitcases, musical instrument cases, handbags, or in belts worn under coats or clothing. Larger items may be concealed and transported in a car or a rifle case. When burglary tools are found on a suspect or in a suspect's automobile, it is advisable to ask the suspect, "Why do you have these items?" The tools may be used in a legitimate job and may not be intended for burglaries at all.

Burglary tools Any of an assortment of tools and picks that may be used in committing a burglary.

Burglars often use a variety of tools to accomplish their work.

Investigating Burglaries

A thorough knowledge of the methods used by burglars is essential to an effective investigation. As in other crimes discussed in this book, a uniformed officer is often the first to arrive on the scene. It is important, then, that he or she have a basic understanding of criminal investigation. This phase of police work should be conducted by an officer who knows both what to do and what not to do in a given situation. During the preliminary stages of a burglary investigation, the investigator should be seeking evidence to show the following:

1. The suspect was actually in the building.
2. The suspect was in the vicinity at the time of the burglary.
3. The suspect has loot or other property from the burglary.

The first element in this list is the most difficult to prove. In the absence of fingerprints or palm prints, investigators should try to find on the suspect or the suspect's clothes traces of physical evidence linking the suspect to the crime scene. The physical evidence could include various materials, such as insulation and metal bits from a safe, as well as roofing materials, plaster, concrete, mortar, brick, glass, wood splinters, paint, and tarlike substances from the scene or from the break-in of the building. Similarly, certain tools or equipment may place a suspect at a particular location. The burglar may have recently burglarized a hardware store to obtain burning equipment or may have purchased tools prior to burglarizing a safe.

Remember that some types of evidence may have latent or microscopic value. For example, in a homicide, a gun found near the body is important as the possible lethal weapon. However, a fingerprint on the weapon or on an ejected bullet casing may prove more incriminating. A drill bit found on a burglary suspect may be a good piece of evidence. But more significant may be the bits of metal clinging to the edges of the bit, should they match the material of a safe that was drilled in an attempt to open it.

Precautions During the Preliminary Investigation

When responding to a burglary call, an officer should be alert for people standing around, fleeing the area, or sitting in automobiles and for suspicious-looking cars parked near the scene. Similarly, officers should be observant of lights, movements, and actions of people in the immediate area. Using a siren en route to a burglary should be minimized or totally eliminated to avoid advertising to the burglar that the police are coming.

During the preliminary stage of a burglary investigation, there are several important procedures to follow, especially if the dispatcher has indicated that the call is for a burglary in progress. These actions include driving slower when approaching the scene, to avoid squealing tires, parking the cruiser a short distance away from the call address; turning down the squelch and volume on the radio—especially on a portable radio; keeping conversations to a minimum and in hushed tones; opening and closing car doors quietly; removing and pocketing ignition keys without jangling them; and using flashlights sparingly and holding them away from the body (to avoid providing a target to a fleeing felon). If the officer will be entering a dark room or building, his or her hat should be off or turned so that the brim will not interfere with vision upward. As a general rule of thumb and depending on different department policies, guns should be drawn but not cocked at this point. Officers should always consult their department policies regarding these last two points.

STATISTICS

According to the UCR, a 13 percent clearance rate was recorded nationwide for burglaries in 1995. Adults were involved in 79 percent of burglary offenses cleared; the remaining 21 percent involved only young people under 18 years of age.

When answering an **alarm call,** a call in response to either an audible alarm or a silent alarm, officers should search the inside of the building after the owner, proprietor, or security company representative has opened it. If K-9 units are available in the area, it is advisable to request their assistance in searching large stores or warehouses during alarm calls.

When responding to **nonalarm calls,** where someone has reported the crime or where the police have discovered it, the circumstances of the case should dictate the procedure required and the decision about whether to search the premises. When there is evidence of forced entry, the officers should search the premises for the burglars and should determine whether they have left. As already advised in Chapter 10, "Robbery," never take anything or anybody encountered during the investigation for granted. That helpful occupant in the house could just as easily be the burglar. Be sure to obtain photo identification of parties found as occupants during a burglary call.

Alarm call Notification of the police by audible or silent alarm that a crime such as a break-in has occurred.

Nonalarm call Notification of the police by citizen alert or direct observation that a crime such as a break-in has occurred.

Conducting a Burglary Investigation

For the most part, the preliminary investigation of a burglary follows the outline described in Chapter 2. This includes (1) apprehension of suspects, (2) protection of the crime scene, (3) searching for evidence, (4) determination of the method of operation, and (5) identification of witnesses, victims, and possible suspects.

Police must use caution when investigating burglary sites.

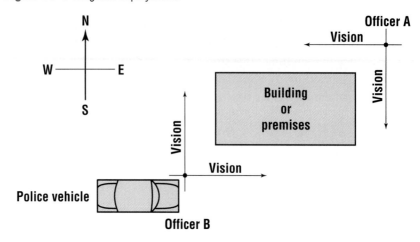

Figure 15–3 Diagonal deployment.

Ideally, a burglary investigation should involve more than a single officer. When the first officer arrives on the scene, he or she should take an appropriate vantage point and await the arrival of back-up units. When two officers arrive at the same time or when the second unit arrives, the officers should secure the premises by using a **diagonal deployment.** In this procedure, each officer places him- or herself at a corner of a building so that two sides can be observed at once. For example, one officer may watch the north and east sides while the other officer watches the south and west sides (see Figure 15–3). Diagonal deployment allows two officers to cover and contain suspects until more officers arrive.

When an officer working alone must check the building immediately, he or she should first drive around the building. Circling the building allows the officer to see any obvious places where a burglar may have broken in. If driving around the building is not possible, the officer should quickly and cautiously circle the building on foot.

When searching the scene of a burglary, officers should seek the manner and method of both entry and exit. The method of entry may have been by cutting a hole in the roof or wall, prying open a window or rear door, breaking a pane of glass, or even using a passkey, shim, or lockpick. Do not draw conclusions about the method of entry if you do not see one. If the entry is unknown, this should be noted in the preliminary report. The crime should be reconstructed, as much as possible, by the investigating officer. Only those facts that can be substantiated through observation of physical evidence, knowledge, or statements by witnesses or victims should be recorded.

A thorough neighborhood canvass may turn up witnesses who heard identifiable sounds, such as those of an automobile, breaking glass, barking dogs, and so forth. These sounds may assist the investigator in fixing the approximate time of the crime and may also provide other leads. The investigator should seek answers to the following questions:

Diagonal deployment A method of arranging officers to both secure and observe a crime scene. Officers arrange themselves so that each can observe two sides of a building at once.

- Who discovered the offense?
- Who was the last person to secure the premises?
- How did the thief reach the point of the break-in?
- Is there any indication of the thief's concealment before the burglary?
- Is the property that was taken insured? If so, for how much? When was the policy taken out?
- Who has keys to the premises, and how accessible are those keys to others?
- Were fingerprints, palm prints, or footprints found at points of entry or exit?
- What property was taken? What is its value?
- Did the thief limit the crime to one kind of property, such as jewelry or electronic equipment, or take all kinds of valuables?
- How did the burglar gain access to secured cupboards, drawers, or dressers? Was force used? Were keys used?
- Was the burglar's search of the premises haphazard or systematic?
- Did the burglar do anything besides search for and steal property?
- Where was the stolen property usually kept by the owner? Who else knew of the property's location?
- When and where was the stolen property purchased? Does the owner have receipts?
- Are photographs of the stolen property available?
- When was the property last seen? Where and by whom?
- Who was the last person to have the stolen property before the burglary?
- Can the owner provide a complete list of all the property that was stolen?
- Can the owner identify his or her property in any way (e.g., serial numbers, identification marks, or other markings)?
- Were any checks or bankbooks stolen during the burglary?
- Are there any fingerprints inside or outside the premises that may need processing? If so, are they being protected?
- Does the victim suspect anyone?
- Can the victim point out any disturbed areas of the premises?

When searching the scene of a burglary, officers should seek the manner of entry and exit.

- Can the victim identify or eliminate as his or hers any items found at the scene?

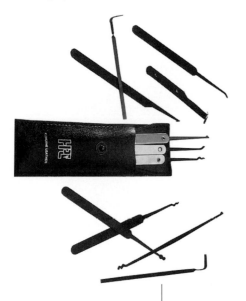

In some jurisdictions, the possession of burglary picks or any burglary tools is a separate crime from burglary.

Investigators should be alert for any unusual events or disturbances observed at the scene. For example, juvenile burglars frequently commit senseless acts of vandalism during burglaries. Similarly, age and other information may be inferred by the types of property stolen. For instance, when valuable jewelry is left behind but cash and stereo equipment are taken, one might infer that the burglars are youthful or at least nonprofessional. Similarly, investigators should carefully consider evidence showing that the burglary may be fraudulent or that the extent of the burglary may be overstated to collect inflated reimbursement from an insurance company. List all articles taken from the location, their quantity and description, and their value. Be sure to inventory all small articles, such as jewelry, coins, or other small objects that might be found on a suspect later.

If tools or implements are found, investigators *should not* attempt to make a comparison by placing an object into a suspected impression on a jimmied window or door. Doing so may contaminate or destroy evidence that might otherwise be useful later in court. The size and type of instrument used can be estimated by measuring the mark, gouge, scrape, or other injury to the door, window, or surface. The damaged area can be photographed and carefully searched for microscopic traces of physical evidence. The investigator should include in his or her notes suspected implements that may have caused the damage. For example, the investigator might write, "gouge probably caused by a 1/4-inch screwdriver" and "a 1/4-inch screwdriver was found at the premises." All evidence should be recorded and secured in the manner previously described in Chapters 3 and 4.

Burglary Suspects and Their Apprehension

Whenever burglary suspects are apprehended, they should be immediately advised of their rights under *Miranda*. The fact that the suspect has been so advised should be recorded in the investigator's notes and report. After the *Miranda* warnings have been given, other actions the investigator should take include, but are not limited to, the following:

- Seize all of the suspect's wearing apparel, including shoes, for lab examination.
- Review each item of property found in the suspect's possession.
- Search the suspect's vehicle (obtain a search warrant or the consent of the suspect).
- Determine the names and addresses of all the suspect's friends and associates.

Figure 15–4 Waiver-of-search form used by some agencies.

I, _____ , have been informed of my constitutional right not to have a search made of my premises without a search warrant, and my right to refuse to such a search. Knowing these rights, I hereby authorize Officer(s) _____
of the _____ Police (or Sheriff's) Department, to conduct a complete search of my residence located at _____ . These officers are authorized by me to take from my residence any letters, papers, objects, and materials which they find, and which they have reasonable cause to believe may be evidence in a criminal proceeding.

This consent to a search and this written permission is being given by me to the above-named officer(s) voluntarily and without threats or promises of any kind.

Signed: _____   Date: _____

Place: _____

Witnessed by: _____

- Record all discovered facts and obtain the suspect's statement.
- Check the records bureau, M.O. files, bulletins, computer databases, and other sources for related or similar crimes.
- Follow up on such items as the suspect's past activities and whereabouts during questionable dates and times.
- Fingerprint and photograph the suspect, and obtain handwriting specimens (especially useful where checks or documents may have been stolen).
- Follow up on any leads that result from any of the previous actions.

Remember that, if a search is to be conducted of a suspect's residence, the suspect's consent and waiver or a search warrant must be obtained. Whenever a suspect voluntarily offers consent to a search of his or her premises, this consent should be recorded in writing with witnesses. Figure 15–4 illustrates a suggested waiver of search that may be prepared for the suspect to sign. Be sure that any such waiver used in your department has been reviewed and approved by the prosecutor's office.

Safe Burglaries

To most people, a safe is a large metal container designed to keep articles secure from fire and burglary. In reality, not all safes provide such dual protection. Generally, safes may be divided into two classifications: (1) fire-resistant safes or fireboxes and (2) burglar-resistant safes or money chests or vaults. A fire-resistant safe, while sometimes providing only minimal protection from burglar attack, is resistant to fire. Such a safe is typically a thin metal shell filled with a fire-resistant material, such as vermiculite, cement, or even sawdust. Locks on fire-resistant safes are more for privacy than security and are usually not very difficult to get past. Fire-resistant safes are typically rated for their ability to resist high temperatures for varying amounts of time.

On the other hand, burglar-resistant safes, money vaults, or money chests are constructed primarily to resist unauthorized entry by burglars. This type of safe is often made of laminated or solid steel and may have dense, heavy insulation intended to make penetration more difficult. While such safes are never *burglarproof,* they do ward off a successful attack from a burglar for a certain amount of time. Locks on burglar-resistant safes are intended to slow entry by an unauthorized individual, rather than merely to provide privacy.

Attack Methods for Opening Safes

Burglars use a number of methods to gain entry into safes. Investigators should have some understanding of these methods, to more readily recognize the skill and knowledge level of the safe burglar. Such knowledge allows officers to better focus the investigation and accurately report the facts of the crime both to their agency and to other police agencies. Burglar-resistant safes may not provide fire protection, and fire-resistant boxes seldom provide adequate burglary protection.

Hand Manipulation   Hand manipulation has all but become a lost art. At one time, it involved opening a combination lock by listening to and feeling the tumblers of the lock as they fell into place. Most safes today are equipped with manipulation-proof locking systems, sometimes involving electronic locking mechanisms. Burglars, however, have found ways to electronically search for and detect the code or combination on even these locking mechanisms.

Punching   In this method, the dial knob of the safe is knocked off and a punch placed on the exposed spindle behind it. The spindle is then driven backward with sufficient force to break the lockbox loose from its mountings. Once accomplished, the handle can be turned and the door opened. Some modern safes are equipped with a secondary lock that automatically engages and secures the safe if the dial is broken off. Punching is a popular technique because it requires little skill or knowledge of safe construction. An experienced burglar can complete a punch attack on a safe in just a few minutes. A disadvantage of punching is the noise made by pounding the punch to break the lockbox. Sometimes cloth or rubber is used to muffle the sound. If such materials are found, they are important pieces of evidence to try to link with a suspect.

Hauling or Carrying Away   This method is most often used by inexperienced burglars or those who are not skilled enough to quickly and quietly open a safe on the premises. Experienced, professional safe burglars can actually open a safe in less time than it takes to haul one away. Once thieves have hauled a safe to a secluded location, they can take as much time as needed to open the safe.

When a safe that was hauled away is recovered, it should be photographed at the place of recovery, and the location of recovery treated like any other crime scene. The investigation should thoroughly seek evidence and materials that may contribute to identifying or linking a suspect to the crime. An outdoor location may provide good physical evidence, such as tire impressions.

Ripping or Peeling   This method is used on fire-resistant safes because of their construction. They typically have a lightweight metal outer shell that can be peeled off the door with a bar, exposing the locking mechanism. Or the sides of the safe can be ripped off with pliers and cutting tools. The insulation material can then be chiseled or cut away and entry gained into the safe. A peel begun in several places before a successful entry suggests a less knowledgeable burglar.

Pulling or Dragging   This procedure works on some older safes but is not often encountered. The burglar places a heavy metal plate with a V shape cut out of it over and behind the dial. The plate has several heavy bolts through it. As the screws are tightened, the V plate lifts and pulls the dial and spindle out of the safe, allowing entry. This method is the opposite of punching.

Chopping   Chopping is a rather crude way to attack a safe. In this method, the safe is turned upside down, and the bottom is smashed with an ax or a sledgehammer. The smashing continues until it has produced a hole large enough to fit a hand through. The burglar then inserts his or her hand and withdraws the contents of the safe.

Torching or Burning   The oxyactylene cutting torch is one of the most effective tools used by a safe burglar. Only certain specially designed steel chests are effectively resistant to it. The small size of acetylene tanks makes this equipment easy to conceal and transport. The torch can be used to burn a hand-sized hole in the side of the safe or to burn around the hinge bolts on the door. In some safes, the burglar can use the torch to cut the locking bolt that holds the door in the locked position.

Drilling   Drilling can be a highly effective means of opening a safe, but it is time-consuming. In some cases, the burglar uses the drill to perforate the door with a series of holes placed close together. This allows the burglar to remove a piece of the door plate, exposing the lock mechanism. In other cases, the burglar drills out the safe bolt. A high-carbon drill bit the size of the bolt or larger is used. The drilling is done through the side of the safe and bores out the bolt. Even if the bolt is only partially drilled, it can be broken with a center punch and a hammer. Once the bolt has been drilled, the door will open.

Using Explosives Even though the penalties for burglaries committed while carrying explosives are typically more severe, some safe burglars do use various explosives, including nitroglycerin, trinitrotoluene (TNT), and various plastic explosives. Burglars who use explosives usually do not work alone. They may have several helpers, each with a special task to do, or simply to serve as lookouts to avoid surprise detection. However, when the explosive charge is detonated, there is considerable noise and potential for detection.

The explosive charge is usually placed in the dial spindle hole after the dial is removed. In some cases, when possible, safes are moved away from the wall before detonation. Doing so prevents the blast from throwing the safe backward into the wall, creating additional noise and wall vibration.

When an investigator encounters signs of the use of explosives in a safe burglary, extreme care must be exercised. Officers should not attempt to neutralize or destroy suspicious materials at the scene of safe explosions. Officers should know and follow their department's procedures regarding encountering explosives and explosive devices.

Investigating Safe Burglaries

Safe burglars usually work in groups of two or more. They are adept at not leaving any traces of their identities at the scene of the

Crime scene photograph of burglarized safe.

crime. Safe burglars regularly wear gloves to avoid leaving any finger-prints. They time their operations with the precision of a fine watch. Safe burglars often case their jobs to obtain information about security systems, guards, possible means of entry and escape, the type and location of the safe and locking mechanisms, the habits of personnel, police patrol patterns, and activities of neighborhood residents.

During the casing of the targeted victim, gang members visit the establishment and observe, among other things, whether or not there are alarm systems on the premises. Sometimes, tools that will be used during the crime are hidden in advance near or in the building. Assignments of gang members, communication equipment, lookouts, transportation, and other details are all taken into account during the planning stages of the crime.

Because safe burglars take such extensive precautions, it is unlikely that any evidence found at the scene will immediately identify the burglar. However, safe burglars do tend to develop a fairly consistent *modus operandi*. Establishing the *modus operandi* can assist the investigator in developing one or more suspects. Thus, evidence at the scene can still be a critical link between suspects and the criminal activity.

Many of the suggestions already offered in this chapter with regard to burglary investigation apply to safe burglary investigation as well. Some of the additional investigative strategies suggested in the following list apply to safe burglaries.

- Prevent unauthorized persons from entering the location. Make a check of the premises, inside and out, to determine the points of entry and exit and the *modus operandi*. Victims or employees may help by pointing out any disturbed areas (articles that have been moved, doors opened or closed, missing items, and so on).

- Attempt to reconstruct the activities of the burglars without disturbing possible trace evidence.

- Sketch and photograph the scene. Include the relationship of physical evidence to the safe, the safe itself, the points of entry and exit, and any damage marks.

- Collect any physical evidence at the scene, including fingerprints, palm prints, footprints, and glove prints; safe insulation material or metal fragments; broken or damaged parts from the safe; discarded or forgotten tools; broken glass, paint chips, and plaster fragments; bloodstains, clothing, and fibers; discarded candy or cigarette wrappers; and any other materials foreign to the premises.

- Interview all persons who have access to the safe or its location. Note the procedures used to secure the safe and the premises.

- Determine the make, size, weight, and serial number of the safe.

National Crime Information Center Tracing and recovering stolen property is much easier using the National Crime Information Center (NCIC) operated by the FBI. Using connecting terminals throughout the United States, local, state, and federal law enforcement agencies can access the NCIC to obtain information on stolen, missing, or recovered weapons; stolen articles, vehicles, and license plates; and stolen, embezzled, or missing securities. Also available are other databases such as the Missing Persons File and the Violent Gang/Terrorist File.

- Check areas adjacent to the premises for possible shoe prints, tire prints, or discarded items.

After the initial investigation has been completed, the following additional investigative steps should be taken:

- Have identifiable stolen property indexed in the records bureau.
- Examine pawnshop and secondhand store records for stolen items.
- Consult personal or department *modus operandi* files for possible leads. Send bulletins to other police agencies, describing the identifiable missing items.
- Question informants about missing property that they might have seen on the street or can be looking for.
- Investigate the whereabouts of known burglars, particularly those whose M.O.s are similar to that in the crime being investigated.

SUMMARY BY LEARNING OBJECTIVES

Learning Objective 1

Burglary is one of the eight crimes that the FBI considers the most serious in American society, and it reports yearly statistics on burglary in its Uniform Crime Reports (UCR). In 1995, burglary made up 21.5 percent of crimes (not including arson) against property.

Learning Objective 2

State statutes precisely define what constitutes the crime of burglary in each state. Generally, these statutes have the following elements in common: Burglary consists of (1) entering a building or occupied structure (2) without the consent of the person in possession (3) to commit a crime therein.

Learning Objective 3

Burglaries can be divided into two general types: residential and commercial. More than two-thirds of all burglaries are committed against residences.

Learning Objective 4

Burglars use a variety of methods of operation, including jimmying doors, tunneling or cutting through walls and roofs, scaling buildings, smashing and grabbing, and casing or hiding out in target buildings. Burglary tools may consist of specialized lock-picking tools or run-of-the-mill household tools, such as screwdrivers, hammers, hacksaws, glass cutters, and tin snips.

Learning Objective 5

Burglary investigations generally follow the same procedures as any criminal investigation. Because some burglaries are well planned and carried out by professionals who leave few clues, a special problem for investigators is collecting physical evidence to identify a suspect and link him or her to the crime.

Learning Objective 6

Safe burglars use a variety of methods to gain entry into safes. Among these are punching, hauling, ripping or peeling, pulling or dragging, chopping, torching or burning, drilling, and explosives. Safe burglars usually work in groups of two or more and are generally adept at not leaving traces of their identities at the crime scene, thus creating a challenge for investigators.

QUESTIONS FOR REVIEW

Learning Objective 1

1. Why must investigators use largely circumstantial evidence for the *corpus delicti* of a burglary?

Learning Objective 2

2. In some states, how much force is required for the crime of breaking and entering?

3. If someone breaks a window and reaches through to steal something, has a burglary been committed? Explain.

Learning Objective 3

4. How would the burglary of a mobile home be classified?

5. If children were caught inside a school at 1:00 A.M., what might the charge be?

Learning Objective 4

6. How does a burglary occur during a party?

7. How do window smashers operate?

8. What sorts of tools are used in burglaries?

Learning Objective 5

9. What type of evidence should an investigator look for at the scene of a burglary?

10. What activities go on during the initial investigation of a burglary?

Learning Objective 6

11. What is meant by ripping a safe?

12. Why do some burglars use hauling as a method of safe burglary?

13. Why are safe burglars so difficult to identify and apprehend?

14. Why do some safe burglars case a location before breaking in?

CRITICAL THINKING INVESTIGATIVE EXERCISE

Consult local newspapers of the past five months. List all the residential and commercial burglaries reported in articles or in the "crime blotter" section. Compile a written summary, using the four activities that follow as a guide, and then compare your summaries with others in the class.

1. Identify any patterns of similarity in the crimes.

2. List any property that the newspaper accounts indicate was stolen; consider whether the type of property taken suggests a pattern.

3. Which of the burglaries, if any, seem to have been committed by juveniles? Explain your answer.

4. List any evidence that the newspaper accounts report as recovered at the scene of the burglaries. Consider the significance of that evidence.

INVESTIGATIVE SKILL BUILDERS

Allocating Time

You arrive at the scene of a burglary, the apartment of a college student. After speaking with the student, you learn that she just returned from spring break and discovered that sometime during the break, her apartment was burglarized. The victim has gone through the apartment and made a list of missing items. These include a stereo system valued at $250, a gold rope necklace valued at $125, an opal ring valued at $75, and an envelope containing $350 cash for next month's rent. The victim indicates that she has apartment insurance but that she is very upset about the burglary and feels very vulnerable.

1. How long should your interview with this victim take? Explain.
2. How much time should you devote to searching for evidence? Explain.
3. What should you tell the victim to make her feel less vulnerable?

Integrity/Honesty

You arrive at the scene of a commercial burglary, where a safe has been ripped open and the contents stolen. While interviewing the store manager, you ask for an inventory of the stolen contents of the safe. He tells you that $1025 in cash and credit card receipts were taken. He also tells you that his insurance has a $500 deductible, so he would like to pad the reported amount by $500 to absorb the deductible. He laughs and says, "The insurance company can better afford to lose the money than I can." What do you tell the manager he should state as the amount of money lost in the burglary?

ENDNOTES

1. Federal Bureau of Investigation, *Crime in the United States,* Government Printing Office, Washington, 1995.
2. Neil C. Chamelin and Kenneth R. Evans, *Criminal Law for Police Officers,* 5th ed., Prentice Hall, Englewood Cliffs, N.J., 1991.

CHAPTER 16

Larceny/Theft

CHAPTER OBJECTIVES

After completing this chapter, you will be able to:

1. Provide an overview of the crime of larceny/theft in the United States.

2. Explain the legal elements of the crime of larceny/theft.

3. List some common types of larceny/theft and describe investigative techniques for dealing with them.

4. Explain how fraud is related to larceny/theft and list some of the common kinds of fraud.

5. Describe the nature of the crime of receiving stolen property and discuss the role of *fences* and other receivers of stolen property in disbursing stolen goods.

KEY TERMS

theft
larceny/theft
grand larceny
petty larceny
shoplifting
employee pilfering
booster device
fence
fraud
hang paper
shill
sting operation

The Nature of Larceny/Theft

Larceny/theft is the most common crime of gain. It is the most frequently reported of the FBI's index crimes. In 1995, over 8 million larceny/thefts were reported (see Figure 16–1), and the distribution of various crimes considered larcenies has remained relatively constant over the past several years. If you look back at Figure 10–2, you will see that larceny/theft made up almost 58 percent of the index offenses reported in 1995. The items targeted in larcenies include everything imaginable, from plastic Big Boy Restaurant mascot figures to pianos to toys to plumbing supplies. Credit cards and checks are regularly stolen and used, and automobile accessories and parts for all makes and models are repeatedly filched. These losses frequently are imposed on consumers in the form of higher prices.

Thieves may be young or old, male or female, rich or poor, employed or unemployed, and from any race, religion, or social status.

Figure 16–1 Larceny/theft crime index totals.

Year	Population	Crime Index Total	Number of Larceny/Theft Offenses
1980	225,349,264	13,408,300	7,136,900
1981	229,146,000	13,423,800	7,194,400
1982	231,534,000	12,974,400	7,142,500
1983	233,981,000	12,108,600	6,712,800
1984	236,158,000	11,881,800	6,591,900
1985	238,740,000	12,431,400	6,926,400
1986	241,077,000	13,211,900	7,257,200
1987	243,400,000	13,508,700	7,499,900
1988	245,807,000	13,923,100	7,705,900
1989	248,239,000	14,251,400	7,872,400
1990	248,709,873	14,475,600	7,945,700
1991	252,177,000	14,872,900	8,142,200
1992	255,082,000	14,438,200	7,915,200
1993	257,908,000	14,144,800	7,820,900
1994	260,341,000	13,989,500	7,879,800
1995	262,755,000	13,867,100	8,000,600

Source: Federal Bureau of Investigation, *Crime in the United States,* Government Printing Office, Washington, 1995.

Thus, it is difficult for an investigator to distinguish a law-abiding citizen from one with larcenous intent. It is important, then, for investigators to learn to recognize certain techniques thieves may use, as well as to know the elements of larceny/theft as defined in their jurisdictions.

Legal Aspects of Larceny/Theft

The word *theft* describes many forms of criminal conduct and is not a common law offense. **Theft,** the taking of property without the owner's consent, is a popular name for larceny and is frequently used as a synonym for the word *larceny.* Larceny/theft takes many forms, but state statutes defining the crime contain five common elements. Generally, **larceny/theft** is

1. the taking and
2. carrying away
3. of personal property
4. of another,
5. with the specific intent of permanently depriving the owner of his or her property.

Each of these elements is subject to slightly differing interpretations. Consequently, the actual legal definition of larceny may vary from one jurisdiction to another, depending on court decisions and interpretations.

Modern statutes, in general, retain the ancient English classification of degrees of larceny, based on a value above or below a specified amount. The values that serve as dividing lines and the penalties imposed for each degree vary considerably across the country. Most modern statutes divide larceny into two degrees: **grand larceny** and **petty larceny.** Generally, grand larceny is considered a felony, while petty larceny is a misdemeanor. What is classified as grand larceny in one state may be classified as petty larceny in another. Some states may use *grand*

Theft The taking of property without the owner's consent; a popular term for larceny.

Larceny/theft The taking and carrying, leading, riding, or driving away the personal property of another with the specific intent of permanently depriving the owner of his or her property.

Grand larceny The taking and carrying away of another's personal property with a value in excess of the cutoff amount in a given jurisdiction, with the intent of depriving the owner of it permanently; generally considered a felony.

Petty larceny The taking and carrying away of another's property with a value below the cutoff amount in a given jurisdiction, with the intent of depriving the owner of it permanently; generally considered a misdemeanor.

HISTORY

In ancient England under the Saxons, simple larceny was originally divided into two sorts—grand larceny, *in which the value of the goods stolen was above 12 pence, and* petit larceny, *in which the value was equal to or below that amount. The offense of grand larceny was subject to the death penalty. The distinction between petit larceny and grand larceny has been modified over time, as has the punishment for the latter.*

theft and *petty theft* as the classifications. Investigators, therefore, should be familiar with the statutes and the definitions of larceny/theft in their own jurisdictions. In some states, grand larceny is classified as any theft involving property valued at $100 or more; thefts of lesser value are classified as petty larcenies. In other jurisdictions, the monetary value in a grand larceny may need to exceed $200. In 1995, 38 percent of larceny/thefts were of property with values over $200; 23 percent ranged from $50 to $200; the remainder were under $50.[1]

In spite of the childhood chant "Finders keepers, losers weepers," keeping found property lost by its rightful owner is a form of theft. Many jurisdictions will award found property to the finder if the actual owner cannot be located. However, a reasonable time and effort must be given to locating the rightful owner and returning the property.

Types of Larceny/Theft

There are many types of larceny/thefts that criminal investigators may encounter. Figure 16–2 shows some of the main categories. We will now discuss some of the more common larcenies and the investigative techniques suggested for each.

Pickpockets and Purse Snatchers

Pickpockets may work alone or in small groups. They are particularly difficult to apprehend, since the art of pickpocketing depends on stealth. A skillful pickpocket is neither seen nor detected by the victim. If, by chance, some onlooker sees the theft occur, the pickpocket may be identified. Purse snatchers are modern versions of pickpockets but tend to lack the finesse often associated with old-world pickpockets. Purse snatchers frequently grab a purse by force and run. Thus, victims of this crime may be injured by the assault. In many jurisdictions, purse snatching is classified as robbery.

Pickpockets sometimes use a bumping technique. During the bumping, they may actually lift the victim's wallet or cash from a pocket. In other situations, the pickpocket may use a razor to slit open a pocket during the bump, causing the wallet to simply fall into the pickpocket's waiting hand. Frequently, valuables are transferred to an accomplice, commonly known as a *tail,* almost as quickly as they are lifted from the victim. Then, should a victim suddenly realize the loss, the pickpocket will not have the incriminating evidence on his or her person. The pickpocket and the tail can meet later and split the take.

Traditional pickpockets are considered to be among the most skilled mechanical criminals. They use many different procedures in their work. The names for different types of pickpockets reflect their techniques:

- Choppers or slitters, who work crowded streets, using razor blades to cut pockets.

- Spitters, who sneeze profusely on their targets and pick their pockets while pretending to clean them off.
- Short workers, who concentrate their activities on public transportation.
- Hugger-muggers or jack rollers, prostitutes who pick the pockets of their johns after transacting their other business. Sometimes an irate accomplice will burst into the room, and in the confusion, the prostitute will pick the john's pocket.
- Toilet workers, who operate in public rest rooms.
- Ticket-line operators, who work ticket lines in airports, stadiums, theaters, and amusement centers.
- Sleepers, who open a purse that has been laid aside and rifle the contents.

In addition, pickpockets use an assortment of other innovative techniques to distract victims and mask their pickpocketing activities.

Pickpockets are drawn to crowded settings, such as amusement parks, shopping malls, parades, concerts, sporting events, railroad and bus depots, airports, carnivals, and bars. Investigators assigned to a pickpocket detail should be alert and observant of potential suspects and victims in such situations. Recognizing known pickpockets from past experience or mug shots can greatly assist investigators. When trying to detect would-be pickpockets, be particularly aware of activities such as the following:

- Individuals moving from place to place for no apparent reason.
- Persons carrying jackets or coats over their arms or newspapers or magazines in their hands.
- Groups of youths who huddle together, split up, and later board the same bus or train separately.
- Persons who seem more interested in the people around them than in the event taking place.
- People who display any unusual or unnatural behaviors.
- People who sit near other people who are dozing or intoxicated, when there are plenty of available seats.
- Individuals who seem to be repeatedly dropping change or keys. They may be intentionally creating a distraction conducive to pickpocketing.

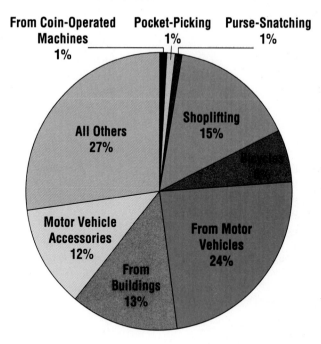

Figure 16–2 Percentage distribution of larceny/theft crime index offenses.

Source: Federal Bureau of Investigation, *Crime in the United States,* Government Printing Office, Washington, 1995.

Shoplifters

Shoplifting accounts for nearly 30 percent of all retail losses in the United States each year. In 1995, shoplifting represented 15 percent of all larceny/theft offenses reported in the FBI's Uniform Crime Reports (see Figure 16–2). Shoplifters may be amateurs or professionals. They may be young or old, and they are not always apprehended. Even when apprehended, they are not always prosecuted. Stores may not prosecute because of fear of losing a good customer, the cost of the court case, fear of being embarrassed in court, or the hope that a simple reprimand will solve the problem.

Shoplifting, taking goods from a retail establishment without paying for them, generally occurs while the person is posing as a customer. Such thievery can be distinguished from the theft of goods from warehouses, factories, and offices by employees, usually referred to as **employee pilfering.** Shoplifting occurs for a number of reasons—not all of which involve monetary gain. If we take a look at some of the general categories of shoplifters, we will see the different motivations for the crime.

The amateur often steals on the impulse of the moment or on a dare. In many instances, a young amateur shoplifter does not even need the stolen item. This sort of amateur shoplifts as a challenge, simply to show he or she can, to gain status in a group, or even to relieve boredom. Some amateurs shoplift simply because the opportunity presents itself. Even some otherwise law-abiding citizens may succumb to an overwhelming urge to "get something for nothing" when they believe no one is watching and no one will be the wiser.

The *modus operandi* of most amateurs is fairly predictable. It usually involves an attempt to conceal merchandise in a shopping bag, purse, pocket, backpack, or coat or under clothing. In some instances, amateurs may simply wear a garment out of the store, either concealing it under their own clothes or leaving their own clothes behind. Switching a price tag or sticker from an inexpensive item with one from an expensive item is another common technique amateurs use (even professionals use this one). Another technique is to place small items in the pockets of garments being purchased or in boxes or packages of items being purchased. If an extra item is detected at the checkout, the thief simply feigns ignorance of how it might have gotten there.

When people think of shoplifting, they tend to think of clothing and other dry goods, jewelry, and expensive luxury items. Yet, a common target of shoplifters

Shoplifting The taking of goods from a retail establishment without paying for them, while posing as a customer.

Employee pilfering The theft of goods from warehouses, factories, and offices by employees.

STATISTICS

In 1995, according to the FBI's Uniform Crime Reports (UCR), 46 percent of larceny/theft arrests were of persons under 21 years of age, and 33 percent of the arrestees were under 18. Females, who were arrested for this offense more often than for any other in 1995, comprised 33 percent of all larceny/theft arrestees. Whites accounted for 65 percent of the arrestees, blacks for 32 percent, and all other races for the remainder.

is meat from supermarkets. Also, cigarettes, baby laxatives (used in the cutting of drugs), and an assortment of other grocery items are regularly shoplifted.

Professional shoplifters tend to be more imaginative than amateurs, and their motive is money or profit. They are also trained in shoplifting techniques. Their crimes are premeditated, executed with care and stealth, and often assisted by special devices and accomplices. Professional shoplifters carry special containers, called booster boxes, with trapdoors into which merchandise can be quickly slipped. The **booster devices** frequently look like common packages of merchandise, or during the holidays, they may be gift wrapped. Specially designed clothing, such as booster skirts, booster coats, and booster bloomers, feature concealed pockets for hiding stolen merchandise. In addition, professionals may wear special harnesses and belts and carry hooks with retractable springs.

Some professionals work in teams. They may even work with accomplices who are employed by the store. One such team effort might involve a version of *tag switching*. The accomplice is usually a cashier who does not question a $5 price tag on a $500 camera or does not ring up all of the items that the other thief has placed on the counter. In another version, one or more accomplices create a disturbance or commotion to distract store personnel while other members of the team grab merchandise and escape with it. An accomplice or accomplices may feign a medical emergency or a domestic argument, or a group may create a general commotion as a cover for the thefts.

Drug addicts are often crime-prone persons because they must constantly seek the means to support their habits. Shoplifting is a means of obtaining items to sell to support their addiction. Often, caught in a desperate situation, drug addicts are capable of using violence to escape apprehension. Others may use burglary or more predatory crimes, such as mugging or robbery, for drug money, but shoplift food. The addict shoplifting for his or her habit will usually "shop" for merchandise with high ticket prices. Such a theft allows the addict to recover more profit when he or she sells the item to a **fence,** a dealer in stolen goods, or to a pawnbroker.

Kleptomania is an irresistible urge to steal—sometimes as a result of an emotional condition. In some cases, kleptomania is a sexually motivated behavior (see Chapter 12). The defense of kleptomania is frequently used for any excessive, repetitive, and apparently unreasonable stealing. Shoplifting caused by kleptomania represents a relatively small percentage of larceny/theft cases. True kleptomaniacs have a serious psychological problem and should be provided with therapy.

Booster device A container, generally a box, with a spring-loaded trapdoor, allowing the professional shoplifter to conceal stolen goods.

Fence Slang term for a professional receiver, concealer, and disburser of stolen property.

Professional shoplifters use a variety of devices to conceal stolen merchandise.

Not all pawnshops intentionally buy or sell stolen property, but some are not very cautious about verifying ownership of property pawned at the shop.

The enormous economic losses sustained from the chronic problem of shoplifting have forced retailers to turn to private security firms and mechanical security devices. Undercover security agents, hidden surveillance cameras, and various electronic tags on products are commonly used to deter and detect shoplifting. Local police agencies, as a rule, are called to the scene of a shoplifting *after* the shoplifter has been apprehended. Criminal investigators, however, may be called on to investigate professional shoplifters or shoplifting teams. This is particularly true when merchants realize they have been struck repeatedly for sizable amounts.

Shoplifting suspects can usually be detected by careful observation. Their strategies, like those of pickpockets, depend on smooth, quick movements; concealment; various types of distractions; and stealth. Persons wearing outerwear inappropriate to the season or carrying objects that could conceal merchandise should be suspect. People holding objects while scanning the store or nervously glancing around should also be monitored.

Fraud

Fraud Misrepresentation, trickery, or deception with criminal intent to deprive someone of his or her property.

Fraud is misrepresentation, trickery, or deception with criminal intent to deprive someone of his or her property. Criminal intent is called *mens rea* in criminal law. Fraud is a less serious crime than larceny/theft or burglary, but it has great economic impact. There are many types of fraud, some of which are more characteristic of business crimes and organized crime. It is the concept that one can get something for nothing. We will limit our discussion to some of the more common forms of fraud that fall into the category of larceny by fraud or deception. Note that fraud differs from larceny/theft in that, in fraud, deceit, not stealth, is used to obtain others' property and goods illegally.

Credit Card Fraud

The enormous availability and use of credit cards has moved this type of fraud to the forefront during recent years. Banks, department stores, furniture stores, jewelry stores, and gasoline companies all issue and honor credit cards. In the 1990s, gasoline credit cards, which once permitted only purchases of service station products and repairs, began changing to more general charge cards. Although one could continue to use the card at the issuing service station, one could also use it as one would any general, bank-issued credit card.

The use of stolen, forged, or unauthorized credit cards or credit card numbers has become a huge illegal business. Companies issuing credit cards are often in states other than the one where the card customer resides. Furthermore, the dollar limit on most cards is usually several hundreds or thousands of dollars. Thus, several years ago, it became a felony to forge, resell, or use a stolen or unauthorized credit card.

Thieves obtain credit cards and credit card numbers by theft—either from the mail or from the card's owner, by fraudulent application to the issuing company, by counterfeiting, or by obtaining or retaining the carbon paper from a used credit card billing form. Some thieves alter credit cards by shaving off the numbers and adhering new ones. Newly issued credit cards stolen from the mail were once highly sought, since they had not been reported stolen or lost and the thief could actually place his or her own signature on the card. To combat this, many issuing companies now require an "activation" telephone call before the card will be accepted by any store. During the activation call, the company requires the caller to know certain security information. This may include the maiden name or birth date of a parent, the card owner's social security number, or some similar secret information.

Check Fraud

Forging checks and writing bad checks are different statutory violations in most jurisdictions. A bad check is one that a person tries to cash when he or she has insufficient funds in the bank to cover the draft. Everyone at some time or another accidentally writes an overdraft on a checking account. This is usually corrected by the recipient's redepositing the check when there are sufficient funds. Or the recipient may ask the issuer to buy the bad check back with cash. However, the occasional overdrawn account is distinguishable from persistently and knowingly writing checks with not sufficient funds (NSF). It is likewise distinguishable from opening a new checking account with a small deposit and proceeding to **hang paper** (write bad checks) all over town, exceeding the amount of the deposit in the account.

Check forgery is the attempt to pass off a false signature on a check as genuine. It may additionally involve the use of forged or stolen identification to convince the victim that the false signature is real. The checks may be stolen from an individual (personal checks) or a business (commercial checks) or may be third-party checks such as payroll checks.[2] Blank checks are often obtained in a burglary.

Hang paper To intentionally write bad checks; slang expression.

STATISTICS

According to the UCR, a 20 percent clearance rate for larceny/theft was recorded nationally and in cities in 1995. Twenty-six percent of the larceny/theft clearances nationally and in cities involved only offenders under 18 years of age; 27 percent of those in suburban counties and 21 percent of those in rural counties involved only persons in this age group.

National Fraudulent Check File Investigating check fraud is difficult because professional bad check passers operate in a city for a short time and then move to another city or state. The FBI's National Fraudulent Check File (NFCF) makes it easier to identify such persons, their patterns of travel, and their techniques. The NFCF also maintains a database of information about check writing standards.

Confidence Games

A confidence game, also sometimes known as a *bunco*, is the obtaining of money or property by a trick, swindle, or device that takes advantage of the victim's confidence in the swindler. The con usually involves a get-rich-quick scheme and uses one of two basic approaches: the con artist either takes the victim for whatever money he or she has at the time or sets up a long con for higher stakes.

Most confidence games, or buncos, have three basic ingredients:

1. Finding a likely victim *(locating a mark),* which means identifying someone with money to fleece.

2. Enticing the mark by making an offer *(the spiel)* that sounds like getting something for nothing, appeals to superstition, or appeals to some aspect of vulnerable human nature *(baiting and setting the hook).*

3. Getting the victim to give up his or her money *(reeling in the mark).*

The confidence artist's business is to stimulate the interest and greed of the victim until his or her reason, judgment, and logic is overwhelmed. Bunco operators are excellent high-pressure salespeople, good actors, congenial people, and experts in psychology and human nature. The basic philosophy of confidence games is that there is larceny in everyone's heart, and some people are able to bring that quality out in others. Of course there are also those old sayings "There's a sucker born every minute" and "You can't cheat an honest man." Perhaps there is more wisdom in some sayings than others.

Bank Examiner Swindle   The bank examiner swindle is a fairly sophisticated con game. It may involve three or more people working in concert to swindle a victim, or *mark*. This con requires some background research. The thieves must learn the mark's name, address, phone number, bank, and latest banking transaction. The con artist contacts the mark, usually by telephone, and identifies him- or herself as a federal bank examiner. The phony bank examiner will then *bait the hook* by offering *the spiel,* saying that there has been a computer malfunction and that he or she needs to verify the latest transaction and the bank balance of the mark's account. After learning the balance, the caller indicates that there is a discrepancy between the mark's records and the bank's. Next, the phony bank examiner explains that he or she is investigating a dishonest teller at the bank who may be tampering with accounts. Now the caller asks for the mark's assistance in catching the dishonest teller—playing on human nature and the desire of many people to play spy or undercover detective. This phase of the con is sometimes referred to as *setting the hook.*

When the victim agrees to help, he or she is asked to go to the bank and withdraw an amount just short of the actual account balance. The mark is told that he or she will be protected at all times by a federal agent, who will watch the withdrawal and make sure the mark returns home safely. After returning home, the mark is visited by a member of the con team. It may be the person who originally called on the telephone or another member. He or she explains that things went exactly as planned and it is now necessary to take the money that was withdrawn into custody as evidence. This end of the game is referred to as *reeling in the mark.*

The con artist will usually write out an official-looking receipt for the money. In some cases, he or she may even promise to redeposit the money in the bank for the mark and may provide the victim with a fake deposit slip. The *agent* will tell the victim that the entire matter must be kept strictly confidential and is not to be discussed with anyone. The victim may even be promised a reward for participating in the investigation. It may take several days or weeks for the mark to learn that he or she has actually been swindled.

Pigeon Drop   The pigeon-drop bunco is typically operated by two people. It is said to be among the oldest swindles on record. The first bunco operator is usually neatly dressed and gifted, or practiced, at persuasion. Upon sighting the potential victim—the pigeon—Operator 1 will "find" a previously planted wallet or envelope so that the victim can see the operator picking it up. The con artist next opens the wallet or envelope and expresses surprise at the contents (all within view and earshot of the pigeon). The bunco operator then looks up to find the victim watching and asks whether the victim saw him or her pick up the wallet or envelope. The victim naturally says *yes*. The operator then tells the victim that the wallet contains a large sum of money, showing the contents briefly.

The contents are either counterfeit bills or some genuine bills mixed with fake currency totaling several thousand dollars. At about this time, Operator 2 happens along, posing as a disinterested bystander. When consulted, Operator 2 suggests that either of the two original parties might have found the envelope. Therefore, they should split the found money—provided they cannot find the actual owner during the next 24 hours. Operator 2 will further suggest that each of the parties put up a specified sum of money as security and to show good faith.

When the victim produces the good-faith money, Operator 1 places it in an envelope and shows it to Operator 2. Using sleight of hand, Operator 2 switches the envelope with an identical one filled with worthless paper slips. The pigeon is allowed to hold both the wallet or original envelope and the second envelope. The three agree to meet at a specified place in 24 hours, and they depart. However, the swindlers go home with the pigeon's money, and the victim goes home with worthless clippings.

Carnival Buncos   *Carnival buncos* refer loosely to several different swindles involving crooked games of chance. Some of the more common ones that investigators might encounter follow.

In three-card monte, the bunco operator uses three playing cards—for example, an ace and two picture cards. The con man coaxes an onlooker into betting that he or she can tell which of the three is a specified card. The cards are turned facedown and quickly moved around. Then the bystander makes his or her selection. Initially, the bystander wins, and usually he or she is a **shill,** or an accomplice of the bunco operator. As the shill continues to bet and win, other onlookers begin to think that this is really an easy win. However, as soon as one of them makes a bet, the bunco operator uses sleight of hand to remove the specified card from the table or inverted box. Thus, it is impossible to choose the correct card.

The switch is made so quickly that no one watching is the wiser. However, in a matter of just a few minutes, a skilled bunco operator can make several hundred dollars (depending on the size of bets). In some cases, the mark is actually permitted to win one or two times, to lull him

Shill   A slang term for a secret coconspirator or accomplice in a confidence game.

or her into a false sense of confidence. The bunco operator may even persuade the mark to place a much larger bet to try to win back his or her money. Naturally, when the mark places a larger bet, he or she will lose.

The shell game works like three-card monte, but instead of cards, the bunco operator uses walnut shells, soda caps, small Dixie cups, or similar objects. Under one of the shells, the bunco operator places a pea or a small ball of some sort. Then, working on a table or an inverted box, the operator quickly slides the caps around the surface. The challenge in this game is to locate the pea (or ball). By the time the operator asks, "Under which cap is the little ball?" he or she has already palmed it. It is, therefore, not under any of the caps or shells. After showing the mark that the ball is not where he or she thought it was, the bunco operator quickly replaces the ball under another cap while revealing it to onlookers. It appears that the person making the wager simply guessed wrong.

Some carnival games of chance are run dishonestly. They may take each victim for only a small amount of money but produce huge overall profits. The standard practice in these crooked games is to entice a customer to try the game—sometimes for free. Part of the lure is big, expensive prizes on display in the game booth. The customer may find the

Even legitimate carnival games of chance require one to play and win many times before being awarded a large prize.

game quite easy when trying it for free and tries it again for money. After winning the game, the customer receives a cheap, tiny prize that was shelved out of sight under the counter. The carnival worker then explains that to get a big prize, you must win many times and trade your prize for a larger one each time your win. Thus, it could be quite expensive to actually win a big prize. Variations on this basic scheme involve rigged games with weighted bottles, under- or overinflated balls and balloons, dull darts, misfiring rifles, and so forth.

Insurance Fraud

Fraud contributes significantly to Americans' insurance costs each year. Phony accident schemes, faked burglaries, exaggerated injuries, and false medical charges all contribute to millions of dollars in losses for insurance companies. For example, someone may intentionally walk in front of a car and make it appear that he or she has been hit or injured. Someone else may claim to have fallen on another's property or in a store. A person may have his or her own car stolen simply to receive the insurance money. A person who reports a burglary may not actually have been visited by a burglar. Some physicians even submit duplicate bills to insurance companies, order unnecessary tests, or upgrade the service bill for treatment not actually rendered.[3] Sometimes insurance swindlers enlist the aid of crooked lawyers and waste hours of court time suing others or insurance companies.

Suspicious claims, even though they may eventually be paid, are usually investigated by insurance companies. In some instances, insurance investigators may need help from law enforcement investigators as well. The nature and scope of the investigation may vary. In some cases, insurance investigators may keep a suspected insurance scam artist under surveillance for days or weeks. In other cases, a quick interview with the alleged victim may reveal false statements or deception.

Consumer and Business Fraud

Many financial and business schemes are perfectly legitimate. However, there are a number that are exploitive and prey on the same human weaknesses as the traditional confidence artist. The following are some common consumer and business frauds:

Bait and Switch   Advertised bargain merchandise lures, or baits, a customer into the store. Once there, the consumer is told that the store had only a single unit of that sale item and it has been sold. However, the salesperson will be happy to sell him or her a more expensive version of the item. The salesperson will even try to convince the consumer he or she is better off with the more expensive item.

HISTORY

In 1963, auditors at the Allied Crude Vegetable Oil Refining Corporation discovered a salad oil scam that Anthony De Angelis had been pulling off to extend the company's inventory of salad oil. De Angelis filled many of the company's oil vats with water, and through a system of underground pipes connecting the phony oil vats, pumped in a layer of oil to float on the water. For nearly 10 years, banks loaned hundreds of millions of dollars to De Angelis to finance worldwide salad oil deals. By the time the auditors discovered the fraud, De Angelis had already sold $175 million of bogus salad oil.

Look-Alike or Sound-Alike Products   Sellers offer inferior products with names that sound like or are packaged like better-quality or higher-priced items.

Misrepresentation or False Advertising   Such frauds involve misrepresentation of product performance, warranty, or quality or the cost of credit. For example, a better product than the one actually for sale is pictured in the advertisement. Or there is a false or misleading promise in the text. For instance, sometimes beef "on the hoof" is advertised for perhaps $1.99 a pound for all cuts. These deals usually require that the consumer buy full sides of beef. Of course, beef on the hoof means a live cow weighed before butchering—including the weight of the head, hide, legs, and hooves. In effect, a buyer may pay several hundred dollars for inedible cow parts. The actual cost of the edible beef received, then, may be $4.00 or $5.00 a pound.

Service Swindles   The basic M.O. for such frauds is to repair a home appliance or an automobile when repairs are not needed or to overcharge for repairs. An alternative is to charge for repairs never undertaken or parts never used or to offer home repairs at what appear to be rock-bottom prices but to never actually complete them.

Misrepresentation of Warranty   Such frauds are intentional failures to provide a consumer with facts about a product's warranty provisions and exclusions. For example, some computer warranties are "carry-in only."

Every year, tens of thousands of people are victims of investment scams. One very popular come-on in 1991 involved Operation Desert Storm. Con operators used patriotism in their spiel to convince victims to invest in phony oil and gas leases. Some 3,500 investors put a total of $50 million into these investments, relying on the promoters' claims that the war would drive up oil prices. The operation was a Ponzi scheme; that is, the early investors were paid with money raised from later investors. The wells were either plugged or not owned by the company making the offer. The scheme collapsed when the supply of new investors dried up.

This means that any repair must be made at a service location, not in the consumer's home. Furthermore, the responsibility and expense for getting the computer to the service location, whether by hand or by mail, is the consumer's.

Ponzi Schemes   Named for Carlo Ponzi, who bilked thousands of Bostonians of their money, Ponzi, or pyramid, schemes offer prospective investors weekly or monthly returns on their investments. Initial investors—the top of the pyramid—do receive the promised return at first. As word spreads, more investors contribute, and additional layers of the pyramid are added. The con artist uses the new investors' money to pay the interest on the older ones'. However, eventually, the interest payments exceed the new capital, and the swindler flees with the remaining investment cash.

Telemarketing and Mail Fraud

Telemarketing fraud and other types of fraud using the telephone have increased in recent years. In one such scam, a telemarketer offers enormous savings for purchasing some high-priced item or dream vacation by credit card. The actual scam is to have the victim tell the caller his or her credit card number. Since no product will ever be delivered, it is easy to offer a sewing machine or jewelry for just a few dollars. Once the caller acquires the victim's credit card number, he or she then uses the account number to make illegal purchases.

Similar scams operate through the mail. (See Figure 16–3.) In some cases, potential victims receive notices that they have been "awarded" a prize. Prizes are described as portable sewing machines, expensive-sounding 35-mm cameras, and so forth. The accompanying letter explains that this is not a contest prize, but a promotional incentive award. All the victim needs to do is send a small amount of money, usually $3 to $10, to cover postage and handling for the award to be delivered. The portable sewing machine turns out to be a cheap, handheld, toylike mending device, and the 35-mm camera is a plastic fixed-lens device worth about a dollar. Victims have reported sending hundreds of dollars over time, convinced that they are actually going to receive an expensive product, such as a new car, television, cash, or trips.[4]

Chain letters are another type of pyramid scheme and are often illegal. Any chain letter that requires payment of money or something

Figure 16–3   Notification of a prize award.

Certificate Of Guarantee

UNISYSTEMS
10000 WESTHEIMER # 150
HOUSTON, TX 77042

Bruce Berg
1000 Winter Ave.
Pittsburgh, PA 15235

CLAIM # 2735267
CTRL # 44132
BONUS # 8546

CONGRATULATIONS
Bruce Berg

This notice is to advise you that you only have 48 hours from receipt to claim your award. You are ABSOLUTELY GUARANTEED at least one (1) of the following four (4) awards for your participation in our National Promotion. To ensure your award you must call NOW!...Our operators are standing by....You must respond immediately...or your award will pass to an alternate recipient.

Our obligation to hold your award will expire and your award will revert to the promotion sponsor if unclaimed. This is the only notice you should receive so please call personally with your claim and bonus number. This is a valid incentive promotion. One call per household. Some restrictions may apply.

Bruce, One of the following Awards is Yours!

1. JEEP WRANGLER - OR - $10,000.00 IN CASH!
2. $3,000.00 U.S. SAVINGS BOND!
3. WORLD CLASS VACATION ADVENTURE!
4. RCA ENTERTAINMENT SYSTEM - OR $1000.00 IN CASH!

CALL TOLL FREE 1-800-555-1111
If Busy Keep Calling
Mon-Fri 9am-7pm(CST)   Sat 10am-3pm(CST)

of value is a violation of federal mail fraud laws. People lose hundreds of dollars every year in chain letter schemes. Earlier investors in the pyramid may receive considerable money or items of value. However, as successive layers are heaped on the pyramid pile, fewer and fewer participants actually receive the promised items. Figure 16–4 shows how a typical chain letter scheme works. Initially, six people are asked to each send a letter to six other people, each of whom must then send letters to six more people, and so on. The letter asks that a specified amount of money be sent to someone farther up the chain. But, as Figure 16–4 shows, the geometric progression of participants will quickly exceed the population of the United States, and even that of the world.

Of course, not all solicitations made through the mail or over the telephone are scams. It is exactly this fact that allows confidence artists to remain successful in these swindles. Other common mail and telephone frauds involve bunco operators masquerading as doctors, lawyers, real estate agents, stock brokers, art dealers, salespeople, parcel delivery agents, and many other service representatives. These various scams usually involve the three basic ingredients of a con game, discussed earlier in the chapter.

Investigating Fraud

Investigating cases of fraud presents challenges to the criminal investigator. Generally there is no crime scene that can be searched for traces of evidence or indications of the offender's *modus operandi*. Information

Figure 16–4 Chain letter pyramid.

No. of Mailings	No. of Participants
1	6
2	36
3	216
4	1,296
5	7,776
6	46,656
7	279,936
8	1,679,616
9	10,077,696
10	60,466,176
11	362,797,056
12	2,176,782,336
13	13,060,694,016

Source: United States Postal Service, Publication 256.

about the crime must come from the victim and witnesses and from any documents or forms used or created by the person committing the fraud.

Investigating any type of check fraud, for example, requires obtaining full details about all checks written and all transactions involved. The check or checks become the main piece of evidence and should be examined and handled like any piece of evidence that is being sent to the lab. Additionally, the names of all bank employees involved in the transaction should be obtained. Interviews with bank personnel may provide a description of the bad-check passer, an address from the identification he or she used, an indication of whether he or she had a vehicle, and a description of the vehicle, if any.

For any crime of fraud, investigators should obtain the following information:

- Description of the offense
- Description of the victim
- Description of the suspect
- Documentary and physical evidence
- *Corpus delicti* of the offense

Receiving Stolen Property

From television and movie police dramas, most people have heard the expression "possession of stolen property" used to describe a criminal offense. More accurately, the crime referred to by that phrase should be "receiving or concealing stolen property." Although statutes vary across the nation, they rarely, if ever, classify mere possession of stolen property as a crime. The reason for this is quite simple. Possession is a fairly weak act and is difficult to justify as a crime in the absence of *mens rea*—criminal intent. On the other hand, the phrase *receiving and concealing* carries with it the inference that one had possession of stolen property with knowledge that it was stolen. Receiving and concealing further implies that there may have been intentional and overt attempts to prevent discovery of the stolen property. These two elements—(1) receiving, buying, or concealing stolen or illegally obtained goods and (2) knowing the goods to be stolen or illegally obtained—constitute the offense of receiving stolen goods.

Fence is the popular name for a go-between who knowingly receives and disposes of stolen property. A fence buys stolen goods from a thief and sells it to others for a profit. Naturally, the amount of money the fence pays the thief is substantially less than the value of the item, and less than he or she expects to resell the item for.

A fencing operation may be small and simple or large and complex. It may consist of one person who buys stolen property from thieves and sells it from the trunk of his or her car. Or it may be a network of fine-art and antique dealers communicating by computer networks. In some cases, a thief works with a fence almost on a consignment basis. In other words, the fence may already have a buyer for a specific item and may arrange for a thief to steal the item. A prearranged price may even be set between fence and thief. In other cases, the thief simply brings anything he or she steals to the fence, hoping a purchase price can be arranged.

Periodically, police agencies establish fencing **sting operations.** Police officers set up a location, such as a store or small warehouse, and go into business as fences. When they have obtained enough evidence on a number of thieves, they obtain arrest warrants and capture the felons. Fencing sting operations often recover a wide variety of products and merchandise, including televisions, radios, credit cards, guns, computers, payroll checks, and savings bonds.

The role of the fence should not be underestimated. The fence is a crucial element in larceny. Without fences and other receivers and concealers of stolen goods, thefts and various larcenies would not be profitable to the perpetrators. The objective in most thefts of merchandise is not the item itself. Rather, it is the money that can be obtained for the item.

Sting operation An undercover operation set up by law enforcement personnel to catch, or "sting," offenders committing a crime; often used to collect evidence against thieves.

Investigating Fences and Other Receivers of Stolen Property

Investigators should maintain contact with the local business community. They should periodically speak to business groups and remind those in attendance to be careful when a supplier offers too good a deal. When investigating possible fences, criminal investigators should pursue the following investigative activities:

- Establish proof that the property was stolen.
- Determine when the property was received by the accused.
- Review records concerning the method of payment, the amount, the place of payment, receipts, and so forth.
- Establish the circumstances of the receipt of the property: from whom, to whom, and when.
- Identify where the property was found, and find out if and how it was concealed.

- Gather evidence that the accused knew the property was stolen.
- Obtain a description of the property, an estimate of its value, and the name and address of the owner.
- Obtain the identity of the person from whom the fence purchased the property.
- Determine the purchase price.
- Gather evidence of the hiding, concealing, or destroying of identification marks.
- Establish the failure to maintain proper records.
- Observe the conduct of the accused, and any statements made, when informed that the property was stolen.

Ways of Preventing Fencing

It has been long established that one way to inhibit fencing is to place identification numbers on products. Not only does this inhibit fences, it also reduces the kinds of items a burglar or thief is likely to steal. When individuals or businesses cannot positively identify their stolen merchandise, it becomes all the more difficult for prosecutors to obtain a conviction of a fence or a thief.

Many manufacturers do make the effort to stencil or stamp identification numbers on their products. However, these precautions are to no avail if the consumer fails to record or register these numbers. Many local police agencies sponsor identification programs. These frequently involve lending an electric etching device to members of the community so that they can etch an identification number on their home appliances, televisions, stereos, and so on. These numbers can be registered with the police and can be used to identify items should they be stolen.

SUMMARY BY LEARNING OBJECTIVES

Learning Objective 1

Larceny/theft is one of eight crimes that the FBI considers the most serious crimes in American society, and it reports yearly statistics on larceny/theft in its Uniform Crime Reports (UCR). In 1995, larceny/theft made up almost 58 percent of crime index offenses.

Learning Objective 2

State statutes define what constitutes the crime of larceny/theft in each state. Generally, these statutes have the following elements in common: larceny/theft consists of (1) the taking and (2) carrying away (3) of personal property (4) of another (5) with the specific intent of permanently depriving the owner of his or her property. Additionally, states may have degrees of larceny, such as *grand larceny* (sometimes also called *grand theft*) and *petty larceny* (sometimes also called *petty theft*). The definitions and penalties for these offenses vary among the states.

Learning Objective 3

The most common types of larceny/theft offenses include thefts from motor vehicles, shoplifting, thefts from buildings, thefts of motor vehicle accessories, thefts from coin-operated machines, purse snatching, and pocket picking. Most larceny/theft cases are solved through experience—working many cases—and by a basic understanding of the motivation for the offenses and of the techniques that both amateurs and professionals often use.

Learning Objective 4

Fraud is depriving someone of his or her property by using misrepresentation, trickery, or deception. It is related to larceny/theft because it is larceny or theft by deception. Fraud can take many forms, including but not limited to the following: credit card fraud, check fraud, confidence games, insurance fraud, consumer and business fraud, and telemarketing and mail fraud.

Learning Objective 5

In most states, receiving, buying, or concealing stolen or illegally obtained goods and knowing the goods to be stolen or illegally obtained constitutes the offense of receiving stolen goods or property. *Fence* is the popular term for a go-between who knowingly receives and disposes of stolen goods. Without fences and other receivers of stolen goods, larceny/theft would not be profitable to perpetrators.

QUESTIONS FOR REVIEW

Learning Objective 1

1. What is the significance of larceny/theft among the crime index offenses?

Learning Objective 2

2. Define *larceny/theft*.
3. Distinguish between *theft* and *larceny*.

4. What are four types of *pickpocket* techniques?

5. Why do some jurisdictions classify purse snatching as robbery rather than larceny?

6. Why do crowded places attract pickpockets?

7. Why should officers be alert to people sitting next to other people who have fallen asleep?

8. What kinds of things should an investigator look for when attempting to apprehend pickpockets?

9. What is a *booster device?*

10. What are some differences between a professional shoplifter and an amateur?

11. What are some investigative techniques for detecting potential shoplifters?

12. What are three basic elements of *fraud?*

13. Explain what is involved in a *pigeon drop.*

14. How does a *bank examiner scam* work?

15. Why is it difficult to prove a criminal case for possession of stolen goods alone?

16. What is meant by the term *fence?*

CRITICAL THINKING INVESTIGATIVE EXERCISE

Divide into three groups. Then, as assigned by your instructor, complete one of the following projects.

1. Research newspapers and magazines to locate published accounts from recent years that describe at least three of the types of fraud discussed in the chapter. Assemble and organize the facts of each case according to the five categories listed in the section titled "Investigating Fraud." Present the cases to the class, informing them how the frauds were perpetrated, investigated, and prosecuted.

2. Contact at least two supermarkets and two department stores to determine their procedures for handling bad checks received from customers. Ascertain if and when the stores involve police, collection agencies, or other organizations. Assemble the information into an oral report to the class on the scope of the problem of check fraud in your community.

3. Contact friends, family members, and classmates, or rely on your own experiences to gather three to five personal accounts of telephone or mail solicitations for an awarded prize. Ascertain the come-ons and what the awardees had to do to gain the prize. Determine if anyone paid a required handling fee or delivery charge for such an award and what the results were. Assemble the completed stories and present them to the class. Discuss what courses of action persons can take when they receive such solicitations.

INVESTIGATIVE SKILL BUILDERS

Servicing Clients and Customers

You arrive at the scene of a disturbance inside a specialty store that sells televisions, radios, and other electronic items. As you walk in, you can hear a man's voice shouting, "Fraud! Crook! You're a swindler." The proprietor at the counter tells you he wants the customer to leave, but he will not. The customer is a man in his seventies who is disgruntled about a clock radio he purchased from the store. The man shouts, "The damn clock won't work. It doesn't do half the things the salesman told me it would do. I want my money back."

The proprietor tells you that the man does not have his receipt and that there are no cash refunds without a receipt. The proprietor points to a sign behind the counter that reads, "No cash refunds without a valid receipt." The customer is visibly upset. He tells you that he has never had any sort of problem like this when dealing with one of the large department stores. He tells you, "That man behind the counter sold me this clock just two days ago, and he knows it." You ask the proprietor if that is true. He tells you that he does remember selling the clock to the man but that rules are rules, and he will not take the clock back. As a police officer, what actions should you take?

Integrity/Honesty

You are a veteran police officer. Your 15-year-old daughter comes home and tells you that she has just gotten a great job that pays $7 an hour. You ask what she is doing, and she tells you that she is making telephone calls to people to inform them that they have been given prize awards. You are confused by her response and, after some additional questions, learn that she is working in a *boiler-room*-style telephone bank for what sounds like a telemarketing scam. Her job is to call people and inform them that they have been selected to receive a special vacation trip to Florida. It is an all-expenses-paid trip, including airfare and hotel accommodations. All the person has to do is send in a refundable $300 deposit to hold the spot. You call a friend on the bunco unit of your department and learn that there are several complaints against this company and an undercover investigation is underway.

1. Do you volunteer your daughter's services to assist in the undercover operation?
2. Do you mention to your friend that your daughter is working for this suspected fraudulent telemarketer?
3. Do you allow your daughter to continue working for the company or risk blowing the undercover operation by forbidding her to do so?

ENDNOTES

1. Federal Bureau of Investigation, *Crime in the United States,* Government Printing Office, Washington, 1995.
2. C. H. McCaghy and S. A. Cernkovick, *Crime in American Society,* Macmillan, New York, 1987.
3. James L. Garcia, "Health Insurance Fraud: A Growing Problem," *USA Today,* Vol. 120, No. 2562, March 1992, pp. 29–30.
4. Nancy Wride, "57 Arrested in Anaheim Fencing Sting," *The Los Angeles Times,* March 25, 1989, p. 19.

CHAPTER 17

Motor Vehicle Theft

CHAPTER OBJECTIVES

After completing this chapter, you will be able to:

1. Provide an overview of the crime of motor vehicle theft in the United States.

2. List some of the common types of motor vehicle theft.

3. Explain the legal aspects of the crime of motor vehicle theft.

4. Discuss some useful techniques for motor vehicle theft investigators.

5. Describe motor vehicle thefts other than automobile theft.

6. Specify certain activities intended to prevent motor vehicle theft.

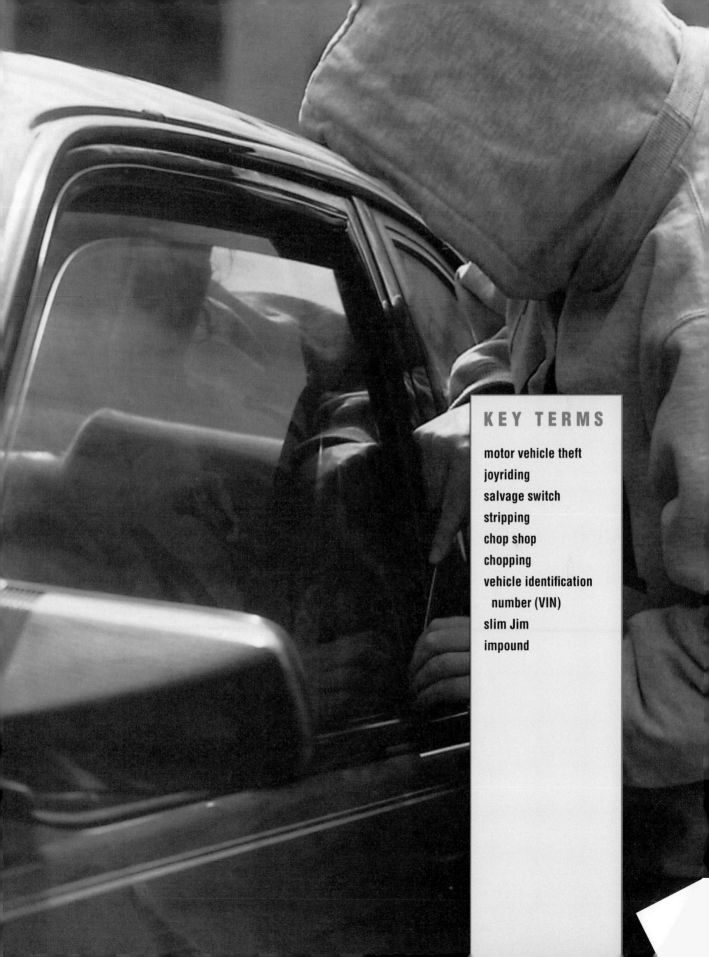

The Nature of Motor Vehicle Theft

As noted in Chapter 16, thefts from motor vehicles are included under larceny/theft in the official crime data of the FBI. **Motor vehicle theft,** however, is a separate category of serious property crime and is itself one of the eight index offenses. The Uniform Crime Reports (UCR) define it as "the theft or attempted theft of a motor vehicle." Included in this category are thefts of automobiles, trucks, buses, motorcycles, construction and farm machinery, aircraft, and recreational vehicles such as boats and snowmobiles. In 1995, there were 1,472,700 motor vehicle theft offenses reported, the lowest total since 1988 (see Figure 17–1). Of all motor vehicles reported stolen during the year, 78 percent were automobiles, 16 percent were trucks or buses, and the remainder were other types. In 1995, motor vehicle theft made up 10.6 percent of all crime index offenses.

Figure 17–1 Motor vehicle theft crime index totals.

Year	Population	Crime Index Total	Number of Motor Vehicle Theft Offenses
1980	225,349,264	13,408,300	1,131,700
1981	229,146,000	13,423,800	1,087,800
1982	231,534,000	12,974,400	1,062,400
1983	233,981,000	12,108,600	1,007,900
1984	236,158,000	11,881,800	1,032,200
1985	238,740,000	12,431,400	1,102,900
1986	241,077,000	13,211,900	1,224,100
1987	243,400,000	13,508,700	1,288,700
1988	245,807,000	13,923,100	1,432,900
1989	248,239,000	14,251,400	1,564,800
1990	248,709,873	14,475,600	1,635,900
1991	252,177,000	14,872,900	1,661,700
1992	255,082,000	14,438,200	1,610,800
1993	257,908,000	14,144,800	1,563,100
1994	260,341,000	13,989,500	1,539,300
1995	262,755,000	13,867,100	1,472,700

Source: Federal Bureau of Investigation, *Crime in the United States,* Government Printing Office, Washington, 1995.

Figure 17–2 Top 20 American cities for automobile theft in 1994.

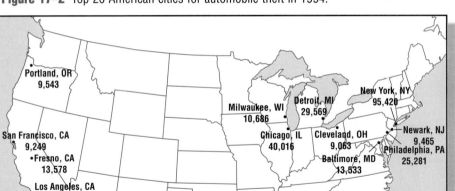

Source: U.S. Department of Justice, Bureau of Justice Statistics, *Sourcebook of Criminal Justice Statistics,* Government Printing Office, Washington, 1995.

Automobile theft has traditionally been considered a problem of larger American cities. However, the theft of and from automobiles is a significant problem in most cities, regardless of size. Figure 17–2 shows the leading 20 American cities with the greatest numbers of automobile thefts, among cities with populations of 100,000 or more.

Methods used to steal cars and frauds connected with stolen and missing cars have become increasingly diverse and complex. Cars have been stolen from every conceivable place: homes, shopping malls, main streets, side streets, parking lots and garages, and even right off the sales floors of dealerships. These thefts cost owners time and money. They also cost the American automobile insurance industry huge sums of money and numbers of personnel hours each year.

Types of Motor Vehicle Theft

Motor vehicle thefts are generally classified by the thief's motive for stealing a vehicle. There is an assortment of motives for stealing vehicles. For the most part, though, these motives may be divided into five major categories: joyriding; transportation; to commit another scrime; fraud; and stripping, chopping, or resale.

Joyriding

Teenagers who steal a car simply to drive around and then abandon it account for most **joyriding.** According to the UCR, teens accounted for 25 percent of all arrests for motor vehicle theft in 1995. Joyriders sometimes work alone, sometimes in small groups. According to teens, their basic motives include getting a free ride, having fun and excitement racing down streets as sport, impressing peers or completing a gang initiation, relieving boredom, and getting a rush. Youthful thieves keep a vehicle for a relatively short time and generally abandon it once it runs out of gas or is immobilized in a wreck, or when they tire of the ride.[1] Joyriders look for easy targets, such as vehicles in which the owner has left keys in the ignition or in a magnetic key box in the wheel well. Because joyriding is a crime of opportunity, it often occurs where juveniles congregate. Several vehicle thefts near such a location may establish a pattern and provide important clues to investigators. In some states, joyriding is a separate offense from motor vehicle theft. Be sure that you know the law in your jurisdiction.

Transportation

Hitchhikers, transients, and runaways who steal cars for transportation are sometimes lumped together with joyriders. There are, however, several distinguishing characteristics. First, the objective of a theft for transportation is usually a specific ride from one point to another, not aimlessly driving around simply for the fun of it. Furthermore, offenders who steal cars for transportation are generally older than joyriders. Finally, a vehicle stolen for transportation is usually kept longer and driven farther before being abandoned than a car taken for a joyride.

To Commit Another Crime

Some offenders steal a car to use as transportation when committing another crime. The robbery of a bank, an armored car, a supermarket, and so on almost always involves the use of a getaway car that has been stolen. Sometimes one stolen car is driven to a second one, or to a legally owned car, to make it more difficult for the police to find the thieves. Other crimes that commonly include the use of a stolen vehicle include kidnapping, burglary, assassination, and murder for hire.

A stolen vehicle used to commit a crime is nearly 200 times more likely to end up in a crash than one driven by a noncriminal. This accident probability is so high for several reasons. First, being chased at high speeds increases the likelihood of an accident. Second, the criminal may be unfamiliar with the roads and road conditions. And third, the driver of the stolen vehicle may be unfamiliar with its operation or unable to handle it under various conditions.

The obvious reason a criminal uses a stolen vehicle to commit another crime is to avoid being detected and identified by witnesses or the police. The criminal is likely to steal the vehicle just before committing the other crime. Doing so provides a short period during which the theft has not been discovered and the vehicle has not been reported as stolen. In some cases, license plates stolen from one vehicle are transferred to another stolen car. With these techniques, the thief hopes to prolong the time before the police can identify the vehicle he or she is driving as stolen.

Fraud

Some fraudulent thefts are actually perpetrated by the owner of the vehicle or someone acting on behalf of the owner. In some cases, an owner or someone acting as the owner's agent drives the vehicle far from the owner's home and burns it or dumps it in a lake or ravine. The owner then files a claim for the "stolen vehicle" with his or her insurer. Sometimes, an owner drives the vehicle to an area of town known for gangs of strippers, who dismantle and sell parts of cars. After waiting a short time, the owner reports that the car has been stolen. When the police finally locate it—if they do—it is likely to be a skeleton of a car, stripped of anything of value. The reason for these fraudulent thefts is usually to acquire money from the insurance company or to obtain a replacement vehicle.

Another fraud commonly associated with automobile thefts is the **salvage switch.** The criminal acquires title to a late-model car by legitimate means. For example, he or she may buy a wreck at a junkyard for a couple of hundred dollars. The offender then disposes of the wreck as salvage or scrap metal, but retains the license plates, registration, and title and various engine and chassis identification number plates. Next, the criminal finds and steals a vehicle of the same make and model as the wreck and replaces the various identification numbers and license plates on the stolen car with those retained from the salvaged wreck. The thief now appears to have all the correct identification plates and ownership documents for the stolen car, which he or she will sell to an unsuspecting buyer.

Salvage switch A switching of vehicle identification number plates from wrecked vehicles to stolen cars of the same make and model..

Stripping, Chopping, and Resale

Stripping and chopping or reselling stolen cars have one commonality. All are techniques professional thieves use to make profits from the theft of a vehicle.

Stripping   Some vehicles are stolen for the purpose of **stripping** them of valuable parts and accessories for resale or for sale to wrecking yards, used car lots, and auto repair shops. Items such as tires, wheel covers, transmissions, motors, wheels, air bags, radios, CB radios, CD and tape players, and even car telephones are attractive to thieves because they generally do not have any identifying numbers and thus are easy to dispose of. In some cases, the thief hunts for a particular make and model of vehicle. If the

Stripping   Illegally removing parts and accessories from motor vehicles to use or sell them.

Some owners burn their cars or arrange to have someone burn them to fraudulently collect payments from their auto insurers.

keys are in the car, it is quickly driven away. If not, the ignition wires are short-circuited to start the engine. In some cases, thieves boldly drive up with a tow truck, hook up the target vehicle, and drive away with it in tow. Once mobile, the stolen vehicle is taken to a secluded area or a garage and stripped of all desirable parts. When the thieves are finished with the carcass, the chassis and unwanted parts are abandoned.

Chopping   A **chop shop** is a place where stolen vehicles are taken for **chopping** or dismantling into parts or accessories that cannot be easily identified, which are resold to repair shops or private citizens. Chop shops often operate out of auto repair shops or wrecking yards that appear to be legitimate businesses. There, stolen vehicles can be quickly chopped, or cut up with torches, and the parts stored without likely detection. Although stripping gangs and chop shops are similar, there are several distinctions. For example, chop shops can remove identifying numbers from the motor and other similarly identified items in the car. Furthermore, they can frequently handle a greater volume of stolen cars, since those that have not yet been chopped can be concealed on the premises. Finally, since the front business is often a repair or salvage yard, parts can quickly become inventory. In some cases, chop shops have special orders and direct a thief to acquire a particular make and model of car to obtain a certain vehicle part.

Chop shop   A place for chopping, or dismantling, stolen motor vehicles into parts and accessories that cannot be easily identified, which are resold.

Chopping   The dismantling of stolen motor vehicles into parts and accessories for use or sale.

Resale   Rather than steal a vehicle for stripping or chopping, some professional thieves steal cars to resell them. In some cases, car thieves actually steal a specific type of car on request from a would-be customer. Others specialize in stealing only certain types of cars. Like other car thieves, they may take a car whose owner has neglectfully left the key in the ignition or clipped to the visor. Alternatively, a resale thief may enter a used-car dealership, pose as a potential buyer, and arrange to test-drive a vehicle. Once the thief leaves the lot, he or she does not return with the auto. Similarly, this sort of thief may answer an unsuspecting car seller's ad in the newspaper. As with the car dealer, the thief arranges to test-drive the car and simply never returns it. Cars may also be stolen by transacting a sale with a bad check.

Few vehicles stolen by professional resale thieves are ever recovered. These thieves are specialists, capable of obtaining not only cars, but false or forged papers for these stolen vehicles. The resale thief may repaint, recover seats, repair any body damage, and match identification numbers to false documents before selling the car to an individual, to a dealer, or at a public auction.

Vehicles manufactured in the United States are very popular in other countries. Mexico and several South and Central American countries regularly receive stolen and altered U.S.-manufactured vehicles for resale. Furthering the potential of exporting stolen vehicles for resale is the fact that other countries offer few effective controls over vehicles crossing their borders. This form of stolen vehicle liquidation has become so popular that in some Caribbean countries as many as 20 percent of all vehicles on the roads were stolen and shipped from the United States.[2]

> ## FYI
>
> A stolen American vehicle often nets double its original price overseas. There, the theft is often erroneously seen as a victimless crime, since American cars are usually covered by insurance.

Legal Aspects of the Crime of Motor Vehicle Theft

Motor vehicle theft is a form of larceny because it is the taking and driving away of a motor vehicle from the owner or possessor with the intent of permanently depriving him or her of it. The law of motor vehicle theft is not well developed. This situation exists despite the importance of motor vehicles in modern society and the large losses suffered each year due to stolen vehicles.

Prosecution for motor vehicle theft varies among the states. In some states, thieves are charged with "grand theft auto." In others, they are prosecuted for "unauthorized use of a motor vehicle" rather than for motor vehicle theft. To combat motor vehicle theft, states have enacted a variety of laws that require stiffer penalties for motor-vehicle-related crimes. For example, in some states, persons who commit the crimes of robbery, burglary, aggravated or sexual assault, eluding police, kidnapping, or manslaughter with a stolen car face longer prison terms than those specified for any of those crimes committed without using a stolen car. In other states, juveniles face mandatory penalties for the first offense in a motor-vehicle-related crime, such as joyriding.

Investigating Motor Vehicle Theft

Once the police receive notification of a vehicle theft, they respond to the complainant, obtain all pertinent information, and write a formal report (see Chapter 9). It is the investigating officer's job to verify all the information obtained about the theft. The investigating officer must also verify that a theft has taken place. In some cases, a report of a stolen automobile will turn out to be nothing more than the owner's misplacing it in a large shopping mall parking lot or garage. In other cases, what starts as a stolen car report, may later turn out to be the unauthorized use of the vehicle by a family member. In still other stolen vehicle cases, investigators may determine that the car has been lawfully repossessed because the owner fell behind on payments. Cars are also reported stolen when they have been involved in hit-and-run accidents or other crimes.

Having accurate information in the theft report does not ensure that the vehicle will be recovered. However, having inaccurate information increases the likelihood that it will not be recovered. You should not take for granted that the person reporting the theft knows the correct license plate number and vehicle identification number (VIN). Check the registration to ensure accuracy. Completeness and accuracy in reporting theft data are essential both to the investigation and to the protection of fellow officers in the field who will be looking for the stolen car. The kind of descriptive data the responding officer should give the dispatcher about the stolen vehicle follows:

- Make and model of the vehicle.
- Year of the vehicle.
- Color or colors of the vehicle.
- Name, address, and telephone number of the owner.
- License plate number and the state that issued it.
- Vehicle identification number (VIN).
- Location and time of the theft.
- Any distinctive characteristics, special equipment, or damage.

Answers to the following questions are also useful in a motor vehicle theft investigation:

- Who was the last person to use the vehicle? If not the owner, what was that person's relationship to the owner?

- Were keys left in the ignition or concealed in a location outside the vehicle?
- Had the vehicle been left unlocked?
- Had the vehicle been left with windows up or down?
- Has the owner kept up with payments on the vehicle?
- Is the owner in financial difficulty?
- Were there any items of merchandise or equipment, or any valuables in the cabin, glove box, or trunk?
- Was the registration, insurance card, or owner's title in the vehicle?

When you are investigating stolen autos, remember that the market for stolen cars changes to meet demand. It is not always the most expensive or best-looking cars that are stolen. Nor do thieves choose autos to steal for the ease or difficulty of taking them. They base their thefts on the ease of selling the stolen vehicles or their parts. As a car gets older, demand for its parts grows, especially if there are a large number of that model of vehicle on the road. Figure 17–3 shows the most popular models of automobiles stolen in a recent year.

Identifying a Stolen Vehicle

Even when a vehicle that matches the make, model, year, and color of a stolen vehicle has been recovered, it may not be the stolen vehicle.

Figure 17–3 Top 25 stolen vehicles in 1996.

1. 1994 Honda Accord EX	14. 1984 Oldsmobile Cutlass Supreme
2. 1988 Honda Accord LX	15. 1995 Toyota Corolla
3. 1992 Honda Accord LX	16. 1987 Chevrolet Caprice
4. 1987 Oldsmobile Cutlass Supreme	17. 1986 Cadillac Deville
5. 1995 Ford Mustang	18. 1985 Oldsmobile Cutlass Supreme
6. 1986 Oldsmobile Cutlass Supreme	19. 1990 Toyota Camry
7. 1995 Honda Accord EX	20. 1988 Toyota Camry
8. 1990 Honda Accord EX	21. 1991 Acura Legend
9. 1989 Toyota Camry	22. 1995 Toyota Camry LE
10. 1992 Honda Accord EX	23. 1991 Honda Civic
11. 1989 Honda Accord LX	24. 1994 Honda Accord LX
12. 1991 Honda Accord EX	25. 1990 Honda Accord LX
13. 1991 Honda Accord LX	

Source: CCC Information Services, Inc.

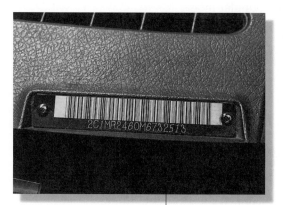

A VIN plate contains a 17-digit number assigned by the vehicle manufacturer and is generally located on the driver's side of the dashboard.

To assure that the right vehicle has been found, the investigator relies on identification numbers affixed to or inscribed on various parts of the car. The most important of these is the **vehicle identification number (VIN).** The VIN is the primary nonduplicated, serialized number assigned by the manufacturer to each vehicle made. This number specifically identifies the motor vehicle.

American automobile manufacturers first began using VINs as the primary means of identifying a vehicle in 1954. Unfortunately, VINs were not uniformly positioned in vehicles. Nor, for that matter, was there a consistent way of attaching the metal plate containing the VIN to the vehicle. The VIN plate might be in the glove box on some models, on the dashboard on others, and even on a doorpost on other models. Similarly, it might be attached by spot welding, screws, rivets, or some sort of plastic fasteners. Because of these inconsistencies, removing or altering a VIN plate was not hard to do.

In 1968, VIN plates on all domestic vehicles and most imports began to be uniformly placed on the left side (driver's side) of the dashboard. In this position, the VIN is clearly visible through the windshield of the car. In 1981, the auto industry adopted a standardized 17-character VIN for all automobiles manufactured or sold in the United States. Before this standardization, VINs varied from 11 to 13 characters. The first 10 characters of the standardized VIN identify the country of origin, manufacturer, make, restraint system, model, body style, engine type, year, and assembly plant. The 11th is a mathematically computed check digit to verify all of the other characters in the VIN. The last 6 characters are the sequential production number of the vehicle.

In 1984 the federal government enacted the Motor Vehicle Theft Law Enforcement Act. The law is an effort to thwart stripping, chopping, and resale of stolen vehicles. It requires manufacturers to put additional identification numbers on up to 14 major automobile parts on certain lines of autos. The parts requiring additional identification are those generally sought by chop shops: engines, transmissions, all doors, hoods, bumpers, front fenders, trunk lids, rear quarter panels, and deck lids, tailgates, or hatchbacks (if present). The car lines chosen for the additional identification numbers are those designated as high-theft lines. The numbers match the 17-character VIN used on the vehicle and must be inscribed on the part or printed on an attached label. The labels must be attached in such a manner that their removal will create significant damage to the part or leave a visible trace of the label. The law carries a fine of $10,000 or five years' imprisonment or both for removal, intentional destruction, or tampering with an identification number on a vehicle or vehicle part.

When verifying a suspected stolen automobile's VIN, look for signs indicating that the metal plate has been changed or disturbed. It is virtually impossible to remove the VIN plate and attach it to another vehicle without leaving some telltale sign. Make sure that the plate is affixed firmly to the vehicle. An authentic VIN plate should fit snugly in place.

Recognizing a Stolen Vehicle

With experience on the street, an investigator develops an instinct or sixth sense about stolen cars. There are no foolproof means of recognizing a stolen vehicle. There are, however, a number of visible and compelling signs that should make an officer suspicious about a vehicle.[3]

- New license on an old vehicle or an old license on a new one.
- Missing plates from either the front or the rear of the vehicle.
- Mismatched plates (in jurisdictions where front and rear plates are required).
- Commercial plates on a passenger car or noncommercial plates on a truck.
- Misaligned numerals or letters on the license plate.
- Broken or missing glass in windows.
- Damage to doors or trunks near locks.
- Punched-out locks.
- Vehicles operated without lights at night.
- Vehicles standing at the side of the road with missing parts.

Vehicles with nonmatching front and rear license plates or plates that have obviously been altered are common indicators of a stolen vehicle.

- Vehicles standing at the side of a road with doors left open.
- Vehicles with what appear to be bullet holes in the glass or body.
- Vehicles parked with the engines left running.
- Vehicles abandoned on streets or in parking lots for several days.

In addition to the preceding visible indicators of a possible stolen car, there are some observable driver behaviors or characteristics that should make an officer suspicious.[4]

- Appearing nervous or perspiring on a cool day or evening.
- Making repeated attempts to move away from the police cruiser.
- Driving in an erratic way (making many lane changes, speeding and slowing up, and so forth).
- Leaving service stations without paying.
- Driving in a reckless or overtly careless way.
- Refusing to stop for minor traffic infractions.
- Being young (perhaps appearing under the legal driving age for the jurisdiction).

If you stop a car that you suspect has been stolen, be cautiously observant in questioning the driver and any occupants of the car. Consider whether the driver is being too polite or cooperative, and observe any other occupants for nervous or evasive behavior. See if the driver seems to know where various documents are or needs to search for them—if they can be produced at all. If the driver's license and car registration are produced, examine them carefully. Have there been any alterations? Can the driver answer questions about his or her age, address, or weight correctly? Are answers given without hesitation? Are there any discrepancies, such as a difference between the address on the driver's license and that on the registration? Was the driver's license issued by the same state as the car's license plate? Finally, have the driver sign his or her name, and compare the sample signature with the signature on the license. If you see any tools in the car that might be used to break into or start a car, ask to see the driver's car keys.

Thieves gain entry to and start vehicles by using a number of different methods. Becoming familiar with these techniques will help you recognize potential or actual thieves when you observe certain behaviors or come across car theft tools. Joyriding teens look for an easy target—an unlocked car, keys dangling from an ignition, or a spare key in a magnetic box attached to the inside of a wheel well. Youths looking for a ride may feel around the wheel wells of cars parked on the street or in a lot until they find such a spare key. If the objective is stripping or chopping the vehicle, thieves in a tow truck may simply whisk the vehicle away.

Like joyriders, strippers, choppers, and resellers appreciate an easy target, but resort to a variety of tools when forced entry is necessary. Some thieves make a crude entry by using a screwdriver, a prybar, or a wire clothes hanger. Other car thieves use a thin but sturdy length of metal known in the trade as a **slim Jim.** This device is slid between the window glass and the door frame and used to unlock the door. Even remote-operated security systems can be breached. Thieves vary the frequency on a remote locking device until they gain entry to the car. When all else fails, the thief breaks a window to gain entry. Once inside the car, the thief then starts the engine by hot-wiring or short-circuiting the ignition system. In some cases, inserting a screwdriver into the ignition breaks the lock housing and exposes the starter wires. Some car thieves use a slide hammer, commonly used to pull dents out of fenders and auto bodies. Forcing the end of the hammer into the ignition allows the lock to be quickly removed and exposes the ignition wires. In other cases, professional thieves have illegally obtained master keys for various automobiles. They simply insert the master key to unlock the car and to start the ignition. A skilled car thief can gain entry to a locked car and start the engine in less than 60 seconds.

> **Slim Jim** A tool, consisting of a sturdy length of metal, used by auto and truck thieves to unlock doors.

When a car is stopped as a possible stolen vehicle or a stolen vehicle is recovered, the police often use state motor vehicle bureaus to check the owner's registration. They also use state driver's license bureaus to try to match the vehicle registration with the driver. Sometimes further checks are required. One valuable source of vehicle theft information is the FBI's National Crime Information Center (NCIC). Vehicle theft investigators can query the NCIC files to learn about stolen vehicles, vehicles wanted in connection with felonies, stolen parts, and accessories, stolen license plates, and drivers' criminal records.

Another resource for vehicle theft investigators is the National Insurance Crime Bureau (NICB). The NICB is a nonprofit organization, not a government agency. It gathers and distributes information about motor vehicle theft. It also helps educate law enforcement officers in investigative techniques of vehicle identification, fraud, and theft. The NICB maintains databases of computerized records that investigators can query to obtain information and leads. Among these databases are a theft file, a salvage file, an export file, and an impound file. Each year, the NICB publishes and distributes to police agencies a manual for identifying automobiles. This manual contains a summary of motor vehicle laws of the states, federal motor vehicle marking standards, information on vehicle identification numbers, and information on domestic and imported vehicles. Every five years, the NICB publishes a similar manual for commercial vehicles and off-road equipment.

Examining Stolen Vehicles for Evidence

The immediate area where a car is recovered becomes the crime scene. On stripped-car recoveries, note the location of the vehicle (on the street, in an alley, in a vacant lot, and so forth) and the direction in which the vehicle was pointing when discovered. Search the area immediately surrounding the vehicle for possible physical evidence or other identifying information that may lead to the thief. In addition, check for any oil or transmission fluid trails indicating the path of travel. Carefully process any property left in the abandoned vehicle. Although the items may belong to the car's owner, they may also belong to the thief. Avoid contaminating any source of possible latent fingerprints (steering wheel, door handles, mirrors, seat adjustment knobs, radio buttons, dashboard, steering column, and so on).

Searching a Stolen Vehicle

After processing the vehicle for latent fingerprints, thoroughly search the vehicle for any trace evidence that might suggest the identity or whereabouts of a suspect. In some cases, as when cars are recovered after being used in a kidnapping or homicide, only crime lab technicians should search the vehicle. When searching a vehicle, never discount anything. Small scraps of paper, burned matches, cigarette butts in ashtrays, supermarket receipts, and so forth may provide useful information for locating a suspect or prosecuting a defendant once apprehended. As with any crime scene, keep accurate notes concerning any physical evidence that is found. Searches of stolen vehicles have produced evidence of narcotics on floor mats, bloodstains on upholstery, and fiber from kidnapping victims' clothing in trunks. Additionally, evidence recovered in the search may lead to the solution of other crimes.

If you know that a vehicle has been involved in other crimes involving narcotics, jewelry, money, or other small articles of value, be sure to search areas of the vehicle that could easily conceal such items. Search inside the air cleaner or oil filter; under or behind the dashboard panel; behind the engine compartment cowling; and inside doors, tires, body panels, and exhaust systems. In short, examine any area of the vehicle that may conceal or might have been used to conceal stolen items.

Disposing of Recovered Vehicles

If a stolen vehicle is to be processed for fingerprints, searched for possible evidence, or examined by a forensic technician, it is **impounded.** Taking the vehicle into legal custody ensures that no unauthorized persons enter or touch the vehicle or any of its contents. If you are the investigating officer when a vehicle is impounded, take an inventory of the car's contents. Make sure the tow truck driver signs the inventory at the scene. Also check to be sure the vehicle is secured at the impound lot

Impound   To take into legal custody.

or garage. An impounded vehicle cannot be released without an official impound release form indicating that it is no longer required as evidence. If, when stopped or recovered, the vehicle is not required as evidence in some other crime, it is stored. A stored vehicle can be released by the storage garage or lot attendant to the owner or the owner's agent.

Whenever a stolen vehicle is recovered, the investigating officer should notify the registered owner. Notification should include telling the owner where the vehicle was recovered and what its current condition and disposition are. If the vehicle is drivable and only being stored, the owner should be informed where it is and how to secure its release. If the vehicle is material evidence in another crime and has been impounded, the owner should be informed of this. The owner also should get some idea of when he or she will be able to retrieve the car.

The officer's final report on the vehicle theft should include information pertinent to the vehicle's use in any other criminal activity or case. Notification of the vehicle's recovery should be made, and noted in the report, to all other interested or involved agencies.

Investigating Other Motor Vehicle Thefts

As previously stated, trucks, buses, motorcycles, construction and farm machinery, aircraft, and recreational vehicles, such as boats and snowmobiles, all fall within the category of motor vehicles. Investigating thefts of such vehicles is similar to investigating auto thefts. Manufacturers and sellers can provide useful information regarding the location of identifying numbers and possible outlets for stolen parts. We will now take a closer look at investigating the theft of one of these types of motor vehicles—motorcycles.

During the past 10 or 15 years, the theft of motorcycles has been increasing along with their popularity. Motorcycles can be stolen easily and dismantled with considerable speed and ease. Because of the motorcycle's relatively small size and weight, it can be quickly lifted onto the back of a truck or into a van and transported away. As with automobiles, the ignition system of a motorcycle is no match for a skilled cycle thief. Also, VINs on motorcycles are not as difficult to remove or alter as on automobiles. Motorcycle VINs are inscribed on fewer parts and can actually be stamped over or altered with relative success.

Motorcycles are typically stolen for stripping or resale. Investigating a motorcycle theft is generally similar to investigating an automobile theft. One of the most effective tools an officer can use to combat motorcycle theft is knowledge. Become familiar with local traffic and safety laws relating to motorcycle operation and equipment requirements. Good local and state traffic regulation and law enforcement help. Current computerized databases allow officers to determine the status of a

Wireless Mobile Data System   For officers on patrol, using a wireless mobile data terminal to simultaneously communicate with the dispatcher and with each other is a plus. Officers on routine patrol can use the system to check on stolen vehicles, verify license information, and generate a warrant check on a driver. The system also advises the dispatcher of a stop and its location.

motorcycle, the rider's right to possession of the vehicle, proper registration, licensing, and identification of the rider and owner.

There are several problems in recovering and identifying stolen motorcycles. First, more than 70 different brands of motorcycles are sold in the United States. As with pre-1968 automobiles, many of these manufacturers have used different numbering systems and locations for identifying the vehicle. Second, motorcycles frequently are registered by the engine number rather than the frame number. Thus, the identification number does not include a model number. In other words, several motorcycles may actually be registered with the same identification number. Additionally, many people fail to register off-road bikes or dirt bikes. When these vehicles are stolen, it is almost impossible to identify them, even when they are recovered. A third problem is that several motorcycles have parts that can be used interchangeably year after year. Thus, parts can be changed and exchanged, making it difficult to locate a cycle's parts once the cycle has been dismantled and distributed.

Today, motorcycle VINs are usually die-stamped into the frame of the motorcycle, although the location may vary between manufacturers.

The VIN can also be found, on most models, on the left and right sides of the headstock, or engine cradle. Finally, most manufacturers also die-stamp a serial number on the engine case itself.

Preventing Motor Vehicle Theft

Generally, the theft of a vehicle requires two things—a desire on the part of a thief, and an opportunity, sometimes inadvertently provided by the owner. Limit the opportunities, and one can expect a corresponding reduction in thefts. In other words, an unlocked car with the key in the ignition is a more likely target for a thief than one with the doors locked and no keys present. A car left with the engine running so that the driver can run into a convenience store, *just for a minute,* becomes a probable candidate for being stolen.

To decrease the opportunity for theft, a number of car manufacturers have installed devices reminding drivers to secure their vehicles. Some of these buzz when keys are left in the ignition or doors are left unlocked as the driver exits the vehicle. Others actually sound a mechanical voice, telling the driver, "Your keys are in the ignition." Some vehicles have automatic systems that can be programmed to lock the doors whenever they are closed.

Automobile security systems are among the many devices motor vehicle owners have installed to prevent motor vehicle theft.

In addition, a number of manufacturers now sell vehicles with various antitheft devices, such as alarms and engine and fuel cutoff devices. Aftermarket devices (those not originally installed by the manufacturer) are also available for older or lower-priced vehicles. These include the boot, a device installed under a front tire to prevent the vehicle from being moved; and the collar, a device to deter penetration of the steering column. Recently, some businesses have been selling official-looking decals for vehicles. These decals suggest that the car is equipped with some sort of alarm or antitheft device. In reality, the car is equipped with a decal. Similarly, one can purchase a small black box (about the size of a package of cigarettes) with battery-operated red and green lights. The device is secured to the dashboard and resembles several aftermarket alarm systems. When switched on, the red light slowly blinks, suggesting that an actual alarm is armed.

Each year numerous law enforcement agencies try to reduce the number of vehicle thefts in their jurisdictions. Some have succeeded simply by educating vehicle owners who reside in the area. They educate people about the importance of locking their cars. Likewise, they stress keeping windows rolled up in a parked vehicle and not leaving keys in the ignition, on the visor, or in hiding places on the outside of the vehicle. Others have increased patrols in high-vehicle-theft areas to reduce crime. In some jurisdictions, officers use tips and informants to discover body shops where vehicles are being stripped and chopped. Some officers routinely visit and inspect local salvage yards for stolen vehicle parts.[5]

Some jurisdictions have set up decal alert programs. To take part in such a prevention program, owners register their vehicles with their local law enforcement agency. An owner agrees to let officers stop the car and question the driver without probable cause if the car is seen on the street during certain hours (such as 1:00 A.M. to 5:00 A.M.). A decal issued by the law enforcement agency identifies the vehicle as registered in the program. Some cities have achieved great success with such programs, having only 0.1 percent of registered autos seized by car thieves.

Many jurisdictions and agencies rely on technology to make recovery of stolen vehicles easier. Their hope is to reduce thefts by deterring thieves who will most certainly be captured if they steal a car. A number of jurisdictions rely on computer networks of the FBI, state, and local police to identify and find stolen vehicles. Some have begun using a revolutionary system for tracking down stolen vehicles and thieves. A small transceiver that acts as a homing device is installed on a vehicle. Each transceiver has its own unique, registered code. If the vehicle is stolen, the owner alerts police, and the homing device is activated. A tracking device in a police car picks up the signal, allowing officers to monitor, track, and recover the stolen vehicle.

SUMMARY BY LEARNING OBJECTIVES

Learning Objective 1

Motor vehicle theft is one of eight crimes that the FBI considers the most serious in American society, and the FBI reports yearly statistics on motor vehicle theft in its Uniform Crime Reports (UCR). In 1995, motor vehicle theft made up 10.6 percent of crime index offenses. Of the motor vehicles reported stolen in 1995, 78 percent were automobiles.

Learning Objective 2

Motor vehicle theft is generally classified by the thief's motive for taking a vehicle. These motives include joyriding, transportation, to commit another crime, fraud, and stripping, chopping, or resale.

Learning Objective 3

State statutes vary in their treatment of motor vehicle theft. In some states, thieves may be charged with "grand theft auto," and in others the charge may be "unauthorized use of a motor vehicle." States have enacted a variety of laws that require stiffer penalties for motor-vehicle-related crimes.

Learning Objective 4

The motor vehicle theft investigator's first job is to determine if a theft has taken place and then to gather and report complete and accurate information regarding the theft. Investigators rely on numbers (especially the vehicle identification number [VIN]) inscribed on the vehicle to identify stolen vehicles. Using their powers of observation and experience, officers can recognize possible stolen vehicles by certain telltale signs on the vehicle as well as by the behavior of the driver and passengers. When a stolen vehicle is recovered, a thorough search must be made both inside and outside the vehicle to gather and preserve evidence, and the owner must be informed of the vehicle's disposition.

Learning Objective 5

In addition to automobiles, motor vehicle thefts can include trucks, buses, motorcycles, construction and farm machinery, aircraft, and recreational vehicles, such as boats and snowmobiles. Investigating these thefts is similar to investigating auto thefts. Manufacturers and sellers can provide useful information regarding type and location of identification numbers, which can vary widely for these types of motor vehicles.

Learning Objective 6

Law enforcement agencies, manufacturers, and various organizations and associations have devised a variety of activities and products to prevent motor vehicle theft. These include educating the public, increasing patrols and inspections, installing mechanical and electronic antitheft devices, and setting up police-citizen prevention programs.

QUESTIONS FOR REVIEW

Learning Objective 1

1. What category of motor vehicle makes up the largest part of all motor vehicle thefts?

Learning Objective 2

2. Into what five major categories can automobile thefts be divided?

3. How might juveniles and professional car thieves differ in their operations?

4. What is meant by *joyriding?*

5. Why might a criminal steal a car before committing a kidnapping?

6. Why might a person burn or hire someone to burn his or her own vehicle?

7. What is meant by a *chop shop?* A *salvage switch?*

8. Why are many stolen U.S. cars resold overseas?

Learning Objective 3

9. Why do charges for stealing motor vehicles vary among the states?

Learning Objective 4

10. List five things that are important to include in a motor vehicle theft report.

11. What are five things to be suspicious of when looking for stolen vehicles?

12. What is a VIN, what is its purpose, and where is it located on most automobiles?

13. How might the information in an automobile theft report be useful for recovering the stolen vehicle?

14. Why should the area immediately surrounding a recovered stolen vehicle be considered a crime scene?

15. Where might an investigator look for latent fingerprints in a recovered stolen car?

Learning Objective 5

16. Why are motorcycles somewhat easy to steal and dispose of?

17. What are some of the factors contributing to the problems in recovering motorcycles?

Learning Objective 6

18. What are some of the measures being taken to deter or apprehend car thieves?

CRITICAL THINKING INVESTIGATIVE EXERCISES

1. Bob Jones parked his 1996 Toyota Camry in front of his home on Long Island, New York, at around 6:00 P.M. At about 12:00 A.M, Mr. Jones happened to look out his window and immediately noticed that his car was gone. He telephoned the police, who arrived about ten minutes later.

   Assume that you are the responding police officer.

   a. What questions should you ask?

   b. What information should you record in your field notes?

   c. What actions should you take after the initial interview?

2. Contact the local police in your area. Gather data that will enable you to profile motor vehicle theft trends in your area during the past 10 years. Use the various types of motor vehicles described in the chapter. Also attempt to classify the thefts according to the five categories outlined in the chapter. Create visuals to illustrate the data, and then write a brief summary of the findings.

INVESTIGATIVE SKILL BUILDERS

Teaching Others

You are an experienced patrol officer. You have been asked to take a rookie on patrol with you and to teach the rookie how to spot suspicious and possibly stolen vehicles.

1. What are the most important things to tell the rookie to look for?
2. What will you tell the rookie to look for regarding drivers?

Integrity/Honesty

Your personal car needs tires, so you go to a local tire store. You have been dealing with this tire store for years and know the owner pretty well. He knows you are a police officer. He tells you that the tires for your car cost $70 each and that you need four. He also tells you that because you are such a steady customer, he has a special deal for you. He explains that he bought an odd lot of these tires from some guy in a truck and that he can sell them to you for $35 a tire. He assures you that these are the same kind of tires as the $70 ones.

1. Do you have any questions for the store owner?
2. Should you look a gift horse in the mouth or simply buy the tires?

ENDNOTES

1. Barry Glassner, Bruce L. Berg, Margret Ksander, and Bruce Johnson, "The Deterrence Effect of Juvenile Versus Adult Jurisdiction," *Social Problems,* Vol. 31, No. 2, 1983, pp. 219–221. See also Cheryl Carpenter, Barry Glassner, Bruce Johnson, and Julia Loughlin, *Kids, Drugs, and Crime,* D. C. Heath, Lexington, Mass., 1988, pp. 187–208.
2. Mary E. Beckman and Michael R. Daly, "Motor Vehicle Theft Investigations: Emerging International Trends," *FBI Law Enforcement Bulletin,* Vol. 59, No. 9, September 1990, p. 16.
3. Nancy E. Hawkins, "Recognizing Stolen Vehicles," *The National Centurion,* Vol. 2, No. 6, July 1984, p. 32.
4. Ibid.
5. G. M. Stern, "Effective Strategies to Minimize Auto Thefts and Break-Ins," *Law and Order,* July 1990, pp. 65–66.
6. Reed Hildreth, "The CAT Program," *Law and Order,* May 1990, pp. 92–93.

CHAPTER 18

Arson and Bombing Investigations

CHAPTER OBJECTIVES

After completing this chapter, you will be able to:

1. Provide an overview of the crime of arson in the United States.

2. Explain the legal elements of the crime of arson.

3. List some common motives for arson.

4. Describe types of evidence that help arson investigators determine that a specific fire occurred and was deliberately set.

5. Provide an overview of bombing incidents in the United States.

6. List the most common kinds of bombs police agencies deal with.

7. Describe some investigative techniques used in bombing incidents.

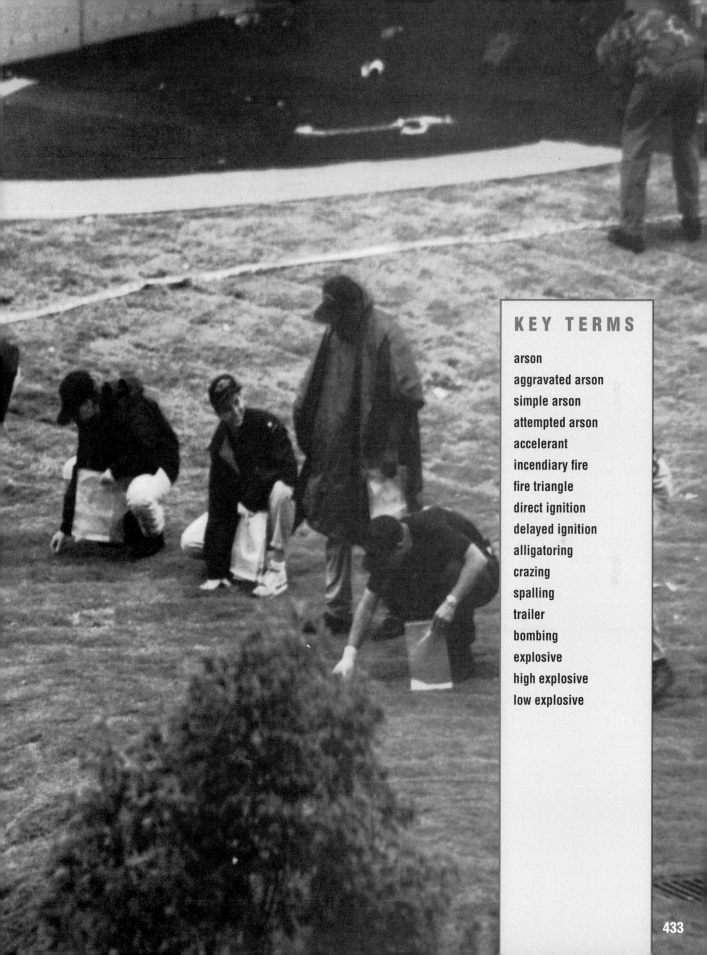

KEY TERMS

arson
aggravated arson
simple arson
attempted arson
accelerant
incendiary fire
fire triangle
direct ignition
delayed ignition
alligatoring
crazing
spalling
trailer
bombing
explosive
high explosive
low explosive

The Crime of Arson

Arson is the last of the index offenses that we will consider. It is one of the most frightening crimes, since it involves the destruction both of property and, potentially, of human lives. Estimates of total property loss each year for all arsons range from $1.5 billion to $5 billion. Even more disturbing are the approximately 800 to 1000 deaths related to arson each year.

Since 1979, the FBI has included arson as a Part I crime index offense in its Uniform Crime Reports (UCR). Only fires determined through investigation to have been willfully or maliciously set are classified by the FBI as arsons. Fires of suspicious or unknown origin are excluded. In 1995, a total of 94,926 arson offenses were reported. This was a decrease of 4 percent from the prior year. In 80,182 of the arsons reported, responding agencies provided detailed information on the type of structure. Figure 18–1 shows this breakdown.

Detection and investigation of arson cases are extremely difficult. One problem is confusion over jurisdiction. Since arson involves fire, one might think it the province of the *fire department* and not the *police department*. In reality, either the police department or the fire department could reasonably claim jurisdiction. Unfortunately, in most areas, neither has sufficient resources alone to investigate this crime as thor-

Figure 18–1 Arson by type of property.

Property Classification	Number of Offenses	Percent Distribution[1]
Total	80,182	100.0
Total structure	42,226	52.7
Single occupancy residential	17,955	22.4
Other residential	7,461	9.3
Storage	3,788	4.7
Industrial/manufacturing	605	0.8
Other commercial	4,322	5.4
Community/public	4,696	5.9
Other structure	3,399	4.2
Total mobile	20,459	25.5
Motor vehicles	19,223	24.0
Other mobile	1,236	1.5
Other	17,497	21.8

[1]Because of rounding, percentages may not add to total.
Source: Federal Bureau of Investigation, *Crime in the United States,* Government Printing Office, Washington, 1995.

oughly as other types of crimes are investigated. Arson investigators from police and fire departments need to cooperate to pool resources and offer the attention required to apprehend arsonists.

Legal Elements of the Crime of Arson

Arson is a combination crime against persons and property. Under common law, arson was defined as the malicious, willful burning of another's house or building. Although some states retain this definition, others have expanded it. Despite variations from state to state, **arson** is generally defined as the malicious and intentional or fraudulent burning of buildings or property. In most jurisdictions, arson broadly covers the burning of all kinds of buildings and structures, as well as crops, forests, farm equipment, and personal property such as boats, cars, or other vehicles. Arson also includes the willful burning of one's own property with the intention of defrauding an insurance company. As with other crimes that derive from common law, *mens rea,* or intent, is an important element of the crime of arson. Proof of intent must show that the act was done voluntarily, knowingly, and purposely.

Some jurisdictions categorize an arson as aggravated or simple. In addition to elements of intentional burning of buildings or property, **aggravated arson** usually includes knowingly creating an imminent danger to human life or a risk of great bodily harm to others. **Simple arson** is the intentional burning of property without creating an imminent risk or threat to human life. In most jurisdictions, aggravated arson is a felony. When a death occurs as a result of arson, the charge may include felonious murder (first-degree murder) as well. In some states, the crime of arson is divided into the first, second, third, and fourth degrees. Many jurisdictions have enacted statutes with more severe punishments for burning schools and other public buildings than for general arson.

In addition to aggravated and simple arson, most jurisdictions include a lesser crime known as attempted arson. The elements of **attempted arson** include demonstrating intent to set a fire and some overt act toward actually setting the fire. For example, pouring gasoline on piles of boxes in a building's basement, but being interrupted before lighting a match, could be interpreted as attempted arson. On the other hand, having several cans of gasoline stored in a well-ventilated garage could not be interpreted as attempted arson.

Motives for Arson

Motive is *not* an element of the crime of arson—nor of any other crime, for that matter. A conviction can be obtained even when the prosecutor is unable to show any motive for the acts of the accused. However, when motive can be shown, it helps a prosecutor's case.

Arson Malicious and intentional or fraudulent burning of buildings or property.

Aggravated arson The malicious, intentional burning of buildings or property and knowingly creating an imminent danger to human life or a risk of great bodily harm to others.

Simple arson The malicious, intentional burning of buildings or property that does not create an imminent risk or threat to human life.

Attempted arson The demonstrated intent to set a fire coupled with some overt act toward actually setting the fire.

Motives can provide compelling explanations for the court or the jury, helping them understand why the accused committed the crime. One researcher suggests that arsonists use fire as a tool to accomplish a specific goal. He divides their motives into two broad categories: *rational* and *irrational*.[1] Rational motives include goals such as revenge or profit. Irrational motives typically are not goals and are related to uncontrollable urges or various mental disorders. As you read through the following list of common motives uncovered in arson investigations, see if you can classify them as rational or irrational.

- Revenge, spite, or jealousy
- Profit: insurance frauding
- Sabotage of a competitor's business
- Terrorism, intimidation, or extortion
- Destruction of evidence of a crime
- Concealment of evidence
- Vanity: to fulfill a hero fantasy
- Securing employment as a guard
- Ensuring selection as a volunteer firefighter
- Landlord-tenant disputes: breaking a lease
- Destruction of records
- Vandalism
- Pyromania
- Fascination with fire
- Other mental disorders
- Suicide

Investigating Arson

Once a fire is out, the investigator must determine where and how the fire started. In other words, was the fire from accidental or natural origins, or was it intentionally set?[2] Initially, the investigator tries to rule out accidental or natural causes unless evidence of one is discovered. In some fires, no evidence can be found that clearly indicates the fire was accidental (e.g., an electrical short, a cigarette dropped on a bed, or faulty heating devices) or natural (such as evidence of a lightning strike or spontaneous combustion). In these cases, the fire may be ruled suspicious or of unknown origin. When any fire-setting device, igniter, or **accelerant** (fire booster) is found near the site, the fire may be classified as an **incendiary fire.** Such evidence is an indication of arson.

Investigating arson differs from investigating crimes previously discussed in this textbook. First among the differences is the unavoidable problem of being unable to secure the crime scene immediately. The determination that the crime of arson has occurred happens either during the fire or after it has been extinguished. During the course of fighting the fire, fire, police, or medical personnel may walk through the crime scene,

Accelerant A booster such as gasoline, kerosene, or paint thinner added to a fire to speed its progress.

Incendiary fire A fire in which a fire-setting device, an igniter, or an accelerant is found.

obliterating evidence of the crime. Subsequently, official personnel examining the origins and causes of the fire may disturb or destroy evidence. Evidence also may be destroyed by the flames themselves.

Typically, investigators begin their investigation of suspected arson by examining the outside of a structure. They look for external causes of a burn or any means of entering the building to set the fire. As with any crime scene, photographs and notes are taken as the investigator examines the exterior of the structure.

Since arson does not have an immediate *corpus delicti,* it is the responsibility of the investigator to show that a specific fire occurred and was deliberately set. Toward this end, the investigator must seek both direct and circumstantial evidence. The first step after securing the scene, then is to determine the origin of the burn. Understanding the nature of fire can assist an investigator in determining its point of origin.

The **fire triangle** is composed of the three basic elements—air or oxygen, fuel, and heat—needed for a fire. One or more of these elements are usually present in abnormal amounts in the area of an arson. Extra *air* or *oxygen* may result from opened vents, windows, and doors or from openings cut in walls or ceilings. Oxygen may also be found in various compounds, such as nitrates, at the arson site. *Fuel* in disproportionate amounts may be observed as stacks of rags, paper, boxes, or other flammable materials piled up at the scene or brought to it. Sparks, flames, chemical reaction, and compression may each cause enough *heat* to ignite a fire. Disproportionate *heat* may result from accelerants, such as lighter fluid, paint thinner, or gasoline, added to the fire after it was ignited.

Direct ignition is simply setting a fire by applying matches or another flame. Gasoline, kerosene, paint thinner, lighter fluid, or other combustible chemicals and materials may be thrown or spread over the part of the structure to be burned. These will cause a more rapid spread of flames and a more complete combustion of the affected area. The fire, however, is immediate and is ignited directly by the arsonist.

Delayed ignition, in contrast to direct, involves the use of some sort of mechanical, chemical, or other timing device. This may be as simple as a cigarette placed in a matchbook or as complex as a radio-activated electronic ignition set off by a telephone call. Delayed ignition is intended to give an arsonist time to escape or to establish an alibi during the time of the fire.

Some delayed-ignition devices, or portions of them, are not entirely destroyed by a fire. The arson investigator should be careful to scrutinize all suspect areas for incendiary materials, equipment, or devices or other means of fire starting.

The crime of arson is generally committed under cover of darkness, at times and in a manner calculated to divert suspicion. Only the arsonist or those acting with him or her are usually present at the scene. The perpetrator hopes that the fire will destroy any incriminating evidence he

Fire triangle The three basic elements—oxygen, fuel, and heat—needed for a fire.

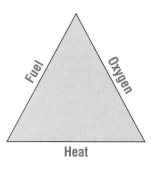

Direct ignition Setting a fire by directly applying a flame.

Delayed ignition Setting a fire indirectly by means of a mechanical, chemical, or other timing device.

or she may leave behind. Arsons are difficult to solve, in part because a timing device can detonate and ignite a fire hours or days later, when the arsonist is miles from the site. This means that the arsonist can set the stage and trigger for a fire and then have an "airtight alibi" for the time of the fire. Naturally, the alibi may be weakened if the prosecution can show that the fire was started with a time-delay device of some sort.

Burn Patterns

The point of origin (place of ignition) and cause of a fire must be determined as soon as possible in an arson investigation. Burn patterns show the effects of burning or partial burning during the fire. These patterns are important elements in determining the point of origin, the spread of the fire, the temperature, the duration, and the presence of accelerants. Frequently, these patterns provide clues to where the fire was ignited. The type of fire, access to oxygen, accelerants, and duration of the burn all affect burn patterns.

V Pattern   Many of us are already familiar with different burn patterns from various activities in life but are simply unaware that we have observed them. For example, if you have ever had a roaring fire in your fireplace, you are familiar with the V-shaped burn pattern left on the back wall of the fireplace. When a fire is unobstructed and has an upward draft, flames tend to fan up and outward, creating a V- or cone-shaped burn pattern similar to the sooty residue left on fireplace back walls. Strong side drafts may distort the cone shape, but when the V pattern can be established, the point of the V usually leads to the source of the fuel in the fire.

Alligatoring   Anyone who has sat by a campfire may recall seeing a blistering that resembled scales on the burning logs. This scalelike pattern, or **alligatoring,** is common on charred wood. Larger, rolling scales or blisters indicate rapid, intense heat; small, flat alligatoring results from low-intensity heat over a long period of time.[3]

Pour or Spill   This pattern appears as a boundary between burned and unburned material. It is caused by pouring some type of liquid accelerant on a floor or surface and then igniting it. For example, imagine you spilled a can of gasoline on the floor of your living room. The gasoline would run out, forming a spill across the floor. If you ignited the gaso-

Alligatoring   A scalelike burn pattern on wood. Large scales indicate rapid, intense heat; small, flat scales indicate low-intensity heat over a long period of time.

line, the burning pattern would immediately follow the spill pattern. Discovering a pour burn pattern is fairly good evidence that an arson has taken place.

Depth of Charring Charring, the dark blackening of burned wood, can indicate the intensity of the heat, the duration of a burn, and the point of origin. One can reasonably expect that the longer a fire burns a piece of wood, the deeper the charring will be. Thus, tracing lightly charred materials to materials with the deepest charring leads to the fire's point of origin. When investigators discover charring of significant depth, it is reasonable to search that area for further evidence of ignition. Finally, the relative depth of charring can provide clues as to how the fire was ventilated, spread, or accelerated. Remember, though, that charring can vary, depending on the type of wood, its moisture content, the use of an accelerant, and the effectiveness of firefighters' efforts in that area of the structure.

Arson investigators sift through the rubble of a fire to determine if it may be classified as an incendiary fire.

Crazing Irregular cracks and lines in glass and ceramic materials produced by rapid, intense heat are known as **crazing.** Crazing into small sections suggests that the item was near the point of origin and the intense heat may have been caused by an accelerant. Larger segments indicate that the item was some distance away from the point of origin.

Crazing Irregular cracks and lines in glass and ceramic materials, caused by rapid, intense heat.

Spalling The chipping, crumbling, or breaking off of cement or masonry by rapid, intense heat is called **spalling.** The fragments may look slightly discolored or chalky.[4] This discoloration, coupled with the presence of certain odors, may indicate the use of an accelerant and probable arson.

Spalling The chipping, crumbling, or flaking of cement or masonry caused by rapid, intense heat.

Smoke If witnesses saw a fire begin, the color of smoke could indicate the material used to start the blaze. Black smoke, for example, indicates that the material may have contained petroleum. On the other hand, white smoke generally indicates that some vegetation, such as straw or dried leaves, was burned. Once the entire structure has begun to burn, it may be difficult to discern from the smoke what materials are burning.

Arson Indicators

Evidence of an accelerant found at the point of origin of a fire is a primary form of physical evidence of an arson fire. As we have seen, burn

The U.S. Postal Service has an investigative agency related to postal operations and illegal activities involving the mails. Postal inspectors carry out the duties of the Postal Inspection Service. As federal law enforcement agents, postal inspectors enforce more than 200 federal statutes dealing with the U.S. Postal Service and the U.S. Mail. Their responsibilities include criminal investigations, audit investigations, and security/administrative duties.

Postal inspectors investigate such crimes as mailbox thefts, robberies of postal authorities, embezzlement, frauds using the mails, and post office burglaries. They also investigate illegal attempts to sell items by mail, obtain funds through fraudulent schemes, and any other violations of postal laws. If anyone uses the mail system illegally to transport firearms, narcotics, obscene materials, or explosive devices, they are likewise the subject of investigation by postal inspectors. Postal inspectors often collaborate with other government agencies and serve on task forces. A postal inspector was part of the Unabomber task force.

Candidates for postal inspector are selected and screened from within the U.S. Postal Service. Applicants must be U.S. citizens, between the ages of 21 and 36. They must have a bachelor's degree and 1 year's work experience. It is desirable that applicants have professional certification in a field such as that of a certified public accountant. Candidates must pass a background suitability investigation and meet certain health requirements, undergo a drug screening test, and have a valid driver's license.

A postal inspector's work requires traveling and frequent absences from home. Inspectors must be willing to accept assignments wherever their services are needed. Because inspectors may be required to respond to all types of emergencies, they are subject to calls at all times. Postal inspectors have the power to make arrests for postal-related offenses, and they carry firearms.

patterns found at the scene may lead an investigator to suspect arson. Additionally, other evidence may lead an arson investigator to recognize a fire as arson.

Multiple Points of Origin   Many arsonists set several fires in a building in widely separated areas to ensure better combustion and more complete destruction.

Odors   Gasoline (the most common accelerant), kerosene, paint thinner, and other flammable liquids have distinctive odors. If used as accelerants, they sometimes leave recognizable odors even after the flames have been extinguished.

Speed and Spread of Fire   The speed at which a fire spreads after its initial discovery may suggest arson. Fires that seem to spread extremely rapidly and engulf major portions of a building or structure very quickly may be considered suspicious.

Holes in Walls or Floors   Arsonists sometimes chop holes in walls or floors to expose raw wood or improve the draft for the fire. They cut holes through ceilings and floors to make the fire travel faster between upper and lower floors.

Alarm Tampering   Destroyed or disabled alarms or sprinkler systems indicate the possibility of arson. In addition, timing devices may be set or **trailers** (paper, rags, or rope soaked in accelerants) may be ignited to bypass or disable alarm or security systems.

Intensity of Heat   The fact that the heat generated by the fire was particularly intense may be a clue that flammable liquids or compounds were added to the burning materials. Likewise, difficulty in putting out the fire may indicate the presence of an accelerant.

> **Trailer**   A material (rope or rags soaked in accelerant, shredded paper, gunpowder, fluid accelerant, and so on) used to spread a fire.

Cooperation Among Arson Investigators

Different agencies, often with joint jurisdiction, investigate suspicious fires. In some larger cities, a suspicious fire may be investigated by special units from the fire and police departments. In some other cities and in unincorporated townships, a suspicious fire may be investigated by the state fire marshal, the state police, the sheriff's department, local fire investigators, or perhaps local town or borough police officers. In addition, insurance investigators may investigate a suspicious fire involving large claims or recently written policies.

As a general rule of thumb, it is the fire department's role to determine the nature and origin of the burning. Lack of trained personnel is a major problem in arson investigation. American firefighters have traditionally been volunteers. In fact, nearly 80 percent of all firefighters in the United States are volunteers.[5] All fire companies require some level of

A trailer (left side of photograph) was used to spread the fire to this barn.

training before allowing anyone to help fight a fire. However, a firefighter's training is typically in survival (for the safety of victims and fellow firefighters) and in managing and extinguishing fires. Little specific training is given in how to investigate causes of fires. Many jurisdictions, therefore, depend heavily on state fire marshals, working in concert with local police agencies, to investigate suspicious fires. The fire marshal's role, however, is generally limited to determining the cause and the point of origin of a suspicious fire. The local police agency follows through on further criminal investigation of the arson. Figure 18–2 shows the basic steps that an arson investigation should follow.

In some jurisdictions, the fire department uses its expertise to investigate suspicious fires. Experienced firefighters have basic knowledge about how fires start, spread, and accelerate. To give this responsibility to the police would be a duplication of effort. Furthermore, fire personnel including the fire marshal—have certain legal authority that police do not. For example, to determine the cause of a fire, fire personnel may enter the fire scene without a search warrant. Furthermore, firefighters may help police agencies by identifying people who regularly seem to be on the scene of suspicious fires.

In addition to the steps outlined in Figure 18–2, the following suspicious persons and circumstances should be taken into account in an arson investigation:

Figure 18–2 Steps in an arson investigation.

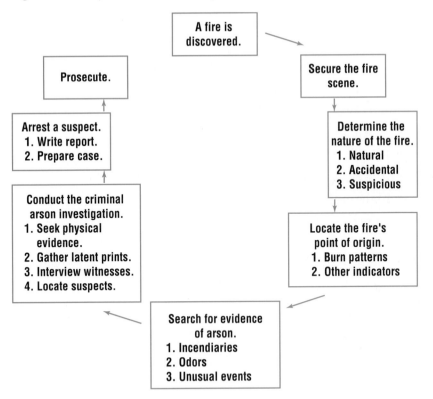

- Presence of familiar faces watching the fire (faces observed at other fires).
- Persons showing undue or excessive interest in the fire.
- Overly helpful or solicitous people.
- Person who discovers the fire and seeks recognition as a hero.
- People with evidence of accelerants on their hands, clothing, shoes, and so on.
- Type and amount of merchandise destroyed in a retail store fire.
- Unusual circumstances, such as removal of specific pieces of furniture or art or items of sentimental value (diplomas, birth or marriage certificates, pets, and so on) prior to the fire.
- Tracks, footprints, fingerprints, or other physical evidence foreign to the scene.
- Receptacles (cans, jars, and so on) containing residue of accelerants or possible latent fingerprints.
- Timing devices or fragments of timing devices.

As in any criminal investigation, witnesses can provide a wealth of information that may lead to suspects and an arrest. The following are some types of information that investigators may obtain from witnesses in the area.

- Time of the fire and general weather conditions.
- What attracted the witnesses' attention to the fire?
- Location at which the fire was burning when first observed.
- The color of the smoke when the fire began.
- Intensity of flames and speed of spreading.
- Any unusual odors detected.
- Possible observation of multiple fires in different locations.
- Any explosions heard prior to the discovery of the fire.
- Observation of anyone fleeing the scene.
- Vehicles seen parked at or leaving the scene around the time of the fire.
- Information about the owner or tenants of the burned structure.

Criminal Bombing

Bombing An incident in which a device constructed with criminal intent and using high explosives, low explosives, or blasting agents explodes.

Bombing incidents, like arson incidents, destroy property and take innocent lives. Bombers include anarchists, racists, militants, religious zealots, hate mongers, criminals, and the mentally impaired. Especially fearsome is the random horror generated by improvised explosive devices detonated from remote sites. The FBI and the Bureau of Alcohol, Tobacco, and Firearms (ATF) gather and coordinate information on bombings reported by state and local public safety agencies. According to the ATF, a **bombing** is any incident in which a device constructed with criminal intent and using high explosives, low explosives, or blasting agents explodes. Bombing incidents are generally divided into explosive bombings and incendiary bombings (see Figure 18–3). Criminal bombing incidents decreased in the United States in 1995, but more people were injured or killed than in the previous year. Property damage from bombing incidents also increased. These increases are the result of the injuries, deaths, and property damage from the bombing of the Murrah Federal Building in Oklahoma City on April 19, 1995.

The main function of any police agency in a bombing incident is to protect human life and property, remove the bomb menace if possible, and investigate and apprehend the bombers or threateners. Explosives is a highly specialized field and disposing of explosives is equally specialized. This portion of the chapter, then, will offer some general information on explosives and some suggested procedures for dealing with bombing incidents. Individuals who have not been specifically trained in explosive materials should never try to disarm a suspected bomb.

Figure 18–3 Bombings by type of incident and device, property damage, and outcome of incident.

	Total Actual and Attempted Bombings	Actual		Attempted		Property Damage (Dollar Value)	Persons Injured	Deaths
		Explosive	Incendiary	Explosive	Incendiary			
1980	1,249	742	336	99	72	12,562,257	160	34
1981	1,142	637	315	92	98	67,082,456[a]	133[a]	30
1982	795	485	194	77	39	7,202,848	99	16
1983	687	442	127	77	41	6,342,652	100	12
1984	803	518	127	118	40	5,618,581	112	6
1985	847	575	102	113	57	6,352,000	144	28
1986	858	580	129	101	48	3,405,000	185	14
1987	848	600	104	102	42	4,201,000	107	21
1988	977[b]	593	156	161	40	2,257,000	145	20
1989	1,208[c]	641	203	243	91	5,000,000	202	11
1990	1,582	931	267	254	130	9,600,000	222	27
1991	2,499	1,551	423	395	130	6,440,000	230	29
1992	2,989	1,911	582	384	112	12,500,000	349	26
1993	2,980	1,880	538	375	187	518,000,000[d]	1,323[e]	49
1994	3,163	1,916	545	522	180	7,500,000	308	31
1995	2,577	1,562	406	417	192	105,000,000[f]	744[g]	193[g]

[a]Includes major bombing incidents resulting in an unusually high number of personal injuries and deaths or substantial damage to property.
[b]Includes 27 incidents involving combination devices.
[c]Includes 30 incidents involving combination devices.
[d]Includes $510 million damage done to the World Trade Center by a bomb on February 26, 1993.
[e]Includes 1,042 persons injured in the World Trade Center bombing.
[f]Includes $100 million damage in the Oklahoma City bombing on April 19, 1995.
[g]Includes 518 people injured and 168 people killed in the Oklahoma City bombing.

Source: U.S. Department of Justice, Bureau of Justice Statistics, *Sourcebook of Criminal Justice Statistics,* Government Printing Office, Washington, 1995.

Explosives

It is important for an arson investigator to understand the fire triangle. It is equally important for a bombing investigator to understand what constitutes an explosive. An **explosive** is any material that produces a rapid, violent reaction when subjected to heat or a strong blow or shock. During the reaction, the explosive gives off large amounts of gases at high pressure. Explosives may be solids, liquids, or gases. All explosives, however, consist of a fuel, an oxidizer (a substance that supplies the oxygen to make the fuel burn), and a detonator (a device that ignites or sets off the reaction). Generally speaking, there are four types of explosives.

Explosive Any material that produces a rapid, violent reaction when subjected to heat or a strong blow or shock.

Primary Explosives These explosives are extremely sensitive to heat. Even a spark of static electricity can cause them to explode. They must be handled in small quantities and are used chiefly as detonators to set off other explosions.

High explosive An explosive material in which the rate of change to a gas is very rapid; explodes only upon the shock of a blasting cap, a detonating cord, or an electric detonator; includes nitroglycerin, TNT, RDX, and plastic explosives.

High Explosives Among materials classified as **high explosives,** the rate of change to a gas is very rapid. That is, the material detonates, or explodes, very rapidly. Liquids and solids change to hot gases that expand with a huge blast of heat and pressure. Included in this category are nitroglycerin, TNT, RDX, and various grades of plastic explosives. High explosives are relatively stable. They explode only upon the shock of a blasting cap to which a fuse is attached, a detonating cord, or an electric detonator. Such explosives tend to have a shattering effect. There is a great deal of fragmenting near the detonation point and less fragmenting farther away. The velocity of high explosives ranges from 3200 to 27,000 feet per second.

Low explosive An explosive material in which the rate of change to a gas is quite slow; the material deflagrates, or burns rapidly, rather than exploding and includes black powder, smokeless powder, and fertilizers.

Low Explosives Among **low explosives,** the rate of change to a gas is quite slow. They deflagrate, or burn rapidly, rather than explode. The most common types of low explosives are black powder and smokeless powder, used to propel ammunition from a gun. Similarly, dust or grain explosions, gas explosions, certain chemical and fertilizer combinations, and volatile vapor explosions are examples of low explosion. Low explosions must be ignited by heat, friction, or a spark. They do not require the shock of a blasting cap or other explosive ignition.

Many agencies use specially trained dogs to search for evidence after an explosion.

Low explosives should not be regarded as low in hazard. Nor should their destructive potential be underestimated. Some of these substances have been used in the most devastating blasts in history. The Oklahoma City bombing in April of 1995, for example, resulted from the explosion of a truck filled with fertilizer, detonated in front of the Murrah Building. The blast destroyed more than one-third of the structure and killed more than 100 people, including 13 children in a day care center. Low explosives are frequently used in blasting operations. They have a *pushing* rather than a *shattering* effect, and a twisting and tearing type of deformation. Velocities of low explosives range from 1200 to about 3200 feet per second.

Blasting Agents   These explosives are the safest and least expensive. They are widely used in industry to shatter rock in excavation and mining. Common blasting agents include dynamite and mixtures of ammonium and fuel oil.

Explosive Accessories

When searching the site of a bombing, an investigator must try to find evidence of the mechanism used to detonate the bomb. A bomber may use the simplest of methods—a flame from a fuse—or a sophisticated remote timing device. Knowing some of the kinds of accessories bombers use can help you know what kinds of things to look for when you investigate a bombing incident.

Blasting Caps   Blasting caps are used to set off, or ignite, high explosives. They contain small amounts of a sensitive, powerful primary explosive. The blasting cap, when ignited, detonates the larger concentration of explosives. Two types of blasting caps are common: electric and nonelectric.

Electric blasting caps, as their name implies, are used where there is a source of electricity. Under certain circumstances, radio waves emitted by a transmitter can detonate an electric blasting cap. Occasionally, caps are connected to lighting circuits. When the lights are turned on, the bomb explodes. Nonelectric blasting caps detonate from the spurt of flame provided by a burning fuse or another flame- or spark-producing device.

Safety Fuses   Safety fuses convey a flame through a medium at a continuous and uniform rate to a nonelectric blasting cap. As their name implies, they allow the person lighting the fuse to seek safety before the blast. In some cases, these fuses may be used for direct firing of a charge, as in the case of blasting powder. Safety fuses often consist of a fine core of special black powder enclosed in and protected by various coverings and waterproofing materials. The speed at which most domestic fuses burn is 30 or 40 seconds per foot. Pressure, degree of confinement, temperature, and moisture all influence the rate of burning of a fuse. Many safety fuses cannot be extinguished by water or by tamping with a foot. If necessary to save a life, and as a last resort, pull the fuse out, or cut the fuse ahead of the burning.

Detonating Cords   Detonating cords are round, flexible cords, similar in appearance to safety fuses. The explosive core of a detonating cord is protected by a sheath of various textiles, waterproofing materials, or plastics. Various coloring and textile patterns differentiate the particular strengths and types of detonating cords. They are used in various ways to detonate high explosives in the same manner as blasting caps.

Electric Squibs   Electric squibs also are known as electric matches. Their function is like that of an electric blasting cap. They may be used to ignite black powder or vaporous gases. The squib provides a spurt of flame or sparks similar to that provided by a burning fuse.

Types of Bombs

There are many types of explosive and incendiary devices that police must deal with. Homemade bombs are the kinds of devices police agencies are most familiar with. These range from crude boxes filled with blasting powder or sticks of dynamite to sophisticated radio-detonated devices of plastic or chemical explosives. The list of materials and chemicals—some commonly found in the home—that can be used to make homemade bombs is unlimited. Contrary to popular opinion, neither commercial explosives nor blasting caps are necessary to construct highly effective bombs. Nor, for that matter, are particularly high levels of knowledge or education required. Considerable amounts of literature, some underground and some openly available in stores, in libraries, and

HISTORY

Although the crude hand-thrown Molotov cocktail has been around for hundreds of years, it got its nickname from its use by the Russians during World War II. Its name, no doubt, came from Vyacheslav Molotov (1890–1986), a Russian revolutionary who helped plan the Bolshevik Revolution of 1917, which brought the Communists to power.

on the Internet, provide information on explosives and bomb construction. A trip to the local hardware and grocery store can provide the raw materials for a devastating bomb.

Pipe Bombs

Black powder or smokeless powder is frequently used to load pipe bombs, one of the most common types of bombs police encounter. A pipe bomb consists of a short piece of pipe, capped at both ends. A small hole is drilled either in one of the capped ends or in the side of the pipe to insert the fuse. The pipe is filled with the powder and sometimes a stick of dynamite to shatter the pipe. Spikes can be wired to the outside of the pipe to increase the shrapnel effect of the bomb. These devices are often ignited by a safety fuse, perhaps with matches and a cigarette taped to the end of the fuse. The safety fuse transmits the flame to the low explosive inside the pipe. When ignited, the low explosive inside the pipe explodes. The gases produced result in a blast and fragmentation of the pipe by the pressure.

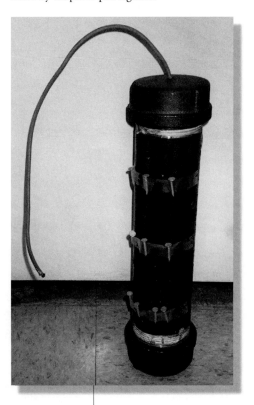

Pipe bombs are common because the materials to make them are easy to get and the bombs are relatively simple to put together.

Recently, potato guns have grown popular among some youths. A potato gun is usually made from a length of PVC tubing large enough to snugly hold an average-sized raw potato at one end. The other end of the pipe is sealed. A small opening is cut in the side of the pipe to insert a vaporous gas, frequently from an aerosol can of hair spray. Through another small opening on the sealed end of the pipe, a sparking device or an electric match (gas grill starters are sometimes used) is inserted. In some cases, a fuse may be used. All openings around the sparking device are sealed with tape or putty. When the sparking device is engaged, the spark ignites the fumes trapped in the pipe, causing an explosion. This explosion propels the potato with significant force, sometimes for distances over 500 yards. In addition to the damage that may be caused by such a projectile, these devices sometimes explode like pipe bombs.

Firebombs

Some bombs are created to induce burning. The crudest of these is the Molotov cocktail. This device is a bottle filled with a flammable liquid, usually gasoline. A saturated fuse of cloth or other thick wicking is inserted into the bottle. The fuse is ignited and the bomb quickly thrown at the target. Some firecrackers can create a similar result.

Letter and Package Bombs

Letter and package bombs are rare but particularly disturbing. They can be sent from a location in New York City to one in Fairbanks, Alaska, and provide little or no warning to the victim. They may be addressed to a particular position in a company—such as "President," "Chairperson," or "Director of Advertising"—or to a public official—such as "Attorney General," "Police Chief," or "Mayor." Sometimes a mail bomb is addressed to a specific person. Letter bombs are often indistinguishable from other mailed letters. Envelopes are of the usual size and color, with names and addresses in the correct places. The envelope may have a return address, but it may be fictitious. Letter bombs vary from about ⅛ inch to ⁵⁄₁₆ inch in thickness and they usually weigh less than 5 ounces. Typically, a letter bomb is triggered by a pressure-release mechanism. Opening the letter releases a floating cocked firing pin—a rod through the center of the envelope. In turn, this detonates the explosives in the envelope.

Package bombs also vary widely in size, weight, shape, and the color of the wrappings. They may arrive disguised as gifts, equipment, books, or other objects. Package bombs may also be sent with some form of special handling, by certified or registered mail, or even by overnight express. Some package bombs operate like letter bombs, with pressure-release mechanisms. Others contain a spring detonating device, held under tension by the package's sealing tape or string. When the package is opened, and the tape or string cut, the spring is released and detonates the bomb. Some package bombs are rigged with a triggering device in the cover or hinge. Opening the unwrapped box triggers the explosion. In some package bombs, a mercury switch is used as the triggering device. Shaking, tipping, or inverting the package causes the mercury to flow, completing an electric circuit and detonating the bomb.

Whenever a letter or package is suspected of containing a possible explosive device, the area should be evacuated and the police department and the Postal Inspection Service notified immediately. Postal inspectors collaborate with federal, state, and local authorities in investigating actual and threatened mail bombs. It is impossible for postal employees to screen all letters and packages for explosive devices. However, mail bombs have certain similarities that have repeatedly shown up (see Figure 18–4). Knowledge of these characteristics of suspect parcels may help prevent a tragedy.

Figure 18–4 Letter and package bomb indicators.

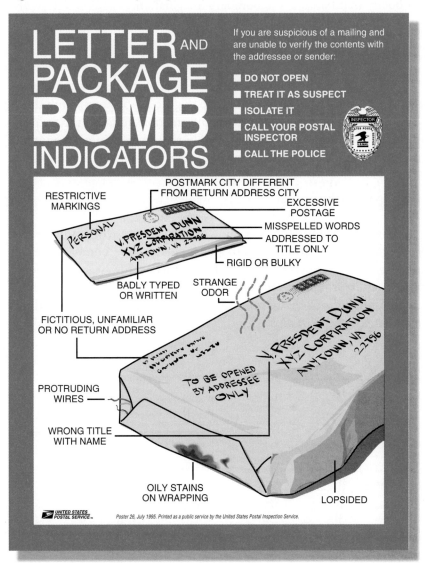

Booby Trap Bombs

Some criminals use bombs as booby traps. The explosion warns the criminal that intruders are near and slows their entry, allowing an escape. The blast may also panic the intruder, scaring him or her away. The explosion may even injure or kill anyone coming near the scene. Detonation of a booby trap bomb may be manual, remote, or timed, or the bomb may be set off by the victim through a hidden trip wire, pressure spring, or plate. Booby trap bombs may be placed in fields and woods surrounding an area of illegal activity (as of illegal drug crops). Or they may be attached to windows or doors of a building or residence (as by a militant antigovernment organization). The only limit on the placement of a booby trap bomb is the bomber's imagination.

Investigating Bombing Incidents

Actions taken in bombing incidents are controlled by the characteristics of the actual or suspected bomb. Figure 18–5 shows bomb threat cards developed by the FBI to gather information in bomb threat investigations. Operating procedures generally should take into account the various skill levels of personnel involved in a bomb incident response.

Searching for Bombs

Bomb searches are typically conducted by two-person teams. Although there are various ways to search an area for a bomb, the search should always be a systematic effort. In other words, searchers should move carefully from one room to another from the top of a structure to the bottom, or from the bottom to the top. Bomb searches should not be undertaken haphazardly.

Figure 18–5 Bomb threat cards.

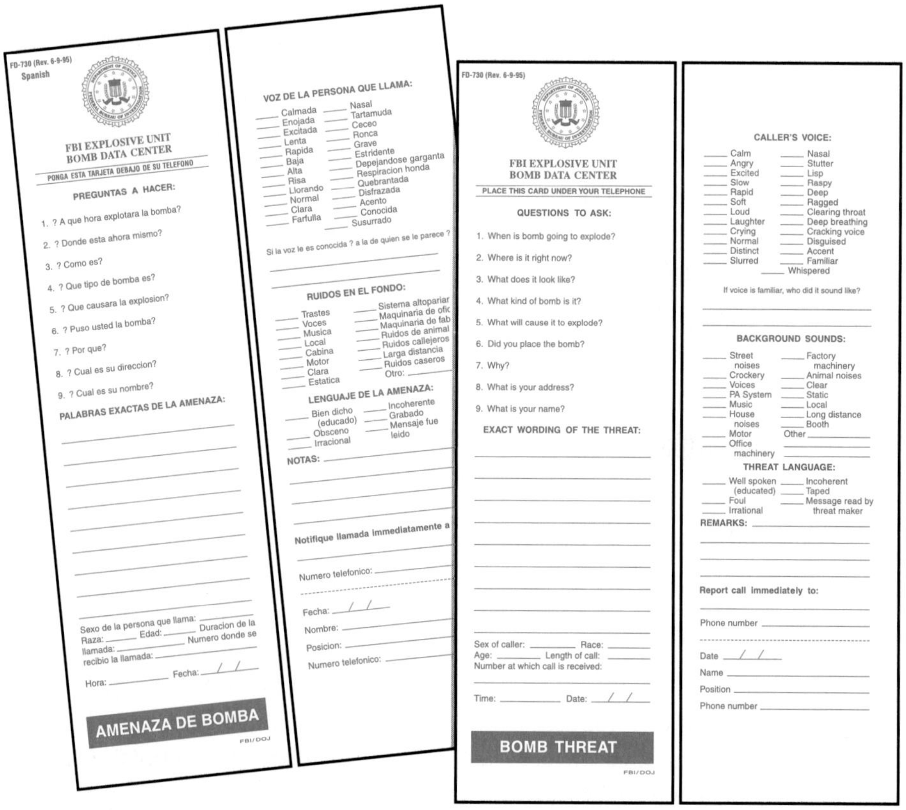
FD-730 (Rev. 6-9-95)
Spanish
FBI EXPLOSIVE UNIT
BOMB DATA CENTER
PONGA ESTA TARJETA DEBAJO DE SU TELEFONO
PREGUNTAS A HACER:
1. ? A que hora explotara la bomba?
2. ? Donde esta ahora mismo?
3. ? Como es?
4. ? Que tipo de bomba es?
5. ? Que causara la explosion?
6. ? Puso usted la bomba?
7. ? Por que?
8. ? Cual es su direccion?
9. ? Cual es su nombre?
PALABRAS EXACTAS DE LA AMENAZA:
Sexo de la persona que llama: ___ Raza: ___ Edad: ___ Duracion de la llamada: ___ Numero donde se recibio la llamada: ___
Hora: ___ Fecha: _/_/_
AMENAZA DE BOMBA
FBI/DOJ

VOZ DE LA PERSONA QUE LLAMA:
Calmada, Enojada, Excitada, Lenta, Rapida, Baja, Alta, Risa, Llorando, Normal, Clara, Farfulla
Nasal, Tartamuda, Ceceo, Ronca, Grave, Estridente, Depejandose garganta, Respiracion honda, Quebrantada, Disfrazada, Acento, Conocida, Susurrado
Si la voz le es conocida ? a la de quien se le parece ?
RUIDOS EN EL FONDO:
Trastes, Voces, Musica, Local, Cabina, Motor, Clara, Estatica
Sistema altoparlar, Maquinaria de ofic, Maquinaria de fab, Ruidos de animal, Ruidos callejeros, Larga distancia, Ruidos caseros, Otro:
LENGUAJE DE LA AMENAZA:
Bien dicho (educado), Obsceno, Irracional
Incoherente, Grabado, Mensaje fue leido
NOTAS:
Notifique llamada immediatamente a
Numero telefonico:
Fecha: _/_/_
Nombre:
Posicion:
Numero telefonico:

FD-730 (Rev. 6-9-95)
FBI EXPLOSIVE UNIT
BOMB DATA CENTER
PLACE THIS CARD UNDER YOUR TELEPHONE
QUESTIONS TO ASK:
1. When is bomb going to explode?
2. Where is it right now?
3. What does it look like?
4. What kind of bomb is it?
5. What will cause it to explode?
6. Did you place the bomb?
7. Why?
8. What is your address?
9. What is your name?
EXACT WORDING OF THE THREAT:
Sex of caller: ___ Race: ___
Age: ___ Length of call: ___
Number at which call is received:
Time: ___ Date: _/_/_
BOMB THREAT
FBI/DOJ

CALLER'S VOICE:
Calm, Angry, Excited, Slow, Rapid, Soft, Loud, Laughter, Crying, Normal, Distinct, Slurred
Nasal, Stutter, Lisp, Raspy, Deep, Ragged, Clearing throat, Deep breathing, Cracking voice, Disguised, Accent, Familiar, Whispered
If voice is familiar, who did it sound like?
BACKGROUND SOUNDS:
Street noises, Crockery, Voices, PA System, Music, House noises, Motor, Office machinery
Factory machinery, Animal noises, Clear, Static, Local, Long distance, Booth, Other
THREAT LANGUAGE:
Well spoken (educated), Foul, Irrational
Incoherent, Taped, Message read by threat maker
REMARKS:
Report call immediately to:
Phone number
Date _/_/_
Name
Position
Phone number

When a search team first enters an area where a bomb may be, the team should stop and stand silently for a moment. Often, bombs are equipped with clockwork timing devices, the sound of which may offer a clue to the explosive's location. The team can then search the room systematically, using a grid pattern, as described in Chapter 3. It should be noted that although a bomb search may be undertaken by local police officers, their task ends upon location of the device. Untrained officers should make no effort to move, remove, or in any way jar a suspicious object.

Disposing of an Unexploded Bomb

When an unexploded bomb or explosive device is located, the police officer's first consideration should be to protect human life and property. The following are some steps the officer should take to both protect and secure the area and aid in the investigation of the attempted bombing:

- Immediately notify qualified bomb disposal personnel, who can evaluate the suspected bomb and take necessary actions.
- Clear the danger area of all occupants to ensure as much safety as possible. Some simple ruse, such as a possible gas leak, may be used as an excuse to evacuate a building without causing panic from fear of a bomb.
- Create a *clear zone* with a perimeter at least 300 feet from the explosive device, and establish a guard to prevent reentry.
- Alert fire department, rescue, and medical emergency units.
- Protect and preserve the scene so that all possible physical evidence can be obtained.
- Note whether the package or object is ticking or making any other audible noise.
- Without touching the object, observe whether it appears to be attached to anything or fastened down. Notify the bomb disposal team about these observations.
- If deemed advisable, remove any flammable materials from the immediate area of the suspected bomb to reduce injury or damage should an explosion occur.
- Shut off power, gas, and fuel lines leading into the danger area if the type of bomb warrants this action. Such action could prevent additional explosions that might add to the damage.
- Set up surveillance of the crowd of spectators to identify possible suspects.
- Photograph or videotape the crowd to possibly reveal familiar faces that have appeared at other bombing sites.

- Interview the person who discovered the suspected bomb. Likewise, interview anyone else at the scene at the time regarding the possible identity of the bomber.
- Canvass the neighborhood immediately around the bomb location. Question individuals about any unknown or suspicious persons they may have seen in the area or possible leads to a suspect's automobile or location.
- Notify the proper agencies when the danger has been declared over.
- Carefully preserve the bomb after it has been disarmed or dismantled and examined for fingerprints or the source of component parts.

FOCUS ON TECHNOLOGY

Bomb Disposal Robot   Remote-controlled bomb disposal robots can safely remove explosive devices and save lives.

Investigating an Exploded Bomb

The primary objects of an investigation following the explosion of a bomb are to (1) establish the nature of the bomb, (2) find out the method of ignition, and (3) obtain any other evidence that may assist in the identification and apprehension of the person or persons responsible. Investigative procedures and considerations include the following:

- Assess the need for immediate response to the scene by explosives specialists.
- Control the scene, including supervision, organization, communications, and coordination of rescue efforts if warranted.
- Determine the degree of urgency (e.g., needs for medical assistance, ambulances, the fire department, and other essential personnel) upon arrival at the scene, based on immediately known facts, visible conditions, and other elements.
- Determine whether power, gas, and fuel lines should be shut off.
- Clear the danger area of all occupants, and establish a secure perimeter to protect the crime scene from all unauthorized people. Allow only essential personnel into the area.
- Carefully remove flammable materials from the area to prevent any further damage.
- Photograph or videotape both the interior and the exterior of the structure, once it is declared safe.
- As in any crime scene, photograph, collect, and document any physical evidence found at the scene. This may include evidence of forced entry, fragments of the bomb itself, portions of the detonating device, or any other relevant evidence.
- As with unexploded bombs, photograph or videotape the crowd gathered at the scene. Interview witnesses and victims, and canvass the areas immediately around the explosion.
- Note cars in the vicinity of the explosion, and record their license numbers. Identify the owners, and interview them as potential witnesses or suspects.
- Search and screen the bombing debris to obtain evidence of the type of container used and the mode of ignition, as well as fragments of components, such as batteries, wire, clockworks, and packaging materials.
- Pay special attention to recovering residue deposits to identify the materials used to create the explosion.
- If a plant or business is the victim of a bombing, consider recently dismissed or irate employees as possible suspects.
- Trace any identified materials found at the scene to their supply sources for possible leads to the identification of the bomber.

- If suspects develop during the investigation, consider such traditional relevant factors as evidence of motive, plan, design or scheme, ability and opportunity, possession of means, fabrication, destruction and suppression of evidence, phony alibis, false statements, and other indications of possible guilt.
- Check local mental institutions for possible bombing suspects.
- Consider previous bombing cases to determine whether they might contribute to the solution of the case under investigation.
- If persons were injured or killed in the explosion, establish their identities and properly notify their next of kin as quickly as possible. Identifying victims may provide a possible reason for the bombing and lead to potential suspects or other valuable investigative information.

SUMMARY BY LEARNING OBJECTIVES

Learning Objective 1

Arson is one of the crimes that the FBI considers the most serious in American society, and it reports yearly statistics on arson in its Uniform Crime Reports (UCR). In 1995, there were 94,926 arson offenses reported. Twenty-four percent of these offenses involved motor vehicles; 22 percent involved residential structures.

Learning Objective 2

State statutes define what constitutes the crime of arson in each state. Generally, these statutes define arson as the malicious and intentional or fraudulent burning of buildings or property. Some jurisdictions categorize an arson as aggravated or simple. In most jurisdictions, aggravated arson is a felony. In some states, arson is divided into first, second, third, and fourth degrees. In addition, many jurisdictions have enacted statutes with more severe punishments for burning schools and other public buildings than for general arson.

Learning Objective 3

Motives for arson can be classified as rational or irrational. Rational motives are goal-oriented and include such goals as revenge, profit from fraud, sabotage, and intimidation. Irrational motives lack direction and include such things as pyromania and vandalism.

Learning Objective 4

Arson is difficult to investigate because valuable evidence is often destroyed in the fire. Investigators study burn patterns to help them determine the point of origin, the spread of the fire, the temperature, the duration, and the presence of accelerants. In addition, certain indicators may lead an investigator to suspect arson. These indicators include multiple points of origin, odors of accelerants, the speed and spread of the fire, holes in walls or floors, alarm tampering, and the intensity of the fire.

Learning Objective 5

Bombing incidents generally are divided into explosive bombings and incendiary bombings. In 1995, explosive bombings made up 79 percent of bombing incidents. There are four types of explosives used in making bombs: primary, low, high, and blasting agents.

Learning Objective 6

Homemade bombs are the kinds of devices that most police agencies deal with. Such bombs include pipe bombs, firebombs, letter and package bombs, and booby trap bombs.

Learning Objective 7

The main function of any police or safety service agency in a bombing incident is to protect human life and property, remove the bomb menace, and investigate and apprehend the bomber. Like arson, a bombing incident is difficult to investigate because valuable evidence is destroyed in the blast. As in any other crime, the bombing site must be preserved, evidence collected and identified, witnesses and suspects interviewed, and reports and follow-up investigations completed.

QUESTIONS FOR REVIEW

Learning Objective 1

1. How does the FBI classify arson?

Learning Objective 2

2. What is the *corpus delicti* of arson?
3. What type of crime is arson in most states?

Learning Objective 3

4. What are four motives for arson?

Learning Objective 4

5. What kinds of evidence may commonly be found at the scene of an arson?

6. What significance does a fire's point of origin have for an arson investigation?

7. What is the relationship between fire and police departments in arson investigations?

8. What factors make arsons difficult to investigate?

9. What can charring of wood indicate about a fire?

10. What conditions cause a V-shaped burn pattern?

Learning Objective 5

11. Define *bombing, high explosive,* and *low explosive.*

12. Is TNT a high or low explosive?

13. How is a safety fuse used?

14. What is an electric squib?

Learning Objective 6

15. Name four types of bombs that a bomb squad would deal with.

16. Why are letter and package bombs so difficult to detect?

17. Why should an officer not touch a suspected bomb found in a building?

Learning Objective 7

18. What is the prime function of the police in bomb matters?

19. What are some actions an officer should perform upon discovering an unexploded bomb?

CRITICAL THINKING INVESTIGATIVE EXERCISES

Divide into two groups, and as assigned by your instructor, complete one of the following activities. Write a group report to present to the entire class.

1. Survey local and/or regional newspapers to identify news stories about arson or bombing incidents that have occurred in your area or state within the past 12 months. If you have to go back further than 12 months to find stories, do so. Assume that your group is a task force set up to investigate local or state arson and bombing incidents. What investigative leads can the group draw from the information provided?

2. Find your state's statutes defining arson and bombing or bomb threatening. Create a chart of the text of the statutes. Then determine who in your community is responsible for investigating arson and bombing incidents and who is responsible for disposing of unexploded bombs.

INVESTIGATIVE SKILL BUILDERS

Interpreting and Communicating Information

You are an officer working dispatch in a medium-sized urban police department. At 11:30 A.M., you receive a telephone call from a man who says, "You have 30 minutes before a bomb goes off at one of the elementary schools in the city. You get to guess which one." There are seven elementary schools in your city, and only six officers on duty during this shift.

1. Who do you call at each school?
2. What do you tell the person at each school?
3. Who else will you notify?

Integrity/Honesty

You are a member of the fire marshal's team investigating a possible arson at a shoe store. As you look around, you see the store manager showing an expensive pair of boots, spared by the flames, to the assistant manager, who is tallying the store's losses for the insurance report. You think you hear one of them say, "I'm sure we can add these boots to the losses." What actions, if any, should you take?

ENDNOTES

1. Frank E. Krzeszowski, "What Sets Off an Arsonist," *Security Management,* January 1993, pp. 42–47.
2. J. D. De Haan, *Kirk's Fire Investigation,* 3d ed., Prentice-Hall, Englewood Cliffs, N.J., 1990.
3. National Fire Protection Association, "Fire Patterns," Sections 921–25, NFPA, Mass., 1995.
4. D. V. Canfield, "Causes of Spalling of Concrete at Elevated Temperatures," *Fire and Arson Investigator,* Vol. 34, June 1984, pp. 324–31.
5. John J. O'Conner, *Practical Fire and Arson Investigation,* Elsevier, New York, 1987.

CHAPTER 19

Organized Crime

CHAPTER OBJECTIVES

After completing this chapter, you will be able to:

1. Provide an overview of organized crime.

2. Discuss some of the major organized crime groups.

3. Describe some techniques useful in investigating organized crime groups.

4. List some major laws enacted to combat organized crime.

5. Discuss the future of organized crime.

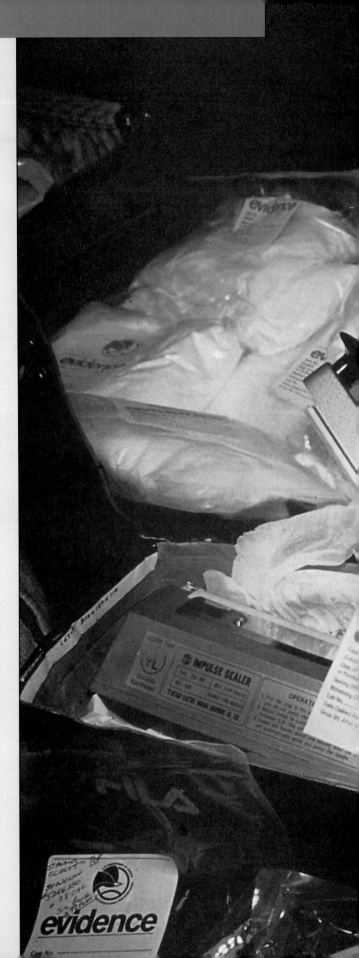

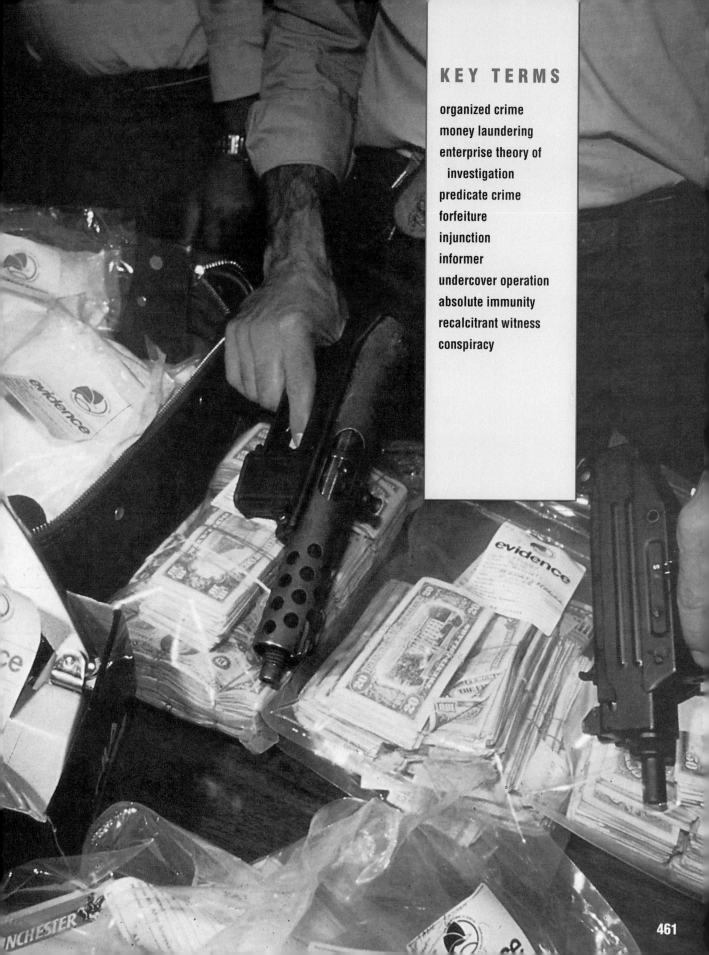

What Is Organized Crime?

The term *organized crime* conjures up images of large men in dark suits, secret rituals, meetings of family members, and gangland killings. This stereotype has commonly been applied to a sophisticated crime organization called *the Mafia* or *La Cosa Nostra* (LCN). The Mafia was made infamous during the 1960s by revelations offered by mobster Joseph Valachi[1] and in the 1970s by Hollywood's release of such popular films as *The Godfather* and *The Valachi Papers.*[2] Today, organized crime includes LCN and many other groups, usually bound by ethnic ties, that engage in supplying illegal goods and services as a business. These goods and services include, but are not limited to, illegal gambling, drug trafficking, loan-sharking, money laundering, credit card fraud, and extortion. Even legitimate businesses are taken over by organized crime groups and used to launder illegal income. Today, the terms "the mob" and "the mafia" no longer refer only to groups such as the Mafia or the LCN. They are synonyms for organized crime groups.

The definition and understanding of what constitutes organized crime varies. The President's Commission on Organized Crime defined it as "a continuing, structured collectivity of persons who utilize criminality, violence, and a willingness to corrupt in order to gain and maintain power and profit."[3] The FBI has defined organized crime as "a continuing criminal conspiracy, having an organized structure, fed by fear and corruption and motivated by greed."[4] For our purposes, we will define **organized crime** as a highly structured, disciplined, self-perpetuating association of people, usually bound by ethnic ties, who conspire to commit crimes for profit and use fear and corruption to protect their activities from criminal prosecution. Most organized crime groups share several basic goals:

- Continuation and propagation of the group.
- Undying loyalty among members.
- Financial gain.
- Power and influence beyond the limits of the group.

Organized crime groups are shrouded in secrecy, wield enormous power, and have fabulous wealth. They may engage in legal enterprises as well as illegal ones, and they frequently use force and intimidation, even murder, to further their goals. Organized crime groups are distorted parallels of career paths and management structures in legitimate business. In other words, organized crime groups operate like business enterprises.

Organized crime groups like the Mafia have a formal pyramid structure similar to that of many corporations. At the top is the leader, or *don.* Below the don are upper-level henchmen and *counselors,* who correspond to upper-level managers in legitimate business structures. Next in the pyramid are lower-level *lieutenants,* who resemble middle

Organized crime A highly structured, disciplined, self-perpetuating association of people, usually bound by ethnic ties, who conspire to commit crimes for profit and use fear and corruption to protect their activities from criminal prosecution.

managers or supervisors. At the bottom are *soldiers* and *button men,* who do the day-to-day grunt work and correspond to line workers in typical businesses. Groups like the Colombian drug cartels have a decentralized structure. They resemble an association of small groups operating under a board of directors composed of the leaders, one from each group.

Organized Crime Groups

Many organized crime groups are offshoots of ethnic gangs that formed out of a need for association, protection, and defense against political, economic, and social isolation. They generally began as small territorial groups involved in petty crime within their own underclass neighborhoods. Individual members formed associations and committed crimes for personal success. Preying on their own communities, they used theft, extortion, gambling, and prostitution as sources of income. As their wealth grew, some groups obtained power, status, and political influence. Successful groups developed an organizational structure as their enterprises grew, and over time, they extended beyond their territories. Even as they expanded, they retained their ethnic characteristics.

We will now take a look at some of the major organized crime groups operating in the United States today. Although these groups are organized along ethnic lines, they make up a tiny fraction of their communities. Most members of immigrant and ethnic communities in the United States are hardworking, law-abiding citizens. They are as outraged by the violence these groups generate as anyone else. They are even the victims who are preyed upon by members of their own ethnic communities.

La Cosa Nostra (LCN)

The LCN is the best-known organized crime group operating in the United States today. The origins of the LCN and of other contemporary Italian organized crime groups, such as the Sicilian Mafia and the Camorra, can be traced to cultural patterns unique to southern Italy and the island of Sicily. Throughout its history, Sicily was ruled by foreigners or outsiders. The Mafia developed as an alternative to these weak outsider governments. Small companies of armed Sicilians, mostly criminals, took the law into

FYI

Organized crime leaders often acquire distinctive nicknames. After beginning his career as a not very successful burglar in the late 1960s, John Gotti turned to hijacking trucks. His career took an upswing, as did his appearance. Gotti began wearing fine, expensive suits and soon was nicknamed *Dapper Don*. Gotti expanded to gambling, loan-sharking, and drug trafficking. Several charges for crimes, including murder, were brought against Gotti in the 1980s. The charges did not stick, giving rise to another nickname—the *Teflon Don*. After one of his underbosses turned state's evidence against him, Gotti was convicted of murder in 1993 and sentenced to life in prison without parole.

their own hands. Wealthy landowners in southern Italy hired armies of these Sicilians as caretakers to oversee and protect their property, as the government was too weak to maintain order. These caretakers developed into tight-knit organizations and began collecting tribute or "protection" from the peasants. The landowners also used the Mafia to put down peasant revolts. Based on their relationship with the landowners and the growth of their power, these groups came to regard themselves as "men of honor" and developed a set of rituals, including a code of silence regarding their activities. The groups became known as *families* and were usually associated with the landowner to whom they were attached.

Mass Italian immigration into the United States began in 1870 and continued well into the first half of the twentieth century. About 80 percent of the immigrants were from Italy's impoverished rural south, with about 25 percent from Sicily alone. The first groups came to New York City, the gateway to America. Soon they spread to other large cities across the United States. Italian gangs formed and began committing many of the same crimes they had committed in Italy. The gangs preyed mainly on their own communities, taking advantage of the immigrants' fear of the Mafia. Most gangs operated under a single leader, fought to guard their territory, and had little, if any, connection with other gangs.

Prohibition (1920–1933) served as the catalyst for the growth of the gangs as well as for uniting opposing ethnic factions. Seeking to improve their profits from bootlegging, gang leaders and groups cooperated to increase the distribution of illegal alcohol into the metropolitan areas the gangs controlled. The Capone gang in Chicago is an example of the power and influence that Italian gangs developed during Prohibition. Al Capone and the members of his gang started as local hoods and rose to become wealthy gangsters who controlled politics as well as crime in Chicago. When Capone was tried for federal tax evasion in 1931, his gang's gross annual income was estimated at $70 million.

When the Great Depression hit in 1929, the Mafia was rolling in money from illegal alcohol. Desperate business owners accepted loans at outlandish interest rates. When the debtors fell behind, their businesses were taken over to repay the loans. In some cases, the Mafia would slowly buy into a legitimate business until it had gained a controlling interest. As the wealth and influence of the Mafia grew, it expanded into other criminal enterprises, such as labor racketeering, narcotics, murder, gambling, loan-sharking, pornography, and extortion.

As the ethnic Italian organized crime groups gained power and influence, friction developed among them. There were several bloody turf wars, ending with a meeting of Mafia bosses in New York in 1931. At this meeting, official codes for governing criminal groups of Mafia origin were set up. Here also, the groups took on the collective name La Cosa Nostra (LCN) and divided the new American Mafia into families, each with its own sphere of influence. A few months later, a commission was set up to assign territories, settle disputes, and exercise internal dis-

Charles (Lucky) Luciano, who conceived the name and idea of *La Cosa Nostra* for the new American Mafia, is led into court in Manhattan in 1936 for sentencing in a prostitution case.

cipline. The commission was originally composed of the five New York families and Al Capone from Chicago. Later it was expanded to include bosses from other families across the country, establishing the bureaucratic structure for which the Mafia is known.

During the remainder of the 1930s, World War II, and the postwar years, LCN consolidated its power and succeeded the Irish, Jewish, German, and other ethnic organized crime groups as the most powerful criminal organization in the United States.[5]

Hispanic Crime Groups

In the early 1970s, cocaine was still a drug for well-to-do jet setters and show business types. Ghetto kids were not yet making fast money selling it on street corners. That began to change as Colombian drug rings organized to increase and control production and distribution of the white powder. Throughout the 1970s, the smugglers gath-

Colombian drug lord Pablo Escobar, killed at age 44 by U.S. backed Colombian antidrug forces, was an early prototype of the new international gangster.

ered power in the cocaine trade, setting up cartels centered around various tight-knit families to control the movement of cocaine into the United States. Of the 20 or so cartels, the most prominent came to be the cartels based in the cities of Medellin and Cali.

The cocaine wars began in south Florida in the late 1970s, when Colombians took control of the drug trade away from Cuban gangs, and spread to Hispanic neighborhoods in places like New York City, Brooklyn, and Hartford, where Dominican and Puerto Rican gangs had small-time drug operations. The Colombians were more willing to deal with Cubans, Dominicans, or Puerto Ricans than with American blacks. Many Hispanic gangs thus became middlemen between the Colombian importers and the black street gangs that sell drugs on the street.

In December 1993, Pablo Escobar, the head of the Medellin cartel, was killed by Colombian antidrug forces. The Cali cartel was able to take over most of the Medellin cartel's market in cocaine trafficking. Like the Chinese triads, the Cali cartel has a superior global network to move raw materials and finished products. The Cali cartel is thought to be the largest supplier of cocaine to the United States and Europe.[6]

Jamaican Posses

The posses, named after the vigilante groups in the cheap European Westerns popular in Jamaica, originated in Kingston, the capital city. The posses rose out of shanty towns to political power by aligning themselves with the major political parties on the island. The gang chiefs, known as "community leaders," became champions of the poor by pressuring the political parties controlling the government to distribute welfare to those in need. Rival parties hired gangs as thugs to influence elections. Gang members exported cocaine and marijuana to the United States to buy guns for political warfare.

In the 1980 election, the political warfare grew especially ugly. Hundreds of Jamaicans died, as gang members working for rival factions fired on political rallies and even police stations. Though put in power by the gang warfare, the new prime minister tried to rein in the gangs. He unleashed the corrupt Jamaican police on the gangs, which had served their purpose but were now a nuisance.

By 1984, many posse members had fled to New York City and Miami, where their flair for violence gave them an advantage over local drug dealers. Posses soon expanded to other cities, including Brooklyn, Philadelphia, Boston, Rochester, Washington, Houston, Dallas, Denver, Detroit, and Los Angeles. The posses' drive to control the crack trade in the 1980s was bloodier than the gang killings of Prohibition days. Posses murdered more than 1400 people in less than five years.[7]

Today, law enforcement officials regard Jamaican posse crack houses and firearms operations as more sophisticated than the operations of any of their contemporary organized criminal competitors. The Jamaican posses strive for an organizational structure similar to that of the Mafia. Many of the middle- and high-level positions in Jamaican posses are filled by criminal fugitives from Jamaica. Lower-level positions are recruited directly from the ranks of urban African-Americans. Because of pressure by law enforcement and Immigration and Naturalization Service officials, the overall structure of posses is not as stable as the structure of some other organized crime groups.

In addition to being motivated by profits from gunrunning and drug trafficking, Jamaican posses are politically motivated. Considerable money from their American criminal enterprises is sent to Jamaican-based posses, who buy local elections on the island. Some wealthy American-based posse members retire to Jamaica and live the life of local "dons." Like other organized crime groups in the United States, American-based posses have begun buying legitimate businesses with profits from their criminal activity.

Asian Crime Groups

Asian crime groups run the gamut from Chinese triads to Viet Ching. These organized crime groups come from areas of the world where civil strife is a part of history. Most of them developed as a response to the chaotic political climate and as a means of social, political, and economic support. Secret societies with elaborate rituals and strict codes of conduct have been a common element of life in Asian countries.

Triads The triads are actually the oldest of the organized crime groups, having come into being in the late 1600s. China was invaded by the Manchus, a tribe from Mongolia who set up the Ching dynasty, which began in 1644 and lasted until 1911. The Manchus had an iron grip on northern China, but in the south they faced continual rebellion. Secret societies sprang up all over southern China. At first their main goal was to overthrow the Ching and restore native Chinese rulers to the throne. As the societies gained the support of the peasants, they also worked to aid the people while still opposing the government. Members of the societies were bound together by an intricate system of secret rituals, oaths, passwords, ceremonial dress, hand signals, and ceremonial intermingling of blood, some of which is still in use today.

By the mid-1800s, after several failed uprisings, the Manchus had the triads on the run. Some fled to Hong Kong, where there were already triad societies, and to North America, where they organized triad groups in Canada and the United States. The British gave the societies the name *triads* because their flags and banners were triangular. Faced with a lack of operating funds, the triads became involved in opium smuggling, extortion, and prostitution. Soon the triads were a distinctly criminal organization, with lesser involvements in social and political activities. This situation remains true today.

Hong Kong is the center of the diverse triad organizations, and groups operate in China, Taiwan, Canada, the United States, and other countries with large Chinatowns that triad members can infiltrate and prey on. Some major triad groups are the 14K, the Wo Group, the Big Four, the Chiu Chow, and the Kung Lok. Under such umbrella groups are networks of triads that work with Chinese street gangs. Triads run drugs, smuggle illegal aliens, make counterfeit currency and credit cards, commit fraud and forgery, and conduct the traditional organized crime activities. Many senior triad members have fronts as legitimate businessmen but continue to operate illegal enterprises.[8]

Tongs Tongs began as benevolent societies set up along family or business lines in major American cities with large Chinese populations. The term *tong* means "meeting hall" or "meeting place" in Chinese. Tongs can trace their beginnings to Chinese triads, are organized along similar lines, and sometimes communicate with each other. During the middle of the nineteenth century, a significant number of Chinese immigrated to the United States. They were lured by advertisements promising high pay and quick fortunes in California. Males were especially welcome to build the railroads and work the mines. Business owners and families of Chinese origin helped the newcomers find jobs, housing, and medical care. In time, they formed their own organizations to provide welfare services, set up rules and regulations, care for the needy, and act as a liaison with the outside, where the newly arrived immigrants were regarded with suspicion by American laborers.

When the California gold rush was over, anti-Chinese sentiment drove out many of the immigrants, who headed east, founding Chinatowns in Chicago, New York, Boston, Philadelphia, and other cities. Chinatowns were divided into districts according to Chinese surnames, and the newly arrived could register with the appropriate tong. Criminal activities such as gambling and prostitution became lucrative businesses and fell under tong control. As the tongs grew, they vied for control of territories and rackets. Legitimate and respectable businessmen joined the tongs just to protect their families and businesses. In 1913, a peace agreement among rival associations stopped the bloody warfare. The

When U.S. officials seize vessels, they often find illegal aliens. Chinese organized crime groups have smuggled tens of thousands of illegal Chinese aliens into the United States.

vice-related activities seemed to disappear, and the tongs seemed to become socially conscious organizations dedicated to bettering the Chinese community.

The mid-1960s brought a change in the image of Chinatowns throughout the United States. The Immigration and Naturalization Act of 1965 allowed Chinese immigration at the same level as for other preferred nations. Chinese immigration, which had been averaging a little more than 100 people a year, suddenly exceeded 20,000 a year. The nation's Chinatowns, already hemmed in geographically, had a hard time absorbing the newcomers. These Chinese immigrants were very different from those of the nineteenth century, who had been descendants of farmers with a tradition of hard work and humility. Many of the newcomers were from the slums of Hong Kong, where triad-linked street gangs were the law and Chinese traditions had long been lost.

The new Chinese immigrants found that life in the United States was not easy. For people who could not speak English, the only jobs were in garment sweatshops or in restaurants, waiting tables. Chinese youth

The term *racket*, as applied to crime, supposedly comes from old-time New York political fund-raising gatherings. They were called rackets because of the noise the attendees made. Later, gangs gave their own rackets, for which merchants and other business owners were forced to buy tickets. The term came to be applied to any enterprise activity resulting in illegal income.

Money laundering The investing of illegally obtained money into businesses and real estate that are operated and maintained within the law.

found it especially hard. Their inability to speak English made them poor students in big-city school systems, where they were often put in classes with students much younger than them. The most insecure coped with these problems by banding together in gangs.

The gangs engaged in robbery, extortion, and other crimes to support themselves and soon were staking out territories. Fearing that the gangs would intrude on their underground gambling and other vice activities, the tongs hired rival gangs to protect their interests. Soon gang wars were raging in San Francisco, New York City, and Toronto. While Chinese gangsters were killing off each other, more level-headed Chinese gangsters were setting up a national Chinese crime syndicate. Taking their cue from the Mafia, these groups hid behind legitimate businesses to launder money from their illegal gambling, extortion, and heroin smuggling. The **money laundering** took many forms, from investing in real estate to having groups of "mules" use cash to buy luxury items to export.

Tongs are involved in many Chinese community functions that help Asian businesses operate, yet many of them are fronts for the criminal operations of organized Chinese crime syndicates. Despite their continued involvement in illegal gambling, extortion, prostitution, and smuggling illegal aliens, drug trafficking is the preferred enterprise for Chinese organized crime syndicates.[9]

Yakuza The Yakuza had their origins in the customs and traditions of the samurai warrior class of ancient Japan. The samurai were known for their extreme loyalty and discipline. By the 1700s, Yakuza gangs had appeared. They were set up in families, reflecting the Japanese tradition of a strong-willed "father" leader who demanded blind obedience from his "children." They capitalized on the traditions of samurai honor and courage while committing crimes, and were considered Robin Hoods. In the late 1800s, they moved into the cities, recruiting members from the ghettos. The social and political upheaval that followed World War II provided the perfect setting for the Yakuza to take over the black market in Japan and to expand their criminal activities. As Japanese people and businesses moved west in post war years, so did the Yakuza.

The Yakuza control Japan's casinos, brothels, white-slave trade, nightclubs, entertainment industry, gunrunning, loan-sharking, drug trafficking, and money laundering. They also practice a unique form of corporate extortion called *sokaiya*. Yakuza members show up at a Japanese corporation and demand a huge payoff. If refused, they threaten to spread damaging rumors about the business. Or Yakuza members may threaten to turn up at a stockholder meeting to spill company secrets, to raise questions about company management, or to create a scene—throw furniture, shout and scream, even slap the chairman of the board. Because the Japanese are so anxious to save face and not be publicly shamed, corporations generally pay up.

The Yakuza are entrenched in Honolulu, San Francisco, Los Angeles, Paris, London, Rotterdam, São Paolo, and other cities worldwide, where they operate in conjunction with other Asian crime groups and with the LCN. Yakuza groups run drugs and arms, launder money, and blackmail Japanese corporations around the world, even trying their luck with American corporations. Some Yakuza are identifiable by their distinctive markings—elaborate body tattoos and missing finger joints, detached in secret rituals to show loyalty.[10]

Viet Ching   At the close of the Vietnam War in the late 1970s, Vietnamese immigrants began immigrating to other countries. Throughout the 1980s, many of these immigrants went to the United States. Among these immigrants were many who were of Chinese ancestry, more commonly referred to as Viet Ching. In America, a number of Viet Ching formed small associations or gangs, and preyed upon Asian communities. Like tongs, these gangs soon were involved in offering protection to local Asian merchants and the drug trade.

Other immigrants from Vietnam included former members of the Vietnamese armed forces and criminals. Many of these men banded together once they arrived in the United States, and formed vicious, strong-arm gangs. Like other Asian immigrant criminals, these Vietnamese gangs preyed largely upon Asian and mostly Vietnamese communities. They were soon involved in the full range of rackets, murder, arson, extortion, and drug trafficking.

Russian Mafia

Life in the Soviet Union equipped many Russian and Eastern European gangsters with skills suited to the scams they have pulled off in the United States and elsewhere in the West. Soviet citizens had to negotiate their way through the vast Communist bureaucracy, with its endless flow of documents, to get a job, to buy a car, to travel, to get medical care—to do just about everything. To survive, criminals had to learn to get around the confines of this totalitarian system. Their tools were bribery, forgery, and counterfeiting. They also had to evade the Soviet police and the dreaded KGB, whose favorite interrogation techniques were beating and torture. Ordinary Soviets, who often used the talents of gangsters to get what they needed, referred to these outlaws as *mafia*, and the name stuck.

Agents lead Russian Mafia crime boss Vyacheslav Ivanov from the FBI office in New York City after his arrest on extortion charges in 1995.

The breakup of the Soviet Union in 1991 brought Russian and Eastern European gangsters out of the underground. They took advantage of the political chaos in all the former republics to invade every area of life. After they had the 15 former Soviet republics under control, they turned their enterprise skills to Western Europe and North America, particularly the United States.

Russian and Eastern European gangs were already operating in North America well before the breakup of the Soviet Union. They operated mostly in New York, Los Angeles, and Toronto. Some smaller groups could be found in Chicago, Boston, Wilmington, Phoenix, San Francisco, and other smaller cities. With the breakup of the Soviet Union and the increased freedom of travel, thousands of Russian gangsters flooded the United States. They hooked up with established Russian and Eastern European gangsters, who knew the language, the American system of law, and the way the system worked. Soon, many had their own criminal networks and were demanding more and more of the criminal pie. This loose-knit collection of gangsters calls itself the *Organizatsiya,* or organization. They are into drug dealing, extortion, kidnapping, bank fraud, counterfeiting, contraband exports, contract murder, and trafficking in dangerous weapons and components. They are forging working relationships with other ethnic organized crime groups, especially the Italian Mafia.[11]

Street Gangs

During the late 1950s and early 1960s, youthful street gangs were problems only in several large American cities. In the beginning, these gangs chiefly fought one another, committed petty crimes, and pulled off small-time extortions. Today, street gangs are involved in murder, drug trafficking, and a host of other serious crimes, all connected to the drug trade. Drug gangs from the nation's largest cities have expanded into medium-sized and small cities, spreading the drug trade and its attendant violence throughout the country.

The most expansive and best organized of these street gangs are the Crips and the Bloods—the African-American street gangs of Los Angeles. These gangs have grown into national organizations that send recruiters into prospective territories (even rural areas) to organize affiliated gang sets. These federations provide an extensive network for the gangs' illegal enterprises, including the manufacture and distribution of crack cocaine, murder for hire, extortion, and the sale of illegal firearms. Identifying the gang federation a member belongs to is not hard. Since the gangs emerged after the Watts riot in 1965, the Crips have worn blue colors, and the Bloods have worn red. Blood gangs can go under any name. Crips gangs usually have the name of the federation in their titles.

The number of street gangs that law enforcement officers must deal with is mind-boggling. In Los Angeles County alone, when Asian, Hispanic, white, and other street gangs are added to the Crips and Bloods, it is estimated that there are more than 1000 gangs. The nature of street gangs makes them extremely difficult to investigate. Their high degree of mobility and fairly fluid organizational structure make them difficult to infiltrate.[12]

Outlaw Motorcycle Gangs

During the 1940s, as American soldiers returned from World War II, free-living motorcycle gangs began to form. Veterans established these clubs, organizing them as paramilitary groups. These early gangs were emulated by more youthful motorcycle enthusiasts and romanticized by movies of the 1950s and 1960s.

Today, there are nearly 1000 motorcycle gangs operating in the United States. Among these, the most influential are Hell's Angels, Outlaws, Pagans, and Bandidos. Hell's Angels are the most well known and the best organized of the groups, with chapters in the United States, Canada, Britain, Germany, France, Brazil, Russia, Japan, and other countries. Outlaw motorcycle gangs are engaged in numerous criminal enterprises, the most frequent and most lucrative of which are drug and illegal firearms trafficking.[13]

Outlaw motorcycle gangs have chapters in many countries.

Investigating Organized Crime

For many years, federal, state, and local law enforcement officials investigated and prosecuted individual members of organized crime groups for such crimes as extortion, fraud, drug trafficking, or murder. The

Computerized Crime Mapping Advances in computer-aided dispatching systems and mapping software programs have made it easier for law enforcement officers to spot crime patterns in neighborhoods and devise creative strategies for fighting them. Video screens display neighborhood diagrams using multicolored dots, ovals, and other symbols to plot everything from shooting locations to drug markets.

convicted felon went to prison, but someone else in the organization was always standing by, ready to carry on in the member's absence, and the crime enterprise continued. Minimum sentences for specific crimes allowed the convicted felons to return quickly to the crime organization, with enhanced stature for having served the sentence and maintained silence about the organization. Furthermore, incarcerating one individual failed to remove the organization's profit from criminal activity. Another aspect of organized crime that protected it from effective prosecution was its corruption of judges, lawyers, politicians, law enforcement officials, financial institutions, and businesses.

Enterprise Theory of Investigation

Since the early 1980s, law enforcement agencies investigating organized crime have relied on the **enterprise theory of investigation** (ETI).

Enterprise theory of investigation An approach to criminal investigation that targets entire crime organizations instead of individual criminals within them.

In an ETI investigation, an entire crime organization is targeted under the Racketeer Influenced and Corrupt Organizations Act, commonly known as RICO. Passed by Congress in 1970, RICO allows a single prosecution of an entire multidefendant organized crime group for all its diverse criminal activities. The crimes do not have to be linked by the same perpetrator or a common criminal conspiracy. Thus, prosecutors can include years of criminal acts in a sweeping racketeering indictment. Prosecutors have used RICO effectively against established, highly structured organized crime groups like LCN. Many states also have enacted their own RICO statutes.

General Provisions of the RICO Statute   The RICO statute is broader than other criminal statutes we have discussed. It does not create individual offenses, but defines a pattern of offenses for which an individual or an entity can be prosecuted. The RICO statute starts out by listing the federal and state crimes that may form the basis of a RICO offense. These include such crimes as gambling, bribery, dealing in obscene matter, dealing in narcotics or other dangerous drugs, mail fraud, witness tampering, and obstruction of justice.

The crimes outlined in RICO are referred to as **predicate crimes** because they constitute a predicate, or basis, for a violation of the statute. The RICO statute requires a *pattern* of racketeering activity. That is, a violator must have committed at least *two predicate offenses* within a 10-year period, one of which took place after RICO became effective. Persons convicted of RICO violations are subject to fines and imprisonment. They are also subject to the punishment for the individual predicate crimes of which they are convicted. All fines are added together, and jail terms must be served consecutively, not concurrently.

Predicate crime   A crime that is a basis of a violation of the RICO statute.

Additional Provisions of the RICO Statute   The RICO statute recognized the profit motive of organized crime and the need to remove the source of the profit. In addition to the fines levied for RICO violations, the statute provides for **forfeiture** of assets acquired directly or indirectly from racketeering activity. Additionally, persons or entities who have had their well-being, their property, or their reputations damaged by the RICO violations can bring a civil action against the violators and sue for damages. Another civil provision of the RICO statute allows the government to obtain an **injunction** to keep members of an organized crime group from controlling a legitimate enterprise, such as a labor union, and using its funds for illegal activities.

Forfeiture   The loss of money and/or property to the state as a criminal sanction.

Injunction   A court order prohibiting a party from a specific course of action; or ordering a party to perform some action.

Investigative Techniques

One very effective technique for investigating organized crime has been the creation of organized crime task forces. Task forces combine resources and personnel from federal, state, and local law enforcement and regulatory agencies to investigate and prosecute organized crime. Some federal agencies that play important roles in investigating organized crime on the national level include the FBI, the U.S. Postal Service, the Secret Service, the Department of Labor, the Securities and Exchange Commission, and the Internal Revenue Service. State attorneys general, district attorneys, and county and city prosecutors can assist law enforcement authorities in investigating organized crime groups that violate state and local laws.[14] Financial analysis, electronic surveillance, informants, undercover operations, pressure from citizens' groups and commissions, and computerized communications and analysis are all tools in the battle against organized crime.[15]

Financial analysis refers to locating and following a financial paper trail. Identifying sources of revenue for large and frequent bank deposits can sometimes lead investigators to organized criminal organizations. The Internal Revenue Service (IRS), naturally, plays a key role in this part of an investigation. Existing IRS codes and regulations provide a means for law enforcement to investigate and analyze the net worth, tax payments (or failure to pay taxes), and general expenditures of an organization.

Electronic surveillance includes the use of wiretaps, concealed video- and audiotaping, and an assortment of other covert strategies. Many investigators regard electronic surveillance as one of the most popular methods of gathering evidence against notorious mobsters. Similarly, **informers,** existing members of criminal syndicates who provide information leading to indictments, as well as evidence and testimony during trials, are a viable weapon against organized crime. Historically, **undercover operations** and infiltrations have been effective—albeit dangerous—in combatting organized criminal activities. Citizens' commissions have been successful at bringing public attention and pressure to bear against organized crime groups.[16]

Furthermore, the use of computer-assisted communications and analysis during investigations has proven invaluable. Computers provide a means of unraveling the intricate fake companies used by many criminal organizations to conceal and launder their ill-gotten money. Sophisticated databases used by the FBI and the IRS give investigators a way to analyze paper trails and coordinate their efforts with other agencies. Furthermore, with advances in electronic banking and money transfer, computers are likely to play a significant role in both the laundering and the concealing of the profits of organized criminal groups. Consequently, investigators will need strong computer skills to compete.

Informer A member of an organized crime group who provides information and testimony for law enforcement investigations and prosecutions.

Undercover operation An investigative police operation designed to secretly uncover evidence against organized crime groups.

Laws to Combat Organized Crime

To defend against the on-slaught of organized crime in America, law enforcement agencies have had to develop creative legal strategies. The laws that have had the greatest impact in this regard are the following:

The Hobbs Act   The Hobbs Act is an antiracketeering act legislated during the 1940s. It has been used to crack down on any activity that interferes with interstate commerce.

The Controlled Substance Act of 1970   The Comprehensive Drug Abuse and Control Act of 1970, popularly called the Controlled Substance Act, created a coordinated and codified system of drug control that would classify all narcotics and dangerous drugs. Another objective was to create a closed regulatory system for the legitimate handling of controlled drugs by physicians, pharmacists, and those involved in the manufacture of pharmaceuticals. The system required legitimate handlers to register with designated state agencies, maintain records, and to make biennial inventories of all controlled drugs in stock.

The Organized Crime Control Act of 1970   The central purpose of this act was to fight organized crime by strengthening legal tools. It provided much stiffer penalties for violations and extended the ways evidence could be gathered.

To encourage witness participation, three things were done. First, **absolute immunity,** a guarantee that the witness would not be prosecuted for any involvement, could be offered. With absolute immunity, as long as a witness complies with the court and testifies, the testimony cannot be used against him or her in any criminal action.

Second, any witness who refused to testify, even with immunity, could be labeled a **recalcitrant witness.** Recalcitrant witnesses could be confined until they chose to testify. The incarceration, however, could not exceed the length of the court proceeding or the full term of the grand jury, including all extensions.

Third, protection was given to witnesses whose lives would be threatened as result of their testifying. The act also stiffened the perjury penalties.[17]

> ## FYI
>
> An investigation by the National Association of Securities Dealers, Inc., and the FBI has revealed that organized crime groups are moving into Wall Street. According to an article in the December 1996 issue of *Business Week*, organized crime groups have established a network of stock promoters, securities dealers, and boiler rooms that sell stock nationwide, using hard-sell tactics. The transactions involve small-capitalization stocks for which promoters quickly drive up the price. Then they get out of the market, leaving buyers with overpriced stocks that they can sell only at a loss. Other securities dealers and traders were said to pay extortion money to organized crime as "just another cost of doing business" on Wall Street.

Absolute immunity   A guarantee that, as long as a witness complies with the court and testifies, the testimony cannot be used against him or her in any criminal action.

Recalcitrant witness   A witness who refuses to testify in a criminal proceeding, even after being offered immunity.

The Bank Secrecy Act of 1970 This act addressed money laundering. The act included a requirement that banks report any transaction of $10,000 or more. Similarly, a bank must report if $10,000 or more leaves or enters the country. Furthermore, citizens must report on their annual tax returns any foreign bank accounts they have.[18]

The Comprehensive Crime Control Act of 1984 This act was another attempt to squelch drug and organized crime activities. In addition to reforms in bail and sentencing, it expanded forfeiture authority and provided amendments intended to aid in the investigation of money laundering.

The Money Laundering Control Act of 1986 Like the Bank Secrecy Act of 1970, this act addressed money laundering. It made money laundering a federal offense. The law made it illegal to cause a domestic financial institution to fail to report transactions of $10,000 or more. This prohibition includes attempts to have financial institutions make false statements by providing them with wrong or misleading information.

The Anti-Drug Abuse Act of 1986 This law greatly expanded federal, state, and local drug abuse control efforts. It created mandatory sentences for certain drug-related crimes and made it a crime to involve juveniles in drug distribution or sales. In addition, the law made it illegal to distribute drugs within 1,000 feet of a school.

The Anti-Drug Abuse Act of 1988 This act was legislated as a complement to the Anti-Drug Abuse Act of 1986. It established a cabinet-level position intended to ease and make more effective federal drug enforcement activities. The position is popularly known as drug czar. In addition to increasing penalties for a number of drug offenses, the law also created mandatory sentences for certain drug-related crimes involving children.

Asset Seizure and Forfeiture Laws The intent of forfeiture is to remove the financial rewards of criminal activity. For example, after Customs arrests a drug smuggler at the airport, the government may seize the private airplane used to fly the drugs in, as well as the trafficker's home, cars, and restaurant, all bought with drug proceeds. Upon conviction, the drug smuggler will lose ownership of these items. Both the Comprehensive Crime Control Act of 1984 and the Anti-Drug Abuse Act of 1986 extended law enforcement's authority to seize profits and property resulting from drug trafficking. In addition, these acts provided a legal means for seizing cash connected with money-laundering activities. Proceeds from forfeitures are funneled back into the fight against crime. Seized boats are sometimes given to law enforcement agencies that need them. Funds from forfeiture are also used to purchase needed equipment.

Conspiracy A crime in which two or more parties are in concert in a criminal purpose.

Conspiracy Laws Simply defined, a **conspiracy** is an agreement between two or more parties to commit an unlawful act by unlawful means. Usually, someone who plans to commit a crime may withdraw from the plan before the act is committed. This is not the case, however, for conspiracy. Once an agreement has been struck, the parties involved are coconspirators, and withdrawal will not allow them to escape the charge of conspiracy.

The Future of Organized Crime

Patterns in organized crime suggest that the traditional bureaucratic organized crime *family* is on the decline. Investigations in many large cities indicate that years of cooperative investigations by federal and state authorities have weakened the Mafia considerably. These investigations, however, may not be the only explanation. Another reason may be that Mafia family heads have been so successful at educating their offspring that the children are not interested in entering the family "business." As these family heads grow older and step—or are pushed—into retirement, there are no younger immediate family members who have been tutored in the business to step in. Instead, some families have had to reach down the bureaucratic structure and elevate lower-level lieutenants, who apparently lack the strength and leadership of the old dons.

Finally, other criminal organizations are seeking control over criminal activities once controlled by the Mafia. These groups, such as the Chinese triads, Jamaican posses, and Colombian cartels, are more ruthless, violent, and brutal than today's *mafiosi.*

The future of investigation of criminal organizations is likely to remain in the area of money laundering and misuses of electronic transfers of funds between financial institutions. Unfortunately, investigators will probably trace human carnage along the same route as they trace the paper and electronic trail to the organizational leaders.

SUMMARY BY LEARNING OBJECTIVES

Learning Objective 1

Organized crime is a highly structured, disciplined, self-perpetuating association of people, usually bound by ethnic ties, who conspire to commit crimes for profit and use fear and corruption to protect their activities from criminal prosecution. Organized crime activities include, but are not limited to, illegal gambling, drug trafficking, loan-sharking, money laundering, credit card fraud, extortion, and murder for hire.

Learning Objective 2

Numerous organized crime groups have emerged in America's cities, neighborhoods, and rural areas. These groups are generally identified by their ethnic origins. These major crime organizations involve, but are not limited to, Chinese, Japanese, African-American, Jamaican, Hispanic, Italian, and Russian criminal enterprises.

Learning Objective 3

Since the early 1980s, law enforcement agencies investigating organized crime have relied on the enterprise theory of investigation. Under the Racketeer Influenced and Corrupt Organizations Act (RICO), entire crime organizations can be prosecuted for all their diverse criminal activities. In addition, investigators use a variety of techniques to enhance investigation and prosecution of organized crime groups, including task forces, asset forfeiture, informants, undercover operations, and computer-assisted communications and analysis.

Learning Objective 4

A number of laws have been passed to assist in the investigation and prosecution of organized crime groups. Among these laws are the Controlled Substance Act of 1970, the Organized Crime Control Act of 1970 (especially the RICO Act provision), the Bank Secrecy Act of 1970, the Comprehensive Crime Control Act of 1984, the Money Laundering Control Act of 1986, the Anti-Drug Abuse Act of 1986, the Anti-Drug Abuse Act of 1988, and various asset seizure, forfeiture, and conspiracy laws.

Learning Objective 5

The future of the United States in regard to organized crime is not promising. The traditional bureaucratic organization of the Mafia is on the decline. In its place is an array of loosely defined organizations from a host of different ethnic groups. These organizations are more ruthless and more creative in devising and perpetrating scams and rackets on the American public.

QUESTIONS FOR REVIEW

Learning Objective 1

1. Where do many Americans get their ideas and images about who is involved in organized crime?

Learning Objective 2

2. How did many organized crime groups originate?
3. What goals do organized crime groups have in common?
4. What is another name for the American Mafia?
5. How did the Colombian cartels originate?

6. How are Jamaican posses political?

7. With what ethnic organized crime groups are *tongs*, *triad*s, and *Yakuza* associated?

8. Why are organized youthful street gangs so difficult for law enforcement to investigate?

9. How did outlaw motorcycle gangs originate?

Learning Objective 3

10. How have federal asset forfeiture laws assisted law enforcement in its pursuit of organized criminals?

11. What does RICO stand for, and how does it assist in the curbing of organized crime?

Learning Objective 4

12. Why can an individual not avoid a *conspiracy* charge by backing out of the crime at the last moment?

13. What effects did the Comprehensive Crime Control Act of 1984 have on organized crime investigations?

14. How might computers assist investigations of organized criminal groups?

Learning Objective 5

15. How would you characterize the future of organized crime groups in the United States?

CRITICAL THINKING INVESTIGATIVE EXERCISES

1. You have just been appointed head of a task force to combat organized crime in your local community. What will be your first goal? What legal means might you use to reach this goal?

2. You are an undercover officer assigned to infiltrate an organized crime group in your local community. What are some things you might try in your effort to infiltrate this group? What safety precautions might you take?

INVESTIGATIVE SKILL BUILDERS

Participating as a Member of a Team

Have your instructor divide the class into three groups. Have each group then designate two representatives to meet with either a prosecutor from your local state's attorney's office or a member of your local police department. At this meeting, the representatives should discuss the kinds of techniques and strategies used to investigate and prosecute organized crime in your community. Have them bring this information back to the group. Using this information and information obtained by group members at the library, prepare a report on strategies for handling organized crime.

Integrity/Honesty

You are the newly elected sheriff of a rural community. You are highly qualified for the position, having served as an investigator for the sheriff's department in a larger community for four years and as chief investigator for five years. Additionally, you hold a master's degree in criminal justice.

During your campaign for sheriff, you made the usual promises to uphold the law and enforce it fairly and impartially. You promised to run the sheriff's office ethically and in a professional manner. As with all campaigns, you had a number of campaign supporters. Some contributed money or services, while others helped with posters and leaflets. Shortly after you were elected, several of the larger contributors came to you and asked if you might have any deputy sheriff's positions for their friends or relatives. You had half expected something like this and, as long as the applicants were qualified, had no trouble hiring several.

Several months later, you make an impressive drug bust. A major drug trafficking ring has been operating in your jurisdiction, and you manage to capture the leader. The man is in his late twenties, but has already developed a reputation as a key player in an organized drug syndicate. Along with $100,000 in cash, you find a kilo of uncut heroin.

The day after the bust, you receive a visit from one of your largest contributors. He tells you that you need to lose the evidence in the drug case and let the suspect go. You are shocked and a little angry that he would even suggest such an action. He tells you that the man you arrested provided the money for your campaign. The man you are talking with was only a front.

1. What should you tell this contributor?
2. What options, if any, do you have?

ENDNOTES

1. Peter Maas, *The Valachi Papers,* Bantam, New York, 1968.
2. Frederick Martens and Michael Cunningham-Niederer, "Media Magic, Mafia Mania," *Federal Probation,* Vol. 49, 1985, pp. 60–68.
3. President's Commission on Organized Crime, *America's Habit,* Government Printing Office, Washington, 1983.
4. *An Introduction to Organized Crime in the United States,* Organized Crime/Drug Branch, Criminal Investigative Division, Federal Bureau of Investigation, July 1993, p. 1.

5. Portions of this section are based on information in *An Introduction to Organized Crime in the United States,* Organized Crime/Drug Branch, Criminal Investigative Division, Federal Bureau of Investigation, July 1993.

6. Material in this section is based on information from the following sources: *An Introduction to Organized Crime in the United States,* Organized Crime/Drug Branch, Criminal Investigative Division, Federal Bureau of Investigation, July 1993; William Kleinknecht, *The New Ethnic Mobs,* The Free Press, New York, 1996.

7. Portions of material in this section are based on information in William Kleinknecht, *The New Ethnic Mobs,* The Free Press, New York, 1996.

8. Material in this section is based on information from the following sources: House Committee on Foreign Affairs, *The Threat of International Organized Crime: Hearing Before the Subcommittee on International Security, International Organizations and Human Rights,* Government Printing Office, Washington, 1994; William Kleinknecht, *The New Ethnic Mobs,* The Free Press, New York, 1996; Antonio Nicaso and Lee Lamothe, *Global Mafia,* Macmillan Canada, Toronto, 1995.

9. Material in this section is based on information from the following sources: *An Introduction to Organized Crime in the United States,* Organized Crime/Drug Branch, Criminal Investigative Division, Federal Bureau of Investigation, July 1993; William Kleinknecht, *The New Ethnic Mobs,* The Free Press, New York, 1996.

10. Material in this section is based on information from the following sources: House Committee on Foreign Affairs, *The Threat of International Organized Crime: Hearing Before the Subcommittee on International Security, International Organizations and Human Rights,* Government Printing Office, Washington, 1994; William Kleinknecht, *The New Ethnic Mobs,* The Free Press, New York, 1996; Antonio Nicaso and Lee Lamothe, *Global Mafia,* Macmillan Canada, Toronto, 1995; Claire Sterling, *Thieves' World,* Simon & Schuster, New York, 1994.

11. Material in this section is based on information from the following sources: *An Introduction to Organized Crime in the United States,* Organized Crime/Drug Branch, Criminal Investigative Division, Federal Bureau of Investigation, July 1993; William Kleinknecht, *The New Ethnic Mobs,* The Free Press, New York, 1996.

12. Some material in this section is based on information in William Kleinknecht, *The New Ethnic Mobs,* The Free Press, New York, 1996.

13. James Davis, *Street Gangs: Youth, Biker and Prison Gangs,* Kendall/Hunt Publishing, Dubuque, Iowa, 1982. See also Larry J. Siegel, *Criminology: Theories, Patterns, and Typologies,* West Publishing, St. Paul, 1992.

14. Material in this section is based on information in the following sources: *An Introduction to Organized Crime in the United States,* Organized Crime/Drug Branch, Criminal Investigative Division, Federal Bureau of Investigation, July 1993; Sue Titus Reid, *Criminal Law,* 3d ed., Prentice Hall, Englewood Cliffs, N.J., 1995.

15. Jay Albanese, *Organized Crime in America,* 2d ed., Anderson, Cincinnati, 1989.

16. Ibid. See also Jay Albanese and Robert D. Pursley, *Crime in America: Some Existing and Emerging Issues,* Prentice Hall, Englewood Cliffs, N.J., 1993.

17. Neil C. Chamelin and Kenneth R. Evans, *Criminal Law for Police Officers,* 5th ed., Prentice Hall, Englewood Cliffs, N.J., 1991.

18. Howard Abadinsky, *Organized Crime,* 2d ed., Nelson-Hall, Chicago, 1985.

CHAPTER 20

White-Collar Crime

CHAPTER OBJECTIVES

After completing this chapter, you will be able to:

1. Explain what is meant by white-collar crime.

2. List some types of white-collar crime.

3. Describe some challenges of investigating white-collar crime.

4. Describe various categories of computer crime.

5. Explain some considerations in investigating computer crime.

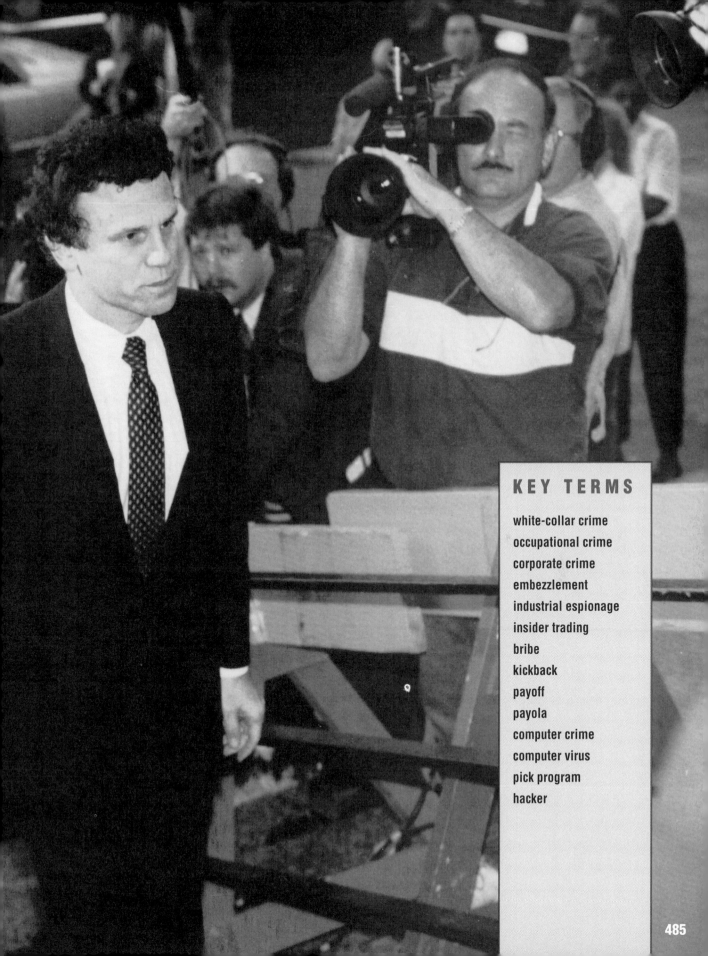

KEY TERMS

white-collar crime

occupational crime

corporate crime

embezzlement

industrial espionage

insider trading

bribe

kickback

payoff

payola

computer crime

computer virus

pick program

hacker

What Is White-Collar Crime?

White-collar crime A nonviolent crime committed by an individual or a corporation that is a breach of trust, confidence, or duty.

Typically, when referring to **white-collar crime,** one is talking about business-related or occupational crime. Edwin Sutherland, a noted social scientist, is often credited with having coined the term in a 1939 address to the American Sociological Society. In this address, and in later writings, Sutherland defined white-collar crime as "a crime committed by a person of respectability and high social status in the course of his occupation."[1] More recently, in a special report issued by the Bureau of Justice Statistics, white-collar crime was defined as "nonviolent crime for financial gain committed by deception."[2]

Taken together, these definitions cover virtually every aspect of white-collar crime. In fact, even certain variations of traditional frauds and larcenies, discussed in Chapter 16, might fit the definition of a white-collar crime. More commonly, however, *white-collar crime* refers to such activities as embezzlement, industrial espionage, insider trading, bribery and extortion, tax evasion, and various corporate crimes. Embezzlement, for example, though it is committed without violence, usually involves more monetary gain than the typical burglary or robbery. In addition, white-collar crime includes virtually any occupation-related law violation, including what some may call mundane office crimes, such as stealing pencils, reams of paper, or rubber bands.

The enforcement of laws concerning white-collar offenses differs from traditional law enforcement. In more traditional street crimes, people are victimized directly or with some degree of immediacy. As a result, the police are summoned to investigate the crime. This places the police in a reactive posture when a crime occurs before they become involved. In white-collar crimes, however, victims are frequently unaware of a crime until long after it has occurred. Therefore, law enforcement and regulatory agencies need to strike a more proactive posture. They must attempt to investigate cases and educate potential victims simply from suspicious circumstances.

Historically, law enforcement has virtually ignored many aspects of white-collar crime. Even convicted offenders have typically gotten off with a fine and a slap on the wrist by the courts. Traditionally, jail time was seldom associated with white-collar crimes. During the past decade, white-collar crimes have become of greater concern to Americans. With the media popularizing such cases as stock manipulations, concealment of savings-and-loan insolvency, and insider trading by figures such as Ivan Boesky and Michael Milken (see chapter opener), Americans have begun to take notice. Even Middle America has grown concerned in the face of such white-collar criminals as television evangelist Jim Bakker, who was convicted of overselling lodging guarantees, called "lifetime memberships," at his Heritage USA religious retreat. In all, Bakker used his television pulpit to defraud $3.7 million from his television congregation. Perhaps the greatest recent example of a white-collar violation of a position of trust occurred in 1995, when Nicholas William Leeson brought down Barings, one of the most solvent and well-respected financial institutions in the world. In a few short months, Leeson allegedly lost more than $1 billion of company money on bad speculative investments.[3]

Nicholas Leeson was convicted in Singapore on two counts of fraud in the financial trading scandal that bankrupted his former employer, Barings Bank.

Identifying White-Collar Crimes

As already stated, white-collar crimes today represent a varied range of activities and behaviors. Persons may act alone or in concert when committing white-collar crimes. The victims of white-collar crimes may be individuals, corporations, or the general public.

White-collar crimes consist of two major categories: occupational crimes and corporate crimes.[4]

Occupational crime The use of one's occupation to illegally obtain personal gain.

Corporate crime Any activity that is undertaken by a corporation for its benefit but violates the law.

The first category, **occupational crime,** includes all offenses committed by individuals in the course of their occupations and by employees against their employers. For example, when a physician bills Medicaid for tests he or she never actually ran on a patient, this physician is guilty of an occupational crime—a white-collar crime. Similarly, a checkout person who steals cash from the register at a supermarket is guilty of embezzlement or theft from his or her employer.

The second category, **corporate crime,** involves "the offenses committed by corporate officials for the corporation and the offenses of the corporation itself."[5] For instance, when a corporation dumps industrial waste into a river or in other ways violates various environmental laws, it is guilty of corporate crimes. During the past several years, sanctions for such crimes have increased. There has also been an increase in green cops, or environmental protection investigators. Green cops are charged with investigating, and on occasion arresting, corporate executives responsible for environmental crimes.

Categories of White-Collar Crime

Another way to look at white-collar crimes is as Herbert Edelhertz did, by dividing these behaviors into four distinct categories: ad hoc violations, abuses of trust, collateral business crimes, and con games.[6]

Ad Hoc Violations Ad hoc violations are illegal activities committed by individuals for personal gain or profit—for instance, tax evasion or various welfare and social service frauds, such as selling food stamps for cash.

Abuses of Trust Abuses of trust include any misuse of authority or malfeasance or public corruption committed by an individual in a place of trust in an organization or government. Examples include embezzlement, graft, bribery, and bestowal of jobs or privileges on those who do not deserve them. Nicholas Leeson's manipulation of purchase orders to cover his failing investments of Barings funds is a further illustration of a violation of trust.

Collateral Business Crimes Collateral business crimes encompass any prohibited activities by which organizations intend to further the business interests of a company—for example, falsifying odometer readings on used cars, attempting to conceal environmental crimes, or using uncalibrated gasoline pumps or weighted scales.

Con Games Confidence games, or con games, discussed in Chapter 16, involve a variety of activities designed to swindle people out of their money or property. These may include fraudulent gold mine sales, sales of phony vacations, and other promises of "something for nothing" that never materialize.

Elements of White-Collar Crimes

In later writings, Edelhertz offered five basic elements of white-collar crimes: intent, disguise of purpose, reliance on the victim's ignorance, voluntary assistance from the victim, and concealment.[7]

Intent   Intent, in white-collar crimes, is the offender's awareness that the activities are wrong or illegal. It does not matter whether the offender knows the specific statutes violated. What is important is that the offender realizes that his or her actions are deceiving the victim in some way.

Disguise of Purpose   Disguise of purpose refers to the offender's conduct while carrying out the scheme. In common street crimes, a wrongful intent is usually followed by some overt and observable action. For example, a bank robbery is planned (intent), and then the robber enters the bank, brandishes a weapon, and declares a robbery. White-collar crimes are seldom that overt. More often, white-collar criminals try to create a facade of normalcy and legitimacy, behind which their actual purpose is hidden.

For example, a loan officer in a bank may file a fictitious loan application, complete with an applicant name, address, job location, credit references, and every other element required for a loan. Thus, the facade of a real loan application has been created. When the loan officer grants the loan, he or she can simply keep the funds. When the funds are not repaid, the loan officer can say that the applicant has defaulted, again creating a facade of normalcy—even against the prying eyes of a bank examiner.

STATISTICS

The National White Collar Crime Center estimates that the yearly cost of white-collar crime ranges from $426 billion to $1.7 trillion.

Reliance on the Victim's Ignorance   Reliance on the victim's ignorance literally means that the victim is unable to see that he or she is being deceived. For example, in the loan officer illustration just offered, it is likely that the offender is confident that his or her fabricated application will be undetectable by other bank personnel and even outside accountants.

Voluntary Assistance From the Victim   Some sort of voluntary assistance from the victim is typically required in most white-collar crimes. This is because not every step in most white-collar crimes is absolutely under the control of the criminal. Most white-collar crimes involve duping or inducing the victim to voluntarily become involved in the crime. Voluntary assistance from the victim may refer to actions on the part of an actual victim who is to be defrauded of money or property. Alternatively, voluntary assistance may come from a kind of intermediate victim. For example, the dishonest loan officer may initially require the assistance of a bank cashier or teller (the intermediate victim) to complete the processing of the phony loan and receive the money from the bank (the true victim).

Concealment   Concealment is the goal of all white-collar criminals to cover up their criminal activities. For example, the loan officer hopes nobody will ever learn that several of the loans he or she authorized were fake. In the back of the loan officer's mind, he or she may even plan to repay the loan before anyone discovers the phony application.

An actual example of concealment may be drawn from the savings-and-loan scandals, which began receiving significant media coverage in about 1989. In 1990, the Government Accounting Office estimated that it would cost at least $325 billion to bail out the insolvent thrifts, or savings and loans, and that it could cost as much as $500 billion over the next 30 or 40 years.[8]

While a considerable number of charges were leveled against various fraudulent savings and loan institutions, many of these charges were for attempts to *cover up* fraudulent behavior or to conceal the institution's insolvency. Of the alleged 179 violations of criminal law reported during the General Accounting Office's examination of savings and loans during 1989, 42 were for concealment activities.[9]

Probably no single categorization can accurately capture all the nuances of white-collar crime. The discussion of white-collar crime typologies here is meant to better familiarize students of criminal investigation with some of the more common types of white-collar criminal behavior. To further this end, let us consider some of the more common white-collar crimes in greater detail.

Law enforcement agencies have many methods of detecting various white-collar crimes. These involve examination of the financial or personal histories of suspected individuals or surveillance of these individuals' activities. If a complainant has summoned the police, the investigation may include such techniques as examining bank and credit records, tax returns, criminal histories, mailing records, box number accounts, and using inside informants. Some of these activities can be undertaken immediately by the investigator. Others, such as searches, undercover investigation, and electronic surveillance, will require official authorization, including warrants.

Types of White-Collar Crime

It is impossible to cover the wide range of white-collar crimes here (see Figure 20–1). In this section, we will discuss some representative types of white-collar crime.

Figure 20–1 Current types of white-collar crime.

- Employee theft (embezzlement and pilferage)
- Cargo theft
- Health care fraud
- Consumer or personal fraud
- Insurance fraud
- Corporate tax fraud
- Computer-related or other high-tech crime
- Check fraud or counterfeiting

- Telecommunications fraud
- Credit/debit/charge/bank card fraud
- Corporate financial crime
- Money laundering
- Savings and loan or stockbrokerage crime
- Mortgage loan fraud
- Coupon and rebate fraud
- Arson for profit

Source: National White Collar Crime Center.

Embezzlement and Employee Thefts

Embezzlement is usually thought of as a theft committed by an individual against his or her employer. Typically, this sort of white-collar crime involves the use of one's position in a business or organization to steal company funds or company property for personal use, gain, or profit. Perhaps when you think of embezzlement, you envision a corporate administrator or a bank executive running off to the Bahamas with the company's or bank's money. To be sure, people in fairly high positions have embezzled huge sums of money. For example, Dorothy Hutton worked as a stockbroker for Merrill Lynch, a respected brokerage house. Yet, in 1991, Dorothy Hutton managed to systematically cheat investors out of $1.4 million, which she used to finance Las Vegas and Lake Tahoe gambling trips.[10]

In 1992, the Phar-Mor discount drugstore corporation disclosed that two of its executives had allegedly embezzled more than half of the company's net worth—approximately $350 million.[11] In a similar corporate embezzlement action in 1994, the Clark Candy company was forced to close its factory in Pittsburgh after alleging corporate mismanagement by its CEO. Allegations were made that nearly $8 million in bank loans had disappeared—bankrupting the candy factory and cheating the banks of their funds.

In June 1995, United Way president William Aramony was sentenced to seven years in prison for his embezzlement of more than half a million dollars of United Way funds.[12] The inclusion of jail time in the sentencing of recent white-collar criminals suggests that society has begun to reexamine the status of such criminals.

Not all embezzlement or organizational theft, however, occurs at the top. Theft by employees may occur at all levels of a business or

Embezzlement The misappropriation or misapplication of money or property entrusted to one's care, custody, or control.

Michael Monus, former president of the drugstore chain Phar-Mor, Inc., talks to the media outside the federal courthouse in Cleveland, Ohio, after being sentenced to almost 20 years in prison for his May 1995 conviction on more than 100 fraud, embezzlement, and tax evasion charges.

company. In addition to money, thefts may include products sold or distributed by the organization and materials and equipment used by the organization. Truck drivers may cut deals with loading dock receiving clerks to steal cartons of products and split the profits. Retail clerks may steal garments by placing them under their own clothing or concealing them in a variety of other ways. Shoe managers may steal cash by juggling the books or falsifying records during storewide markdowns. Factory workers may steal an assortment of products or equipment by putting them out with the trash and returning later to recover the stolen items. In short, there are virtually no limits to the ways employees can embezzle or steal from their employers.

Industrial Espionage

Industrial espionage
Espionage work undertaken in corporate and industrial areas to keep up with or surpass competitors.

Another fairly common form of white-collar crime is **industrial espionage.** This type of white-collar criminal activity may include industrial spies, who infiltrate a company by posing as workers. It may also include computer experts who breach even sophisticated computer security systems to gain entry to corporate computer systems. Once in the company's computer, files and records can be looted, altered, or destroyed. Besides high-tech industries, other large companies are subject to industrial spying. Toy companies are in constant competition to produce toys that capture the largest shares of the industry market. Advance information about a forth-coming toy can give a competitor the opportunity to knock off a similar, competing toy. This has long been true for the garment industry as well, where designers carefully guard their new designs until they are publicly shown.

In industrial espionage cases, investigators should carefully consider the complainant/victim as a possible suspect. Complainant/victims of industrial espionage sometimes have ulterior motives for reporting or staging a crime. For example, a fashion designer may have his or her designs insured and may be seeking to defraud the insurance company. Investigators should inquire about the possibility of insured losses in all cases of industrial espionage.

Insider Trading

Recently, **insider trading** in stocks and bonds has become a serious criminal problem. Insider trading typically involves a corporate executive with direct knowledge or market-sensitive information about a tradable stock who uses this information for personal gain. The information may involve advance knowledge of a corporate takeover, information about financial problems faced by a corporation, or any other confidential information that might affect stock sales.

In recent years, federal courts have expanded the scope of insider trading to include people working in many kinds of financial institutions, such as banks and savings and loans, who abuse confidential information on pending corporate actions. The abuse may be employees' using the information for their own gain or sharing it with others, who use it for their gain. These sorts of practices violate federal trade codes.

The problem for law enforcement investigations involves distinguishing a good stock tip from insider information. Many stockbrokers call their clients with tips on stock that they have been watching and believe will soon go up in value or split. Such information, when accurate with any consistency, is what gives brokerage houses good reputations. However, a tip from a source who has confidential information about a company or its financial standing may be a criminal act.

Insider trading An employee's or manager's use of information gained in the course of his or her job and not generally available to the public to benefit from fluctuations in the stock market.

Bribery, Kickbacks, and Payoffs

Bribery, kickbacks, and payoffs may occur between individuals, businesses, and government agencies and representatives, in both the pri-

For 23 years, the fugitive American financier Robert Vesco lived in opulent self-imposed exile, first in Costa Rica, then in the Bahamas, and finally in Cuba. Vesco was charged in 1972 with stealing $224 million from Investors Overseas Services, Ltd., a Swiss-based mutual fund. Using his investors' money, he traipsed around in the tropics, eluding law enforcement officials by paying off politicians and government leaders. Hoping to foster goodwill with the United States, the Cuban government announced in June 1995 that Vesco would be extradited.[13] In August 1996, however, a court in Havana handed down a sentence of 13 years in prison for Vesco's role in a shady investment deal. Vesco had misled foreign investors by making them believe that a plant-based drug known as TX was being produced in Cuba, but it was not.[14]

vate and the public sectors. Typically, this sort of white-collar crime involves at least one person in a position of authority. It may be a government official, such as a police officer or administrator, a town council member, the mayor, or a member of the governor's staff. Or it may be a business official, such as a buyer for a department store, a contractor, or even a security guard.

While similar in nature, bribes, kickbacks, and payoffs are not identical. A **bribe** is the payment of cash, goods, or services to someone, in exchange for a special service, product, or behavior. Bribes are sometimes confused with extortion. The difference is in who initiates the arrangement. If someone in a position of authority or control demands money, goods, or services from another party in exchange for something, the crime is extortion. On the other hand, if one party asks another to use a position of authority or control to the first party's advantage, in exchange for money, goods, or services, it is a bribe.

Kickbacks involve an agreement between two or more parties that one of them will pay money in exchange for receiving a contract or job. For example, a contractor may arrange with a city manager to receive a large city building contract in exchange for paying the city manager a large sum of money. The city manager may in turn owe a kickback to others, such as city council members who agreed to give the contractor the contract. Or a home health care company may pay kickbacks to physicians in return for referrals to its services.

A **payoff** is the receiving of compensation or money from an individual in exchange for some favor. In some ways, it is similar to a bribe.

Bribe The payment of cash, goods, or services to someone in exchange for some special service, product, or behavior.

Kickback The payment back of a portion of the purchase price to the buyer or a public official by the seller to induce a purchase or to improperly influence future purchases.

Payoff The receiving of compensation or money from an individual in exchange for some favor.

Payoffs can occur in any industry. In the late 1990s, for example, there were allegations that the music industry was using payoffs to get selected videos on the air. These allegations were reminiscent of the **payola** scandals of the 1950s and 1960s, in which disc jockeys got payoffs to play certain records while excluding others.

Tax Evasion

Perhaps the most common form of white-collar criminality is tax cheating or tax evasion. Many average American citizens do it by underreporting their income, claiming false deductions, inflating the amount of charitable contributions, and so forth. In some cases, underreported income may simply be an error. In other cases, it is a deliberate attempt to avoid paying tax. An important element of tax fraud is *willfulness.* Tax evasion is enormously difficult to prove and successfully prosecute. Furthermore, it is difficult to discern between careless or unintentional underreporting of income and willful tax evasion. The IRS estimates that more than $120 billion in taxes goes uncollected each year because individuals underreport their income or fail to report all sources of income.[15]

Corporate Crime

Corporate crimes are crimes committed for the benefit of a legitimate business organization or enterprise. Corporate crime may take many forms, including price fixing, bribery and kickbacks (discussed previously), tax evasion or other tax violations, assorted frauds, environmental crimes or concealments, and a variety of other criminal activities.

Since the beginning of the nineteenth century, certain business practices have been defined in the law as illegal. These include restraint of trade, deceptive advertising practices, misrepresentations and frauds against banks, sales of phony stocks and securities, dangerous or faulty manufacturing of foods and drugs, and environmental pollution, as well as the unlawful use of patents and trademarks.[16]

During the latter portion of the nineteenth century, public concern grew concerning the development of corporate monopolies. These monopolies threatened to eliminate free trade and competition in the American economic market. In an effort to protect free enterprise in America, a number of federal regulations were enacted. Among the earliest was the Sherman Antitrust Act (1890). This legislation made it illegal to restrain trade and forbade the formation of monopolies. In addition, it made price fixing—collusion between large corporations to set artificially high, rather than competitive, prices—a felony, with a maximum corporate fine of $1 million. The legislation further provides for the levying of private treble-damage suits by victims of price fixing. In other words, a company injured by price fixing could receive three times the actual losses it incurred.

For the most part, like many aspects of white-collar criminality, corporate violations are policed by various regulatory agencies. For instance, the Federal Trade Commission, established in 1914, is responsible for examining many corporate trade practices. In all, there are more than 50 federal regulatory agencies with varying degrees of police power over corporate violations of law.

Regulatory agencies have a variety of sanctions that they can impose on errant corporations: fines, recalls, decrees and unilateral orders of compliance, injunctions, financial penalties, and even jail time for CEOs and other corporate leaders.

Investigating White-Collar Crime

As suggested in the preceding pages of this chapter, white-collar crimes encompass a wide variety of offenses. Also, white-collar crimes are generally very difficult to prevent—let alone detect. When they are detected, they may not always be reported to the police. Thus, some white-collar crimes, even when detected, are often handled unofficially by the corporate victim, or the employer of the white-collar criminal. In other cases, however, white-collar criminality is detected and investigated.

On the federal level, detection of white-collar crimes is left chiefly to administrative departments and regulatory agencies. In determining whether to pursue criminal or civil violations, these agencies typically consider the seriousness of the offense, the intentions of the offender, and the offender's prior record.

The Department of Justice receives any evidence of criminal activity, and if necessary, the FBI may be asked to conduct an investigation. Some federal agencies have their own investigative branches. For example, both the IRS and the U.S. Postal Service have investigative/enforcement branches. Federal investigations of many white-collar crimes are reactive, coming only after a complaint has been filed with the agency.

The investigation of white-collar crimes requires patience, imagination, the willingness to ask for help from other agencies, and increasingly sophisticated computer and technology skills.[17] Advances in technology have increased the need for investigators to improve their knowledge of computers and accounting. Many federal law enforcement agencies prefer or require 12 to 17 credits in accounting for entry-level agent positions.

At the state and local levels, the investigation of white-collar crimes is often messy, lengthy, and inefficient. Jurisdictional disputes may arise between the state attorney general and local prosecutors, and a lack of technical expertise among investigators may further hamper investigations.[18]

There is evidence that local investigators working in concert with local prosecutors can successfully pursue and prosecute white-collar criminals.[19] Unfortunately, many prosecutors do not regard white-collar criminal activity as a serious problem. Benson, Cullen, and Maakestad found that white-collar crimes were more likely to be prosecuted at the local level if substantial harm had resulted and no other agencies were willing to take action. Provisions of the RICO statute (Chapter 19) are sometimes used in prosecuting white-collar crimes.

Frequently, white-collar crime investigation and law enforcement is left in the hands of corporations themselves. Many large corporations spend millions of dollars each year on internal audits and investigations that uncover employees guilty of white-collar offenses.

Many law enforcement agencies across the nation have begun to recognize how widespread white-collar crime has become. In some jurisdictions, local, state, and federal law enforcement agencies and prosecutors' offices have teamed together to detect and apprehend white-collar criminals. By joining together, the agencies increase their personnel power, share resources, and find experts with the technological or other skills needed for a specific investigation.

Computer Crime

When computers first began emerging in the 1940s, most were complex, large (sometimes filling an entire room), and difficult, if not impossible, for the average person to operate. Computer engineers used complex languages such as Fortran to create operational programs. Even when computers were used in business settings, probably few corporate managers had the skills to use the cumbersome and complex machines themselves.

Today, with the advances in menu- and icon-driven user-friendly programs, the ease of computer use has made great leaps. The general population has grown more computer-literate over the past several years. That includes both honest, law-abiding citizens and dishonest, criminal ones. It is not surprising, then, as researchers frequently note, that with the explosion in the amount of computer equipment available to the public and the numbers of people who know how to use it, computer-related crimes are increasing.[20] Some people have begun referring to computer-related crime as *cybercrime* and to the people who perpetrate it as *cybercriminals*. Because of this increase in computer-related crimes, it is important for investigators to have a working understanding of common computer-crime terms. Figure 20–2 lists some of the more common computer-crime-related terms and their meanings.

For many types of computer crimes, all one needs is a personal computer (PC) equipped with a modem, the right software, and the desire to commit a crime. Regardless of security programs and passwords, designed to limit access via telephone, large corporate and governmental computer systems are still vulnerable to intrusion and tampering.

Figure 20-2 Common terms related to computer crimes.

Antivirus program	A program designed to detect a *computer virus* that has attached itself to a program on a disk or hard disk. Most antivirus programs contain a subprogram intended to *cure* the program by removing the virus.
Backdoor	A glitch in a computer system that permits someone entry without proper code or password. Sometimes such entry can be made by gaining entry to an unsecured segment of a program and opening a window between the unsecured and secured segments.
Browsing	The unauthorized examining of someone else's data after unlawful entry into another's computer files.
Computer virus	A program designed to attach itself to some other program and to attack and destroy the program. Sometimes, viruses are designed to *ride* one program into a system but to attack and destroy data or memory in the computer's main drive. Some viruses are simply obnoxious, rather than really destructive. In this case, they may cause a computer to automatically shut down, or to show disks as blank even when the data are still present.
Data diddling	A procedure sometimes used by insiders. Involves placing false information into a computer, as in placing a false name on a payroll or paying a fraudulent bill.
Fraud	As it relates to computer crimes, fraud represents any use of trickery, deception, or falsification involving computers to obtain money, services, or property.
Hacking	The illegal entry into a computer system, usually through trial and error, or systematically by using a random-digit program, a modem, and an automatic caller.
Impersonation	In computer-related crimes, the unauthorized use of someone's identity, code, or password. It is sometimes associated with calling card or voice-mail frauds as well.

Computers operated by the U.S. Department of Defense, various defense contractors, utility companies, universities, hospitals, research institutes, banks, and an assortment of Fortune 500 companies have all been invaded by hackers. Sometimes the hackers are teenagers who want to get in simply to show that they actually did it! Sometimes, however, the invasions have more sinister purposes. They may be part of some governmental or industrial espionage plan or simply a criminal means of obtaining services or money.

Masquerading	Like *impersonation,* an unauthorized use of someone else's identity, code, or password.
Picks	These are programs designed to break through or bypass security locks and safeguards intended to prevent unauthorized duplication of software.
Program piracy	The unauthorized copying of commercial programs.
Salami slice	The establishing of an unauthorized account in a company's or bank's computerized records. At regular intervals, small amounts, perhaps only fractions of a cent, are placed in the unauthorized account. Sometimes these transfers go unnoticed for long periods, because the amounts are covered by rounding figures. These pennies and fractions of pennies can eventually amount to many hundreds of thousands of dollars.
Superzapping	The use of repair, diagnosis, or maintenance programs to sidestep antitheft programs on a corporate computer system. Although some manipulation of the program may be necessary, once inside, the *superzapper* is soon able to control the system's operations.
Trapdoor	A phenomenon similar to a *backdoor.* Usually, however, trapdoors are intentionally left by a computer programmer so that he or she can gain entry, no matter what antitheft or security measures may be added later.
Trashing	The taking of information from discarded printouts, computer disks, or tapes. This can sometimes uncover important information and may occur in governmental or industrial espionage cases.
Trojan horse	A hidden program that may lay dormant until a particular program is called up or a particular time or date occurs in the computer clock and calendar. Then the Trojan horse program awakens. Sometimes Trojan horses contain computer viruses. Other times they run specific program tasks or data manipulations.

For example, a number of years ago, a computer operator for Wells Fargo, one of the leading bonded money movers in the United States, electronically transferred several million dollars into his own Swiss bank account. The transfer occurred on a Friday afternoon and was not discovered until Monday. The thief had nearly three full days to escape to Switzerland. He has never been apprehended.

Until recently, the criminal justice system has not addressed the criminal misuse of computers. In 1979, the U.S. Department of Justice

Corporate investigators work for companies other than investigative firms. Generally they are private investigators who work for large corporations and report to a corporate chain of command. They conduct internal or external investigations. External investigations can consist of preventing criminal schemes, thefts of company assets, and fraudulent deliveries of products by suppliers. Investigators may also investigate the business practices of a company's competitors or check out an executive candidate or a prospective overseas partner. In internal investigations, they may ensure that expense accounts are not abused and apprehend employees who are stealing.

Corporate investigators generally specialize in some aspect of business. Investigators who specialize in finance, for example, may be hired to investigate the financial standing of companies or individuals. They generally develop confidential financial profiles of individuals or companies who may be parties to large financial transactions. An asset search is a common type of procedure in such an investigation. Computers are an integral part of a corporate investigator's work. They allow investigators to affordably gather massive amounts of information in a short period of time. Investigators can access dozens of on-line databases containing financial records, motor-vehicle registrations, credit reports, association memberships, and other information.

Many corporate investigators enter from the military or law enforcement jobs and apply their experience as law enforcement officers, military police, or government agents. Most corporate investigators must have a bachelor's degree, preferably in a business-related field. Some corporate investigators have masters of business administration or law degrees, while others are certified public accountants. The hiring process may require a criminal history check, a personal interview, an ethics interview, a practical test, verification of education claims, and license review. Additionally, investigators hired by larger companies may receive formal training from their employers on business practices, management structure, and various finance-related topics.

defined **computer crime** as "any illegal act for which knowledge of computer technology is essential for its perpetration, investigation, or prosecution."[21] More recently, a National Institute of Justice report indicated that there are five distinct categories of computer crime:[22]

- Internal computer crimes
- Telecommunications crimes
- Computer manipulation crimes
- Support of criminal enterprises
- Hardware or software thefts

Internal Computer Crimes

This category of crime includes any alteration of an existing computer program that causes it to operate in a manner other than that for which it was designed. This includes changes in programs that result in sudden losses or deletion of data, lockouts of legitimate users, deterioration of memory sectors, and so forth. These sorts of problems are caused by what are generically called **computer viruses.** Computer viruses literally attach themselves to some other program when that program is placed in a contaminated computer. Usually, viruses are transferred from one computer to another when a user shares programs on disks or signs on to a computer bulletin board. If an infected computer is discovered soon after a virus has attached itself, it can be *cured* with any of a number of commercial *antivirus* programs. Unfortunately, if the virus is discovered too late, it can ruin the data and memory sectors of a computer's hard disk.

Computer virus   A computer program, usually hidden within another computer program, that inserts itself into programs and applications and destroys data or halts execution of programs.

Telecommunications Crimes

Telecommunications crimes involve illegal access to or use of computer systems over telephone lines. They may involve the use of a random-digit program to determine a valid access code for a computer system, or the misuse of toll-free numbers, calling-card numbers, and voice-mail systems. In addition, telecommunications crimes include the misuse of computer bulletin

FYI

Cryptography, the technology that scrambles messages and data so that eavesdroppers or snoopers cannot read them, was for many years the province of military and intelligence agencies. About 20 years ago, however, cryptography was combined with computer technology to provide encryption software. The public now had an inexpensive shield of privacy for electronic data. This capability has spawned a debate regarding the privacy of electronic data. On one side are private computer users, who maintain their right to protect and safeguard their computer files from intrusion. On the other side are law enforcement agencies, who maintain their right to protect society from abuses that might be hidden in encrypted data.

boards or the creation of underground bulletin boards to carry out criminal activities. These may include sale or solicitation of child pornography, drugs, or stolen property, or even murder for hire. During recent years, terrorists have even begun to use bulletin boards to send and receive messages and to provide members with information about law enforcement activities. For example, after the tragic bombing at the 1996 Summer Olympic Games, many Americans were shocked to learn that instructions for constructing a pipe bomb were readily available on a number of computer bulletin boards.

As technology advances, so do the ways criminals adapt to these innovations. An example of this can be seen in increases recently in the illegal use of stolen calling-card numbers and the theft of calls from commercial voice-mail services.

Most of us are familiar with voice mail. Typically, a recorded message gives the caller a menu of numbers to press on a Touch-Tone phone to reach an intended calling destination. In some cases, one may need the extension number of someone in particular to bypass or exit the voice-mail system. If the intended party is not available, the voice-mail recording tells the caller how to leave a message in a *voice mailbox*. These systems allow the owner of the voice mailbox to call in and, using a tone or password code, retrieve his or her voice-mail messages.

Criminals, however, have discovered ways to commit voice-mail fraud, usually against businesses equipped with toll-free numbers.[23] A caller leaves a personal, nonbusiness message for another person in a business's voice mailbox, using a toll-free number. Then, when the other person retrieves the message, he or she can return the personal call, again using the company's toll-free number. The loss will be reflected in the long-distance telephone bills the company receives at the end of the billing cycle. These bills can be staggering, especially when the fraud involves overseas calls.[24]

Variations on this fraud involve obtaining and using voice-mail code numbers. Frequently, voice-mail systems include a remote code that allows a member of the company to make a long-distance call through the system, in a manner similar to a calling card. If this code is learned by an unscrupulous person, it may be misused or even sold. Corporations have sustained losses exceeding $1000 from such frauds in just the first few hours following the report of a stolen corporate calling card or code number. In one case, the loss to the corporation exceeded $220,000 after only 13 hours of fraudulent use.[25]

Many state statutes define fraud as the *obtaining of money, property, or services by trick, deception, or false pretense*. Therefore, the unauthorized use of toll-free numbers, calling codes, and calling cards can be prosecuted. Since voice-mail fraud may cross several jurisdictions and may even involve international calls, state and local prosecutors must sometimes work with a federal prosecutor to process a case.

The unauthorized use of automated teller cards or credit cards with personal identification numbers (PINs) may also fall in the category of telecommunications crimes. Although various safeguards have been taken to reduce the unauthorized use of bank accounts and credit lines through automated teller machines (ATMs), it continues to be a serious criminal problem.

Computer Manipulation Crimes

These types of crimes involve changing data or creating records in a system for the specific purpose of advancing some other crime. For example, in 1994, the chief administrator of a large Pennsylvania hospital wrote false bills to the hospital and then authorized them to be paid. The bills were entered into the hospital's computer information system and went undetected for four years, until a routine audit uncovered them as fraudulent.

Superhacker Kevin Mitnick was arrested by the FBI in 1995 after a two-year cat-and-mouse game in which he breached computer networks nationwide to steal thousands of computer files and credit card numbers.

Support of Criminal Enterprises

Computer programs are an aid not only to legitimate businesses, but to illegal ones as well. For instance, criminals can use computer-based account ledgers to keep track of their drug business or the profits and expenses of an auto theft ring. Computers may even be used by criminals to maintain information or to simulate a planned crime.

With the additional technology of color laser printers and various graphics programs, computers can be used to create counterfeit concert, theater, and sporting event tickets, certificates of authenticity, stocks, and even money. As computer and printing technology expands, so do the possibilities of illegal behaviors.

Hardware and Software Thefts

The theft of computers, monitors, and other hardware devices seems rather uncomplicated. Theft of software, however, has a number of more subtle shades of ambiguity. Software piracy is a serious problem because it is relatively easy to accomplish. It involves the unauthorized duplication and distribution of software programs. Software companies lose millions of dollars a year to this type of crime. While some software companies have put safeguards, or locks, on their programs, intended to prevent unauthorized duplication, these efforts are not always successful. It is a simple task to obtain a **pick program** designed to bypass the security measures intended to prevent duplication. Adding to the problems related to this type of crime are the attitudes of many consumers of commercial programs. Many do not recognize the problems caused by making a duplicate program for a friend. Others do not believe it is a crime if no fee is charged for the duplicate program. Still others rationalize that the high cost of programs entitles them to make copies. Especially worrisome are illegal **hackers** who gain access to or enter others' computer systems to steal secrets or money.

> **Pick program** A computer program designed to bypass security measures against duplication of electronic files.

> **Hacker** A person who is proficient at using or programming a computer.

The lack of clear and unambiguous definitions of computer crimes is a problem for law enforcement agencies. Further, several different categories of computer crime may overlap, creating a potential problem in determining charges. Finally, computer illiteracy and computer fears in police departments hinder some investigations and prosecutions.

To resolve some of these problems, criminal investigators should become more familiar with computers, computer jargon, and methods of computer crime. Investigators should begin to develop contacts and resources they can turn to when faced with various computer crime problems. Clearly, computer crimes will become more prevalent in the future.

Investigating Computer Crime

When a report of a computer crime is received by a police agency, the department's report policy is initially followed. The investigator assigned to the case interviews the complainant to determine whether a crime has been committed. Once it is determined that a crime has been committed, and what the crime is, the usual investigative procedures continue to offer an investigator guidelines.

Other people or employees may provide information regarding the crime or possible suspects. Investigation of computer crimes is similar to investigation of other internal organization crimes. It typically begins at the lowest levels of employees and continues to the highest levels of administration. Investigators should remember that *any* of the people interviewed could be in collusion with one another to commit the crime. Caution should be used when trying to eliminate possible suspects.

A special audit or a repair order may have brought the crime to the attention of the authorities, as in traditional embezzlement cases. Borrowing from such cases, investigators should determine which employees might have had access to or reasons to be involved with computer operations related to the computer crime.

Because evidence in computer crime investigations may be electronic records, which are easily lost or destroyed in error, it is critical that investigators move cautiously. The general principles of investigation for computer crimes are similar to those for other crimes. However, if an investigator is not conversant with computer *lingo* or comfortable with and knowledgeable about computer hardware, he or she should seek the assistance of a computer specialist. In fact, investigators may have to become *cybercops* and carry laptop computers along with their badges and weapons.

After the initial investigation and report, officers should develop a plan for the continued investigation of the crime. Although the investigation may deviate from this plan along the way, guidelines will assist officers in their follow-up investigation. The plan should include the names and telephone numbers of computer consultants, if any are to be used in the investigation. It should indicate the nature of the crime, any persons suspected of being part of the crime, the type of hardware or software involved, any witnesses, the personnel needs of the investigation, and an estimate of how long the investigation may take. The nature of the crime should include whether it is a local, state, or federal law violation. The appropriate prosecuting attorney should be contacted and his or her aid solicited if needed.

Seizing a computer as evidence must be undertaken very carefully. Many computer criminals are capable of booby-trapping their computers. Touching a certain key on the keyboard, or even switching the computer on or off, could easily set the trap in motion and destroy evidence. Whenever an officer finds a computer involved in a crime and must seize it, he or she should follow certain guidelines.[27] These guidelines are presented in the Focus on Technology feature.

When investigating a computer crime in a large organization, it is sometimes necessary to develop an undercover operation. It is essential that the officers participating in this operation actually have the computer knowledge they need to remain under cover. Sending in officers who cannot blend with others in the organization is equivalent to sending them in wearing blue police uniforms. Furthermore, having those computer skills will permit the officers to recognize evidence when they find it.

The process of conducting interviews and interrogations in a computer case is essentially the same as in any other investigation. The rights of the suspect during searches or seizures of evidence are also the same.

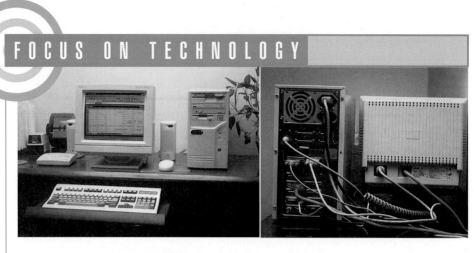

Seizing a DOS- or Windows-Based Computer

1. Never touch the keyboard. If the computer is off, leave it that way.

2. If the computer is on, without touching anything, photograph the entire area, including cable and connector hookups and what appears on the screen.

3. Carefully remove any disks in any of the disk drives and tag, secure, and record them as evidence.

4. If the computer is on, disconnect the plug from the wall to turn it off. Do not use the On/Off switch.

5. Place a virus-free bootable disk in each disk drive, replug the computer into the wall receptacle, and turn on the computer.

6. Using a utility program on the bootable disk, park the hard drive head in a neutral position so that data will not be damaged in transport. Do not use the machine's Park command. Remove the bootable disks.

7. Place a blank disk in each of the disk drives and seal each with evidence tape.

8. Turn off the computer and remove the plug from the wall. Remove all the connecting cables, taking care to label how they are connected to the computer.

9. Take into custody anything in the area related to the computer. This may include disks; peripheral equipment such as keyboard, a mouse, or an external CD-ROM drive; printouts; and discarded items in the wastebasket. Keep disks away from magnetic fields.

10. Thoroughly inspect the area around the screen and keyboard before moving the computer. Look for labels, tags, or notes containing number series or terms that may be passwords or cryptographic keywords. Collect all such items as evidence.

Among the major problems in investigating computer crimes is the need to determine if the crime was committed by someone within the organization or by someone outside it. It is important to determine exactly what the crime is. Given ambiguities in the classification of computer crimes, a victim within the organization may have to determine if it would better serve justice to handle the crime internally or through the criminal justice system.

Finally, a serious problem facing the investigation of computer crimes is the reluctance of some victims to prosecute a computer felon. Many large corporations, financial organizations, and even government agencies fail to report such crimes or fail to pursue prosecution of offenders. They often fear negative publicity. A large corporation may not want it known that a hacker was able to bypass its computer security strategies and gain entry. A financial organization, such as a bank, may be even more reluctant to have its depositors learn that someone broke through and *diddled* (altered or in some way manipulated) the depositor accounts.

SUMMARY BY LEARNING OBJECTIVES

Learning Objective 1

White-collar crimes are nonviolent crimes, committed by individuals and corporations, that are a breach of trust, confidence, or duty. The basic elements of a white-collar crime are intent, disguise of purpose, reliance on the victim's ignorance, voluntary assistance from the victim, and concealment.

Learning Objective 2

A variety of crimes can be considered white-collar crimes. Among these are embezzlement and employee thefts; industrial espionage; insider trading; bribery, kickbacks, and payoffs; tax evasion; and corporate crime.

Learning Objective 3

White-collar crimes are generally very difficult to prevent, let alone detect. Even when they are detected, they may not always be reported to law enforcement officials. Some are often handled unofficially by the corporate victim or the employer of the white-collar criminal. In other cases, white-collar crime is investigated by law enforcement agencies.

Learning Objective 4

Computer crime is a crime committed with or against computers. It can include internal computer crimes, telecommunications crimes, computer manipulation crimes, support of criminal enterprises, and hardware and software thefts.

Learning Objective 5

Because evidence in computer crimes can be easily lost or destroyed, it is critical that investigators move cautiously. The general principles of investigating computer crimes are similar to those for other crimes.

QUESTIONS FOR REVIEW

Learning Objective 1

1. Define *white-collar crime*.
2. Name the four categories into which Edelhertz divided white-collar crime.
3. What are Edelhertz's five basic elements of white-collar crime?

Learning Objective 2

4. What is meant by *embezzlement?*
5. How might an employee steal from his or her employer?
6. What is *industrial espionage?*
7. Why might a dress manufacturer commit industrial espionage?
8. How does *insider trading* operate?
9. Why is *insider trading* a crime?
10. What is the difference between *bribery* and *extortion?*
11. What is meant by the term *payoff?*
12. What are three examples of *corporate crime?*

Learning Objective 3

13. Why should local, state, and federal investigations of white-collar crimes be team efforts?
14. Why are many white-collar criminals never prosecuted?

Learning Objective 4

15. What is meant by *telecommunications crimes?*
16. What is meant by *computer manipulation crimes?*

Learning Objective 5

17. Why are computer crimes difficult to investigate?
18. Why are computer crimes increasing?

CRITICAL THINKING INVESTIGATIVE EXERCISES

1. Using the following checklist, consider how secure the computer system is in your college or university. You will need to contact the computer support center at your school to answer some of these questions. Once these questions have been answered, develop a plan for improving the security of the system.

   a. Is someone in charge of security for the system?

   b. Are there measures to protect all users' output?

   c. Are codes or passwords used to limit access to the system?

   d. Are there any provisions for securely destroying (for instance, shredding or incinerating) output that is not picked up by users?

   e. Have there been any unauthorized uses of the computer system in the past 10 years?

   f. Has the system ever contracted a virus?

   g. What safeguards have been taken against viruses?

   h. Are errors made by staff members at the computer support center categorized by type or frequency?

   i. What sanctions are imposed on staff when repeated errors are made?

2. Using newsmagazines or newspapers in your library, locate four different instances of white-collar crime (not four stories about the same crime). After reading these stories, answer the following questions about each:

   a. What type of white-collar crime is discussed?

   b. How was the crime detected?

   c. What agencies were involved in the investigation?

   d. What sanctions, if any, were discussed or imposed?

INVESTIGATIVE SKILL BUILDERS

Using Reasoning

You are a criminal investigator in a medium-sized rural community. One of the larger chain department stores in your town has contacted you about employee pilferage. You meet with the store's security manager, John Gilligan, who explains the problem.

Mr. Gilligan tells you that, in the past week, he has found high-cost price tags in the garbage and a number of low-cost items without tags on the shelf. He reasons that someone has been switching tags and buying expensive items for low prices. He believes that it is an employee, since he found the tags in the back-room garbage bin. He has totaled the tags he found, and they amount to $7,857.

1. Is Mr. Gilligan correct in reasoning that the theft is being undertaken by an employee or employees?

2. How might you determine which employee or employees are involved?

3. How might the thieves make a monetary profit on this theft?

Honesty/Integrity

You are filling out your income tax forms for the year. You remember that you attended the Academy of Criminal Justice Sciences national meeting. Since this meeting relates to your position as chief of police in a medium-sized department, expenses for it are tax-deductible. You have an envelope with all your receipts for airfare, hotel, conference registration, and food. The receipts total $845. You also have a statement from your department indicating it reimbursed you $600 for this trip. Should you deduct the full amount of receipted expenses? Explain your answer.

ENDNOTES

1. Edwin Sutherland, *White Collar Crime,* Dryden Press, New York, 1949, p. 2.

2. Bureau of Justice Statistics, *Federal Offenses and Offenders: White Collar Crime, a Special Report,* Department of Justice, Washington, 1987, p. 1.

3. Daniel Pedersen, William Underhill, Marc Levenson, Tony Clifton, Melissa Roberts, Steven Strasser, and Peter McKillop, "Busted!" *Newsweek,* March 13, 1995, pp. 37–47.

4. Larry J. Siegel, *Criminology,* 5th ed., West Publishing, Minneapolis/St. Paul, 1995.

5. Marshal Clinard and Richard Quinney, *Criminal Behavior Systems: A Typology,* Holt, Rinehart and Winston, New York, 1973, p. 117.

6. Herbert Edelhertz, *The Nature, Impact and Prosecution of White Collar Crime,* National Institute of Law Enforcement and Criminal Justice, Washington, 1970.

7. Herbert Edelhertz et al., *The Investigation of White Collar Crime: A Manual for Law Enforcement Agencies,* National Institute of Justice, Washington, 1977, pp. 21–25.

8. O. Johnston, "Government Accounting Office Says S&L Cost Could Rise to $500 Billion," *Los Angeles Times,* April 7, 1990, pp. 1, 28. See also Henry H. Pontell and Kitty Calavita, "Bilking Bankers and Bad Debts: White-Collar Crime and the Savings and Loan Crisis." In Kip Schlegel and David Weisburd (eds.), *White-Collar Crime Reconsidered,* Northeastern University Press, Boston, 1994.

9. General Accounting Office, *Thrift Failures: Costly Failures Resulted From Regulatory Violations and Unsafe Practices,* Report to Congress, General Accounting Office, T-AFMD-89-4, June 1989.

10. Michael Siconolfi and Robert Johnson, "Broker Grandmother Accused of Losing Clients' Cash at Baccarat," *Wall Street Journal,* August 29, 1991, pp. C1, C11.

11. Frank E. Hagan, *Introduction to Criminology,* 3d ed., Nelson-Hall, Chicago, 1994.

12. Anne Gearan, "Former United Way President Gets Seven Year Sentence," *The Indiana Gazette,* June 23, 1995, p. 7.

13. Howard Chua-Eoan, "The Predator's Fall," *Time,* Vol. 145, No. 25, 1995, pp. 36–38.

14. Pascal Fletcher, "Cuban Court Gives Vesco 13 Years," *USA Today,* August 27, 1996, p. 5A.

15. Internal Revenue Service, *Tax Reporting Data, 1992,* Internal Revenue Service, Washington, 1994. See also Alan Murray, "IRS in Losing Battle Against Tax Evaders Despite Its New Gear," *Wall Street Journal,* April 10, 1984, p. 1.

16. Hagan, op. cit.

17. Arthur G. Sharp, "White-Collar Crime: More Resources Needed to Combat Growing Trend," *Law and Order,* Vol. 42, No. 7, 1994, pp. 91–96.

18. Ibid.

19. Michael Benson, Francis Cullen, and William Maakestad, "Local Prosecutors and Corporate Crime," *Crime and Delinquency,* Vol. 36, 1990, pp. 356–72.

20. Jay S. Albanese, "Tomorrow's Thieves," *The Futurist,* September/October 1988, p. 26; Walt W. Manning and Gary H. White, "Data Diddling, Salami Slicing, Trojan Horses . . . Can Your Agency Handle Computer Crimes?" *The Police Chief,* April 1990, pp. 46–49; Clyde M. Stites, "PCs: Personal Computers, or Partners in Crime?" *Law and Order,* September 1991, pp. 161–65.

21. D. B. Parker, *Fighting Computer Crime,* Scribner, New York, 1983, p. 23.

22. C. H. Conley and J. T. McEwen, "Computer Crime," *NIJ Reports,* January/February 1990, Vol. 218, pp. 2–7.

23. Ronald R. Thrasher, "Voice Mail Fraud," *The FBI Law Enforcement Bulletin,* Vol. 63, No. 7, 1994, pp. 1–4.

24. Ibid.

25. Ibid.

26. Bob Baum, "Thieves Cash in With Stolen Card," *The Indiana Gazette,* February 11, 1995, p. 22.

27. Stites, op. cit. A similar but more extensive listing of activities to do when securing computer equipment appears as Appendix A in Michael G. Noblett's article, "Computer Analysis and Response Team (CART): The Microcomputer as Evidence," *Crime Laboratory Digest,* Vol. 19, No. 1, 1992, pp. 10–15.

CHAPTER 21

Narcotics and Dangerous Drugs

CHAPTER OBJECTIVES

After completing this chapter, you will be able to:

1. Offer definitions of narcotics and dangerous drugs.

2. Identify and describe some common types of dangerous drugs.

3. List and discuss other dangerous drugs.

4. Discuss legal aspects of narcotics and dangerous drugs.

5. Specify some procedures related to illicit drug investigations.

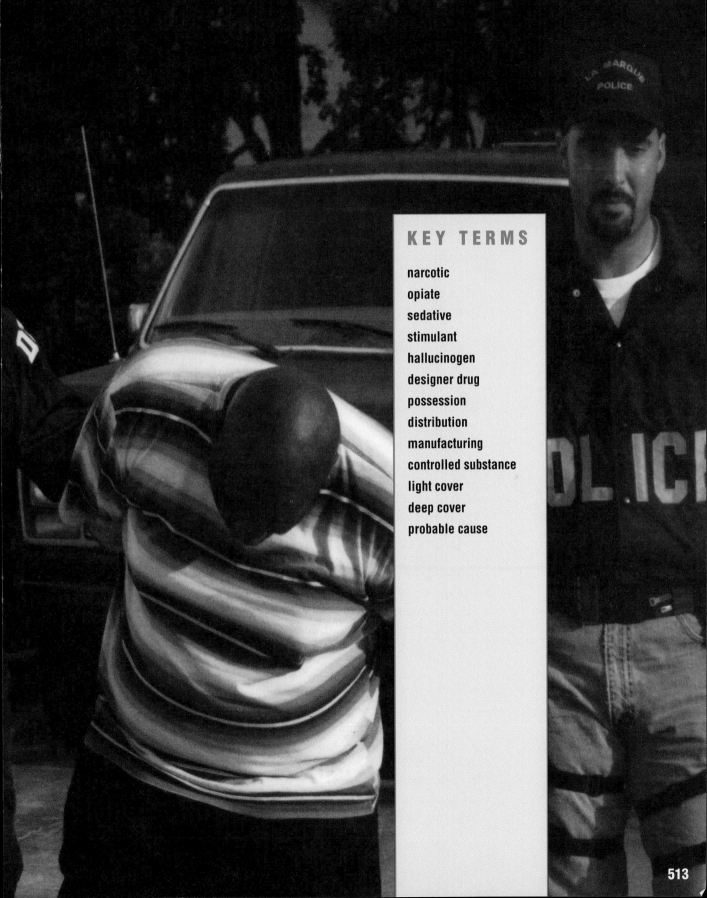

KEY TERMS

narcotic
opiate
sedative
stimulant
hallucinogen
designer drug
possession
distribution
manufacturing
controlled substance
light cover
deep cover
probable cause

Narcotics

A t one time, the term *narcotic* referred to a variety of substances inducing altered states of consciousness and derived from distillations of the opium poppy plant *(Papavar somniferum).* In today's common and inconsistent parlance, the term **narcotic** is used for any drug that produces a stupor, insensibility, or sleep.[1] As a consequence, narcotics could include substances ranging from alcohol to heroin to crack cocaine.

In legal matters, *narcotic* may designate any drug that is allegedly dangerous, is heavily abused, or has a high potential for abuse.[2] Therefore, substances such as marijuana, cocaine, PCP, amphetamines, and barbiturates have all been considered, along with heroin and other opium derivatives, in narcotics regulations.

Properly defined, narcotics include *only* the natural derivatives of *Papavar somniferum,* having both analgesic and sedative properties, and any synthetic derivatives or compounds of similar pharmacological structure and action.[3] The actual range of drugs accurately labeled *narcotics* can be limited to two specific categories:

1. *Natural narcotics* (compounds derived directly from *Papavar somniferum*): opium, morphine, and heroin.

2. *Synthetic narcotics* (compounds possessing similar pharmacological structures and properties): Dilaudid, Percodan, codeine, methadone, Demerol, Darvon, Talwin.

Taken together as a group, natural and synthetic narcotics differ widely in their uses, effects, and addiction potential. Any substance that is derived directly or indirectly from opium is classified as an **opiate.** Addiction to opiates is an actual physical dependence. It is augmented by the development of a tolerance requiring larger and larger amounts of the substance to avoid withdrawal symptoms. Manufacturers and distributors of medicinal opiates are stringently controlled by the federal government through laws designed to keep these products available only for legitimate medical use. Those who distribute these drugs are registered and monitored by federal authorities and must comply with specific record-keeping and drug-security requirements.

Narcotic Drug Abuse

The abuse of narcotic drugs dates back to ancient times. Their use today is still a serious problem. The appeal of morphinelike drugs (heroin, codeine, Percodan, Hycodan, Dilaudid, and so on) lies in their ability to reduce sensitivity to both psychological and physical stimuli and to produce a state of euphoria. These drugs dull fear, tension, and anxiety. A person under the influence of morphinelike narcotics is usually lethar-

Narcotic Any drug that produces a stupor, insensibility, or sleep.

Opiate Any of the narcotic drugs produced from the opium poppy.

gic and indifferent to his or her environment and personal circumstances. Chronic use leads to both physical and psychological dependence. Tolerance develops, and ever-increasing doses are needed to achieve the desired effect. As the need for the drug increases, the addict's activities become increasingly drug-centered. Drug-suppressed desire for food and growing cravings for the drugs frequently result in protein deficiencies in chronic narcotic abusers.

When deprived of morphine or heroin, the addict usually experiences the first withdrawal symptoms shortly before the time of the next scheduled dose, or *fix*. Complaints of cramping and vomiting and demands for the drug increase in intensity and peak 36–72 hours after the last fix. Less severe symptoms, such as watery eyes, runny nose, yawning, and perspiration, tend to appear about 8–12 hours after the last dose. Thereafter, the addict may fall into a restless sleep.

The longer the addicted person is without drugs, the greater and more violent his or her withdrawal becomes. Restlessness becomes irritability and insomnia. Individuals may experience gooseflesh, chills, tremors, and violent muscular contractions. These withdrawal symptoms typically reach their peak at 48–72 hours after the last fix. The addict becomes weak, depressed, nauseated, and cramped. Vomiting, stomach cramps, and diarrhea are common. Heart rate and blood pressure become elevated. Chills alternating with flushes and excessive sweating are also common symptoms at this point of withdrawal. Pain in the bones and muscles of the back and extremities occurs, as do muscle spasms and kicking movements—perhaps the source of the expression "kicking the habit." The withdrawal discomfort at this point becomes so severe that many addicts become suicidal. The withdrawal runs its course, and most residual symptoms disappear in about 7–10 days. How long it will be before physiological and psychological equilibrium returns is unpredictable. Fear of withdrawal symptoms drives addicts to lie, cheat, steal, and turn to prostitution to obtain money to purchase their next dose of drugs. Figure 21–1 shows the effects of some illegal drugs.

Categories of Drugs

Narcotics and various other controlled substances vary in their effects on people. For the most part, drugs can be divided into four categories based on their manifest effects.

Narcotics   Narcotics are drugs with a depressant effect on the central nervous system. Euphoria and a general feeling of warmth and well-being are frequently associated with their use. Narcotics are used to relieve pain and induce sleep. Prolonged use of narcotics results in both

Figure 21–1 Some effects of illegal drugs.

| Drug Type | Short-Term Effects | | Duration of Acute Effects | DEA View of Risk of Dependence |
	Desired	Other		
Heroin	• Euphoria • Pain reduction	• Respiratory depression • Nausea • Drowsiness	• 3 to 6 hours	• Physical: high • Psychological: high
Cocaine	• Excitement • Euphoria • Increased alertness, wakefulness	• Increased blood pressure • Increased respiratory rate • Nausea • Cold sweats • Twitching • Headache	• 1 to 2 hours	• Physical: possible • Psychological: high
Crack cocaine.	• Same as cocaine • More rapid high than cocaine	• Same as cocaine	• About 5 minutes	• Same as cocaine
Marijuana	• Euphoria • Relaxation	• Accelerated heartbeat • Impairment of perception, judgment, fine motor skills, and memory	• 2 to 4 hours	• Physical: unknown • Psychological: moderate
Amphetamines	• Euphoria • Excitement • Increased alertness, wakefulness	• Increased blood pressure • Increased pulse rate • Insomnia • Loss of appetite	• 2 to 4 hours	• Physical: possible • Psychological: high
LSD	• Illusions and hallucinations • Excitement • Euphoria	• Poor perception of time and distance • Acute anxiety, restlessness, sleeplessness • Sometimes depression	• 8 to 12 hours	• Physical: none • Psychological: unknown

Sources: NIDA, "Heroin," *NIDA capsules,* August 1986; DEA, *Drugs of abuse,* 1989; G.R. Gay, "Clinical management of acute and chronic cocaine poisoning: Concepts, components and configuration," *Annals of emergency medicine,* (1982) 11(10):562–572 as cited in NIDA, Dale D. Chitwood, "Patterns and consequences of cocaine use," in *Cocaine use in America: Epidemiologic and clinical perspectives,* Nicholas J. Kozel and Edgar H. Adams, eds., NIDA research monograph 61, 1985; NIDA, James A. Inciardi, "Crack-cocaine in Miami," in *The epidemiology of cocaine use and abuse,* Susan Schober and Charles Schade, eds., NIDA research monograph 110, 1991; and NIDA, "Marijuana," *NIDA capsules,* August 1986.

psychological and physiological dependence. Also, tolerance to dose level occurs over prolonged use, requiring the user to increase dosage to obtain the same effects.

Sedatives   **Sedatives** are used to allay irritation or nervousness. Sedatives can create a lethargic and sleepy feeling in the user, but may also produce a general feeling of calm and well-being. When sedatives are used over long periods, the user may develop a tolerance and require larger doses to produce the same sense of relaxation. Both psychological and physiological dependence may result from prolonged use.

Stimulants   **Stimulants** are drugs or other substances that increase the activity of tissues (such as the central nervous system), thereby affecting the physiological processes of the body. Stimulants may remove inhibitions and produce a feeling of zest and excitement. Some stimulants produce a euphoric sense of well-being and energy. Like sedatives and narcotics, when used repeatedly over time, stimulants may produce both psychological and physiological dependence.

Hallucinogens   **Hallucinogens** are drugs or substances capable of altering perceptions and producing hallucinations. Hallucinogens may produce the perception of heightened senses and visualization of vivid colors. They may also produce exaggerated feelings of fear or terror, or visions of monsters or terrifying imagined situations. Repeated or extensive use of hallucinogens may produce psychological dependence. Additionally, hallucinogens have been known to produce *flashbacks,* or hallucinogenic images and states of mind, even months after use has ended.

Sedative   A drug used to allay irritation or nervousness; creates a lethargy in the user, but may also produce a general feeling of calm and well-being.

Stimulant   A drug with a stimulating effect on the central nervous system, causing wakefulness and alertness while masking symptoms of fatigue.

Hallucinogen   A drug causing changes in sensory perception to create mind-altering hallucinations and loss of an accurate sense of time and space.

Types of Narcotics

Most people take drugs for the effects they produce. As we saw earlier, the effects may be mood changes, excitement, sedation, relaxation, pleasure, stimulation, or pain reduction. Most illegal drugs are consumed for their mind-altering effects.

Heroin

Heroin is an odorless crystalline white powder. In the United States, heroin is frequently sold in glassine packets, sometimes called *decks,* or in capsules, referred to as *caps.* The darker the heroin's color, the more impurities it contains. Heroin is the chief opiate

FYI

Although opium is no longer widely abused in the United States, its by-products are. Morphine is made from opium, and heroin is made from morphine. The three drugs have similar effects. However, heroin is the strongest, and opium is the least powerful.

abused in the United States and many other countries. Generally, heroin is injected.

Heroin acts as a depressant to the spinal cord. Tolerance for this drug builds up faster than for any other opiate. Consequently, the danger of drug dependency is considerably greater. Heroin has come to be considered by many as the most dangerous and enslaving drug on the drug scene.

By the time heroin reaches its market of users on the street, it has usually been diluted, or *cut* or *stepped on,* considerably. Heroin reaching the United States ranges from 20 to 80 percent pure. Deaths from heroin overdoses are not uncommon. Sometimes death occurs because the user is unaware that the drug is more pure and potent than on previous occasions. Investigators should also be aware that addicts may be murdered, for a variety of reasons, by being given a hot shot of heroin, or a nearly pure concentration of heroin. In some situations, addicts die because of an allergic or toxic reaction to materials used by the dealer to dilute the heroin. Powdered milk, sugar, or quinine are commonly used to cut heroin. However, talcum powder has been used on occasion, with lethal results. Talcum powder is inert and cannot be absorbed by the human body. When injected intravenously with heroin, it travels the arterial system until it eventually forms blockages. Depending on their location, these blockages may cause loss of limbs or death.

Heroin remains a serious narcotic addiction in the United States. Studies have estimated that as many as 750,000 Americans are addicted to this drug.[4] An even larger number of people may be controlled, occasional users not actually addicted to heroin.[5] The 1980s were marked by a surge in the use by addicts of crack cocaine. The 1990s, however, showed an alarming resurgence in heroin's popularity among addicted Americans.

Heroin is not well absorbed if taken orally. Users, therefore, usually administer the drug by intravenous injection. In the United States, some addicts combine cocaine with heroin, snorting, injecting, or even smoking the combination. In other countries, notably England, "chasing the dragon," or smoking the fumes of heroin oil, has been popular since the 1970s.[6]

After processing, heroin is packaged and sold by the kilo, approximately 2.2 pounds. The initial purchaser of pure heroin expects to cut it at least three times before further sale. In other words, for every kilo purchased, the principal, or wholesale, distributor will dilute the heroin to 6.6 pounds. Principal distributors may pay $25,000, $30,000, or more for a

STATISTICS

According to the Drug Enforcement Agency (DEA), South American (primarily Colombian) heroin accounted for 62 percent of heroin seized in the United States in 1995. This was a dramatic shift. In 1989, most heroin (96 percent) seized in the United States originated in Southeast or Southwest Asia. In 1993, when the DEA developed procedures to identify South American heroin, South American heroin accounted for just 15 percent of seizures.

single kilo of nearly pure heroin. The price variation occurs because of market fluctuations. These are caused by pressure brought by federal drug enforcement efforts and varying levels of cooperation with the governments of countries where poppies are grown or heroin laboratories are hidden.

Wholesale distributors sell the cut heroin to middle-level traffickers, usually by the pound, at prices ranging from about $10,000 to $20,000 a pound. This middle-level trafficker will also dilute the heroin and will sell the product to dealers by the ounce, at prices ranging from about $500 to $1000. The price variation at this stage is generally related to how adulterated the heroin has already become.

Dealers again cut the heroin and put it into smaller bags for street sale. Decks and caps are prevalent methods of packaging for street sales. These packages may be sold by street dealers, who work for the dealer or work for themselves after purchasing the packages from the dealer. By the time the addict purchases the heroin from the street dealer, it has been reduced to about 4–10 percent of its original potency. The profit potential along most of heroin's distribution process is enormous. The original kilo of heroin, with all the adulterations at each level, may have been stepped on 20 or 30 times. This has produced a total of 44–66 pounds of heroin at the street level. At a price of about $50 a gram, the total return on the original kilo soars to more than $1.5 million dollars!

Criminal investigators should be aware that many heroin addicts are predatory criminals. During the sequence of buying and selling at the street level, drug peddlers may be hijacked, robbed, or ripped off. This may result in violence, additional crimes, and, in some cases, homicides. Addicts also involve themselves in a variety of other criminal activities to obtain money to maintain their habit and avoid the onslaught of withdrawal.

Because heroin is chiefly injected intravenously, needle marks or tracks may be observed on an addict's body. Investigators should be aware that these tracks may be observed in a variety of places on the body, but are most often in places that are easy to reach. Veins in the elbow folds, along the forearms, on the backs of the hands, and on the legs are the most common. However, repeated injection of a vein results in its eventual collapse, further resulting in the scarring referred to as *tracks*.

On some addicts who attempt to conceal their addiction, injection marks may be found between the toes or under the tongue. Tracks indicate previous use of the drugs. They do not usually indicate recent use. Recent use can some-

The scarring patterns that result from collapsed veins on a heroin user are commonly called tracks.

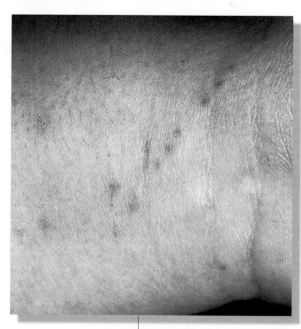

times be detected by finding a series of small scabs, which usually last about a week or ten days. These scabs are due to small localized infections brought about by unsterilized injection outfits, generally unclean conditions when injecting the heroin, and various impurities in the drug itself.

Cocaine

Cocaine, made from the coca plant, is a white, odorless, crystalline powder resembling snow, Epsom salts, or camphor. As an analgesic, it has been largely supplanted by synthetic drugs. Its medical applications are now mainly restricted to operations of the ear, eye, nose, and throat. Its medical use was popular because it constricted the blood vessels and limited bleeding in anesthetized areas.

Illicit cocaine is typically adulterated to about half its total volume with various sugars and local anesthetics. Amphetamines and other drugs with stimulant properties may also be used. As with heroin, the cost of the drug and the potential for enormous profits increase the likelihood of cutting the drug at various levels along the distribution process. The major source of cocaine in the United States is South America.

The effects of cocaine include stimulation of the central nervous system and increases in heart rate, blood pressure, and body temperature. Because of its central nervous system effects, the drug is habit-forming. The pleasure effects of cocaine are mixed with mild hallucinations. A commonly reported hallucination is that of insects crawling on the skin. Cocaine remains a serious danger because it can produce paranoia and anxiety, and an overdose can result in death.

Cocaine has a fairly fast effect. When inhaled through the nose, it goes to the back of the nasal cavity, combines with mucus, and drips down the back of the throat. The nose and upper gum become numb and then the high begins. If the drug is mainlined, or taken intravenously, all of the infections associated with heroin use can occur, including abscesses and hepatitis. Some heroin addicts combine heroin and cocaine in one injection. This has been called a *speedball*. The effects of the two drugs are directly opposite, and the body is seriously abused by their combined use—sometimes to the point of death.

Freebasing Cocaine   Freebasing cocaine involves separating the base of cocaine from its hydrochloride powder. Cocaine is dissolved in a solution of distilled water and calcium carbonate or lactose. The mixture is stirred or shaken to completely dissolve the cocaine. Next, several drops of ether are added to the solution, and the mixture is shaken again. The cocaine is attracted to the ether, while the other additives and impurities are attracted to the calcium carbonate or lactose solution.

The newly formed ether-cocaine solution separates from the larger solution in a manner similar to oil separating from water. The ether-cocaine solution rises to the surface. By using an eyedropper, one can suction off the ether-cocaine solution and place it in a container to allow the moisture and ether to evaporate. The resultant crystals will be smoked and will produce a more potent high, since the concentration of base cocaine is much greater now that it has been freebased. The evaporation process may occur naturally or may be accelerated by adding heat. However, since ether is an extremely flammable and volatile chemical, heating the ether-cocaine solution can be dangerous.

Crack Cocaine   Crack cocaine, contrary to popular belief, is neither *freebase cocaine* nor *purified cocaine.* As Inciardi and McElrath point out, some of the confusion about what crack cocaine is results from the different ways the word *freebase* is used.[7] As a noun, *freebase* refers to a drug, a cocaine product converted to the base state from cocaine hydrochloride after adulterants have been chemically removed. Crack cocaine, however, is converted to the base state without removing the adulterants. As a verb of action, *freebase* means to inhale vapors of cocaine base, of which crack is but one form. Finally, crack cocaine is anything but pure. When crack is processed, the baking soda used in the process remains as a salt and actually reduces the overall purity of the cocaine product. Crack gets its name, in fact, from the cracking sound that the residue of baking soda often makes when heated.

Crack cocaine can easily be produced in a dealer's kitchen. The process involves mixing cocaine, water, and baking powder. This solution is slowly heated until all the moisture has evaporated. The remaining *cookie* of combined cocaine and baking powder is then broken into small

FYI

Coca plants are harvested from two to six times each year. The leaves are soaked with solutions to chemically extract coca paste. This paste, or crude cocaine, is then shipped to illegal laboratories in various countries, including the United States, for processing into cocaine.

pieces, which are placed in small containers or wrapped in plastic wrap and sold for as little as $5 or $10. These bits, or *rocks,* as they are commonly called, are placed into pipes and ignited, and the cocaine fumes are inhaled. Crack cocaine is substantially less expensive than powdered cocaine, creating a much wider, and unfortunately more youthful, market for the drug.

Since crack cocaine, like freebase cocaine, is a concentrate of the base cocaine, it is considerably more potent than powdered cocaine. The DEA estimates that 75 percent of those who try crack cocaine will become addicted with as few as three uses. Moreover, they estimate that as many as half of all people who try crack may become addicted after only a single use.[8] Crack cocaine has maintained its popularity with users because it produces a high similar to but much more intense than that of powdered cocaine.[9]

Morphine

Morphine is the principal alkaloid of opium. It was discovered in 1806 by F. W. A. Serturner. Morphine is converted from crude opium by a fairly simple process of boiling and filtering. Opium is placed in water and heated until it breaks down into a liquid. Next, chemicals are added to the solution to filter out impurities. This results in a chemical separation of the morphine base from the original opium-and-water solution. Because morphine is a condensed extract of opium, it is significantly more potent. It is usually estimated to be three times stronger than opium.

In its natural state, morphine is not readily soluble in water. Therefore, it is treated with sulfuric acid. The resultant, morphine sulfate, is quite soluble and is the most common form used. Morphine is white and comes in three main forms: powder, cubes, and ⅛- and ½-grain tablets. The texture is very light, similar to that of chalk dust. Peddlers adulterate the powder with milk sugar, cutting the potency considerably. The drug is taken orally or intravenously. Most addicts prefer intravenous injections because the effects are more immediate and pronounced. The improvised hypodermic *outfit* is the same as that used to inject heroin.

Codeine

The alkaloid codeine can be found in crude opium in concentrations from 0.7 percent to about 2.5 percent. It was identified in 1832 when discovered as an impurity in a batch of morphine. Codeine is commonly found in a variety of legally controlled medical preparations sold in the United States. It is the least addictive of the opium derivatives and very similar in appearance to morphine (a white crystalline powder). The narcotic is used illicitly in the same manner as morphine and heroin. Since codeine is commonly found in combination with aspirin, Tylenol, and various cough syrups, it is occasionally used by addicts deprived of their regular source of heroin. Its primary effects include dulled perception, straying attention, and a general lack of awareness of surroundings. When withdrawal symptoms do occur, they are usually less severe than from more potent drugs, such as heroin or morphine. Abusers generally obtain codeine by stealing it from drugstores or feigning illness to acquire prescriptions for medications that contain codeine.

Percodan

Percodan (oxycodone, dihydrohydroxycodeinone) is extremely important in medicine as an analgesic (painkiller). The addictive potential of dihydrohydroxycodeinone, the narcotic ingredient of Percodan, is somewhere between morphine and codeine, but the drug is much closer to morphine in its effects. Percodan and codeine are taken orally by some addicts when heroin is not available. Addicts may also dissolve Percodan tablets in water, filter out the insoluble binders, and inject the active drug intravenously.

Methadone

In response to a shortage of morphine during World War II, German chemists synthesized methadone. Although chemically unlike morphine or heroin, it produces many of the same effects. It can be administered orally or by injection. While methadone does not produce the euphoric high sought by heroin users, a similar tolerance and dependency does occur. Withdrawal symptoms, however, develop more slowly and are less severe than in withdrawal from morphine or heroine. But, methadone withdrawal symptoms may be more prolonged. Methadone was introduced in the United States in 1947 as an analgesic. Commercially, it has been distributed under such names as Dolophine Hydrochloride, Amidone, and Methadone.

Since the 1960s, methadone has been widely used in the detoxification of heroin addicts and in methadone maintenance programs. Methadone treatment maintains an addict's physical and mental dependency on a drug, but is intended to keep the user away from the criminal behavior necessary to support a heroin habit. Unfortunately, many heroin addicts who miss the euphoric sensation revert to heroin abuse.

Other Dangerous Drugs

To be truly prepared to undertake the duties of a criminal investigator, it is important to understand certain dangerous drugs other than narcotics. Identifying drug offenders requires a broad understanding of a number of the most common drugs of abuse in America.

Stimulants

Drugs classified as stimulants directly stimulate the central nervous system, producing excitation, a feeling of alertness, and sometimes a temporary rise in blood pressure and respiration. A typical abuse cycle may begin with the lawful use of a stimulant for some legitimate reason. After using the drug for a while, the individual begins to depend on its effects. In addition to cocaine, commonly abused stimulants include nicotine, caffeine, amphetamines, phenmetrazine, and methylphenidate.

Tolerance to stimulants occurs quickly, and abusers may require larger doses to obtain comparable results. When taking large doses of stimulants, the abuser may need to take depressants (discussed later) to get to sleep. This cycle of uppers and downers puts enormous stress on the body. Symptoms of chronic stimulant abuse include grinding the teeth, touching or picking at the face, rapid speech patterns, confusion, and—in some cases—paranoia. As tolerance increases, the possibility of a toxic overdose increases.

Depressants (Sedatives and Hypnotics)

The barbiturates, made from barbituric acid, constitute the largest group of sedatives. Their effects are opposite from those of stimulants. They are the most frequently prescribed drugs to induce sleep and to reduce daytime tension and anxiety. They are known as hypnotics and are commonly referred to as sleeping pills. Because of their sedative effect, they are also called *downers* by drug users. People can legally buy and use these drugs only with a doctor's prescription. However, abusers sometimes feign sleep problems to obtain prescriptions. This group of drugs depresses the central nervous system and relieves anxiety. Barbiturates are valuable when used properly but extremely dangerous when abused.

Repeated use of barbiturates can be addicting. Signs of physical dependence appear with doses well above therapeutic levels. Withdrawal from barbiturates is especially dangerous and is characterized by convulsions and delirium. Chronic use produces slurred speech, staggering, loss of balance, and irritability. Overdoses of barbiturates, particularly in conjunction with alcohol, result in unconsciousness and death.

Barbiturates are often diverted from legitimate channels. Popular brand-name depressants bear trademarks or other identifying symbols. Their trade names are usually recognizable by the ending *al,* for instance, Seconal, Nembutal, Amytal, and Luminal. Individual barbiturates are distinguished from one another by the colors of the gelatin capsules in which they are packed. Frequently, barbiturates are nicknamed on the streets by their capsule colors. Seconal capsules, for example, are sometimes referred to as *reds* because of their red color, Nembutal capsules are sometimes called *yellows,* and so forth.

Glutethimide (Doriden) Glutethimide, when introduced in 1954, was incorrectly believed to be a nonaddictive barbiturate substitute. The sedative effects of this drug begin approximately 30 minutes after its ingestion. Its effects, however, may last as long as 8 hours. Since the effects of the drug can last so long, it is difficult to treat or reverse an overdose. Recently, glutethimide has been illicitly used with codeine tablets to give a heroinlike effect. Street names for this potentially lethal combination include *dors and 4s* and *Ds and Cs.*

Methaqualone Methaqualone is chemically different from barbiturates and unrelated to glutethimide. It does, however, have similar sedative-hypnotic effects (drowsiness, motor/speech dysfunctions, and so forth). Although it does not have as strong a knockout effect as barbiturates, it does produce a "drunken" intoxication, and its effects can be dangerously increased by combination with alcohol.[10] Originally, methaqualone was mistakenly thought to be safe and nonaddictive and to have aphrodisiac qualities. Actually, it has caused many cases of serious poisoning and has also been implicated in highway accidents and hazardous driving. Large doses cause coma and may be accompanied by thrashing or convulsions. Methaqualone has been marketed in the United States under various brand names, such as Quaalude, Parest, Optimil, Somnafac, and Sopor.

Tranquilizers

Tranquilizers were originally developed as medical aids to psychotherapy for mental patients. Larger doses and more potent tranquilizers continue to be used in this manner. The benzodiazepines (Valium and Librium), however, are more often prescribed by physicians for general anxiety and as antidepressants.[11] Although tranquilizers are not usually part of illicit drug traffic, they are sometimes diverted from the prescription industry, pharmacies, hospitals, and even family medicine chests, for sale on the streets. Even when not diverted to the illicit drug market, tranquilizers are sometimes seriously abused as prescription drugs, and strong dependence on them can become a serious problem.

In the mid-1990s, a new tranquilizer surfaced. This drug, commonly called the *rape drug* or *ruffys,* is actually a powerful Valiumlike drug called Ruhibnol. The drug is slipped into the drinks of unsuspecting young women at parties and in bars. The drug quickly causes the victim to feel slightly dizzy and often nauseated. The would-be rapist then helps the young woman home, where she soon falls into what physicians sometimes refer to as a *twilight state*. In a twilight state, a person is neither fully asleep nor fully awake. During this period, however, the victim is helpless to ward off a sexual assault and often remembers the attack only as a dream.

Hallucinogens

Hallucinogens, also referred to as psychedelics or consciousness-expanding drugs, are capable of distorting perception of objective reality. Alterations of time and space perception, illusions, hallucinations, and delusions may be either mild or overwhelming, depending on the dose. The effects experienced after taking hallucinogens are not related solely to the drug. They are also modified by the emotional state, mental attitude, and environment of the user. The results of taking hallucinogens, then, are very variable. One might experience a very pleasurable high, see bright and beautiful colors, hear music and sounds as never before, and feel calm and relaxed. On the other hand, one might just as easily have a "bad trip," during which one might see frightening monsters or believe one was being attacked. The most commonly abused hallucinogens are LSD 25 (lysergic acid diethylamide) and PCP (phencyclidine).

LSD 25 (Lysergic Acid Diethylamide) In 1938, Dr. Albert Hofmann, a biochemist at Sandoz Laboratories in Basel, Switzerland, first synthesized LSD from a dark purple fungus named *ergot*. On an April afternnon in 1943, Dr. Hofmann accidentally inhaled an infinitesimal amount of the new compound. He recognized its perception-altering properties and repeated his intake a few days later to confirm his findings.[12]

Since then, LSD has become known as one of the most powerful drugs abused on the drug scene. An average dose of LSD is a tiny speck, perhaps 30 or 40 micrograms, or about the amount one could place on the tip of a pin. The effects of LSD may last 8–12 hours. Users may place the LSD on a cube of sugar, on a blotter, or in food or drinks. Inmates have been known to receive letters that have had their corners dipped in LSD. By sucking a corner, the inmate ingests the drug. Along with mental and perceptual effects, the user may have dilated pupils, a flushed face, chills, and perhaps a rise in temperature and heart rate. Like other hallucinogens, LSD does not produce physical dependence and is not considered addictive, although many users regularly use it.

PCP (Phencyclidine) Phencyclidine—or, as it is commonly called, PCP— was originally produced as an animal tranquilizer and anesthetic. It affects a number of different neurotransmitters and may function as a stimulant, a depressant, or an analgesic. An extremely powerful drug, PCP can produce irrational and disoriented reactions, hallucinations, feelings of invulnerability, speech difficulty, and frightening death feelings. High doses may produce psychosis, convulsions, coma, and death. The actual effects of PCP are sometimes influenced by the user's expectations and emotional state.

In the drug vernacular, PCP is referred to as *angel dust* or simply *dust*. It dissolves readily in water and, as a street drug, may be both adulterated and misrepresented as something it is not. Often, PCP is misrepresented as THC, the psychoactive ingredient in marijuana. It has also been sold as LSD or other hallucinogens.

The prevailing patterns of street-level abuse are oral ingestion of the drug, alone or in combination with other drugs, and smoking the drug after it has been sprinkled on parsley, marijuana, or tobacco—in the vernacular, after these items have been "dusted."

Reported experiences of the effects of phencyclidine seem so unpleasant that one wonders how PCP has become so popular. In low doses, the experience usually proceeds in three stages: changes in body image, sometimes accompanied by feelings of depersonalization; perceptual distortions, infrequently evidenced as visual or auditory hallucinations; and feelings of apathy or estrangement. The experience often includes drowsiness, inability to verbalize, and feelings of emptiness, weightlessness, or "nothingness." Reports of difficulty in thinking, poor concentration, and preoccupation with death are common. Common signs of PCP use include flushing, profuse sweating, involuntary eye movements, loss of muscle control, nausea, and vomiting. In addition, people under the influence of PCP are sometimes irrational in their behavior and very violent, and they seem to have extraordinary strength.[13] Users of PCP feel the effects about 2–5 minutes after smoking a small amount. When PCP is taken orally, the onset of effects takes somewhat longer. The high, once begun, may continue for 4–6 hours, but the user may not feel normal for 24–48 hours.

Other Hallucinogens   In addition to LSD 25 and PCP, a large number of synthetic and natural hallucinogens present problems of varying degrees to law enforcement. These include mescaline (peyote), psilocybin and psilocyn ("magic mushrooms"), and dimethyltryptamine (DMT).

Mescaline   Mescaline, which is derived from the buttons of the peyote cactus, has been used for centuries by various Southwestern Native American tribes and Indians of Central America in religious rites. Generally ground into a powder, peyote is taken orally. Because of its bitter taste, the drug is often ingested with tea, coffee, milk, orange juice, or some other beverage. Mescaline is available on the illicit market as a crystalline powder, in capsules, or as a liquid in ampules or vials. A dose of 350–500 milligrams of mescaline produces illusions and hallucinations for 5–12 hours. Like LSD, mescaline is not likely to produce physical dependence but may result in psychological dependence.[14]

Psilocybin and Psilocyn Also derived from plants, psilocybin and psilocyn are obtained from *Psilocybe* mushrooms, generally grown in Mexico. Like mescaline, they have been used in Indian rites for centuries. During the 1960s, they were discovered by hippies interested in so-called mind-expanding drugs and were nicknamed *magic mushrooms* or *shrooms*. Their effects are similar to those of mescaline, except that a smaller dose, 4–8 milligrams, is ample to produce hallucinatory effects for about 6 hours. In addition to the actual mushrooms, psilocybin and psilocyn are available in crystalline, powdered, or liquid form. Again, these drugs do not produce physical dependency, although chronic users have been known to develop a tolerance to them.

Dimethyltryptamine (DMT) Dimethyltryptamine (DMT) is a short-acting hallucinogen found in the seeds of certain plants native to the West Indies and parts of South America. The powdered seeds have been used for centuries as a snuff, called *cohoba,* in religious ceremonies to produce a state of mind that the Haitian natives claimed enabled them to communicate with their gods. Chemists in illegal labs have also produced DMT synthetically. The drug is not taken orally. Rather, its vapor is inhaled from the smoke given off by the burning of the ground seeds or powder mixed with tobacco, parsley leaves, or marijuana. The drug can also be injected. The effects of a single dose of 60–150 milligrams last only 45–60 minutes and are mainly hallucinations. While the drug may cause psychological dependence, it has not been proved to cause any physical dependence.

Cannabis (Marijuana)

Although sometimes considered a mild hallucinogen, cannabis should actually be put in its own category *(Cannabis sativa)*. Cannabis is among the most commonly abused drugs, and grows in almost all parts of the world. At one time, cannabis was a leading cash crop for America, second only to cotton. It was used to produce hemp rope and linens and other textiles. Today, its cultivation, though illegal, is once again becoming important in some areas of the United States. The northwest United States is the regional capital of indoor marijuana cultivation. Drug-related cannabis products include marijuana, hashish, and hash oil.

Marijuana Marijuana is a dried plant material obtained from the Indian hemp plant *Cannabis sativa.* It has limited medical use in the United States, and that use remains largely experimental, rather than approved. In addition to the use of the plants in the production of rope, linens, and bags, the sterilized seeds of marijuana are occasionally used commercially in various bird seed mixtures. Marijuana grows as a shrublike plant 4–20 feet tall. In full bloom, the plant's leaves are a dark green, similar to the hue of evergreen trees, on the outside and a lighter green on the undersurface. The leaves of the plant have 5 to 11 leaflets or fingers (always an odd number). These leaflets are 2–6 inches long, slender, and pointed almost equally at both ends, with sawlike edges and pronounced ridges running from the center diagonally to the edges. The green plant has a slightly mintlike odor, is sticky to the touch, and is covered with fine hairs that are barely visible to the naked eye.

The female of the species contains an abundant amount of delta-9-tetrahydrocannabinol (THC), which is the actual narcotic element of marijuana. Marijuana varies in strength, depending on where it is grown, whether it is wild or cultivated, whether it is smoked or eaten, and which portion of the plant is used (for instance, leaves, seeds, stems, or resin).

For use as a drug, the leaves and flowering tops (buds) of the plant are dried in indirect heat. They are packaged in compressed bricks similar to miniature bales of hay. The bricks may be square or slightly oblong in shape and weigh 1 kilo (about 2.2 pounds). The bulk price for a kilo may range from about $1500 to more than $2500, depending on several factors, including the quality of the marijuana, the type of marijuana it is, its source (for instance, Colombia, Mexico, or domestic), and the part of the country where it is to be sold. The marijuana will be subdivided during the distribution process, reaching street sales at weights of about an ounce or less. At current street prices, a single ounce of high-quality marijuana may cost as much as $350.

There are several ways of using marijuana. The most prevalent method in the United States is to smoke it, usually as a cigarette. In the past, marijuana cigarettes have been called *reefers, joints, sticks, jays, weed, Mary Jane,* or *numbers.* The most common terms for marijuana today include *grass* and *pot,* although some of the terms from earlier times remain. Marijuana may also be smoked in ordinary or water pipes, or in special marijuana pipes called *bongs.* Occasionally, users may make a tea from the twigs and/or ground seeds, or marijuana may simply be added to various foods and eaten.

The immediate effects of marijuana on the smoker are best described as a kind of intoxication, or high. The overall effect is that of a mild depressant, resulting in drowsiness, reduced nervous system activity, and slowed reaction time. With higher THC content, the effects may be more dramatic, including sensory distortion. Marijuana is not physically addicting, and there is no withdrawal if one suddenly stops using the drug. However, considerable psychological dependence is possible from prolonged use of marijuana.

Hashish Hashish, or *hash,* consists of the THC-rich resin scraped from the leaves and buds of the marijuana plant. The resin is dried and compressed into small blocks. The color of hash typically ranges from a brownish tan to a dark brown. Hash is cut into small cubes and sold by weight. Because of the high concentration of resin, hashish is often five or six times as potent as marijuana leaves. Hash is usually smoked in pipes, although it, too, can be used in foods.

Hash Oil   Hash oil is a dark, amber-brown, syrupy concentrate of resin produced by a process of repeated extractions. Samples of hash oil have been found to contain as much as 60 percent THC. A drop or two of this oil on a cigarette is easily equal in psychoactive effect to smoking an entire marijuana cigarette. Hash oil may also be smoked, by placing a small amount in a glass pipe and heating the oil until it fumes. These fumes can then be inhaled by the smoker.

Designer Drugs

Designer drug   Substance produced in clandestine laboratories by adding or taking away something in an existing drug's chemical composition.

Designer drugs are so called because they are created in the laboratory by adding or taking away something in an existing drug's chemical composition. Because the new substance no longer has the same composition as the original, it may escape federal regulation until its danger is recognized and it is added to the schedule of controlled substances.

The practice was first observed in the 1960s, when it was used on a small number of tranquilizers. However, during the 1980s and 1990s, the trend in designer drugs was more toward producing synthetic narcotics—for example, a synthetic heroin that is up to 1000 times more potent than natural heroin. Designer drugs have also included analogs such as MDMA, or ecstasy, which combines an amphetaminelike rush with a hallucinatory experience, and nexus, which combines the hallucinogens DMT and 2c-B.

Police now take no chances when they raid illegal drug labs and protect themselves from dangerous chemicals when gathering evidence.

Along similar lines to the designer drugs is smokable methamphetamine, or ice. Ice is a freebase form of methamphetamine (speed). Ice is called by many street names, including *L.A. glass, hot ice, super ice,* and *L.A. ice.* Typically, ice is smoked in a glass pipe or a cigarette. Ice may be nearly clear and look like a piece of cracked ice taken from the freezer. In this case, the ice was produced with a water base and will burn quickly. Some ice has a yellowish tint. Such ice is oil-based and tends to burn slower and longer than water-based ice. The high received from smoking ice generally lasts 8–30 hours, as compared with a crack high of 8–20 minutes.[15]

Ice is much cheaper to make than crack cocaine and is both deadlier and more addictive than crack. The physiological effects of smoking ice include a rapid heartbeat, increased blood pressure, extreme energy, sleeplessness, euphoria, and possible seizures that can occur as soon as 6 seconds after one puff of ice. Pupils of the eyes contract, and smokers sometimes spike fevers as high as 106°, causing brain damage. Extended use of ice can be fatal.

Inhalants

Though not generally considered part of the illicit drug trade, inhalants have been a serious problem for many law enforcement agencies. A number of common household solvents, cleaners, and aerosols have been used primarily by teenagers to obtain a high. Other materials used frequently by juveniles include gasoline, paint, and freon. Vials of amyl or butyl nitrite have become a commonly abused inhalant among some homosexuals who believe it produces an extended orgasm.[16] In addition, some contemporary youths inhale freon from air conditioners to obtain a high—often with deadly results.

Legal Aspects

Federal and state laws define drug offenses. Specific drug laws and penalties, therefore, vary between levels of government and from one jurisdiction to another. Drug investigators should be aware of their local community ordinances as well as state and federal drug laws.

Categories of Drug Offenses

Generally, drug offenses fall into three categories: possession, distribution, and manufacturing of dangerous and/or illicit drugs.

Possession A drug offense that consists of having a controlled drug on one's person or under one's control, as in one's house or vehicle.

Distribution A drug offense that consists of selling, trading, giving, or delivering illicit drugs, regardless of whether one stands to profit from the transaction.

Manufacturing A drug offense that includes any activity to cultivate, harvest, produce, process, or manufacture illegal drugs.

Controlled substance A drug or substance whose use and possession are regulated under the Controlled Substances Act.

Possession **Possession** or use laws prohibit having a controlled drug on one's person or under one's control, as in one's car or house. Most states prohibit possession of a controlled substance in other than expressly permitted circumstances, such as when prescribed by a doctor. Some states also separately prohibit drug use or being under the influence of a controlled substance. Specific provisions and levels of proof to differentiate simple possession from possession with intent to sell vary among the states with such laws.

Distribution The charge of distribution may be imposed on an individual for any exchange of illegal drugs between two or more parties. Generally, distribution offenses include sale, trade, gifts, and delivery of unlawful drugs, regardless of whether one stands to profit. Typically, the charge of **distribution** of a drug is considered more serious than mere possession.

Manufacturing **Manufacturing** offenses include any activity to cultivate, harvest, process, produce, or manufacture illegal drugs. Some drugs, such as LSD25, PCP, and methamphetamine, can be produced by amateur chemists in illegal labs. Similarly, cocaine is processed from coca paste in illegal laboratories, and crack cocaine is processed in kitchen labs. Marijuana, in contrast, requires no special processing and is used in its natural state as an agricultural crop.

The Controlled Substance Act

The Controlled Substance Act (CSA), Title II of the federal Comprehensive Drug Abuse Prevention and Control Act of 1970, requires federal law enforcement agencies to control the abuse of narcotics and other dangerous drugs and chemical substances. Since its enactment, many states have used the CSA as a model for their own laws. The CSA is intended to place certain controls on a variety of drugs and chemical substances. Also, the CSA provides criteria for determining if a substance should be controlled. Finally, the CSA provides procedures for bringing a substance under control.

In its criteria for controlled-substance inclusion, the CSA uses five categories, called schedules (see Figure 21–2). A drug's placement on one schedule or another is determined by its medical use, potential for abuse, and likelihood for causing dependence. The Department of Health and Human Services and the DEA may add to, delete from, or change the schedule of controlled substances. The major role played by the DEA is to determine whether a substance has the potential for serious abuse. When the DEA determines that a drug or chemical should be classified as a **controlled substance,** it also determines on which schedule the item should be listed.

Figure 21–2 Federal schedules of controlled substances.

Federal law schedules drugs according to their effects, medical use, and potential for abuse.

DEA Schedule	Abuse Potential	Examples of Drugs Covered	Some of the Effects	Medical Use
I	Highest	Heroin, LSD, hashish, marijuana, methaqualone, designer drugs	Unpredictable effects, severe psychological or physical dependence, or death	No accepted use; some legal for limited research use only
II	High	Morphine, PCP, codeine, cocaine, methadone, Demerol®, benzedrine, dexedrine	May lead to severe psychological or physical dependence	Accepted use with restrictions
III	Medium	Codeine with aspirin or Tylenol®, some amphetamines, anabolic steroids	May lead to moderate or low physical dependence or high psychological dependence	Accepted use
IV	Low	Darvon®, Talwin®, phenobarbital, Equanil®, Miltown®, Librium®, diazepam	May lead to limited physical or psychological dependence	Accepted use
V	Lowest	Over-the-counter or prescription compounds with codeine, Lomotil®, Robitussin A-C®	May lead to limited physical or psychological dependence	Accepted use

Source: Adapted from DEA, *Drugs of Abuse: 1989.*

Federal Anti-Drug-Abuse Legislation

Major initiatives against drug abuse on the federal level were undertaken in the 1980s (see Figure 21–3). The first half of the decade emphasized legislation to reduce the supply of illegal drugs. This effort included aggressive internal enforcement of drug laws through drug and asset seizures and the cutting off of supplies. The second half increased spending for prevention and treatment. The legislation also focused on any use of illegal drugs and on individual users.

Investigating Illegal Drug Cases

The investigation of illicit drug cases involves generally the same basic investigative practices applied to other criminal violations. However, the nature of this type of case requires specialized investigative approaches and skills.

Figure 21–3 Major recent federal anti-drug legislation.

The 1984 Crime Control Act
- Expanded criminal and civil asset forfeiture laws.
- Amended the Bail Reform Act to target pretrial detention of defendants accused of serious drug offenses.
- Established a determinate sentencing system.
- Increased Federal criminal penalties for drug offenses.

The 1986 Anti-Drug Abuse Act
- Budgeted money for prevention and treatment programs, giving the programs a larger share of Federal drug control funds than previous laws.
- Restored mandatory prison sentences for large-scale distribution of marijuana.
- Imposed new sanctions on money laundering.
- Added controlled substances' analogs (designer drugs) to the drug schedule.
- Created a drug law enforcement grant program to assist State and local efforts.
- Contained various provisions designed to strengthen international drug control efforts.

The 1988 Anti-Drug Abuse Act
- Increased penalties for offenses related to drug trafficking, created new Federal offenses and regulatory requirements, and changed criminal procedures.
- Altered the organization and coordination of Federal anti-drug efforts.
- Increased treatment and prevention efforts aimed at reduction of drug demand.
- Endorsed the use of sanctions aimed at drug users to reduce the demand for drugs.
- Targeted for reduction drug production abroad and international trafficking in drugs.

The Crime Control Act of 1990
- Doubled the appropriations authorized for drug law enforcement grants to States and localities.
- Expanded drug control and education programs aimed at the Nation's schools.
- Expanded specific drug enforcement assistance to rural States.
- Expanded regulation of precursor chemicals used in the manufacture of illegal drugs.
- Provided additional measures aimed at seizure and forfeiture of drug trafficker assets.
- Sanctioned anabolic steroids under the Controlled Substances Act.
- Included provisions on international money laundering, rural drug enforcement, drug-free school zones, drug paraphernalia, and drug enforcement grants.

Source: U.S. Department of Justice, Bureau of Justice Statistics, *Drugs, Crime, and the Justice System,* Government Printing Office, Washington, 1992.

Illicit drug cases require special knowledge and familiarity with narcotics and other dangerous drugs and their applicable laws. Because of the increasing menace of drug abuse, and the violence that has become commonly associated with the drug trade, drug suppression has become a primary mission of many law enforcement agencies. As suggested in Chapter 19, organizations specializing in drug importation and distribution have used violence to protect their markets in the United States.

The dollar amounts involved in the drug trade are so enormous that human life has been made to seem insignificant by contrast. Therefore, extreme caution must be taken by officers involved in any drug investigation.

Drug investigations may include open investigations, undercover field investigations, and even stings. During an undercover investigation, an officer may assume the role of a drug buyer or dealer to gather evidence against drug distributors. Drug investigations typically involve several stages, which begin when information reaches the police about the possibility of drug activity. During the preliminary stages of the investigation, officers must verify that the information is correct and that illicit drug activity is occurring or has occurred. Considerable care is required during this stage

of the investigation, since not all sources of information are always reliable. Information may be verified through the use of standard surveillance techniques (see Chapter 8). In addition, street test kits are available to help an officer determine probable cause for arrests by identifying certain drugs. Once it has been established that unlawful drug activity has occurred, the investigation can proceed along a number of lines. Among these may be undercover operations and the use of informants.

Undercover Drug Operations

The term *undercover* has been used as a generic label for decoy work, sting operations, and police intelligence-gathering efforts.[18] According to George Miller, there are actually two types of undercover work: light cover and deep cover.[19] Both types are useful in drug investigations. **Light cover** drug investigations involve donning various costumes and assuming roles during a regular shift of duty. Having donned these disguises, officers spend time on the streets, gathering information about drug deals and dealers. They may even attempt to set up narcotics purchases, or *buys*. At the end of that day's shift, they return to the police station, change out of their disguises, and go home.

Deep cover, on the other hand, involves an officer's entirely submerging him- or herself in the role of an underworld figure. To a large measure, the officer becomes the person he or she pretends to be. The duration of a deep cover operation may be several days, weeks, or months. The officer's primary responsibility during a deep cover drug operation is to locate key figures in the drug distribution network and collect incriminating evidence against them.

During light cover operations, officers may operate in teams, with an ample number of back-up officers observing the undercover officer's activities, ready to move in to assist. In deep cover operations, however, the greatest protection for the officer is secrecy. Often, deep cover officers do not report even to superiors at regular intervals. Instead, they sporadically contact a superior or supervisor to advise them of the progress of their assignment. Undercover drug investigators face many risks including increased use of automatic weapons by drug dealers, increased violence

Light cover An undercover police operation that extends only as long as the officer's tour of duty.

Deep cover An undercover operation that may extend for a long period of time, during which the officer totally assumes another identity.

by foreign nationals involved in drug trafficking, handling informants whose allegiance may be confused, and the lure of big-money deals.[20] Additionally, undercover officers may have to feign friendships with criminals or even commit crimes to maintain their cover.

Informants and Other Aids

The use of informants to obtain information, leads, or evidence in police work is common practice. In drug cases, informants may also be useful for arranging introductions to drug dealers or distributors. The use of informants should be undertaken cautiously. Informants may lead investigators to information and arrests. However, especially given the enormous profits being made in the illegal drug trade, an unreliable informant could just as easily lead an investigator into a trap.

When conducting drug buys, whether working with an informant or using other methods, there are a number of things officers should bear in mind. These include the following:

- Learn to recognize the characteristic behavior of illicit drug users and physical symptoms resulting from the use of narcotics and dangerous drugs.
- Become familiar with the paraphernalia used in preparation and use of illicit drugs: hypodermic needles, pipes, bongs, beakers, ampules, vials, and so forth.
- Learn street jargon relating to narcotics and other dangerous drugs.
- Learn to recognize the telltale marks and punctures on the arms and bodies of drug users; conditions or appearance indicative of illicit drug use.
- Avoid conducting buys inside private residences, garages, or other enclosed structures. Besides reducing the back-up and arrest team's ability to get to you quickly, making buys in such places may also cause the loss of evidence.
- Always maintain control over the buy situation. Tell the suspect how the deal will be set up, where it will occur, when parties will meet, and so forth. It may be wiser to lose the arrest than to allow yourself to be compromised by letting the suspect set the rules and a trap.
- Do not flash buy money in crowded areas. While you may be concentrating on a potential drug arrest, other offenders may be seeking mugging victims.
- Be sure to turn off the overhead dome light in your vehicle before going to a buy location. When the light goes on as you open the door, you become an illuminated target.
- Always be certain that everyone on the back-up team knows the signal to come in.

- Attempt to arrange the arrests after the deal has been completed, rather than during the actual buy. This will allow you to leave the scene and move from potential danger.

Probable Cause and Searches

Drug investigators must have a clear understanding of the laws regarding illicit drugs, particularly search and seizure laws. In addition, officers must understand the legal elements of probable cause for search and arrest. Specific criteria for establishing probable cause vary slightly from one jurisdiction to the next. There are, however, a number of broad general guidelines to follow. Courts have generally held that **probable cause,** also called *reasonable suspicion,* is evident if a person of average intelligence and foresight (ordinary prudence) would be led to believe that a crime has been committed.[21] In other words, probable cause may exist even when there is some doubt. But for the arrest to be lawful, more than a mere suspicion that a crime has been committed is necessary.

Whenever possible, the best way for an officer to search a person, vehicle, or premises is with a search warrant issued by a magistrate. Such a warrant means that a magistrate has received information from a sworn affiant that probable cause exists to believe that the fruits or instrumentation of a crime are possessed by an individual or present at a particular location.

There is no special trick to effectively searching persons, property, premises, or vehicles. Illicit drugs may be found in a variety of places or containers. The predominant rule in all searches is to be extremely methodical and thorough. In all instances, the officer must be certain that the search has been undertaken lawfully. This means (1) there is valid, willing, voluntary consent, offered either orally or in writing (the courts will review consent searches to make sure the consent was freely and clearly given and without duress or coercion), (2) there is a search warrant (obtained by demonstrating probable cause to a magistrate or judge), or (3) the search is incidental to an arrest and is limited to the area under the offender's *immediate control. Under immediate control* typically means approximately within arm's reach. If the officer desires a more extensive search, a warrant is required.

Searches of Persons   Searches of persons can occur for several reasons. First, officers may search for weapons in the interest of self-protection. These *stop-and-frisks,* or *Terry-stops,* derive from the case of *Terry v. Ohio.*[22] This case involved a trio of suspects who were stopped and searched while apparently casing a store for robbery. The officer, Detective McFadden, did, in fact, find that two of the three men were carrying pistols. Both Terry and one of his associates were arrested and convicted on concealed weapons charges. Terry appealed on the grounds that the search was illegal and the evidence of the gun should have been suppressed at trial.

Probable cause   Reasonable grounds for belief that a person should be arrested or searched or that a person's property should be searched or seized.

The Supreme Court did not agree with *Terry*. Instead, the high court ruled that police have the authority to detain a person briefly for questioning even without probable cause if they have reason to believe the person may have been involved in a crime. This detention does not constitute an arrest; however, the officer is entitled to frisk or pat down the individual to ensure the officer's personal safety.

A second type of search of a person, usually incidental to an arrest, is made to check for both weapons and other contraband.

Officers should be aware that suspects have been known to conceal illicit drugs on or in various parts of their bodies and clothing. Searches of the body include hair, ears, mouth (under the tongue), body cavities, groin area, tape on the body, soles of the feet, and between toes. Other areas that should be searched are hats and hatbands, hat linings, coats or jackets, ties, belts, socks, and shoes (soles and heels). In some cases, a drug smuggler may ingest balloons or condoms filled with narcotics. The acid in the suspect's stomach will eventually cause the balloon to deteriorate, releasing the drug and likely killing the smuggler. When this is suspected, it is important that the smuggler be convinced to regurgitate the balloons as quickly as possible. Although most balloons may be successfully passed, drug couriers frequently die when drugs in balloons rush into their systems after stomach acids have dissolved the containers.

Searches of Vehicles   The question of the scope of a lawful search that follows an arrest is of particular concern with respect to automobiles. Discussion of vehicle searches frequently begins with consideration of *Carrol v. United States*.[23] In this case, the Supreme Court established clear distinctions among searches of people, vehicles, and premises. Basically, the Court held that a warrantless search of a vehicle was legitimate, provided the officer had probable cause to believe the vehicle contained evidence or contraband.

The scope of a vehicular search can be better understood by following the rationale set forth in *Chimel v. California*.[24] In the *Chimel* case, officers arrested a man without a warrant. While holding the man in one room of his home, the police proceeded to search the entire three-bedroom house, including the garage, attic, and workshop. The Supreme Court held that searches incidental to arrest are limited to the area within the arrestee's immediate control, or that area within which he or she might reach a weapon.

As applied to the search of a car, courts have repeatedly held that if probable cause has been established, vehicles can be searched without warrants because vehicles can be quickly moved out of the jurisdiction where the warrant would be sought and applicable. However, the scope of these searches was originally limited to the cabin and immediate reach of the occupants.[25]

In 1991, the Supreme Court further extended the scope of searches with respect to automobiles. A general rule for determining the scope

The Drug Enforcement Administration (DEA) is responsible for enforcing laws concerning all narcotic drugs. It controls the registration provisions of federal drug laws, combats illegal drug traffic, and regulates distribution of dangerous drugs. The agency also determines the quantities of narcotics permitted in the United States for medical purposes.

The initial requirements are U.S. citizenship, availability for assignments in the United States and at foreign posts of duty, and being between the ages of 21 and 36. All applicants must also pass vision and hearing tests, be in excellent physical condition, and have a valid driver's license. A DEA special agent candidate must have a four-year college degree, and professional experience in law enforcement or the military is preferred. Like FBI special agent candidates, DEA special agent candidates must complete a polygraph examination, drug abuse screening, psychological suitability assessment, and an exhaustive background investigation. Those successfully completing the requirements go through a training period and pass a physical fitness test to be appointed DEA special agents.

Agents may conduct complex criminal investigations, carry out surveillance of criminals, and infiltrate illegal drug organizations. They may work closely with confidential sources of information to collect evidence leading to the seizure of assets gained from the sale of illegal drugs. Being a DEA special agent is a difficult and dangerous job. At one time or another, agents will work undercover, and their duties will take them throughout the world.

---

of a motorist's consent to a search of his or her car was established. Also, the Court simplified the rules concerning warrantless searches of vehicles and of containers found inside a car. The Court declared that a person's general consent to a search of the interior of an automobile justifies a search of any closed container found inside that vehicle that might reasonably hold objects of the search. Therefore, an officer, once he or she receives general consent to search a car, does not need to ask permission to look inside each closed container.[26]

The Court's decisions do not alter the rule that a search of a vehicle incident to an arrest must bear a reasonable relation to the particular

Officers of the U.S. and Haitian coast guards stand watch over drugs seized from a Colombian sailboat near Port-au-Prince in March of 1997.

arrest. For example, in arresting for a traffic violation, the officer cannot conduct an incidental search, since no fruits, instrumentalities, or contraband are usually connected with traffic violations. If, however, during the course of a lawful traffic stop, the officer observes contraband, weapons, burglary tools, or other illegal items in plain sight, the situation changes. Once observed, the items may be seized, and probable cause may be established for a more extensive search of the vehicle, including its trunk or other areas of concealment.

Vehicles have often been used to transport and conceal narcotics and dangerous drugs. A variety of places within, outside, under, and as part of the vehicle have been used to conceal contraband. Illicit drugs have been found in the ashtrays, in the glove compartment, in the steering column, in compartments concealed in or under the dashboard, beneath the seats, in the car's upholstery, in door panels, in the engine compartment, in the hollows of tires, in a specially constructed gas tank with a false bottom or compartment, on the undercarriage (welded, taped, or tied), in bumpers, under fenders, and in other places limited only by the imagination and patience of the officer.

Searches of Premises In conducting a lawful search of a premises, search sections or rooms in a systematic, thorough manner. Tools and equipment that may be useful in searching include a camera, a measuring tape, screwdrivers, wrenches (for plumbing traps), a light (flashlight or portable floodlight), an extension cord, a shovel, and a metal rod for probing flower beds or places indicating soil disturbances. The searchers should look into, around, under, and through all objects, containers, materials, and places of possible concealment. A recorder should be appointed to take notes of any evidence found during a search. If drugs are found, ask the suspect (if present) what they are, get an admission of ownership, and keep notes of exact conversations. Both the searcher and the recorder should mark any found evidence. The officer finding the evidence should keep it until turning it over to the crime laboratory for technical examination and identification. The name of the manager or landlord of the residence should be obtained for report purposes.

Drugs have been secreted in a number of places. Suggested places to search for illicit drugs include the following:

- Bathroom medicine cabinets (pill bottles labeled *aspirin* may not actually contain aspirin).
- Hampers of dirty clothes (check individual articles of clothing).
- The undersides of washbowls.
- Under the toilet lid.
- Inside the toilet tank and in the float ball.
- The cardboard tube of the toilet paper roll.
- Lipstick tubes and other cosmetic containers.
- Baby powder containers, toothpaste tubes, shaving cream cans, and so on.
- Tissue boxes.
- Face cream (object may be submerged) or hollowed-out bars of soap.
- Behind wall and light fixtures, in air ducts, in doorjambs, and in the hollow of doors.
- Areas behind blinds and under floor coverings.

Other places include the kitchen and food storage areas. Illicit drugs may be concealed in various foods—tea, coffee, flour, sugar, chips, beans, grains, and others. Drugs may be concealed in kitchen appliances or taped to their backs or bottoms. Cabinets, sinks, and even garbage disposals should all be examined as possible places of concealment. Searches of bedrooms, the living room, and other parts of the house should include clos-

Laser Rangefinder   Investigators use a high-accuracy laser unit to measure the inside of trailers and containers without unloading them. It is then easy to compare the inside and outside dimensions of suspect containers to locate hidden compartments that might contain illegal drugs. By not having to unload cargo to take measurements, more inspections can be conducted.

ets, clothing, furniture, wall hangings, televisions and radios, and areas beneath rugs and carpeting and behind loose moldings, as well as in bedposts, mattresses, pillows, and stuffed toys and in and under playpens, baby cribs, dressers, and changing tables and in containers hung from windows. Any object may be a potential place of concealment of drugs, and none should be overlooked. Basements, areas beneath houses, porches, stairs, attics, and garages are also used to conceal contraband. When searching the grounds around premises, it is important to look for indications of recently disturbed shrubs or earth. It may also be helpful to locate well-traveled paths or areas leading to air vents or other hiding places evidenced by obvious foot-traffic impressions.

Investigators should also be mindful of booby traps (see Chapter 18). Particularly where drugs are concerned, it is not uncommon for criminals to place explosive charges in unexpected places. When an unsuspecting officer moves an object, turns a switch, or even walks in the wrong place, the explosive may be detonated. For example, it is not difficult to remove the glass bulb from a lightbulb and fill it with a small quantity of gasoline. If the base is replaced on the bulb and carefully sealed with silicon (to prevent the gasoline from seeping), a simple explosive has been made. When the bulb is placed in a socket and switched on, the gasoline will ignite and explode.

Arrest Situations

When patrol officers witness what they believe may be a drug buy, they may not want to immediately make an arrest. Instead, it may be more fruitful to obtain as complete a description as possible of both parties and any vehicles involved. There is no urgency in making the arrest, because it is very likely that the drug buyer and seller will continue to meet and conduct business over time. If the buy is observed and the officer has probable cause, he or she does have the legal authority to make a drug arrest. In many cases, however, it is more prudent to simply observe and gather information. Whenever drug arrests are planned or made, certain procedures should be followed:

- Use sufficient personnel to handle the arrest safely.

- In addition to arrest warrants, have a search warrant if possible; be mindful of the legal limits of the search.

- Brief all participating officers on the part each is to play during the arrest and the search.

- Move quickly and simultaneously on all locations.

- If circumstances justify it, use force to enter a premises, and locate the suspects quickly. It takes only seconds to flush evidence down the toilet or otherwise destroy evidence.

- As soon as a suspect is in custody, handcuff his or her hands behind the back; advise the suspect of legal rights; conduct the search; if necessary, call in a doctor for an internal body search.

- If available, use drug-sniffing dogs to search the premises.

- If a suspect has needle marks, photograph them.

- Check names, addresses, and telephone numbers found in a suspect's effects for investigative leads about associates and possible meeting places.

- Request crime laboratory analysis of all materials and substances believed to be or contain drugs.

- Consider blood and urine tests of suspects where advisable.

Learning Objective 1

The term *narcotic* is used to describe any drug that produces a stupor, insensibility, or sleep. It includes in its meaning substances ranging from alcohol to heroin or crack cocaine. In the legal sense, a narcotic is any drug that is allegedly dangerous, is heavily abused, or has a high potential for abuse.

Learning Objective 2

Most people take drugs for the effects they produce. Most illegal drugs are consumed for their mind-altering effects. Among these drugs are heroin, cocaine, morphine, codeine, Percodan, and methadone.

Learning Objective 3

In addition to narcotics, there are other dangerous drugs that are among the most commonly abused drugs in America. These include stimulants, depressants, hallucinogens, marijuana, designer drugs, and inhalants.

Learning Objective 4

Federal, state, and local laws define drug offenses. Specific drug laws and penalties vary, but offenses generally fall into these three categories: possession, distribution, and manufacturing of dangerous and/or illicit drugs.

Learning Objective 5

Investigating illicit drug cases generally involves the same basic practices as investigating other crimes. However, the nature of drug cases requires special approaches and skills. These specialties include knowledge of drugs, their effects, and applicable laws; undercover drug operations; use of informants; and understanding of search and seizure laws.

QUESTIONS FOR REVIEW

Learning Objective 1

1. Define *narcotic*.
2. What are the four major categories of drugs?
3. From what plant do *opiates* derive?

Learning Objective 2

4. How do heroin addicts obtain their drugs?

5. Which is considered stronger, morphine or heroin?

6. What category of drug is cocaine?

7. What is freebasing?

8. How is crack cocaine different from run-of-the-mill powder cocaine?

9. What are the contents of a speedball?

10. From what is codeine derived?

11. How do addicts administer Percodan?

12. How is methadone used to treat heroin addicts?

Learning Objective 3

13. What are the physical effects of the use of stimulants?

14. What kind of drug are sleeping pills?

15. How are different types of barbiturates distinguished?

16. Which hallucinogens are most frequently abused?

17. Describe the effects of drugs from the category hallucinogens.

18. How might cannabis be useful to medical science?

19. What does hash oil look like?

20. What is a *designer drug?*

21. What are some of the dangers of the drug called *ice?*

Learning Objective 4

22. What are the three primary parts of the Controlled Substance Act?

23. What is meant by the crime of *manufacturing* drugs?

Learning Objective 5

24. What are the main differences between *light cover* and *deep cover* drug investigations?

CRITICAL THINKING INVESTIGATIVE EXERCISE

Divide into two groups to present a debate on the question, Should drugs be legalized? One group should gather data and prepare arguments to give this answer: Yes, legalizing drugs would solve the drug problem. The other group should prepare to give this answer: No, legalizing drugs would be dangerous.

INVESTIGATIVE SKILL BUILDERS

Participating as a Member of a Team

Divide into three or four teams of about seven or eight members. Identify a team leader in each group. Next, assign one or two members of each team to contact the local police chief, state's attorney, and mayor. The team members should ask each official how he or she would stand on a bill in the state legislature that would make growing marijuana for personal use legal. Have the team representatives learn as much of each figure's viewpoint as possible. Finally, each group should produce a report that includes team members' views about the legalization of marijuana in light of the viewpoints offered by the chief, the state's attorney, and the mayor.

Integrity/Honesty

You are an off-duty police officer attending a college football game. In front of you are four reasonably well-dressed college-age men. Their behavior is fairly appropriate for the setting of a football game. However, at halftime, you notice that one of the men has taken a reasonably large *joint* (marijuana cigarette) out of his pocket and is lighting it. The men pass the joint to one another. At one point, one of the men notices that you are watching. He smiles as he turns to you and asks, "Would you like a toke?"

1. How do you respond to the offer?
2. Do you identify yourself as a police officer?
3. Do you make any arrests? Explain.

ENDNOTES

1. James A. Inciardi, *The War on Drugs,* Mayfield Publishing, Palo Alto, Calif., 1986.
2. Ibid.
3. Ibid.
4. "Heroin Comes Back," *Time,* February 19, 1990, p. 63.
5. Norman E. Zinberg, "Nonaddictive Opiate Use," in James Inciardi and Karen McElrath (eds.), *The American Drug Scene,* Roxbury Publishing, Los Angeles, 1995, pp. 147–58.
6. Marc A. Schuckit, "Chasing the Dragon," in James Inciardi and Karen McElrath (eds.), *The American Drug Scene,* Roxbury Publishing, Los Angeles, 1995, pp. 144–46.
7. James Inciardi and Karen McElrath (eds.), *The American Drug Scene,* Roxbury Publishing, Los Angeles, 1995, p. 161.
8. Thomas A. Constantine, "Drug Wars," *The Police Chief,* Vol. 57, No. 5, 1990, p. 37.

9. James Gordon Knowles, "Dealing Crack Cocaine," *FBI Law Enforcement Bulletin,* Vol. 65, No. 7, July 1996, pp. 1–7.

10. Ronald L. Akers, *Drugs, Alcohol, and Society,* Wadsworth Publishing, Belmont, Calif., 1992.

11. Ibid.

12. Sidney Cohen, *The Beyond Within,* Atheneum, New York, 1964.

13. Drug Enforcement Administration, *Drug Enforcement,* Department of Justice, Washington, 1975.

14. Ibid.; see also Akers op. cit.

15. Susan Pennell, "'Ice': DUF Interview Results From San Diego," *NIJ Reports: Research in Action,* September 1990, pp. 12–13.

16. Erich Goode, *Drugs in American Society,* 3d ed., Knopf, New York, 1989.

17. Anita Timrots, Benjamin H. Renshaw III, and Sue A. Lingren, *Drugs and Crime Facts, 1994,* Bureau of Justice Statistics, Department of Justice, Washington, 1995.

18. Gary T. Marx, "The New Undercover Police Work," *Urban Life,* Vol. 8, 1980, pp. 399–446.

19. George I. Miller, "Observations of Police Undercover Work," *Criminology,* Vol. 25, 1987, pp. 27–46.

20. Michael D. Lyman, "Minimizing Danger in Drug Enforcement," *Law and Order,* September 1990, pp. 143–47.

21. Bruce L. Berg, *Law Enforcement: An Introduction to Police in Society,* Allyn and Bacon, Boston, 1992.

22. *Terry v. Ohio,* 392 U.S. 1 (1968).

23. *Carrol v. United States,* 267 U.S. 132 (1925).

24. *Chimel v. California,* 395 U.S. 752 (1969).

25. *South Dakota v. Opperman,* 428 U.S. 364 (1976); *New York v. Belton,* 453 U.S. 454 (1981).

26. *Florida v. Jimeno,* 59 L.W. 4471 (May 23, 1991).

CHAPTER 22

Terrorism

CHAPTER OBJECTIVES

After completing this chapter, you will be able to:

1. Describe the nature of terrorism.

2. Provide an overview of terrorism in the United States.

3. Discuss some of the major domestic terrorist groups in the United States.

4. Detail legal aspects of terrorism.

5. Describe some antiterrorist activities.

6. Discuss the role of local law enforcement with regard to terrorism.

KEY TERMS

terrorism
hate group
domestic terrorism
terrorist incident
suspected terrorist
  incident
terrorism prevention
survivalist training
international terrorism
INTERPOL
terroristic threat
counterintelligence
crisis negotiation team

Terrorism in Perspective

As suggested throughout this book, law enforcement investigators must deal with a wide assortment of crimes, criminal types, and violent interpersonal behaviors. In addition, law enforcement investigators deal with crimes that have a political motivation, including those categorized as *terrorism*.

From a law enforcement perspective, *terrorism* is a rather elusive term to accurately define and understand. It is a term laden with emotions, one that in most law enforcement communities conjures images of bombs and threats of violence, kidnapping, and murder. The public reaction to the term is similarly negative, involving an uneasiness about personal safety. When terrorist acts fall within certain guidelines, they may not be the problem of local police alone, but rather of the FBI in concert with local agencies. This chapter will consider some of the key points concerning investigations of terrorist acts. It should be understood, however, that the length and breadth of this chapter are insufficient to encompass all facets of terrorist behavior or the role police may play in its investigation.

There are a variety of ways terrorism might be defined. Most definitions, however, follow lines of political philosophy and offer little meaning relevant to investigation. For the purposes of investigation, we will define **terrorism** along lines similar to those suggested by the Vice President's Task Force on Combating Terrorism:

> [Terrorism] is the unlawful use or threat of violence against persons or property to further political or social objectives. It is generally intended to intimidate or coerce a government, individuals or groups to modify their behavior or policies.[1]

In short, terrorism involves any behavior that employs force or threats of force to achieve a political end. From a legal standpoint, terrorism is not by itself the crime. Rather, terrorism is a way of describing the nature of certain kinds of fairly traditional criminal acts. These might include murder, kidnapping, rape and torture, arson, and bombing. When these crimes are used—together or separately—to create a general climate of fear and terror, terrorism has occurred.

Political terrorists differ from other types of criminals. Many persons who commit violent crimes are compelled to do so because of some emotional disturbance or mental deficiency. Others are motivated by a variety of factors, including revenge, profit, hatred, and the need to silence witnesses or associates. Political terrorists, however, often cannot be neatly placed in one of these categories.

Terrorism The unlawful use or threat of violence against persons and property to further political or social objectives. It is generally intended to intimidate or coerce a government, individuals, or groups to modify their behavior or policies.

STATISTICS

According to the State Department, about 21 percent of world terror is aimed at the United States.

Eight people died and 4,700 were injured in the March 1995 nerve gas attack by terrorists in a Tokyo subway.

Political terrorists are motivated by their philosophical (sometimes religious) and ideological beliefs. They are zealots frequently willing to sacrifice their own lives or the lives of others for the cause they believe in.

Terrorism in the United States

Until recently, many Americans did not view political terrorism as a serious threat to safety in the United States. Naturally, they were aware of such political acts of terrorism as the 1972 murders of Israeli athletes during the Olympic Games in Munich; the Americans seized in 1979 in the U.S. embassy in Iran and held for more than a year; the 1981 assassination of Egyptian President Anwar Sadat; the 1983 terrorist attacks on U.S. Marines in Beirut, Lebanon, which left 241 military personnel dead; the terrorist-caused crash of Korea Air Lines Flight 858 in 1987, which left 115 passengers and crew members dead; and the terrorist bombing attack on Christmas 1988 that caused Pan American Flight 103 to crash in Lockerbie, Scotland, and killed 270 people. In many of these and other terrorist assaults, American lives were lost. Yet Americans felt safe sleeping in their homes at night and walking through their shopping malls during the day. That is, of course, until 1993, when Americans were shaken awake to the perils of political terrorism with the bombing of the World Trade Center in New York City.[2]

But even this wake-up call was soon neatly fit into the comfortable contours of foreign political terrorism. After all, the suspects in the case were all from the Middle East. Furthermore, anti-American terrorism has persistently occurred in other nations, and its occurrence on American soil was viewed by many as inevitable. For many Americans, the realization that they, too, were vulnerable to such violence came in April of 1995, with the bombing of the Alfred P. Murrah Federal Building in Oklahoma City.

This incident received enormous media coverage as the first major case of domestic terrorism. That is, it was terrorism by Americans against other Americans on U.S. soil. It was not, of course, the first case of domestic terrorism witnessed by law enforcement agencies. Throughout the 1970s, police had confronted such terroristic acts as the bombing of the Army recruitment office on White Hall Street in New York City, for which the then-notorious student activist group the Weathermen claimed responsibility; the bombing of Hearst's Castle in southern California, believed to be the work of the Symbionese Liberation Army; and assorted robberies, bombings, and other crimes alleged to have been committed by the Black Panthers. During the 1980s, the United Freedom Front claimed responsibility for ten bombings of corporate and mil-

On February 26, 1993, a bomb exploded in the basement garage of the World Trade Center, killing 6 persons and injuring 1,040 others.

itary targets in the New York City area, and police dealt with various domestic right-wing groups, such as the white supremacist group The Covenant, the Sword, and the Arm of the Lord.[3]

During the late 1980s and early 1990s, terrorist incidents were witnessed at abortion clinics across the United States, as were incidents involving self-styled patriot groups. These patriot groups were largely antifederalist groups that often endorsed defying federal regulations and law. In addition, the Unabomber, whose bombs had killed 3 people and injured 23 over an 18-year period had again become active during the 1990s. In April 1996, federal agents seized Theodore Kaczynski, a former college professor, as the suspect in the Unabomber case. Beginning in 1994 and escalating in 1996, a rash of mysterious fires assailed black churches across the South. Various **hate groups** have been investigated in these arson cases.[4]

Even terrorist activities in foreign countries, when perpetrated against Americans, began to be viewed through awakened eyes. For example, the bombing of the Khobar Towers complex in Dhahran, Saudi Arabia, in 1996, which killed 19 Americans and injured hundreds of other people, drew considerable attention from Americans.[5] In fact, several FBI evidence response teams were immediately sent to Saudi Arabia to investigate this bombing.

Finally, the history of America has been checkered with the use of terrorist tactics by assorted hate groups, such as the Ku Klux Klan and various neo-Nazi and white supremacist groups.

Domestic Terrorist Groups

The face of **domestic terrorism** began to change in the mid-1990s. There was a decline in traditional left-wing extremism and an increase in activities among extremists associated with right-wing groups and special-interest organizations. (See Figure 22–1 for a seven-year tally of terrorist-related incidents.) The full list of groups involved in domestic terrorism is beyond the scope of this textbook. Instead, we offer the following descriptions to familiarize the reader with some of the major categories of current terrorist groups and their basic characteristics.[6]

Left-Wing Groups

These groups advocate liberal, often radical, measures to effect change in the established political order. During the 1960s and 1970s, left-wing groups formed to protest the war in Vietnam or as centers of action in the Black Power movement. Groups disillusioned with the federal government's involvement in the war in Vietnam and civil rights

Hate group A group antagonistic toward various minority groups in the United States.

Domestic terrorism An unlawful violent act directed at elements of the U.S. government or population by groups or individuals who are based and operate entirely within the United States and Puerto Rico without foreign direction.

Terrorist incident A violent act, or an act dangerous to human life, in violation of the criminal laws of the United States or of any state, to intimidate or coerce a government, the civilian population, or any segment thereof, in furtherance of political or social objectives.

Suspected terrorist incident A potential act of terrorism in which responsibility for the act cannot be attributed at the time to a known or suspected terrorist group or individual.

Terrorism prevention A documented instance in which a violent act by a known or suspected terrorist group or individual with the means and a proven propensity for violence is successfully interdicted through investigative activity.

Figure 22–1 Terrorism in the United States.

Year	Terrorist Incidents	Suspected Terrorist Incidents	Terrorism Preventions
1989	4	7	16
1990	7	5	1
1991	5	4	1
1992	4	0	0
1993	12	7	2
1994	0	0	1
1995	1	2	1
Total	33	25	22

Source: Department of Justice, Federal Bureau of Investigation, *Terrorism in the United States, 1995,* Government Printing Office, Washington, 1996.

policies at home wreaked havoc. Arson, bombings, demonstrations, and violence of all types became commonplace. Student-based groups such as Students for a Democratic Society (SDS) and more militant splinter organizations, such as the Weather Underground Organization (WUO), used terrorist acts to make their voices heard.

This same era also witnessed the growth of the militant, antiwhite Black Panther movement and groups such as the Black Liberation Army (BLA). As the United States wound down its involvement in Vietnam in the early 1970s, terrorist attacks from residual groups focused on symbols of American imperialism and what many of these groups saw as the capitalist exploitation of Third World nations. The new targets became financial institutions, banks, corporate offices, and military facilities.

Left-wing terrorism has declined in recent years. This decline may be due to the arrest of many leftist group leaders during the 1980s and the rejection of communism as a viable economic and political system by many national governments in the 1990s. Among current groups with a left-wing orientation are the African National Ujammu, Ansaru Allah Community, United Freedom Front, and Dar-U1 Movement. Although Puerto Rico voted to remain a U.S. commonwealth in 1993, extremist groups such as the Armed Forces of National Liberation (FALN) and the Macheteros are still willing to plan and conduct terrorist acts to draw attention to their desire for independence.

Right-Wing Groups

Of recent concern to law enforcement officials are the activities of right-wing terrorist groups. Right-wing groups are conservative, favoring

554   Chapter 22 *Terrorism*

traditional views and values. They distrust government activism and oppose sudden changes in the established order. Terrorist groups characterized as right-wing are generally conservative, racist, antigovernment, and survivalist and promote the advancement of the white race. Some espouse fundamentalist Christian beliefs. Among these are such groups as the Ku Klux Klan, Posse Comitatus, the Aryan Nation, neo-Nazis and skinheads, and citizen militias and patriot groups.

During the 1970s and 1980s, law enforcement agencies became aware of a network of right-wing groups operating in the United States. These groups maintained a steady stream of racist, antifederalist, and conservative religious beliefs and rhetoric. Law enforcement officials were already familiar with the right-wing activities of the Ku Klux Klan and the American Nazi Party, but the new groups were far more radical. Many of them maintained paramilitary **survivalist training** to be prepared to protect themselves from agents of the federal government. Many groups and individual members of such groups stockpiled automatic weapons, explosives, and even hand-fired missiles.

Members of radical right-wing groups do not regard themselves as terrorists. Rather, they style themselves as "patriots," "tax protesters,"

Survivalist training A type of training in which separatist groups practice guerrilla warfare tactics to prepare to protect themselves from law enforcement officials or other agents of the government.

A common element of citizen militia training is instruction in shooting a weapon.

"citizen militias," and "constitutionalists." They believe that the country is headed toward disaster and that they must be ready to fight to protect their inalienable rights. During recent years, they have become more outspoken against the federal government, expressing their belief that it has become too invasive and restrictive.

The most militant of the right-wing groups are the citizen militias and patriot groups, who continue to attract supporters. They dress in combat fatigues, carry assault weapons, and participate in paramilitary maneuvers and guerrilla training. Formal militia groups have been reported in at least 22 states. Membership estimates for each state vary, but they range from as few as 50 to as many as several thousand. The larger organizations are located in the Midwest and West, with notable groups in Michigan, Montana, Idaho, Texas, Arizona, Alabama, Mississippi, Georgia, Pennsylvania, and Ohio.

HISTORY

April 19, the date of the bombing of the Murrah Building in Oklahoma City in 1995, has significance for members of militia and patriot groups. On April 19, 1775, the Battle of Lexington, the first battle of the Revolutionary War began. On April 19, 1993, the siege of the Branch Davidian compound by federal agents at Waco, Texas, ended. When Timothy McVeigh rented the Ryder truck, he used a forged driver's license whose date of issue was April 19, 1993. And on April 19, 1995, Richard Wayne Snell, a member of the white supremacist group The Covenant, the Sword, and the Arm of the Lord, was executed for the murders of a Jewish business owner and a black police officer.

One antigovernment, antitax group based in Montana and calling itself the Freemen held law enforcement officers at bay for nearly three months in 1996. On March 25, federal agents arrived with warrants for the arrest of several people at a ranch that had been lost in a tax foreclosure. Members of the group had been charged with defrauding banks and other companies of $1.8 million and with holding seminars for 800 people on how to conduct fraud. The indicted persons refused to surrender to the authorities. On March 28, several members were charged with threatening local law enforcement officials. During the three-month standoff, a number of occupants, including some minors, came out of the complex without incident. The remaining holdouts came out on June 13. When they appeared in court the next day, some were defiant, denying that the court had any jurisdiction over them.

Extremist right-wing groups feed on fear and spread paranoia. Many militia members believe that the U.S. government is part of a conspiracy to create a "new world order." They resent the involvement of the United Nations in international affairs. According to believers, in this new order, existing international boundaries will be dissolved, the United States will be overtaken by armies of the one-world government, and the world will be ruled by the United Nations. Many believe that signs on the interstate are actually coded to provide directions for invading armies.

Other militia supporters believe that the federal government is either too powerful or simply illegal. Their antigovernment stance has resulted from the changing political environment of civil rights legislation, environmental legislation, and gun-control legislation and from clashes between militia members and law enforcement officials. Many are so fed up with the federal government that they are ready to take up arms to overthrow it.

Estimates suggest that those who are arming themselves against the day when United Nations tanks roll across the nation's heartland to establish the one-world government, may alone number as many as 100,000. If you add all the people in as many as 40 states who accept the patriot rhetoric about a sinister and conspiratorial out-of-control federal government, businesses put out of business by environmental regulations, and all the unemployed who blame their plight on federal policies, the numbers may rise to about 12 million.

One extremist fringe religious movement uniting many of the white supremacist groups calls itself the Christian Identity Movement. Members of this group maintain a steady stream of anti-Semitic, white racist, fundamentalist Christian, and antifederalist rhetoric and beliefs. Right-wing groups in this movement are bound together by a shared hostility against Jews and nonwhites. They believe Jews have taken control of the economic structure of America and have put a stranglehold on the purse strings of white Christian Americans. This conspiracy theory has led believers of the movement to advocate the overthrow of the federal government. Other believers resent educational and job opportunities federally mandated for nonwhites that they think should go to white Christian Americans. Moreover, followers believe that nonwhites are destroying America by making it racially unpure.

> # FYI
>
> **O**ne product of the militia movement is common law courts. These courts—which have no legitimate authority—consist of self-appointed judges and juries who sometimes issue fraudulent indictments and warrants.

Special-Interest Groups

These groups seek resolution of specific issues rather than widespread political changes. Examples include groups which espouse terrorism to promote environmental issues or animal rights. Among them are such groups as the Animal Liberation Front, Up the IRS, and the Earth Night Action Group. Also included in this category are extremist antiabortion groups who attack abortion clinics and their personnel. The causes these groups promote may not be criminal, but the means—violence and destruction—they use to attain their goals are. They differ from traditional law-abiding special-interest groups in their use of criminal activity and violence to achieve their goals.

International Terrorist Groups in the United States

International terrorism
An unlawful use of force or violence by a group or individual who has some connection to a foreign power or whose activities transcend national boundaries, against persons or property to intimidate or coerce a government or the civilian population, to further political or social objectives.

The United States has long been resented in some countries around the world. Critics of the U.S. government say it has supported dictators who helped American companies operating in their countries or who shared America's dislike of the Soviet Union. With the dismantling of the U.S.S.R., America became the world's only superpower and thus a target of much of the world's bitterness and frustration. Americans were frequent targets of terrorism, but most incidents took place overseas. Most Americans felt little threat from **international terrorism** on a daily basis. The bombing of the World Trade Center in New York City by radical international terrorists in 1993 changed all that. Americans realized that the United States was still unpopular among other nations and that foreign terrorists could now operate within the once-safe boundaries of the 50 states.

Foreign terrorists view the United States as a priority target, an attractive refuge from prosecution, and a staging area for obtaining funds and support for their activities. America's open society makes it possible for terrorists and their supporters to live in and travel freely throughout the nation. There are a number of international terrorist groups in the United States whose allegiance stems from their ethnic ancestry in the Middle East. Many of these groups oppose Jewish organizations in the United States or are antagonized by America's support of Israel.

Formal terrorist groups such as the extremist Egyptian Al-Gama'at Al-Islamiyya, the militant Islamic Hezbollah (also called the Party of God and the Islamic Jihad), and the Palestinian terrorist HAMAS (Islamic Resistance Movement) are believed to be conducting criminal activities as well as military-style training in the United States in support of their groups' objectives. In addition to these formal groups, there are loosely affiliated individuals and groups who view the United States as both a target and a staging area. They take advantage of the advanced technology available in America, travel undetected, and manage to get around U.S. laws. Investigation of international terrorist groups usually requires communication and cooperation with INTERPOL and the law enforcement agencies of other countries.

Legal Aspects of Terrorism

The federal government has taken the lead in combating terrorism. Unlike most state and local law enforcement agencies, federal agencies have the funds, personnel, special skills, and jurisdiction to effectively lead investigations of most serious cases of terrorism. Nonetheless, several larger cities, such as Los Angeles, New York, and Chicago, have established special counterterrorist intelligence and investigative units. Some state police agencies also have small units or specially trained officers to handle local cases of terrorism and to work on task forces with federal and municipal officers.

For domestic cases of terrorism occurring in the United States, the U.S. Attorney General has the principal responsibility for coordinating law enforcement activities. This is accomplished through the Federal Bureau of Investigation (FBI); the Bureau of Alcohol, Tobacco, and Firearms (ATF); and, to a lesser extent, several other federal law enforcement agencies.

Outside the United States and its territories and possessions, the State Department is the primary coordinator of activities when Americans are the subject of terrorist acts. The State Department, however, is not a law enforcement agency nor in any way a specialist in the gathering of antiterrorism intelligence or strategies for combating terrorist activities.

Since 1984, **INTERPOL,** an international policing agency, has had a special group, the Provisional Terrorism Unit, that brings law enforcement skills and authority to international terrorism investigations. This unit places all of Interpol's resources—communications, intelligence, and support services—related to terrorism and terrorist activities at the disposal of member nations.[7]

As more and more domestic terrorism has been confronted at the state level, state governments have begun adopting laws designed specifically to cope with terrorist activities. However, since each state's experience has been slightly different, their efforts and laws differ too. All states continue to enforce conventional laws that are violated in the course of what might be called a terrorist crime. These include robbery, assault, murder, kidnapping, extortion, and use and possession of explosives and weapons. In addition, several states have passed specific terrorism legislation.

Most states have avoided the creation of specific terrorism statutes, since they usually require the state to demonstrate the additional dimension of political or social motivation. In conventional criminal prosecution, as mentioned in other places in this book, motive is not part of the *corpus delicti* required to obtain a conviction. Many states may include in their charges the offense of terroristic threat. Statutes against **terroristic threats** are not usually aimed at the possible political or social motivation for a crime. They are directed, instead, toward the nature of the activity undertaken by the offender and, therefore, are easier to work with.

INTERPOL An intergovernmental organization of law enforcement authorities from about 200 countries. Its official name is the International Criminal Police Organization. It works to ensure and promote cooperation and mutual assistance among members.

Terroristic threat The unlawful threat of injury or death to manipulate an individual into doing something.

Antiterrorism Activities

Among other antiterrorism strategies used by the United States government is its tireless effort to gather counterintelligence. **Counterintelligence** involves obtaining information about potential terrorist activities while they are still being planned. Federal agencies, as well as several state and large urban police agencies, compile intelligence on people and groups they believe have serious potential for future criminal involvement in terroristic activities.

Gathering counterintelligence involves a number of sources and types of information. It may include information obtained by snitches and paid informers or offered voluntarily by disillusioned former group members. It may include information gathered in undercover operations in which officers infiltrate suspect groups, or from various forms of surveillance. Investigators from these agencies can use the information gathered to plan specific operations, to assess the actual threat presented by a specific individual or group, and to share with other agencies in the area.

In many ways, the major difference between investigating an act of criminal terrorism and a conventional crime is the use of intelligence. Many terrorist groups operating in the United States today are large and fairly well organized. They may operate interstate over large areas. Records held by various levels of law enforcement on the activities of these groups may represent the raw data needed for apprehending offenders. Naturally, this will require strong communication links and coordination of various law enforcement organizations and agencies.

There are some problems, however, in maintaining the kinds of files that law enforcement agencies may find useful as intelligence data. Agencies should be aware of these problems to avoid violating the constitutional rights of suspects. For example, one cannot maintain surveillance or maintain police records on individuals merely because they may support a group that espouses an anarchistic philosophy.

To maintain a file on an individual or a group, it is necessary to first develop sufficient probable cause to believe that a crime involving the individual or group has occurred or is about to occur. Considerable care must be taken to avoid infringing on citizens' rights to free speech by alleging that they are making terroristic threats. A fine line exists between some groups and their radical fringe elements that claim to be working

FYI

In 1984, Congress established the Counter-Terrorism Rewards Program. The program offers substantial rewards—up to $2 million—for information preventing acts of international terrorism against U.S. citizens or property or leading to the arrest or conviction of those responsible for such acts. The reward level is up to $4 million when U.S. civil aviation is targeted by terrorists. The U.S. government protects in strict confidence the identity of those providing information, and in some cases, those individuals and their families may be relocated for their safety.

CAREER FOCUS: FOREIGN SERVICE SPECIAL AGENT

Special agents of the Bureau of Diplomatic Security are responsible for the security of Foreign Service personnel and property and sensitive information throughout the world. They are also responsible for protecting the Secretary of State, certain foreign dignitaries during their visits to the United States, and others designated by the Secretary of State. Major job responsibilities include protective services, criminal investigations, background checks, managing security programs for Foreign Service posts, and administrative, training, and liaison functions. The Foreign Service is part of the U.S. Department of State.

Applicants must be citizens of the United States, must be at least 21 and not more than 37 at the time of their appointments, must have at least a bachelor's degree from an accredited college or university, and must have one year of specialized experience. Although not a requirement, foreign language ability is desirable. Applicants should have a valid U.S. driver's license and be able to pass a defensive driving course during initial training.

Candidates must be willing to travel to a variety of overseas posts, many of which are remote and unhealthful or have limited medical support. Applicants must meet rigorous medical fitness standards and must undergo a thorough background investigation to determine their eligibility for a security clearance and their suitability for appointment to the Foreign Service. Agent candidates must be willing to carry firearms and must qualify with firearms during initial training and periodically thereafter. Applicants must be fit for strenuous physical exertion and be able to pass periodic physical fitness tests. Candidates must successfully complete all aspects of the training program. After a probationary period not to exceed four years, the special agent becomes a permanent employee.

Entry-level salary is normally at the third step of Foreign Service, grade FP-6. In 1997, the salary range at this grade level was $30,046 to $36,953. With satisfactory performance, special agents can be promoted to the FP-5 level. Beyond the FP-4 level, special agents are considered for promotion annually in competition with others in their specialty.

Antiterrorism Activities

for the same philosophical ends. For example, there are a number of environmental groups that strongly advocate careful harvesting and replacement of forested trees. Most could not accurately be labeled environmental terrorists. Yet, there are some overzealous environmentalists who use explosives to destroy lumbering equipment, interrupt the harvest of forests, and intimidate workers. Some have even booby-trapped trees with spikes, causing the deaths of workers.

Speaking generally, investigating terrorist activities requires techniques similar to those used in investigating organized criminal groups (see Chapter 19). These techniques include, but are not limited to, locating and identifying coconspirators, arranging surveillance, and prioritizing investigation of conventional crimes involved in the terrorism.

Local Police and Terrorism

Once a terroristic act has occurred, a patrol unit from the local police is likely to arrive first on the scene. As in any arrival to a crime scene, officers must be alert and cautious as they arrive and exit their vehicles. The crime scene should be immediately secured, and witnesses, victims, and possible suspects should be identified as quickly as possible. The arriving officers should advise headquarters of the situation and any additional personnel or services required.

Once the officer determines from an assessment at the scene that terrorists are involved, the officer should notify headquarters. If hostages are involved, the department's hostage negotiator (if one is available) should be contacted. If the local agency does not have the necessary specialists, the state and federal agency offices in the area should be immediately consulted. While some larger police agencies may have specialists in incendiary and explosive devices, most smaller agencies do not. Similarly, many smaller agencies do not have specialists in dealing with terrorists or conducting hostage or terrorist negotiations. It is important for local agencies to recognize their own limitations and to seek assistance from appropriate agencies.

As in other criminal cases, crimes of terrorism require careful and accurate record keeping. The record should begin with the first notification of the police. This may often be a threat of violence or notification of a kidnapping, with demands from the kidnapper. The activities investigators should undertake include the following:

- Record the time and date the threat was received, who received the threat, and how it was received.
- Indicate the character of the threat (e.g., bombings, arson, kidnapping, or murder).

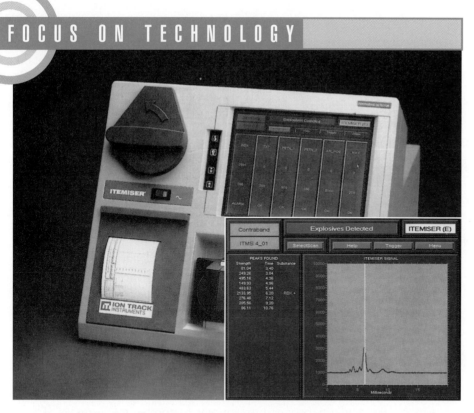

Trace Explosives Detector   An explosives trace detection system traps traces of vapors or particles given off or left behind by explosives. These trapped samples are evaporated and drawn into the detection system where they are analyzed. An audible alarm and screen display indicate the presence of explosives. This process takes less than three seconds to complete.

- Identify the target and time of the terroristic threat.
- Determine what prompted the threat.
- Determine any organizational ties of the threat maker.
- Record any telephone conversations, and examine the tape for background noises and telltale characteristics of the threat maker.
- If the threat is written, avoid handling the document with ungloved hands. Determine who has already handled the document, and secure samples of their fingerprints. Have the document examined by the forensic lab to identify possible fingerprints or other identifying marks.
- If the threat was in person, question the reporting individual, and obtain a description of the threat maker.

Crisis negotiation team
A group of specialists trained to defuse potentially dangerous situations.

When officers arrive at the scene of terroristic activity, they may not immediately realize that it is not a conventional crime. In other words, a bank robbery may be an attempt to obtain money for a radical political group's efforts and hence, in a broad sense, a terroristic activity. The arriving officers, however, are likely to see the event as merely another bank robbery. It is appropriate to work the scene as one would any other robbery. However, once it is determined that the crime may be classified as an act of political terrorism, the proper officers or agencies should be notified. For example, in some large departments, there may be officers assigned to a **crisis negotiation team,** specialists in defusing potentially dangerous situations. Smaller departments may need to contact state level enforcement or the local office of the FBI.

Suspect Background Information

As suggested earlier, terrorist investigations rely heavily on intelligence data, and on cooperation among a number of agencies. These efforts frequently produce great amounts of data requiring considerable personnel hours and computer-assisted analysis. Among the elements of information likely to emerge are various potential suspects.

History demonstrates that persons involved in terrorism often have previous law violations. Careful attention should be given to examining various records and the background characteristics of potential suspects. We have previously discussed information sources that may prove helpful in locating suspects or obtaining evidence of criminal involvement. These sources include *modus operandi* files, arrest records, employment records, motor vehicle records, and utility records, to name just a few.

Physical Evidence

One of the most important elements of terrorist-related investigations is the collection and preservation of physical evidence. In both the 1993 New York City World Trade Center bombing and the 1995 bombing of the Murrah Federal Building in Oklahoma City, it was physical evidence that led investigators to suspects. In the first case, a fragment of a truck axle led ATF investigators first to a rental agency and then to a suspect. Similarly, wreckage from the rented truck used to house the fertilizer/explosives in the Oklahoma bombing case led investigators to arrest Timothy McVeigh as the prime suspect and later to locate Terry Nichols as a coconspirator and Michael Fortier as a prosecution witness.

The search for physical evidence in terrorism cases should extend from the physical crime scene to surrounding areas and to locations where a suspect may have conducted surveillance or concealed him- or herself before or during an incident (e.g., an arson or bombing). Because terrorist activities frequently involve more than one person, it may be important to establish each coconspirator's activities and whereabouts during the terrorist event through physical evidence.

Procedures for appropriate collection of evidence were covered in Chapter 4. However, it should be noted that during terrorist investigations, items that may seem unrelated to the crime may actually prove critical later in the case. A can of Coke may ultimately lead to a suspect if investigators trace the manufacturer's identification code and locate the town, and even the store, where the can was purchased. By examining minute debris and the detonating device left by the bomb that brought down Pan American Flight 103 over Lockerbie, Scotland, authorities were able to identify the most likely suspects.

In addition to items that may have been touched or accidentally left by the terrorists, materials used in bombs or devices may offer clues. Parts of these contrivances may be traced to their sources—often right to the retail level. When a series of bombings or arsons have occurred, materials found at the scenes may be linked to show a common origin. Many establishments maintain records of their transactions. By locating the retailer of an item used by a terrorist, one may actually identify a suspect.

A twisted piece of truck axle found near the Oklahoma City bombing site gave investigators a vital first clue in the investigation that led to a verdict of guilty against Timothy McVeigh on June 2, 1997.

SUMMARY BY LEARNING OBJECTIVES

Learning Objective 1

Terrorism is the unlawful use or threat of violence against persons and property to further political or social objectives. It is generally intended to intimidate or coerce a government, individuals, or groups to modify their behavior or policies.

Learning Objective 2

Until recently, many Americans did not view terrorism as a serious threat. The realization that they were vulnerable to the violence of political terrorism came with the bombing of the Murrah Federal Building in Oklahoma City in April 1995. The Oklahoma City bombing was not the first case of domestic terrorism witnessed by law enforcement agencies in the United States.

Learning Objective 3

Terrorist groups operating in the United States can be classified as left-wing, right-wing, special-interest, and international.

Learning Objective 4

From a legal standpoint, terrorism is not in itself a crime. Terrorists commit crimes such as murder, kidnapping, rape, arson, and bombing. When these crimes are used to bring about political or social change, terrorism has occurred. Law enforcement officials consider terrorism a crime, and terrorists criminals. Capturing and prosecuting terrorists generally involve interagency cooperation.

Learning Objective 5

Federal and state governments use a variety of strategies to combat terrorism. One of the most important is counterintelligence, the gathering of data on people and groups that have a serious potential for future terrorist activities.

Learning Objective 6

Local police officials are generally the first to respond to a terrorist incident. The same investigative precautions and procedures that apply to any crime apply to a terrorist incident. One of the most important elements of investigating a terrorist-related event is the collection and preservation of physical evidence.

QUESTIONS FOR REVIEW

Learning Objective 1

1. What is *terrorism?*

Learning Objective 2

2. Why have Americans believed they were invulnerable to terrorist attacks?

3. Why didn't the bombing of the World Trade Center in New York City frighten Americans as much as the bombing in Oklahoma City two years later?

4. Why has left-wing terrorism declined in the United States in recent years?

5. What do many of the right-wing militia groups have in common?

6. How are special-interest terrorist groups different from political terrorists?

7. Why do international terrorists target the United States?

8. Why does the FBI tend to investigate terroristic activities?

9. What is Interpol, and what role does it play in terrorism investigations?

10. What is a *terroristic threat?*

11. What is the major difference between investigating conventional criminals and investigating political terrorists?

12. In what ways are investigations of terrorism similar to those of organized crime groups?

13. How are crime scenes handled by patrol units that arrive at a terrorist event?

14. Why might a terrorist group rob a bank?

15. What sorts of records might be helpful in considering suspects in a terroristic crime?

16. Why might one examine the employment records of a business that has been the target of terrorism?

17. How is physical evidence important to an investigation of terroristic activity?

18. How can even minute bits of physical evidence be helpful in a terroristic bombing case?

CRITICAL THINKING INVESTIGATIVE EXERCISES

1. You are working dispatch, and a phone call comes in reporting a bomb threat.

   a. What will you need to do?

   b. What questions will you ask the caller?

2. Using a variety of resources, write a paper examining the policies and arguments of a political activist group. The group may be an animal rights group, an environmental preservation group, a right- or left-wing group, or a separatist group. If the group has a history of using terrorist tactics, be sure to document them. The report should be at least five pages long and should clearly present the group's ideological stance and political orientation.

INVESTIGATIVE SKILL BUILDERS

Working With Cultural Diversity

You have just begun work as an investigator for a larger city police department. Your partner is of Asian decent, but you are not sure exactly what her ethnicity is. You and your partner are called to a section of town known locally as Little Vietnam, where a robbery has taken place. When you arrive, another Asian officer is already interviewing the proprietor in Vietnamese. You repeatedly hear the term *Viet Chin* mentioned by the storekeeper. You are aware that this is a fairly organized gang of men of Vietnamese decent who have been terrorizing local merchants for protection money. Your partner looks at you and asks, "I don't suppose you speak Vietnamese, do you?" You reply, "No."

1. Should you ask your partner at this point what her ethnicity is?
2. Should you ever ask your partner what her ethnicity is?
3. Should you have answered her question with, "No, I don't, but don't you?"

Integrity/Honesty

You and a partner have been called to the scene of a terrorist hostage situation. A terrorist has taken a kindergarten class hostage, along with its teacher. There are 26 children in the class. Originally, the terrorist was demanding the release of political prisoners named on a list he provided to the hostage negotiation team already on the scene. The terrorist has also demanded a helicopter and $2 million in cash. The terrorist has threatened to kill a child every 15 minutes until his demands are met. To show he means business, he sends the teacher out and shoots her in the back as she walks toward the police. Fifteen minutes later, he sends out a small boy, whom he also shoots in the back. The SWAT team moves in and manages to apprehend the terrorist. You and your partner take the terrorist into custody and are asked to transport him to headquarters.

After your partner has driven several blocks from the crowds and ambulances, he turns into an alley and stops the car. Before you can even ask what he is doing, he has gotten out of the driver's seat and is in the backseat with the terrorist. He immediately begins beating the handcuffed man with his nightstick.

1. What is your immediate response?
2. What actions will you take when you get to headquarters?

ENDNOTES

1. *Vice President's Task Force on Combating Terrorism,* Government Printing Office, Washington, 1986, p. 2.

2. Priscilla Painton, "Who Could Have Done It?" *Time,* March 8, 1993, p. 33.

3. Marcia M. Trick, "Chronology of Incidents of Terrorism, Quasi-Terroristic, and Political Violence in the United States, January 1965 to March 1976," in *National Advisory Committee on Criminal Justice Standards and Goals, Disorders and Terrorism: Report of the Task Force on Disorders and Terrorism,* Department of Justice, Washington, 1976.

4. Jeffrey Ian Ross and Ted R. Gurr, "Why Terrorism Subsides: A Comparative Study of Canada and the United States," *Journal of Comparative Politics,* Vol. 21, 1989, pp. 405–20.

5. Christopher Dickey, "Terrorism: Target America," *Newsweek,* July 8, 1996, pp. 22–25.

6. Material on the major categories of terrorist groups and their characteristics is based on information from the following sources: Department of Justice, Federal Bureau of Investigation, *Terrorism in the United States, 1995,* U.S. Government Printing Office, Washington, 1996; Benjamin Netanyahu, *Fighting Terrorism,* New York: Farrar Straus Giroux, 1995; *International Terrorism,* Hearing Before the Committee on International Relations, House of Representatives, June 20, 1995, Government Printing Office, Washington; David Van Biema, "Militias: The Message From Mark," *Time,* Vol. 145, No. 26, 1995, pp. 56–61; Jill Smolowe, "Enemies of the State," *Time,* Vol. 145, No. 9, 1995, pp. 56–58.

7. James Overton, "Interpol's Perspective on International Terrorism and Drug Trafficking," In R. Ward and H. Smith (eds.), *International Terrorism,* University of Illinois, Chicago Circle, 1988.

Glossary

Numbers in parentheses indicate the chapter in which the term is introduced.

ABC surveillance   A three-officer foot surveillance in which Officer **A** follows the suspect and in turn is followed by Officer **B.** The third surveillant, Officer **C,** normally walks on the other side of the street opposite the suspect. (8)

Absolute immunity   A guarantee that, as long as a witness complies with the court and testifies, the testimony cannot be used against him or her in any criminal action. (19)

Accelerant   A booster such as gasoline, kerosene, or paint thinner added to a fire to speed its progress. (18)

Action stereotyping   The misreading of common or stereotypic behaviors of people at or near a crime scene who may actually be the offender(s). (10)

Adhesive-tape technique   A method of collecting microscopic evidence in which transparent tape is used to cover an area to which physical evidence such as fibers may have adhered. When the tape is pulled off, the evidence will adhere to the sticky surface of the tape. (4)

Adipocere   A whitish gray, soapy or waxy substance that forms on the surface of a body left for weeks in a damp location. (14)

Administrative law   The body of law created by administrative agencies in the form of rules, regulations, orders, and decisions, sometimes with criminal penalties for violations. (1)

Admission   A voluntary statement by an accused person containing information and facts about a crime but falling short of a full confession. (6)

Affected words   Words that have negative connotations in certain contexts in a given culture. (6)

Aggravated arson   The malicious, intentional burning of buildings or property and knowingly creating an imminent danger to human life or a risk of great bodily harm to others. (18)

Aggravated assault   An unlawful attack on another person with the intention of causing severe bodily harm. (see Felonious assault) (11)

Alarm call   Notification of the police by audible or silent alarm that a crime such as a break-in has occurred. (15)

Alcoholic robber   A person who robs to sustain an addiction to alcohol or who attributes criminal actions to the influence of alcohol. (10)

Alibi   A defense offered by a suspect or defendant that attempts to prove that he or she was elsewhere when the crime in question was committed. (6)

Alligatoring   A scalelike burn pattern on wood. Large scales indicate rapid, intense heat; small, flat scales indicate low-intensity heat over a long period of time. (18)

Anatomical dolls   Dolls or puppets with sex-appropriate genitalia used in interviews with suspected child victims of sexual abuse or assault. (12)

Apprehension   The act of seizing or arresting a criminal offender. (5)

Arrest report   A police record created to document the events surrounding an arrest. (9)

Arson   The malicious and intentional or fraudulent burning of buildings or property. (18)

Asphyxiation   Death due to a lack of oxygen and an excess of carbon dioxide in the blood. (14)

Assault   An unlawful attempt or threat to commit a physical injury to another through use of force. (11)

Attempted arson   The demonstrated intent to set a fire coupled with some overt act toward actually setting the fire. (18)

Autoerotic asphyxiation   The seeking of sexual gratification by near asphyxia. (14)

Automated fingerprint identification system (AFIS)   A computerized system for scanning, mapping, storing, searching, and retrieving fingerprints. (7)

Aware hearing   A technique of listening and actually hearing what is being said, without interrupting the speaker. (6)

Baseline method   A sketching method that takes measurements along and from a single reference line called a baseline which can be established by using a length of string, a chalk line, or some other convenient means. (3)

Battered child syndrome   The group of injuries suffered by physically abused children. (11)

Battery   Once used to refer to the actual carrying out of the threat of physical harm in an assault; today, in most jurisdictions, it is synonymous with *assault*. (11)

Blackmail   The unlawful demand of money or property under threat to do bodily harm, to injure property, to accuse of crime, or to expose disgraceful defects; commonly included under extortion statutes. (13)

Bloodstains   Dried spills or drops of blood. (4)

Blood-typing   Method of classifying blood into four major blood groups—A, B, AB, and O. Another factor, called the *Rh factor,* also helps determine a person's blood type, which is positive or negative for the Rh factor. (4)

Bombing   An incident in which a device constructed with criminal intent and using high explosives, low explosives, or blasting agents explodes. (18)

Booster device   A container, generally a box, with a spring-loaded trapdoor, allowing the professional shoplifter to conceal stolen goods. (16)

Bore   The hollow, cylindrical chamber or barrel of a firearm. (4)

Bribe   The payment of cash, goods, or services to someone in exchange for some special service, product, or behavior. (20)

Bulb   The rounded area at the end joint of every finger and thumb. (7)

Burglary   Entering a building or occupied structure, without the consent of the person in possession, to commit a crime therein. (15)

Burglary tools   Any of an assortment of tools and picks that may be used in committing a burglary. (15)

Cadaveric spasm   A rigidity of certain muscles that usually occurs when the victim is holding something at the time of death and the hand closes tightly around the object; sometimes a sign of suicide. (14)

Carjacking   The robbery of a car with the driver and/or occupants still in it. (10)

Case law   The sum total of all reported cases that interpret previous decisions, statutes, regulations, and constitutional provisions that then become part of a nation's or a state's common law. (1)

Chain of custody   Proof of the possession of evidence from the moment it is found until the moment it is offered in evidence. (2)

Child abuse   Physical harm, including sexual abuse, or emotional harm to children. (11)

Child molesting   A broad term encompassing any behavior motivated by an unnatural sexual interest in minor children. (12)

Chopping   The dismantling of stolen motor vehicles into parts and accessories for use or sale. (17)

Chop shop   A place for chopping, or dismantling, stolen motor vehicles into parts and accessories that cannot be easily identified, which are resold. (17)

Circumstantial evidence   Evidence of other facts from which deductions can be drawn to show indirectly the facts to be proved. (2)

Citizen's arrest   An arrest by a private citizen, as contrasted with a police officer, permitted under certain circumstances, generally for a felony or misdemeanor amounting to a breach of the peace. (11)

Classification   A method of organizing fingerprints. (7)

Clear   To solve a criminal case by arresting at least one person, charging him or her with the crime, and turning him or her over to the courts for prosecution. (10)

Close surveillance   Surveillance conducted while remaining very close to the subject. (8)

Cognitive interview   An interviewing technique that helps victims or witnesses mentally put themselves at the crime scene to gather information about the crime. (6)

Commercial burglary   A burglary committed at a place of business or commerce. (15)

Commercial robbery   The robbery of a commercial location such as a bank, service station, restaurant, or convenience store. (10)

Common law   Principles and rules of action based on usage and custom in ancient England and incorporated into colonial American laws and subsequent state statutes. (1)

Comparison description   A physical description in which a victim or witness notes similarities and differences between the suspect and another person, whose characteristics are known. (2)

Compass point method   A sketching method that requires a protractor or some method of measuring angles between two lines. One point is selected as the origin and a line extending out from the origin becomes an axis from which angles can be measured. (3)

Competency   The quality of evidence or its fitness to be presented to assist in determining questions of fact; a requirement for admissibility in court; also used to describe a witness as legally fit and qualified to give testimony. (2)

Complacency   Unconcern resulting from having grown accustomed to a given pattern of events or behavior. (11)

Complainant   An individual who seeks satisfaction or action for an injury or for damages sustained. It may be the victim of a crime or someone who acts on behalf of the victim. (6)

Complaint   A formal allegation by which a legal action is commenced against a party; a request for police action in some matter. (6)

Complaint report   A police report written to document events surrounding misdemeanors and miscellaneous incidents. (see Incident report) (9)

Composite description   A description obtained by compiling separate, slightly varying descriptions into a whole. (2)

Computer crime   A crime committed with or against computers.

Computer virus   A computer program, usually hidden within another computer program, that inserts itself into programs and applications and destroys data or halts execution of programs. (20)

Concentric fractures   Irregular, but concentric, circular crack patterns in the broken glass around the point of impact. (4)

Conchoidal fractures   A series of curved lines along the edge of broken glass that form right angles with one side of the glass, forming a shell- or cone-shaped pattern. (4)

Confession   A voluntary statement—written, oral, or recorded—by an accused person, admitting participation in or commission of a criminal act. (6)

Conspiracy   A crime in which two or more parties are in concert in a criminal purpose. (19)

Contact wound   A wound created when a gun is fired while being held against the skin of the victim; typically found in self-inflicted wounds and execution-type murders. (14)

Contributing to the delinquency of a minor   An act or omission that contributes to or tends to make a child delinquent. (12)

Controlled substance   A drug or substance whose use and possession are regulated under the Controlled Substances Act. (21)

Convoy   The following of a subject by multiple individuals. (8)

Cop speak   Specialized vocabulary, or jargon, used by police. (9)

Corporate crime   Any activity that is undertaken by a corporation for its benefit but violates the law. (20)

Corpus delicti   All the material facts in a crime showing that a crime has been committed. Latin for "body of the crime." (2)

Counterintelligence   The activity of gathering political and military information about foreign countries and institutions to prevent terrorist attacks. (22)

Crazing   Irregular cracks and lines in glass and ceramic materials, caused by rapid, intense heat. (18)

Crime   An offense against the public at large, proclaimed in a law and punishable by a governing body. (1)

Crime index   A collection of statistics in the FBI's Uniform Crime Reports on the numbers of murder, rape, robbery, assault, burglary, larceny-theft, motor vehicle theft, and arson crimes reported in a calendar year. (10)

Crime of opportunity   A crime that is committed, with little or no planning, as the opportunity presents itself. (5)

Criminal homicide   The wrongful killing of a human being without justification or excuse in the law. There are two degrees of the offense—murder and manslaughter. (14)

Criminal investigation   The lawful search for people and things to reconstruct the circumstances of an illegal act, apprehend or determine the guilty party, and aid in the state's prosecution of the offender. (1)

Criminalist   A person specifically trained to collect evidence and to make scientific tests and assessments of various types of physical evidence. (3)

Criminal jackets   Official police records of criminals. (8)

Criminal law   The body of law that, for the purpose of preventing harm to society, defines what behavior is criminal and prescribes the punishment to be imposed for such behavior. (1)

Crisis negotiation team   A group of specialists trained to defuse potentially dangerous situations. (22)

Cross projection method   A sketching method in which the ceiling appears to open up like the lid of a hinged box, with the four walls opening outward. Measurements are then indicated from a point on the floor to the wall. (3)

Cults Religious or quasi-religious groups generally considered extreme, with followers that sometimes act in an unconventional manner. (5)

Custody Detainment by a police officer; a situation in which a person feels he or she is not free to leave. (2)

Dactylography The scientific study of fingerprints as a means of identification. (7)

Date rape Forced sexual intercourse that occurs between friends or acquaintances or while a couple is on a date; also called *acquaintance rape.* (12)

Deductive reasoning The drawing of conclusions from logically related events or observations. (1)

Deep cover An undercover operation that may extend for a long period of time, during which the officer totally assumes another identity. (21)

Defendant In criminal law, the person who is accused of a crime. (1)

Defense wound A wound on the hand or forearm of a victim who has attempted to fend off an attack. (14)

Delayed ignition Setting a fire indirectly by means of a mechanical, chemical, or other timing device. (18)

Designer drug Substance produced in clandestine laboratories by adding or taking away something in an existing drug's chemical composition. (21)

Diagonal deployment A method of arranging officers to both secure and observe a crime scene. Officers arrange themselves so that each can observe two sides of a building at once. (15)

Direct ignition Setting a fire by directly applying a flame. (18)

Distribution A drug offense that consists of selling, trading, giving, or delivering illicit drugs, regardless of whether one stands to profit from the transaction. (21)

DNA profiling A procedure in which DNA is extracted from biological evidence samples gathered from crime scenes and from comparison samples collected from victims and suspects. The DNA samples are analyzed and compared to determine whether or not they could have had a common origin. (4)

Domestic assault Any type of battery that occurs between individuals who are related or between individuals and their significant others. (11)

Domestic terrorism An unlawful violent act directed at elements of the U.S. government or population by groups or individuals who are based and operate entirely within the United States and Puerto Rico without foreign direction. (22)

Domestic violence statute A state law that outlaws physical violence against any family member; responding officers serve as the complainant in domestic situations under certain circumstances. (11)

Drug-addicted robber A person who robs to sustain an addiction to some type of illegal drug. (10)

Due process of law The rights of people suspected of or charged with crimes as prescribed in the U.S. Constitution, state constitutions, and federal and state statutes. (1)

Dying declaration A statement given by a victim at a crime scene, in anticipation of death. It is admissible as evidence. (2)

Elimination prints Fingerprints taken of all persons whose prints are likely to be found at a crime scene, but who have a lawful reason to have been there and are not suspects. (7)

Embezzlement The misappropriation or misapplication of money or property entrusted to one's care, custody, or control. (20)

Employee pilfering The theft of goods from warehouses, factories, and offices by employees. (16)

Enterprise theory of investigation An approach to criminal investigation that targets entire crime organizations instead of individual criminals within them. (19)

Evidence Any item that helps to establish the facts of a related criminal case. It may be found at the scene of the crime, or on the victim, or taken from the suspect or the suspect's environment. (3)

Evidence report A report written about the evidence found at a crime scene; usually an evidence inventory is attached as part of the report. (9)

Exclusionary rule The rule that evidence that has been obtained in violation of constitutional guarantees against unlawful search and seizure cannot be used at trial. (2)

Excusable homicide The killing of a human being without intention and where there is no gross negligence. (14)

Explosive Any material that produces a rapid, violent reaction when subjected to heat or a strong blow or shock. (18)

Extortion The obtaining of money or property from another by wrongful use of actual or threatened force, violence, or fear, or under color of official right; refers to such acts by public officials. (13)

Felonious assault   An unlawful attack on another person with the intention of causing severe bodily harm. (see Aggravated assault) (11)

Felonious homicide   Wrongful killing of a human being without justification or excuse in the law; there are two degrees of the offense—murder and manslaughter. (14)

Felony   A relatively serious criminal offense punishable by death or by imprisonment for more than a year in a state or federal prison. (1)

Felony murder   The killing of a person during the commission or attempted commission of a felony other than murder. (14)

Felony report   A police record created to document the events surrounding a felony crime. (9)

Fence   Slang term for a professional receiver, concealer, and disburser of stolen property. (16)

Fingerprint   An impression created by the friction ridges on a person's hands and feet. (7)

Fire triangle   The three basic elements—oxygen, fuel, and heat—needed for a fire. (18)

Fixed surveillance   Close watch on a subject or object from a single location such as in a building or vehicle. (8)

Follow-up report   A report written during the secondary level of a criminal investigation. (see Supplementary report) (9)

Forcible rape   Sexual intercourse against a person's will by the use or threat of force. (12)

Forensic entomologist   A person who specializes in the study of insects in relation to determining the location, time, and cause of death. (14)

Forensic pathology   A specialized field of medicine that studies and interprets, in relation to crime investigation, changes in body tissues and fluids. (14)

Forensic specialist   A person specifically trained to collect evidence and to make scientific tests and assessments of various types of physical evidence. (3)

Forfeiture   The loss of money and/or property to the state as a criminal sanction. (19)

Form section   A boxed section of a police report form, designed for fill-in and check-off of information. (9)

Fraud   Misrepresentation, trickery, or deception with criminal intent to deprive someone of his or her property. (16)

Friction ridges   Minute, raised lines on the outer surface of fingertips, palms, toes, and heels. (7)

Grand larceny   The taking and carrying away of another's personal property with value in excess of the cutoff amount in a given jurisdiction, with the intent of depriving the owner of it permanently; generally considered a felony. (16)

Grid search pattern   A search pattern that consists of two strip searches, the second perpendicular to the first. It allows the area to be viewed from two angles. (3)

Hacker   A person who is proficient at using or programming a computer. (20)

Hallucinogen   A drug causing changes in sensory perception to create mind-altering hallucinations and loss of an accurate sense of time and space. (21)

Hang paper   To intentionally write bad checks; slang expression. (16)

Hate group   A group antagonistic toward various minority groups in the United States. (22)

High explosive   An explosive material in which the rate of change to a gas is very rapid; explodes only upon the shock of a blasting cap, a detonating cord, or an electric detonator; includes nitroglycerin, TNT, RDX, and plastic explosives. (18)

Homicide   The killing of one human being by another. (14)

Hostage   An innocent person held captive by one who threatens to kill or harm the person if his or her demands are not met and who uses the person's safety to negotiate for money, property, or escape. (13)

Hostage negotiator   An individual specially trained to deal with persons holding hostages. (13)

Hot pursuit   The crossing of jurisdictional lines to chase a suspect. (2)

Identification   A process in which physical characteristics and qualities, especially fingerprint information, are used to definitely know or recognize a person. (5) (7)

Impound   To take into legal custody. (17)

Incendiary fire   A fire in which a fire-setting device, an igniter, or an accelerant is found. (18)

Incest   Sexual intercourse between persons who are so closely related that their marriage is illegal or forbidden by custom. (12)

Incident report   A police report written to document events surrounding misdemeanors and miscellaneous incidents. (see Complaint report) (9)

Indecent exposure Exhibiting the private parts of one's body in a lewd or indecent manner to the sight of others in a public place. (12)

Index offense One of the eight crimes (murder, rape, assault, robbery, burglary, larceny-theft, motor vehicle theft, and arson) that the FBI considers the most serious which are combined to create the crime index. (10)

Inductive reasoning The making of inferences from apparently separate observations or pieces of evidence. (1)

Industrial espionage Espionage work undertaken in corporate and industrial areas to keep up with or surpass competitors. (20)

Informer A member of an organized crime group who provides information and testimony for law enforcement investigations and prosecutions. (19)

Injunction A court order prohibiting a party from a specific course of action; or ordering a party to perform some action. (19)

Insider trading An employee's or manager's use of information gained in the course of his or her job and not generally available to the public to benefit from fluctuations in the stock market. (20)

International terrorism An unlawful use of force or violence by a group or individual who has some connection to a foreign power or whose activities transcend national boundaries, against persons or property to intimidate or coerce a government or the civilian population, to further political or social objectives. (22)

INTERPOL An intergovernmental organization of law enforcement authorities from about 200 countries. Its official name is the International Criminal Police Organization. It works to ensure and promote cooperation and mutual assistance among members. (22)

Interrogation Questioning to obtain information from persons suspected of being directly or indirectly involved in a crime. (6)

Interview Questioning to obtain information regarding a person's knowledge about a crime, suspect, or event. (6)

Intrafamily violence Any type of violent behavior that occurs within a family. (11)

Invisible print A latent print not visible without some form of developing. (7)

Jimmy A prying tool of any sort, used to force open a door, window, or lock. (15)

Joyriding The temporary taking of a motor vehicle without the intent of permanently depriving the owner of the vehicle; generally undertaken by juveniles. (17)

Justifiable homicide The killing of another in self-defense or defense of others when danger of death or serious bodily injury exists. (14)

Kickback The payment back of a portion of the purchase price to the buyer or a public official by the seller to induce a purchase or to improperly influence future purchases. (20)

Kidnapping Taking another person from one location to another against that person's will, by using force or coercion. (13)

Larceny/theft The taking and carrying, leading, riding, or driving away the personal property of another with the specific intent of permanently depriving the owner of his or her property. (16)

Latent print An impression transferred to a surface by sweat, oil, dirt, blood, or some other substance on the ridges of the fingers; it may be visible or invisible. (7)

Leading surveillance The procedure of watching and following a subject while remaining ahead of the subject. (8)

Lewd and lascivious behavior with a child Touching any part of a child to arousal; appealing to or gratifying the sexual desires of either the child or the perpetrating adult. (12)

Light cover An undercover police operation that extends only as long as the officer's tour of duty. (21)

Lindbergh law Federal antikidnapping legislation passed in 1932. (13)

Line of communication A channel for communicating with another party. (13)

Livor mortis A dark discoloration of the body where blood has pooled or drained to the lowest level; also called *postmortem lividity.* (14)

Low explosive An explosive material in which the rate of change to a gas is quite slow; the material deflagrates, or burns rapidly, rather than exploding and includes black powder, smokeless powder, and fertilizers. (18)

Manslaughter The unlawful killing of another without malice. It may be voluntary—upon sudden heat of passion—or involuntary—in the commission of an unlawful act. (14)

Manufacturing A drug offense that incudes any activity to cultivate, harvest, produce, process, or manufacture illegal drugs. (21)

Materiality The importance of evidence in influencing the court's opinion because of its connection with the issue; a requirement for admissibility in court. (2)

Miranda warning A cautionary statement to suspects in police custody, advising them of their rights to remain silent and to have an attorney present during interrogation. (2)

Misdemeanor A less serious crime that is generally punishable by a prison sentence of not more than one year in a county or city jail. (1)

Modus operandi (M.O.) The method of operation that a criminal uses to commit a crime. Latin term for "mode of operation." (5)

Money laundering The investing of illegally obtained money into businesses and real estate that are operated and maintained within the law. (19)

Motive A wrongdoer's reason for committing the crime. (5)

Motor vehicle theft The theft or attempted theft of a motor vehicle. (17)

Moving surveillance The observation of a subject while moving on foot, in a vehicle, or in an aircraft. (8)

Murder The unlawful killing of a human being by another with malice aforethought. (14)

Mutual consent Willing participation by both parties in sexual acts. (12)

Narcotic Any drug that produces a stupor, insensibility, or sleep. (21)

Narrative section A lined or blank section of a police report form designed for detailed descriptions and accounts of events. (9)

Nonalarm call Notification of the police by citizen alert or direct observation that a crime such as a break-in has occurred. (15)

Occupational crime The use of one's occupation to illegally obtain personal gain. (20)

One-consenting-party rule A legal principle that permits the audio recording of a two-party conversation if one party has consented. (8)

Opiate Any of the narcotic drugs produced from the opium poppy. (21)

Opportunistic robber A person who steals small amounts of property or cash whenever the opportunity presents itself. (10)

Organized crime A highly structured, disciplined, self-perpetuating association of people, usually bound by ethnic ties, who conspire to commit crimes for profit and use fear and corruption to protect their activities from criminal prosecution. (19)

Payoff The receiving of compensation or money from an individual in exchange for some favor. (20)

Payola A payment to a disc jockey for a favor such as promoting a favorite recording. (20)

Pedophile An adult who is sexually attracted to children or performs sexual acts with children. (12)

Penal code A collection of state statutes that define criminal offenses and specify corresponding fines and punishment. (1)

Perimeter box surveillance A vehicle surveillance technique that involves four cars and allows surveillants to maintain coverage even if the subject suddenly turns at an intersection. (8)

Persuasion Motivating and convincing a person to offer information or to comply with a request. (6)

Petty larceny The taking and carrying away of another's personal property with a value below the cutoff amount in a given jurisdiction, with the intent of depriving the owner of it permanently; generally considered a misdemeanor. (16)

Physical stereotyping A misconception that a criminal is a certain type of person. (10)

Pick program A computer program designed to bypass security measures against duplication of electronic files. (20)

Pie, or wheel, search pattern A search pattern in which the area is divided into pie-shaped sections, usually six in number. Each section is then searched, usually by a variation of the strip pattern. (3)

Plastic print A type of visible print formed when substances such as butter, grease, wax, peanut butter, and so forth that have a plasticlike texture are touched. (7)

Polygraph A device that assesses deception by the person responding to questioning by measuring changes in various physiological data, such as respiration, depth of breathing, blood pressure, pulse, and changes in skin's electrical resistance; lie detector. (6)

Possession A drug offense that consists of having a controlled drug on one's person or under one's control as in one's house or vehicle. (21)

Precedent A decision in a court case that furnishes an example or authority for deciding subsequent cases in which identical or similar facts are presented. (1)

Predicate crime A crime that is a basis of a violation of the RICO statute. (19)

Preliminary investigation Fact-gathering activities that take place at the scene of a crime immediately after the crime has been reported to or discovered by police officers. (2)

Prima facie **evidence** Evidence good and sufficient on its face to establish a given fact or chain of facts and, if not rebutted or contradicted, to be proof of that fact; Latin for "on the surface." (2)

Probable cause Reasonable grounds for belief that a person should be arrested or searched or that a person's property should be searched or seized. (21)

Procedural law The body of law that prescribes the manner or method by which rights and responsibilities may be exercised and enforced. (1)

Professional robber A person who has incorporated robbery into a lifestyle and robs as a means of economic support. (10)

Property report A specific report directed toward documenting property taken or damaged in a crime. (9)

Prosecutor Name given to the government as the party that accuses a person of a crime. (1)

Psychological profiling A method of suspect identification that seeks to identify an individual's mental, emotional, and personality characteristics as manifested in things done or left behind at the crime scene. (5)

Radial fractures Cracks that start at the center of the area where the object struck the glass and radiate outward creating a slightly star-shaped pattern. (4)

Ransom Money, property, or other consideration paid or demanded in exchange for release of a kidnapped person. (13)

Rape An act of sexual intercourse or penetration of the victim's vagina, without consent from the victim, and against the victim's will by force, coercion, or duress. (12)

Rape kit An evidence kit used in many hospital emergency rooms to secure physical evidence specimens in rape cases. (12)

Rapport A relationship of mutual trust and emotional affinity that develops between an interviewer or interrogator and the person being interviewed or interrogated. (6)

Reagents Substances used to detect or test for the presence of blood, or other substances. (4)

Recalcitrant witness A witness who refuses to testify in a criminal proceeding, even after being offered immunity. (19)

Rectangular-coordinates method A sketching method that involves measuring the distance of an object from two fixed lines at right angles to each other. It is often used to locate objects in a room. (3)

Relevancy The applicability of evidence in determining the truth or falsity of the issue being tried; a requirement for admissibility in court. (2)

Repression The act of suppressing or preventing an action from taking place. (5)

Residential burglary A burglary committed at a dwelling place, whether occupied or vacant. (15)

Residential robbery A robbery in which the target is a person in a private residence, hotel or motel room, trailer or mobile home, or other attached areas of a residence. (10)

Restraining order A court order requiring a person to do or refrain from doing a particular thing. (11)

Rigor mortis A stiffening of the body after death that disappears over time. (14)

Robbery The unlawful taking or attempted taking of another's personal property in his or her immediate possession and against his or her will by force or threat of force. (10)

Rules of evidence Rules of court that govern the admissibility of evidence at trials and hearings. (2)

Salvage switch A switching of vehicle identification number plates from wrecked vehicles to stolen cars of the same make and model. (17)

Sedative A drug used to allay irritation or nervousness; creates a lethargy in the user, but may also produce a general feeling of calm and well-being. (21)

Sex crime Any of an assortment of criminal violations related to sexual conduct. (12)

Sexist language Insensitive, politically incorrect language used in reference to gender or gender issues. (9)

Sexual seduction Sexual intercourse between an adult and a willing minor. (12)

Shill A slang term for a secret coconspirator or accomplice in a confidence game. (16)

Shoplifting The taking of goods from a retail establishment without paying for them, while posing as a customer. (16)

Simple arson The malicious, intentional burning of buildings or property that does not create an imminent risk or threat to human life. (18)

Simple assault The intentional causing of fear in a person of immediate bodily harm or death. (11)

Situational stereotyping False or mistaken conclusions from the appearance of certain situations. (10)

Slim Jim A tool consisting of a sturdy length of metal, used by auto and truck thieves to unlock doors. (17)

Smudging Gray ring around a gunshot wound resulting from the deposit of gunpowder after a gun blast at close range. (14)

Spalling The chipping, crumbling, or flaking of cement or masonry caused by rapid, intense heat. (18)

Spiral search pattern A search pattern typically used in outdoor areas and normally launched by a single person. He or she begins at the outermost corner and walks in a decreasing spiral toward a central point. (3)

Stalking Intentionally and repeatedly following, attempting to contact, harassing, or intimidating another person. (11)

Standard of comparison A model, measure, or object with which evidence is compared to determine whether both came from the same source. (3)

Stationary surveillance Close watch on a subject or object from a single location such as in a building or vehicle. (8)

Statutory law The body of laws passed by legislative bodies, including the U.S. Congress, state legislatures, and local governing bodies. (1)

Statutory rape Sexual intercourse with a minor, with or without the minor's consent. (12)

Stimulant A drug with a stimulating effect on the central nervous system, causing wakefulness and alertness while masking symptoms of fatigue. (21)

Sting operation An undercover operation set up by law enforcement personnel to catch, or "sting," offenders committing a crime; often used to collect evidence against thieves. (16)

Street robbery Any of an assortment of robberies that occur in street settings. (10)

Striations Marks, lines, or scratches on the hard surface of an object such as a bullet. (4)

Stripping Illegally removing parts and accessories from motor vehicles to use or sell them. (17)

Strip search pattern A search pattern in which the space to be searched is divided into a series of lanes. One or more searchers proceed up and down each lane, continuing until the area has been completely searched. (3)

Substantive law The body of law that creates, defines, and regulates rights and defines crime and its penalties. (1)

Supplementary report A report written during the secondary level of a criminal investigation. (see Follow-up report) (9)

Surveillance The secret observation of people, groups, places, vehicles, and things over a prolonged period to gather information about a crime or criminal. (8)

Survivalist training A type of training in which separatist groups practice guerrilla warfare tactics to prepare to protect themselves from law enforcement officials or other agents of the government. (22)

Suspected terrorist incident A potential act of terrorism in which responsibility for the act cannot be attributed at the time to a known or suspected terrorist group or individual. (22)

Synopsis A summary or abstract of a larger body of writing, such as a police report. (9)

Tagging Writing a word or symbol on a wall to identify a person or a group such as a gang. (5)

Tattooing The burned skin around a gunshot wound, resulting from hot gunpowder from a gun blast at very close range. (14)

Ten-print card A card or form on which fingerprints are transferred along with other personal data and then filed for future retrieval. (7)

Terrorism The unlawful use or threat of violence against persons and property to further political or social objectives. It is generally intended to intimidate or coerce a government, individuals, or groups to modify their behavior or policies. (22)

Terrorism prevention A documented instance in which a violent act by a known or suspected terrorist group or individual with the means and a proven propensity for violence is successfully interdicted through investigative activity. (22)

Terroristic threat   The unlawful threat of injury or death to manipulate an individual into doing something. (22)

Terrorist incident   A violent act, or an act dangerous to human life, in violation of the criminal laws of the United States or of any state, to intimidate or coerce a government, the civilian population, or any segment thereof, in furtherance of political or social objectives. (22)

Theft   The taking of property without the owner's consent; a popular term for larceny. (16)

Third degree   The use or threat of physical force, mental or emotional cruelty, or water or food deprivation to obtain a confession. (6)

Toxicological screening   An examination of body tissue or fluids for poisons or other toxins. (14)

Trademark   A distinctive characteristic by which a criminal becomes known. (5)

Trailer   A material (rope or rags soaked in accelerant, shredded paper, gunpowder, fluid accelerant, and so on) used to spread a fire. (18)

Triangulation method   A sketching method that requires measuring the distance of an object along a straight line from two widely separated, fixed reference points. (3)

Undercover operation   An investigative police operation designed to secretly uncover evidence against organized crime groups. (19)

Vehicle accident report   Police record created to document the events surrounding a vehicular accident. (9)

Vehicle-driver robbery   Robbery of an object of value in or attached to a vehicle or from the driver of the vehicle. (10)

Vehicle identification number (VIN)   A nonduplicated, serialized number assigned by a motor vehicle manufacturer (of autos, especially) to each vehicle made. (17)

Visible print   A fingerprint found at a crime scene that is immediately visible to the naked eye. (7)

White-collar crime   A nonviolent crime committed by an individual or a corporation that is a breach of trust, confidence, or duty. (20)

Wipe ring (smudging)   A gray ring around a gunshot wound, resulting from the deposit of gunpowder by a gun blast at close range. (14)

Zone search pattern   A search pattern in which the area is divided into four quadrants, each of which is then examined using one of the other patterns. (3)

Index

Bullets, as evidence, 75–78
Bump-and-stop carjackings, 248
Bureau of Alcohol, Tobacco, and
    Firearms (ATF)
    bombings and, 444
    domestic violence and, 270
    records of, 199
    terrorism and, 559
Burglary(ies), 362–381
    blood as evidence in cases of, 66
    commercial, 366
    definition of, 365
    fibers as evidence in cases of, 72
    glass as evidence in cases of, 74
    legal aspects of, 365–366
    methods of, 367–368
    paint as evidence in cases of, 74
    residential, 366
    of safes. See Safe burglaries
    tools used for, 369
Burglary investigations, 369–375
    conducting, 371–374
    preliminary, precautions during,
        370–371
    of safe burglaries, 378–380
    suspects in, 374–375
Burglary tools, 369
Burning. See also Arson
    safe burglary by, 377
Business fraud. See Consumer fraud

Cadaveric spasm, 337
California v. Behler, 137
California v. Prysock, 136
California v. Stewart, 134
Cameras, robbery investigations and,
    256
Capone, Al, 242, 301, 464, 465
Carbon monoxide poisoning, 352
Careers
    as corporate investigator, 500
    as DEA special agent, 539
    as foreign service special agent, 561
    as police detective, 10
    as postal service inspector, 440
    as regulatory agency investigator, 27
Carjacking, 247–249, 310–311
Carrion insects, time of death and,
    339–340
Carrol v. United States, 538
Carrying away, safe burglary by, 377
Car theft. See Motor vehicle theft
CARTs (Computer Analysis and
    Response Teams), 505
Case law, 5
CAT (Combat Auto Theft), 428

Cellular telephones, for report writing,
    209
Central-pocket loop fingerprint pattern,
    163
Chain letter schemes, 402
Chain of custody, 26
Charring, depth of, arson and, 439
Check fraud, 393–394
Chemicals, for developing invisible
    prints, 170–171
Chem Print method, for developing
    invisible prints, 171
Child abuse, 270–271
Child molesting, 285, 286–287
Child Protection Act of 1984, 286
Children. *See* Child sexual abuse;
    Juveniles
Child sexual abuse, 284–293
    categories of, 285–286
    characteristics of people committing,
        286–287
    investigation of, 287–293
Child stealing, 311–312, 316
Chimel v. California, 538
Chinese crime groups, 467–470
Chopping
    of automobiles, 416
    safe burglary by, 377
Chop shops, 416
Circumstantial evidence, 32
Citizen militias, 555–556
Clarity, of reports, 212
Classification, of fingerprints, 160
Clearing offenses, 243
Close surveillance, 191
Clothing
    collection guide for, 86
    for identifying homicide victims, 336
Cocaine, 516, 520–522
    crack, 516, 521–522
    freebasing, 521
CODIS (Combined DNA Index
    System), 288
Cognitive interviews, 125–126
Combat Auto Theft (CAT), 428
Combined DNA Index System
    (CODIS), 288
Commercial burglaries, 366
Commercial robberies, 246
Common law, 3–4
Common law courts, 557
Commonwealth v. Albright, 176
Communication, lines of, 311
Comparison descriptions, 23
Compass point method, for sketching
    crime scenes, 49

Competency, of evidence, 33
Complacency, in assault investigations,
    266
Complainants
    definition of, 126
    interviewing, 126–128
Complaint(s), 126
    nonspecific, 127, 128
    specific, 127
Complaint reports, 219–220
Completeness, of reports, 211
Composite descriptions, 23–24
Comprehensive Crime Control Act of
    1984, 478
Comprehensive Drug Abuse Prevention
    and Control Act of 1970, 477, 532
Computer(s)
    for report writing, 209
    seizing, 506
Computer Analysis and Response Teams
    (CARTs), 505
Computer crime, 497–499, 501–508
    computer manipulation, 503
    definition of, 501
    hardware and software thefts,
        503–504
    internal, 501
    investigating, 504–507
    to support criminal enterprises, 503
    telecommunications, 501–503
    terminology for, 498–499
Computer imaging, for suspect
    identification, 255
Computerized crime mapping, 474
Computerized polygraph testing, 152
Computer printer comparison
    specimens, 81–82
Concentric fractures, in glass panes, 73
Conchoidal fractures, in glass panes, 73
Conciseness, of reports, 212
Confessions, 147–152
    definition of, 147
    guidelines for taking, 148–150
    legality of, 134–136. *See also* Miranda
        warning
    polygraph and, 150–152
    truth serums and hypnosis for taking,
        152
Confidence games, 394–398, 488
Conspiracy laws, 478–479
Consumer fraud, 398–400
    bait and switch, 398
    look-alike or sound-alike products,
        399
    misrepresentation, 399
    Ponzi schemes, 400

reflective ultraviolet photography, 268
for report writing, 209
for surveillance, 198
thin-layer chromatography, 76
trace explosives detector, 563
ultra-violet light, 76
video monitors, 24
Telecommunications crimes, 501–503
Telemarketing fraud, 400–402
Telephone(s)
cellular, for report writing, 209
extortion threats by, 315–317
Telephone numbers, in reports, 215
Ten-print card, 166
Tented arch fingerprint pattern, 163
Terrorism, 548–566
antiterrorism activities and, 560–562
definition of, 550
domestic groups, 553
international groups in United States and, 558
left-wing groups and, 553–554
legal aspects of, 559
local police and, 562–565
physical evidence and, 564–565
prevention of, 554
right-wing groups and, 554–557
special-interest groups and, 557–558
suspect background information and, 564
in United States, 551–553
Terry-stops, 537–538
Terry v. Ohio, 537–538
Theft. *See also* Larceny/theft
definition of, 387
flammables as evidence in cases of, 83
Thin-layer chromatography, 76
Third degree, 145
Threats
during interrogation, 143
terroristic, 559
Time, in reports, 216
Timepieces, time of death and, 340
Titles of persons, in reports, 214–215
Tone, for interrogation, 139–142
Tongs, 468–470
Torching, safe burglary by, 377
Toxicological screening, 346
Trace explosives detector, 563
Tracks, 519
Trademarks, 108

Trailers, arson and, 441
Transportation, motor vehicle theft for, 414
Triads, 467–468
Triangulation method, for sketching crime scenes, 48
Truth serums, for interrogation, 152
Typewriter comparison specimens, 81

UCR (Uniform Crime Reports), 242–243, 250, 403
Ulnar loop fingerprint pattern, 163
Ultraviolet light, 76
Ultraviolet photography, reflective, 268
Undercover operations, 476, 535–536
Understating, for interrogation, 144
Uniform Crime Reports (UCR), 242–243, 250, 403
U.S. Attorney General, terrorism and, 559
United States v. Dockery, 137
United States v. Lane, 137

Valachi, Joseph, 462
Validation questions, 144
V burn pattern, 438
Vehicle(s). *See* Motor vehicle theft; Motor vehicle(s); Motor vehicle theft investigations
Vehicle accident reports, 232–233, 234
Vehicle-driver robberies, 247–249
Vehicle identification numbers (VINs), 12, 420–421
Vehicle surveillance, 190–191
Vehicular manslaughter, 353–356
Vesco, Robert, 494
Video monitors, 24
Video surveillance, 193–194
Videotapes, of crime scene, 44–46
Viet Ching, 471
Vignera v. New York, 134
VINs (vehicle identification numbers), 12, 420–421
Violence, intrafamily. *See* Intrafamily violence
Visible prints, 167
Visual inspection, for identifying homicide victims, 336
Vollmer, August, 101
Voluntary manslaughter, 326–327
Vucetich, Juan, 161

Warranty misrepresentation, 399–400
Watches, time of death and, 340
Westover v. United States, 134
Wetterling, Jacob, 300
White-collar crime, 484–508
bribery, kickbacks, and payoffs, 493–495
categories of, 488
computer crime. *See* Computer crime
corporate, 495–496
definition of, 486
elements of, 489–490
embezzlement and employee thefts, 491–492
industrial espionage, 492–493
insider trading, 493
investigating, 496–497, 504–507
tax evasion, 495
Whorled fingerprint pattern, 163–164
Wipe ring, 349
Witnesses
biased, 130
children as, 132
deceitful, 131
descriptions given by, 254–255
eyewitnesses, 129
frightened, 130
hostile, 130–131
interviewing, 128–132
mature adults as, 132
recalcitrant, 477
reluctant, 129
silent or disinterested, 129–130
timid, 131
unreliable, 130
willing, 129
young adults as, 132
Women, battering of, 267, 269–270
Words, affected, 141
World Trade Center bombing, 447, 552, 558, 564
Written words, ritualized crimes and cults and, 108–110

Yakuza, 470–471
Young adults, interviewing, 132

Zone search pattern, 53–54

Photo Credits